Heroes of the French Epic

A Selection of Chansons de Geste

'Take me to the fields
Whence none return, but where great singers
Sing their songs forever. Take me now . . .'

Heroes of the French Epic

A SELECTION OF *CHANSONS DE GESTE*

Translated by
Michael A. H. Newth

THE BOYDELL PRESS

First published 2005
The Boydell Press, Woodbridge

1 84383 147 3

The Boydell Press is an imprint of Boydell & Brewer Ltd
PO Box 9, Woodbridge, Suffolk IP12 3DF, UK
and of Boydell & Brewer Inc.
668 Mt Hope Avenue, Rochester, NY 14620, USA
website: www.boydellandbrewer.com

A catalogue record for this book is available
from the British Library

Printed from camera-ready copy supplied by the translator

This publication is printed on acid-free paper

Printed and bound by.
Athenaeum Press Ltd, Gateshead, Tyne & Wear

For Sue

'Seor, dulce amie,
Bone fud l'ore que jo te pris a per.'

Chançun de Willame ll. 945-6

Contents

Preface

This volume contains translations of six of the best epic poems to have survived from medieval writing in French. The original works belonged to a form of public entertainment known generically as *chanson de geste* (literally 'song of deeds'), of which some ninety or so examples still exist in their manuscript copies today.

These surviving song-tales are themselves the literary culmination of a long tradition of 'heroic chanting' in France, inspired originally by the historical deeds and legendary exploits of the great Frankish king and Western emperor Charlemagne (742–814) in his role as Defender of the Christian Faith. Orally composed, the first epic chants evolved a narrative construction which was heavily reliant upon mnemonic techniques and devices. Stereotyped themes, episodes and motifs were interwoven in strictly accented lines made up largely of formulaic expressions, and strung together in a ballad-like structure of verses monorhymed by assonance.

Received enthusiastically by the Frankish barons, whose delight in combat they reflected, these early chants were also welcomed, accommodated and nourished by the Church, which fostered their development along the pilgrimage routes to important shrines, such as that of St James at Compostella in north-western Spain. Reworkings of the old chants and original songs were subsequently written down by *trouvères* (poets, usually of good birth and education) and presented by *jongleurs* (itinerant musicians), who sang or recited them to the accompaniment of a *vièle*, a forerunner of the viol, in private halls, public places and even within the precincts of the Church. In this way the *chanson de geste* genre came to provide the chief means of cultural and imaginative expression in the French language from the eleventh up to the middle of the twelfth century.

It remains unknown whether the original panegyrics surrounding Charlemagne, well-documented as being sung among the people in the ninth, tenth and eleventh centuries, began, as has been variously suggested, as soldiers' songs, bardic laments, ecclesiastical chronicles or actual poems of hagiographical or epic nature, in Latin or in the vernacular. What *is* clear, however, is that the masterly level of sustained Epic diction achieved in the *Chanson de Roland*, the earliest complete written *chanson de geste* that we possess today, reflects and consummates a long legacy of prior oral composition within the genre.

The *Chanson de Roland*, by general consent the first masterpiece of French vernacular literature, is thought to have been composed in its present form towards the end of the eleventh century, at a time when the interests of both Church and State were united and galvanised into violent action against a common enemy by the preaching of the First Crusade in 1095. The song's narrative tells of the betrayal and defeat of Count Roland of Brittany, presented as Charlemagne's own nephew, at the Pass of Roncesvalles (French: *Roncevaux*) in the Pyrenees. Against a background of religious zeal and feudal loyalty, scenes of personal conflict and national combat are skilfully sustained upon a high level of emotional intensity by the poet's mastery of the genre's rhetorical devices. Despite its highly fictionalised rendering of a well-documented historical event (the ambush and slaughter of the emperor's rear-guard by heathen Basques in August 778), the enormous influence of this one epic tale upon the whole social and artistic consciousness of medieval France is hard to overestimate. Its tone matched so exactly the contemporary fervour aroused by Pope Urban II's crusading rhetoric and its content so movingly established and celebrated the enduring ideal of Christian martyrdom in battle against God's foes. Few of the *chansons de geste* that survive today do not owe something to the history and artistry preserved in the *Chanson de Roland*. Well over half of them deal directly with the life and deeds of Charlemagne or of those with whom he travelled to and from Roncesvalles. Several deal directly with the adventures of the emperor's barons specifically before of after the doom of that day, drawing to a greater or lesser extent upon the episodes, characters and themes of the *Roland* and describing them with an identical poetic art.

The deeds of the crusading knights subsequently inspired and continued to be inspired by a succession of *chansons de geste*, some celebrating contemporary heroes such as Godfrey of Bouillon, his brother Baldwin and Tancred of Sicily (e.g. the *Chanson d'Antioche, Chanson de Jérusalem, Les Chétifs* and *Le Chevalier au Cygne*). One of the finest of the later, so-called 'secondary' epics, known today as the *Chanson d'Aspremont*, was written in Sicily or Calabria during the preparations for the Third Crusade, which set out from Messina in 1191.

The religious sentiment which pervaded the majority of the earliest epic compositions, providing the moral fulcrum on which the drama and humour of their narratives turned, is expressed most succinctly in the *Roland* itself:

> *'Pagans are wrong and Christians are right'* (1.1015).

The Pagan foes, known indiscriminately as Saracens, Arabs, Africans, Turks, Persians and Slavs, were defined in the first generation of written epics only in terms of their ignorance of or opposition to Christianity, and their narrative function was to bear the physical and moral discomfort and discomfiture thereof. The early *trouvères* endowed their epic heroes' opponents with names, physical features, religious practices and a general deportment both on and off the battlefield which parodied both the Christian and the chivalric ideals. Collectively, the Moslems were portrayed as exotic 'evil others', who worshipped Mahomet as the foremost deity in a hierarchy of deities, which were replaceable both on and off the battlefield by graven images. The Pagan rank and file were lampooned for their cowardice, their general light-headedness, their brittle obedience to their leaders and fickle adherence to their religious faith. The Moslem leaders were shown to lack little in terms of bravery, but lacking the True Faith, their exaggerated boasts and taunts were there to be punished by the noble and righteous French with curt or elaborate *Schadenfreude*.

The written *chanson de geste* genre flourished in France for approximately two hundred years (c.1100–1300). Performed across the country before audiences of differing and changing tastes its content and tone were altered accordingly. The deeds of regional heroes like William of Orange, Girart of Vienne and Aymeri of Narbonne were exploited in addition to those of Charlemagne. As actual Crusader, pilgrim and trader contact with the Moslems increased, so the depiction of the 'Saracen other' became more complex, more individualised and, sometimes, more sympathetic, with the introduction of stock characters such as 'the Christian convert', 'the skilful physician' and 'the amorous princess'. Episodes of romance were included in response to the growing popularity of the tales of 'courtly love', of Breton lay and Arthurian legend, which the more literate and literary aristocracy wished increasingly to read privately, not hear publicly. Female characters in general began to participate to a greater extent in the intrigue of the plots, advancing, and in some cases dominating the narratives by their physical, moral and intellectual attributes. The character of the amorous Saracen princess in particular, smitten with love for a Christian knight and fired with the uncompromising zeal of the newly converted, added a new dimension of sensuality and humour to the songs – the sensuality inherent in the princess's foreign origin and 'exotic' beauty, the comedy apparent in the aggressive energy she was shown to bring to all tasks, some of them traditionally masculine to Christian ears and eyes, and in the invective she loosed and the plots she hatched against the Saracen enemy, her own kith and kin, in pursuit of her romantic goals. The tastes of non-aristocratic audiences were also increasingly accommodated by the introduction of comic elements in the form of social, racial and even religious satire. To begin with, a slapstick 'kitchen humour' became embodied in the creation of a stock character who may be called a '*churl-hero*'. This figure, possessing inordinate physical strength, extreme fondness for food and drink, and an obsessive attachment to an unconventional weapon and way of fighting, stood in obvious burlesque of the noble knights. In extension of the disdain accorded the 'Pagan other' in the earliest *chansons de geste*, any non-French warriors became targets of raillery and ridicule. Saxons, Danes, Germans and especially Lombards were lampooned for their ugliness, dress and manners, miserliness and, above all, cowardice. Priests and monks were derided for their verbosity, selfishness, treachery, niggardliness and, again, cowardice. The profusion of these comic elements in the thirteenth and fourteenth century 'epic' compositions attests not only to an extensive vogue for this kind of humour among both popular and noble audiences, but also to the aesthetic influence on the genre of the contemporary rise into social prominence of the *bourgeoisie*.

Successful songs were continued either backwards or forwards in time and new tales containing the youthful exploits or last days of particular heroes or the deeds of their ancestors or descendants were added to the *jongleurs'* repertoires. At the height of their popularity, towards the end of the twelfth century, all the epic tales were grouped by the performers themselves into three main cycles, each named after the one legendary figure which united them in some way – Charlemagne (the cycle of the King), Garin de Monglane and Doon de Mayence. The Garin de Monglane cycle – also known as the William of Orange cycle or the cycle of the Aymerides – is a group of twenty-four surviving *chansons de geste* dealing with the exploits of an illustrious family, each generation of which is driven from home by its father to seek fiefs and glory in the south of France and in Spain. The Doon de Mayence cycle is also known as the cycle of rebellious barons, a small group of otherwise unrelated songs which detail the bellicose exploits of regional Carolingian barons, not in conflict with the Infidels but with their own central monarch or with each other.

During the thirteenth century the twelve-syllable alexandrine line ousted the ten-syllable line and consonance replaced assonance in the monorhymed verses. The stanzas (called *laisses*) themselves, seeking descriptive rather than dramatic effects, became more chapter-like in length and purpose, and the old mnemonically-inspired epic formulas lost their syntactic flexibility, emotional functions and, finally, their narrative pulse. Great cyclic manuscripts, however, containing up to seventeen *chansons de geste*, continued to preserve and rehandle the subject-matter of the earliest and/or most successful poems. 'Historical' compilations, in verse, such as the *Chronique rimée* of Philippe Mousket in 1260, began to collect and codify the Charlemagne legends contained in the epic tales. Prose compilations and adaptations of the best of them began to appear in the middle of the fourteenth century (e.g. the *Myreur des Histors* of Jean d'Outremeuse, 1340) and continued through to the mid-fifteenth (e.g. *Les Croniques et Conquestes de Charlemaine* of David Aubert, 1458), and into the early decades of the age of printing.

The influence of the *chansons de geste* upon the literature of other countries was widespread, significant and enduring. Adaptations, imitations and translations of many of the Old French epic tales survive extensively in Danish, English, German, Italian, Norwegian and Welsh manuscripts. The Norwegian prose compilation called *Karlamagnús Saga* (1230–1250) contains many of the songs whose French originals are either lost today or preserved only in much later copies. *Chansons de geste* plots, in fragment or in entirety, and some of their main characters, in reputation or in action, appear in the works of such everlasting poets as Wolfram von Eschenbach, Dante, Chaucer and Shakespeare. The Franco-Italian adaptations of the 'songs of deeds' are significant not only by their considerable number. Some, like the fourteenth century version of *Aliscans*, and *Aspremonte*, dated 1509, both currently in the possession of the Biblioteca Nazionale Marciana in Venice, are virtual copies of their French originals and bear witness not only to the enduring popularity of certain Old French epics and their legends but to the survival of the genre itself in Italy. Others, such as *L'Entrée d'Espagne* (c.1300), and its continuation *La Prise de Pampelune* (1328) and *La Spagna* (c.1365), are original poems by Italian authors and link the last epic poetry in France to the first epics of the Italian Renaissance and beyond. In addition, the derivative prose works of Andrea da Barberino (1370–1431), in particular his *I Reali di Francia*, a large compilation of Charlemagne legends, were the major source for the *Orlando Innamorato* of Boiardo in the fifteenth century and the *Orlando Furioso* of Ariosto in the sixteenth. In their own right, da Barberino's tales were read extensively up to the nineteenth century, which itself saw a revival of interest among scholars and poets of the Romantic school in medieval literature in general and in the legends surrounding Charlemagne in particular.

The poems selected for this volume are taken from all three Old French epic song cycles and, apart from their individual merits, display the complete range of themes, episodes and character-types which were the life-blood of the *chanson de geste* genre. Against a common background of religious zeal and feudal honour they tell of perfect knights and rebel barons, of loyal and lascivious ladies, of grumbling 'greybeards' and high-spirited youngsters, and of the craven and the noble-hearted. In narrative length they range from the fragmentary to the novel-like, and in line-length from the octosyllabic through the decasyllabic to the alexandrine. In tone they vary from the crude to the elevated, from the brusque to the graceful, from the grimly realistic to the playfully satiric. Their diction ranges from the colloquial to the highly dignified, commonly within the same poem, not uncommonly within the same stanza. Together they offer examples of composition within the genre across one hundred years, and do, to some extent, I think, reflect the general development in form, narrative feature and social function of the surviving *chansons de geste* during the main period of their popularity.

In making the translations I have tried, above all, to preserve most of the formal properties of the original texts. The *chansons de geste* of whatever period are still oral-based poems and the performance-driven qualities of such verse (the mesmeric effect of formulaic diction, the affective powers of assonance, rhyme and rhythm) need to be recreated in verse and *declaimed* (at least inwardly!) by the modern 'reader', if something of the fine and full effects of this fascinating art-form is to be appreciated today. Of necessity, such an approach to translation is taken at the sacrifice of some literal accuracy, but I would ask those scholars who find these versions too free, to consider whether a prose translation of any piece of verse is, in essence, a 'stricter' translation at all.

It would appear that, in actual performance, all the lines in every stanza of the same *chanson de geste* were chanted to the same brief melodic phrase, like a litany. Most of the earlier songs were written in ten-syllabled lines, grouped together in stanzas of irregular length. The final syllables of all the lines in one Old French epic stanza were originally assonanced together, but in later poems they were fully rhymed. This full rhyme, which is easy to achieve in French, is impossible to copy in English, and so I have used the traditional assonance patterning for all six tales contained in this collection. The occasional rhyme occurs, of course, but is, usually, fortuitous. The assonance changes with each stanza and is commonly masculine but occasionally feminine. A feminine ending is one in which the stressed syllable that carries the assonance is followed in the original poem by an unaccented **e**: (e.g. baronn**ie**, fol**ie**); a masculine ending is one in which it is not so followed: (e.g. bar**on**, donj**on**). This additional unstressed syllable does not count in the scansion of the line. Thus, in the translations, not only do words like *brave* and *jail* assonate, but so do *barons* and *madness*. The lines themselves are strictly measured with a strong internal accent. There is a break in the line after the fourth syllable (or occasionally after the sixth), and the final syllable before this caesura may once again be either masculine or feminine and may vary from line to line.

While preserving the medieval verse-structure as much as possible, I have also tried to accommodate the needs and expectations of the modern readers of these tales. I have maintained a uniform past tense in narration that does not reflect the indiscriminate mixture of tenses to be found in all of the originals. I have created many more run-on lines than occur in the Old French, and have, more radically, but again for the ease of modern reading, divided each text artificially into numbered sections, to indicate narrative episodes which are discernible but not distinguished thus in the manuscripts or any editions thereof.

These translations are primarily intended for general readers, for scholars and students of history or of comparative literature, and for readers of modern French who may not often venture beyond the formidable frontiers of the Renaissance writers. The individual introductions and select bibliographies provided for each poem have been prepared alike to serve primarily the needs and interests of these groups. It is also hoped, however, that this volume will be useful to scholars and students of Old French itself, for classroom or individual purposes. The surviving *chansons de geste* offer a fascinating insight into the matters and manners of their times. As art, they form a vital and varied but comparatively neglected body of verse, the literary achievements of which have been represented almost exclusively, and to some extent atypically, by the *Chanson de Roland*. The translations contained in this volume will hopefully contribute to a wider appreciation of the information, excitement, pathos, humour and wisdom to be found within this poetic *corpus*, while providing an echo of its enthralling, atavistic art form of epic chant.

I am indebted to Richard Barber and the editorial board at Boydell and Brewer for their belief and collaboration in the realisation of this long project. My warm thanks go also to Clifford Aspland and John O. Ward, my academic mentors in Sydney, and to Dr Sarah Kay at Cambridge, for their encouragement of my work. I am very grateful to the Board of Regents at Arizona State University for granting me their permission to revise for this volume my earlier translation of "*The Song of Girart of Vienne by Bertrand de Bar-sur-Aube: A Twelfth-Century Chanson de Geste.*" MRTS Volume 196 (Tempe, AZ 85287), copyright Arizona Board of Regents for Arizona State University. The collaboration of my friends Margarita Wilson and Gary Heap upon the compilation, respectively, of the Glossary and Maps included in this volume, has also been much appreciated. Finally, and most importantly, I thank my wife Sue, for her unfailing moral and practical support.

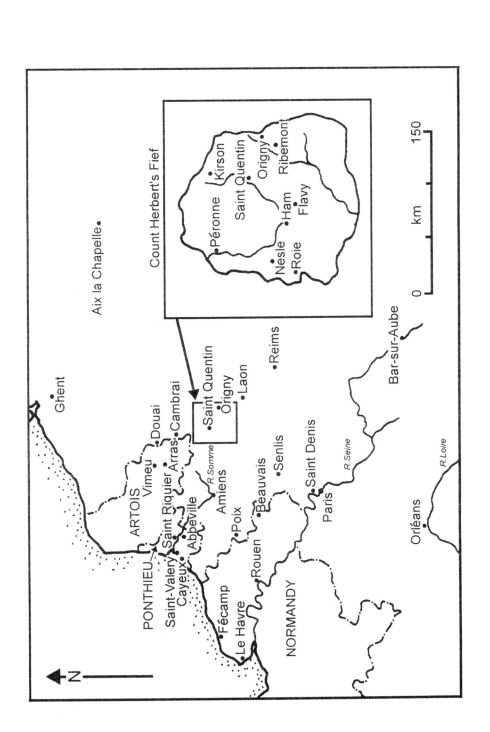

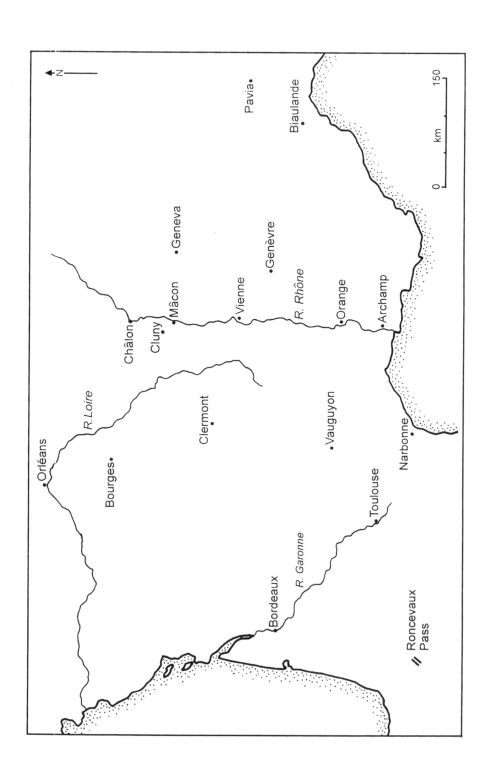

GORMONT AND ISEMBART

(c.1070–1100)

Introduction

The Old French epic fragment known today as *Gormont et Isembart* contains an imaginative account of the victory won by the French under the leadership of King Louis III over an army of Northmen at Saucourt-en-Vimeu on August 3, 881. In the poem, whose authorship is unknown, but which is considered to be one of the earliest *chansons de geste* to have survived in its written form, King Louis is presented as Charlemagne's own son, Louis the Pious, while his Pagan adversary, King Gormont, can be readily identified with the Viking King Gudrum, who founded the English Danelaw. The central character of the extant fragment, however, and almost certainly of the entire original poem, the renegade Christian knight Sir Isembart, is impossible to identify with any historical prototype. His name does not appear in any ninth century Carolingian manuscript.

According to the *Vita Alfredi*, written by Bishop Asser of Sherborne (d. 910), the Viking King Gudrum arrived in England in 870, defeated Alfred the Great the following year, but was in turn defeated by him in 878. In 879 he and his troops retired to Cirencester in Gloucestershire, where they made contact with a second party of Northmen raiders. This army it was which subsequently set out for France, devastated Ponthieu and Vimeu – regions around the mouth of the Somme in Picardy – burned the abbey of Saint-Riquier at Centule, then met defeat at Louis' hands in Saucourt. These events are referred to in the *Anglo-Saxon Chronicle* for the years 880 and 881:

'880: In this year the army went from Cirencester into East Anglia, and settled there and shared the land. And the same year the army which had encamped at Fulham went overseas into the Frankish empire to Ghent and stayed there for a year.'

'881: In this year the army went further inland into the Frankish empire and the Franks fought against them.'

Gudrum himself never left England, but according to the chronicle of Aethelweard, supported such raiding parties from secure bases in East Anglia until his death in the year 890.

Artistic Achievement

It is certainly regrettable that a mere 661 lines, depicting one of the final acts in what must have been a considerably longer narrative, are all that survive today in the one manuscript held at the Royal Library of Belgium in Brussels. The strong characterisations, the witty dialogues and the skilfully created dramatic background, against which the private passion of the apostate hero Isembart is played out in lyric lines of lament, despair and prayer, reveal the artistry of a highly talented and original poet.

The fragment opens in the mêlée of the final battle where, until his death some four hundred lines later, the narrative is dominated by the personality and deeds of the pagan King Gormont. Without devoting a single line to a physical description, the poet succeeds in presenting him as one of the genre's most frighteningly impressive opponents of Christianity, through the extraordinary and brutal valour of his actions and through the venom of his every word. In a succession of single combats he withstands, on foot, a series of mounted charges by the knights of France. The originality of this manoeuvre is matched by that of his stinging war-boasts (or *gabs*), which comprise racial and religious insults, heavy sarcasms, ironic gibes, and a range of witty wordplay unmatched in any other surviving full-length epic verse-tale of medieval France. The combats themselves are described in varied but precise detail – despite its brevity *Gormont and Isembart* employs a military vocabulary as rich as that of any other *chanson de geste*.

With Gormont's death (line 395), the narrative structure of the poem changes as the poet explores and exploits the dramatic and lyric possibilities inherent in the personality of his most original character, the anti-hero Isembart. Having revolted against his liege lord, King Louis, forsaken his homeland and abjured his Christian faith (hence his sobriquet of 'The Renegade' in the poem), he has entered the service of the Pagan king and persuaded him to conquer France. At Gormont's death, he then becomes the leader of the Pagan's demoralised forces. The poet's skill lies now in his ability to convincingly move his audience from a sense of outrage to a feeling of pity, and then finally to an approbation of Isembart's morality and actions on personal, national and religious levels. Our disapproval of his original revocation of fealty is tempered by Isembart's touching lament at his benefactor's death, and by his gallant leadership of a doomed and disrespectful rabble. Our affront at his attack upon fellow Frenchmen is softened by his own admission of their superiority, and our revulsion at his attack upon his own father is immediately quelled by the poet's deft explanation of its unwittingness. Finally, the audience's most enduring antipathy – that engendered by his treacherous desertion of the Christian faith – is transformed abruptly into a sense of heartfelt loss at Isembart's death. He confesses his sins, and dies indeed as an almost Christ-like figure. Cut down unrecognised by four of his countrymen, he forgives them for all – and, for all, is himself forgiven.

The poet's finest artistic achievement, however, lies in his able and original handling of the single most important and striking formal ingredient of all early *chanson de geste* composition, namely the so-called 'epic formula' or 'formulaic expression.' These stereotyped verbal constructs, usually of both four and six syllables in length, but in *Gormont and Isembart* composed exclusively and uniquely of the former, allowed the early performers/poets to create an epic diction that was able to operate on three narrative levels. The simplest formulas, no doubt mnemonically inspired, are one dimensional, and act purely as the building-blocks of the song to state an action, sketch a person, object or scene, express an emotion, to describe a combat or to deliver dialogue: e.g. *he drove the steed* (lines 16, 119, 200), *he struck so well* (lines 19, 50, 122, 183, 231, 342), *the best of kings* (lines 29, 129) *from front to back* (lines 26, 75, 150, 458), *so help me God* (lines 208, 221) *with ringing voice* (lines 2, 32, 131, 154, 255, 355, 584). A second level, one of semantic amplification, is achieved through the use of syntactic combinations that tend to intensify rather than simply to qualify the narrative phrase. These verbal constructs usually appear in the hemistich, most frequently in this poem as 'noun+adjective' and 'verb+verb' formulas: e.g. *the fight was hard* (lines 9, 42, 66, 138), *on grass of green* (lines 56, 505) *he ripped and wrecked* (lines 21, 169, 457). The affective power of these formulas is then increased, when used in combination by the poet either in whole-line or even double line blocks:

> *The fight was hard, the fray was harsh* (l. 164)

> *The fight was hard, the fray was fierce*
> *And great indeed the battle's grief;* (ll.9-10)

> *How fine you were! How fair of face!*
> *How blithe your looks, how bright your gaze!* (ll.481-2)

The frequent and cumulative employment of these stylised combinations of formulaic expressions still manages to achieve a mesmeric effect upon the modern reader, much as it must have done upon the original audiences of the poem:

> *The fight was hard, the fray was fierce*
> *And great indeed the battle's grief;*
> *Sir Walter Mans spurred up with speed,*
> *A duke, the son of Erneïs;*
> *He saw the Moor upon the peak*
> *And if he'd spurned the chance to meet,*
> *He would have held his honour cheap;*
> *With shining spurs he drove the steed*
> *And crimson blood went spurting free;*
> *Against the Moor he aimed his spear*
> *And struck full-tilt upon his shield;*
> *He broke the boards, he cleft them clean;*
> *He ripped and wrecked the coat beneath;* (ll.9-21)

It is, however, the extreme and unique syntactic flexibility of the old chanters' formulas which gives them their greatest narrative strength. When used in combination with the changing assonance of successive *laisses*, plot progression can be accomplished both in short verses, where the same sorts of actions are repeated in so-called 'parallel' *laisses*, (the first seven combat verses of *Gormont and Isembart* are an example of this technique) and in longer verses where the narrative is embellished with description in the place of action. Alternatively, the narrative can be arrested and considerable dramatic and lyric effects achieved, when the same sorts of emotions are repeated and thereby intensified, once again by combining the flexible formulas with an altered end-assonance. The affective powers of this formalised adaptability in laments, and in the ritualised descriptions of duel and death, are quite extraordinary. In *Gormont and Isembart* the speeches and laments occasioned by the Pagan King's death exemplify this technique of 'similar' *laisses* at its best. The above techniques can be seen to even better advantage in the surviving epic tales from the twelfth century written with a decasyllabic line, where the extended flexibility of the four-syllable formula to one of six in the second hemistich allows for an almost unlimited range of 'melodic' invention to be achieved. The versification of *Gormont and Isembart* is archaic – *laisses* of octosyllabic lines occurring elsewhere only in very early poems such as the old Provençal *Alexandre* and *Chanson de Sainte-Foi*, which date back to the eleventh century. It is quite possible, however, that the eight-syllable line may have been the common measure of the very first, orally composed and presented, *chansons de geste*, of which *Gormont et Isembart* affords us today a unique glimpse. When read aloud, the poem certainly has a more primitive ring to it than any other surviving epic verse-tale from medieval France. Its composition is, however, anything but artless. Its narrative is choc-a-bloc with formulaic phrases that fit simply and densely into place, creating a persistent and ponderous effect that matches skilfully and exactly the unremitting bleakness of this fragment's particular theme. Uniquely in Old French epic, the unknown poet of *Gormant et Isembart* employs an assonating quatrain after *laisses* 1, 2, 3, 4, 6 and 7, which serves as a refrain each time the Pagan king disposes of a French champion. Moreover, lines 609-12 constitute a similar assonating quatrain which serves to underline the gradual completion of the Pagan rout. Both quatrains rhyme internally *aa bb* and are surely intended to complement each other.

Sources and Influences

Although there is undoubted originality in the poet's handling of conventional *chanson de geste* compositional elements, there is also considerable similarity between his application of verbal formulas, motifs and episodes traditional to the genre and that of the poets of the *Chanson de Roland* and the *Chançun de Willame*. Whether or not the poet of *Gormont et Isembart* was consciously imitating certain successful features of earlier versions of these two more famous verse-tales cannot really be known, but it seems more likely that any such similarities in descriptions of weapons, horses and combats, in the appreciation of Pagan leaders and deprecation of their followers, in the frequent employment of boasts, taunts, laments and prayers, were part of the long oral tradition of epic chanting and thus common material for the first recorders and then for the writers of the genre to draw upon.

The surviving *Gormont et Isembart* is probably a rehandling of an earlier poem which Hariulf, a monk of the abbey of Saint-Riquier in Ponthieu, Picardy, heard sung near his abbey in the second half of the eleventh century. In Chapter 20 of Book 3 of his Latin chronicle of the abbey, which he completed in 1088, Hariulf writes that during the reign of Louis III the Pagans, commanded by their King Guaramundus and the Frankish traitor Esembardus, devastated Ponthieu and burned down the church of Saint-Riquier. Louis, he says, defeated them, but died shortly thereafter. Hariulf declares that he is only summarising these events as "they are found in the chronicles and sung daily by the local folk." Apart from the names of both leaders, Gormont and Louis, and those of the old fiefs containing Saint-Riquier, Saint-Valéry and Cayeux, the only other precise historical and geographical reference in the poem is to Cirencester as the starting-point of Gormont's invasion. Hariulf's chronicle makes no mention of Cirencester, but it seems likely that Anglo-French poets of the Conquest age were aware from Old English sources of the legend of Garmund's or Wermund's capture of this town in Gloucestershire, and that an Anglo-Norman poet or a French poet with knowledge of the English legends combined it with the legend to which Hariulf refers and wrote *Gormont et Isembart*. The unique fragment of the copy we now possess is written in Anglo-Norman hand and dates from the thirteenth century.

Louis III's victory at Saucourt had inspired as early as 881 itself the Old High German *Ludwigslied*, generally considered the first extant German historical ballad. It is clear from the text that the *Ludwigslied* was written by a churchman before the death of King Louis, which occurred in August 882. There is general critical agreement, however, that there is no connection whatsoever between the composition of the *Ludwigslied* and that of *Gormont et Isembart*.

The *Chronique rimée* of Philippe Mousket, written around 1260, contains in its lines 14,053-296 a complete version of the Isembart story, of which the present fragment preserves the *chanson de geste*'s concluding scenes only, and develops the by then hackneyed theme of the king's injustice to his rebellious barons. A century later Mousket's story was rewritten in verse and then, in 1405, put into prose at the request of Marguerite de Joineville, and made part of the romance *Lohier et Mallart*, which survives in a German translation made for Marguerite's daughter, Elisabeth of Lorraine. In the inventory for the library of Philip the Good, made in 1420, appears the entry *Livre de Ysambart*, and in a book census carried out in Burgundy around 1467 the same volume is recorded as *Le Livre de Yzembart*, its opening line being the 'classic' *chanson de geste* invocation: '*Or entendez seigneur baron!*'

Note to the Translation

This translation is based on the definitive edition of the poem, that of Alphonse Bayot, first printed in 1931. I have tried to preserve all the formal properties of the original, including the poet's unusual predilection for the distich and the quatrain. I have, however, maintained a past tense in narration, which does not reflect the seemingly indiscriminate mixture of tenses used in the manuscript. The occasional lines placed in parentheses represent my own attempts to 'second-guess' the copyist, whose manuscript has become damaged at those points.

GORMONT AND ISEMBART

1. Gormont's stand

[KING GORMONT THEN, the bravest Moor,]
Cried out and said, with ringing voice:
"You've come to grief for good and all!
He's little help, this God of yours!"

On striking down the worthy count,
Towards his men he drove the mount;
His lance-head then he faced about
And grasped the shield they passed him out.

THE FIGHT WAS HARD, the fray was fierce,
And great indeed the battle's grief;
Sir Walter Mans spurred up with speed,
A duke, the son of Erneïs;
He saw the Moor upon the steep,
And if he'd spurned the chance to meet,
He would have held his honour cheap;
With shining spurs he drove his steed
And crimson blood went spurting free;
Against the Moor he set his spear
And struck full-tilt upon his shield;
He broke the boards, he cleft them clean,
And ripped and wrecked the coat beneath;
Against his ribs the lance-head pierced,
But not one drop of blood appeared;
King Gormont took no injury
And hurled in turn a dart of steel:
From front to back the weapon sheared
And struck a German at his rear –
It slew them both upon the field;
The best of kings, the noblest Peer
Who in this world had lived and breathed,
If in the Lord he had believed,
With ringing voice rejoiced indeed:

11

"These Christian folk are fools, it seems,
Who cannot wait to joust with me!
Not one shall boast when night is here:
I'll kill them all or make them yield!"

On striking down the worthy counts,
Towards his men he drove the mounts;
His lance-head then he faced about
And grasped the shield they passed him out.

ABOVE CAYEUX, around the chapel,
The fight was hard and fierce the battle;
[If you had seen King Gormont stand there]
He struck and slew, he gored and gashed them!
Each man he met he stripped from saddle,
And dressed anew in death's apparel!
Thierry of Termes spurred at him
Upon his bay, Castile-bred stallion;
He drew his rein at Gormont's standard
And struck so well the shield he carried
He broke the boards, the buckler shattered;
But his spear too split into fragments,
And Gormont drew his sword from scabbard
And struck it through his helmet's panels;
The head flew right, and, dropping, landed
On grass of green at Gormont's ankles;
With ringing voice he hailed him gladly –
The French there heard him all too sadly:
"This God of yours is such a bad one,
He cannot save his bravest vassals!"

On striking down the worthy count,
Towards his men he drove the mount;
His lance-head then he faced about
And grasped the shield they passed him out.

ABOVE CAYEUX, upon the grass,
The fight was hard, the battle harsh;
Behold the count of Flanders charge
Across the ground full-tilt and fast!
He saw Gormont the Moor at last

And on his shield he struck him hard;
He broke the boards, he split the targe,
And hauberk white he cleft apart –
But did the flesh beneath no harm;
Then Gormont hurled his wyvern-dart:
From front to rear the weapon carved
And struck the ground behind its mark;
His body fell, its spirit passed,
And Orient's lord, Gormont, remarked:
"What fools they are, this folk of France!
What foolish hope bides in their hearts,
When at my shield they aim their lance!
Not one shall boast when day is dark!"

On striking down the worthy count,
Towards his men he drove the mount;
His lance-head then he faced about
And grasped the shield they passed him out.

THE FIGHTING FLARED and flamed again
As Eudon came, count of Champagne;
With Chartres and with Blois he claimed
Château-Landon in Gatinais;
An Arab steed he rode that day,
On Gormont's shield his lance to lay;
He struck and smote its black away
And hauberk white he cleft of mail;
But Gormont's flesh he failed to scathe,
So drew his sword, made in Kolane;
On Gormont's helm three blows he rained
And stunned the Moor, who stooped and swayed;
He would have killed him then, I'd say,
When at his horse an Irish knave
Cast forth a dart that found its aim;
Said Gormont: "Ah, now that's a shame!
Back in Etampes you should have stayed!
Your Moorish horse is more than lame!
For months you'll not ride him again!
Right here with me you'll have to stay:
Upon this heath your head you'll lay!"
He cast a dart, both strong and straight,

But this time God was there to aid:
The Frenchman's flesh he failed to scathe,
And Eudon turned in his escape.

THE FIGHTING FLARED and flamed afresh
As on all sides the battle spread;
See Poitou's count divide the press
Upon his steed of white and red!
He saw Gormont upon the crest,
And if he'd spurned to joust him then,
He would have held his honour dead;
He drove his steed with such duress
Its crimson blood flew right and left;
On Gormont's shield his shaft was set
And struck its bands of iron so well
He broke the boards, the buckler cleft;
The burnished coat he ripped and wrecked
But failed to scathe King Gormont's flesh,
Who drew his sword of graven edge
[Then brought it down with brutal strength]
And cleft the count from brow to belt;
The best of kings, the best of men
That ever was of heathen bred,
With ringing voice cried out and said:
"For good and all you've met your end!
Your God on High was little help!"

On striking down the worthy count,
Towards his men he drove the mount;
His lance-head then he faced about
And grasped the shield they passed him out.

THE FIGHT WAS HARD and fierce the battle,
As on all sides men clashed and clamoured;
A Norman count spurred forth his stallion,
The lord of Rheims; it was this baron
Who at Fécamp first built the abbey;
He sent no spy, he sent no vassal,
But went himself to joust the Arab;
One lance's length he threw him backwards,
And had the shaft itself not shattered,

So Saint-Denis' own charter has it,
That blow would have laid low the Savage!
But Gormont hurled his wyvern at him:
From front to rear it sheared a passage,
Then bursting out his back, it battered
A Lombard lad of noble standing;
Their bodies fell, their spirits vanished;
With ringing voice King Gormont ranted:
"What fools they are, this Frankish rabble!
What reckless pride, what mighty madness,
To show their face and then attack me!
Not one shall boast tonight of valour:
They'll die or lie in mortal anguish!"

On striking down the worthy counts,
Towards his men he drove the mounts;
His lance-head then he faced about
And grasped the shield they passed him out.

THE FIGHT WAS HARD, the battle wild;
Behold Ernault of Ponthieu shire!
Saint-Valéry was his by right,
And at the Moor he'd sworn to strike!
He hit his shield and split it wide
And ripped and wrecked the byrnie's hide;
He drove the spear against his side
And forced the flag, atop it tied,
Against his ribs and out behind;
The crimson blood flew left and right,
As Ernault said: "Yes, here am I!
This ground, and lands around are mine;
I serve no lord or other knight,
Except Lord God, Who never lies,
And Louis, who is France's Sire!
This charge it was my lance supplied!"
"I felt it well!" the Moor replied:
"But where you dwell, I'll dwell nearby!"
He gripped his blade of golden gripe
And struck so well the helmet bright
From brow to belt he split the knight,
Whose body fell and soul took flight;

With ringing voice the Pagan cried:
"You've come to grief for good this time!
He's little help, this Jesus Christ,
Who on the Cross was judged to die
By foolish Jews, and crucified!
Do you still think He rose on High
And has the power to save your life?
What kind of help can He provide,
Who could not save His own poor hide!
By good Apollo, like you, He died!"
At this, the gallant Hugh arrived,
The one whose visit I've described!
And when he heard our Lord reviled,
His heart was filled with darkest spite;
He drove the steed he sat astride
Until he reached King Louis' side;
He hailed him then and spoke his mind:
"Ah, noble King of gallant line,
Have you beheld this Antichrist
Who slays us all before your eyes
And slights the Lord with slanders vile?
It fills my heart with darkest spite!
So help me God, Who never lies,
Though I should die, I'll not decline
From striking him in joust or fight,
Whatever fate awaits me, Sire!"
The Emperor at once replied:
"But, come now, Hugh, my brother fine,
Will you as well desert my side?
If you are slain alike, then I've
No comrade left, nor friend alive."

2. Hugh's challenge

GOOD HUGH REPLIED: "I must, my lord;
My sire was brave and his before,
And I myself am nobly born
And should be bold in deed and thought!
So help me God, the Lord of all,
No mortal hand shall halt my course:
I'm off to smite that blighted Moor!"

The King leant down to seize his horse,
But Hugh swayed right and, letting fall
His horse's rein, he spurred it forth,
Then used his spear to reach the fore;
He rode like none of mortal born,
But thundered like a raging storm,
Not stopping till he reached the Moor;
He struck so well his buckler's boards
He split them wide and broke them all;
But his own spear was snapped and shorn,
So gallant Hugh withdrew his sword
And smote his helm with such a force
That Gormont fell upon all fours;
He would have killed him then, I'm sure,
But Pagans rushed to his support;
As Gormont stood, Hugh flung a taunt
Which gave the Moor no joy at all:
"Sir Hugh it is who's stopped you short –
The same man whom you've seen before,
Inside your camp in Louis' cause;
In maiden's dress your meal I brought –
A peacock served upon a board:
But something shocked and locked your jaws!"
Said Gormont: "All is fair in war,
And you deserve a fair reward!
Before you've worn this ground much more,
I'll pay you warmly, rest assured!"
His spear aloft, a blow he scored
On Hugh's left side, where flesh was torn
Which wet his horse's cloth with gore
And forced brave Hugh to sway and fall.

WITH RINGING VOICE the Moor exclaimed:
"You boast too much, you foolish knave!
I know you, Hugh, make no mistake:
You graced my tent the other day
And placed a peacock upon my plate,
But stopped my mouth some magic way,
Except from grunting some foolish phrase;
Then, shamefully, you stole away
My champion's best destrier!

But rest assured, I'll make you pay –
I'll lay you dead upon this plain;
Not one more 'yes' or 'no' you'll say:
No doctor in the world today
Shall save you now from mortal pain;
This God of yours – He's little aid!"
"Your words are wind!" said Hugh the brave:
"My acton's all that's felt your blade;
My fur-lined coat you've somewhat frayed,
But don't you fret – we'll meet again!
You'll see me riding through the fray
And crying out my Monarch's name,
Brave Louis, son of Charles the Great!
How glad are they our flag sustains!
How sad are they of Pagan ways!"
Hugh leapt upon his feet and raised
His shining spear: my friends, in faith
He would have slain the Moor, I'd say,
When at him leapt an Irish knave!
Hugh struck him down with all his rage:
At Gormont's feet he met his fate;
Remounting then his Gascon bay,
Hugh rode around the field of fray;
His gonfalon, unfurled, he waved,
And cried aloud his Monarch's name,
Brave Louis, son of Charles the Great!
How glad were they his flag sustained!
How sad were they of Pagan ways!
Across the field he turned his rein
To joust Gormont the Moor again:
He struck his rounded shield so straight
That Gormont's knees both hit the plain;
But as Hugh turned, all Gormont's hate
Impelled his spear at brave Hugh's waist
And felled him on the sandy plain.

HUGH STOOD UPON the field, for twice
King Gormont's spear had struck his side;
And then his horse ran off in fright;
When Isembart, the rebel knight,
Beheld his old horse running wild,

One thought alone ran through his mind:
If he could gain it, using guile,
He'd rather lose his limbs and life
Than lose that horse a second time!
So, speeding up, with all his might
He used the grip upon his pike
And tried to halt the horse's flight;
He failed, my friends, although he tried,
Because it held its head too high!
Then Hugh himself moved up to try:
He stalked the horse with lengthy strides,
And as the steed came speeding by,
He grasped its reins, all golden-bright,
Then gripped the bows and swung astride;
From crossbows shafts flew left and right
And archers shot and troops arrived,
But, striking blows, he broke their lines
And drew back, somewhat, from the fight;
His wounds wept blood without respite:
His heartbeat stopped – he fell and died;
Friends, what a loss, was that one's life,
For Hugh, he was a noble knight
And always brave in battle's strife;
Across the field his faithful squire
And nephew too, his sister's child,
Young Gontier, fought with all his might;
At Saint-Riquier the charter writes
That seven days had not gone by
Since Hugh had armed him as a knight;
So when he saw his liege lord die,
His grief was great, his rage alike;
In angry haste he reached his side
And grasped his horse and held it tight,
Then gripped the bows and swung astride;
He held aloft his sword of iron,
Whose blade was chipped and coated by
The crimson blood of heathen lives;
He saw the Moor upon his rise
And struck so well the helmet's stripes
He slit its straps of leather hide;
Strong Gormont's knees, they buckled wide,

As in reproof good Gontier cried:
"Gormont, you are a king by right,
But do you know again the squire
Who stood at Hugh the envoy's side,
Within your tent, a few days by?
I stole a cup of gold, which I
Presented to Saint-Riquier's shrine;
For setting his fine church on fire,
You well deserve to pay the price!"
King Gormont gave him this reply
With ringing voice and stinging pride:
"Away from me, you snivelling child!
I'm from a proud and princely line,
Whose great prowess is richly prized!
I will not fight today with squires!"

3 . Gormont's death

WHEN LOUIS, KING of all the French,
Saw all his knights and all his friends
Lose limb or life to Gormont's strength,
His grief was great, his woe unchecked:
"Lord God above, alas for them!"
The King of all the Frenchmen said:
"I must have been bereft of sense
To not oppose this Fiend myself
In single fight before the rest;
I am a King, and he no less;
One combat would have been the best;
Whichever one had gained success,
So many knights would not have bled,
And such prowess lie maimed or dead;
Brave St Denis, assist me yet!
From you I hold my mighty realm
And bow the knee to no one else
Except Lord God on High Himself;
Brave St Riquier, I need your help!
This villain burned the church you bless,
But I'll rebuild and raise its *flèche*
By thirty-seven feet, I pledge!

Saints, bless my horse and guide its steps
Towards the Moor, this Fiend from Hell!"
He spurred his mount, when this was said,
As Gormont hurled three spears ahead;
God's mercy saved King Louis' breast
As all three failed to scathe his flesh;
But Louis' rage grew more intense:
He sent no sign of his intent,
But raised his pike above his head
And struck the Moor with such prowess
He split apart his pointed helm
And hauberk's coif from edge to edge,
And cleft the Moor from brow to belt;
He split apart and fell down dead,
As Louis' pike, alike, fell next;
With such a will King Louis went
To strike, he almost fell himself,
But held on just, hands tightly clenched
Around his sturdy stallion's neck;
Yet what a weight his hauberk lent,
And helm of green upon his head,
And banded shield about his neck!
And what a weight they added, when
He seized his pike from where it fell,
Six inches long from edge to edge;
He gave his life to save his men,
For as he sat upright again,
Beneath his feet the stirrups bent
And leathers stretched three fingers' length:
He sat up with such savage strength,
He burst the lungs inside his chest;
In thirty days he died, my friends;
And what a loss was Louis' death:
He was of knights the noblest bred,
Forever brave in battle's stress,
And wise in counsel of Christian men;
The song says this, and it's correct:
No lawful heir's ruled France since then.

THE MOORS, ON SEEING Gormont die,
Turned round towards the port in flight;

The Renegade heard all their cries
And spurred back to their flag to find
King Gormont dead, upon the rise;
Across his corpse he swooned three times:
"Alas!" he cried, "Those fates were right,
That said if I took Gormont's side,
I'd soon be caught or lose my life;
Now I know well their words were wise."

4. Isembart's stand

THREE DAYS THE FIGHT endured between
King Louis' force and Gormont's fiends,
Then, on the fourth, that faithless breed
Of Pagan Moors began to flee
Across Vimeu and Ponthieu's fiefs
To allods in Saint-Valéry;
The Renegade heard all their shrieks
And spurring forth, hailed all and each:
"You craven Moors, where can you flee?
Upon this land you'll find no peace!
You have no kin or comrades here
To offer you a safe retreat!
Turn back, I say, and follow me,
And we'll avenge our great Emir,
Our leader, lord of all Leutice,
Who gave us lands with hands so free,
And fur-lined coats of grey and cream,
And castles, forts and mighty keeps."
The Moors, however, paid no heed,
And turned in flight towards the sea;
When Isembart beheld them leave,
The Renegade felt rage so deep
He almost went berserk with grief;
He made his stand upon the field
And struck a knight known as Seguin,
Full cousin to King Louis he;
His pike ran through and cleft his shield,
Then ripped and wrecked the mail beneath;

With all the force of shining steel
He ran him through from front to rear,
Which slew and threw him from his steed;
Then two more French of high degree
Were slaughtered by The Rebel's spear,
Before he spurred across the field.

KING GORMONT, DEAD upon the grade,
Lay bathed in blood, his mouth agape;
Sir Isembart, upon his way,
Turned rein to where the Moor was lain
And swooned with grief and bitter pain;
Friends, hear the great lament he made:
"Strong Emperor, ill-starred your fate!
I told you, time and time again,
At Cirencester, in your domains,
The French had valour in their veins!
And on the boat you heard me say
That fierce would be the force you'd face –
And now you've learnt the truth too late,
About this fine and gallant race!
No others born could be as brave
Or ever take their lands away!
Ill-starred your fate, good king and great!
How fine you were! How fair of face!
How blithe you were! How bright your gaze!
And now – how bleak and black a change!
Ah Louis, Sire, how strong to save
And serve sweet France you were today!
How dear a price this Prince has paid!
But I must lead the force he raised,
While I may still gird on my blade."
Both all and each once more he hailed:
"Where can you flee, you stranded strays,
Without a king, in country strange?
Turn back with me along these lanes
And seek revenge for Gormont's sake,
[Who gave us all the wealth we've gained]
In silver, gold – our soldiers' wage,
And fur-lined coats of cream and grey."

Their fears forgot, the Moors obeyed
And turned to fight on lane and plain;
King Louis' ranks were strict and straight,
The King himself in pride of place,
When once again the Pagans came;
So many blows their blades exchanged!
So many spears were shorn in twain!
So many Moors, on country lanes
And grass of green found bloody graves!

TO GORMONT'S FLAG, upon the crest,
Where now that Satan lay in death,
From every side those Pagans pressed:
"Upon your faith, well-born and bred
Sir Isembart, don't fail us men!"
"I never will," the Frenchman said,
"As long as I have life and strength!
Do not despair, but fight your best!"

5. Louis' noblesse

FOUR FURTHER DAYS the fight went on
Beyond the death of King Gormont;
For Isembart remained that long
With Moors some forty thousand strong;
Among the French they charged non-stop
And slaughtered scores upon the spot;
King Louis' ranks were chosen from
Ten thousand of the best he'd got;
Among the Moors they charged non-stop
And slaughtered more upon the spot
Than I could say or tell you of;
King Louis climbed the crest ere long
And found the Moor where he had dropped
When slain by him in righteous wrath;
Most nobly he bemoaned the loss:
"Alas," he said, "Emir Gormont,
Ill-starred your birth, fine champion!
Had you believed in our Lord God,
A better man no land could want!"

Then Louis showed his royal bond:
He bore back to his tent Gormont,
[Upon his breast a shield embossed.]

KING LOUIS FOUND King Gormont dead,
Beside his flag, upon the crest;
Most nobly then he made lament:
"Ill-starred your birth and your prowess!
Had you known God, Who made all flesh,
A better man no land had bred!"
Then Louis showed his great noblesse:
He bore the Moor back to his tent,
A rounded shield upon his breast;
Then, riding back among the press,
He found Count Hugh, who'd bled to death;
Young Gontier knelt beside his head,
Who'd been his squire and still was yet;
Inside a fur they wrapped him well
Upon a Gascon stallion's neck,
And bore him thus to Louis' tent;
The King held firm the rings himself;
They laid him down upon a bed
That faced the place the Moor lay dead.

6. Isembart's death

THE FRAY WAS FIERCE, and, on one side,
Sir Miles the Sturdy fought this time
With Isembart in single fight;
He would have claimed Sir Miles's life,
When old Bernart himself arrived,
The Rebel's father, the charter writes,
And smote a blow so fierce and wild
Upon his shield he split it wide;
But Isembart returned the spite:
He split his father's buckler wide
And slit the mail of burnished iron;
From hide to heart he drove his pike
But failed to scathe the flesh inside:
The father fell, the horse ran by,

And Isembart reined in the prize;
While Bernart stared, he swung astride
And never asked for leave or right!
My friends, it was a sinful crime
For Isembart to fell his sire –
But both men fought unrecognised!
If he had known, he would have tried
To touch his heart quite otherwise;
[But now, my friends, behold him ride]
And cut a swathe through Louis' knights!
Each man he met was checked mid-stride
And, once addressed, not once replied,
Unless the Lord restored his life.

THE FIGHT WAS HARD and fiercely fought;
The Pagans yelled with ringing voice:
"Ah, Isembart, you have forsworn
Your Christian Faith and Gormont's cause!
These Frenchmen fight with mighty force!
Ill-starred we came to Ponthieu's shore,
To lands you said we'd take by storm!
In all of this you've played us false!"
But Isembart harangued them all:
"You faithless Saracens and Moors!
You wretched race of herded hordes!
For every Frenchman here, I'm sure
There're thirty men of you, and more!
Defend your sorry selves, therefore,
If you would live to see the dawn."
And so they did, when thus he talked.

THE FIGHTING FLARED and flamed afresh,
As on all sides the battle spread;
But all the Moors gave way at length,
Worn out with pain and strain and stress,
And all with hunger hard oppressed;
They turned in flight to flee the French,
Who raced and chased right after them;
Without their boats, at anchor left
When they'd arrived upon their quest,
Not one would have escaped from death.

As startled deer dart over moorland,
Those Irish rogues fled over shore-land;
In hot pursuit on rapid horses
Rode Louis and his loyal forces.

THE PAGANS FLED in scattered groups,
But Isembart remained, unmoved,
Surrounded by two thousand troops;
The man he struck bade life adieu,
For pointed helm was little use,
Nor hauberk white: his pike ran through
And split them, brow to belt, in two;
[Four Frenchmen then spurred into view,]
The first three counts, the fourth a duke;
The first one split his buckler through,
The others speared his hauberk smooth
And scathed his flesh with three great wounds,
As from his horse they hacked him too;
They knew not who he was, in truth,
And galloped on in hot pursuit.

WHERE THREE PATHS CROSS the Renegade
Fell down at last, in mortal pain;
Within a glade, well-leafed for shade,
He called to mind the Lord God's name,
Then spoke aloud so fine a phrase,
His soul, I'd say, was surely saved:
"St Mary, fairest, blessed Maid
And Mother of Lord God," he prayed:
"Ah! I was told before we sailed,
By Pagan Moors who read the fates,
That if I came to these domains,
I would be either caught or slain;
Their words were wise, that much is plain!
Lord, help me now," the Rebel prayed,
"Who on the Cross were cruelly nailed
And on that Friday died to save
All those who heed the Christian Faith:
Who in that blessed grave were laid,
Whence three days later You rose again;

As You did this, in truth, I say,
Have mercy on my soul this day!
Forgive them, Lord, those barons brave
Who've slaughtered me for Your love's sake!
St Mary, fairest, blessed Maid
And Mother of Lord God," he prayed:
"Please ask your Son to show His grace
Upon this lamb that went astray."
Then Isembart saw in a dale
An olive-tree well-leafed for shade;
He struggled down with utmost strain
And sat upon the grass of May;
Towards the East he turned his face
And, falling down, said: "Mine the blame."
Then raised himself a little way...

THE SONG OF WILLIAM

(c.1100–1120)

Introduction

The *Chançun de Willame*, considered by some to be the finest surviving Old French epic poem after the *Chanson de Roland*, is preserved in only one thirteenth century manuscript copy, held currently at the British Library in London. The copy itself presents a reworking of older material from two different sources, the first of which may even predate the *Chanson de Roland*, and both of which establish its narrative as a foundation work of the William of Orange epic cycle. This group of poems celebrates the legendary exploits of an illustrious family which, during the times of Charlemagne and of his son, Louis the Pious, led important campaigns against the Saracens in the South of France and in Spain. Up to seventeen of the corpus are contained, in legendary sequence, in the great cyclic manuscripts of the thirteenth and fourteenth centuries, and together they exhibit some of the noblest, funniest and most realistic writing in Old French literature.

The central character of the anonymous work that we possess, Count William of Orange, can be identified with the historical Count William of Toulouse, who was a grandson of Charles Martel and hence a cousin of Charlemagne himself. After the disaster of Roncesvalles in 778 the Emperor established the realm of Aquitaine, which was administered by nine counts, one of whom was replaced in 789 by Count William of Toulouse. In 793 a Saracen army under Hixem I invaded the Midi region of France, set fire to the outskirts of Narbonne and made for Carcassonne. At the head of a small band of men, William of Toulouse met with this force on the banks of the river Orbieu; the Christians were defeated but inflicted sufficient casualties upon the enemy for them to return to Spain with their booty. Intent on revenge, the Franks opened up a campaign which, starting in present-day Catalonia in 796, culminated in 803 with the siege and capture of Barcelona. According to the *Vita Hludovici*, composed by a monk known as the Limousin Astronomer, the French attack utilised three battalions: while King Louis himself stopped at Roussillon with the first, Botstagnus, Count of Gerona, took the second and laid siege to the town; the third, William among them, was sent some distance from Barcelona to prevent outside help from reaching those inside the town. Engaging the enemy, Count William again fought with outstanding valour and forced the Saracen troops, sent from Cordova, to return to the west of Spain. Upon his own return home, Count William of Toulouse entered Aniane as a monk in 804, founded the monastery of Gellone, later to be called Saint-Guilhem-du-Désert in his honour, and retired there in 806. He died on May 28, 813, was canonised in 1066, and is venerated on May 28.

The *Chançun de Willame* was probably first written down in the early years of the twelfth century, and presents, in condensed form, a poetic biography of the Count during that decade of 793–803. In the course of the intervening centuries, however, the names of places have been transmitted imperfectly or transposed intentionally, the exploits of William have undergone considerable embellishment, and the long and largely unknown oral traditions of epic chanting have created an elaborate legendary lineage for this hero-turned-saint, who himself emerges with a new name – that of William Hooknose, the Count and Marquis of Orange.

Although in their transformation from fact to fiction there is nothing but contradiction, inconsistency and downright fantasy in the several legends concerning William and his family and the places where they lived and fought, there is well-documented and substantial evidence of the growth and dissemination of these legends themselves. In a Latin elegy called *In honorem Hludowici*, written in 827, only fourteen years after the Count of Toulouse's death, one Ermold the Black portrays a swashbuckling William taking the lead in the conquest of Barcelona, and refers in two lines to the popularity of his deeds 'among the common folk.' The so-called *La Haye* fragment, dated between 980 and 1030, is a Latin prose exercise which describes the siege of Gerona by Charlemagne's forces, among whom are the knights Bertrandus, Bernardus, Ernaldus and Wibelinus. Although these four fighters have no historical authenticity, they can readily be identified as Bertrand, Bernart, Hernaut and Guielin, nephew and three brothers of the epic Count William Hooknose. It is certain that by 1125, when the monks of Gellone composed their *Vita Sancti Wilhelmi*, dedicated to William of Toulouse, his legend had already been the subject of many a *chanson de geste*. In chapter 5 of their *Vita*, before telling of William's monastic life, mention is made of his fight with the Saracen king Theobaldus outside the gates of Orange, and of his subsequent governorship of the town. Given that the historical William never conquered Orange, which was never in Saracen hands during Charlemagne's reign, and given that there could never have been a Moorish king with the Germanic name of Theobaldus anyway, it seems certain that the monks must have incorporated this information from the material related in the *chanson de geste* called *La Prise d'Orange,* a performance of which they allude to at the start of their own 'biographical' work.

The characters whom the unknown author of the *Chançun de Willame* inherited from the traditions of epic chant are, for the most part, a mixture of pure and impure fiction – a composite of competing personalities which were confused and then fused with the dominating legend of the Count of Toulouse. The exploits of some sixteen other historical Williams, for example, were eventually credited to the tally of the epic Marquis William himself. Count Vivien, the martyr-knight, whose agonising death on Archamp field and the subsequent revenge that it prompts form the first half of the present poem, is probably patterned on both Vivianus of Tours, who died fighting the Bretons in the army of Charles the Bald in 851, and a certain Venantius, a fifth century Gallic convert, who was killed fighting the Pagans during a siege of the city of Arles. Whereas Vivianus's body had no proper burial, Venantius was laid to rest in the famous cemetery at Arles, called Aliscans (Archamp in the present poem). Although William's parents, brothers and plentiful nephews in the poem have no proven identity with any historical figures or merging of figures, some of them are thought to correspond with illustrious members of the House of Narbonne during the eleventh and twelfth centuries. It seems fairly certain that the historical prototype of Lady Guibourc can be found in the Count of Toulouse's first wife, called Witburgh. The Pagan counterpart of Louis the Pious, Desramed the Emir, can also be identified with the Arab leader Abd-Er Rahman, who invaded Gaul in 732, took possession of Bordeaux and was subsequently defeated by Charles Martel. The churl-hero Renewart, however, whose fantastic and humorous exploits dominate the second half of the poem, is undoubtedly a figure of purely bardic creation.

Exactly why and how the historical William's deeds at Barcelona should have been transferred to the epic William's battle at Archamp-on-the-sea (which it is not), remain a mystery, as does the relocation of his seat of power from Toulouse through Barcelona to Orange. Accuracy, consistency, or even feasibility in matters geographical are goals for which the majority of *chanson de geste* poets, performers or recorders seem rarely to have striven. The thirteenth century scribe who has joined the disparate Vivien and Renewart stories into his copy of the poem makes little attempt to unify any narrative or stylistic elements of his two sources, and there are consequently so many contradictions and confusions in the manuscript as we have it, that most scholars have divided their appreciation of the text into that of the *Chançun de Willame* proper (ll.1–1980) and that of the *Chançun de Rainouart* (ll.1981–3554).

Artistic Achievement

In neither section of the poem as we now have it is there the unity of plot or tone which characterises the written genre's great progenitor, the *Chanson de Roland*, and which makes that work such an outstanding example of sustained epic diction. The mood and style of the *Willame* are much more like those of the great majority of the extant Old French epics, bearing the heavy imprint of their oral tradition, and varying, often jarringly to our   modern sensibility, from the elevated to the humorous and the downright crude. This sense of unevenness strikes any *reader* of the poem first, and is unfortunately accentuated by the extremely corrupt nature of the surviving copy itself – well over half the lines in the manuscript are defective in either length or assonance, and frequently in both. However, the writing is imbued with the energy, comedy and realism which pervade the whole William of Orange cycle, and exhibits frequent moments of great profundity and narrative skill.

The two halves of the one work which has come down to us are given some cohesion by the strong and sympathetic characterisation of Count William throughout and by a certain consistency in his interaction with a small but diverse cast of credible and interesting personalities. The human strengths and weaknesses with which the original poets have endowed him render him perhaps the most engaging figure created in the whole genre. We admire his innate cheerfulness, his bravery, decisiveness and sheer effrontery when fighting or escaping from the Saracens, and we are moved by his faithfulness to his wife Guibourc and to his nephew Vivien, both of whom deserve it, and to his liege-lord King Louis, who does not. We can only sympathise with the contempt he feels for his selfish sister, King Louis' wife, for the cowardly knights and turncoats in his own army and for certain of his heathen adversaries, and with his own frustration at the ungrateful monarch he defends and the fickle barons whom he has served and who will not serve him in his need. We can identify with his depressions and with his confessions of self-doubt, but above all we can love him for his ability to laugh in the face of danger and at himself. William Hooknose, the hero, is three hundred and fifty years old, a wise and experienced leader, loved or feared by high and low, and held in awe by friend and enemy alike. He is strong enough to outwit the Saracens and to stand up to his liege lord King Louis, yet at times he is no match for the wit and gentle mockery of his wife Guibourc, or that of his young nephew Gui, or even that of the untutored, pole-swinging kitchen-boy Renewart.

It is in the exploitation of this discrepancy between heroic outlook and human behaviour that much of the comedy of situation and incident, which borders on parody, and which is such a feature of all the Orange cycle of poems, arises. In both halves of the poem it helps to define and develop the personalities of all the protagonists. Guibourc, Count William's wife, and Gui, his nephew, are both noble and worthy partners of William the hero, but are also presented humorously and movingly as foils to William's old age. The portrait of Guibourc is particularly well drawn. A convert to Christianity, she is an energetic, enterprising, loyal and witty wife who helps to belie and gently belittle William's weaker moments. She prepares huge meals for her husband and commends his healthy appetite as an innate proof of his self-doubting vigour. She assembles on her own initiative an army of thirty thousand men and lies brazenly to them about William's achievements in order to enlist their support. She offers them inducements of beautiful maidens, while telling William that if he does not bring back her nephew Guischard alive, she herself will withhold all conjugal favours. The loyalty and love which William openly displays towards his convert queen illustrate one of those rare occasions in the *chanson de geste* corpus where the Saracen Princess motif complements the epic tone of the narrative into which it is introduced. The essence of Guibourc's personality, her energetic fidelity, represents a quality totally lacking in that of the only other female character in the poem, Count William's unnamed sister, the French Queen, whose slothful self-indulgence and carping ingratitude are themselves presented in obvious contrast to the merits of William's wife. Lord Gui, the fifteen year old brother of Count Vivien, is too young for the rigours of battle. He is inexperienced but has all the eagerness and audacity that inexperience lends, and it is precisely because young Gui is both unprepared but ready for anything that his character comes alive as both a charge and a comfort to his ageing uncle, according to the latter's changing moods. Whenever Gui, in his blunt effrontery, seems to be challenging his uncle's 'heroic' authority, William very humanly interprets this juvenile exuberance as a brash attack upon his own person. The amusing yet serious conflict of the 'generation gap' is thus ever present in their exchanges:

> *"But who will rule my borders when I die?*
> *I have no son of my own loins and line."* ...
>
> *"In faith, my lord, I've never heard the like!*
> *For I would rule your borders, if you died,*
> *And serve Guibourc with all my heart and mind;*
> *No evil I could guard her from would thrive,*
> *For she has cared for me throughout my life."*
> *On hearing this, the Count groaned at the child*
> *And answered him in tones of bitter spite:*
> *"You are more fit to sit beside the fire,*
> *Than on the seat that rules my mighty shires!"*
>   (ll. 1434–54)

William's retort betrays a certain touchiness about his age and capabilities, and, in the battle of wits between the two, young Gui holds the upper hand. He is a coldly logical young man whose curt replies to all of William's protests become his *leit-motif* in the poem. Neither the battle nor the wit is all one-sided, however. When William spots the runaway youth dwarfed by both his steed and his weapons, he calls out, mockingly:

> *"Who is that well-armed boy*
> *Perched on a horse among you, riding tall?*
> *He's short on men who brought that one to war!"*
>   (ll. 1616-18)

William's criticism of the boy's immaturity is shown to be partly justified when, during the second battle on Archamp, young Gui loudly laments his hunger and thirst. In retrospective mood he misses the loving-kindness and regular meals that he received from Guibourc's hands, and William, busy in the field, must take time out to find him something to eat and to drink. On another occasion Gui, showing his ignorance and disregard for the rules of battle, decapitates Desramed the emir whom William has maimed and laid helpless on the field – an action which again invokes William's wrath, and which again Gui must talk his way out of. It is to William's credit, however, that he recognises young Gui's potential. Single-handedly he frightens away twenty thousand Saracens who feel that they have been struck by lightning or, equally frightening, that Count Vivien has come back to life. Gui does in fact save William from certain death, as he told Guibourc he would, and William embraces him as the new great hope of the family:

> *He beckoned Gui to come to him and kiss him;*
> *Three times they kissed, then William told his kinsman:*
> *"In truth, my boy, your words display much wisdom;*
> *Though still a child, you have a warrior's spirit;*
> *To you indeed may all my lands be given!"*   (ll. 1476-80)

Despite the all-pervading presence of Count William Hooknose, it is true to say that the central character of the poetic structure in the first half of the poem is his nephew Vivien, and in the second half the youth Renewart. The two characters would appear at first glance to have nothing whatsoever in common, there being nothing but tragedy attached to the fate of the first and nothing but comedy attached to the behaviour of the second. If viewed, however, as figures representing two extreme positions across a broad spectrum of Christian faith, we can appreciate both of them as the two most symbolic characters, if therefore the two least capable of arousing our empathy, in the whole work as we have it. Vivien's relationship with his uncle distinguishes itself completely from that of the other characters in the first half of the poem. Whereas the latter offer perspective, the former is as one-dimensional as the ideal it represents. It is the ideal relationship between the vassal-knight and the liege lord, and as such can be compared with that of Roland and Charlemagne in the *Song of Roland*. The parallel seems valid and intentional. With both Roland and Vivien, faith in their liege lord and in God is absolute, hence their courage is complete in itself. If Roland's character succeeds more as an artistic creation, it is partly because Vivien is even more the perfect knight, who combines the bravery of a Roland with the wisdom of an Oliver. He is free of that pride of Roland's which made him eager to join battle without the proper and needed support from his lord. Vivien repeatedly requests Thibaut to summon William, so that Christianity as a whole may triumph. His stubborn and lonely resistance upon Archamp is not that of the arrogant fighter, too proud to acknowledge any human defeat, but that of a model Christian, whose pledge to God binds him to a passion of unrelenting severity unmatched by any other knight. His agonising, lonely and lowly death in the first battle on Archamp field render him a Christ-like martyr to his extreme vision of faith and faithfulness. In an evident parallel to Christ in Gethsemane, the young count shrinks one instant from his inevitable fate:

"Sweet Mary mild, most ever blessed Maiden,
As you, in truth, bore Jesus Christ our Saviour,
Protect me now with your most gracious favour
From death this day among Desramed's Pagans."
This said, at once young Vivien bewailed it:
"That was a foul and foolish way of praying,
To try and save myself from mortal danger,
When our Lord God Himself refused the same thing,
Who suffered death upon the Cross to save us
From mortal woes and all the wiles of Satan."   (ll. 813-22)

This identification with Christ of the 'tragic' hero on the point of death is one of several thematic similarities between the first half of the *Chançun de Willame* and the contemporaneous epic fragment *Gormont et Isembart*, and it is in such artistic details that the religious inspiration of the earliest *chansons de geste* is overtly shown.

It is not difficult, likewise, to sense the presence of the *Chanson de Roland* in the dramatic structure of the *Chançun de Willame*. As in the *Roland*, the story falls into two halves which tell of the death and subsequent avenging of a proud, young, much loved nephew and knight. Vivien, like Roland, is betrayed and left to die – but only after a succession of duels celebrate his heroic martyrdom and herald the inevitable victory of the Christian cause. The poet of the *Willame*, however, makes at least as much of the theme of kinship's bonds as that of religious fervour. William's loss at Archamp is more of a family loss than a Christian loss. His family's presence at Louis' court helps him secure the aid he needs to avenge this loss. His motive to avenge is the loss of a nephew and the liberation of kinsmen, not the loss of a kingdom and the liberation of a faith. The worthiest reward he can give to Renewart, who achieves all of this for him, is to baptise him and then to have him wed his favourite nephew's widow.

A rich vein of realism, which sets the first half of the *Chançun de Willame* apart from almost every other *chanson de geste*, pervades the entire section, running through almost all of the battle scenes, which are described in the most gruesome detail, shaping the cruel and crude comedy directed at the cowardly knights and Pagan adversaries, and underlying the gentle humour which sustains the relationship between Count William and his wife. Guibourc is a more admirable than laughable Saracen princess, yet the combination of 'virile' energy with which she defends her palace, acting as seneschal, butler and suspicious gate-keeper, and 'exotic' sensuality inherent in her character-type, still raises a wry smile and adds another layer of humour to the first half of the surviving work.

Most scholars agree that the *Chançun de Willame* proper ends at line 1980 of the surviving manuscript, and that the remaining 1574 lines, relating principally to the exploits of a kitchen-boy of royal blood called Renewart, are a scribal addition, probably folkloric in their origin, and should be distinguished as the *Chançun de Rainouart*. There are certainly a number of inconsistencies in the complete narrative as we have it to support this claim. William's residence is given as Barcelona in the first half of the poem and as Orange in the second. Vivien's cousin and companion Girart dies in the first half of the poem but appears as one of the prisoners released by Renewart in the second. The scene between William and the pagan Alderufe in lines 2134–63 replicates almost exactly that between William and Desramed the emir in lines 1920–49. On a formal level, the lengthening of the *laisses*, or verse structures, as the text progresses, betrays two different artistic modes. The strong dramatic possibilities of the short assonating *laisse*, where the changing assonance of successive verses can be used with the syntactic flexibility of the epic formulas to create crescendos of emotion, are used to fine effect in the scenes between Vivien and the cowardly counts, William and Guibourc, William and Louis, William and Vivien, and William and Gui in the first half of the poem. On the other hand, the antics of Renewart in the second are detailed in descriptive verse-blocks of up to one hundred lines, where the assonance is often replaced by a full rhyme which plays no emotional role, and where the change of rhyme is at times almost chapter-like in its infrequency and in its function. Actions themselves become extenuated, secondary episodes interpose, descriptions become objective and self-important, and characters proliferate.

Because of the humorous incidents associated with his massive *tinel* or carrying-pole trimmed to a club, because of his trade as a kitchen-helper, his inordinate physical strength, slow-wittedness, naiveté, absent-mindedness and preoccupation with food and drink, Renewart, whose antics dominate the last one thousand lines of the text, can be viewed as both a comic and a burlesque figure. He is filled with the zeal of the newly converted Christian, although he has never been to church and is not even baptised. He yearns to slaughter as many heathens as he can, although he knows himself to be the son of the pagan emir Desramed. His unusual attempts to achieve this noble goal contrast sharply with the chivalric ideal and provoke laughter among the knights in the poem – and, no doubt, provoked laughter among both the aristocratic and popular audiences originally. He refuses to ride a horse and misuses conventional armour and weapons. His pole, even when held like a lance, kills both rider and mount. He champions a rank of runaways, refuses all courtesies and certainly gives none himself. The endowment of Renewart with noble parentage is a convenient, if not entirely convincing, poetic touch. It creates a tenuous connection between the two disparate sources of the current text, as Renewart is revealed as Guibourc's long-lost brother, and therefore brother-in-law to the hero of the entire song cycle. It also provides valid psychological motivation for Renewart's rough treatment of his fellow menials and fellow warriors, who constantly taunt him. More artfully, it allows him the social mobility required by the narrative to associate with and provoke mirth among the entire cast of Christian and Pagan characters.

Despite their substantial differences from each other, both halves of the song that has come down to us offer fine examples of poetic craftsmanship which the carelessness of the thirteenth century copyist has not destroyed. The emotive force of formulaic diction, so overpowering in the *Roland*, is used equally well in the scenes of battle and death in the *Willame*. The 'parallel' verses in which Girart lays down his arms are as skilfully wrought as those in which Roland says farewell to his sword:

> *"Alas, great spear, how you oppress my arm!*
> *What help are you to Vivien at Archamp,*
> *Who in great pain is fighting to the last?"*
> *Down on the field he cast away the lance.*

> *"Alas, great shield, how you oppress my neck!*
> *What help are you to Vivien near death?"*
> *Down on the field he cast it from his breast.*

> *"Alas, good helm, how you make my head ache!*
> *What help are you to Vivien the brave,*
> *Who fights for life on Archamp field this day?"*
> *Down on the field he cast the helm away.*   (ll. 716-26)

Likewise, the similar verses in the *Renewart* section of the poem, where William views the empty halls of his castle and the ruin of his lineage, contain some of the loveliest lines to be found in all of the genre that we possess today.

Like the persistent and mysterious invocation *'AOI'*, which concludes many a laisse in the manuscript of the *Chanson de Roland*, an abrupt refrain *'Evening of Monday'* occurs at the end (mostly) of thirty-one verses in the *Chançun de Willame*, changing three times to *'Evening of Wednesday'* and seven times to *'Evening of Thursday'*. These irregular, dissonant interjections add a certain dramatic force to the tale, and may also represent a praiseworthy attempt by the much maligned copyist to create a link between his disparate sources, by providing at least a logical time sequence and length for the campaign of battles at Archamp.

Sources and Influences

The sources of both halves of the *Chançun de Willame* as we have it today are highly conjectural. From its themes, versification techniques and formulaic diction, the first part of the surviving work appears closer in its poetic conception to the *Chanson de Roland* than does any other extant *chanson de geste*, and may have been directly inspired by a version of that famous legend. It may equally, however, have grown independently out of the oral and largely unknowable traditions of tenth and eleventh century heroic chanting. What seems certain is that the British Library manuscript has preserved one of the oldest surviving examples of medieval French epic poetry, and a copy of the foundation poem of the William of Orange song cycle. Despite the fantastic geography of the work, which suggests that an association with pilgrimage routes in southern France played little part in its genesis, some critics have sought to give a definite historical background to the poem. Indeed the *Annales Engolismenses* and the *Revelationes Audradi Modici* (c.853) describe in detail the campaign of Charles the Bald in 851 against the Bretons, and chronicle how Vivianus of Tours took over command of the army when the king had left, and how he was beaten and slain.

As stated earlier, the source or sources of the Renewart section of the poem are thought to be folkloric. There is no connection whatever between the Vivien and Renewart sources and it is quite incongruous in the surviving copy that Vivien should be avenged by Renewart, an unrelated kitchen-boy, rather than by his liege lord and uncle William. Analogies have been drawn between Renewart's revenge and the Atonement Theme in European folk-tales, while his actual character may be derived from the popular theme of a scorned young man winning universal esteem and the hand of a fair princess. There were probably at least two reasons for the introduction of a Renewart type – a churl-hero – by the *trouvères* into the chivalric gallery of *chanson de geste* protagonists. The first was to add a comic dimension, both of humour and satire, in an attempt to widen the appeal of the songs to a more popular audience. The second was to add a social dimension, and may well have reflected the contemporary rise of the *bourgeoisie* into prominence. Although there is little in the *Chançun de Willame* to characterise Renewart as a symbol of the people and a champion of the poor, as he undoubtedly is in several later epics, his obvious successes with his lowly pole, and his leadership of the rank of cowards, are testimonies perhaps to this poetic purpose and certainly of an artistic potential.

As we have seen, the poem translated here has been preserved in only one manuscript, outside of the cyclic tradition of its fellow William poems, and no prose continuations of it have been traced. However, the influence of the characters, themes and episodes that it or its original(s) introduced to the Orange cycle and to the whole genre itself can hardly be overestimated. During the Middle Ages, both inside France and across her borders, the fame of Count William was surpassed only by that of Roland, Oliver and Ogier the Dane. Twenty-four surviving *chansons de geste* deal with either the Count himself or with his legendary relatives, ancestors or descendants, and these poems themselves constitute one quarter of all the Old French epic tales that we possess. Four songs deal directly with Vivien's valour, and with the battle of Archamp, later called Aliscans. Of these the finest is *The Song of Aliscans*, in which the comic and social role of Renewart are skilfully sustained through 5,400 lines of primary plot and secondary intrigues. The four best known poems of the William cycle today are the shorter *Coronemenz Loois*, *Charroi de Nîmes* and *Prise d'Orange*, which chronicle William's rise to power, and the longer *Moniage Guillaume,* which tells touchingly and humorously of Count William's last years spent as a monk. In *Girart de Vienne*, the fifth poem contained in this present selection, its author transforms his title character, most certainly an historical figure, into the legendary great-uncle of the genre's William of Orange. However, it is through the introduction of the two characters of Renewart and Guibourc, that the *Chançun de Willame* or its source(s) can be credited with establishing the prototypes of the two stock figures which were to dominate all but a handful of the later epics – namely those of the comic 'churl-hero' and the amorous 'Saracen Princess.'

Renewart himself plays such an important role in several subsequent works that he may be said to have inspired his own song cycle. Like him, most of the other plebeian figures in the later *chansons de geste* display a fondness for victuals, possess great strength, and have a great attachment to an odd weapon. The most successful among these many literary successors are Robastre the ploughman in *Garin de*

Monglane, *La Chevalerie Doon de Mayence* and *Gaufrey*; Gautier the ploughman in *Gaydon*; Fromer the mariner in *Gaufrey*; young Richier the bastard in *Hugues Capet*; Hervis and Rigaut, father and son in *Garin le Loherain*, and Varocher in *Macaire*. Though the appearance of some of these characters is only episodic and obviously intended as brief comic relief, in *Gaufrey* and *Gaydon* it dominates the action. In *Hugues Capet*, where the bourgeois Hugh, son of a butcher, works his way up to become King of France, the social dimension of their role, glimpsed in *Willame* and revealed in *Aliscans*, is given the limelight. Renewart's all-conquering pole itself initiates a tradition of the 'unconventional weapon', which floods not only the later epics, but spills over into the *romans d'aventure* and touches even the age and pages of Rabelais. In *Gargantua*, Chapter 27, for example, Picrochole's men are decimated by brother Jean des Entommeure's use of his 'baston de la croix'.

Created by the *trouvères* in direct response to the growing popularity of the female-dominated *roman courtois*, the character-type of the Saracen Princess, smitten with love for a Christian knight, and fired with the zeal of the newly converted, finds its first embodiment in William's wife in this song. The romantic and comic dimensions of Guibourc's role in the *Willame* are developed charmingly by the unknown poet of *Aliscans*, but are expanded to absurdity by the authors of the thirteenth century epics. The romance is inherent in Guibourc's foreign sensuality, the comedy latent in the aggressive energy she brings to all tasks, some of them traditionally masculine, and in the plots she hatches against the Saracen enemy, her original kin. Guibourc's own appearance in the *geste Renewart*, and those of her many literary descendants, exploit to the full these two character traits. Among her more successful reincarnations are the characters of Floripas in *Fierabras*, Claresme in *Gaydon*, Flordepine in *Gaufrey*, the unnamed wife of the Emir in *Aspremont*, the Queen in *Les Enfances Renier*, and Princess Agaiete in *Guibert d'Andernas*. In epics like *Anseis de Mes*, *Simon de Pouille*, and *La Prise de Cordres et de Sebille*, the energy of Guibourc in the *Willame* degenerates, however, into the aberrant antics of women cast in a military role, which is probably intended as burlesque; it gasps its last in the novel-like romantic fantasy of a fourteenth century epic such as *Tristan de Nanteuil*, where the heroine Blanchandine earns fame for knightly feats, gives birth to a child, and then is completely metamorphosed into a man and becomes a father!

The legend of William of Orange certainly spread to Italy, where there are five extant manuscripts of an Italian prose text called *I Nerbonesi* which date from the fourteenth, fifteenth and sixteenth centuries, and in which the events featured in the *Chançun de Willame* are retold in their turn. There are three poems of *Willehalm* and *Rennewart* and a prose text in Middle High German, the *Willehalm* of Wolfram von Eschenbach being the best and most famous. Ironically, although the one copy we have of the *Chançun de Willame* is written in Anglo-Norman dialect, there is no evidence to suggest that the legend of William had any impact at all in England or on writing in English during the Middle Ages or later. Rare indeed are the literary collections such as Andrew Lang's *Book of Romance* and A. R. Hope Moncrieff's *Romance and Legend of Chivalry*, in which the famous deeds and family of this hero of medieval story-telling have been revealed to the English-speaking public. On the other hand, William (Guglielmo) and Renewart (Rinoardo) appear immediately and exclusively after Charlemagne and Roland as the *chanson de geste* heroes contemplated in Dante's vision of Paradise (*Divine Comedy*, Canto 18, 47).

Note to the Translation

The *Chançun de Willame* has been edited several times since it was bought from the private library of Sir Henry Hope Edwards in 1901 by George Dunn, who published a private edition of two hundred copies in 1903. The earliest scholarly editions attempted to 'normalise' the extremely corrupt text by 'correcting' its language and versification, most notably and successfully that of Hermann Suchier in 1911. The most critically acclaimed edition, however, that of Duncan McMillan, was published by the *Société des Anciens Textes Français* in 1949–50, and presents the manuscript without any unnecessary alterations. The edition made by Nancy Iseley, published by the University of North Carolina Press in 1961, does likewise. The most recent edition is that of Philip E. Bennett (Grant and Cutler, 2000), which is complemented, in a companion volume, by a thorough analysis of the poem's development from legend to text, and of its artistic merits. I have based my translation upon the Iseley edition, partly because it offers easy access to the poem for general readers, and partly because of its excellent glossary prepared by Guérard Piffard. In the interests of fluency, I have however assumed a normalised text, like Suchier's, maintaining a uniform past tense in narration and a strict syllable count within each line.

I am grateful to the University of North Carolina Press for its formal permission to translate from LA CHANÇUN DE WILLAME, edited by Nancy V. Iseley. Revised edition published 1961. Copyright © by The Department of Romance Languages and Literatures, University of North Carolina at Chapel Hill.

THE SONG OF WILLIAM

1. How Desramed the Moor invaded Archamp

FRIENDS, WILL YOU HEAR of bitter frays and battles:
Of Desramed, a Pagan king who challenged
Our Emperor, King Louis, and his barons,
Till William with greater force attacked him
And slaughtered him most gloriously at Archamp?
So many times he threw the Pagans backwards
And lost the best of all his men and vassals,
His nephew too, Sir Vivien the gallant,
Which filled his heart with everlasting sadness;
Evening of Monday.
Henceforth begins the song of William's valour!

KING DESRAMED set forth from Cordova;
He steered his fleet along the ocean's path
To the Gironde, his forces fully armed,
And pillaged there each port his warships passed.

HE SEIZED THE LANDS, he laid the borders waste;
He stripped the shrines of relics they contained;
He dragged away their noble knights in chains;
On Archamp field his fury fell one day.

ONE KNIGHT ESCAPED the Pagan's cruel stroke;
He rode to tell the Count of Bourges, Thibaut,
Who at that time was in his town of Bourges;
He found him there, inside the town he owned,
With Esturmi and Vivien the bold,
And new-dubbed knights, some seven hundred souls,
Each dressed alike in heavy hauberk-coats;
The knight arrived to tell his tale of woe.

47

2. *How Thibaut of Bourges received the news*

THIBAUT THE COUNT was coming back from vespers;
His nephew, Esturmi, walked at his elbow,
With Vivien, Count William's good nephew,
And new-dubbed knights, some seven hundred henchmen;
Thibaut was drunk, so drunk he'd lost his senses,
And by the hand his nephew held him steady;
The knight arrived to tell his tale of terror:
"God save Thibaut as he returns from vespers!
I have grim news of Desramed to tell you:
His fury fell this day on Archamp meadow."

"KING DESRAMED has come from Cordova;
He's steered his fleet along the ocean's path
To the Gironde, his forces fully armed,
And pillages your fief at every pass."

"HE'S SEIZED THE LANDS and laid the borders waste;
He's stripped the shrines of relics they contained;
He's dragged away your noble knights in chains;
Beware, my lord, lest they are led to Spain!"

"WHAT SHALL WE DO, good men?" Count Thibaut cried;
"Ride forth at once!" the messenger replied.

"SIR VIVIEN," he said, "what shall we do?"
"We cannot well do less!" replied the youth.

"THIBAUT, MY LORD," said noble Vivien,
"You are a count and held in high respect
By every lord that coastal land has bred;
Heed my advice and none will love you less:
Send envoys forth and summon all your friends!
Do not forget Count William himself:
In any fight his wisdom is the best
For guarding well and guiding ranks of men;
If he arrives, we'll vanquish Desramed."

"DON"T THINK OF THAT, my lord," Esturmi cried:
"Within this land, wherever Pagans strike,
The people call on William each time;
Though you arrive with twenty thousand knights,
And William rides up with only five,
Or three or four, a sum of paltry size,
And though you fight and beat the Moors outright,
The folk thank *him* for rescuing their lives;
Whoever goes, *he* gains the praise and prize;
We'll vanquish them, alone, I swear it, sire!
Your name and fame shall match Count William's pride!"
"My noble lords, I beg you," Vivien cried,
"We cannot beat the Moors with so few knights!
Send forth, I say, for William the wise,
Who is the best at leading men in fights;
We'll beat the Moors, if William arrives."
Said Esturmi: "This course is ill-advised,
For foreigners each day hold William high
And all our men rank lower in their eyes."
"He only speaks this way," Thibaut replied,
"Because he dares not come with us and fight."

SAID VIVIEN: "You know that is a lie!
For there is none of mother born to life,
Beyond the Rhine or any ocean's tide,
In Christian lands or Pagan realms alike,
Who dares to fight great battles more than I –
Save William Hooknose, the first of knights,
My own uncle, with whom I do not vie;
I do not set my worth at William's price."
Evening of Monday.

THEN THIBAUT SAID: "Bring wine again to me
And let me drink with my own Esturmi!
Before the dawn we'll seek out this Emir:
Folk all around will hear the Pagan screams,
The clash of shields, the shattering of spears."
The butler brought more wine to him in brief
And Thibaut drank, and so did Esturmi;
Count Vivien went to his lodge to sleep.

3. How Thibaut and Vivien set out for battle

THEN ALL THE MEN of Thibaut's fief assembled;
At break of dawn ten thousand stood in helmets;
Thibaut himself woke up in his high bedroom,
Opening a window to let the fresh air enter;
The sky was clear, the land was not, however:
He saw it heave with byrnies and with helmets
Of Pagan Moors, that wretched race of devils:
"God!" said Thibaut, "What can this vision beckon?"

"HAVE PITY, MEN, for love of Jesus Christ!
Some eighteen years have come and gone since I
First held this town and ruled the lands close by;
I never saw before so many knights
Who did not know which way to turn and ride!
Whatever towns or fortresses you strike
Will know defeat as soon as you arrive!
The lands you waste, what woe they will abide!"
"I know such talk," brave Vivien replied:
"Thibaut was drunk last night from his red wine;
Now he has slept his senses have revived;
We shall await Count William this time."
The men were mute who'd muttered low that night;
But most ashamed were those who'd boasted high.

COUNT VIVIEN the noble spoke again:
"I recognise such ravings, by my head!
Thibaut was drunk last night, but now he's slept
We shall await Count William himself."
Young Esturmi weaved through the throng of men;
He took Thibaut by his right hand and said:
"Do you recall, upon the vespers bell,
The bitter news that came of Desramed?"
Said Thibaut: "Have I sent for William yet?"
"No, lord, there is no time for him to help."

"YOU'LL HAVE THE FIEND around your neck ere evening,
If you delay for William to reach here."
Thibaut replied: "In that case, let us leave it."

He called for arms and his attendants heeded:
They helped him don his byrnie bright and gleaming.

UPON HIS HEAD they laced a helm of green,
Then at his side girt on his blade of steel,
As by the grip he grasped his mighty shield;
Within his hand they set a cutting spear,
And to the ground its pure white pennon streamed;
They brought him out his swift Castilian steed
And on the left he mounted up the beast;
He rode forth to a postern-gate to leave,
Ten thousand men in helmets at his rear;
King Desramed they sought on Archamp field.

4. How Thibaut left Vivien upon the field

FROM NOBLE BOURGES they left, with Thibaut leading
Ten thousand men, in armour bright and gleaming,
For Archamp field and Desramed the heathen:
But friends, they had a feeble lord in Thibaut;
Evening of Monday.
They came at length to Archamp on the seaboard.

THIBAUT LOOKED OUT across the open ocean;
He saw the sails of twenty thousand boats there
And said aloud: "I see their camp below us."
Said Vivien: "No, that cannot be so, lord;
That is a fleet of further Moors approaching!
If they are here, their camp will be much closer."
Then he rode on and saw out in the open
The poles of some five hundred tents in total;
Said Vivien: "This is their camp, I know it."
Thibaut spoke forth, the lord of Berry's holdings:
"Sir Vivien, ride up that ridge and over,
To estimate their fighting strength this moment,
How many men they have on land and ocean."
Said Vivien: "You should not make me go, lord;
I should, instead, charge down, my visor lowered,
Upon their field and strike the villains boldly –
For this is how Count William has shown me;
So help me God, I'll never spy on soldiers!"

"MY LORD THIBAUT," brave Vivien said then,
"You are a count and held in high respect
By every lord this coastal land has bred;
Ride up that ridge and estimate yourself
How many men on land and sea they've sent;
If you have men sufficient in their strength,
Then ride against these Moors and fight with them;
We shall prevail, with God Almighty's help;
But if you think we lack sufficient men,
Then hide your force along this valley's length
And send off messengers to summon friends;
Do not forget Count William himself;
In any fight his wisdom is the best
For guiding men and using their prowess;
If he arrives, we'll vanquish Desramed."
Thibaut replied: "Your words are wisely said."
He spurred his horse and climbed the ridge's crest;
He scanned the shore, along the water's edge,
And saw it filled with barges right and left,
With rapid skiffs and ships with armoured decks;
The sky was clear but not the land ahead;
Forgetting all in fear of certain death,
He spurred his steed back down the ridge again
To tell the news to all his waiting men.

"MY NOBLE HOUSE, what will become of us?
One thousand men they have against our one!
We shall be slain if we don't turn and run:
To save our lives let us escape at once!"

"SIR VIVIEN, with this rock-face to hide you,
Conduct our force along this deep divide here,
So that the Moors now coming cannot sight you;
If he dares come, Count William can fight them!"
Evening of Monday.
"I'll not attack without the Count beside me."

SAID VIVIEN: "You offer bad advice!
You've seen the Moors and they have seen our lines;
If you withdraw, it will be judged a flight;
Our Christian Faith will always bear the slight,

While Pagan ways will be more praised and prized;
Stand firm, my lord, and we shall win this fight;
Then you may set your worth at William's price:
You claimed to be his equal man last night."
Evening of Monday.
"With William's prowess your own may vie!"

FIVE THOUSAND SCORE of King Desramed's host
Were in those ships and boats upon the coast;
They saw Thibaut, who stood there on the slope,
And knew him from the marks his buckler showed.

THIS MADE THEM SURE that hidden in the valley
Were all his friends and many of his vassals.

Evening of Monday.
THE SARACENS from Saragossa's fiefs
Approached the shore, five thousand score at least;
Each bore a white, bright hauberk of the East
And wore a helm of Sargossa green:
With floral coils the golden frontals gleamed;
Their swords were girt, their burnished blades hung free,
As by the grips they grasped their sturdy shields;
In their right hands were cutting darts and spears;
Beneath their thighs were swift Arabian steeds;
They disembarked upon the shingle beach
And occupied the land beneath their feet;
A mighty war they'd journeyed forth to seek:
What sorry words they caused; what sorry deeds!

THE DAY WAS CLEAR, the morning fair and fine;
The sun shone bright and broadly in the sky;
The Pagans crossed an ancient wood in lines
And shook the ground wherever they rode by;
The golden jewels set in their helms of iron
Shone with a glow that bathed the trees in light;
If you had seen those Moors surge forth to fight,
You would recall what hardy men were like;
Sir Vivien showed Esturmi the sight.

"SIR ESTURMI, I see the Pagans coming;
The steeds they ride are bred so full of running
That they can race for fifteen leagues cross-country
And then return unflagging and untroubled;
On Archamp field this day the weak will stumble;
This very hour their vanguard will confront us;
The haughty now shall not protect the humble,
Nor father save his son, nor any other;
So let us trust Almighty God above us,
Whose strength is more than all of Satan's number;
We shall prevail, if we display our courage."

THEN THIBAUT SAID: "Sir Vivien, what now?
The Pagan van will come this very hour!"

"GOOD ESTURMI, what now?" he asked again:
"How can each one of us escape from death?
If we remain, our lives are at an end;
Let us escape so we may save ourselves!"
"That is a cur's advice!" said Vivien;
Thibaut cried out: "I will not heed what's said
By any kin of mine which shames myself,
Or by deceit brings ruin on my head."

"SIR ESTURMI, tear up your gonfalon,
So we may not be known as we ride off;
Our flag would bring the Moors to us in flocks!"
Said Esturmi: "Most gladly, lord, by God!"

THE COWARD RAISED his lance aloft at once
And laid the shaft upon his saddle's front;
With both his hands he tore the banner up.

HE STAMPED IT IN the mud beneath his feet;
Thibaut the count grasped hold of his great spear;
He turned the butt into the air and leaned
Its iron tip upon his saddle's rear;
With both his hands he tore the banner free
And stamped it in the mud beneath his feet:
"White flag, may you be struck by lightning-streaks,
Before the Moors through you may strike at me!"

Sir Vivien spoke forth: "How sad a speech!
Now we shall lack both flags on Archamp field."

5. How Vivien took allegiance from the French

"MY WORTHY LORDS, how shall we prosper hence
On Archamp field, with neither standard left?
Both Count Thibaut and Esturmi have fled,
And see, the Moors are very close ahead!
And when our men, in groups of five or ten,
Take on five score or fifty score of them,
We shall have none to rally all our men,
Or any flag to rally round ourselves;
A lordless folk has no hope of success;
Depart from here, you worthy knights well-bred,
For I cannot endure it to be said
That worthy men like you were left for dead;
As for myself, I'll face the grievous press,
And not turn back, for I have made a pledge
To never flee for any fear of death."
The French replied – hear what they said, my friends:

"SIR VIVIEN, you have our liege's forebears
And well can lead us band of Frenchmen forward;
You are the son of Count Beuvon of Cornbut
And his fair wife, Count Aymeri's own daughter;
Your uncle is Count William the war-lord;
Who more than you can guard and guide our forces?"
Said Vivien: "By God, I thank you warmly;
But in your words there lies one thing to thwart us:
You're not my men: no pledge was ever sworn to;
You could desert and bear no censure for it."
When this was said they lifted up their voices:
"No, lord – do not say that! We swear henceforward,
Upon the Faith that Jesus in His glory
Brought down to earth in ancient days and taught us,
That while you live we shall not fail your orders."

"AND I PLEDGE YOU, by Jesus, King of kings,
And by the Grace which flowed and showed in Him

When He was maimed and slaughtered for our sins,
To stand by you, though I lose life or limb."
When this was said he showed his flag forthwith.

INSIDE HIS HOSE bright red he put his hand
And, drawing forth a pure white silken flag,
He clipped it on his lance with three gold clamps;
His right arm raised, he held his lance-head back,
And round his fist the streamers fell and flapped;
He spurred his steed, which sped to the attack,
And struck a Moor upon his buckler's bands;
From edge to edge the sturdy boards he cracked
And cleft the arm that held on to the straps;
He split the breast and made the heart-strings snap,
And through the spine his mighty spear he rammed;
Down on the field he flung the villain flat
And cried: "Mountjoy!" the war-cry of the Franks.

6. How Girart punished the cowardly knights

AS FINEST GOLD divides itself from silver,
So did the bold from those of lesser spirit;
With Count Thibaut the cowards fled there quickly,
While stouter hearts stayed gallantly with Vivien
And struck the Moors where they were thronged the thickest.

AS FINEST GOLD from silver soon divides,
So did the bold from those of lesser mind;
The stouter hearts all swore to stay and fight,
And struck the Moors together with such might
That no one there could name the bravest knight;
But as they struck Count Thibaut took to flight
Along the road to Bourges and Berry shire,
Till he arrived at where four roads combined;
Four robbers there were hanging side by side;
The beams were low, their gallows short and wide,
And Thibaut's horse rode under, passing by;
One corpse's boot struck Thibaut's mouth inside
And he was filled with so much pain and fright
That he befouled the cloth beneath his thighs;

He felt the mess upon his left and right
And raised his leg to thrust the cloth aside;
Pursuing him, he saw Girart, a squire:
He cried: "My friend, pick up that cloth of mine!
With finest gold and precious stones it's lined;
One hundred pounds in Bourges would be its price!"
But brave Girart was knowing and replied:
"What should I do with booty all begrimed?"

THE NOBLE SQUIRE Girart cried out aloud:
"Thibaut, my lord, wait briefly for me now,
Then you may say back in your shire and town
That I stayed here while you escaped a rout;
I doubt that you will see me past this hour,
For I shall stay with Vivien the count:
He is my kin and small is my renown;
But I have wealth, well hidden in the ground,
And you must learn where this is to be found,
So, when I die, no quarrelling breaks out."

COUNT THIBAUT WAS a fool in his next action:
For Girart's sake he reined his rapid stallion;
When Girart came he grasped his neck and grappled
The count to ground, who fell right off his saddle
And struck his head against his helmet's strapping.

THEN GIRART PUT his hand to Thibaut's neck
And grasped the count's great buckler from his breast;
Gold bordered it all round and to excess:
The central boss was all of gold as well;
A Magyar lord first bore this buckler when
It was a prize of Vivien's prowess
On Gironde's banks, when he consigned to death
King Borrel's sons and Alderufe the Red;
He took away this mighty buckler then
And gave it to his liege lord William,
Who gave it on to Count Thibaut the wretch;
A worthy hand at last held it again!
He seized his coat, of strongest chain-mail meshed,
And his good sword with its sharp point and edge.

GIRART REARMED himself upon the way
And swapped his horse for Thibaut's destrier;
Thibaut got up, his head still in a daze,
And looked around and found squire Girart's jade;
He seized the rein and, mounting straightaway,
He thought at once of his escape again;
He looked ahead and saw a huge stockade
Of sticks so strong he could not lift one stake,
Nor leap across, so tall they were and great;
Nor did he dare to cross the valley-trails –
For he could hear the Pagans in the dales;
Upon a hill he saw some ewes at graze,
And through their flock he tried to flee away;
His stirrups struck and spiked a sheep of grey!

HIS STIRRUPS STRUCK and stuck a sheep to him;
He dragged the thing both up and down the hills,
And when at last he came to Bourges' bridge,
Its head alone was sticking to the tip!
Evening of Monday.
No man of wealth won such a spoil as this!
No pauper stood to lose so rich a thing.

I'LL TELL YOU MORE of squire Girart, the vassal;
As he returned to Archamp at the gallop,
He looked ahead and saw Esturmi's stallion;
That worthy steed had been abused so badly
It scarcely bore the weight still in its saddle,
But Esturmi still spurred it notwithstanding;
Girart rode up and hailed him in this manner:
"Sir Esturmi, whatever is the matter?"
And he replied: "Take heed and flee the battle!"
Young Girart said: "Turn back and face the challenge!
If you do not, I swear you'll wish you had done!"
"That I will not!" cried Esturmi in answer;
Squire Girart said: "You'll stay, whatever happens!"
He spurred his horse and with his lance attacked him;
He broke the shield and ripped his coat to tatters;
He drove the shaft and three whole ribs he shattered;
A full lance-length he knocked him from the saddle,
And, felling him, he hurled this insult at him:

"BE GONE, YOU WRETCH, in shame and pain immortal!
You shall not boast to Count Thibaut henceforward
That if you fled, no worthy man would halt you!
For evermore Count William will scorn you,
And Vivien, and all who hear your story!"
Evening of Monday.
"Nor Vivien, nor William will support you."

7. How the French were slaughtered

GIRART RODE BACK to Archamp on the sand;
His shield was bright, both at the front and back:
Of beaten gold was all the shoulder-strap,
And both the ties and all the outer tasse;
God never placed in line a finer man
Than Girart was when he rejoined their ranks;
He charged the press with all the strength he had
And smote a Moor upon his byrnie's back;
Right through his spine the solid spear he rammed;
He struck him well and flung him dead with that:
"Mountjoy!" he called, the war-cry of the Franks.

HE STRUCK ONE MORE upon his double targe;
From edge to edge he split it all apart
And cleft the arm with which the shield was clasped;
He smote the chest and struck him through the heart;
Right through the spine he rammed the solid shaft
And flung him dead full-length upon the grass;
"Mountjoy!" he called, the war-cry of King Charles;
In their distress the French beheld Girart.
Evening of Monday.

BRAVE VIVIEN urged on his noble force:
"Advance, my lords, with your most worthy swords!
Display your strength against this throng of Moors,
For I have heard the King's or William's horn:
If either comes, this battle will be short."
His men obeyed; they raised their swords and poured
Across Archamp to face the fierce assault;
They met Girart and greeted him with joy.

BRAVE VIVIEN addressed him and inquired:
"When were you dubbed a knight, Girart, good squire?"
"Not long ago, my lord!" the lad replied.

SAID VIVIEN: "Do you know where Thibaut is?"
And Girart told what happened on the roadway;
The count replied: "Enough of what you've told me;
Your tongue should not dishonour one born nobly."

"COME FORTH, GIRART, and fight by my right hand!
We'll strike as one and you shall bear our flag;
If you are near, I'll fear for nothing bad."
How well that day they led their gallant Franks!
Two royal friends, together they attacked
And took great toll of King Desramed's ranks.
Evening of Monday.
But they were doomed without Count William.

SIR VIVIEN looked out on Archamp plain:
Before his eyes he saw those barons brave,
The best in France for fighting bitter frays;
Upon the ground so many dead were lain
He wrung his hands and rent his beard for pain;
His eyes wept tears which streamed across his face;
How much he grieved for strong-armed William's sake:
"Ah, gallant lord, where is your strength today?
How much we miss your wisdom and your aid –
Too much, indeed, for all these nobles slain!"

"MY WORTHY MEN, by God Who guards us all,
Do not lose heart or will for this assault,
But let us wait for William, my lord:
If he arrives, we shall defeat the Moors!"
Evening of Monday.
"Alas for us that he was not informed!"

UPON THE HILL some thirty bugles brayed;
In serried ranks some seven hundred stayed;
There was not one without a bloodied blade
From striking blows already in the fray.

AND ERE THEY LEFT they'd strike so many others!
Count Vivien rode round and saw among them
Three hundred men of his own shire and country;
There was not one whose reins were not all ruddy,
Whose saddle-bows and cloth were not all bloody;
They clutched the guts disgorging from their stomachs,
To stop their steeds from treading them asunder;
On seeing this, brave Vivien cried humbly:
"What can I do to help you, noble brothers?
No man on earth can cure or give you comfort."

"FOR JESU'S SAKE, I beg of you, brave men:
Do not ride home to die in your own beds!
Who will avenge our comrades' slaughter then?
There is no lord in all King Louis' realm
Whom your own sons would give one moment's rest,
Once they had learned he'd brought about your deaths;
No rock or wall, no palisade or hedge,
No fort or tower, no ancient ditch's depths
Would hide him then or halt their swords' revenge;
While we still live, let us avenge ourselves!"
And they replied: "Brave lord, as you think best."
They seized their spears and spurred their destriers
Straight down a hill to face the Saracens;
With all their zeal they fought the Moors afresh.

THEY FOUGHT THE MOORS afresh with all their zeal;
Dismounting then upon the grass of green
They saw their dead and injured, far and near;
If you had seen the skill they showed and speed
In bandaging the wounds of all they reached;
The broken-armed snapped off a length of spear
And bound it tight to give themselves some ease;
They drank the wine they found across the field;
Those finding none drank water from the streams,
The stronger there all sharing with the weak,
And helping men who had no lord or liege;
When this was done they sought their fallen peers.

OF THEIR OWN RACE they found some seven hundred;
Between their feet the guts spilled from their stomachs;

From every mouth the crimson blood went running
Upon the grass across their broken bucklers;
Their cheeks were white, their faces set with suffering,
And every eye was turned awry or upward;
They moaned and cried, then died, one then another;
On seeing this, the other knights said humbly:
"What can we do to help you, noble brothers?
No man on earth can cure or give you comfort."

SAID VIVIEN: "My lords, for Jesu's sake!
Behold the Moors, that evil, heathen race,
Who've slain your sons and brothers here the same,
Your nephews too and friends who never failed!
They've sought no truce nor any treaty's claim;
While we still live, let blood for blood be paid!
St Stephen and the host of martyred Saints
Are no more blest than any man this day
Who dies for God on Archamp's bloody plain."
His men replied: "Brave vassal, lead the way!"
They mounted up, and, spurring off in haste,
They reached the field and smote those renegades;
With all their strength they struck with spear and blade
And slew at once some fifteen thousand knaves.

THE MOORS struck back with rage and torment wondrous:
Of Vivien's men they left him but one hundred.

HOW SORROWFUL would any warrior be
Who led ten thousand men upon the field,
And then had just one hundred left to lead,
One half of whom bore wounds or injuries!
Sir Vivien was such a one as he.

"SIR VIVIEN, how shall we prosper hence?"
And he replied: "We'll fight them to the death!
May God the Lord protect us with His strength
And send my liege Count William and his men,
Or King Louis, the Emperor, himself."
They all replied: "God prosper this request!"
They struck again with Vivien at their head
And laid at once one thousand Pagans dead;

The Moors struck back with rage and torment dread:
Of Vivien's men but twenty knights were left –
And these withdrew along a mountain's cleft.

"SIR VIVIEN, how shall we prosper more?"
"What can I say, save what I have before?
We shall prevail, so help us God the Lord!"
But some replied: "He's cast us from His thoughts!"
And others said: "Sir Vivien's at fault,
Who wants to lead just twenty men to war
Against five hundred thousand well-armed Moors!
If they were pigs to hunt, or savage boars,
Within a month we'd not have killed them all."
Said Vivien: "I recognise such talk:
It is your fields and vineyards you recall,
Your well-armed towns, your fortresses and forts,
And wives you have back in your homes and halls;
Who thinks of these does no brave deeds at all;
Depart, my lords, I give you leave henceforth!
But I shall stay on Archamp's bloody shore,
Nor shall I leave, for I have pledged and sworn
To never flee from any fight or war;
I shall prevail with Jesus and my sword."

"I BEG YOU, FOR the love of God, good men,
Do not return to die in your own beds!
See all around your comrades cut to shreds:
While they still had the joy of life and strength,
They stood with us to fight till their last breath;
And you know well the pledge you made to them;
You should not break a promise to the dead!
But I shall stay, though you may all have fled;
I shall not leave, for I have sworn a pledge
To never flee for any fear of death."
When this was said all twenty left, except
Girart the squire; no other men were left;
Those two remained to face fierce Desramed;
Two shields alone would face the fight ahead.
Evening of Monday.
Two shields alone were left to face the end.

THROUGH PAGAN HILLS those twenty rode away;
In front of them they saw their homeland plains;
Between the two they could not see one space
Which was not filled with evil heathen knaves;
At every pass their spears and helmets blazed;
Now when they saw that there was no escape,
That through the Moors they'd never ride unscathed,
They stopped their steeds and, turning round the reins,
They rode them back to Vivien again:

"LORD, REST ASSURED that we remain your vassals!"
Said Vivien: "I welcome you most gladly!"
"If you retreat, we likewise shall not tarry;
If you advance, we too shall show our valour;
Do what you will, we score shall be your shadow!"
Said Vivien: "Good men, I greatly thank you."
He turned and looked at Girart, his companion,
And spoke these words in their own native language:

8. How squire Girart rode for Count William

"GIRART, MY FRIEND, are you still hale and whole?"
"Yes, lord," he said, "in body and in soul."

"THEN TELL ME, FRIEND, how sturdy are your weapons?"
"In faith, my lord, they are both sound and ready,
As fit a man who's fought in countless mêlées
And will again, if there is need to ever."

"TELL ME, GIRART, how sturdy is your strength?"
And he replied he felt his strongest yet.

"TELL ME, GIRART, how sturdy is your horse?"
"He's fit and fine, and keen to run, my lord."

"GIRART, MY FRIEND, then will you dare to ride
To William by moonlight this same night?"

"WILL YOU RIDE FORTH to tell him this, my friend:
That he should think of Saragossa, when

He fought the Moor called Alderufe the Red;
His Magyar force were beating William's when
I joined the fight with my three hundred men;
I cried 'Mountjoy!' and cleft the Pagan press,
And turned the fight to William's success;
I struck the Moor called Alderufe to death
And took the heads of Borrel's sons all twelve;
I took away this mighty buckler then
From Alderufe the Magyar king himself
And gave it to my liege Count William,
Who gave it then to Count Thibaut the wretch;
A worthy man now bears it round his neck;
Say all of this and summon him to help!"

"GIRART, MY FRIEND, tell William my liege lord
To bring to mind the city of Limenes,
The mighty port that perches on the seaboard;
And Fleury, which I stormed for him and seized it;
Say all of this and summon him to seek me!"

"YOU MUST SAY THIS to William the faithful:
Let him recall the fight King Turlen gave him,
And how I rode some thirty times against him;
I slew five score and fifty of his Pagans
Who were the best and bravest of his nation;
And when our King turned round and rode for safety,
I climbed the mound with two hundred retainers
And cried 'Mountjoy' and won him back the day there;
I lost Raher, my friend, on that occasion,
Whose memory, each living moment, pains me;
Say all of this and summon him to save me."

"YOU MUST SAY THIS to William the Frank:
Let him recall the mighty fight he had
Beneath Orange against Tiebault the Slav,
A mighty fight won by our Christian band;
I climbed the mound with Bernart of Brabant –
My uncle and a very gallant man;
Bertrand that day stood firm at my right hand,
Among the best of our most gallant clan;
With Lord God's help and with the Norman flag

I won the field for William to have,
And stooped the pride of proud Tiebault the Slav;
Now let him come to Archamp's bloody sands
And in our grief bring comfort as he can."

"YOU MUST SAY THIS to Gui my younger brother:
He should not fight until his fifteenth summer,
But for my sake let him seize arms and come here
To fight with me in this fierce, foreign country."

"YOU MUST SAY THIS to Guibourc, my dear lady:
Let her recall the care and education
She gave to me for fifteen years unfailing;
Tell her she must ensure that it's not wasted
And that she sends her husband here to aid me;
If she does not, no other's hand will save me."

GIRART SAID: "LORD, I'll leave you with regret."
"Do not say that! It is to bring me help!"
They parted then, those kindred souls and friends;
Their grief was great, they made no joke or jest;
From both men's eyes fell tears of tenderness.
Evening of Monday.
Dear God above, why did they part just then?

GIRART TURNED BACK along a hillock's bend;
For five whole leagues he met so many men
That he could not proceed one yard unchecked,
But had to fell each Saracen he met,
To cleave a foot, cut off a fist or head;
And when he left the Pagan throng and threat
The noble horse beneath him fell down dead.

WHEN BRAVE GIRART escaped the Pagan fields
His noble horse fell dead beneath his feet;
For fifteen leagues the land was gripped with fear
And he found none with whom his tongue could speak,
Nor any horse on which he could proceed;
So on he pressed, on foot and full of grief;
The day was hot, as May in summer's heat;
For three whole days he'd had no food to eat;

His thirst was fierce and nowhere found relief:
For fifteen leagues no ford there was or stream,
Save those of salt close by him on the beach;
His weapons' weight oppressed him then indeed;
My worthy friends, hear how he chided these:

"ALAS, GREAT SPEAR, how you oppress my arm!
What help are you to Vivien at Archamp,
Who in great pain is fighting to the last?"
Down on the field he cast away the lance.

"ALAS, GREAT SHIELD, how you oppress my neck!
What help are you to Vivien near death?"
Down on the field he cast it from his breast.

"ALAS, GOOD HELM, how you make my head ache!
What help are you to Vivien the brave,
Who fights for life on Archamp field this day?"
Down on the field he cast the helm away.

"ALAS, HAUBERK, how much you burden me!
To Vivien the brave what help are we,
Who in great pain is fighting and great grief?"
He pulled it off and cast it on the field;
Girart the squire shed all his battle-gear,
Except his sword, whose shining blade of steel
Was crimson now from pommel's point to peak;
In blood and guts its scabbard-case was steeped;
Upon his sword he leaned, its blade unsheathed
To grip the ground in striving to proceed;
From dusk till dawn he plodded plains and peaks:
How hard he ran down all the valleys deep!
How hard he climbed up all the mountains steep!
Each step he took was measured by the steel
In his right hand, as on its point he leaned;
He would not stop till William his liege
Was told the news of Vivien's great need:
How at Archamp, with twenty men to lead,
He strove to halt King Desramed's whole fleet;
One thousand Moors had fallen to his zeal.

9. *How Vivien was defeated*

SIR VIVIEN had only ten men more;
They asked of him: "What shall we do henceforth?"
"For our Lord's sake, keep fighting!" he implored:
"You all have seen young Girart riding forth
For William or Louis in their halls:
Whoever comes, we shall defeat the Moors!"
"Then lead us on, brave count!" they cried in joy;
Those ten and he moved out to strike once more,
But bore the brunt of such a fierce assault
That none survived where ten had stood before:
His shield alone defied Desramed's force.
Evening of Monday.
His shield alone defied them one and all.

HIS SHIELD ALONE was all that stood between them
As, countless times, he rushed headlong to meet them;
His spear alone laid low one hundred heathens;
The Pagans said: "We'll never see him beaten,
Unless we slay the destrier beneath him."

"WE NEVER SHALL defeat this noble vassal,
Unless we slay the steed beneath his saddle."
And so they chased through every hill and valley,
And lay in wait like hunting-men to trap it;
Across a field a host of Moors rode at it
And loosened spears and sharpened darts and arrows
Which struck the shanks and flanks of Vivien's stallion;
The shaft-lengths would have filled an open wagon;
And then a knight from Barbary attacked him:
The horse he rode beneath his thighs was rapid;
In his right hand a cutting dart he carried;
He shook it thrice then in a trice it landed;
The byrnie's hide on Vivien's side it shattered
And thirty rings down on the ground it scattered;
In Vivien's side a mighty wound it battered
And his right arm let fall his white gonfalon;
Friends, never more would he lift up that banner.
Evening of Monday.
No more in life would he lift up a standard.

HE PUT HIS HAND behind his back to find
The Pagan's shaft and wrenched it from his side;
He struck the Moor right through his byrnie's hide;
From front to back the spear ran through his spine
And with this blow he threw his foe from life.

"BARBARIAN, base rogue, go to your death!"
Said Vivien and flung the felon dead:
"You'll never see again the land you left,
Nor ever boast again of your prowess
In having slain one more of Louis' men."
He drew his sword to strike the Moors again.

WHICHEVER MOOR he struck on helm or hauberk
Was cleft in half and to the ground went falling:
He called aloud: "St Mary, I implore you,
Send Louis here or William the war-lord!"
He prayed aloud while they all moved towards him.

"MAJESTIC GOD, Who gave me breath to breathe,
And Who,Yourself, took on humanity,
And for our sins endured the Cross's grief:
You dwell on High in Holy Trinity;
You made the earth, the Heavens and the seas,
The sun and moon; You ordered forth all these,
Then made Adam and Eve that Man might be;
As this is true, as truly I believe,
I beg you Lord to arm my soul with steel,
Lest my weak self should ever think to flee
From any fight against Your enemies!
May I be true until my soul is free!
Lord, with Your grace, confirm my pledge and plea!"

"SWEET MARY MILD, most ever blessed Maiden,
As you, in truth, bore Jesus Christ our Saviour,
Protect me now with your most gracious favour
From death this day among Desramed's pagans."
This said, at once young Vivien bewailed it:
"That was a foul and foolish way of praying,
To try and save myself from mortal danger,
When our Lord God Himself refused the same thing,

Who suffered death upon the Cross to save us
From mortal woes and all the wiles of Satan."

"MY LORD, I SEEK no shield from mortal blows,
For You Yourself sought no respite from those;
But Lord, bring here Count William Hooknose
Or Louis, King of lovely France, my home;
With William's help we shall defeat the foe;
Men are alike; not many stand alone,
Except my liege Count William Hooknose;
For I am strong in body and in soul,
And my prowess may match my uncle's blows;
But near and far his name and fame have grown;
If he were here at Archamp on the coast,
He would have won this battle-field, I know;
Wretch that I am, I could not manage so."
Evening of Monday.
"What do they want with me, this faithless folk?"

THE HEAT WAS STRONG, like summertime in May;
He'd fought them long, not eating for three days:
His need was fierce and very hard to take,
As was his thirst, so many hours unslaked;
Out of his mouth the crimson blood escaped,
And from the wound his left side had sustained;
The streams were far, nor did he know the way;
For fifteen leagues there was no pool or spray,
Save those of salt which ran off from the bay;
But through the field a muddy trickle drained
Across a rock which ridged beside the waves;
The Pagan steeds had fouled it when they came,
And then its brew was mixed with blood and brains;
To such a stream Sir Vivien made haste;
To such a stream as this he stooped his face
And drank his fill of water foul to taste;
The Pagans came; they hurled their spears and rained
Great blows at him upon the shore and shale;
They could not break or breach the byrnie's mail
That bound his front and back in sturdy chains;
But all elsewhere, on legs and arms the same,
In twenty spots and more they found their aim;

With boar-like strength Sir Vivien stood again
And from its sheath he drew his shining blade;
With great prowess a strong defence he made,
To keep the Moors, like hunting-dogs, at bay;
The draught he drank was bitter gall to taste,
And soon his guts could not support the bane:
From mouth and nose they spewed it forth again;
His grief was keen, his eyes were dim and glazed;
He could not see to make a stand or stay;
Then by the Moors once more he was waylaid;
From every side their soldiers struck and aimed
Their spears at him and cutting darts steel-made;
His quartered shield was crushed so out of shape
It served no more to guard his head and face;
Down on the field he tossed the shield away;
On seeing this, Desramed's knights assailed
Sir Vivien with all their heart and hate.

THEY HURLED THEIR SPEARS and wyverns sharply-tipped;
On front and back his hauberk's hide they hit,
And their sharp iron cut through the chain-mail rings
And all his breast was splintered with the bits;
Upon the ground his bowels burst and split;
No mortal man could suffer more than this!
He prayed to God for mercy on his sins.

SIR VIVIEN went straying through the field;
His helm was crushed upon its nasal-piece;
His guts had burst and spilt beneath his feet;
With his left arm he grasped them in his grief,
While in his right he held his sword of steel,
All crimson now from pommel-point to peak,
In blood and guts the scabbard-casing steeped;
His blade unsheathed, upon his sword he leaned;
The pangs of death soon seized him hard indeed;
He only stood by leaning on his steel;
To Jesus Christ he made one last appeal
For William to come to him, his liege,
Or Louis, King of lovely France the sweet.

"ALMIGHTY GOD, our Everlasting Lord,
Who of the Virgin Mary's womb were born,
Who died for us upon the Cross's boards,
The One True God, in Trinity adored:
I beg of You to guard my soul henceforth,
Lest my weak self should ever form the thought
Of taking flight from any heathen Moors!
May I be true until my soul is Yours!
Lord, with Your Grace uphold the pledge I've sworn;
Send here to me Count William, my lord;
His ways are best in any fight or war;
He knows well how to use and save his force."

"ALMIGHTY GOD, Whose glory knows no end,
I beg of You to let no mortal threat
Allow the thought to enter in my head
Of taking flight from any fear of death."

AGAIN A KNIGHT from Barbary attacked him;
He dropped the rein and goaded his fast stallion
To smite the head of Vivien the gallant;
He split his skull and all his brains were scattered.

THE PAGAN KNIGHT swooped down upon him swiftly;
Between his thighs a mighty horse he'd ridden,
While in his hand a mighty wyvern swinging;
Upon his head he smote the gallant Vivien
And split his skull and all his brains went spilling;
Upon his knees Sir Vivien was smitten;
Friends, what a loss when princes fall like this one!
From every side they seized upon him quickly
And cut him down to drop upon the shingle;
Not wishing then to leave him there, they gripped him
And by a path beneath a tree they hid him –
They did not want his corpse found by the Christians;
And now, my friends, I'll tell again of Girart,
How he arrived to tell his news to William.
Evening of Monday.
The Count was back in Barcelona city.

10. How Girart was received in William's hall

IN BARCELONA TOWN the Count was back;
He had returned from fighting an attack
Against Bordeaux upon the Gironde's banks,
Whereby he'd lost great numbers from his ranks;
Girart arrived to tell the news he had.

COUNT WILLIAM had just come back from vespers;
Within his hall, upon its highest level,
His wife Guibourc and he looked out together;
Across a hill he scanned the fields and meadows
And saw Girart in far Archamp's direction,
His bloody blade in his right hand extended;
Upon its hilt his weary way he wended.

SAID WILLIAM: "Sweet sister, lovely wife,
How blest the day I took you for my bride!
More blessed still the day you were baptised!
I see a man who plods across the rise;
In his right hand he holds his blade of iron;
I tell you this, I know without a lie
That he has fought a battle for his life!
He's come to me for help in battle's strife;
Let's meet with him and hear what's on his mind."
So both Guibourc and William the wise
Climbed down their steps until they reached outside;
They met Girart when he at last arrived;
They looked at him and recognised the squire;
Then, nothing loath, Count William inquired:

"GIRART, GOOD YOUTH, what news have you to tell us?"
Girart replied: "I have much that is dreadful."

"KING DESRAMED has come from Cordova;
He's steered his fleet along the ocean's path
And pillages his way deep into France!"

"HE SEIZES LANDS and lays the borders waste;
He treats the shires as his desires dictate;
From every hall he drags your knights in chains

Aboard his ships, lamenting and enraged;
Think well, my lord, how you may bring them aid."

"KING DESRAMED has come from his own realm
To waste your lands and take them for himself;
Count Thibaut and Sir Esturmi both went
With Vivien the brave to halt his men;
One fights them still, the other two have fled."
"God," said the Count, "that is brave Vivien."
"You are not wrong, my lord," young Girart said:
"He summons you, through me his messenger,
To help him now in grief and great distress."

"HEED THIS, MY LORD, from Vivien the faithful:
You should recall the fight King Turlen gave you,
And how he rode some thirty times against him;
He slew five score and fifty of his Pagans,
And when our King turned round and rode for safety
He climbed the mound with two hundred retainers
And cried 'Mountjoy!' and won him back the day there;
He lost Raher, his friend, on that occasion,
Whose memory, each living moment, pains him;
He summons you to help him in grave danger."

"HEED THIS, MY LORD, from Vivien the fearless:
You should recall the city of Limenes,
And Breher too, which perches on the seaboard,
And Fleury, which he stormed for you and seized it;
To Archamp field he summons you his liege lord."

"HEED THIS, GUIBOURC, who are his dearest lady:
You should recall the care and education
You gave to him for fifteen years unfailing;
For Jesu's sake, ensure it is not wasted
And that you send your husband there to aid him!
If you do not, no other's hand will save him."

"HEAR THIS AND HEED, Lord Gui, his younger brother:
You should not fight until your fifteenth summer,
But now you must, for one born of your mother,
To save his life in that fierce, foreign country!"

SAID WILLIAM: "Will I find him alive?"
"Why question thus?" the fair Guibourc replied:
"Ride forth at once – your questioning wastes time!
God help you, William, if he should die!"
On hearing this, he turned his head aside;
For pity's sake the tears fell from his eyes,
And past his nose the warm drops fell alike;
Down to his belt they wet his beard of white;
He called Guibourc and thought to test his wife:
He had in mind to put her heart on trial,
To see how much she loved his family's lives;
When speaking thus his words were true and wise:
"Sweet sister, friend, for love of God on High,
Three days alone have come and gone since I
Myself returned from fighting for my life
With my own men at Bordeaux on the brine;
And I have lost too many of my knights;
The lands I guard have borders far and wide,
And many men would have to reunite,
And I myself am worn with woe and tired;
This well may prove a waste of strength and time;
Famed Vivien is fighting in his prime;
He cannot look for my support this time;
He will prevail without me by his side."
To hear these words drove Guibourc almost wild;
She fell to ground; she kissed his feet and cried
From her heart's depths, protesting as she sighed:
"Ride forth at once! Your waiting wastes the time!
In your good care my own nephew shall ride,
Who is Guischard, whom you have dubbed a knight."

"IN YOUR GOOD CARE my own nephew shall leave,
Who is Guischard, whom I hold very dear;
Two days ago you dubbed him knight indeed;
If he should die, you'll lie no more with me!"
He gave his word, though he would be aggrieved
At bringing back at all this Pagan peer:
For he renounced Lord God on Archamp field.
Evening of Monday.
With his last breath he lost eternal peace.

GUIBOURC HERSELF served young Girart with water;
When this was done she brought a towel for him;
She bade him sit high up in the great hall there
And brought him forth a whole shoulder of boar's meat;
He grasped the haunch and ate it without pausing.

SHE BROUGHT GIRART a bread-cake sifted fine,
And brought him then a mighty mug of wine;
Girart ate up the boar's meat in a trice
And in two draughts he drained the mug of wine –
Not one small drop he offered William's wife,
Nor raised his face from eating all the time;
Guibourc looked on and to her lord she cried:
"By God, this youth is one of yours all right!
A leg of pork just whets his appetite,
And with two draughts he drains a mug of wine!
I'm sure he'll give his neighbours lusty fights
And never flee a battle all his life!"
"For pity's sake, by God, my worthy wife!
He was in need and great was his desire;
He's had no food for three whole days and nights!"
His bed was made; they bade him then retire;
Evening of Monday.
His bed was made; they bade him sleep a while.

GIRART STOOD UP and finished with his meal;
His bed was made; he went to take his ease;
Most willingly fair Guibourc served his needs
And stayed with him until he fell asleep,
Commending him to God Almighty's keep;
Girart slept on until the night was near,
Then from his bed he leapt most gallantly
And cried: "Mountjoy! Brave knights, mount up your steeds!"
He asked for arms and servants brought him these;
The Count stepped forth to knight him for his deeds.

UPON HIS BACK they laced a noble hauberk,
Then laced a helm of green upon his forehead;
About his waist Count William girt a sword-blade,
While Girart grasped a mighty shield they brought him;
They led him forth one of their finest horses

And by the left he leapt upon the war-horse;
Fair Guibourc held the stirrup steady for him,
Commending him to God's good care henceforward.

11. *How William first fared on Archamp field*

FROM HIS GOOD TOWN, when daylight turned to evening,
The Count set off with Sir Girart and leading
Knights fully armed and thirty thousand liegemen
To Archamp field and Desramed the Heathen;
They journeyed through the cold night air, unspeaking
Till break of dawn and light of day appearing;
When they arrived at Archamp on the seaboard,
The Moor had won; the French were fled or beaten;
He'd taken spoils, the dead men's armour seizing,
And ridden back to rest with all his people
Inside their ships and barges iron-sheeted;
The wind had dropped and so they could not leave there;
But all their lords, their captains and their leaders,
Had gone to scout the dry land in the meantime;
A league or more they'd ridden from the beaches,
When William the Count rode up to meet them
With well-armed knights and thirty thousand liegemen,
One half of whom were very keen to greet them
With blows of iron to show their strength of feeling!
They cried: "Mountjoy!" and moved to strike them fiercely;
Those Pagan lords were helpless to receive them:
They had no arms to counter blows or deal them;
They turned in flight towards the shore, retreating
Inside their ships and sundry other sea-craft;
They seized their arms and roused themselves to wield them.

THE SARACENS were from Seguna's land:
Five thousand score beneath Desramed's flag,
Each bearing mail and wearing helmets spanned
With fronts of gold and esses of gold-band;
They girt their swords about their flanks and shanks,
And grasped their shields to grip them by the straps;
Their cutting spears they clutched in their right hands;

Beneath their thighs fleet Arab steeds they had;
They rode them out upon the grit and sand
And sallied forth upon the solid land;
What evil hours they boded for the Franks:
How fierce a fight they gave Count William!

A MIGHTY WAR they waged which raged most heavy
And unrelieved from Monday until Wednesday;
It did not end, nor for one hour it lessened,
Till Thursday night, just as the sun was setting;
Each day it went the fighting was relentless
On either side, for heathens and for Frenchmen;
But William, at last, was left defenceless.
Evening of Thursday.
Two shields alone were all he had to help him.

WITH TWO ALONE the Count maintained the struggle:
One was Girart, whose heart was filled with courage,
While Guibourc's nephew Guischard was the other;
Friends, will you hear of those two noble cousins,
And how they both were parted from their uncle?

FRIENDS, WILL YOU HEAR of those two noble boys,
And how they both were parted from their lord?
Towards the left Sir Girart turned his horse,
But, stumbling down, it threw him by the shore;
His coat of mail was tangled in the fall
And down the dunes some thirty heathens poured;
With flashing spears and shining, sharpened swords,
They wounded him in thirty spots and more;
As death drew in, he cried aloud and called
His uncle's name, who heard and turned his horse;
He slaughtered ten and forced the others forth;
To young Girart he said with gentle voice:

"GIRART, MY FRIEND, if you were borne from here,
And your great wounds were bound, tell me, brave peer,
Would you survive and could your wounds be healed?
Or do you think that your life's end is near?"
Girart replied: "My lord, let all that be!
I do not want to bind my injuries

Or to be borne away from Archamp field;
No mortal hand can save or comfort me!
But if my lord could set me on my steed
And lace on me once more my helm of green,
And place on me once more my mighty shield,
And set my hand upon my sword of steel,
And let me drink a wine-sack to the lees,
Or, if you've none, a draught from that dark stream,
I swear to God that I should live and breathe
Till I have sold my wounded body dear,
From which the blood flows forth so forcefully."
The Count replied: "You have not long, I fear."

Evening of Thursday.
COUNT WILLIAM dismounted his fine destrier;
He took Girart by his right hand and elbow
And raised him up to sit upon the meadow;
His cheeks were pale, his look was dark and deathly;
Beneath his brow his eyes had turned already;
His head was drooped across his byrnie's leather;
His helm had dropped upon his chin and breast-bone,
His head was down, his soul half-way to heaven;
Said William: "No mortal hand can help you."
How sad it is when such brave men are severed!
What mortal eye could see and not regret it?

FRIENDS, WILL YOU HEAR of Guischard now, the Moor,
And how he too was parted from his lord?
His horse fell down beneath him on the shore,
And, as he fell, his coat of mail was caught;
Then down a dune some thirty heathens poured
And wounded him in thirty spots and more;
He cried for help and loudly uttered forth
His uncle's name, who heard and turned his horse;
He slaughtered ten and made the rest withdraw;
On riding up, he spoke aloud his thoughts:

"GUISCHARD, MY FRIEND, if you were borne from here
And your great wounds were bound, could you be healed,
Or do you think that your life's end is near?"
Guischard replied: "My lord, leave me in peace!

I do not want my wounds bound up to heal,
Or to be borne away from Archamp field;
But if some friend could set me on my steed,
I'd never fight for you again, my liege!
Just let me drink a wine-sack to the lees,
Or, if you've none, a draught from that dark stream,
Then watch me leave for Cordova the sweet,
And nevermore uphold the Christian creed!
I cannot serve a God I cannot see!
If I had not abjured my old belief,
I would not see these wounds all over me,
From which the blood flows forth so forcefully."
Said William: "A curse on you, you fiend!
While you were hale and hearty and well pleased,
You loved the laws of Christianity;
But now that death treads closely on your heels,
You cannot move, your spirit is so weak!
I have no wish to bear you from this field!"

Evening of Thursday.
COUNT WILLIAM leaned from his horse, extending
His hand to seize the hand of Guibourc's nephew;
He set the youth behind him on his destrier.

A KNIGHT FROM BARBARY sped down the valley;
Between his thighs he rode a rapid stallion;
In his right hand a cutting dart he carried;
He shook it thrice then cast it in his anger;
Upon the left of Guischard's hip it landed,
And half a foot inside his flesh it carried;
Behind the Count it killed Guischard the vassal;
The body slumped and started sliding backwards;
On seeing this, the Count strained hard to catch it
And haul it back before him on the saddle;
With his right hand he pulled the evil arrow,
Then smote the Moor upon his buckler's panels;
He struck him well and flung him on the gravel;
He didn't flee, but William left the battle;
In front of him the dead Guischard he carried.
Evening of Thursday.
He didn't flee, but neither did he tarry.

12. How William was consoled by his wife

GUIBOURC THE FAIR did not forget her lord;
When William Hooknose set forth for war
On Archamp field with Desramed the Moor,
She summoned forth her liegemen from their halls:
Some thirty thousand came, the song records,
And half of those who answered to her call
Were dressed and armed to take the field by storm;
When they arrived, at once she called them forth
And sat them down to feast at William's boards;
The jongleurs sang their tales and songs of yore,
While she herself brought wine and served them all;
Then, as she leaned against a marble wall,
She looked out of a window there and saw
Her noble lord approaching on his horse;
Across the bows, before him, lay the corpse,
And Guibourc thought of Vivien, and all
The joy she felt turned quickly to remorse;
She cried aloud: "I've much to do, my lords!
My husband comes! Down from the hill he draws;
A dead man lies before him on his horse;
Across his saddle-bows he's laid the corpse:
It is brave Vivien – of this I'm sure!"
"My lady, no! Do not say that, Guibourc!"
Cried all the knights and barons with one voice.

"FOR GOD'S SAKE THEN, my lords, who can it be,
Brought back this way from Archamp's bloody beach,
If not the King, who is my husband's liege,
Or Vivien, the nephew he holds dear?"
"My lady, no; don't say that it is these;
It is perhaps the minstrel that he keeps;
In all of France none sings as well as he,
Nor in a fight strikes blows so bold and keen;
He can recite the songs of all the deeds
That Clovis did, the first king who believed
In God our Lord to rule in France the sweet;
And of his son, Flovent, the fighter fierce,
Who waived his right to all of France's fiefs;
He sings of all the worthy kings there've been,

Right up to King Pepin and his fair Queen;
He sings of Charles, of Roland and the Peers,
Of Girart of Vienne and all his breed,
Who were his ancestors and family;
And he himself is very brave indeed;
Because of this, his wondrous minstrelsy,
And winning deeds in countless battles' heat,
Your noble lord has brought him from the field."

"FINE LORDS OF FRANCE, for love of God, I beg you
To give me leave so I may bid him welcome;
He is my lord, I must go to attend him!"
She hurried off and, hastily descending
Towards the gate, she turned the key of metal;
She opened up to let her husband enter;
He looked at her and then he asked this question:

"MY LOVE, SINCE WHEN have you become my porter?"
"Upon my faith, my lord, it's but a short time!
My noble lord, your company is smaller."

"SWEET FRIEND OF MINE, since when do you guard doors?"
"Upon my faith, not long at all, my lord!
My noble Count, your company is small."

"MY LOVE, BEHOLD your nephew Sir Guischard;
You never shall see Vivien, brave heart!"
Guibourc the fair held forth both of her arms
And she received the body of Guischard;
The load was great and tumbled from her grasp –
Her woman's strength could not perform the task;
The body slumped and sprawled upon the grass;
The tongue rolled out and lolled and hung aslant.

Evening of Thursday.
Guibourc looked down and saw her Pagan nephew;
His cheeks were pale, his look was dark and deathly,
And in their rims his eyes had turned already;
His head was drooped across his byrnie's leather;
His helm had dropped upon his chin and breast-bone;
As Guibourc wept Count William said gently:

"BY GOD, GUIBOURC, you weep and you do right;
At France's court they said, in times gone by,
That you were wed to William, a knight
Of great prowess, unmatched in any fight;
But now you are a wretched weakling's wife,
A craven Count who turns his back in flight
From any fray and brings back none alive!
You soon shall cook and bake by your own fire,
And share your hall no more with barons high!
My nephew fair, brave Vivien, has died;
Whoever grieves, my arm has lost its might,
And honour's name shall nevermore be mine."
Tears filled his eyes and Guibourc wept alike;
But when she heard her husband's cries and sighs,
She put, in part, her own grief from her mind,
And, speaking out most lovingly, replied:

"COUNT WILLIAM, my lord, attend to me!
Most sad it is that any man should weep,
And grief indeed that any man should grieve!
Among your race the case has always been
That when they fought for honour with their steel,
They often died upon the battlefield;
Far better you should die on Archamp's beach,
Than that your heirs should suffer by your deeds,
And when you died still bear the infamy!"
On hearing this, he hung his head in grief;
Tears filled his eyes and spilled upon his cheeks;
And then he spoke to her he held most dear
These tender words in his own native speech:
"Sweet sister, friend, fair wife, attend to me!
Whoever grieves, I have much cause to weep;
Three hundred years and fifty more have been
Since from my mother's womb this life I've breathed!
I am too old for warfare and too weak!
What God once granted me has run its lease –
Long years of youth, gone now, no more to be!
And now the Moors hold my prowess so cheap
That when I come they neither turn nor flee;
King Desramed has dealt my men defeat;
He's taken spoils and stripped their bodies clean,

And with his Moors has boarded ship to leave;
The lands I rule have borders far afield,
And many men would have to reconvene,
And if I went once more to Archamp field,
The Moors may well have started out to sea;
My arm has lost its might, whoever grieves,
And honour's name no more belongs to me."
He wept again, but Guibourc wiped his tears:
"Ah, husband, lord, attend my pledge and plea!
Allow me, lord, to make a lying speech
To thirty thousand men, assembled near,
One half of them already armed and keen
To take the field by storm and strike with speed!"
"Where are these men? Come, tell me truthfully,
Beloved wife, my friend, my sister dear!"
"They're in your hall, all sitting at a feast!"
How William laughed and quickly left his tears!
"Go then, Guibourc! Say anything you please!"
So back she went, most lightly on her feet,
And singing too, instead of shedding tears;
The knights looked up and asked her, all and each:
"Who was it then, Guibourc? What did you see?"
"Much, worthy men, that filled me with good cheer!
My noble lord has come back home to me,
And, God be praised, he took no injuries;
And he has won the battle in the field
And slain the Moor Desramed, the Emir;
But in one thing his cause has come to grief:
He has lost all his noble knights and peers,
Who were the flower of France's chivalry;
And they have slain famed Vivien the fierce;
In Pagan lands or Christendom's demesne
No truer knight was ever born than he,
For championing the blessed Christian creed
And cherishing the law with all his zeal;
Go to Archamp, my lords, for God and me!
The Pagan boats lie damaged on a reef;
The winds have dropped, they cannot put to sea;
Down in a cave, beside a cove and creek,
Ten thousand Moors have sheltered, and with these
Is all the gold and silver of your peers,

And all the arms stripped from them on the field;
My lord was left alone and had to leave –
But if you go to Archamp on the sea,
This plundered wealth may surely be retrieved;
What's more, my lord holds large domains in fief,
Which, if you go, he'll give you willingly!"

"AND ANY MAN with land who wants a wife,
I have five score and sixty more inside,
Princesses all of peerless mien and mind;
By William's grace I've raised each from a child;
They sew my silk each day with rowels fine;
Come with me now and choose the one you like!
My lord will give you land, and I a wife,
If you will go and win them in the fight!"
How many men rushed forth to choose a bride,
Who at Archamp were fated soon to die!
Evening of Thursday.
Guibourc brought water to her husband's side.

HE TOOK HIS SEAT among the lower tables:
He could not move for grief up to the greater;
She brought him boar, and with no more delaying
He grasped the meat and ate it without waiting;
He could, because it was well cooked and tasty.

SHE BROUGHT TO HIM a loaf of bread most fine,
And then two cakes baked freshly on the fire;
And then she brought a peacock, huge in size,
And afterwards a mighty mug of wine
Which her two hands could scarcely hold upright;
Her husband ate the bread up in a trice,
Then both the cakes baked freshly on the fire,
And all the haunch of roasted boar alike;
In two great draughts he drained the mug of wine;
He cleaned the plate, he drained the goblet dry,
No crumb or drop he offered to his wife,
Nor raised his face from eating all the time!
Guibourc looked on and shook her head and smiled,
Although with tears still welling in her eyes;
These tender words in William's tongue she cried:

"Almighty God, Who made me see the light,
And unto Whom this sinner's soul of mine
Shall be returned when Judgement Day arrives:
He who can eat a loaf of mighty size,
And then two cakes baked freshly on the fire,
And then a haunch of boar in just two bites,
And then can eat a peacock in a trice,
And in two draughts can drain a mug of wine,
Will surely give his neighbour lusty fights
And never flee a battle all his life,
Or bring reproach upon his kith and kind!"
"Sweet sister, friend, I thank you, worthy wife!
But who will rule my borders when I die?
I have no son of my own loins and line."
At this, young Gui got up from by the fire,
His nephew and Beuvon of Cornbut's child,
Born to a daughter of Aymeri the wise,
A nephew born on William's own side
And brother of brave Vivien the prized;
Not yet fifteen, his stature still was slight;
He had no beard, no hair upon his hide,
Save on his head, which he had had for life!
He strode across and at his uncle's side
He hailed him thus and with these words replied:
"In faith, my lord, I've never heard the like!
For I would rule your borders, if you died,
And serve Guibourc with all my heart and mind;
No evil I could guard her from would thrive,
For she has cared for me throughout my life."
On hearing this, the Count groaned at the child
And answered him in tones of bitter spite:
"You are more fit to sit beside the fire,
Than on the seat that rules my mighty shires!"

"YOU ARE MORE FIT to sit among the cinders
Than on the seat that rules my lands and cities!
Nor does my wife have need of your assistance!"
On hearing this, young Gui replied with wisdom:
"In truth, my lord, I've never heard such mischief!"
"You wretch, why turn the blame on me?" cried William;
"I'll tell you why, but first I must consider –

For it is wrong for any loving Christian
To speak in heat and overstep the limits;
Why rail at me for being young and little?
The biggest man was little to begin with!
And by the Cross, my lord, I tell you this much:
There is no man in any Christian kingdom,
Nor any knight who fights for his religion,
Who, when you die, might come to seize and pillage,
With Vivien dead and Guibourc without issue,
Whom I'd not fight until his life were finished!
Then I would rule your lands and all your cities,
And take good care of Lady Guibourc's wishes."
On hearing this, the Count was filled with pity,
And from his eyes the tears flowed down his visage;
He beckoned Gui to come to him and kiss him;
Three times they kissed, then William told his kinsman:
"In truth, my boy, your words display much wisdom;
Though still a child, you have a warrior's spirit;
To you indeed may all my lands be given!
Sweet sister, friend, take care of him, I bid you."
Evening of Thursday.
Fifteen he was and heir to William's riches.

COUNT WILLIAM got up from his good meal;
The bed was made so he could take his ease;
His worthy wife caressed him tenderly;
My friends, there was no wife in Christ's demesne
Who championed His laws with greater zeal
Or cherished more the blessed Christian creed
And loved and served her husband more than she!
She stayed with him till he was sound asleep,
Commending him to God Almighty's keep;
Then back she went to join those at the feast;
The Count slept on until the night drew near,
Then from his bed he leapt most gallantly
And cried: "Mountjoy! Brave knights, bestride your steeds!"
He asked for arms and servants brought him these.

UPON HIS BACK they laced a noble hauberk,
Then placed a helm of green upon his forehead;
About his side Count William girt his sword-blade,

Then grasped a shield and gripped it by the cord-straps;
He clasped his spear, whose tip was sharply-pointed;
Embracing him, his wife bowed down before him,
Commending him to God, our mighty Warden.

13. How young Gui joined William on the field

BEFORE HIS TOWN, as daytime turned to evening,
The Count set off upon his steed and leading
Knights fully armed and thirty thousand liegemen
To Archamp field and Desramed the Heathen;
Within the town, alone, bode Lady Guibourc;
Inside her rooms she took young Gui the fearless,
And both of them, as long as they could see him,
Commended him to God Almighty's keeping;
But when he'd gone the youngster burst out weeping;
Guibourc looked on and asked her nephew sweetly:
"Young Gui, my friend, what makes you now so tearful?"
"My lady fair, I have good cause for grieving;
I'm just fifteen, and so am held so cheaply
That I am kept from fighting with the heathens;
How shall I earn my heritage and fiefdom
If not in war on Archamp's bloody beaches?
Beyond the hill I see my liege lord leaving
To fight the Moors, accompanied so meanly
That he has not one life-long friend to cheer him,
Except Lord God, Who is the world's Redeemer."
Fair Guibourc said: "Hush now, for love of Jesus!
You are too young, my lord, and too unseasoned
To bear the trials and hardships you would meet there –
The sleepless nights, the long days without eating,
The awful blows, the battles harsh and fearsome;
What's more, the Count has placed you in my keeping,
So you must stay, for all your tears and pleading,
Or I shall lose the love there is between us!"
Young Gui replied: "These reasons have no reason!
For I can lie and tell him when I reach him
That I escaped from you by force – believe me,
As I believe in my own self and Jesus,
If I don't go to Archamp on the seaboard,
You'll nevermore see William your liege lord;

But if I go, I'll bring him back still breathing!"
Guibourc replied: "Brave youth, then I release you!"

THEY CLOTHED HIM IN their smallest coat of mail,
Then on his head their smallest helm was laced;
They girt a sword, a short but worthy blade,
Then round his neck a little shield was draped.

FAIR GUIBOURC BROUGHT the youth a little shaft:
The wood was strong, the tip was very sharp;
Its pennon flapped across his hand and arm.

GUIBOURC LED OUT her saddle-horse Balzor;
Its seat was good, but all the straps were short:
It had not served a warrior before!
Gui mounted up, while Guibourc held the horse,
Commending him to God Almighty's ward.

YOUNG GUI WAS SMALL, the saddle-horse was large;
Above the bows he showed but half a yard;
Below the cloth his spurs hung half a palm;
Men twice his age were not his peer by half!

GUI LOOSED THE REIN and spurred along the road;
But half a yard he showed above the bows;
But half a palm his stirrups hung below;
In Jesu's care fair Guibourc bade him go
To join the squires and fight their heathen foe.

ALL THROUGH THE NIGHT young Gui rode with the squires,
Until the dawn and early morning's light;
When they all came to Archamp on the tide,
The Count moved forth to speak with all his knights;
He called his lords and barons to one side
And they convened to hear him speak his mind;
In their own tongue with ringing tones he cried:

"YOUR DUTY CALLS, my noble lords and barons;
I do not steal your hunting-dogs and pack-hounds,
But give you mine whenever you would have them;
Nor do I take your hunting-hawks or falcons,

Or do you harm through any word or action;
When fathers die, I bless their sons so gladly
That widows have no reason to be anxious;
My men don't come to seize their goods and chattels,
But help their sons in any way they can do;
I care for them and knight them as my vassals
To keep their lands exempt of fees and taxes;
I give them land from my own fiefs and allods;
God curse me if I profit from their sadness!
Now, in return, support my battle-standard!"
They all replied: "Most willingly we shall do!
While life is left, you shall not find us lacking!"
Evening of Monday.
All men should serve a lord of William's valour,
And be prepared to die for him in battle.

HE LEFT THEM WHEN their pledges had been sworn,
And went to speak with all his vavasors;
He summoned them together, then he called
In their own tongue upon them, one and all:
"Good vavasors, my honoured, noble lords:
King Desramed the Moor has struck our shores;
We cannot let his evil flourish forth
Or look away and let it prosper more!
My worthy men, I tell you now therefore
That he has slain a knight I deeply mourn:
Famed Vivien, the gallant-visaged lord;
Beyond the Rhine or any foreign port
Of Christendom or Pagan lands abroad,
No better knight than he was ever born
For championing the blessed Christian cause,
Or cherishing and fighting for the law;
Strong, noble knights, you may be very sure
That no one else in any Christian court
Could call upon such vavasors' support,
Save Louis, who holds all of France in ward,
Our noble King, our rightful liege and lord;
Against his worth I neither vie nor vaunt;
So hear me well, my trusted knights true-born!
No mighty fight can ever be well fought
Without strong vavasors all standing sure,

And nimble youths not shirking from the toil
With sturdy knights experienced in war."
He looked at them and saw Gui on his horse;
He asked aloud: "Who is that well-armed boy
Perched on a horse among you, riding tall?
He's short on men who brought that one to war!"
They all replied: "What do you ask us for?
You ought to know your nephew Gui, my lord!"
On hearing this, the Count looked down, distraught,
And from his eyes the tears began to fall;
With all his heart he cursed his wife Guibourc:
"A curse on you, sweet sister, for this fault!
Young Gui, it seems she's cast you from her thoughts."
On hearing this, wise Gui made this retort:
"You're very wrong to blame your wife, my lord;
You left me in a woman's care by choice;
It was not hard to leave that care by force!"
Said William: "What do you blame me for?"
"I'll tell you why; but let it wait, my lord;
Down in their boats bide all those heathen Moors
Who've slain a knight we both most deeply mourn,
Famed Vivien, the gallant-visaged lord;
It is on them that your ill-will should fall!"
"Nephew, in truth, there's wisdom in your talk;
Though still a child, you have a warrior's voice;
When I am dead my land shall all be yours;
But there's one thing which troubles still my thoughts:
You are too young, my boy, and far too raw
To bear the trials and hardships to be borne:
The sleepless nights, the long days eating naught,
The awful blows struck in the fierce assault;
Upon that hill up there I'll have you brought
And guarded well by twenty of my force –
Now lost to me before they've even fought:
Upon the field they would have helped me more."
Young Gui replied: "I've never heard such talk!"
Said William: "What do you blame me for?"
"I'll tell you, since you've asked me to, my lord:
Do you regard the Love of God so poor
That He Who gives to great men His support
Will not uphold alike the weak and small?

There's none so great who wasn't small when born!
Today I'll strike with this, my girded sword,
And prove my worth and strength before you all;
My honour and my family's shall stand tall!"
Said William: "There's wisdom in your talk;
Gui, use your spurs and exercise your horse –
I want to see how you bear arms for war."

GUI LOOSED THE REIN and spurred across the field;
Just half a yard he showed above the seat;
Just half a palm his stirrups hung beneath;
Upon his left he raised his pennon free;
Across his arms the falling fringes streamed;
He raised it high and flew it in the breeze,
Then reined his horse to halt within four feet;
He spun its tail across the grass of green
To point its head at William his liege;
The Count exclaimed: "You should be good, young Gui!
Your father was and all your noble breed."

"COME, NEPHEW GUI, and ride at my right hand,
Your pennon raised beside my battle-flag;
With you to help, I fear for nothing bad!"
And so they rode to battle, lord and lad,
Two royal friends on Archamp's bloody land;
What woe they'd sow among those Pagan ranks!
Evening of Monday.
Had Gui not gone, they'd not have made it back.

14. How young Gui fared on Archamp field

KING DESRAMED had won, the French were beaten,
The first time that Count William had been there;
He'd taken spoils, the dead men's armour seizing,
Then ridden back to rest among his fleet there;
The wind had dropped and so they could not leave there;
Their overlords, their captains and their leaders,
A thousand score of King Desramed's heathens,
Had ridden forth for pleasure in the meantime;
A league or more they'd ridden from the beaches;

They'd brought a feast and, ready then to eat it,
They sat in rows about to start their feasting;
Then William came, most keen to join their mealtime,
With well-armed knights and thirty thousand liegemen,
Prepared to serve cold cuts for their repletion!
They cried "Mountjoy!" and charged the tables freely;
The Pagans cried: "Brave knights, mount horse to meet them!"
They all leapt up to face our Frenchmen fiercely,
And only those who couldn't move stayed seated;
They left their wine, their bread and meat uneaten,
Their golden plates, their cloths, their rugs and beakers;
But none of them could match Count William's greeting!
They turned in flight right back to where their fleet was
And raced aboard their galleys iron-sheeted;
They dressed for war, their arms and armour seizing,
And then once more they rode ashore to meet him.

COUNT WILLIAM may well have won that battle,
With Jesu's help and his own mighty valour,
But Desramed the Moor lay in an ambush
With fifteen kings whose names I'll tell you gladly:
Encas was one, another was Ostramas;
Then Butifer the bold and mighty Gamas,
Turlen Dosturges and his nephew King Alfay.

NUBLES OF INDIA, the Persian Ander,
Morans and Cabuel and Aristragot;
Strong Varians, King Salvain and Clamador.

THE FIFTEENTH was Nubia's king, called Thomas;
Each one of them had brought one thousand warriors
Who swallowed men like leopards or like monsters;
Without regard they rushed ranks in a body –
If one was felled another led them onward.

THE FRENCH SUSTAINED great loss of life again;
Bertrand was caught and hauled away in chains,
With Guielin and Count Giscard the brave,
Renier the bold and Walter of Termes;
They bound them tight and dragged them all away
Inside their ships at anchor on the bay;

The Count was shocked, and helplessly he gazed
As all his men were slaughtered or enslaved;
With all his strength the Count maintained the fray,
With nephew Gui beside him all the way.

THE DAY WAS CLEAR, the morning fine and bright;
The sun beat down and made their armour shine;
The sunbeams struck the shield of Gui the child
And tender tears ran freely from his eyes;
The Count looked up and asked him on the ride:
"What troubles you, young Gui, my nephew fine?"
"That's quickly told, my lord," the lad replied:
"I miss the care of fair Guibourc, your wife,
Who served me food as soon as day was light;
For now's the hour she fed my hunger, sire,
Which is so great that I shall surely die!
I cannot wield my arms to offer fight,
Or lift my lance or guide my horse's stride
To help myself or harm Desramed's knights;
To your distress and to the Moors' delight,
This is the day that I shall surely die!
My hunger's such that I shall lose my mind;
If only I had stayed at Guibourc's side!"

"MY HEART HAS STALLED, and so has all my courage!
I cannot help myself or harm another;
I cannot wield my arms to strike or struggle;
I'll die this day, to your dismay, good uncle!"

"MY EYES, UNCLE, are dimming in my head!
My arms have failed and so has all my strength!
My hunger's such that I shall lose all sense;
I miss Guibourc, the worthy wife you wed,
By whose sweet hand each morning I was fed;
I'll die this day, my lord, to your distress!
What suffering will strike your vassals then!
If I had food, I could escape from death."
"If only I could find some," William said;
Morning of Wednesday.
Dear God, if he could find some wine or bread!

"SIR WILLIAM, what will become of me?
My heart has stalled, I swear it faithfully;
I cannot wield my arms or lift my spear,
Or spur my horse Balzor or check its speed;
If I should die, to your distress and grief,
There's little left of our great family."
Said William: "I am hard-pressed indeed!
But can you ride back to that farm where we
Surprised the Moors on Monday at their feast?
Their cloth was spread but many chose to leave,
And left behind what could not turn and flee!"
"Do you mean wine, my lord, and bread and meat?"
"Go there, my boy!" cried William, his liege:
"Go, eat some bread and drink what wine you need,
Then help me here upon this fearsome field!
I need you, lad – do not abandon me!"
They parted thus, Count William and Gui.

Morning of Wednesday.
They parted thus and then Lord Gui the youth
Rode for a farm to find himself some food;
Across the land the Moors rode in pursuit,
But he escaped beyond their reach and view.

WHEN THEY COULD SEE that Gui had quite outstripped them,
They watched him go with curses and misgivings:
"This one will seek what Girart sought to bring us,
When he came back and brought the Count back with him:
He's off to France to seek their King's assistance;
Let us return to Archamp field and win it!
Let none of them still left return home living!"
And back they charged to find the Count and kill him;
Young Gui meanwhile had found the farmstead quickly
And, leaping down from Balzor's back and stirrups,
He ate some bread, in truth a very little,
But found some wine and drank a gallon swiftly;
Remounting then, he hurried back as bidden;
King Desramed and all his Moorish minions
Advanced meanwhile upon the Count to kill him;
On seeing this, that worthy knight and Christian

Cried out: "Mountjoy!" and galloped in their middle!
With just his lance he took the lives of sixty!

THEY PRESSED HIM HARD on every side and part;
They cast at him their wyverns and their darts,
Their cutting spears, their falchions and their shafts;
Between his thighs they slew his horse Liart;
Behold him, friends, down on his feet at last!
He drew his sword to fight them, stout of heart.

THEY PRESSED HIM HARD on every side and reach;
They cast at him their shafts and cutting spears;
So many struck upon his quartered shield
He couldn't stop it falling to his knees;
They beat him down with blows from head to heel
So that he lay outstretched upon the beach;
They struck him more with lances and with spears
But couldn't breach his coat of sturdy steel;
Out of his mouth the blood ran down his beard;
He cried aloud: "Come soon, fine nephew Gui!
If you would prove your valour, come to me!"
The youth just then was coming from his meal;
The cry was loud and struck the youngster's ears.

THE CRY WAS LOUD and, riding down the hillside,
He heard it well and charged his mount there swiftly
To smite a Moor right on his buckler's middle;
He split it wide and smashed the boards to splinters
And ripped the coat of sturdy mail to ribbons;
He flung the Moor upon the floor and killed him;
He cried: "Mountjoy! My lord, are you still living?"
Upon his shield he struck another villain;
He split it wide and smashed the boards to splinters
And ripped his coat of sturdy mail to ribbons,
The tunic too, and then the breast within it;
He flung the Moor upon the floor and killed him;
He cried: "Mountjoy! My lord, are you still living?"

UPON HIS SHIELD another Moor he battered;
From band to boss he splintered all its panels

And in his throat the Moor took all the fragments;
Gui's mighty spear drove through him to the gravel;
It broke his spine and bared it to the marrow;
The blow went through his shoulder-blades and backbone,
And when he fell Gui's sturdy lance was shattered;
He gripped his sword and drew it from the scabbard.

HE DREW HIS SWORD and like a worthy knight
He raised the blade and pointed it on high;
He struck a Moor upon his helmet's iron
And split it through down to the nasal-spike;
He cleft the coif and cracked the skull inside;
The blow was huge, as huge as he could strike,
And to the waist clean through the Moor was sliced,
The saddle split and then the horse's spine;
Upon the ground both man and horse were piled;
On seeing this, the Saracens took fright;
Each said to each: "That was a lightning-strike!
Count Vivien the brave's come back to life!"
They turned in flight and left the field of fight,
And, when they did, Count William could rise:
A foot-soldier without a horse to ride!

MY FRIENDS, IT WAS a wonder of our Lord,
That one young lad turned twenty thousand Moors!
They turned in flight and fled back to the shore,
As William leapt to his feet once more;
Both Gui and he gave chase with flashing swords.

THEY TURNED IN FLIGHT and fled towards the sea,
As William once more leapt to his feet;
Both Gui and he gave chase with flashing steel;
Count William went running down the field,
And, seeing this, Gui spurred across to speak:
"My lord," he cried, "mount up this worthy steed!
With willing heart your wife gave it to me!"
So Gui got off for William, and he
Jumped up at once and then said angrily:
"In faith, my lad, that was a foolish speech!
You said before that you escaped her keep,
And now you say she gave you her own steed!

Who gave you leave to blame my wife to me?"
"A curse on that, my lord!" replied young Gui:
"Ride on its back and head straight for the sea!
The Moors may well have left with all their fleet!"
On saying this, once more he raised his steel.

15. How King Desramed was slain

BRAVE WILLIAM rode through the field of battle,
His visor down, his sword drawn from the scabbard;
His feet hung loose below the young boy's saddle;
The stirrups beat against his calves and banged them;
He held his sword between the blade and handle
Upon the bow before before his saddle's padding;
Beneath his thighs good Balzor gently cantered,
While noble Gui jogged in the horse's track-marks,
Knee-high at times in pools of crimson lagging;
Beside the field in ambush lay Desramed,
His features smeared with mud and blood-bespattered;
But William observed him by his manner;
The Pagan thought their spears had done such damage
That William would fall if he attacked him,
And he'd resolved upon a daring ambush;
So up he leapt and grasped the horse he had there;
He slipped the rein from its right foreleg's ankle
And gripped his spear, which was both sharp and massive;
Straight from the ground he leapt astride his stallion;
He spurred its sides and rode the horse straight at him.

THE COUNT LOOKED UP and saw him on his horse:
His body swayed, his spear was brandished forth;
Before his face the Count raised up his sword;
The Pagan King looked at him then and stalled
His horse's stride and slowed it to a walk;
Gui called aloud: "Count William, my lord,
I beg of you to step down from Balzor
And let me have my Arab steed once more,
So I may joust against this evil Moor!"

"COUNT WILLIAM, my lord, I beg you, please,
To let me have once more my Arab steed,
So I may joust against this foreign fiend!"
Said William: "That was a foolish speech!
Lad, do you dare to claim first blow from me?
Since I began to bear arms in the field,
No mother's son dared make so bold a plea,
Not even Louis, who is my King and liege!
If I can strike with my good sword of steel,
I'll soon avenge the blows and woes I feel!"

Wednesday it was; AS DESRAMED rode in,
The Count struck hard upon his helmet's rim
And smote to ground the right hand side of it;
The Moor was stooped by such a fearsome hit
And grasped his steed to stay astride and live;
But, as the Count rode through, in passing him,
He swung and cleft his whole leg at the hip;
His body slewed the other side and slipped;
Count William put forth his hand and gripped
The passing reins upon that horse of his,
Then came to Gui and offered him the gift.

THE SARACEN, struck down upon the field,
Beheld the Count lead off his noble steed
And raised aloft a wild lament indeed:
"Alas, Balzan, how much I held you dear!
From my own shire and shore I led you here;
Who owns you now has not the skill to bleed
Or shoe you well or tend you properly!"
Said William: "Let this lamenting be,
And think instead how your own leg may heal!
Your horse's care can well be left to me!"
He came to Gui and offered him the beast.

THE PAGAN'S HEART was filled with raging spite:
"Alas, Balzan, fine steed, ill-starred your life,
Your lovely limbs and your majestic stride!
You've borne me well to where I've lost my thigh;
Upon your back I've won so many fights!
You have no peer in any horse alive;

A bitter loss you are to Pagan knights!"
Said William: "I care not for your sighs!"

BRAVE WILLIAM rode on across the field;
Upon his right he led the Pagan's steed
And offered it to his young nephew Gui;
He called aloud: "Mount up this noble beast
And lend me yours, fair nephew, if you please;
I like the horse; it suits me well indeed;
You have this horse which was the Moor Emir's!"
"With all my heart," said Gui, "but let me keep
The saddle there which first belonged to me!
You have the one upon the Pagan's steed."
The Count replied: "I willingly agree."
Then swung to ground to swap them each for each.

WHILE WILLIAM was busy with the swap,
The Pagan sighed and writhed upon the spot;
Gui drew his sword and cut his head clean off;
On seeing this, the Count was filled with wrath.

"AH, WRETCHED YOUTH, what arrogance is this?
How dare you strike a lord bereft of limb?
In highest courts they'll censure you for this!"
Young Gui replied: "A curse on such a thing!
Though he had lost a leg that carried him,
He still had eyes that he could see us with,
And genitals to breed more gentiles with!
He could have reached his heathen home and lived;
And then, one day, some son or heir of his
Would seek us out with all his evil skill;
To save myself I'll never flinch one inch!"
Said William: "There's wisdom in your wit;
Though still a child, you have a warrior's will;
When I am dead, you'll rule my lands forthwith."
Wednesday it was,
When William beat Desramed the king.

16. How Vivien died and Gui was captured

THE COUNT RODE ON, across that field of fight;
His heart was filled with bitter rage and spite;
He broke the straps upon his helmet bright,
And hung his head in anguish out of mind;
With crimson blood his noble flag was grimed;
A mighty loss he found of all his knights;
Upon his right Gui followed, far behind;
Beside a pool brave Vivien he spied,
Where flowed a fount whose falls went beating by,
Beneath an olive tree both broad and high;
His hands of white were crossed upon his sides;
He smelled more sweet than any balm or spice;
Some fifteen wounds had rent his body wide –
Of any one the greatest lord alive,
A king or count, or captain, would have died;
How sadly now our Count bewailed his life:
"Sir Vivien, ill-starred your heart!" he cried:
"So brave to serve, so daring and so wise!
Now you are dead, where shall I find your like?
I have no sons, nor worthy kin or kind."

"SIR VIVIEN, ill-starred your youth so splendid,
Your lovely limbs, your cheek and chin so gentle!
I dubbed you knight in my own hall at Termes;
For love of you to others I presented
One hundred swords, one hundred shields and helmets;
I see you now struck down on Archamp meadow,
Your pallid breast and body split and severed,
And all these men of yours slain in the mêlée;
May God the Lord in His great mercy bless them,
Who governs all below from His high dwelling!"

WHERE FLOWED A FOUNT whose falls were fleet and fresh,
Beneath a mighty olive's bough widespread,
Beside a pool he found Count Vivien;
With fifteen wounds his body was all rent –
The least one would have bled a prince to death;
In tender tones the Count made this lament:

"Sir Vivien, ill-starred the great prowess
And proud resolve that God placed in your breast!
I dubbed you knight in my own town Termes,
And there you gave your life to God and pledged
To never flee from any foe you met;
You always strove to keep your word since then,
And now, for this, I see you hacked to death;
Tell me, fine lord, can your tongue still confess
And know the name of God Omnipotent?
If you believe that on the Cross He bled,
Then in my pouch I have some holy bread
Which God's own hand at holy mass has blest;
If you could taste one morsel of it yet,
You need not fear the harrowing of Hell."
When this was said the youth regained some sense:
He raised his gaze to see his uncle there,
And his fair lips said this with his last breath:
"Ah, noble lord, fine liege, I know this well:
God is the Truth, the Life and Light of men,
Who came to earth to save mankind from death;
Born of the Maid in blessed Bethlehem,
Upon the Cross He suffered in our stead;
When Longinus's lance had pierced His flesh,
From His fair side both blood and water bled
On blinded eyes and made him see again;
He begged for grace and gained it there and then;
Now I lay all my sins and weaknesses
Before His grace and everlasting strength;
Fine uncle, lord, give me a little bread!"
"Ah!" said the Count, "Blest hour that gave you breath!
He who believes shall surely live again."
To wash his hands he found the fountain's edge,
Then from his pouch he took some holy bread;
He laid a crumb on Vivien's tongue, and then
The youth strove hard to swallow it; then, friends,
His soul rose up and left his body dead;
The Count looked on and, seeing this, he wept;
He raised the youth upon his piebald's neck
To bear him back and lay him to his rest;
But once again the Count was soon beset
By fifteen kings whose names I know full well:

King Mathamar and two kings of Avers,
One Bassumet, another Desramed,
Soldan the Black and strong Eaduel,
King Aelran and his son Aelred;
King Sacealme, Alfam and Desturbed,
Golias, Andafel and Wanibled;
They struck as one, and their united strength
Upon his shield well-nigh thrust him to death;
When William saw he could not counter them,
He laid the corpse back on the ground and then,
Commending it to God, he turned on them;
In frenzied haste they struck with blows so dread
That by brute force they drove apart both men,
Lord from the lad whom he had loved the best;
And then the Moors surrounded Gui as well
And brought his horse, the Moor's Balzan, down dead;
Upon the ground young Gui was overwhelmed;
How sad it is, the fall of such prowess!
All wielding swords, three hundred rushed him next
And, seizing him, they bound his arms and legs;
The Count looked on and cried with deep regret:
"Dear God, Who dwells in Trinity most blest,
Who rules the earth and Heavens overhead,
How all my fame has fallen to its end!
How brought to naught my clan most nobly bred!
And you are caught, young Gui, my worthy friend!
God help you now, Who suffered death Himself
On Good Friday to save all Christian men!"
Inside their ships they dragged young Gui with them;
The Count looked on, whose heart was filled with dread;
With all his rage he charged the Pagan press
And slew fifteen and wounded sixty men
Of whom not one would ever walk again.

17. How William slew Alderufe the Pagan

Evening of Monday.
THE FRENCH WERE DEAD or led away in chains;
No man on horse remained, no horse remained;
The Count alone was left on Archamp plain,
Bereft of all except Lord Jesu's aid;

Then, on his right, one Alderufe by name,
Rode up to him and stared him in the face:
"You're not Bertrand or William," said the knave,
"Nor Guielin nor Walter of Termes,
Nor Guischard, nor Girart whom they obey;
You do not look like any of that race!"
The Count replied: "I ought to, in all faith!"
"By my right hand, I care not either way!
Be who you may, this is your dying day!
Palermo's gold won't save you from your fate."
The Count replied: "God's will is what prevails."

"BRAVE SARACEN, since you are keen to fight me,
First tell me here what I have done to spite you;
For any wrong I'm ready to requite you;
I give my word, a pledge you can rely on."

SAID ALDERUFE: "I blame the war-lord William
For his defence of Christian men and women
Within this realm, and spreading false religion!
Whoever bears the cross of Christ is guilty;
It's of no worth to be baptised a Christian;
God dwells above but Lord Mahom is with us;
God gives us warmth, Mahomet gives us winter;
God sends the rain, Mahomet grows grass with it;
To live down here a man needs our permission,
Mahomet's too, who governs all the living."
The Count replied: "You lack both wit and wisdom!
But what is more, your words are sacrilegious!
I challenge you for your pernicious thinking!
Lord God is more than any living thing is!"
Both turned about then charged their horses swiftly;
On either's shield the lance of each went hitting,
And edge to edge both split apart and splintered;
Their coats were rent, their mail was ripped to ribbons;
The Count was felled with both his legs uplifted,
And Alderufe fell too, his body spinning;
No help to them were saddles or surcingles;
Against the ground their helmet-points went sticking;
Up in the air their tumbled feet went kicking!

KING ALDERUFE was very bravely bred,
A worthy knight, a man of mighty strength –
But he shunned God and so his soul was dead;
He served Beelzebub, Pilate the wretch,
And Antichrist, Bagot and Tartaren,
And Astarut the old who dwells in Hell;
He was the first to gain his feet, but when
The Count was up his strength was nothing less;
He swung the blade which Charlemagne had held;
The Saracen was strong and tall as well,
His body long, and high his head and neck:
The blade fell short; it struck his thigh instead
And from his trunk it cut off all his leg;
It fell to ground on one side of him there,
And he dropped too, he couldn't help himself;
The Count called out: "Why should I strike again?
Bereft of limb, your strength is profitless!"
Then he beheld the Moor's horse Florescele,
And, seizing it, he mounted in one step
And struck the spurs against the horse's flesh;
With force and strength it reared on its hind legs:
"Ah," said the Count, "the Lord has blest my quest!
How well He aids all those who serve Him best!
Who trusts in Him will always have success!
This horse, I think, will serve me to the end!"

Evening of Monday.
SAID WILLIAM: "The Lord has blest me so!
This horse is worth Palermo's wealth of gold."
He grasped Balzor and slit the horse's throat;
No sooner done, he said in tender tones:

"ALAS, BALZOR, to kill you was unjust;
So help me God, you never failed me once,
In any way, at night or daytime, but
I did it so that no foul Saracen
Could mount your back and use your strength on us!"
He turned his mount and, changing tone and tongue,
He spoke in Hebrew, African and Hun,
In German, Greek, Armenian and Dutch,
And all the tongues he'd learnt to speak when young:

"You craven Moors, may Mahom fail your trust!"
On Florescele, and speaking to them thus,
He tricked the Moors and slaughtered scores of them.

COUNT WILLIAM rode forth in fiery fettle,
A gallant knight of noble strength and temper;
King Alderufe, meanwhile, lay on the meadow;
On looking up, he saw his horse had left him:
"Ah, Florescele, fine war-horse," he lamented,
"I could not find a finer charger ever!
Desramed's mount you were before he perished;
I won you back, resaddled you and led you
To fight again for me and for our empire;
Now you are caught and all my fame has ended!
Count William, I curse you and condemn you!
How fine a mount you've robbed me of, you devil!
If only you knew how to keep and tend him!
He has no peer in Christendom or elsewhere:
No Pagan land has ever bred one better;
Lord, pity me and give him back, I beg you!
Four times his weight in Arab gold I'll send you,
The finest gold that any mine could render."
The Count heard this and laughed beneath his helmet:
"Fool king, think first of how your leg is severed!
Go make a crutch so you can stand up steady,
And on your stump go fit an iron peg-leg!
Leave me to care for your good horse's welfare,
Like any man well used to it already –
Thank God above, I've kept and cared for many!"

"AH, FLORESCELE, sweet-natured horse of mine,
I never saw a horse that was your like!
The wind is not as swift as you in stride,
Nor any bird as fleet as you in flight;
You've carried me to where I've lost my thigh;
I've lost you too, and all my valour's pride."

Evening of Monday.
On hearing this, the Count, his sword aloft,
Approached the Moor and cut his head clean off;
Then Pagans from Palermo raced across

With Nicodemians and Africans
And Pagans from the land Superbia;
They chased the Count back to his town Orange;
He neared its gates, then found them barred and locked!

18. How William gained entrance to Orange

HE HAILED THE PORTER hastily and grimly:
"Friend, open up the gates, and do it quickly!"
"And who are you?" "I am your liege lord William!"
The porter said: "In truth, you'll not come in here
Until I go and ask my noble mistress."
"Then, brother, go! Do not delay or dither!"
The porter climbed the steps of marble swiftly:
"My lady wise, as Jesus is my witness,
Before the gates a fierce knight seeks admission!
He's very big, and strong of limb and figure,
And so fierce-faced I dared not scan his visage;
He says he is your husband Hooknose William,
But I did not unbolt the bar or lift it,
For he's alone and has no other with him;
And such a horse he has between the stirrups!
You will not find in any Christian kingdom
Or Pagan realm a horse that matches this one;
The knight himself bears Saracen equipment."
The lady said: "I'll know if it is William,
And, if it is, we surely shall admit him!"
Guibourc herself went down the staircase swiftly
And, moving forth, she said bravely and briskly:
"Who are you, knight, who come seeking admission?"
"You know me well," he said, "my lady Guibourc!
Before you stands your husband Hooknose William!"
But Guibourc said: "Sir knight, don't try to trick me!
You are well skilled in that, you Pagan villains!
By all you've said so far I'll not admit you,
For I'm alone, no other knight is with me;
And if you were my husband Hooknose William,
You'd have with you my liegemen and your kinsmen,
Frenchmen of France, its barons and its princes!
And all around the jongleurs would be singing,

And we would hear the rotes and harps of minstrels."
"Wretch that I am, alas!" said Hooknose William:
"It was my wont to travel with such spirit!
My lady wise, you know with your own wisdom
That men are rich as long as Lord God wishes,
And then are poor once more if He should will it;
From Archamp field beside the sea I've ridden,
Where I have lost my nephew, noble Vivien;
And young Bertrand was captured and imprisoned,
Sir Bernart's son, who rules Brabant's fair cities;
And Guielin and famed Giscard are with him."
Along the road his wife saw in the distance
A horde of Moors in arms approaching thither;
From France the sweet they'd cut a swathe of pillage;
They'd set on fire at Tours St Martin's minster,
And knocked to ground the mighty tower built there;
In chains they'd dragged one hundred captives with them,
And with stout sticks unceasingly they hit them,
And with their whips and stinging scourges whipped them;
His wife saw this and wept at once for pity:
"Sir knave, if you in truth were Hooknose William,
In Jesu's name you would defend those Christians
And seize the wealth that raiding-gang has pillaged!"
"Ah," said the Count, "I've never heard such mischief!
This is a test that in return she gives me,
And, live or die, I must do as she bids me!"
And so he turned and spurred the horse he'd ridden,
More fleet of hoof than any bird of wing was;
The Moors, in joy, beheld his looming figure:
"I see our liege!" each said to all his kindred:
"King Alderufe, Palermo's lord, has finished
The great assault he planned for Orange city!
The gods be praised, who bring him back uninjured,
Alive and well from William the villain!
Well should we praise the gods of our religion,
Mahom, Bagot, Apollo, Macabeus!"
But all this time, while their delight continued,
The Count drew in, intent upon his mission!
The very first he met, when riding in there,
He hewed of head, and then with swift precision,
A second, third and fourth fared little different;

Fifteen in all he slew before he'd finished;
Some Pagans said: "This is an evil spirit!"
But others said: "No! You are wrong – and guilty!
Our captain's wrath is aimed at your contingent,
For you were not at Archamp's battle with him,
And we all were and fought with him to win it!"
Then all those Moors and Saracens relinquished
Their evil gains and fled there panic-stricken;
The Count looked on and offered God thanksgiving;
He freed the French and gave them back their riches.

THE COUNT SPURRED OFF his war-horse to the right,
One Corberan of Oliferne to strike;
He split his shield and slit the hauberk's hide;
One lance's length he flung the Moor from life;
His wife looked on, and from her window's height
She spoke again, with warmer words this time:
"That blow of yours was truly William-like!
Ride back to me and to my gate, sir knight!"

THE NOBLE COUNT turned round and back he rode:
"My Lady, now will you draw back the bolt?"
She said: "No sir, so help me God, I won't,
Unless you show the wound upon your nose
Which William my hook-nosed husband shows
From when he fought and slew the Slav Tiebault!
For many men are equal to behold,
When on their steeds they strike their lusty blows;
I have no guard, and I am here alone,
Save for the man whom you have seen below."
"No more of this!" said William and groaned:
"What pains this day I've had from friend and foe!"
He raised his helm, inset with precious stones,
And let it fall back on his shoulders, so
His wife could see the visage loved and known;
So Guibourc looked and knew it for his own;
With tender sighs her tears began to flow:
"Unlock the gates, good guard, and be not loath!
This is indeed my liege lord true and bold!"
Evening of Monday.
They opened up and welcomed William home;
He'd longed for this a long, long time ago!

19. How William lamented his loss of men

COUNT WILLIAM dismounted by the hall;
Guibourc herself stood there to take his horse
And led it down below inside a stall;
She stripped its reins and saddle first of all,
Then gave it feed, good oats to eat, before
She covered it with rugs to keep it warm;
Then she returned to hug and kiss her lord,
And asked him in a fair and courteous voice:

"WHAT HAVE YOU DONE, my lord, with all the men,
Four thousand seven hundred that you led?"
"In truth, my love, the Moors have slaughtered them;
With bloody mouths across Archamp they're spread."
"What have you done, my lord, with Vivien?"
"In truth, my love, the Moors tore him to death."
On hearing this, his wife filled with distress:
"And brave Bertrand, where is that nephew then,
Son of Bernart, who in Brabant was bred?"
"Sweet sister, friend, he fought his very best
In fifteen jousts, unflinching in the press;
The sixteenth joust, with overwhelming strength,
They brought him down, though up he leapt again;
He drew his sword and thrust his shield ahead
And drove his blade against their sides and legs;
But he was caught by all those hounds from hell;
By hand and foot they bound and led him hence,
And, as I watched, aboard their boats they went;
I could not save or help our nephew then."
Fair Guibourc said: "Bertrand, alas, my friend;
My grief is great; I loved you long and well."

"WHAT HAVE YOU DONE," she asked him after that,
"With little Gui, the fair and gallant lad?
I gave to him King Mabun's battle-flag,
The battle-steed of Oliver the Gasc,
The mail and helm of King Tiebault the Slav."
"In truth, my love, he fought with all he had,
In fifteen jousts, unflinching, with our flag;

And he did well until the sixteenth clash,
When he was caught as all of them attacked;
They led him hence, bound fast by feet and hands,
And, as I watched, aboard their boats they ran;
I could not save or even help the lad."
Fair Guibourc said: "For little Gui, alas!
I loved him well and now my heart is sad."

"MY HUSBAND, LORD, what have you done with Walter,
And Guielin and noble Renier also?"

"IN TRUTH, MY LOVE, the Moors have those as well;
In captives' bonds they hold them on their decks."

"GOD," SAID GUIBOURC, "how great a loss and crime,
If this is so and none is left alive!
But come, my lord, come wash your hands and dine;
I've had a feast prepared since morning's light;
Now you must eat for all four thousand knights,
Their men-at-arms and all their worthy squires."
"Ah, wretched me," Count William replied:
"Not two whole days have run their course since I
Rode out to fight with fifteen thousand knights;
Now I am here with two men by my side;
How far my fame has fallen in that time!"

HE GRASPED THE SLEEVE of his good wife Guibourc
And climbed the steps inside his marble hall;
There was no man to serve their needs at all –
Guibourc herself brought water back and forth,
And then a towel for William her lord;
They both sat down, but at the lowest boards:
The highest one they shunned in their remorse;
He saw the seats, the tables and the forms
Where all his lords were wont to sit before;
Now he saw none at ease within his court,
None playing chess or backgammon for sport,
And he bemoaned as one most nobly born:

"ALAS, GREAT HALL, how long you are and wide!
How well adorned on each and every side,

How well endowed by my most blessed wife!
Alas for you, great tables, raised so high!
I see you spread with linen-cloths so fine,
Your dishes filled and all your platters piled
With hunks of meat, with pastries and with pies!
You'll fill no more those hungry men of mine
Whose bloody mouths on Archamp's meadow lie!"
At this he wept and Guibourc swooned outright;
He raised her up, to soothe her if he might:

"GUIBOURC, MY LOVE, you have no cause to weep,
For you have lost no friend or kinsman dear;
I am the one who must bewail and grieve,
For I have lost my noble family!
Now I shall flee to some far-distant fief,
To St Michael in Peril by the Sea,
Or St Peter's in Rome on Nero's field,
Or to the plains where I may disappear
And take the vows that holy hermits keep,
And you the veil inside a nunnery."
"My lord," she said, "we may do this indeed –
When we have lived our lives together here!"

20. How William rode to Laon for royal help

"SIR WILLIAM, I urge you in God's name
To mount your horse as soon as morning breaks
And make your way to Louis, who maintains
His court at Laon; he owes you much, in faith!
Request him there to help us with all haste;
If he will not, return this fief straightway –
Be damned if you should keep it one more day!
Both you and I will join him in that case,
And we shall eat at his expense and pains,
And take our share of his bread every day!"
Said William: "I'm loath to leave this way,
But your advice has always been well made
And helped me much at many a time and place."
The Count moved off to take what rest he may;
At dawn's first light he mounted horse in haste.

"SWEET SISTER, FRIEND, your counsel I accept;
To Louis' hall at Laon I'll ride unchecked
And ask him there to lend and send us help;
But if the Moors observe that I have left,
The Saracens with their united strength
Will seize this hall and all that it protects;
Who will defend its walls and all its wealth?"
"My lord," she said, "the Lord our God Himself,
And ladies more than thirty score of them!
White hauberk hides will be their battle-dress,
Their heads adorned with green and pointed helms!
And we will stand upon the battlements
And hurl down stones and sticks and spears as well!
God willing, lord, it soon will have an end,
When you arrive with Louis and the French."
"Ah," cried the Count, "may God defend you then,
Who bides on high and bids his will to men!"

THE COUNT SET OFF and Guibourc wept with pity;
He led a squire who only was a stripling,
So young indeed he'd not seen fifteen winters;
So long his spear that he could scarcely lift it;
Along the ground his shield dragged as he gripped it,
And, as he rode, from side to side he slithered;
The Count looked on and, filled with heart-felt pity,
Relieved the lad of each piece of equipment;
And when they met with trading-folk or pilgrims,
Or journeyed past a fort or through a city,
He handed back the spear and buckler quickly
Till they were past, then once more lent assistance;
He wept all day for brave Bertrand in prison,
For Gui the youth and gallant-hearted Vivien,
And, grieving thus, his journey he continued
As far as Laon, where he dismounted swiftly;
Fine Spanish gold it was his wont to bring them,
And many men, in vain, ran to assist him;
For thirty men, let well alone for sixty,
He had no wealth, nor did they gain sufficient
Between them all to buy one glove with this time.

21. How William fared at King Louis' court

WHEN WILLIAM beheld the knights' dismay,
Who'd hastened forth in hope of gold or gain –
For he was wont to give them rings from Spain –
He said: "My lords, don't blame my sorry state!
My stock of gold and silver still is great,
Back in Orange, my city prized and praised;
But, by the Lord, I've none of it today,
For I've just come from Archamp on the waves,
Where I have lost Sir Vivien the famed;
The brave Bertrand was dragged away in chains
With wise Renier and Walter of Termes,
And Guielin and Giscard, fair of face;
Within Orange my wife is without aid;
She calls on you to help her, for God's sake."
But when they heard the losses he'd sustained,
Without delay they dropped his horse's reins
And turned their backs and quickly walked away;
Inside their hall they went and to their plates;
Count William would learn upon that day
How wealth is deaf to poverty's complaint,
And how good works may earn a paltry wage.

"WHERE IS THE COUNT?" asked Louis of his Peers;
They all replied: "Upon the steps, my liege;
The Devil's work has brought him to us here,
For, as he says, he's fared most evilly!"
The King replied: "My lords, let all that be;
You should not mock so fine a Count as he;
Go down at once and bring him here to me!"
"Since you command it, Sire, most willingly."
The Count strode forth to meet the King, his liege,
Who, kissing him, first bade him sit and eat;
When he had done the King began to speak:
"My loyal lord, how have your fortunes been?
I have not seen you now these seven years;
You would not come, I know, without good need."

He said: "My lord, you shall know all in brief:
I had secured so well my Spanish fief
That no man born of mortal flesh I feared;
Then Vivien the famed asked me to lead
My barons of Orange to his relief;
He was my blood, I could not but agree;
I took some seven thousand knights and peers;
Not one of them returned alive with me;
Famed Vivien lies dead upon the beach
And brave Bertrand was dragged off on a leash,
Son of Bernart who rules the Brabantines;
And Guielin was caught and little Gui;
Within Orange my wife remains besieged;
I call on you to rescue her, my liege!"
But Louis' face was turned away in grief:
For Bertrand's sake the King began to weep.

"KING LOUIS, LORD, my hardships have been many,
And I am worn with strain from struggles heavy;
Within Orange my wife has no protection;
For Jesu's sake, I call on you to help her!"
"I am not sure of this," King Louis said then:
"I will not go this time, nor will my levies."
Cried William: "God curse who breaks his pledges!"
He drew his glove of golden-threaded leather
And threw it down at Louis' feet in menace:
"King Louis, lord, your fief herewith I render!
I will not keep six inches of it henceforth!
Let someone else enjoy it at your pleasure."
There in the hall some fifteen knights were present
Of William's clan, his brothers, uncles, nephews,
Who would not fail their kinsman then or ever;
Upon one side was Poitier's Count Reynold,
His eldest sister's son, one of his nephews;
In ringing tones he started to address him:
"Fine uncle, no, by all the powers of Heaven!
Brave hero's son, retain the fief you merit!
So help me God, Who is our great Protector,
There is no man on earth who will prevent me
From bringing you four thousand knighted Frenchmen
On rapid steeds with bright arms at the ready!"

Said William: "Thank God there's one to help me!
Accursed the man who scorns a worthy nephew!"

ACROSS THE HALL stood Hernaut of Gironde
And William's father Aymeri of Narbonne,
And Count Garin, who ruled the town Anseune;
Each said aloud: "How shameful and how wrong,
If we should leave our kinsman to be lost!"
Said Aymeri, his father, of Narbonne:
"No King or count shall hinder me, by God,
From bringing him some seven thousand strong!"
"Four thousand I," said Garin of Anseune.

BEUVON, COUNT OF Commarchis city cried:
"And I shall stand by my good brother's side;
I'll not be stopped by any man alive
From bringing him four thousand of my knights."
"And I'll bring three," white-haired Hernaut replied:
"And I'll bring two," said brave Guibert the child;
Count Baldwin, lord of Flanders, spoke his mind:
"Count William, my lords, is brave and kind;
He loves his peers and neighbours all alike
And brings them aid whenever needs arise;
I'll not be stopped by any man alive
From bringing him one thousand men to fight;
Let us beseech King Louis' grace and try
To gain his help in aiding William's plight."

TOWARDS THE KING those noble lords drew nearer;
Count Baldwin was the first of them to speak there:
"True Emperor, for God's sake we entreat you:
See William! He stands before you weeping;
His skin is bruised beneath his Eastern bliaut;
This was not done by cowardice or weakness;
Within Orange, alone, is Lady Guibourc,
And now the hordes of Syria besiege her,
Palermo Moors and heathen Tabarians;
If Orange falls, they'll capture all that region,
Then they will cross Saint-Gilles and pass on freely
To capture Paris, then Saint-Denis' own precincts!
A curse on him who'd serve you then as liege lord!"

The King replied: "Then I shall go, and lead there
Some thirty thousand knights in levied legions."
"No, do not go, my lord!" the Queen beseeched him:
"Lady Guibourc was born and bred a heathen
Who knows the arts and every act of evil;
She's skilled in herbs and how to mix and heat them;
She'll poison you or take your life, believe me!
William will rule with Guibourc as co-regent,
And I'll be left a lost and grieving creature!"
To hear these words set William's anger seething:
"What did you say? God curse your interference!
You wretched Queen, last night you drank too freely!
The King knows well I never have deceived him;
The cruel blows that you have heard me speak of
Were real enough at Archamp on the seaboard!"

"YOU WRETCHED QUEEN! You stinking chatter-crow!
Thibaut had you, that filthy, feckless rogue,
And ill-faced Esturmi, who were supposed
To guard Archamp from any Pagan foe!
They fled the field and left Vivien alone;
One hundred priests and more have cracked your bones
And ridden on your back, this much I know,
And not once did you want your handmaid close!
You wretched Queen! You stinking chatter-crow!"

"IF YOU WERE CUT in two, it would be fitter,
Since by your deeds all France has been belittled!
When you are sat by your warm fire in winter
And eat your fill of fine and spicy chicken,
You drink your wine from goblets finely-lidded,
Then go to bed the best bedecked of women,
Your legs aloft, well laid upon the linen;
What lusty blows your lecher-lovers give you –
While we awake with aching heads and grimly
Ride forth to take the lusty blows and hitting
Upon Archamp and come back bloody-visaged!
Be in no doubt: if your mad talk continues,
I'll need no help to split you down the middle!"
He drew his blade one full foot and six inches,
But Aymeri, his sire of Narbonne city,

Stepped forth at once and spoke these words of wisdom:
"Sir William, no further! I forbid you!
Though curse her birth, the Queen is still your sister!"
King Louis said: "Well spoken, worthy Christian,
For it is clear that something has bewitched her!
Sir Count, though I myself may not go with you,
I'll summon here at break of dawn and give you
A thousand score with spear and sword uplifted."
"Lord Emperor, my hearty thanks," said William.

22. How Renewart joined forces with the Count

THE EMPEROR called all his knights together;
With his own seal he signed the urgent message
And sent it forth to all parts of his empire;
Within a week one thousand score assembled
Beside the force brought to the Count already
By his own kin from lands in their possession;
Then Louis called the Count into his presence:
"My noble lord," he said, "at your requesting
I've summoned forth these knights and their attendants."
The Count replied: "May God in Heaven bless you!
Now give me leave to journey back, I beg you."
Upon a hill the Count had set his tent up,
And from the King's own kitchen ran a fellow
Dressed all in rags, with no shoes and no leggings;
His feet were huge and newly freed from fetters;
His shoulder bore a pole both huge and heavy;
No man alive but he could hold or heft it;
To William he ran and thus addressed him:
"My noble lord, my will is to attend you
And fight for you on Archamp's bloody meadow;
I'll slaughter Moors and Saracens a-plenty!"
Said William: "Your will will be well tested!
You look like one who likes his food at vespers,
And who, at dawn, is loath to leave his bedding!"
Said Renewart: "My lord, you are in error!
If you take me to Archamp's coastal meadows,
I shall do more than fifteen of the best ones
Among those peers whom you have here or elsewhere."

Said William: "A noble boast, young fellow!
I'll have you armed to fight with proper weapons."
Said Renewart: "Except this pole, I'll never
Bear other arms, so please the Lord of Heaven,
Nor climb astride a horse's back, God help me!"
Then, running back to seek his master's blessing,
He said: "My lord, I've worked for you at length here,
But now it's time to show I can do better!
Count William will take me to the mêlée
At Archamp field, which lies upon the headland."
His master said: "He'll not, you foolish beggar!
You'll never bear the hungry days unending,
Nor all the trials and hardships to be met there;
And you will miss the wines and meads you cherish,
The bread and meat and all the kitchen's plenty,
And you will die in misery most wretched;
And I would grieve, for I have reared you gently!"
Said Renewart: "Your words are vain and empty;
There's nothing here for me that will prevent me
From leaving it to fight where fighting beckons."
On hearing this, his master moved directly
Towards the youth to thwart what he had threatened;
But with his pole he thwacked the cook so deftly
He knocked him flat upon the fireside's embers;
Before he stood his beard was singed and severed!
Said Renewart: "Good man, lie there at leisure,
And you can guard this household here for ever;
If something's lost, then it is you they'll question."
Across the hill he ran in the direction
Where William had had his tent erected;
He asked and asked till someone deigned to tell him
Where Wiliam's kitchen was, wherein he entered
With water-pails and got the camp-fire ready;
He was well skilled and earned the praise of many;
They gave him mead and mugs of wine well-peppered;
They filled his cup till he had lost his senses
And then they stole the pole that he so cherished;
On waking up, he couldn't find his weapon,
And cursing fate, he fell to great lamenting:
"Ah, woe is me, why was I born so wretched?"
The pranksters laughed and carried on their jesting

Till Renewart looked at them all and bellowed:
"You sons of whores, have you purloined my treasure?"
He ran at them with all his rage and temper
And, grabbing two, he banged their heads together
With such brute force their eyes burst from their temples;
A third one said: "I'll fetch your pole directly!"
Said Renewart: "You'll not escape my vengeance!"
So two of them went with him to a shed there,
But could not budge the pole for all their efforts;
When Renewart could see where it was buried,
With just one hand he raised it up and swept it
Around his head and threatened every Gentile:
"Now I've my pole, there's nothing will protect you!"

COUNT WILLIAM woke up when dawn appeared;
He bade his horns blown lustily indeed
And sixty more called back across the field;
The mighty din cleared Renewart's dull ears
And in a daze he started from his sleep;
In haste to go he left behind his beam
Without a thought until they reached a stream;
Before the French he tried its depth and steeped
His visage in its waters cold and fleet;
Then from the wine his wits began to clear
And straightaway he thought about his beam;
He turned around to run back where he'd been,
As William said, on seeing him retreat:
"Friend Renewart, are you so quick and keen
To get back to your kitchen-spits and grease?
Before you left I said how it would be,
How you would not endure the trials you'd meet!"
"No, noble lord! That thought is far from me;
But back in camp I've left behind my beam!"
"You foolish rogue, let that poor lumber be!
I'll have one more cut down from these good trees
To fit your back, one long and strong and sleek!"
But Renewart replied: "God! No, my liege!
No wood on earth could make a pole its peer;
I've had that pole for more than seven years,
In Louis' hall, down by the fire with me!
It's never split nor lost one splintered piece!"

Said William: "Then it shall be brought here."
Said Renewart: "Now that's a noble speech!"
The Count looked round and saw a Fleming near,
A handsome knight, his body strong and lean,
Well mounted on a swift and sturdy steed;
He ordered him to go and bring the beam:
"Most willingly," he said, "at your decree."
He spurred in haste to where their camp had been,
Where, stepping down, he tried to lift that beam –
He cursed it soon and turned to let it be!
He mounted horse, returning with all speed,
Not stopping once until he met his liege:
"Fine friend, where is young Renewart's good beam?"
"Fine lord, I couldn't budge the thing," said he:
"A curse on him who left it in the field,
His mother too! A curse upon all three!"
Said Renewart: "Then I must go – it seems
It will not come by any mortal means
If my own arms do not perform the deed!"
Said William: "I'll wait no longer here!
If you go back, it's all the same to me,
But join our ranks before the night is here!"
So Renewart ran back with rapid leaps –
A Gascon steed would not have matched his feet –
And laughed with joy when he beheld his beam;
In just one hand he raised it with great ease,
And though the French pressed on with their best speed,
Young Renewart stood waiting in a field
Before the French had all passed through that stream!
Count William called out, when he appeared:
"Tell me, my friend, have you retrieved your beam?"
"Yes, noble lord, thanks be to God it's here!
St Mary's grace has brought it back to me!
The Moors shall pay most dearly for their greed:
Now I've my pole, not one of them shall flee!"

Evening of Monday.
CRIED RENEWART: "Be neither loath nor laggard!
If we are slow, when we arrive for battle
The Pagans from Superbia and Africa
And Nicodemia will all have vanished!"

The French all said: "This peasant is a madman!
He wants a fight – may God give him a bad one!"
For in their hearts the cowards heaved with anguish,
While braver men sat firmly in the saddles
Of their swift-paced, Castilian-bred war-stallions.

23. How Renewart was greeted in Orange

THE COUNT RETURNED across the dales and hillsides
And over heights, loath now to lag or linger;
At last he came to his beloved city,
Upon the stones dismounting from his stirrups;
Before the hall his wife Guibourc stepped quickly
And lovingly she welcomed him with kisses,
And then she asked: "How have you fared, Sir William?"
"No way but well, so please you, Lady Guibourc!
One thousand score and more have journeyed with me
Whom Louis, at his court in Laon, commissioned,
As well as men sent by my loyal kinsmen;
Thank God the Lord, two thousand score I bring you!"
"And not the King?" "No, Lady, great's the pity;
At royal Aix he lies, struck with a sickness."
Fair Guibourc said: "I swear you made him sicken!
If he's struck down, may he not rise unbidden!"
The Count replied: "May Jesus Christ forgive you!"
He strode inside his palace marble-pillared,
And Renewart, his pole well clutched, went with him;
Inside they thought he was some forest brigand,
And many there were frightened he would kill them!

THE COUNT STRODE UP his steps of marble made,
And Renewart, his pole well clutched, the same;
Fair Guibourc looked intently at his face,
Then hurried to her lord with this to say:
"Fine husband, lord, who is that youngster, pray,
Who bears a pole across his shoulder-blades?"
"Good wife," he said, "he is a willing knave,
A youth whom God has thought to bring my way."
"And have we need to fear him?" she exclaimed:
"No, not at all! Address him unafraid!"
So, leading him inside a private place,

She asked: "My friend, where were you born and raised?
What realm is yours, what family and race?"
And he replied: "I'm from the land of Spain;
I am a son of Desramed the great
And Orabel from far across the waves."
"What are you called?" "Renewart is my name."
On hearing this, she knew him straightaway;
Fair Guibourc sighed and said with tearful gaze:
"That name is very dear to me, in faith;
For once I had a brother named the same;
I'll have you dubbed a knight for his name's sake,
And given arms and noble destriers."
Said Renewart: "Except this pole, I'll take
No other arms, by God in Heaven's Grace,
Nor climb astride a horse on any day!"

"FAIR BROTHER, FRIEND, I'll have you dubbed a knight
And given arms and noble steeds to ride!"

"GOOD LADY, NO!" thus Renewart implored her:
"There's not one thing that I hate more than horses!"

"MY FRIEND," SHE SAID, "then you shall wear a sword,
So, come what may, if that stout pole of yours
Should break apart or splinter or be shorn,
Then you may use this blade upon the Moors!"
And he replied: "That much I'll have with joy!"

FAIR GUIBOURC BROUGHT the sword-blade forth to give him;
Its hilt was gold, incised with black and silver;
She girt it on as Renewart stared stiffly;
He did not know that Guibourc was his sister,
Nor would he know until their ranks were thinner,
The battle won and all the fighting finished.

THE COUNT BADE ALL his servants serve a dinner
To fill the knights with cheer and with new vigour;
So Renewart moved off inside the kitchen,
His sword still on, and went to turn the spits there;
The cooks were pleased, for he was very skilful;
They gave him wine and mead and stronger spirits,

They filled his cup till he was weak and witless;
Guibourc herself did not forget her kinsman,
But in the hall prepared a bed to fit him,
Just as she did for her good husband William;
In tender tones she called him, like a sister:
"Fair brother, friend, rest in this bed, I bid you!"
Then she lay down next to her husband William;
And Renewart looked at the bed, as bidden,
But did not prize the comfort it would give him,
And he ran back to sleep down in the kitchen;
The pranksters there gave his thick hair a singeing
And set alight his bedding with some cinders;
On starting up, he smelt the burning linen
And leapt aloft just like a top sent spinning!
He roared with rage, his ringing voice uplifted:
"Ah, woe is me! What rogues have dared this mischief?
I am Desramed's son, the ill-starred issue
Of fair Orabel's womb, his Eastern Princess!
Ill-starred the hour my eyes beheld Count William,
Who brought me here away from Louis' city,
The hearth and heart of France's noble kingdom!
The Count's own men esteem my worth so little
That they have burnt my beard and singed my whiskers!"
Those rogues, meanwhile, began to laugh and snigger,
Till Renewart stared hard at them, grim-visaged:
"You sons of whores, did you scorch me, you villains?
You will regret you ever tried to trick me!
Unless I fail, you will not leave here living!"
He swung his pole and slew four in an instant;
He swung again and, running off, a fifth one
Was hit so hard across the back and kidneys
His spine was cleft, then with his foot he kicked him
Straight in the heart and split it down the middle;
Then Renewart went back inside the kitchen;
He locked the doors so he could sleep unhindered,
Then laid his head on one corpse for a pillow;
He thrust his pole beneath his ribs and midriff
And slept as sound as some upon a quilt-bed!

BRAVE RENEWART got up before the dawning;
He left the hearth and went along the hallway;

He cried: "Mountjoy! Brave knights, bestride your horses!
When we arrive at Archamp on the water
The Saracens will all have fled before us!
We'll not regain the moment if we loiter!"
The French cried out: "You rogue, leave off your roaring!
Accursed the hour that you were ever born in!
The cock has cried twice only yet this morning!"
Said Renewart: "But I have cried an order!
I am a Prince and will be heard henceforward!
Now by the faith that I have pledged and sworn to,
If you do not arise and heed my warning,
I'll make quite sure you all pay dearly for it!"
He raised his pole and struck a roof support-beam
Straight through the grain, destroying one whole storey;
Above their heads the whole roof shook unsurely
And almost brought the walls of the whole hall down!
The French, in fear, leapt from their sleeping-quarters:
One thousand lost their shoes in the disorder
And couldn't find the clothes each one had worn there!
They saddled up their swift and sturdy war-steeds
And in the dark rode fifteen long leagues forward –
And black it was, with no sign of the dawn-light!
Friends, how they cursed brave Renewart in chorus:
"May God, the Lord of Miracles, destroy him,
This wretched rogue, this boorish, brainless pauper,
Who has us out at such an hour on horseback!
He should be whipped and flayed for what he's caused us!"
But William replied: "My lords, I warn you:
Though he is mad, you should not mock or taunt him!
For any one of you, however dauntless,
Who laid a finger on him, would be slaughtered!"

THEN WILLIAM led forth the force of France
Until they came to Archamp field at last.

24. How Renewart turned cowards into heroes

SAID WILLIAM'S BROTHER, Beuvon of Commarchis,
And his fine father Aymeri of Narbonne:
"Brave countrymen and fellow knights stout-hearted:
The finest war is one that's done the fastest!"
The French replied: "We swear by our dead fathers
To strike so hard with all our swords and lances
That, though we die, France will be feared hereafter."
When this was said they roared "Mountjoy!" in answer,
The battle-cry of mighty Charlemagne;
They raised their spears towards the Moors, advancing.

THE HOST OF FRANCE had followed William's lead
And come at last to Archamp on the sea,
Where they beheld the mighty Pagan fleet:
"My worthy lords," said William the fierce,
"We've journeyed far and now you all can see
The mighty host of Pagandom's Emir;
Now we must go and show the wrath we feel
For those who shame and blame our Christian creed!
But if there's one of you who will shame me
When in this fight at Archamp on the sea,
Then in God's name and mine I bid him leave
And make his way back home to France the sweet."
On hearing this, some thanked the Lord indeed
And in a crowd those cowards all convened;
The Count's support this way was much decreased,
As some turned round already in retreat;
They asked their leave from William their liege
And he deigned not deny them all or each;
But I don't think they travelled far afield –
For Renewart waylaid them by a stream
They had to cross beside a great ravine;
Across his back he bore his mighty beam;
He said: "My lords, please tell me why you're here?"
"The Count has said that some of us may leave;
Come with us too and bring your trusty beam!
So many Moors and Saracens we've seen
That none of us will live or flee their zeal!"

Said Renewart: "You rogues lie in your teeth,
And by God's Faith you'll pay for such a speech!"
He rushed them then and pay they did indeed,
For with his pole he slew more than fourteen
And made the rest turn back at twice the speed!
Brave Renewart approached the Count to speak:
"Sir William, one moment, if you please!
These runaways, these cowards that you see,
Shall be my troops, my force, my men of liege:
Place them and me in your front ranks to field
The cutting edge of all the Pagan spears."
Said William: "I willingly agree!
So help me God, they'll have small chance to flee!"
My friends, those men, so cowardly and weak,
Did noble deeds henceforth on Archamp field
And served the Count with honour in his need.

25. How Renewart rescued William's nephews

COUNT WILLIAM struck first with all his might,
As glorious God inspired his band of knights,
And brave Beuvon of Commarchis alike,
And Aymeri and Hernaut bearded white,
And Renewart, who swung his pole on high;
Three hundred Moors he slew in his first strike;
And all the day they battled fierce and wild,
And on and on throughout the dark of night
Until the dawn and morning's early light;
A stream of blood flowed through the field so wide
It would have turned a strong young ox aside;
Young Renewart at midday scanned the sky
And saw the sun high overhead and cried:
"The Devil this! Shall we do naught besides
Attack and slay more heathens all the time?
Their sum, it seems, has grown three times in size!
If I were back in Louis' hall, where I
Was kitchen-boy and cook in times gone by,
Then by this hour I'd already have dined
And drunk my fill of Louis' claret wines!
I'd be asleep and warm beside the fire!
The Moors shall pay for all this with their lives!"

"COUNT WILLIAM, stay here, and while you wait
I'll make my way down there to Archamp bay,
Where I can see their ships at anchor lain;
I'll break their boats and smash their boards away!
When we have done and won this bitter fray
The Moors will run back to their ships to sail
Away from us across the Spanish main!
By God above, I'll not have them escape!"
The French replied: "How fierce a speech and brave!
Good Renewart, God bless the hour you came!"
So Renewart ran down towards the waves;
But as he did a Pagan rode his way:
From Cordova he was, called Ailrez,
Well mounted on a swift-paced destrier;
The youngster's pole upset him all the same:
It broke his bones and drove his breath away;
Straight through the spine it split his horse in twain;
Then in the ship of strong King Ailrez
He found his men, some seven hundred knaves,
And smote them all and felled them straightaway;
Bertrand the count was captive there, in chains,
And, seeing this, he looked at him, amazed:
"Sir knight, my lord," said Count Bertrand the brave:
"Heroic son, who wield a wooden mace,
God bless the house where you were born and raised!
Are you a Moor or of some Christian race?"
Said Renewart: "I serve the Christian Faith;
But who are you? Speak up without delay!"
"I'm William's nephew! Bertrand is my name."
"I know him well," said Renewart again:
"From Louis' hall he took me when I came
Out of the kitchen where I had lived enslaved."
"Good Renewart, release me from my chains!
Count William will love you all your days!"
Said Renewart: "I will, Bertrand, but wait!
Behind those screens I see some Moors afraid
To meet with me or greet my wooden mace!
So it and I must welcome them, I'd say!"
Young Renewart strode down the planks and plates
And stalked those Moors across the whole deck-space!
With just one blow he broke their backs and brains

Then, turning back, he helped Bertrand to break
The rope and chains around his neck and waist;
He laid the count down gently, like a babe;
Bertrand looked up and spoke to him this way:
"Brave Renewart, you have unbound my chains;
Now save the rest, for God our Maker's sake!"
"What, are there more?" asked Renewart the brave:
"Yes, truly, four whom you should love the same:
Renier the wise and Walter of Termes,
And Guielin and Guiscard fair of face."
"Bertrand, my lord, can you steer ships of sail?"
"Yes friend, I can; I learnt in former days;
But we'd not move this mighty galley's weight
If we'd a crew of seven hundred slaves!"
Said Renewart: "Don't speak too soon – just wait!
A sluggard's deeds will earn a paltry wage
And never live in song or people's praise!"
He drove his pole deep in the sand and shale,
Then pushed it hard and made the whole ship shake;
He almost raised the whole boat in the air!
Bertrand ran off to hold the rudder straight!
The Moors looked on, incensed with grief and rage;
They cast their spears, their stones and sharpened stakes,
But Renewart heaved closer, unafraid;
He leapt aboard another ship and aimed
His mighty pole with all its deadly weight;
He flattened all who ventured in his way;
Three thousand jumped in fright across the rails!
Said Renewart: "You've made a bad mistake!
You'd meet your fate much quicker, if you stayed,
Than drowning thus among the ocean's waves!
You sons of whores, you'll have a lowly grave!"
He saw the counts and broke their captives' chains;
Bertrand spoke forth and hailed him once again:
"Brave Renewart, you have unbound my chains,
And others' too, God bless you with His Grace!
Now think, I beg, of our good destriers,
And armour too in which we were arrayed;
Then you shall see the blows that we can make!"
Said Renewart: "There's plenty here, I'd say:
The Moors have brought enough and more today!"

He raised his head just as a Pagan came
Well mounted on a swift-paced destrier;
The youngster's pole upset him just the same;
It broke his bones and drove his breath away;
Straight through the spine he split his horse in twain;
Bertrand spoke forth: "Your blow has gone astray!
I'll never mount upon that destrier!"
Said Renewart: "My lord, one moment, pray!"
He looked aside and saw King Overtez
And smote him hard with his great wooden mace;
He broke his bones and drove his breath away;
Straight through the spine he split his mount again;
"If this goes on, I'll not be armed today!
You could well kill four thousand in this way!"
Said Renewart: "You don't know what you say!
This pole is big – I can't control its weight;
My strength's enough to lift it up and aim,
But when on high it starts to fall again
I cannot stop it then in any way
To give a smaller blow than those it makes!"
"Then will you heed my counsel, in that case?"
"Fine lord, I'd bless your hour of birth always!"

BERTRAND SPOKE ON: "Did you not once consider
That your strong pole could kill by thrusting with it?"
Said Renewart: "Kill with a thrust – what wisdom!
You speak the truth – upon my faith, I didn't!"
He looked ahead and saw there in the distance
King Corduel who rode his courser thither;
Young Renewart, pole up, ran forth to hit him,
Then thrust the pole and broke his bones to splinters;
From nose and mouth his crimson blood went spilling,
And when his feet had slithered from the stirrups,
Up leapt Bertrand to mount his courser swiftly;
Then Renewart made sure the rest were given
Good, rapid steeds, good arms and fine equipment;
Bertrand the count addressed him then in this way:
"Brave Renewart, you've freed us all from prison;
Now lead us forth to our fine uncle William!"
Said Renewart: "I'll show you well and willing;
Stay close to me, Bertrand, and you his kinsmen!"

Then he began to strike the Moors so quickly
That none of them could flee before he hit them;
Throughout their ranks, whose sum the record gives us,
The youngster's pole cut such a swathe from swinging
That four wide carts could meet and pass unhindered.

BERTRAND SPURRED OFF upon his horse of war;
No coward he, nor was his courage small;
He moved to strike King Malagant the Moor;
He split his shield and slit the hauberk's coils;
He flung him dead one lance-length from his horse
And told him this: "Wretch! We have met before!
I knew your face and those fine clothes of yours;
Upon your ship you showed me no remorse!"

THEY RODE AND FOUND the Count upon a hill;
In fond embrace Bertrand and he both kissed,
Then William, the hook-nosed Count, said this:
"My nephew fine, who freed you from their ships?"
Bertrand replied: "Fine uncle, one most fit
For fame, so young and strong and proud he is!
I bless the hour that he was born to live!
By his own hand three thousand Moors were killed
And then he smashed their fleet of ships to bits!"
Cried William: "How much I'd cherish him,
If he had wit to match that strength of his!"
Evening of Monday.

26. How Renewart won the day for William

COUNT WILLIAM held Bertrand in embrace,
And Guielin and Walter of Termes,
And wise Girart and Giscard fair of face;
What joy they brought to William again!
But then loomed up a wicked Pagan knave,
Palermo's lord, King Gloriant his name;
What grief and loss he'd caused the French that day;
Young Renewart rushed forth and swung his mace,
Which cracked his skull and crushed it all away;
In fifteen spots it splattered forth his brains;

Said William: "You should and shall be raised
To knighthood's rank, with land and noble maid
To be your wife – God curse me if I fail!"

FROM TOP TO TAIL behold the valour born
And bred from Aymeri of Narbonne's loins!
Not one lies now in graveyard or in vault,
For all were slain on mighty plains of war;
Behold, my friends, Tabur of Canaloyn –
God curse the soul of such a vicious Moor:
His frame was big, but stooping and deformed,
And hairy as a bear, with long-toothed jaws!
He bore no weapons except his fangs and claws;
Young Guielin he saw and galloped forth
With jaws agape to greet and eat the boy
Like a ripe apple – or this is what he thought!
But Guielin's sharp spear drove in his groin,
A mortal wound, had not the shaft snapped short;
Count William himself lent his support
And with his spear struck Tabur with such force
It snapped as well and into three was shorn;
His hide was tough, naught pierced it through at all;
Both Guielin and William drew their swords
And hacked and hewed while Tabur's great mouth yawned
Back at their blades and bit the steel and gnawed
With fangs galore, which may God curse him for!
He'd have our men, of this he was quite sure,
With harder hide than any armour worn
Or any weapon borne – except, of course,
The swinging pole of mighty Renewart!
Behold him, friends! From deep down in a gorge,
When he beheld the beast he hastened forth,
As did the Moor, without delay or halt,
His jaws agape to swallow man or boy!
But Renewart attacked his head and scored
Nine mighty blows, then felled him with one more!
Four leagues away the people heard the noise
As Tabur writhed in death with howls and roars;
And when those Moors and Magyars heard it all
They were aghast to know they'd lost Tabur!

WHEN WILLIAM beheld the monster perish
He raised his hands in thanks towards the Heavens;
To Renewart he said: "May Jesus bless you,
And guard your days from mortal pain or peril!
No lance or spear, I say, are worth a penny!
Your wood's worth more than any man-made weapon!"

THIS BLOW WOULD HAVE laid low the Moors at once,
But the Emir of Balan's realm rode up:
He bore no arms except a flail of wood;
His skin was wrapped in four deer-hides at once;
A hood of mail and helmet bound his skull;
His mighty flail came from a holm-oak's trunk,
And hit so hard upon our French when swung
That it slew more than any mangonel
With seven rocks to aim with would have done;
On seeing this, Count Hugh filled with disgust
And spurred his steed, which galloped at the touch;
With lance in hand he struck the Moor in front;
If he'd struck rock, he would have had more luck!
The Pagan swung his flail at him at once
And left to right sheared through the shield and struck;
Beneath his thighs Hugh's slaughtered war-horse slumped;
Hugh left the fight – my friends, he had to run;
"Alas!" he cried, "Alas for Bertrand's son
And William's cousin, the mighty lord of Laon,
Forced by a Moor from Archamp field to run!"
The French all cried: "At last they've summoned up
The Antichrist, Bagot or Tartarun,
Or from Hell's depth ancient Beelzebub!
Brave Renewart, where are you and your club?
Without your strength we shall be overcome!"
Then Renewart ran down a hill at once,
Where two strong kings had fought him well enough,
King Mathanar and then King Feraguz,
But, thanks to God, he'd slain them both and won;
His worthy pole was covered with their blood;
Count William was never so in luck!
He said: "I feared that you were lost to us!
Behold this fight, whose like there never was!
A living fiend strikes with a flail of wood

So viciously that none can bear the brunt!"
"Then give me seven shields," said Renewart,
"And seven coats that I may wear as one,
And seven helms to strap upon my skull!"
He gripped his pole and went to face him thus.

THE VICIOUS MOOR saw Renewart arrive:
In his own tongue he called to him and cried:
"The Devil this! Are you a Christian knight,
Who bear a club like that into a fight?
No Christian man before you bore the like!"
Said Renewart: "I am indeed baptised;
And if you don't renounce Mahom for Christ,
Apollo's tricks and old Tervagant's lies,
I'll teach you too that our God has the right!"
He ran at him, his pole held like a knight,
And like a lance he thrust at him to strike
Upon his brow, and just above the eyes
He made a gash more than six inches wide;
But curse the Moor if he was hurt thereby!
It did not harm one bit his awful might,
Nor did it curb his proud and fierce desire.

HE SWUNG HIS FLAIL at Renewart instead;
Six of his shields he sheared from edge to edge;
Of seven shields he bore but one was left;
Young Renewart leapt back full fifteen steps;
He would have died if it had flicked his flesh.

YOUNG RENEWART was sly and very brave;
Behind the Moor a rapid turn he made
And struck the Moor so hard upon his nape
That both his eyes were driven from his face;
Before the French he flung him to his grave;
But then, behold the strong King Aildrez,
The uncle of young Renewart, in faith;
Upon his back he bore an iron mace;
He had attacked four hundred French that day
And from his hands not one of them escaped;
Now he had made Count William his prey –
But Renewart ran up and barred his way:

"My lord, fight me! I stand in William's place!"
"Away with you and let me be, you knave!
I will not speak with villains of your age!
Just show me where Count William awaits,
So I may strike and slay him with my mace!"
Said Renewart: "Your challenge comes too late!
By heathen hands this morning he was slain:
See there! He lies in death upon the plain;
His helm of green and studded shield remain."
"You harlot's son, is this the truth you say?"
"Yes, lord! What's more, I'll let you share his fate!"
As Renewart charged forth his strong arms raised
His mighty pole high up into the air;
And Aildrez likewise swung high his mace;
The Pagan's helm took all the pole's great weight –
But it was strong, with polished steel ablaze,
And Renewart's sleek pole was glanced away;
Said Renewart: "Now I am put to shame!
I must strike harder still or lose my fame!"
So in his wrath he raised the pole again
And struck a blow with all his strength and rage:
The Moor was crushed and crashed down to his grave,
While through its spine his horse was split in twain;
A full six feet the pole lodged in the plain,
Then in three bits it shattered from the strain;
Had they subdued all Christendom's domains
And won back lands the length and breadth of Spain,
The Pagans' joy would not have been as great!
Like starving dogs who see at last their prey,
They rushed to seize good Renewart the brave;
He braced himself most bravely for the fray;
He bore no lance or spear to lend him aid,
But showed his fists and raised them strong and straight:
And every back that bent he went to break,
And every breast that stooped to him he staved,
And every eye that blinked he dashed away:
"He is a living fiend!" the Pagans wailed:
"He is much worse than when his pole was safe!
The devil come and take him to his fate –
No mortal man will send him to his grave!"
He loosened then the belt-knot at his waist,

And saw the hilt of that same worthy blade
Girt on before by Guibourc, fair of face;
He filled with joy and drew it from its case;
He looked ahead and saw strong King Forrez:
Upon his helm he struck him straightaway
And split the wretch in half from wits to waist,
While through its spine his horse was split in twain;
Hilt-high the sword embedded in the plain;
Said Renewart: "By God, I am amazed
So small an arm can cut so sweet and straight!
God bless the soul who girt it at my waist!
Each worthy man should carry four the same,
So he may use one more, if one should break!"

THE PAGANS CRIED: "We must have lost all sense,
To tarry here and face a certain death!
Men, let us flee to reach the sea again,
Where all our boats are moored in readiness!"
But Renewart had changed their trim so well
That none of them were ready – all were wrecks!
The Pagans fled and still he slaughtered them;
Before he'd done two thousand Moors lay dead;
The rest turned tail till none of them were left.

27. How Renewart was rewarded for his deeds

THE FRENCHMEN CALLED their fighting to a finish,
For they could find no heathens left for killing!
They'd won so much in Pagan gold and silver
That they would live for evermore as rich men;
They told their squires to guard it well and bring it,
Then blew their horns and turned their horses quickly
Towards Orange, returning in high spirits;
When they arrived they washed and sat for dinner,
But quite forgot that Renewart was missing;
How they would rue that they rode off so swiftly!
So, as those squires brought back the loot as bidden,
Young Renewart lamented in self-pity:
"Unhappy me! O most ill-blest of children,
King Desramed's own son, the blighted issue

Of fair Orabel's womb, his Eastern princess!
I have not been baptised to be a Christian,
Nor prayed to God inside a church or minster,
But I have fought and won this fight for William;
And yet the Count considers me so little
That he refrains from asking me to dinner;
So I shall leave for Spain and in that kingdom
I'll serve Mahom and worship his religion;
And, if I wish, I shall be crowned a king there
And rule the land in Durester's fair city,
From Babylon to Port Durazzo's limit;
My staff shall be a pole, for I consider
No other arm compares one penny with it!
And I'll return one day to this fair city,
And on that day shall do to all within it
As I have done on Archamp field to win it!"

"YOU BACHELORS and squires, you worthy people,
I leave you all to God the Lord's safe-keeping!
As I turn back to foreign lands and heathen,
Go to Orange, and when at last you reach there,
Repeat my words so William may hear them,
But for God's sake greet Lady Guibourc sweetly:
There's none on earth whom I esteem more dearly."
And they replied: "We'll do as you entreat us."
And so they came to fair Orange and greeted
The Count this way: "Sir William, please hear us!
Brave Renewart and his strong arm are leaving!"
The Count replied: "You rogues, why do you tease me?"
"Lord, we do not; we speak with truth and reason;
He has sped off to Spain, full of ill-feeling;
He never was baptised or christened either,
Nor led to church so he might pray to Jesus;
He will be crowned a king, if he so pleases,
And rule the land in his fair town Durester,
From Babylon to Durazzo the sea-port;
He will return one day to this fair region
With all his host, one hundred thousand heathens;
His mighty pole shall be the rod that beats us,
For on that day he swears that he will treat us
As he has done this day on Archamp's beaches."

Said William: "That would be very fearful;
If any man can stop him yet from leaving,
He shall receive much wealth when next I see him;
And any man who brings him back to me here
I shall endow with many of my fiefdoms;
My noble lords, pursue him, I beseech you!"
"Your will is ours," said all his knights and liegemen;
Four thousand men seized arms and armour keenly;
In coat and helm they mounted horse to leave there;
They hastened forth and saw him in a field there,
Approaching fast upon a city's precincts;
On looking up, he saw them rush to meet him
And didn't know if they meant good or evil;
He glanced around and saw a cabin near him,
And ran to lift its corner-posts up cleanly,
Then broke the ridge inside its roof to pieces;
Across his back he laid the largest beam-end
And turned to face the Frenchmen as they reached him:
"My lords," he said, "why have you come to see me?"
"Count William has sent us here to greet you
And make amends for treating you so meanly
As to forget to ask you to his feasting."
Said Renewart: "It's too late now for speeches!
A curse on me if I'll heed such a weak one
Before I see his knights fall dead beneath me!"

AMONG THOSE KNIGHTS was one called Guinebolt,
A brother of Alealme of Clermont;
Now, like a fool, he raised his voice aloft:
"By God, you rogue, we shall outlive your wrath!
We'll drag you back to William's tower to rot!
You put to death my brother Guinebald,
Who singed your beard down in the kitchens once;
By all the faith I owe St Simeon,
If it were not for fair Guibourc, by God,
I'd ram my lance right through your lungs straight off!"
Said Renewart: "You have a wicked tongue!
You will regret you wagged it once too long!"
He raised his beam and ran at Guinebolt;
He howled and growled then smote his helmet-top,
Struck out his eyes and turned his brains to broth.

Evening of Monday.

SAID RENEWART: "You took my lightest blows,
But still are dead – as for the rest, who knows?"
The rest turned round and scattered down a slope;
Their horses fell, their spears flew from their hold.

HE RAISED ON HIGH the ridge-piece from the cabin;
It swung aloft, then down to earth came crashing!

HE SPLIT THE HEADS of any who delayed;
Back in Orange the Count stood at his gate,
His noble wife held in his fond embrace;
He said aloud: "Our knights are in great haste!
Strong Renewart's the reason, I dare say!"

Evening of Monday.

THE FRENCHMEN CRIED: "Alas that we agreed
To halt or hold that timber-swinging fiend!
He's killed five score unshriven by a priest!"
Said William: "Then I must go, it seems!"
He took with him Guibourc, his convert Queen,
And Guielin and Walter of Termes,
And Giscard and Girart, who led at least
Three hundred French who bore or wore no steel;
They met the youth upon a hillock's peak;
Guibourc it was who moved the first to speak:
"Brave Renewart, I beg you to receive
The rich amends of William my liege!"
"By my right hand, I willingly agree;
But had you not yourself asked this of me,
I would have split his head from brow to beard
And dashed his brains with this good wood I wield!
But I forgive him now the villainy
Of not inviting me to share his feast."
The French all said: "Then cast aside your beam!"
Said Renewart: "I shall do, willingly!"
He cast it then for over half a league;
Above three hundred Frenchmen's heads it sheered;
They cheered with joy when he had tossed it free!
One hundred ran to bear it from the field!

NOW RENEWART and William were one;
They made their peace between them with great love,
Then side by side returned to town at once;
You can be sure they feasted soon enough!

THE PALADIN Bertrand brought him some water,
While Guibourc brought a towel and stood before him;
Count Walter of Termes obeyed his orders.

WHEN RENEWART had feasted well and dined,
Guibourc spoke first and graciously enquired:
"Good Renewart, for sake of God on High,
Can it be true that you are not baptised?"
"No, I am not, by God," the youth replied,
"Nor have I been to church to pray to Christ."
"Then I shall see to both," Count William cried,
"So you may lead a new and blessed life!"
Said Renewart: "I thank you greatly, sire."
They went at once to good St Omer's shrine,
Where they filled up a tub so great in size
That four farmhands could bathe at ease inside!
The youth was held by William and his wife,
And by Bertrand, the valiant and wise,
The finest flower of all sweet France's knights;
Friends, you can guess their gifts were very fine:
One thousand pounds in gold and coin combined,
One hundred mules and rapid steeds to ride!
The Count gave him some seven forts besides,
And Ermentrude the maid to be his bride,
And all the lands of Vivien who died;
Once more Guibourc was first to speak her mind.

GUIBOURC WAS MOVED to speak her mind again:
"Brave Renewart, for God our Saviour's sake,
How did you come to leave your native place?"
He said: "Pay heed, and you shall hear the tale:

"MY FRIENDS," HE SAID, "this is my honest story:
My father left for Meliant one morning
With his good friend the Almanzor of Dorant;
He left me with Apolicant, who taught me;

He too rode off one morning as the dawn broke
And told me not to stir out of my quarters
Till he'd returned from worshipping Tervaugant;
I never did obey my teacher's orders
And so I left and raced along the shoreline
With every haste and started to play ball there;
Then I laid eyes on all the galleys moored there,
And full of prank and pride I climbed aboard one;
But then a wind, a tempest, roared and bore me
At mighty speed far out upon the waters;
I saw a ship with merchants on its foredeck
And my boat battered theirs, I couldn't halt it!
One hundred bits and more my boat was torn to;
I would have drowned without the help they brought me:
Inside a barge four crewmen heaved and hauled me;
They took me then across a foreign border
And set a wreath upon my head and called me
A wretched waif, a slave-child to be auctioned;
But there was not one wealthy lord who saw me,
No Roman, German, Breton count or Norman,
Who could afford the price they wanted for me;
Then through the fair the French King came on horseback,
And in his eyes a handsome youth he thought me
And bought me for one hundred marks in coinage;
He set me on an ambling mule and brought me
To Laon, his town, and to his royal court there;
He asked me then if I had noble forebears,
And I replied, without a lie or falsehood,
I was a son of Desramed the Moor king;
And when he heard that my descent was royal,
He feared my father and all my family for it;
He bound me to his cook's domain and orders
And then he took an oath to God and swore it,
That I would serve no better trade henceforward;
For seven years that kitchen was my quarters,
Where I was cold, but had good food to warm me;
Then William took me to Archamp's slaughter,
Where I have slain some thirty kinsmen for him!"
On hearing this, fair Guibourc moved towards him:
"Embrace me, child! Your sister stands before you!"
Evening of Monday.

"Count William, are you my brother-in-law, then?
If I had known of this on Archamp's shoreline,
Though I did much, I would have done much more there!"

CHARLEMAGNE'S PILGRIMAGE

(c.1150–1175)

Introduction

The single thirteenth century manuscript which had preserved this short but cleverly wrought poem disappeared from the Royal Library of the British Museum in 1879. Its text is known to us today thanks to a first 'faithfully copied' edition of it made by Francisque Michel in 1836, and to a much less conservative but very timely one undertaken by Eduard Koschwitz in 1879 itself. The poem is written in Anglo-Norman dialect, and, according to most scholars, was originally composed in France at some time in the third quarter of the twelfth century. Its narrative begins and ends at the great abbey of Saint-Denis, which, in the twelfth century, stood just outside the city wall to the north of Paris, and became, from 1140 onwards, under its Abbot Suger, the centre of religious, artistic and political life in France. Each June the abbey was the scene of a great fair and holiday known as the Lendit, which celebrated the centre's relics of the Passion, and its crowds could well have been the first audiences to be entertained and instructed by this highly satirical but essentially 'epic' tale.

Although the poem describes a pilgrimage and a journey of Charlemagne to Jerusalem and to Constantinople respectively, it is quite certain that the historical emperor never set foot in either town. There is considerable evidence to suggest, however, that at the time of the composition of the *Pèlerinage*, the legend and firm belief that he had done so were both well established and widely promoted. Between the years 972 and 1000 an Italian monk, Benedictus de Sancto Andrea, while translating certain fragments of Eginhard's *Vita Karoli*, transforms the emperor's embassies to Jerusalem and Baghdad into personal journeys made by Charlemagne to the Holy Sepulchre and to the Emperor of Byzantium. In 1095 the knights of the First Crusade were sent and went off to war in the firm belief that they were following in the footsteps of Charles the Great. The monks of Saint-Denis themselves composed a text at the end of the eleventh century which was called *Descriptio qualiter Karolus Magnus clavum et coronam Domini a Constantinopoli Aquisgrani detulerit qualiterque Karolus calvus hec ad sanctum Dyonisium retulerit* ('a description of how Charles the Great brought the nail [of the Cross] and the crown [of thorns] of our Lord away from

Constantinople to Aix-la-Chapelle and of how Charles took them then to Saint-Denis'). This chronicle tells of the emperor's expedition to Constantinople at the request of the emperor Constantine, who had given shelter to the Patriarch of Jerusalem after this latter's expulsion from the Holy City by the Saracens. In their narrative the monks of Saint-Denis tell how Charlemagne defeats the Pagans, restores the Patriarch, is received warmly in Constantinople and returns to Saint-Denis with holy relics, which he deposits at Aix-la-Chapelle, and which are later taken to Saint-Denis by Charles the Bald.

Church records indicate that in 1108 a fragment of the Holy Cross was accepted by the authorities at Notre Dame in Paris, and that, in the following year, a commemorative procession to the place called the Lendit was instituted. It seems, therefore, quite likely that the monks of Saint-Denis, whose abbey was located along the processional route, wrote their *Descriptio* in order to authenticate their own relics of the Passion, and to take a greater part in the Lendit fair by instituting a procession of their own. One the one hand then, the anonymous author of the *Pèlerinage de Charlemagne* may well have been a *jongleur*-poet who, on hearing one of the Lendit sermons, collaborated with the chronicler-monks of Saint-Denis to create an entertaining attraction for the fairground patrons as well as for the more pious pilgrims observing the relics at Saint-Denis during this June festival.

On the other hand, some scholars have suggested that the *Pèlerinage* is a political satire, parodying the disastrous pilgrimage undertaken by Louis VII during the Second Crusade (1147–1149). There are, in fact, many passages in the poem where the parallel between Louis' actual behaviour on that occasion and Charlemagne's imagined antics would have been clear to the Parisian public in the 1150s, and several obscure passages in the poem obtain some clarification if this connection is made. The contrast between Charles's boast of conquest at Saint-Denis and his timorous behaviour at Constantinople, for example, may well be a caustic commentary on the historical fact that Louis' barons were forced to pay homage and swear fealty to Emperor Manuel of Constantinople in 1147. The foolhardy criticism made by Charlemagne's wife at the beginning of this *chanson de geste* could indeed have been inspired by the reported complaints of Louis' lively wife, Eleanor of Aquitaine, that she had 'married a monk rather than a king'. The same number of pilgrim-soldiers follow Charlemagne in the poem as followed King Louis in 1147, along a very similar route. The episode in the song where Charles and his Twelve Peers are mistaken for Christ and His Apostles may be seen as a further satirical comment on Louis' holy preoccupations as opposed to his military prowess. The extravagant war-boasts made by Charles's barons in King Hugo's palace, which constitute the artistic centre-piece of the *Pèlerinage*, are quite possibly a literary echo of the frustration voiced by the body of Louis' forces, which culminated in their actual demand for an attack on Constantinople in 1147. Louis' political humiliation and his army's humble return to Paris in 1149, with little of value except for certain holy objects, could certainly have been received in Paris in an atmosphere where popular satire of the events (or non-events) would flourish.

Artistic Achievement

Whatever its inspiration, the *Pèlerinage de Charlemagne* is certainly the earliest extant Old French epic composition to reveal an essentially comic intent. In its brief but richly crafted narrative structure the poet combines a clever parody of both the themes and diction of the two main literary genres of his day, namely the *chanson de geste* and the *roman courtois*, to achieve a biting burlesque of the venerable emperor Charlemagne and of the 'epic' ethos itself. Skilfully illustrating a procedure somewhat tediously imitated in several later poems, he transforms the father figure of the 'songs of deeds' from a gallant leader into a gullible loon, and from a proud supporter into a pompous exploiter of his Faith.

The work's opening scene, set amid the sacred splendour of Saint-Denis itself, establishes the poet's satiric intent, both in character and tone. Roused neither by human plea nor divine summons, but by the bristling of a bruised ego, the emperor sets forth upon a personal quest against a non-hostile fellow-Christian. He takes with him an oddly chosen, non-traditional Twelve Peers, whose un-epic departure is highlighted at once:

> *They bore no shields or lances, or swords upon their hips,*
> *But ash-staffs tipped with iron and pilgrims' belted scrips;* (ll. 79-80)

These heroic figures of French chivalry are indeed endowed by the poet throughout the narrative with the stock epithets befitting their epic status – they are *'companions brave and bold'* (l. 111), *'his gallant band of men'* (l. 254), *'his gallant Frenchmen'* (l. 400) and *'that worthy band of friends'* (l. 784). Such standard descriptions become immediately comic, however, when used as dogged formulas to highlight these particular heroes, who shed not one drop of blood, who behave like boorish rustics amidst the opulence of Constantinople, who are literally swept off their feet in King Hugo's revolving palace, and who scramble up a pine-tree to escape a flood. Similarly, though described in the time-honoured way as *'the Great'* or *'the Fierce'*, Emperor Charlemagne demonstrates, in fact, neither of these attributes during his 'pilgrimage'. He is the Frenchmen's leader, but only in bluster and folly. He cuts a far from fierce figure, for example, when, seated upon an ambling mule, he meets the object of his quest, King Hugo, who is seated upon a golden plough, driving his oxen. Indeed, the succession of scenes which depict the contact between West and East, the contrast between Charles's warriors and Hugo's courtiers, all serve to reinforce the basic satiric standpoint of the Western emperor's cultural inferiority.

The unheroic behaviour of the Frenchmen and their leader finds its comic apotheosis at the centre of the poem, in its longest single episode, which is that of their war-boasts or *gabs*. One of the brightest jewels in the crown of the Old French epic genre, the traditional war-boast of the gallant hero provides the traditional *jongleur*-poet with the opportunity to display a wide range of rhetorical skills, from the sarcastic or witty insult to the lyric or pithy panegyric. The narratives of *Gormont and Isembart*, *The Song of William* and *Raoul of Cambrai* in this selection each provide examples of such 'paralleled' verses, where one protagonist pauses to relish the discomfiture of an opponent and/or the triumph of his own bravery. The poet of the *Pèlerinage*, however, once again succeeds in using a convention of epic diction to achieve a new, comic result. His brave French boasters are drunk, and frightened, and lying on their backs on their beds. Their boasts, comic enough by their extravagance, are almost all intended to offend the authority of their host, King Hugo, who has, in fact, behaved impeccably towards them. The 'heroic' world of these bellicose jests is, however, turned upside down by the poet, who turns the vaunters into the victims themselves – for King Hugo has left a spy inside their room, who comments wryly on each utterance before he tells all to his master. The warrior Charles is bested by the courtly Hugh and the traditional 'discomfiture of the enemy' motif is given a comic twist – the jesting heroes must actually perform their boasts, or *they* die!

At the same time, the author of the *Pèlerinage* uses and/or abuses certain standard features of *roman courtois* composition to lighten and deepen his essential parody. On one level, certainly, Charlemagne's journey can be viewed as a courtly quest. Challenged, the high-born hero departs into unknown and exotic regions at the inspiration of a fair lady. Yet *this* hero departs not out of love, but out of spite, and *this* quest's fair inspiration runs a fair risk of decapitation should it fail. The destination of the quest is King Hugo's city of Constantinople, which provides the setting for well over half of the poem, and is indeed the idealised city of the courtly romance poems. The tall-towered buildings are surrounded by luxuriant gardens and peopled with honest citizens. The sophisticated courtiers lead a leisurely life centred around a magical palace of magnificent opulence and cunning automatons. The gallant French, led on by the freshly-named Charles 'The Great', arrive on ambling mules, and their immediate reactions of sarcastic jealousy to all they see detract again from the epic reputation of them all. Their fierce-faced leader is thrown to the floor when Hugo's palace begins to revolve, and then he asks, somewhat pathetically, when 'normality' will be restored. Wined and dined splendidly by the Eastern emperor, Charlemagne's response is to lead the drunken war-boasts, blather excuses to an indignant Hugo, abuse his privileged relationship with the Almighty, so movingly celebrated in the *Chanson de Roland*, then seek out personal safety in the branches of a tree. But the humour created in these scenes is not all one-sided, as the artificiality and over-sophistication of certain manifestations of the 'courtly' ethos are lampooned too. King Hugo's daughter, albeit Christian, becomes a parody of the traditional 'amorous Saracen princess'. The finest flower of this courtly culture, she succumbs with a naive readiness to the earthier marvels of Count Oliver's epic lust, only to be spurned for Charlemagne's company at the end of the poem. For all their art and artifice the marvellous palace and city of the Eastern king do fall to the uncouth war-boasts of the French, when, through the medium of the Passion's relics, God's favour is pronounced and produced. Yet even during his eventual victory this Charlemagne is not a winner. He gloats churlishly over Hugo's 'defeat', which neither monarch by their actions has deserved, and his original quest succeeds in a merely physical way – he is, as his queen had doubted, indeed superior to King Hugo – by fifteen inches in height, when wearing a crown.

The pious aspect of Charlemagne's pilgrimage provides the poet with a third dimension for his satiric humour. Charlemagne's God-driven dreams, so powerful an inspiration for imperial action in several earlier, and later, *chansons de geste*, seem more like glib excuses for self-aggrandisement when he sets out for the Holy City in this poem. The piety of his whole pilgrimage to Jerusalem is also parodied by the abuse the Frenchmen make of their reception there. Mistaken in the Temple for God among His Apostles, Charles relishes the moment to accept the title of 'The Great' from the Patriarch, then to request gifts in the form of relics of the Passion. These relics are subsequently either abused or overworked, and, in Constantinople, both. Ironically enough, no doubt, for the original Lendit audiences, the poet selects these sacred relics, the very objects of their own pilgrimages, to provide his most daring mockery of the mighty Charles. For God, Who halted the sun's course to give the emperor his ultimate victory over the Infidels in *The Song of Roland*, is now petitioned by him, in these relics' name, to provide what is, this time, a totally undeserved retribution and deliverance. The legendary king's subsequent triumph is a mockery of his traditional contract with God. In the *Pèlerinage de Charlemagne* Charles uses God's support for his own, unworthy ends; but support for his religious status as the great Defender of Christianity is undermined by the poet's cutting wit.

The common threads of all humour – exaggerations, crossed purposes, mistaken identities and surprises – are skilfully woven into the comic fabric of this triple parody. Usually one element is allowed to dominate the scene, as in the opening exchange, where Charles's pomposity is completed deflated by the queen's candour, or during the conversations that take place in the Temple at Jerusalem, when Charles is mistaken for the Lord God Himself. It is the artist's best achievement, however, that he is able to sustain the richness of his narrative texture by the simultaneous interplay of several comic devices. The extensive verses containing the ill-fated war-boasts offer the best example of this talent, but the shorter dialogues between Charles and the Patriarch, Charles and King Hugh, and between Count Oliver and the princess, also illustrate this comic talent.

The blend of epic, courtly and religious diction creates a well-balanced narrative in itself, which both relieves and sets into relief the poet's comic tilt and thrust. The formal structure of the poem also reflects a thoughtful artist. The change of assonance provided by verses which, in the main, are of short and regular length, facilitates a fluent and fast-moving performance. The *Pèlerinage de Charlemagne* is the earliest extant *chanson de geste* to be written in the alexandrine metre. With the caesura after the sixth syllable, the well-balanced, almost slick lines which result give the whole narrative a jocular lilt well-suited to the poet's satiric purpose.

Sources and Influences

Three versions of a journey by Charlemagne to the East are preserved in the thirteenth century Old Norse compilation called the *Karlamagnús saga*. The first of these is a serious account of such a pilgrimage, epic in tone, and thought to be an abbreviated translation of an Old French poem possibly older than the *Roland* itself. Several scholars have suggested that Constantinople represents the Celtic Otherworld Kingdom, and that King Hugo's palace can be compared with the Magic House of the Celtic

Otherworld literature. Although there may indeed be some justification for admitting Celtic or Breton *motifs* as the background for several of the extravagant boasts made by the French in Hugo's palace, the descriptions in the *Pèlerinage* of the mechanical marvels there and of the opulence at Constantinople in general, can also be found in well-known Latin texts prior to 1150, and appear frequently in the reports of French pilgrims' visits to Byzantium.

Branch VII of the Norwegian *Karlamagnús saga*, called *Jorsalaferd*, contains a translation of a French text very similar to the *Pèlerinage*, made in the middle of the thirteenth century. Again, in Branch X of the same saga, a third version of the story can be found, dating this time from the late thirteenth or early fourteenth century, and deriving from the *Speculum Historiale* of Vincent of Beauvais. The plot of a Castilian poem related in the *Chronicon Mundi* of Archbishop don Lucas de Tuy in 1236 is also almost identical to that of the *Pèlerinage de Charlemagne*. In French literature itself, the text of an intended continuation of the present poem is preserved in a poem from the end of the thirteenth century called *Galiens li Restoré*, and also in the cyclic compilation known as *Guerin de Monglane*, which was published in prose right up to the nineteenth century. Another French *chanson de geste*, called *Simon de Pouille*, derives its inspiration from the text of the *Pèlerinage*. In this thirteenth century poem the French set out upon another, specifically military expedition to Jerusalem and Constantinople. The *Roman de Charlemagne*, written around 1300 by Girart d'Amiens, retells the life of the great emperor, recounting in its turn the legend of his journey to the East, as does the vast prose compilation of 1458 called the *Croniques et conquestes de Charlemaine*, attributed to David Aubert.

Note to the translation

This translation is based on the edition of Burgess and Cobby published by Garland in 1988. In general I have followed their readings of corrupt or difficult lines, and am indebted to their prose translation and thorough analysis of the poem. For fluency's sake I have maintained a strict twelve-syllable line with either male or female ending before the caesura of each verse, which the original does not.

CHARLEMAGNE'S PILGRIMAGE

1. Charles's anger

ONE DAY KING CHARLES the Frenchman, at Saint-Denis the shrine,
Picked up and put his crown on and made the Cross's sign;
He girt his sword about him, its pommel golden-bright,
With all his dukes and lords there, his barons and his knights;
The Emperor looked round him and saw the Queen his wife:
She wore her crown in splendour most beautiful and fine;
Then by the hand he took her beneath an olive wide
And spoke directly to her, his voice aglow with pride:
"My Lady, have you ever seen any man alive
Who wore his crown or sword-blade with better grace than I?
I still shall conquer cities with such a lance as mine!"
The Queen did not speak wisely, but foolishly replied:
"O Emperor," she told him, "you set yourself too high,
For I do know another who makes a finer sight
Each time he puts his crown on to wear before his knights!
When *this* king puts his crown on, he looks the more refined."
When Charles the Frenchman heard this, he filled with bitter spite:
Because the French had heard it, he turned his face aside:
"Where *is* this king, my Lady, and what's his name?" he cried:
"We both shall put our crowns on and wear them side by side;
Your friends and your advisers shall all be there, and I
Shall call my knights to witness, from every shore and shire;
If all of them confirm it, then I'll admit you're right:
But you will pay most dearly if I find out you've lied –
For I shall cut your head off with my own sword of iron!"
"O Emperor," she answered: "Do not be angry, Sire!
This king may well be richer in gold and coin alike,
But he has much less courage, less valour and less might
To strike great blows in battle and put a foe to flight!"
When she beheld her husband, so angry and so wild,
She gladly would have fallen before him, all contrite.

"FOR LOVE OF GOD, have mercy, fine Emperor!" she said:
"I am your wife – I only said what I did in jest!
My lord, if you command me, I'll prove my innocence
By swearing on the Bible or by a trial or test;
Or from the tallest tower in Paris town I'll step,
To show you very clearly I never thought or meant,
By word or thought whatever, to shame you or distress!"
"You won't!" said Charles, "But tell me this monarch's name instead!"
"O Emperor," she answered, "I don't remember well!"
Said Charles: "You will directly, or, on my oath, I pledge,
I'll call this very moment for you to lose your head!"

THE QUEEN COULD NOT escape – she knew it at that moment;
She gladly would have stopped, but now she couldn't hope to:
"Do not think me a fool, O Emperor!" she told him:
"Of King Hugo the Strong I've heard such stories spoken;
He's Emperor of Greece and of Constantinople;
He rules all Persia too, as far as Cappadocia;
From Antioch to here they say there's none more noble,
Nor any band of knights like his, except your own one."
"Upon my oath," said Charles, "I'll seek the truth and know it!
If you have told a lie, your own life will be over!"

SAID CHARLES: "UPON my faith, you've set my anger seething;
My love and my goodwill you have forgone completely;
I truly think that you should lose your head for treason:
My Lady, do not doubt the power that I wield here;
I shall not let this rest until my eyes have seen him."

2. Charles's pilgrims

THE EMPEROR proceeded and, in his crown of state,
Laid treasure rich and royal before the altar-rails,
Then to his Paris palace he turned and went again;
He went there with Count Roland and Oliver the same,
With William of Orange and Duke Naimon the brave,
With Ogier, duke of Denmark, Gerin and Bérenger,
And Turpin the archbishop, Hernaut and Count Aimer,
Bernart, the lord of Brabant and Count Bertrand the brave,
And knights more than a thousand, all born in France and raised:

"My lords," said Charles the Frenchman, "pay heed to what I say:
So please God, we shall journey to kingdoms far away –
Jerusalem we'll visit and God the Lord's domain,
Where I will pray and worship His Holy Cross and Grave;
Three times I have seen visions and now I must obey;
And I will seek a monarch whom I have heard much praised;
Load seven hundred camels with gold and silver weight,
For seven years to sojourn and tarry in that place!
I'll not return, I tell you, until I've seen his face."

THE KING OF ALL the Frenchmen prepared his knights forthwith,
And all those going with him he lavishly equipped –
Pure gold galore and silver he gave to them in gifts;
They bore no shields or lances, or swords upon their hips,
But ash-staffs tipped with iron and pilgrims' belted scrips;
Both front and rear their war-steeds were shod then for the trip,
As servants padded saddles on sumpter-mules, then filled
Their saddle-bags with silver and bright gold to the brim,
With vessels and with money and sundry other things:
Equipment, golden faldstools and tents of shining silk;
At Saint-Denis the abbey the king took up his scrip,
And Turpin the archbishop blessed all his men and him;
Then Turpin took his own scrip, then all the Frenchmen did;
On ambling mules and sturdy they mounted with a will
And rode forth from the city, their manner bright and brisk;
So Charles, at God's own bidding, went on his pilgrimage;
The Queen was left there weeping, both sore at heart and sick;
The King rode on till reaching an open plain, at which
He turned his mule to one side and hailed Bertrand with this:
"How fine a sight this army of wandering pilgrims is!
Before us rides a vanguard with eighty thousand in!
A man who leads that many must be a mighty King!"

3. Charles's arrival in Jerusalem

THE EMPEROR rode forward with all his mighty host:
Before them rode a vanguard of eighty thousand souls;
They left sweet France behind them; through Burgundy they rode,
Then through Lorraine, Bavaria and Hungary they strode,
Then rode on through Romania, its mountains and its slopes,

Through woods and forest country till reaching Greece below;
Then, crossing Laodecia, where mighty waters flow,
The Emperor spurred onwards through Troy, along the roads
Among the Turks and Persians and that accursed folk,
Until they reached the country where Jesus suffered so,
And saw the ancient city – Jerusalem the old;
The day was fine and sunny, so, camping in a grove,
They went inside the church there and offered gifts of gold,
Then turned back to their campsite, companions brave and bold.

HOW NOBLE WERE the presents of Charles and all his army!
The church wherein they entered had painted marble arches,
Beneath which was an altar to God our blessed Father;
Our Lord Himself said Mass there, and the Apostles chanted:
The twelve chairs they had sat in are still set in an arc there,
A thirteenth in the centre, enclosed and set apart there;
Charles went inside its portals, inspired and joyful-hearted,
And when he saw the chair there he did not stop advancing,
But sat himself down in it, to bide a while in calmness,
And all Twelve Peers around him sat in the rest regardless!
No man before had sat there or ever did thereafter!

WITH ALL ITS WONDROUS beauty King Charles was greatly cheered;
He saw the whole church painted in colours bright and clear,
With martyrs and with virgins and great majestic scenes –
With water fleet and flowing and fishes of the sea,
With courses that the moon takes, and all the yearly feasts;
The King's face was uplifted, its look severe and fierce,
When suddenly a Jew came and stared in disbelief:
On seeing Charles the Frenchman, his body shook with fear;
He dared not look upon him, his gaze was so severe,
And, almost falling over, the Jew turned round to flee;
He climbed the marble stairway and hastened forth to meet
The Patriarch himself there, and thus began to speak:
"My lord, come to your chapel and fill your fonts for me,
For I want to be christened – baptised in your belief!
Just entering your church there, I saw twelve counts appear,
And with them a thirteenth one, whose like I've never seen;
This one is God Himself, sir – I truly do believe;
He and His Twelve Apostles have come to see you here!"
The Patriarch made ready, on hearing this, to leave,

And called forth from the city his priests in all their gear:
They donned their albs and copes then, obeying his decree,
And left in great procession, their master in the lead;
When Charles the Frenchman saw him, he got up from his seat,
And doffed the hat he'd worn there and bowed before him deep;
They kissed each other warmly and then each questioned each;
The Patriarch said firstly: "What land is yours, fine liege?
No man before your coming has dared to enter here,
Unless he had my orders, or if he had my leave."
"Sir, I am Charles the Frenchman: I come from France the sweet;
And through my strength and valour twelve kings have met defeat;
Now I seek a thirteenth one of whom I've heard men speak;
The love of God has brought me to see and sojourn here,
The Cross and Grave of Jesus to worship faithfully."
The Patriarch responded: "Sir, you are brave indeed,
And you've sat in the same chair where God Himself has been;
Be called now CHARLEMAGNE, the King without a peer!"
The Emperor responded: "Much thanks for this indeed!
You have here holy relics – please give me some of these,
Which back to France I'll carry to glorify the Creed."
The Patriarch responded: "Aplenty you'll receive!
St Simeon's own arm here you'll have immediately,
St Lazarus's head too I'll bring for you in brief,
And blood from blessed Stephen, who died for his belief."
In turn King Charlemagne pledged friendship long and dear.

THE PATRIARCH continued: "A blessing on your quest!
In seeking the Lord God here, you have deserved the best;
I'll give to you such relics as no lands else possess:
The shroud of our Lord Jesus that He wore on His head,
When in His Grave they laid Him and left Him there for dead;
The Jews they left to guard Him bore swords of burnished edge,
But, on the third day rising, as He before had said,
He came to His Apostles to cheer their hearts again;
I'll give to you the nail-spike that pierced His foot, and then
The crown of thorns they made Him and thrust upon His head;
And you shall have the chalice which He Himself has blessed,
And willingly I'll give you the silver bowl as well,
Inlaid with gold, and gleaming with precious stones inset;
And you shall have the knife which He held when breaking bread,
And hairs of good St Peter, both from his beard and head."

In turn King Charlemagne pledged always to be friends,
And all his body trembled with joy and tenderness.

THE PATRIARCH continued: "A blessing on your visit!
Lord God has led you to me, this is my firm conviction;
I'll give to you such relics as have great power in them:
Some milk of Virgin Mary's which nourished Christ the infant,
When He came down from Heaven to live on earth here with us;
And some of Mary's clothing we have, and I shall give you."
In turn King Charlemagne pledged friendship long and willing,
And gladly took the relics when they were all delivered;
The relics had great power, which straightaway they witnessed:
For near them lay a poor man, an old, bed-ridden cripple,
Whose every joint was swollen and every bone was brittle:
He leapt up of a sudden and never felt such vigour!
The Patriarch, observing the wonder of God's spirit,
Set every church-bell ringing in all parts of the city;
The King had made a casket – no better one existed:
One thousand marks he melted of Arab gold to build it;
He sealed it off securely and bound the whole thing rigid
With closely-fitted ribbons of thickly-plaited silver;
He placed it in the convoy of Turpin the archbishop;
The King was filled with gladness, as was each baron with him.

FOR FOUR WHOLE MONTHS they stayed, within the town abiding,
The King and his Twelve Peers, that worthy band of knighthood;
And high they lived, and well, for Charles the King was mighty;
They founded there a church to blessed Mary plighted:
It's called The Latin Church by those who still reside there
And in it sell their silk and serge and linen likewise,
And cinnamon and ginger, and sundry other spices,
And many goodly herbs, too many to describe them:
But God is still in Heaven, and His revenge will strike them.

4. Charles's departure from Jerusalem

THE EMPEROR of France, he made a lengthy stay,
Then took aside his host and spoke to him this way:
"Fine sir, give me your leave no longer to delay;
I must return to France, the kingdom whence I came;

My stay here has been long and long I've been away
From all my knights at court, who know naught of my fate;
Accept one hundred mules with gold and silver laid!"
The Patriarch replied: "Don't press me, Charlemagne,
For all my treasure here is yours for pleasure's sake!
Let all your Frenchmen have as much as each can take,
But in return defend our world from Pagan knaves
Who would destroy us all, together with our Faith!"

"DO YOU KNOW WHAT I bid you?" the Patriarch said then:
"To slaughter every Pagan who holds us in contempt!"
"I will," said Charlemagne, and gave his word and pledge.

"I'LL SUMMON ALL my forces, as many as I may,
And with all haste I'll take them and make my way to Spain."
And this he did, good people, and kept the word he gave;
In Spain Count Roland perished, the Peers Twelve the same.

THE EMPEROR of France, he stopped and stayed at length,
Then he recalled his wife and all that she had said,
And left to seek the king whom she had praised the best;
Until he found that man, he swore he'd never rest!
That night, back in their camp, he told this to the French,
And all were filled with joy on hearing of his quest;
When morning came, at dawn, as soon as light would let,
They saddled up their mules and piled them high with wealth,
Then each one mounted horse and on their way they went;
To Jericho they rode, and many palms they held,
And cried, with ringing voice: "Ride on, with Jesu's help!"
Upon a rested mule the patriarch was set,
And led them all the way, as long as light was left;
King Charles's men, that night, took their repose in tents,
And nothing they required failed ever to be fetched;
When morning came, at dawn, as soon as light would let,
Each man bestrode his horse, and set off once again;
The Patriarch hailed Charles, and to him thus he said:
"My lord, let me return, while you continue hence."
The Emperor replied: "As God and you think best!"
The two of them embraced and parted thus, and then
The Emperor led on his gallant band of men;
The relics had great power through which God showed His strength:

Each time they reached a flood, at once the waters ebbed,
And eyesight was restored to all the blind they met;
They made the dumb to speak, and lame to walk again.

5. The Frenchmen's arrival in Constantinople

THE EMPEROR rode onward with all his band of knights;
They rode across the ranges and Abilant's great heights;
They passed the Rock of Guitume and left its plains behind,
Then saw Constantinople, a city great and fine,
Its belfries topped with eagles, its domes all shining bright;
For one whole league in distance, upon the city's right,
Were groves adorned with laurels and planted through with pines,
And blooming with laburnum, with rose and eglantine;
They found inside the gardens some twenty thousand knights,
Sat round in silken garments, from top to toe attired
In mighty skins of marten and ermine furs of white;
At backgammon and chess-games they played to pass the time,
And some of them had falcons and goshawks at their side;
And three thousand fair maidens, in orfreys golden-bright,
And sundry silken garments, made up a comely sight
As, clinging to their lovers, they sported in delight;
Upon his ambling donkey King Charlemagne arrived;
He called his nephew Roland and said to him, aside:
"My friend, where is King Hugo? His might can't be denied!"
He called out to a knight there and asked him, with a smile:
"My friend, where is King Hugo I've journeyed far to find?"
The knight at once responded: "Ride on from here a while,
And you will see him sitting beneath an awning high."
The Emperor rode forward, not wasting any time,
And found King Hugo working, as with a plough he plied:
The yokes were both a-gleaming with gold all shining-bright;
The axles and the ploughshares were made of gold alike;
King Hugo wasn't walking, with goad in hand to strike,
But had a strong mule ambling upon his left and right,
And on a chair all golden he sat there all the while;
Upon a noble cushion the emperor reclined,
Of oriole its plumage, of Persian silk its pile;
His feet were on a faldstool incised with silver white,
His head was nobly hatted, his hands well gloved alike;

Four poles were raised around him to carry and to tie
The fine, grey silken curtains which draped him on all sides;
Of finest gold he carried a royal rod upright,
And drove his plough and ox-team with such address and style
That each one of his furrows was an exact straight line;
Upon his ambling donkey King Charlemagne arrived.

THE MONARCH DROVE his plough, to get his day's work over;
King Charlemagne rode up along an ancient roadway
And saw the hanging silk and all the shining gold there;
He hailed Hugo the Strong with honest heart and open,
And Hugo looked at Charles, his face so fierce and noble,
His slim and slender trunk, his mighty arms and shoulders:
"May God protect you, lord! How is it that you know me?"
"I come from France the sweet," King Charles replied and told him:
"My name is Charlemagne, my nephew is young Roland;
Jerusalem I've seen and am returning homeward;
I wanted to see *you*, and your brave band of nobles."
The strong King Hugo said: "Some seven years ago now
I heard the stories told to me by foreign soldiers,
Of how no king on earth had knights to match your own ones;
Stay with me here a year – but if you want to only!
I'll give you silver, gold, and noble cloths and clothing –
Your men can take as much as their pack-mules can shoulder!
Now I'll unhitch my beasts in friendship's sign and token."

THE KING UNYOKED his oxen and left his plough at rest;
The beasts grazed in the meadows and higher up as well;
King Hugo took his donkey and gently rode ahead;
"Lord," said King Charlemagne, "this plough that you have left
Is built of gold more richly than I could ever guess:
I fear it will be stolen, if there's no guardsman left."
At once King Hugo answered: "Good monarch, never fret!
I've never had a robber within my kingdom yet;
The plough could stay untouched there for seven years on end!"
Said William of Orange: "By good St Peter's breath!
If it were in the country where I and Bertrand dwell,
It would be hacked and hammered and stripped away to shreds!"
King Hugo spurred his mule on and gently rode ahead;
He came beneath his palace, and when he saw her there,
He bade his wife get ready, and having dressed herself,

She then prepared the palace: its hall with silk was decked;
Then Charlemagne arrived there with all his gallant men.

6. The Frenchmen's reception at Hugo's palace

THE EMPEROR dismounted by marble white and gleaming,
And hastened to the palace, up hallway steps, to see there
Some seven thousand courtiers, and all of them were seated
At backgammon and chess-games, to pass the time more sweetly,
All dressed in cloaks of ermine and coats of Persian weaving;
And not a few, but many, came running out to meet them,
Who took hold of their horses and sturdy mules to lead them
Inside the stalls and stables, where they were nobly treated;
King Charles beheld the palace, its mighty wealth perceiving:
Of purest gold the tables, the chairs and benches reared there;
The hall was blue of border and to the eye most pleasing,
With rich and noble paintings upon the walls and ceiling,
Of birds in flight and serpents and sundry other creatures;
The hall itself was vaulted and self-enclosed completely,
Most skilfully constructed and firm in every feature;
The column in the centre was striped with silver seaming,
And flanked with marble pillars one hundred more, and each one
Inlaid upon its frontal with finest gold and dearest;
A statue of two children stood there, of copper beaten,
Who to their lips each lifted a white horn for this reason:
If any breeze or wind-gust blew inland from the seashore
And struck against the palace, upon its western reaches,
It set the hall revolving until the palace seemed like
The spokes upon a chariot as on and on the wheel goes!
And then those white horns sounded and pounded forth as clearly
As any drum or thunder or mighty bell set pealing;
Both children faced each other and looked with laughing features,
And truly you'd have thought them to be alive and breathing!
King Charles surveyed the palace, its mighty wealth perceiving,
And all of his possessions he valued then most cheaply,
And thought back to his wife whom he'd threatened so severely.

"MY LORDS," SAID CHARLEMAGNE, "this palace is most fine;
Not mighty Alexander, nor aged Constantine,
Nor Crescentius the Roman constructed one its like!"

No sooner had he spoken, when from the sea nearby,
Across the port towards them he heard a wind arise;
It swept up to the palace and struck it on one side
And set it into motion – a gentle, quiet wind,
Revolving like a windmill, with everyone inside!
Both statues blew their horns then and gave each other smiles,
And truly you'd have thought then that they were both alive;
It was a joy to hear them hallooing clear and high,
And those who did thought truly they'd come to Paradise,
Where Angels sing with voices so gentle, sweet and mild;
But this one was a storm-wind, with snow and hail alike:
It roared towards the palace, increasing all the time;
The windows of the palace were made of crystal tiles
Cut out of quartz the colour of lapis lazuli;
Inside, the room was peaceful, as tranquil and as fine
As days of May in summer, with sunshine warm and bright;
Outside, the storm was grievous and terrible to bide;
Charles saw the palace turning and quivering to life,
But, unadvised beforehand, he didn't then know why,
And sat down on the marble – he couldn't stay upright,
Nor could his Frenchmen either, and all were tossed awry!
With both hands, very quickly, they shielded heads and eyes,
And said to one another: "We're in a sorry plight!
The palace doors are open, but we can't go outside!"

CHARLES SAW THE PALACE turning, both quietly and gently,
His barons didn't dare to, and kept their heads well buried!
At this the strong King Hugo before them all went stepping
And said to all the Frenchmen: "Please don't let this distress you!"
"My lord," said Charlemagne, "Does this go on for ever?"
The strong King Hugo answered: "Lord, wait a while, I beg you!"
And as the daylight faded, the storm began to lessen;
The French regained their footing and dinner soon was ready;
Charles sat down at the table with all his gallant Frenchmen,
As did the strong King Hugo, he and his wife, together
With their most lovely daughter, of fair hair, and complexion
As white as any flower that blooms in summer meadows;
Count Oliver, he loved her as soon as he beheld her!
"Ah, would to God," he whispered, "in His majestic Heaven,
That back in France or home in the town of Dun I held her,
For then I'd take my pleasure in full with her at leisure!"

Between his teeth he whispered, so no one knew he'd said it;
No food the Frenchmen asked for did Hugo fail to fetch them,
And venison and boar's meat were served to them in plenty,
And wild geese and crane-meat and peacocks spiced with pepper;
And wine and mead they brought them – their cups were never empty;
And then the *jongleurs* chanted to rotes and to *vièles*;
Most nobly and most richly the Frenchmen all made merry.

WHEN IN THE ROYAL PALACE their feasting had been made,
The seneschals came forward and cleared the cloths away;
The squires, from every corner, forsook their seats in haste,
And went straight to the stables to tend their mounts again;
At this the strong King Hugo called out to Charles the Great,
And to one side withdrew him, his Peers Twelve the same;
He took his hand and led him within a room inlaid
With crystal gems and painted with floral scenes ornate;
A glittering carbuncle shone with a burning flame,
Set into a stone pillar since King Goliath's day;
A dozen beds of copper and metal met their gaze,
With pillows all of velvet and silken overlays;
Four carts and twenty oxen would scarce have moved their weight;
The thirteenth in the middle was most ornately made:
Its feet were solid silver, enamel all its rails;
Its coverlet was fashioned by one Maseuz by name,
A noble-blooded spirit to whom King Hugo gave
A guerdon that was greater than an emir could pay;
And Charles, he should have cherished a host who had displayed
Such honour in his service, such bounty in his grace.

7. The Frenchmen's bedroom-boasts

THE FRENCH WERE IN their bedroom and gazed upon the beds,
Then each of them selected the one that pleased him best;
The mighty monarch Hugo had more wine brought to them,
But he was wise and cunning, alert and circumspect:
Within their very bedroom, beneath a marble step,
Inside a hollowed space there he placed one of his men,
Who all night through could watch them by looking through a vent;
The ruby glowed so brightly that he could see as well
As on May days in summer with sunshine overhead;

Meanwhile the strong King Hugo had joined his wife in bed,
And Charles and all his Frenchmen were lying down at rest;
His marquises and counts then began to boast in jest:
The French were in their bedroom – the wine was in their heads!

THEY SAID TO ONE another: "How lovely all this is!
How noble is this palace, how beautiful and rich!
If only God in glory, by His majestic Will,
Had destined Charlemagne to own or buy all this,
Or win it all in battle by force of arms and skill!"
King Charlemagne answered: "I'll make my boast forthwith!
There is no youth in service to Hugo, mighty king,
In all of this fine household, however strong or quick,
Though he strapped on two helmets and hauberks double-stitched,
And sat astride a war-horse however fresh or swift,
If I had Hugo's sword with its golden-pommelled hilt,
Whose helmets I'd not hammer till their best panels split,
And send their jewels flying and slit his coat to bits,
And split the felt and saddle on any horse of his;
My sword shall strike the meadow and still it shall not stint:
A full lance-length I'll drive it within the ground until
No mortal man can stir it from where I've stuck it in!"
"By God," the spy responded, "your muscles must be big!
How foolish was King Hugo to lodge you here, I think!
If I should hear this evening more folly from your lips,
Then at first light tomorrow I'll have you all dismissed!"

SAID CHARLES: "FINE NEPHEW Roland, the second boast is yours!"
"Just as you wish, fine uncle, and willingly, my lord!
If you request King Hugo to lend me his own horn,
Then out upon the plain there I'll gallop on my horse;
My breath shall be so sturdy, and such a wind I'll cause,
That in this mighty city, so brimming and so broad,
I'll leave no gate-post standing, nor any gate or door,
No steel nor any copper, however strong at all,
Will not be crushed and crumpled beneath the wind I'll roar!
Their king will be a hero if he can venture forth
And stop the great wind scorching his whiskers off by force,
And curling from his collar those furs that he adores,
And turning inside outward that ermine cloak he wore!"
"By God," the spy responded, "how foul and fierce a taunt!
How foolish was King Hugo to have you here at all!"

THE NOBLE COUNT continued: "Sir Oliver, your boast!"
"Most willingly," he answered, "if Charles would have it so!
Let Hugo take his daughter, of hair so fair and gold,
And place us in her bedroom in one bed on our own;
If I do not possess her one hundred times all told,
Then have my head tomorrow – I'll let you, on my oath!"
"By God," the spy responded, "you'll falter first, I hope!
You've spoken words of outrage, and when King Hugo knows,
Each day he lives henceforward he'll hate you as his foe!"

"AND YOU, MY LORD archbishop, will you join in our vaunting?"
"Indeed," good Turpin answered, "since Charles himself exhorts me!
Let Hugo take tomorrow the best three of the horses
Which he has in his city, and make a circuit for them;
When they are at full gallop, upon that plain before us,
Then from the right hand side here you'll see me rushing forward
And leap astride the last one, the other two ignoring;
I'll have with me four apples, and while King Hugo's horses
Are running round the circuit without a rein to halt them,
I'll juggle all four apples and toss them back and forth there;
If one of them escapes me, or from my hand goes falling,
Then Charles may pluck my eyes out – I'll let him, I assure you."
"By God," the spy responded, "this boast is fine and courtly,
For it contains no outrage to Hugo or his fortunes."

SAID WILLIAM of Orange: "Attend the boast *I'll* give you!
Do you see that great sphere there? I never saw one bigger:
Behold the gold and silver the mighty thing has in it!
Some thirty men have laboured so many times to shift it,
But couldn't even budge it, so big and heavy is it;
Tomorrow, when the dawn breaks, with one hand I will lift it,
And then, my friends, I'll roll it right through this palace building
And topple forty fathoms and more of wall down with it!"
"By God," the spy responded, "I don't believe this insult!
Curse Hugo if he doesn't compel you to commit it!"

THE EMPEROR continued: "Ogier shall make his taunt,
The Danish duke who labours so nobly in our cause!"
"Indeed," the brave man answered, "since you permit me, lord;
Do you observe that column which holds up all this hall,
Which on this very morning we saw swing back and forth?

Tomorrow you will see me embrace it with such force,
No matter what its strength is, I'll crush it till it falls,
And all this mighty palace will topple to the floor!
Whoever stays inside here will not escape at all;
The king will be a madman if he does not withdraw!"
"By God," the spy responded, "how mad and bad a thought!
May God forbid you ever to undertake this vaunt!
How foolish was King Hugo to give *you* bed and board!"

THE EMPEROR continued: "Your boast, Naimon the duke!"
"Indeed," the brave man answered: "My hair is white of hue,
But ask the king to lend me his hauberk bright and new!
Tomorrow, when I've donned it, and tied and laced it through,
I'll twist and turn and shake it in front of all of you
So strongly that, no matter how tough its steel should prove,
The rings will fall like corn-stalks – I'll shake the whole lot loose!"
"By God," the spy responded, "you're old and hoary too,
But underneath your muscles must be both trim and true!"

THE EMPEROR continued: "Your boast, Lord Bérenger!"
The count replied: "Most gladly, since you desire the same!
Let Hugo's knights tomorrow take off their swords and place
Their pommels in the ground there, embedded and arranged
So that their blades point upwards; and when they're all in place,
I'll climb the tallest tower, and then, without delay,
I'll hurl myself down from it upon those naked blades!
I'll crush the blades together, and as they bend and break,
One blade will strike another and shatter it again;
But you'll not find me wounded or hurt in any way:
Not one will pierce me gravely or leave me with a graze!"
"By God," the spy responded, "this man has lost his brains!
If this boast is accomplished, he has an iron frame!"

THE EMPEROR continued: "Bernart, now make your boast!"
The count replied: "Most gladly, since you command me so;
Do you see that great river which sweeps the banks below?
Tomorrow I shall make it completely overflow
And flood each field and meadow for you to all behold;
Its depth will fill the cellars of all this city's folk –
King Hugo's population will be completely soaked!
And he will have to climb up the tallest tower he owns

And stay there, not descending until I tell him so!"
"By God," the spy responded, "This man is mad, I know!
How foolish was King Hugo to let you in his home!
At dawn's first light tomorrow you'll all be made to go!"

"MY UNCLE'S BOAST shall follow!" called out aloud Bertrand;
"Upon my faith, most gladly," said Hernaut of Gironde:
"Let Hugo take four loads of some heavy leaden blocks
And melt them all together in mighty cauldron-pots!
Then let him take a barrel, both wide enough and long
To fill it with the liquid and have it reach the top;
I'll sit right in the middle till nones has come and gone,
And when the lead has settled and all its flow has stopped,
And when it is well hardened, you'll see me sway and rock
Till all the lead around me has shattered with the shock;
Not one whole lump I'll leave there the weight of a shallot!"
"This is a wondrous war-boast!" the spy said in response:
"I've never heard of any whose body was that strong!
He has a frame of iron, if he can pull that off!"

"NOW MAKE YOUR BOAST, Sir Aimer!" the Emperor continued;
The count replied: "Most gladly, since it is you who bids me;
I still possess a headpiece with almandine for trimming,
Whose panels are of fish-skin wrapped with a golden ribbon;
Tomorrow, when King Hugo is seated at his dinner,
And when I've put this hat on and dressed myself up in it,
I'll drink up all his claret and finish all his fish up!
Then I'll come up behind him and strike him with such vigour
He'll sprawl across the table before he knows what's hit him!
Then watch me pull his beard off and pluck his royal whiskers!"
"By God," the spy responded, "this man's a crazy villain!
How foolish was King Hugo to let you lodge here with him!"

"BERTRAND, NOW MAKE your war-boast!" the Emperor said next;
The count replied: "Most gladly, since that is your behest;
Tomorrow, with three bucklers, all sturdy edge to edge,
I'll climb up to the top of that ancient pine-tree there;
Then you will see me strike them together with such strength,
And toss them in the air there, while making such a yell,
That all around the city, for four leagues' length and breadth,
No woodland stag whatever, no deer in forest-depths,

No savage beasts or roe-deer or foxes will be left!"
"By God," the spy responded, "that is a wicked jest!
How angry will the king be to learn of your intent!"

THE EMPEROR continued: "Gerin, now make your vaunt!"
The count replied: "Most gladly, in front of one and all!
I'll need a spear tomorrow, the strongest, longest sort,
So heavy that a rustic be charged to bear it forth;
Its shaft should be of sorb-wood, one ell of iron its point;
On top of Hugo's tower, upon its marble vault,
Place one upon the other two single denier coins;
Then I'll go pacing backwards one league in length or more,
Then, if you watch me closely, you'll see my lance-head soar
From tower's base to summit and strike one single coin
So sweetly that the second is not dislodged at all!
Then I shall be so rapid, so fleet of foot and sure,
That I'll race through the doorway that leads inside the hall
And catch the spear I cast with before it hits the floor!"
"By God," the spy responded, "this boast beats all before –
It sheds no shame whatever upon the king my lord!"

WHEN ALL THE COUNTS had boasted, they fell asleep and slept;
The spy, hid in the chamber, heard everything then left
To reach the royal bedroom where Hugo lay at rest;
He found the door was open, and so approached his bed;
King Hugo saw him coming, and straightaway he said:
"So tell me what they're doing, fierce Charles and all the French!
Did you hear them discussing if friendship is their end?"
"By God," the spy responded, "that word means naught to them!
All night you were the butt of their mockery and jest!"
And he retold exactly the boasts they had expressed,
And when King Hugo heard them, how sad he was and vexed!

8. King Hugo's challenge

"KING CHARLES WAS VERY FOOLISH, upon my faith," he cried,
"When with such gay abandon he mocked both me and mine!
Within my marbled bedrooms I lodged them all last night!
Well, if they can't accomplish the boasts as they described,
Then I shall cut their heads off with sword-blades burnished bright!"

More than one hundred thousand he summoned of his knights
And gave them all the order to don their coats of iron;
So, clad in cloaks, and bearing their sword-blades at their side,
They came inside the palace and sat around their sire;
When Mass had been conducted, Charles left the local shrine,
Returning to the palace with all his barons fine;
The Emperor was leading, which, as their liege, was right,
And in his hand he carried an olive-branch entwined;
But when King Hugo saw him, from far away he cried:
"Charles! Why did you insult me and mock me with your gibes?
Within my marbled bedrooms I lodged you all last night;
You shouldn't have thought lightly of mocking me and mine!
Well, if you can't accomplish the boasts that you described,
Then I shall cut your heads off with sword-blades burnished bright!"
King Charlemagne heard this, and fearing for his life,
He looked at all the Frenchmen and told his barons fine:
"Last night we drank too deeply of claret and of wine:
I think that in our chamber the king had placed a spy!"

"LAST NIGHT YOU LODGED us all," said mighty Charlemagne:
"You gave us wine to dine and more besides thereafter;
Our custom, back in France, in Paris and in Chartres,
Is that, when knights retire, they vie in boasts and laughter,
And some good things are said, and some mad things, I grant you;
Now let me speak at once to my brave knights and hardy,
Then gladly I'll respond with pledges to your charges."
"In truth, the crime's too great!" King Hugo said in answer:
"By my white beard and faith, I swear, when you depart here,
You will not boast again to anyone hereafter!"

9. The Frenchmen's response

KING CHARLES turned up a pathway, the Peers Twelve the same;
Beneath a vaulted archway they gathered in all haste,
And Charles the King said sadly: "Great woe has come our way!
We all drank too much claret and too much wine the same,
Then made the most of war-boasts that we should not have made!"
He asked then that the relics be brought out and displayed,
And all knelt down before them, confessing each their blame;
They called on God in Heaven, upon His power and Grace,

To save and to protect them from Hugo's wrath that day,
Whose heart had turned against them and filled with angry rage;
Then lo! God made an Angel appear before their gaze:
It came to Charlemagne and raised him with this phrase:
"Fear not, King Charlemagne, but heed what Jesus says:
The boasts you made last evening were mad and bad to make:
Lord Jesus Christ commands you to mock no man again –
But go now and perform them – not one of them will fail!"
When Charlemagne heard this, his joy was very great!

THE FRENCHMAN CHARLEMAGNE stood up to his full height
And, with his hands uplifted, he made the Cross's sign;
And then he told his barons: "Put all your fears aside!
Come with me to King Hugo up in his palace high!"

"MY LORD," SAID CHARLEMAGNE, "this much must be admitted:
Last night in marbled chambers you lodged us after dinner,
And from the wine and claret some drank beyond their limit!
But when you parted from us, your own wrong you committed,
For you left in the chamber a spy to look and listen!
We know of such a country where it would be considered
To be an act of treason to do the thing you did here!
We shall perform the war-boasts – of your, not our volition!
Whomever you have chosen both should and shall begin them!"
"Well," said the strong King Hugo, whose choice was not an ill one,
"Count Oliver stands near me, who foolishly predicted
That he would have my daughter one hundred times by midnight!
Let courts call me a coward, if I do not submit her!
If I don't give her to him, my honour is but little!
But if he once should falter, through lack of manly vigour,
My polished sword will strike him and smite his head off swiftly!
Both he and all your Peerage are destined to be killed here!"
King Charles, he smiled to hear this, who trusted in God's wisdom,
And added to the judgement: "A curse on who'd acquit him!"
All day the Frenchmen dallied in pleasure and high spirits,
And nothing that they asked for took any time to bring them,
Until the day grew darker and night fell on the city;
Inside her room well curtained with walls of silks and linens,
King Hugo led his daughter, the fair and lovely princess;
Her face was white and pallid as any summer-lily;
Then Oliver came in there, his face aglow with grinning;

The maid was very frightened to see his laughing visage,
And yet she was most courtly and said with noble spirit:
"Lord, did you leave your homeland to come and kill us women?"
But Oliver responded: "Fear nothing, lovely sister,
For I've no will to harm you – just trust in me a little!"

THE COUNT LAY IN the bed there, the princess at his side;
Then, turning her towards him, he kissed the maid three times,
And said, in courtly fashion, for she was most refined:
"My lady, you're a Princess, of beauty rich and high;
Despite the boast I uttered, be in no fear or fright:
In truth, I've no intention of sating my desire."
"My lord, have mercy on me!" the lovely maid replied:
"If you bring shame upon me, you will destroy my life!"
Said Oliver: "My fair one, your will I will abide,
But you must help acquit me in strong King Hugo's eyes;
I seek no other sweetheart, in truth I'd make you mine."
She was a courtly maiden and pledged her faith alike;
That night he did it to her no more than thirty times;
The next day, as the dawn broke, the king at once arrived;
He called out to his daughter and took her to one side:
"Fair daughter, did he have you one hundred times last night?"
"My lord and king, yes, truly, he did," the maid replied;
You do not need to wonder if Hugo's face went white!
He came where Charles was sitting inside the hall and cried:
"He must be a magician! The first has saved his hide!
I'll find out if the others have told the truth or lied!"

THE KING WAS HEAVY-HEARTED to hear the boast fulfilled;
He said to Charlemagne: "The first has saved his skin!
I'll find out if the others can do as well as him!"
"Whichever man you've chosen, is ready to begin!"
"Here's William, the son of Count Aymeri – let him
Pick up that sphere of metal that stands here in our midst,
And, if he cannot throw it, as in his boast he did,
My polished sword will strike him and lop his lying lips!
Both he and all your Peerage have little time to live!"

COUNT WILLIAM saw clearly that it was *his* turn now,
So, taking off his mantle, whose beaver-pelts were brown,
Among the cloths of silk there he threw it on the ground,

Then hurried to the spot where the sphere was to be found;
With just one hand he raised it and swung it with great power,
And then he sent it rolling before the watching crowd;
It toppled forty fathoms of wall, then more fell down,
Not through the strength of William, but God Almighty's power
And love for Charlemagne, who'd brought them to that town.

KING HUGO FILLED with sadness to see his palace wrecked;
He said to all his men there; "How foul and fell a jest,
Not worthy of a hero, in faith I must confess;
These men are all magicians who have come here in stealth
To steal my kingdom from me, and all that I possess!
I'll find out if the others will do as well as them!
If one of them should falter, by God, I pledge again
That from my windy pine-trees they'll all hang by the neck
Upon a sturdy gallows – and naught shall help them then!"

"MY LORD," SAID CHARLEMAGNE, "shall we fulfil more boasts?
Whichever man you've chosen will start, and nothing loath!"
"Well," said the strong King Hugo, "there's Sir Bernart, the bold
And oldest son of Aymeri, who boasted, so I'm told,
That he could make the river, which sweeps the vale below,
Leap right out of its channel and fully overflow
And flood inside the city and soak the city-folk –
And I should have to climb up the tallest tower I own
And stay there, not descending until he told me so."

BERNART THE COUNT saw clearly *his* turn had come this time;
He said to Charlemagne: "Now pray to Jesus Christ!"
Then, turning to the river, he made the Cross's sign,
And God performed a wonder, the glorious Lord on High:
He raised that mighty river until it burst its sides
And flooded through the meadows in everybody's sight,
And flowed inside the city and filled its cellars high
Till all King Hugo's people were soaked and none was dry!
Inside his tallest tower the king fled for his life,
And fierce-faced Charlemagne climbed up an ancient pine,
Both he and all his Peerage, that worthy band of knights;
They all prayed God in Heaven to pity them their plight!

10. Charlemagne's triumph

ATOP AN ANCIENT PINE-TREE King Charlemagne went
With all his Peers together, that worthy band of friends!
He heard, in his high tower, King Hugo's loud lament:
How he would give Charles treasure and go to France himself
And there become his vassal and hold his realm in pledge;
When Charlemagne heard it, then pity filled his breast:
For we should all show mercy on those who show regret;
And so he prayed to Jesus to make the flooding end;
For love of Charlemagne, God showed His mighty strength –
The waters left the city; across the plains they ebbed
Right back inside their channel and filled their banks again,
So Hugo, from his tower, was able to descend;
Beneath a shady fruit-tree he came to Charles and said:
"True Emperor, I know now that God must love you best!
I shall become your vassal and hold my realm in pledge;
With tribute and with treasure I'll go to France myself."
King Charlemagne answered: "Shall we fulfil more jests?"
Strong Hugo swiftly answered: "No more for now!" he said:
"If they are all accomplished, my woes will never end!"

"MY LORD," SAID CHARLEMAGNE, to Hugo, strong and proud:
"You have become my vassal! Your men have heard the vow!
Today we must make merry and celebrate the hour,
And both of us together must wear our golden crowns!
For love of you I'm ready to put my own on now!"
"I too, my lord," said Hugo, "for you and your renown;
And we shall walk together within these palace grounds."
King Charles set on his head then his mighty golden crown,
And Hugo bore his own one – a little lower down,
For Charles was fifteen inches the taller, brow to brow!
The Frenchmen gazed upon them and all agreed, aloud:
"Our Lady Queen spoke wrongly and in a foolish hour;
 King Charles is very worthy – he's shown his greater power;
In every land we enter the honour will be ours!"

CHARLES WORE HIS CROWN of gold inside Constantinople,
And Hugo wore his too, and stood a little lower!
The Frenchmen gazed on both and all agreed most boldly:

"Our Lady Queen spoke false and in a foolish moment,
When she held up to scorn such prowess as our own is!"
They walked in fine parade within the grounds enclosed there,
And Hugo's wife herself was in her crown, and holding
Her daughter by the hand, of hair so fair and golden –
Who saw Count Oliver and gladly would have spoken
And welcomed him with warmth, her friendship clearly showing;
She would have kissed him too, but feared the king's reproaches;
They went inside the church to which the cloisters opened,
Where Turpin led the priests, with noble heart and holy,
In singing Mass, where all left offerings and tokens,
Then went back to the hall in joy and high emotion.

THE FRENCH WERE IN the palace, and when the meal was ready,
And squires had set the tables, they all sat down together;
No food the Frenchmen asked for did Hugo fail to fetch them,
And venison and boar's meat were served to them in plenty,
And wild geese and crane-meat and peacocks spiced with pepper;
And wine and mead they brought them – their cups were never empty;
And then the *jongleurs* chanted to rotes and to *vièles*
Till, hailing Charlemagne, King Hugo thus addressed him:
"My city's mighty treasure I place here at your pleasure!
As much as each can carry, I'll give to every Frenchman!"
The Emperor responded: "No more of this – I tell you,
I would not and I will not deprive you of one penny!
My men have more of wealth than they can bear already!
But give to us your leave – for we must go directly."
"My lord," the king responded, "I do not dare prevent you!"
So to the marble mount-blocks they led their mules and held them;
King Charlemagne hailed him: "At your command, farewell then!"
They kissed and wished each other God's blessing and protection.

11. The Pilgrims' return

WHEN ALL THE FRENCH had eaten, they made no more delay,
So to the marble mount-blocks their mules were led and laid,
And, mounting happy-hearted, the men set on their way;
At this King Hugo's daughter ran forward, unrestrained,
To Oliver, whose clothing she clutched as she exclaimed:
"My love and my affection I give to you this day;

If you will take me with you, then I am yours to take!"
Said Oliver: "My fair one! My love for you remains –
But I am off to France now with my lord Charles the Great!"

THE GALLANT CHARLEMAGNE was happy and content
To conquer such a monarch and no blood to have shed;
Who should I spin my story to any greater length?
They passed through all the countries and sundry foreign realms
Till they came back to Paris, that worth town, and went
To Saint-Denis directly and to the shrine again;
The gallant Charlemagne lay prostrate on its steps
And, having prayed to Jesus, he raised himself, and then
He placed upon the altar the nail and crown, and sent
The other holy relics throughout his kingdom's breadth;
The Queen was in the church there, and fell down to repent;
The King shed all his anger against her disrespect:
The sepulchre he'd worshipped had shown him love's largesse.

RAOUL OF CAMBRAI

(c.1180–1190)

Introduction

Raoul de Cambrai is not only one of the finest Old French epic tales, it is one of the best medieval poems composed in any language to have come down to us today. The complete poem survives in only one manuscript copy, held currently at the Bibliothèque Nationale in Paris. Its latest editor, Sarah Kay, concludes that this one copy was made by two scribes working in different halves of the thirteenth century. Generically the poem belongs to the song cycle of 'rebellious barons' (see Preface p. xiv). Historically, the composition of such works during the eleventh and twelfth centuries is thought to have reflected an early contemporary resistance to the weakening Frankish monarchies of pre-Capetian France, and a subsequent baronial resentment at the re-imposition of royal authority during the reign of King Philippe-Auguste (1180–1223).

The full text of *Raoul de Cambrai* is a classic example of its cyclic kind, showing three reworkings of legendary material associated with a rebellious 'Raoul figure', whose historical inspiration comes from the violent deeds and early deaths of at least two so-named pre-Capetian French counts. In the year 896, according to the *Annales Vedastini*, one Raoul, son of Baudoin of Flanders, seized Péronne and Saint-Quentin in northern France, burning the abbey of the latter town to the ground. King Eudes restored the lands to Herbert of Vermandois, who then slew this Raoul in a battle. Some fifty years later, a second Raoul is credited in the *Annals* of Flodoard with a similar feat and defeat:

'In the year 943 Count Herbert died and was buried by his sons at Saint-Quentin; then, when they learnt that Raoul, son of Raoul de Gouy, was advancing to invade their father's lands, they attacked and killed him: this news greatly saddened King Louis.'

As often happens in the *chansons de geste*, during the centuries between the creation of oral chants surrounding the deeds of certain historical personalities and their eventual written record, there arises a confusion and subsequently a fusion between characters, and more significantly in the case of *Raoul de Cambrai*, between character-traits, which produces a composite hero contrived to accommodate the individual writer's poetic purpose.

The present poem claims as its original author one Bertolai of Laon, who as a soldier-poet among the anti-Raoul forces allegedly composed an eye-witness account of the battle in which this famous anti-hero was slaughtered:

> *'Ybert, he swore to cede them not one step,*
> *And every one of all his liegemen pledged*
> *To stand by him till all their blood was shed:*
> *"What loyalty, by God!" young Bernier said:*
> *"A curse on him, I say, who first relents*
> *Or breaks his word and flees before the press!"*
> *Then Bertolai said he would write a geste,*
> *The like of which no jongleur chanted yet.*
>
> *THIS BERTOLAI was very wise and brave;*
> *Both born and bred in Laon itself and raised*
> *Of noble stock, of highest rank and race;*
> *He saw it all, he witnessed all the fray*
> *And wrote this song, whose like was never made,*
> *And which I've sung in countless halls of state,*
> *Of Guerri, called 'The Red', and fair Aalais,*
> *And Count Raoul, the liege lord of Cambrai,*
> *Whose godfather was bishop of Beauvais.'*   (ll.2259-75)

Whoever the composer of the original epic chant may have been, it is clear that the author of its eventual written reworking had an unusually thorough knowledge of the epicentre of its narrative action, namely the abbey at Origny. This fact has led to the suggestion that Bertolai's continuator was perhaps one of the *trouvères* or *jongleurs* who attended Saint-Géri abbey in Cambrai during its annual '*fête des jongleurs*' celebrations.

In *Raoul de Cambrai*, the central character, a child at his father's death, is deprived of his inheritance by King Louis, who is, in fact, his own uncle. Promised, but subsequently not given, the first fief then to fall vacant, he is forced to assert his claim in a violent way against his neighbours, the sons of Vermandois. If the inspiration for the creation of a *Raoul* legend lies in the tenth century, with popular sympathy for a local lord and resentment of a central monarch, (who at that period had the legal right to appoint the successor to a fief), and if the impetus for its continuation can be found in the ongoing discrepancy between law and justice during the reign of King Philippe-Auguste at the end of the twelfth (when all fiefs were legally hereditary), its enduring fame as a powerful and moving narrative must be attributed to the poem's intrinsic artistic achievement. *Raoul de Cambrai* still speaks to us today because it presents a very skilful portrayal of a tragic, universal human type, which is that of a good but passionate man goaded by the whimsy of others to a bad end.

Artistic Achievement

Raoul de Cambrai is at once one of the most brutal yet beautiful poems of the Middle Ages. In its well-crafted verses the unknown author presents a small cast of strong, regional characters swept up and finally swallowed in a vortex of tragic events set in motion by a careless central monarch. Deprived of his own inheritance, then grudgingly awarded someone else's, the tale's central character is forced into conflict not only with a neighbouring clan, but with his own mother, his lifelong companion, and with the Church. Written with a sparse but unsparing realism, the narrative is a tragedy of relationships in crisis, of warring wills which all, from their own standpoint, have right on their side. The poet's greatest achievement lies in his ability to use the simple stylistic techniques of the earliest *chansons de geste* to arouse and sustain our sympathy for essentially flawed protagonists – a reckless 'anti-hero', a paternal 'evil angel', and a bastard son who slays his one benefactor.

The tragic figure of the young count of Cambrai is surely one of the best-drawn and most moving portraits of heroic character in general, and of that very recklessness which constitutes the essence of 'heroic' temperament in particular, that Western literature of any era has produced. A winning, brave and generous youth, with a just cause to begin with, Raoul is doomed to misfortune because of the unthinking, unblinking nature of his courage. More complex than the reckless pride of Roland in the genre's greatest tale, young Raoul's impetuous ardour drives him to be savagely unjust to others, and, worse still, to be heedless of his Faith. Misled by his liege and uncle, King Louis, spurred on by his paternal uncle Guerri the Red, admonished and cursed by his mother Fair Aalais, then deserted by his companion Sir Bernier, Raoul's great heart is driven to undertake deeds of heartlessness equally as great. His conscience, however, again unlike that of Count Roland at Roncesvalles, is a tortured one, as its ties of fealty, family and friendship are tested to the breaking-point, as is, indeed, our own sympathy for him, by each twist and turn of the plot.

Guerri the Red is one of those irascible veteran warriors, proud patrons of their regional clans, whose frustratingly endearing characteristics, a volatile mixture of mature wisdom and ageing folly, enliven several of the best-written *chansons de geste* – one thinks immediately of old Girart d'Eufrate in the stirring *Song of Aspremont* and of Garin de Monglane in the following tale of this collection, *Girart of Vienne*. Each fiercely protective of their family's honour and torn alternately between a life-long delight in combat and the accumulated prudence of their years, they succeed only in giving mixed messages to the hot-headed scions of their house. In each case, it is the fragility of their own warrior-egos, once vaunted and now taunted, which furnish the narrative with its moments of crisis and resolve. Unlike either Girart or Garin, however, Red Guerri shares equally in the tragedy that his temperament helps to create. A noble and valiant knight, he is admirably protective of his brother's son, to the extent that he sacrifices both of his own in defence of his nephew's rights. His memorable speeches, at moments of pivotal significance in the narrative, act as catalysts to Raoul's brooding thoughts and brewing emotions, producing actions well beyond their own original strength.

The character of Bernier, Count Raoul's protégé, squire and companion, is the third unusually complex creation of this original poem. The true 'hero' of the complete *Raoul* opus, his tragedy is one of conflicting duties. On the one hand he owes allegiance, both moral and legal, to Raoul, whose mother transplanted him from the shadow of bastardy into the sunlight of her son's companionship, and who then himself promoted and knighted him in Paris as his squire and his vassal. On the other hand, Bernier remains the son of Count Ybert of Vermandois, whom Raoul would dispossess, and of Marsent, abbess of Origny, whom Raoul, in one of his rages, burns to death. Relieved of his feudal obligation only when Raoul strikes him in the face, Bernier's moral conflict remains intense while Raoul lives, and then interminable when he slays his lifelong friend in defence of his own family's honour. His personal dilemma is articulated throughout the entire poem with a throbbing refrain of despair.

The original text of the *Raoul* story translated here is written with an artistic austerity, in terms of both story and structure, which harks back to the oldest, orally composed *chansons de geste*. Only the unknown author of *The Song of William* shares, at certain moments, the same bleak focus of the present poet's narrative vision. The scenes in which he describes both personal arguments and collective combats, and in which he presents the pivotal moments of his plot – the burning of Origny abbey, the cruelty of his anti-hero's deeds and his eventual death – are written with an unflinching realism, in relentless spasms of emotion-charged verses driven by the rhetorical pulses and impulses of his art-form's formulaic diction.

Sources and Influences

As stated earlier, the only manuscript which has preserved the complete story of *Raoul de Cambrai* is a composite text, consisting of three reworkings of a ninth and tenth century story. All three reworkings themselves are thought to date from the reign of King Philippe-Auguste (1180–1223). The sources of the earliest reworking, the only one translated in this volume, cannot be identified now. It is certain, however, that the manuscript now held at the Bibliothèque Nationale in Paris does not contain the poem in its original form – it is, in fact, a recast in rhyme of an assonanced model or prototype to which reference is made extensively in the *Waulsort Chronicle* (c.1150) and briefly in the *Ensenhamen* of Guerau de Cabrera, which also dates from the middle of the twelfth century. Among the epic tales themselves, the tragedy of the Count of Cambrai is alluded to in *Les Saisnes* (c.1200), *Les Enfances Vivien* (c.1225) and in *Aubri le Bourgoing* (c.1250). It is interesting to observe that both in these later *chansons de geste* and in the earlier *Waulsort Chronicle* there are two important narrative differences from the surviving poem of *Raoul*. In these other works Raoul's motive for attack is actual encouragement from the King, who wants revenge for imprisonment at Vermandois hands. Raoul is, however, shown in an unfavourable light throughout the entire narratives. The re-evaluation of Raoul's heroic status as witnessed in these texts, may attest to another, earlier and variant form of his story, although Kay describes in all some fourteen surviving literary works whose composition is either contemporary with or subsequent to the three reworkings preserved in the Bibliothèque Nationale manuscript, and in which "Raoul is invoked not as a character within a plot, but as an instance of madness, atrocity, or pride – a vivid impression of violence, and thus a kind of literary shorthand for it, rather than a fixed and coherent narrative" (*Raoul de Cambrai*, lxi). This symbolisation in itself, however, offers ample evidence of the widespread and enduring success of the original author's artistic achievement.

Note to the Translation

The tale of *Raoul de Cambrai* translated here is based upon the most recent edition of the complete *Raoul* manuscript, made by Dr Sarah Kay and published by Oxford University Press in 1992. I am indebted to Dr Kay's scholarship, not only for my general understanding of the whole poem, but also for its guidance in the re-composition of several missing lines from the damaged beginning of the text. The Paris manuscript runs to some eight and a half thousand lines in total, and is unique among its surviving peers in that it presents the first half of its narrative in rhyme, while its second half is copied in the more ancient, assonanced form. Most scholars have concluded that the thirteenth century copyists' intention to recast an assonanced original into rhyme was thwarted for some reason at this middle point in their task. My translation finishes, however, at line 3541 of her edition, with the death of Raoul, which was clearly the climax of the original *chanson de geste*, and turns this first part of the poem back into its original, certainly assonanced form.

RAOUL OF CAMBRAI

1. Raoul's birth

NOW HEAR A SONG of fine and fierce prowess!
You all have heard before, I'm sure, my friends,
Those other bards, whose pride is to present
Their newest songs – but they forget the best!
I'll tell of knights whose valour was immense:
Of old Raoul who ruled Cambrai so well
That he was called 'The Rending-Iron' back then;
He had a son who was a prince of men,
Named after him and with his father's strength:
How fierce a war on Herbert's clan he led –
Until the day young Bernier struck him dead!

TO MISS THIS SONG would be a sad mistake –
So hold your peace and let me tell the tale
Of Guerri, called 'The Red', and fair Aalais,
And young Raoul, the liege lord of Cambrai,
Whose godfather was bishop of Beauvais;
How fierce a war with Herbert's clan he waged!
Pay heed, my friends, to deeds of love and hate!

THIS SIRE I'VE NAMED, Raoul 'The Rending-Iron',
Was very brave and fierce of heart and mind;
He served the King so well, when in his prime,
That in return the King's reward was high:
He gave to him Cambrai, the town and shire,
To be his fief, and gave him then a bride
Of peerless grace in everybody's eyes;
At Louis' court their vows were said and signed;
Their wedding-feast, as you may hear, was fine;
Raoul lived on till all his hair was white,

187

Then left the world in God's good way and time;
The fair Aalais, his good and noble wife,
Was filled with grief when her great husband died;
Their barons bore his shrouded corpse to lie
Within the church of St Géri nearby;
In truth, my friends, when Raoul left this life,
The fair Aalais was carrying his child.

RAOUL THE RENDING-IRON, as I have sung,
That worthy knight, was blessed and buried thus;
In truth, my friends, when all his days were done,
The fair Aalais was carrying his son
Within her womb till God's good time should come;
When he was born what joy there was among
The men-at-arms, the knights and everyone!
How many tongues rejoiced which soon enough,
Believe me, friends, were stricken sad and dumb!
When he was born she wrapped her infant up
In buckram-cloth both rich and soft to touch;
When this was done she summoned forth at once
Two noble lords – Thibaut, I know, was one,
The other one, I think, was Acelin:
"My lords," she said, "come forward, for God's love!
To Beauvais town ride with the rising sun!"

THE FAIR AALAIS was generous and loving:
She laid her son upon a purple cover
And summoned forth two lords of noble courage:
"To Beauvais town ride with tomorrow's sunrise!
Its bishop there, Lord Gui, is my own cousin."
So they set out next morning, as instructed,
Not stopping once until they saw the turrets
Of Gui's great hall, all gleaming in the sunlight;
Geoffrey of Lavardin was this man's brother.

THEY CLIMBED THE STEPS and soon they came inside,
Both carrying their charge by left and right;
On seeing Gui, the bishop praised and prized,
With noble grace they greeted him and cried:
"May God the Lord, Whose Judgement Day is nigh,
Guard and protect his bishop here in Christ!

Thus says Aalais, our Lady fair and wise,
Who was the wife of Raoul Rending-Iron;
The Count has died and left this world behind,
But with an heir to comfort his fair wife:
With loving heart she sends him to your side
To be baptised before his kith and kind."
On hearing this, Gui made the Cross's sign
And praised the Lord in His majestic might:
"Well-bred Countess," he said, "God be your guide!
With no delay this child shall be baptised."
Inside his church he bade the font filled high
And oil and cream brought forth to bless the child;
Then he himself put on his priest's attire.

TO CHURCH AND FONT good Bishop Gui made haste
And blessed the babe for whom his love was great;
For Rending-Iron, his worthy father's sake,
He named the child at once Raoul the same;
That noble man, Lord Gui, made no delay,
But clothed the child befitting its new name;
A foster-mother there, most fair of face,
Was clothed alike in furs of white and grey;
The messengers took up the child again
Then took their leave and rode back to Cambrai,
Where Aalais and red-haired Guerri remained;
Inside the hall no jest or joke was made,
But young Raoul was welcomed back that day
And cherished much henceforth and nobly raised,
Day after day, by fine and fair Aalais,
Till three years passed, according to the tale.

2. King Louis' mistake

THE FAIR AALAIS was generous and kind;
But learn, my friends, the sadness of her life:
The endless feud against Count Herbert's line!
The King of France had in his court a knight
Called Giboin of Le Mans by low and high,
Who served him well with his good sword of iron;
In many wars he orphaned many a child;

He served the King with all his strength and pride,
And with success, as well he should and might;
Now, in return, he sought a fitting prize,
And all the lords who lived beyond the Rhine
Said he should have the fief of Cambrai shire,
And Geoffrey's widowed cousin to be his wife,
The fair Aalais, and rule her knights alike;
By God, Whose hand turned water into wine,
How many men still living then would lie
Sprawled out in death, because of that advice!

KING LOUIS HEARD his barons speak their mood,
And all his men, without exception, moved
That fair Aalais and all of Cambrai too
Should go to Sir Giboin for service true;
And he agreed, most wrongfully, thereto;
He gave the glove to Giboin as a proof,
And he, in turn, knelt down to kiss his shoe;
The King, who held all France beneath his rule,
Said thereupon: "My trusted friend, in truth
A mighty fief in brief shall be your due;
Upon these terms I give Cambrai to you:
I do not wish to rob the boy Raoul,
But he is young and you must guard the youth
Till he bears arms and knows their proper use;
The town shall be his fief, without dispute,
But all its shire I offer now to you."
Sir Giboin said: "My lord, I'll not refuse,
If I may have the land and lady soon."
To covet these, my friends, he was a fool;
How many men still living then he doomed!
The fair Aalais, whose face outshone the moon,
Would not have him, though all her limbs were hewn!

KING LOUIS MADE a great mistake indeed,
When he agreed to split his nephew's fief;
And Sir Giboin was wrong himself to seek
Another's land in payment for his deeds –
A shameful death was all that he received;
King Louis bade his envoy then appear
And said to him: "Go saddle up your steed!

Attend Cambrai, my noble sister's seat,
And tell her this: I have this day decreed
That she shall wed the worthy and the fierce
Sir Giboin of Le Mans, who has no peer
For bravery from here unto the East!
He has received all Cambrai shire in lease
And will depart to join her there in brief
With his own lords and all their company;
Each one of them is kith or friend to me
And should be met by her in love and peace;
Her dower-land, the town, is hers to keep,
But of the shire she'll have no share or fee."

WHEN THIS WAS SAID the envoy turned in haste
To saddle up and mount his destrier;
He left the court and hurried to Cambrai;
On reaching there, he galloped through the gate
And spurred towards St Géri's straightaway;
There in the square he found the fair Aalais
With many knights and lords of her domain;
Dismounting then, he tied his horse's reins
And greeted her in royal Louis' name:
"May Lord our God, by Whom the world was made,
The sky, the land, and all that they contain,
Bless you yourself and all you love the same –
So says the King whom all of France obeys."
"And you, my friend," she answered, full of grace:
"What message sends the King my brother, pray?"
"In Jesu's name, I'll tell you without fail:
Our mighty King decrees that you must take
Sir Giboin of Le Mans, well-bred and brave,
To be your lord and lord of your estates."
On hearing this, Aalais cast down her gaze;
She heaved a sigh and tears rolled down her face;
She cried aloud and said in her dismay:
"The King was mad to grant him all Cambrai!
Raoul, my son, must have it back again
The very day his knighthood's vows are made
And he can prove in court his rightful claim!"
Red-haired Guerri at once rode off in rage
To see the King; my friends, alas the day!

KING LOUIS WAS ill-counselled and at fault
When he agreed with all his other lords
To give Cambrai to Giboin of Le Mans;
Red-haired Guerri rode off at once to court,
And when the King confirmed the deed, he roared:

"I CHALLENGE THIS and am prepared to fight
In Raoul's name with my own blade of iron!"
"If you insist in this," the King replied,
"Then you must bring to court Raoul the child,
Who is but three and still to be a knight!"

"TRUE EMPEROR," entreated Red Guerri,
"Will he be robbed of his good father's fief
Because he cannot ride a horse at three?
By all the faith I owe you as my liege,
One thousand knights, I swear, will cease to breathe,
Before Sir Giboin of Le Mans succeeds!
True Emperor, I'll make this very clear:
If that man's seen inside Cambrai or near,
He'll lose his head, this much I guarantee!
And you will bear the blame and shame indeed:
Raoul's your nephew too! How could you dream
Of robbing him to feed another's greed?"
The King replied: " Sir Guerri, let this be!
The gift was made and cannot be retrieved!"
Loath now to stay, Red Guerri turned to leave –
God woe the day and way he left his liege:
Upon the stones his barons were convened,
All set to mount upon their noble steeds,
When, calling out, he said to all and each:
"Men lithe of limb, prepared to fight and bleed,
Bestir yourselves and seize your arms of steel!
For by the Lord, Who bore the Cross's grief,
I'd rather lose each limb I have than see
My nephew robbed, while I have breath in me!"

RED-HAIRED GUERRI was in a dreadful rage:
He seized his reins and rode back to Cambrai,
Dismounting there upon the square in haste;
The fair Aalais was there to see and came

To welcome him and hear if he had made
The King relent, or if his plea had failed:
"I will not lie," he answered straightaway:
"The King persists and says he will not change,
For he has pledged the shire of Rending-Blade
To Giboin of Le Mans, God curse the knave!
Your dowerland, the town, you may retain,
So says the King who governs France this day."
Aalais replied: "Would I were in my grave!
I'd rather cast my body to the flames
Than see a cur usurp my husband's place!
But I must live to see my young son raised
To be a knight and right the wrong again."
Red Guerri said: "Well spoken, brave Aalais!
I'll stand by you while blood flows in my veins!"

RED GUERRI SAID, as one to courage born:
"While I'm alive I'll not neglect your cause!
Where is your son, my nephew young Raoul?"
At this request two young men went and sought
The boy inside and then they brought him forth;
Just three years old he was, the song records;
He wore a cloth of Eastern silk and bore
A crimson cloak of buckram rich and warm;
In all the world there was no finer boy;
Red Guerri took him by the hand to walk,
And, as he did, he sighed with sad remorse:
"Fair lad," he said, "but still so young and small!
King Louis pays no heed to you at all;
Behind your back he barters what is yours!"
The child replied: "Good uncle, rest assured,
If I may live to bear my father's sword,
I'll win it back upon my steed in war!"
"Indeed, my boy, a thousand score shall fall
Before you'll lose one foot of Cambrai soil!"
Inside, they called for water to be brought,
And then they washed and sat down in the hall.

AALAIS THE FAIR and fearsome Red Guerri,
With all their knights, sat in the hall to eat;
The seneschals attended them with zeal,

Each one well trained in serving every need;
Fair-faced Aalais, when all the cloths were cleared,
Gave costly furs to every man of liege;
Red-haired Guerri then sought and took his leave
And hastened to Arras, his family seat;
And then, my friends, there passed a dozen years,
Wherein the town and shire remained at peace;
When Raoul of Cambrai had turned fifteen,
He was a youth as noble as could be –
So all his men and marquises agreed.

3. Raoul's companion Bernier

BELOVED AALAIS, so fair of face and figure,
Beheld her son grow up in strength and vigour
Till fifteen springs had followed fifteen winters;
Now in her fief a nobleman was living,
Called Lord Ybert, a man of fearsome spirit;
A bastard son he had, who as an infant
Was called Bernier the day that he was christened;
He was a boy of loving disposition
Whom fair Aalais had raised since he was little;
Between the boys a loyal bond existed
Through all the years that they had shared as children;
So when Raoul was sent to court that springtime
He took Bernier to stay in Paris with him;
He met this way the richest in the city,
And served them wine and claret at their dinners;
My worthy friends, it would have show more wisdom
If young Raoul had slain him to begin with:
For in the end it was Bernier who killed him!

4. Raoul's service

AALAIS BEHELD HER SON grown up at last
And knew that he was ready to bear arms –
I'll tell you now of how that came to pass;
She sent off men to Louis, King of France,
Reminding him, her brother, of the past:

Her son had served the term that he had asked,
Now he must knight and give Raoul his chance,
To right the wrong of Giboin of Le Mans.

AND SO IT WAS that Louis dubbed him knight;
He summoned all his marshals to his side
And said: "Bring arms and armour all of iron!"
To young Raoul he said: "My nephew fine,
You're big and strong I see, thank God on High."

THE KING INDEED cared greatly for the boy;
He gifted him a helm which was a Moor's
Whom Roland slew upon some Rhenish shore;
He placed it on a double-hauberk's coif,
Then said to him: "Good nephew, rest assured,
This ancient helm belonged once to a Moor:
No weapon made can shatter it at all;
May He Who at that wedding-feast of yore
Made water wine, inspire you evermore."
Young Raoul said: "I swear to you, my lord,
That I shall give no peace, here or abroad,
Both night and day, to foes of His and yours."
Upon that helm, my friends, the noseguard bore
A ruby rich by which the wearer saw
Through darkest night the way that lay before.

THE KING GIRT ON his sword both strong and heavy,
Its pommel gold and all the hilt together;
The smith Galant gave all his skill and pleasure
In gorges dark to forging it of metal;
Save Durendal, which was the best sword ever,
Young Raoul's blade was better made than any;
No armour made could counter it, nor weapon;
And such an arm for him was made to measure,
For he alike was strong and fierce of temper;
If only he had been less rash and reckless,
No vassal born to rule could have been better;
But this one fault would prove a fatal blemish –
Unbridled men must bide a heavy penance.

THEN LOUIS GAVE Raoul his rapid steed,
Its saddle gold, both at the front and rear,
And finely carved with nobly-postured beasts
And with all kinds of other scrolls replete;
The horse was draped in buckram rich and sleek,
The saddle with a silk cloth from the East,
Which fell in folds towards the ground beneath;
Raoul leapt up at once, his manner fierce;
He grasped the straps of his new, shining shield:
Its boss had gold above it and beneath;
No cutting thrust could pierce it in the least;
And then he seized his golden-glowing spear:
Five golden nails secured the banner's sweep;
He charged his horse as one well-born to lead,
Then reined it in so close to Louis' feet
That one glove's width was all that intervened!
The French all said: "How fine a youth indeed!
How well he'll fight for all his father's fief!"
How many grins would turn to groans of grief –
As you shall hear, if you will hold your peace!

SO YOUNG RAOUL was dubbed and armed a knight,
And for some years he stayed at Louis' side;
The Emperor, of heart and courage high,
Befriended him as his own kith and kind,
And made him seneschal of France in time,
As you have heard and we all know is right;
From Paris to Ponthieu no lords were shy
Of sending him their sons or their young squires,
Their nephews or their cousins first in line;
For Sir Raoul befriended all alike,
He welcomed, kept and clothed all who arrived,
And gave them all good Arab steeds to ride;
His enemies, however, filled with spite,
Like Sir Giboin, who had received the shire
Of all Cambrai – which was a fateful prize
With Raoul grown and hating him on sight;
Red-haired Guerri was soon to give advice
Which led the pair to start that bitter strife
Wherein both men and many more would die.

AT LOUIS' SIDE for several years he stayed,
Until the hour that I shall tell of came;
One Eastertime it was, when Christians pray
And celebrate upon successive days;
Raoul stepped forth from Saint-Denis' great nave,
Where he had gone to offer prayers and praise;
Upon that square of such renown and fame
The knights began to sport in fencing-games,
To show their skill and while the hours away;
But sporting turned to spite the more they waged,
Until two lads lay on the precinct slain;
Both youths were sons of Ernaut of Douai.

WHEN BOTH OF THEM lay on the precinct dead,
Ernaut of Douai's sons, the two of them,
The blame was laid on Raoul for their deaths,
For all the lords and Louis' barons said
That he began the bout wherein they fell;
Ernaut swore then a hatred without end
Until such time as he might take revenge;
How many days and years elapsed till then
I do not know, nor ever have I read;
But I know this: without the Lord God's help,
He'd rue the day he thought that they should fence!
How much it grieved brave Guerri, called 'The Red',
And rightly so, it seems to me, my friends,
For those two deaths made many enemies
And trials for him till he turned white of head!

HOW SAD IT WAS when both those lads were buried;
At Pentecost, when Christian men make merry,
The King held court with fitting royal splendour;
He hailed Raoul, whom he most dearly cherished,
And said to him: "I bid you, noble nephew,
To serve my feast with spiced wine from the cellars."
"Most gladly, lord," Raoul replied directly:
"You are my liege, your service is my pleasure."
The wine was brought to Bernier and together
They served the lords so generous a measure
That none of them could say they were neglected!
The following day, young Bernier was presented

Before Raoul, who with the King's own blessing,
First dubbed him knight then gave him noble weapons;
Upon his back he placed a coat most splendid,
Then on his head a gold-embellished helmet,
Then girt a sword which he himself presented;
Bernier at once leapt up astride his destrier.

AS SOON AS HE was mounted on his steed,
How fine a knight he looked and was indeed!
He seized the straps of his gold-banded shield
And grasped the grip of his well-sharpened spear;
Five golden nails secured its banner's sweep;
He charged the horse for everyone to see;
Upon the square were many knights and peers,
And they all said: "How fair a knight and fierce!
Although a son of unwed parents, he
Is of a brave, well-bred and mighty breed."
"Praised be the Lord for that!" Raoul agreed:
"Believe me, lords, I have no doubt or fear
Of dubbing him with arms of shining steel,
And honouring alliances he keeps."
But time would come when young Raoul would grieve
For this and more, as you will shortly hear;
"Sir Bernier," said Raoul, adept in speech,
"For love of me and so the King may see,
Ride out and strike a quintain in the field!"
Bernier replied: "I willingly agree!
So help me God, I will not fail to heed
This first request that you have made of me!"
So in the field two hauberks damascened
Were set on posts and strapped with buckler-shields;
Bernier called out, in ringing tones and clear:
"My lord Beraut, please listen to my plea!
May I ride forth in your good company?"
Beraut was rich, and a most noble liege;
He said at once: "With all my heart, indeed!"
And led him forth, his pleasure plain to see;
So great a blow he struck those quintain-beams
As never hence a bastard's son would deal!
His lance went through both buckler-shields and sheared
The hauberks' mail and ripped them seam to seam;

One stake was hit and split in many a piece
As Bernier's lance drove through from front to rear;
He turned his horse as all the Frenchmen cheered;
What wondrous praise he won from all and each,
And many a gaze from ladies who were near.

SIR BERNIER STRUCK the quintain more than firmly,
Then turned his steed before them all and spurred it;
How fine he looked, how nobly tall and sturdy!
Dismounting then, though with his spurs still girded,
He knelt before Raoul and said with fervour:
"My lord and friend, how far you have preferred me!
I swear henceforth to be your man and serve you;
No heir of mine shall ever bear the burden
Of my disgrace through treason or desertion;
But, in the name of God the Lord, I urge you
To live in peace with all the sons of Herbert."
Raoul heard this, the end of which disturbed him;
Towards his lodge he turned with all his servants
And many lords whose names I've never learned of;
In Louis' hall they strode, all dressed in ermine,
Where Guerri stood, whose hair to white was turning,
To gain at last the goal of Raoul's service:
How many men the King's response would murder!

5. Raoul's demand

RED GUERRI SPOKE, whose hair was turning white:
"In truth, my lord, I must speak forth my mind;
Raoul the youth has served you far and wide
And in reward gained nothing as a knight
From you the King nor any friend alike;
Give back to him at least the Cambrai shire,
The land that was his father Rending-Iron's!"
"I cannot give it back," the King replied,
"I gave it to Giboin – though, truly, I
Regret indeed the pledge I swore and signed;
It grieves my heart and has done countless times;
But it was made on all my lords' advice."
Red Guerri said: "And we must pay the price!
By St Géri, I swear this is not right!"

With every haste he left the King to stride
Down from the hall with anger in his eyes;
Raoul himself was playing chess meanwhile,
Like any man with no ill on his mind,
When suddenly his arm was wrenched awry
By Red Guerri, who ripped his robe and cried:
"You harlot's son!" – which was an awful lie –
"You feckless rogue, is playing games your life?
The land you own is now about the size
You need to rub and scrub a sumpter's hide!"
Raoul jumped up, at this, with such a cry
It shook the hall and all the walls inside,
And every lord could hear him as he cried:
"Which reckless rogue robs me of what is mine?"
Red Guerri said: "It is, without a lie,
The King himself, who should defend our rights!
In Louis' court your honour is reviled!"
On hearing this, young Raoul's blood was fired;
This fierce exchange was overheard meanwhile
By two knights raised by Raoul Rending-Iron,
And Bernier too, attending them with wine;
All three of them rushed forward in surprise,
Then off they went to see the King, all five;
Not one of them knelt down when they arrived,
And Raoul spoke with Guerri by his side.

SIR RAOUL SPOKE with anger in his breast:
"True Emperor, by St Amant the blest,
You know that I have served you long and well,
But you have made me no reward as yet:
Now render me the land I have been pledged,
Which Rending-Iron, my noble father, held."
"I cannot grant you that," said Louis then,
"I gave it to Giboin for service met;
Milan's great wealth won't buy it back again."
On hearing this, Red Guerri cried and said:
"Then I shall arm and ride against his men;
I'll hound this thieving Giboin to his death!"
He called Raoul a weak and faithless wretch:
"By all the Saints whom sinners seek, I pledge,
If you don't seize the land your father left

Before the sun tomorrow night has set,
This hand of mine will no more bring you help!"
How many lords would meet their bloody deaths
Because of what Raoul would utter next:
"True Emperor, you know, above all else,
That it is right for any dead man's wealth
To pass at once to his first son and heir;
By St Amant, I should lose all respect
Among the world, if from this moment hence
I let my shame grow greater, as I let
Another man take my inheritance!
By Him Who made the Heavens overhead,
If I set eyes on Giboin now, I pledge
That my own sword will speed him to his end!"
On hearing this, the King hung down his head.

6. King Louis' compromise

SIR GIBOIN OF Le Mans sat in the hall;
The threats he heard put fear into his thoughts,
And in his cloak he broached the Emperor:
"I am most badly done by here, my lord;
You gave Cambrai to me with pledges sworn,
But now it seems your promises fall short;
A haughty count has stridden in your court,
Who is Raoul, a richly-clad young lord,
And, as we know, a nephew too of yours,
And also of the fierce Guerri Le Sor;
In all this land I have no friend or force
Who could stand up against them in my cause;
I've served you well with my Viana sword
And never gained one denier in reward;
Now I must leave on my Norwegian horse
With less to show than when I came before;
How all the lords of Germany will talk,
And all the counts of France from south to north:
I've served you well and shall return with naught!"
On hearing this, the King was moved, and called
Upon Raoul, his golden glove held forth:
"Fine youth," he said, "by God Who gave us laws,

Leave him your land for two or three years more,
Upon such terms as I shall now endorse:
If in that time, from here to Vermandois,
From royal Aix to Senlis, or from Laon
To Orléans, there dies a landed lord,
Then you shall have his titles, fiefs and forts;
You will not lose by this in land or coin."
On hearing this, Raoul delayed no more;
With Red Guerri's support he hurried forth
To seize the glove – and start his fateful course.

RAOUL AT ONCE addressed Guerri the Red:
"Good uncle, lord, I know you are my friend;
I will not fail your trust in me again."
Because of this, his father's fief was swept
Up in a war which slaughtered countless men!
He asked the King to grant him hostages,
And, ill-advised, the King selected them
From all at court who were adjudged the best;
Two score there were who swore the fateful pledge;
Friends, how they grew to rue what they had said!
The King picked out Lohier and Anseis,
And Jociaunes, and Gerard and Gerin,
Herbert of Maine, Geoffrey Anjou, and then
Henri of Troyes and young Gerard, who held
The town Senlis towards Beauvais itself;
He named Gaudin and Galeran as well,
And Count Berart of Quercy, says the *geste*;
Raoul himself lacked nothing in intent:
Inside the hall he had rich relics sent
Of Saints he loved – Firmin of Amiens,
St Peter and St Augustine the blest;
King Louis called no priest but pledged again
To give Raoul the riches and the rents
Of any fief whose Count first met his death.

THE KING GAVE HIM Olivier and Ponçon,
And then Garnier and then the brave Othon,
Then Amauri and noble Lord Droon,
Old Riquier and Almeria's Foucon,
And Bérenger and his uncle Samson;

He named these men to bind his word and bond;
In Louis' hall they swore to him and God
That they would stand as solemn witness of
The pledge he made to give Raoul the rod
Of any fief whose lord died first, from Laon
To royal Aix, Soissons to Orléans;
Raoul had cause, I don't say he did not,
But Louis' pledge was madly made and wrong,
To forfeit land that he knew nothing of;
How many men would pay for that ere long!
Raoul was wise to ask for such a throng
To witness what the King had started off.

SOME FORTY HOSTAGES the King made over
To Guerri's charge, who took them and who told them
That they must swear to bear their witness boldly;
Hugh of Hantonne was one, Gerin of Auxois,
Richart of Reims and Simon of Péronne,
Droon of Meaux, Savaris of Verona,
Estout of Langres and Duke Eudon of Bourbon,
Who ruled all Burgundy upon his throne there,
The noblest knight as far as Barcelona;
The King himself swore on his crown as token
That young Raoul would not lose what he owed him.

THE EMPEROR, so powerful and dread,
Before them all called forty witnesses
To hear the pledge made at Raoul's behest:
That any fief whose lord first met his death,
From Vermandois to Île-de-France itself,
Should be Raoul's, whoever this might vex –
Raoul should want for nothing from this pledge;
But later on he broke his word, my friends:
His rashness led to countless liegemen dead,
And forty lives left hanging by a thread!

7. King Louis' dilemma

WITH HOSTAGES enough for satisfaction,
The matter stayed a long time as it had been –

One year and fifteen days, the record has it;
Raoul rode back to Cambrai and fair Aalais,
And in the time that I have said elapsed then,
Count Herbert died, a rich and mighty baron,
Well-bred and wise, with many close companions;
All Vermandois was his, and fiefs attaching:
Roie and Péronne, Origny with its abbey,
And Ribemont, Saint-Quentin too, and Clary –
How lucky he who has so many allies!
On hearing this, Raoul was filled with gladness;
Without delay he mounted his fine stallion
And summoned all those hostages to back him;
Among them rode red-haired Guerri of Arras;
Some seven score in all were dressed in mantles
And rode away until they came to Paris;
They went to claim the gift their King had sanctioned:
How many men would die from its retraction!
Raoul had cause, I've learned, in all this matter;
The King it was who wronged a noble vassal:
How many men are ruined by a bad one!
So Raoul's band arrived outside the palace;
Beneath the olive-trees they left their saddles
And strode inside to have their pledge enacted;
Upon his throne they found King Louis sat there;
The King looked up and saw his forty barons
Behind Raoul, whose face was blithe and handsome:
The youth spoke up: "May God, Who bore the Passion,
Both bless and keep King Louis, our strong Champion!"
The King himself felt neither strong nor happy:
"God guard you too, Who dwells on High," he answered.

YOUNG RAOUL SAID, as one well-bred and brave:
"I will not hide what I have come to say:
Reward me now, your nephew, in good faith;
A count has died, Count Herbert is his name;
All Vermandois he held beneath his sway;
Grant me at once his titles and estates;
Before us all you pledged me this exchange,
With hostages to guarantee the same."
But Louis said: "Nephew, I must refrain!
The noble count you speak of bred and raised

Four noble sons, who all are highly praised;
You could not find four finer knights than they;
If I should take their lands for you to claim,
Each lord of mine would censure me with blame
And never come when summoned to my aid,
Nor ever serve or honour me again;
And what is more, young Raoul, in this case
I have no wish to take their land away
And injure four for only one man's sake."
On hearing this, Raoul first stood amazed;
But then he felt the scorn those words contained
And, turning round, he stormed away enraged;
He did not halt till in the hall of state
He saw some lords who'd pledged their word that day,
And charged them all because their oaths had failed.

RAOUL THE COUNT was bitter and aggrieved;
He summoned forth Droon and Geoffrey, he
Who ruled Anjou, but shuddered through with fear!
He summoned too Gerart, Herbert, Henri,
Samson of Troyes and Bernart white of beard:
"Step forward, lords, I beg you all and each!
Since you were sworn as hostages to me,
I'll welcome you tomorrow, as agreed,
Inside my tower, by blessed St Géri!
You'll have your share in all I have of grief!"
On hearing this, the blood left Geoffrey's cheeks:
"My friend," he said, "what does such menace mean?"
Raoul replied: "I'll tell you, noble peer:
Count Herbert's died, the lord of Origny,
Of Saint-Quentin, of Péronne and Clary,
Of Ham and Roie, of Nesle and Flavy;
But do you think that I have gained his fiefs?
The Emperor has failed his pledge and me."
The hostages each answered with this plea:
"Grant us a truce, so we may go and speak
With Louis now, and learn the way and means
That he intends to save us in our need."
Young Raoul replied: "I grant you this reprieve."
And so they left, and Bernier left with these,
To find the King with every haste indeed;

Count Geoffrey was the first one there to plead:
"True Emperor, our pledges have been breached!
Why did you make us hostage to this fiend,
The fiercest heart that ever coat concealed?
Count Herbert's died, whose valour had no peer,
And now Raoul demands his mighty fief!"

COUNT GEOFFREY SPOKE and pleaded with his lord:
"True Emperor, our pledges are forsworn!
You were too rash to pledge Raoul at all
Another's land, however great or small;
Now Herbert's died, who ruled all Vermandois,
He has the right to it – the wrong is yours!
Give him the fief which we stood hostage for!"
"God," said the King, "I shall be more than galled
If just for one I lose the love of four!
By God, Who made Edessa's statue talk,
This gift of mine shall cause more pain than joy!
Unless some pact by marriage can be wrought,
How many men will pay for it henceforth!"

KING LOUIS SPOKE with troubled heart and heavy:
"Come forward then, Raoul, my noble nephew!
Possess the fief, but with this one concession:
My knights and I will never save or help you."
Raoul replied: "I ask for nothing better."
On hearing this, Bernier stood up directly
And cried aloud before the whole assembly:
"Count Herbert's sons are knights of noble temper,
All rich in wealth and richer still in friendships;
Their land is safe from you to its last penny!"
On hearing this, across the hall the Frenchmen
Said each to each, the greater and the lesser:
"Raoul is young but shows a grown man's mettle
In this exchange for Rending-Iron's possessions!
The King's resolve will start a war so dreadful
That many wives will rue the lives it ended!"

SIR BERNIER SPOKE, the brave and noble-minded;
He cried aloud to be well heard and sighted:
"True Emperor, I beg you, by St Simon,

To think again if you have acted wisely;
Count Herbert's sons have done no wrong to spite you;
Within your court they should be treated rightly;
Why do you give their land away so lightly?
May God Himself condemn them, if they idly
Allow Raoul to take it without fighting."
"I quite agree," said Louis in replying:
"He's gained a gift of his, not my, desiring;
He shall not have my flag to fly beside him."

8. Raoul's intransigence

SIR BERNIER SPOKE, to Count Raoul this time:
"I am your man; this I shall never hide;
But for my part I urge you not to try
And seize their land; I know, without a lie,
That Ernaut of Douai has fifty knights
Who have no peer in any land or shire;
Accept a pact, but do not start a fight;
I'll stand by you, if they denounce your right;
For love of you I'll seek some compromise."
"I won't consider that," Raoul replied:
"The gift is made; I'll not give back what's mine!"
Bernier replied: "I'll say no more till I
Have seen how fierce an answer they supply."

WHEN RAOUL SAW the matter go so well
That in the court his plea had been upheld –
With Louis loath to break his given pledge –
As young Bernier tore at his hair, perplexed,
He stood his ground, then turned around and went;
As trumpets trilled he mounted horse and left
The King behind with nothing further said.

WITH EVERY HASTE he rode his horse away
And spurred it hard until he reached Cambrai;
Dismounting both before their lodging-place,
Young Bernier had a sad and downcast gaze,
For he had crossed the lord he should obey;
He sought to sleep before he drank or came

Within the hall or castle-keep again;
He had no wish to clash with fair Aalais;
As Raoul stepped on Cambrai's stones again
His mother came, Aalais, the fair of face,
And kissed his mouth and chin in her embrace.

AALAIS, SO FAIR of visage and of form,
Embraced her son and welcomed him once more;
He kissed her cheek, then hand in hand they walked
The steps and stairs to their ancestral hall;
Once there, she said a word well heard by all:
"Fine son of mine, I see you strong and tall,
A seneschal of France, praise God the Lord!
I am amazed at Louis in his court –
For you have served him long and well, I'm sure,
And yet the King has made you no reward;
It's time indeed he did so and restored
Each foot of land your father held before,
Brave Rending-Iron, the husband I adored;
The Mansel knight hangs on to what is yours;
I am amazed that for so long you've borne
With this disgrace and have not slain its cause!"
On hearing this, Raoul was filled with gall:
"For grace, by God Who never fails!" he roared:
"I have reward, and it is far from poor:
Count Herbert's died, of this you may be sure,
And I have gained his titles, lands and forts."
Aalais, she sighed and then replied: "My boy!
For many years I raised you here in joy,
But rest assured, the lord who gave Péronne,
Saint-Quentin, Nesle, Flavy, Ham and Roie,
And Origny and Clary's well-stocked walls,
Invested you with early death, I'm sure!
Forget this gift, for love of God the Lord!
The Rending-Iron, who sired you of his loins,
And he who's died, were bosom friends of yore,
And side by side fought countless mighty wars;
They never fought between themselves at all;
By all the Saints of Ponthieu's shire and shore,
Nor shall their sons, if you will heed my voice."
But Raoul said: "I will not let this fall,

For all the world would say I was at fault,
And all my heirs would bear the shame henceforth."

"MY NOBLE SON," Aalais the fair said then,
"I nourished you with milk from my own breast:
Why do you strike my heart with such distress?
The lord who gave Péronne and Péronnelle,
The towns of Ham and Roie, Flavy and Nesle,
Invested you, I'm sure, with early death!
Whoever sought to fight a war with them
Would need rich steeds, rich armour and rich men!
I'd rather be a slave or nun myself
And see you poor, than not see you again!
This land will burn, if you spurn what I've said!"
With jutting jaw Raoul swore nonetheless
By God born of the Maid in Bethlehem,
That he would not forgo King Louis' pledge,
No matter now how many barons bled,
How many brains were dashed or bodies rent.

AALAIS THE FAIR, of tender face and meek,
Stood in her fur, a minevered pelisse;
She told her son, although she disagreed:
"My noble son, if you won't let this be,
Call forth the lords of Arrouaise at least."
"Most willingly, but if they're loath to leave,
Then by the faith I owe St Hilary,
If I return alive from Herbert's fields,
I'll wrench their eyes and limbs out while they breathe,
Then hang them high upon the gallows-tree!
Those still alive will have good cause to scream."
"God!" said Aalais, "This doesn't comfort me!
When you depart, red-haired Guerri must lead!"

"MY WORTHY SON," said noble-visaged Aalais,
"Do not begin so long and wrong a battle!
Count Herbert's sons are worthy knights and vassals,
All rich in wealth and richer still in allies;
Do not destroy God's churches and His chapels!
For Jesu's sake, do not harass the hapless;
My worthy son, tell me the honest tally

Of men you have to plunder all you plan to."
"Five hundred score and more will soon be rallied;
Red Guerri's hand will bear aloft our banner;
The lords of Arrouaise won't dare be absent,
However much they may dislike the matter."
"God!" said Aalais, "This augurs very badly."

"GOD," SAID AALAIS, "by Your most holy name,
I'd never say Red Guerri isn't brave
And wise and true with every breathe he takes;
In his strong hand your battle-flag is safe,
And will subdue the land along your way;
But I doubt much the men from Arrouaise:
If you take ox or sheep to eat, then they
Will roar as fierce as lions after prey;
But take the field and they will moan and wail,
And when it comes to striking blows, turn tail
And leave you there in terror of your fate;
Count Herbert's sons will neither flinch nor quail:
When they see you alone, bereft of aid,
They'll cut your head clean off with their sharp blades,
And I, fine son, by all St Simon's faith,
Will die of grief which nothing will assuage."
Raoul replied: "You speak to no avail,
For by the Lord Who suffered for our sake,
I do but go to claim what Louis gave;
An empire's gold won't stop me now, Aalais."

"RAOUL, FINE SON, I say of what I'm sure:
The men of Arrouaise are craven boors;
If you win goods of any worth or store,
Then they will follow you on foot and horse;
But do not arm a single one for war:
They would not wield whatever arm they bore,
But run away, whatever loss it caused;
You would not have an army worth a straw;
Count Herbert's men are not like that at all;
They'll cut you down, that is the long and short,
And what is more, with their sharp-bladed swords
They'll cut the heart out of your bloody corpse."

"RAOUL, FINE SON, by God our Judge on High,
You should not start a war that isn't right;
What will become of Sir Bernier, your squire?
You raised him here, then dubbed him as a knight."
"God's truth, Aalais, I saw his other side;
Before the King he challenged what was mine;
When I made plain that he would pay the price
If he spoke out against me one more time,
He told me then that he would let things lie
Till it was time to let the lance decide,
But, if need be, he'd take his uncles' side."
On hearing this, Aalais was filled with spite;
In ringing tones she wailed aloud and cried:
"I knew it well! And now I will not hide:
This man's the one who will destroy your life
And slaughter you, if chance and means arise;
Raoul, fine son, I urge you to be wise,
To make your peace with those of Herbert's line
And sign a pact which compensates your pride;
Respect their land and they will yours alike,
And help you then to fight your proper fight –
To drive the Mansel knight from Cambrai shire!"
On hearing this, he almost lost his mind;
He swore to God, the Judge of all mankind,
That he would not for all the world comply:
"A curse on any noble," he replied,
"Who when his honour calls him forth to fight,
Runs first to ask a woman for advice!
Attend your rooms and spend your ease, such knights!
Go drink your draughts until you bloat your sides,
Then eat your fill and drain your cellars dry;
You are not fit for any other life!"
On hearing this, Aalais began to cry:
"Fine son," she wept, "you've turned my world awry!
I've served you long and well in times gone by;
When all the French were set to sell your rights
And marry me, when your dear father died,
To Sir Giboin, who soldiered for a price,
I shunned at once to wed and bed the swine;
I brought you up the darling of my life,
Till you could mount upon your steed and ride,

And then bear arms and fight for what was right;
I sent you then to court escorted by
Four hundred lords, you know this is no lie,
All noble men with happy hearts and light,
With double-hauberks on and helmets bright;
The Emperor was glad when you arrived;
He had no wish to see our house decline,
But dubbed you knight and helped your fortunes thrive
Till you became a seneschal in time;
Your enemies grew angry at your rise,
While all your friends were happier to find
That in their need your aid would turn the tide;
But now you wish to claim the towns and tithes
Of lands which never were your kith and kind's;
And if my tears won't make you change your mind,
Then may the Lord, Whose Judgement Day is nigh,
Not keep you safe but curse your enterprise!"
This curse of hers worked all too well in time;
As you will hear, he lost his limbs and life.

FAIR AALAIS' HEART was filled with dark dismay;
She cursed her son and left the hall of state;
She went inside St Géri's church to pray;
With arms outstretched before the cross she lay
And called to God, Who never lies or fails:
"Lord Jesus Christ, Who bore the Cross's pain,
And took the blow from Longinus's blade,
Who on Good Friday shed Your blood to save
Our sinners' souls, as this is true, I pray:
Bring back my son alive, unharmed and hale;
How wrong I was to curse him and his fate;
Ah, woe is me! His life has been my grace!
If he should die, then I am sore afraid
I'd end my life with some sharp dagger's blade."
On saying this, she left the holy nave
And, looking up, saw Red Guerri the brave;
She hastened forth and seized his horse's reins:
"My lord, what brings you riding here today?
What plot or plan has brought you to Cambrai?"
Said Red Guerri: "I will not lie, Aalais;
It is your son, his proud and stubborn ways;

No man alive who criticised or blamed
A word of his, would be his friend again!"

RED GUERRI'S WORDS in no way reassured her;
He sought Raoul and called out when he saw him:
"Fine nephew mine, what will you do henceforward?
Will you give up this war on Herbert's borders?"
The youth replied: "What madness are you talking?
I'd rather lose my arms and legs than forfeit."
Throughout Artois he summoned all his forces
And called on all the Arrouaise to join him,
And so they did, not daring to ignore him;
Ten thousand strong they came there to support him;
You should have seen them crowd the gates and portals,
Their backs aglow with gold and silver hauberks!
Aalais looked on, bereft of senses almost:
"My mind is numbed with grief," she groaned forlornly:
"Count Herbert's sons will summon all their forces,
A mighty host, and, if it comes to warfare,
It cannot end without a heavy slaughter."

THE FAIR AALAIS stood in the city centre;
She saw a stream of Spanish stallions enter
The city-gate called Galeran Tudela,
So many knights on saddles so resplendent!
She'd prayed inside the chapel of St Géri,
And, coming out, she sought her son's attention:
"For Mary's sake, fine son, what folly tells you
That you will gain from such a gang of peasants?
These men from Arrouaise aren't worth a berry!
They're very strong when filling up their bellies,
But I have heard that when a battle beckons
They're all as soft as cheese in summer weather!"
On hearing this, his heart heaved with displeasure;
From breast to throat it leapt, his anger swelling;
With jutting jaw held in his hand he bellowed:
"My mother dear, you sing a dreary descant!
I swear upon our Lady of Nivele,
I'd rather be a servant's serf forever
Than not attack Péronne and Péronnelle,
The towns of Ham and Roie, Flavy and Nesle;

The King himself, the lord of all the Frenchmen,
Within his hall gave all to me with pledges;
Ten thousand men will lie across the meadows
With broken brows and frozen brains and entrails,
Before I'll cede one inch of those possessions."
"God!" said Aalais, "Your heart's as hot as hell-fire;
You'll burn to death with courage so untempered!"

"MY NOBLE SON, don't treat me so with scorn;
Though I am old and all my hair is hoar,
I've yet to lose my sense as you have yours!
Pay heed to me – do not proceed with war!"
On hearing this, he sweated like a boar
And called Guerri, his fierce-eyed uncle, forth:
"Without delay assemble all our force!
Let such a war be waged on Herbert's soil
That churches there are burned in countless scores!
Ignore Aalais – her wits are weak and worn;
She blames the men who've come to my support,
Yet they have stood in countless fights before
And never been defeated or outfought!"

9. Raoul's departure

RAOUL SET OFF and rode with all his knights;
He left Cambrai and fair Aalais alike;
Through Arrouaise he rode, which was his shire,
With Red Guerri his uncle by his side,
On noble steeds and both well armed with iron;
To Vermandois they rode and, once arrived,
They seized the herds, which ruined countless lives,
And burnt the crops and set the farms alight;
How sick at heart was Bernier at the sight:
To see the lands of all his kith and kind
Go up in flames, his anger drove him wild;
Each time they struck, Bernier remained behind
And showed no haste in his desire to fight.

RAOUL CALLED FORTH Manecier and summoned
Droon the count and Sir Gautier his brother:

"Without delay select four hundred others;
Take up your arms and on good horses hurry
To Origny before tomorrow's sunset;
Erect my tent inside the church for cover
And let its porch and cloisters house my sumpters!
Within the crypt prepare my food for supper
And let my hawks perch on the crosses hung there!
Make ready at the altar for my coming
A splendid bed where I may sleep in comfort:
I'll rest my back against the cross's upright
While all my squires make merry with the nuns there!
It is my wish to raze the place to rubble,
Because I known the sons of Herbert love it."
His men replied: "We cannot fail your summons."
So, hastily, they gathered as instructed,
Then mounted horse, well armed for any trouble
With swords of steel for every man among them,
A shield and lance and hauberk woven double;
For Origny they rode across the country;
As they approached the bells rang from the turrets
And they recalled our Lord, the God of Justice:
Their wildest then had cause to pause abruptly
And showed no wish to desecrate or plunder;
They pitched their tents with leafy trees above them
And took their rest until the morning's sunrise;
They made their camp as carefully constructed
As if they planned to spend a whole twelve months there.

BELOW THE TOWN a lovely woodland thrived,
And there it was they pitched the tents that night
And took their rest until the dawn arrived;
Raoul rode up about the hour of prime
And cursed them all in anger as he cried:
"You sons of whores, you low, deceitful swine!
How base of you! Why did you dare decide
To disobey a strict command of mine?"
"Have mercy, lord, for love of Jesus Christ!
We are not Jews or bandits," they replied,
"To desecrate or plunder holy shrines!"

THE COUNT BEGAN to grow more rash and reckless:
"You sons of whores," he called the men he'd sent there,
"I bade you pitch my tent inside their dwelling:
Within the church I told you to erect it!
Who gave the word that you should pitch it elsewhere?"
Said Red Guerri: "Raoul, you grow too headstrong!
It isn't long since you were dubbed with blessings,
But you won't last if God should turn against you!
This place is loved by all God-fearing menfolk –
Its holy shrine should not be disrespected;
The meadow here is very green and pleasant,
And see how clear the river is and gentle!
Erect your tent and post your vanguard's sentries
To thwart attacks on us from all directions."
Raoul replied: "Fine uncle, at your pleasure;
I'll leave it thus, as you advise discretion."
They took the rugs and spread them on the meadow,
Where Raoul lay and leaned upon his elbows;
He summoned forth ten knights and all together
They hatched the plan which had so bad an ending.

10. Marsent's appeal

RAOUL CRIED OUT: "To arms, my noble knights!
Let Origny bear witness to our might!
I'll never love the man who lags behind!"
His men obeyed, not daring but comply –
Three thousand strong they were, the record writes;
They seized their arms and mounted horse to ride;
They struck the town and cast their spears inside;
The city-folk strove hard to save their lives,
While Raoul's men came closer all the time;
They felled the trees which lined the city's sides,
As all the nuns were coming from their shrine,
Their psalters clasped, and singing as they filed,
Each one of them of noble birth and high;
Marsent was one, and Bernier was her child:
"Mercy, Raoul," she cried, " for love of Christ!
You will be blamed and shamed if we should die;
Have you come here to kill weak womankind?"

MY WORTHY FRIENDS, Marsent was Bernier's mother;
She held a book as ancient as King Solomon,
And said a prayer to God the Lord of Justice,
Then clasped Raoul, his glowing hauberk clutching,
And cried aloud: "My lord, by God above us,
Where is Bernier the brave and noble-blooded?
I have not seen my son for many a summer."
Raoul replied: "In God's name, he's among us;
In our main tent he sports with friends and others;
From here to Rome no vassal has his courage,
And it is he who prompted me to come here
And challenge Herbert's sons – for he cares nothing
If they are left with no more than a button!"
Marsent replied: "Then he is false and cunning,
For it's well known that they are all his uncles;
If they are robbed, then woe betide the culprits!"

"RAOUL, MY LORD, will plea of mine persuade
You to withdraw and take these men away?
For we are nuns, by all Bavaria's Saints,
No hand of ours shall ever wield or wave
A lance or flag to send you to your grave."
He said: "In truth, you are a cunning jade!
I'll make no pledge to whoring chambermaids,
To those who've been a prostitute by trade,
A slut and slag for any man to take!
I saw you sell yourself to Count Ybert –
Your body's price was cheap enough to pay –
By good St Peter, any rogue or rake
Could have you for a pittance, night or day!"
"God!" said Marsent, "How could you speak this way?
How could you throw such insults in my face?
I never was a whore or as you say;
I was indeed the mistress of a brave
And noble lord, whose son I'm proud to claim;
I bear no shame, thanks be to Jesu's grace,
Which flows on those who serve His holy name."

"RAOUL, MY LORD," Marsent went on to speak,
"You can destroy and slaughter us with ease,
For we're too weak to handle arms of steel;

No hand of ours shall ever wave or wield
In our defence a lance-head or a shield;
Our livelihood and all we have to eat
Is in this shrine which we attend and keep;
The stores we have are gifts from Origny;
High lords and knights hold our good convent dear
And send us gold and silver for its needs;
Reprieve our hearth and leave our church in peace!
Go take your ease in our most pleasant fields;
If you agree, my lord, you shall receive
Enough good food for all your men of liege,
And all your squires shall have enough to feed
Good hay and oats to all your horses here."
"By St Riquier," he said, "since you so plead
Your plight, it shall not fall upon deaf ears!
I pledge a truce, whoever this may grieve."
Marsent replied: "I thank you heartily."
As Raoul left on his fleet-footed steed,
Bernier arrived, whose honour had no peer;
He'd come to see his mother proud and dear;
He had great need to speak with her indeed.

RAOUL RODE OFF in haste towards his tent;
Bernier arrived, who was most richly dressed,
And left his steed to greet his mother there;
She kissed her son, her arms around his neck,
Embracing him three times, her joy unchecked:
"Fine son, I see you are a knight," she said:
"God bless the Count who honoured me so well!"
"And bless you more for earning his respect!
But there's one thing I need you to confess:
Why have you come to fight your father's men?
They'll all be yours upon your father's death,
If you show sense and they see your prowess."
"I swear by good St Thomas," Bernier said,
"I'm loath to fight, for all of Baghdad's wealth;
But Raoul's worse than Judas was himself;
He is my lord, by whom I'm clothed and fed;
He gives me steeds and silks of Eastern thread;
For fiefs of gold I cannot fail my pledge
Till all can say 'Bernier, you've done your best'."

"Son," said Marsent, "you cannot well do less;
Obey your lord and God will guide the rest."

11. Origny's destruction

THE SPACIOUS TOWN of Origny was loved
By Herbert's sons and all around it was
A palisade which they had helped construct –
Though for defence it wasn't worth a glove;
Below the town there was a field in front,
Where tournaments were held and jousting done;
The ford it had was given to the nuns
And there they grazed their oxen safe enough,
For no man dared provoke Count Herbert's sons;
Raoul chose there for his pavilion;
Its poles shone gold and silver in the sun,
And it could hold four hundred men when up;
But three of them, the very worst of them,
They spurned its shade, spurred on by plunder-lust!
Too near was Origny, its wealth too much,
Though its allure would prove a fatal one;
All three were caught by ten fierce citizens
Who slaughtered two with crowbars and with clubs;
The third one fled to save his skin and skull;
Straight back to camp, not stopping once, he flung,
And from his steed upon the mead he swung
And kissed the shoe of Count Raoul at once;
With weeping face and terror on his tongue
He cried aloud for vengeance, saying thus:
"God curse you in your battles yet to come,
If you don't first avenge the evil done
By these too rich and haughty citizens!
Their scorn for you and any man is such
That if they catch you too they've sworn to cut
Your head clean off – my lord, I heard as much!
Montpellier's gold won't ransom you enough;
I saw my brother and then my nephew slump
Beneath their blows, then cruelly slain and dumped;
By St Riquier, had I not turned and run,
Those villains would have slain all three of us."

On hearing this, Raoul's whole visage flushed;
He cried aloud: "My worthy knights, rise up!
It is my will that Origny be crushed!
Since I am spurred to war, by God above,
I'll make quite sure they pay for it in blood!"
On hearing this, his liegemen ran and rushed
To arm themselves – what else could they have done?
As I have heard, ten thousand was their sum;
Towards the town they spurred their mounts and plunged
Straight through the moats to make a swifter thrust;
They swung the steel held in their hands and struck
That palisade and smashed it all to stumps;
They crossed the moat beside the pond and lunged
Towards the walls with fierce intent and rough;
The citizens themselves were stunned and stung:
Their palisade had saved or helped them none.

THE PEOPLE SAW their shattered palisade
And their most brave began to feel afraid;
They all withdrew to ramparts stoutly raised
And threw down stones and mighty, pointed staves –
And many men were slaughtered then or maimed;
Within the town no able man remained
But climbed the walls to keep their city safe;
They swore to God, and in His power's faith,
That if Raoul was caught, they'd make him pay!
How well they strove, the young ones and the aged;
Raoul looked on and swore with deepest rage
That if he did not kill them all, his name
Would not be worth henceforth a wisp of hay;
He cried aloud: "Men, set the town ablaze!"
And, hearing this, they willingly obeyed,
For they had come to war in hope of gain;
How badly kept the pledge Raoul had made
To good Marsent, the abbess of that place;
How wickedly he greeted them that day!
He burned the town till not a thing remained;
How sick at heart, my friends, was young Bernier,
To see the town of Origny in flames.

RAOUL WAS FILLED with anger at the stand
That Origny had made to his attack;
He swore to God that he would not hold back
For all the wealth held in the See of Rheims,
From razing it before the day elapsed;
He called for fire and squires tossed burning brands;
The houses burned, the floorboards all collapsed;
The barrels burned, their hoops split through and snapped;
The children burned, the young girls and the lads,
In agony and evil out of hand;
The day before Raoul had promised that
They wouldn't lose the meanest cloth or rag;
And now they burned as Raoul turned quite mad;
They fled to church, but no respite they had;
If only they had forced him from their land!

12. Marsent's death

IN ORIGNY, that spacious town and great –
Count Herbert's sons had loved it so they placed
Marsent therein, the mother of Bernier,
With some one hundred nuns to serve the Faith –
Raoul, Count of Cambrai, in reckless rage,
Had set alight each building, street and lane:
The houses burned, the floorboards all gave way;
The wines were spilled, the cellars filled like drains;
The bacon burned, the larders sagged and gave;
The bacon fat fuelled even greater flames
Which reached the convent tower, so proudly raised,
And soon the roof crashed down upon the nave;
Between the walls there raged so fierce a blaze
That all the nuns had no hope of escape;
They burned to death in torment unallayed;
Marsent, she burned, the mother of Bernier;
Clamados burned, the daughter of Renier;
Their burning flesh was smelt upon the air
And every knight shed tears for pity's sake;
When young Bernier beheld their awful fate,
His grief was such he almost went insane;
If you had seen how with his shield upraised

And sword unsheathed, he ran towards the blaze!
The flames escaped from every door and space;
No man could reach within a javelin's range
Of anyone, so fearsomely they raged;
Bernier broke in, along a marbled way,
And saw the corpse of Marsent where she lay;
The tongues of flame licked all around her face;
Upon her breast her psalter was in flames,
And it was then he said: "I am too late!
No human hand will help Marsent again;
Ah, mother mild, you kissed me yesterday!
Yet as a son I was of no avail –
I could not help or save you from your fate;
God rest your soul, Whose Judgement never fails!
And may you burn in Hell, Count of Cambrai!
No longer shall I serve you or your name;
I shall not think my honour worth a grain
If I do not avenge this wicked shame!"
He grieved so hard that, letting fall his blade,
He swooned three times upon his destrier;
He turned away to seek Red Guerri's aid
And wise advice; but nothing could be changed.

BERNIER WAS FILLED with bitter spite and grief;
To seek advice he turned to Red Guerri:
"What should I do, by God our loyal Liege?
My lord Raoul has served me wickedly;
He's burnt to death the mother I held dear,
Noble Marsent, abbess of Origny;
The very breasts with which she suckled me,
I saw them burn, by blessed St Géri."
Said Red Guerri: "This saddens me indeed;
For love of you I too am much aggrieved."

13. Raoul's contempt

THE KNIGHTS AND MEN returned to all their tents;
Bernier spurred off with anger in his breast,
Dismounting then his stallion swift of step;
His vassals came to take his boots and wept

With all his friends on seeing his distress;
In noble tones he said to all of them:
"Good men of mine, hear my complaint and pledge:
My lord Raoul has served me with contempt,
For he has burned my mother here to death!
I pray to live until I've had revenge!"
The Count returned, his rampage at an end;
When all was done one hundred nuns lay dead;
He leapt beside his tawny steed and then
His vassals came with those who loved him best;
They took his helm, of green and gold all blent,
Ungirt his sword of sharp and shining edge,
And then his coat of double-mail well-meshed;
His quartered tunic underneath was rent;
No fairer knight there was in France, my friends,
Nor one as fierce or proud in his prowess.

UPON THE GRASS at his pavilion's entrance
He leapt to ground beside his rapid destrier;
His vassals came and took away his weapons;
His tunic's vest had ermine round the edges,
And when disarmed he looked more fair than any;
He bade at once his seneschal attend him,
Whose service was, to both of them, a pleasure;
The fellow came as soon as he was sent for:
"Prepare some food and do not stint the measure:
Roast peacock and some swan with lots of pepper,
And then we'll have good venison a-plenty;
The worst of men shall come and fill his belly;
I will not be the laughing-stock, I tell you,
Of any lord for any city's treasure."
On hearing this, the other stared in terror,
Then crossed himself three times at this transgression:
"What are you thinking, lord, by all that's blessed?
Will you defy the Holy Church's lessons,
And baptism and God Himself in Heaven?
For it is Lent, when Christians fast together;
That solemn day, Good Friday, sad and splendid,
When sinners praise the Cross of our Redemption;
And as for us poor wretches whom you've led here,
We've slaughtered nuns and burned the Lord God's dwelling;

We never shall be reconciled with Heaven,
Unless His grace forgives ours sins already!"
On hearing this, Raoul flung round with menace:
"You harlot's son!" he cried, "Mind where you meddle!
Why did the folk of Origny offend me?
Two men of mine were slaughtered by their sentries;
Are you amazed that I exacted vengeance?
But I forgot the day, I must confess it."
He said no more, but asking for a chess-set
He left, ill-pleased, and sat down in the meadow.

RAOUL SET DOWN the chess-board and he played
As one well skilled in every move to make;
He moved his rook with speed into the game
And with his pawn he took a knight straightway;
He was, indeed, about to check and mate
The noble lad who'd sat with him to play,
When up he leapt, with bright and shining face,
And, being hot, threw off his cloak of grey;
He called for wine and ten young men of brave
And noble birth supplied him with the same.

HE CALLED FOR WINE to cool his body down;
Some fourteen lads, all clad in ermine gowns,
Ran forth to see his order carried out;
One noble youth, born in Saint-Quentin town,
Son of Ybert, who was a palace-count,
Caught up at once a cup filled to its brow
And golden brim with wine a spicy brown;
With this in hand he knelt before the Count;
You could have worn a war-horse to the ground
Before Raoul replied with word or sound;
The young lad swore by good St Firmin's shroud
That if his lord refused to drink it now,
Then he would pour the wine and spices out.

WHEN RAOUL SAW the boy and heard his cry,
He quickly seized the goblet full of wine:
"Fair brother, friend, by God Who never lies,
I swear I didn't see you there," he cried;
Not waiting more, he raised his voice on high:

"Now hear me well, good, noble knights of mine!
By this good wine raised here before your eyes,
And by my sword upon this rug of white,
And by the Saints who served Lord Jesus Christ,
I swear to you I'll humble Herbert's line –
Just like this cup, I'll drain each brother dry!
By St Géri, in faith, I swear that I
Shall harry them with unrelenting spite
Until they flee across the sea in fright!"
"In Jesu's name," Bernier at once replied,
"If you did this, then it would be a crime;
For by the Lord Who governs all our lives,
Count Herbert's sons are brave and worthy knights,
With ties of blood to fifty more besides,
Who each have pledged to fight until they die
For all the rest, if ever that's required."

14. Bernier's departure

RAOUL SPOKE FORTH, his temper high and fierce:
"Now hear me well, good knights of noble breed:
I swear by God, Who judges all and each,
Count Herbert's sons shall soon have cause to fear!
I'll bleed them dry of every penny-piece
And leave them not one foot of all their fiefs
To dwell upon alive or dead beneath!
I'll make them flee in fright across the sea!"
Once more Bernier leapt up at this to speak:
"Raoul, my lord, your life is lived between
Great deeds of fame and deeds of blame indeed!
Count Herbert's sons, I must and will repeat,
Are noble knights and men to be esteemed;
If you succeed in forcing them to flee,
You will not rule their tenants here in peace;
I know full well I am your man of liege –
Yet what a poor reward I have received:
My mother's church you've burned at Origny,
With her inside, beyond all mortal reach,
And now you'd slay my father and his peers!
Are you amazed that I am so aggrieved

And wish to help the kinsmen I hold dear?
I will avenge all outrage done to me!"
On hearing this, Raoul was filled with spleen,
And in reply spoke most abusively.

HE SPOKE AGAIN, his cheeks aglow with wrath:
"You harlot's son," he swore, "son of Marsent!
I know full well whose side you're really on!
Your father is Ybert of Ribemont:
You serve me now to hurt me later on;
My barons tell to you each plan we plot;
A bastard's tongue should never wag so long;
St Simon's blood! I tell you, mongrel dog,
I've half a mind to cut your head clean off!"
"How fine a fee!" cried young Bernier, "By God,
How fine a fee indeed for all I've done!"

BERNIER REPLIED, both loud and clear his voice:
"I have no kin or brother here, my lord;
My father's name is known to one and all;
My mother was a lady nobly-born."

"RAOUL, MY LORD, I swear to what I'm saying;
My mother was the daughter of a brave knight
Who ruled the length and breadth of all Bavaria;
But she was wooed, to her great sorrow later,
Within that realm until the suitor claimed her
And married her before God's congregation;
But then, before the King of all the nation,
He raised his sword and slew two lords he hated;
An awful war broke out with no abating,
And he escaped to Gaifier of Spoleto,
Who knew his worth and willingly retained him;
He never saw my mother's face again, lord;
He never deigned to ask his friends for favours."

"MY MOTHER HAD no husband and no friends,
And still no peer on earth for loveliness;
My father held a high position then,
And took her by brute force, as I learned hence;
He did not marry her, I must confess."

"RAOUL, MY LORD," said young Bernier once more:
"Ybert, my father, took fair Marsent by force;
He bedded her when she was lorn and poor,
And forced his will on hers and did it all;
I cannot say he married her henceforth:
He took to wife another at the court;
He offered her Joifroi, whose hand she scorned;
She took the veil – which was a better choice."

"RAOUL, MY LORD, you sin against the Heavens,
For you have burned my mother in God's dwelling!
God, let me live until I have my vengeance!"
On hearing this, Raoul said, with his head down:
"You harlot's son, you dark, deceiving devil!
If it were not for God and pity's blessing,
I would have torn you limb from limb already!
I'll do it yet – there's no one to prevent me!"
Bernier replied: "How evil is your friendship!
I always loved and served you and upheld you;
How vile a fee I see my service merits;
If I had on my bright and burnished helmet,
Then I would fight on foot or horseback any
Armed nobleman in proof of this contention:
True bastards are the men God disinherits!
Not even you, who are so rash and reckless,
Would strike me then, for all of Rheims's treasure."
On hearing this, Count Raoul swung his head up
And, seeing that his hunting-men had left there
A length of spear, which was both long and heavy,
He snatched it up with all his rage and frenzy
And struck Bernier as both men came together;
The blow was such that blood ran from a head-wound
And swiftly turned his coat of ermine redder;
On seeing this, his anger swamped his senses;
With all his rage he seized him and they wrestled;
He would, in truth, have soon assuaged his temper,
But all the knights came rushing up to wrench them
Apart again, before the brawl turned deadly;
Young Bernier called upon his squire directly:
"Bring straightaway my hauberk and my weapons,
My worthy sword and my strong, banded helmet;
I'll leave this court at once, with no farewelling!"

RAOUL WAS WILD, his temper high and dread;
But when he saw young Bernier so distressed,
And saw the blood go streaming from his head,
He was appalled and quite beside himself:
"My lords," he said, "advise me for the best;
Bernier has left with anger in his breast!"
His worthy knights replied in concert then:
"He has good cause, my lord, to be upset!
His blade of steel has served you long and well,
But you have paid his wages with contempt!
You've burned Marsent in church till she was dead,
And struck his head so hard it split and bled!
May God on High, Who judges all, condemn
Whoever blames his yearning for revenge!
But make amends – perhaps he will accept!"
Raoul replied: "I'll do as you have said;
In Jesu's name, Bernier, fair brother, friend,
Before my men I want to make amends!"
"What recompense could any man accept?
Because of you my mother burned to death;
Because of you I have a broken head;
But by the One to Whom we both confess,
You will not see me take your recompense
Until this blood that I see running red,
Runs back to fill the wound whence it was shed;
When I see that, then I may well relent
The great revenge I'll have upon you yet!
I'll not be bought for all Montpellier's wealth!"

IN TUNIC CLAD Raoul knelt on the meadow;
On Bernier's face he looked with great affection
And with largesse he lovingly addressed him:
"Come on, Bernier," he said, "my comrade ever;
Will you not take amends and have this settled?
It's not because I fear you'll strike against me,
But that I may remain the friend you cherished;
For by the blest St James of Compostella,
I'd rather lose the blood from my own breast here,
Or take a wound that spilled forth all my entrails,
Or lose my hall itself, than lose your friendship;
For the Emir who governs rich Tudela,

Or for our King himself, I'd do no better;
I say this, by the Virgin Maid, to tell you
That I cannot do more to recompense you;
From Origny itself as far as Nesle,
Full fifteen leagues, I specify the measure,
One hundred knights shall bear their saddles tethered
Around their necks, as I shall yours, I pledge you!
I'll lead Baucent, my own Castilian destrier,
And every man or maid I meet I'll tell them:
'I bear this saddle of Bernier's as a penance.'"
His knights all said: "Now that's a noble gesture;
Whoever baulks at this, rejects your friendship."

RAOUL SPOKE ON with great humility:
"Bernier, my friend, your valour has no peer;
Take my amends and let this hatred be."
Bernier replied: "What childish games are these?
The gold of Aquilance won't purchase me
Until this blood, that still is running free,
Runs back inside the wound you did to me;
No settlement shall ever be achieved
Until I wreak revenge upon your deeds!"
Raoul replied: "Then this is sad indeed,
For we must part in bitterness, it seems."
Guerri spoke up at this, his mood extreme:
"By God, bastard, you spur us with your heel!
My nephew here has pledged more than he need!
From this day on, wherever you may be,
Know well your death is written on my spear!"
Bernier replied: "Rely no more on me!
Your nephew's blow will lead to endless grief."

15. Vermandois' army

THROUGHOUT THE RANKS how great a cry was made!
See young Bernier, whose face with valour blazed!
He bound his head with cloth of silk and laced
His hauberk on, well meshed with iron mail,
And then his helm and then his worthy blade;
He mounted horse, a steed of dapple-grey,

Then round his neck a spotted shield he draped
And grasped his spear, its pennon swiftly raised;
He blew his horn in one long-winded wail;
Five knights of his came round him straightaway,
Five knights who held their lands in vassalage;
To Bernier's call they all rode up in haste,
Not failing him for life nor limb, I'd say;
How sad a sight when they all rode away!
To Ribemont they rode without delay,
Where Count Ybert, whose beard was white with age,
Stood looking from his well-paved hall of state,
With many knights who lived in his domains;
His gaze was fixed upon a pleasant vale
When suddenly he saw his son Bernier;
At once he knew his retinue and paled;
He said aloud: "My worthy men and brave,
I see my son approaching through the dales;
Each knight of his is armed from head to tail!
They look prepared for trouble, come what may;
Now we shall hear why Raoul of Cambrai
Has left his shire to lay our borders waste!"

YBERT THE COUNT, of fearsome heart and temper,
Turned round at once to heed the call of vespers;
Bernier arrived, he and his knights together;
The castle's squires came forward to attend them,
And then they asked: "By God the Lord of Heaven,
Do you have news of Count Raoul's intentions?"
He answered: "Yes, I come with news a-plenty,
But all so bad I know not how to tell it;
Those men of you with lands to be defended
Had better lace your helmets on already:
His plan it is for Herbert's clan to perish,
To drive his sons from all of their possessions,
Or, if they're caught, to cut their limbs and heads off!
May God above, in His great love, protect us!"
Before the hall they took off Bernier's helmet
And saw the blood still bleeding from his head-wound;
On seeing this, how many men lamented!
With vespers done, Ybert returned and gently
Embraced his son and warmly bade him welcome;

He saw the gash that ran across his temple
And stared in shock at such a bloody blemish;
So stunned he was he almost lost his senses:
"Fine son," he said, "by Riquier's blood, the blessed,
Am I too old to ride a steed, God help me?
Who dared to raise his hand in hate against you
While I can still wear armour and bear weapons?"
"My liege himself it was in wicked frenzy:
The Cambrai Count has made us all his enemy;
He's ridden here to drive us into exile,
Claim all our lands and leave us not a penny;
He's burned the town of Origny already –
I saw Marsent, who had no peer or better,
Burnt in her church, on purpose, not in error;
I raged at him and, in his fearsome temper,
He swung a shaft of apple-wood to fell me;
He split my head – the blood ran to my belt-knot;
I'll not deny he offered to do penance,
But I could not consider or accept it;
I've hurried here, good father, for your blessing
And your advice; this outrage calls for vengeance."
On hearing this, Ybert's own curse fell heavy.

YBERT REPLIED, whose hair and beard were white:
"Bernier, my son, I will not tell a lie:
I know the tale of many people's lives;
Say what you will, a man of reckless pride,
Though reasoned with, will always fall in time;
The wealth he gains in seven years of guile
Is lost within one day of rash desire;
When you were small and lived here as a child,
We cared for your with all our main and might;
But when you grew and led a young man's life,
You left us then and with a foolish mind
You loved Raoul, his honeyed words and wiles,
And made your way to Cambrai at his side;
You served his will, and how well he's replied:
He's beaten you like some old hack he rides!
I've cut you off from any wealth of mine –
You'll not receive one penny when I die."
Young Bernier's blood, at this, began to rise:

"Fine father, lord, for pity's sake," he cried,
"Reclaim me now so I may do what's right;
I'd rather have stood bare on Russia's ice
Than see the church of Origny alight,
And know Marsent, my mother, was inside,
And many more who perished in the fire –
Five score in all – not one of them survived;
By all Pavia's Saints, I tell no lie:
When I spoke out before my men and knights
To Count Raoul about his wicked crime,
He struck my head so fiercely in his spite
The crimson blood bled in my ears and eyes."
Ybert the count was in no mood to smile;
He swore to God and His Son Jesus Christ:
"Alas indeed that he began this strife,
That fair Marsent, you mother, should have died!
Raoul the cur has robbed her of her life!
How many shields our spears will split aside!
How many coats of mail we'll rip awry
Before that dog shall overrun our shires!
No man alive could say he has the right:
The right is ours to see he is defied;
He has destroyed most foully what is mine;
If I do not defend the land and lives
Put in my hand, then I should be reviled;
Count of Cambrai, a curse upon your pride!
You gave your word at Origny and lied!
You told the nuns to have no fear or fright,
Then burned them all to death as you drank wine!
The Devil's loose, if God lets you survive
And sunders not the ground that you bestride!"

YBERT WAS FULL of bitter rage and hate,
But lovingly he looked upon Bernier:
"Fine son," he said, "do not be so dismayed;
By Him Who judges all our days and ways,
Raoul, I swear, will soon be made to pay!"
When this was said the table-cloths were laid
And every knight, in his appointed place,
Sat down to eat – although the count refrained:
He only toyed with what was on his plate;

His knights and men began to remonstrate:
"Eat, noble lord, for God of Judgement's sake –
On Easter Day no Christian should dismay!"
"I cannot start to eat," the count exclaimed:
"When I behold my son, who to his waist
Is wet with blood, then I am filled with rage;
Raoul must hold my honour in disdain,
To send him home with blood upon his face!
You older men must keep our ramparts safe,
The mighty tower and noble hall the same;
You younger men and noble squires make haste
To saddle up each one his destrier,
For we must ride without one moment's waste!"
"Don't leave me here!" cried out the young Bernier;
"I must, my son, for by St Riquier,
You're badly hurt – so take your ease and wait:
You need to rest and heal that ugly graze."
But once again he cried: "Don't bid me stay,
For by baptism's oil I'll disobey;
Though I lose limb or life, I'll not refrain
From seeking out swift vengeance for my shame!"
When this was said they mounted straightaway
Then rode all night without a stop or stay;
They came to Roie before the break of day.

THEY CAME TO ROIE before the light of morning,
And straightaway dismounted from their horses;
Ybert the count without delay went forward,
Well-armed indeed, his spotted shield before him:
Already laced his white and sturdy hauberk,
Already girt his sharp and shining sword-blade;
They strode along until they reached the ford there;
The watch-in-chief was in his tower and saw them;
He cast a stone, not waiting any orders,
Which almost struck Ybert upon the forehead –
And, had it struck, it would have sent him sprawling!
Before his horse it splashed upon the water;
The watch called out: "Who are you? With what forces?
I threw the rock, and if it missed, I warn you
My bow is drawn, its arrow aimed towards you!"
Ybert replied: "Unstring your bow, good warden!

I am Ybert, the son of him we mourn for;
Inform Eudon, your fierce and fearless war-lord,
My brother dear, whose hair and beard are hoary,
And bring him here! I wait most keenly for him!
I need him now, as never yet or more so!"

"WHAT IS YOUR NAME?" called out again the watch:
"Fair brother, friend, you'll know it well ere long:
I am Ybert, the lord of Ribemont;
Go and inform my brother, Lord Eudon,
And bring him here, for by St Simon's cross,
A greater need than now there never was!"
"God bless us all!" the watch cried in response,
And to his lord the worthy man ran off.

THE WATCH RAN OFF with no delay to reach
Sir Eudon's room where he was still asleep;
He rapped the ring and Eudon's guard appeared;
When Eudon woke and saw the watchman's fear,
He said: "My friend, by God our trusty Liege,
Speak up at once! Is help required from me?"
"As never yet, my lord, from what I see;
Outside our walls is someone you hold dear –
He said his name was Count Ybert to me."
On hearing this, Eudon leapt to his feet,
Put on his robe, an ermine gown, and seized
His coat of mail and laced his helm of green;
Against his side he tied his burnished steel;
This done, his seneschal, called Tierri,
Led forth his horse, a noble Arab steed;
Eudon leapt up, and seizing forth his shield,
He grasped his lance, its pennon flapping free,
And left his hall with all address and speed.

EUDON RODE DOWN the sloping ground in haste,
Not stopping till he reached the barricade
Where Count Ybert and all his knights had stayed:
"What brings you here, fair brother?" he exclaimed:
"Are you in need at such a time of day?"
"In truth, our need will never be as great:
The King has waived our right to these estates

In favour of young Raoul of Cambrai!
Raoul has brought ten thousand men our way;
We must defend or lose all our domains;
Send word to all our allies straightaway!"
Eudon replied: "There's many who will aid;
But I'm convinced this is some jest you make;
I cannot think, for all the wealth of Spain,
That he would be so reckless as to raise
A force of men to fight us face to face!
Red Guerri is no foolish youth or knave –
He'd not have urged or backed so wild a claim."
Ybert replied: "It's folly to debate!
Raoul has set all Origny ablaze,
And all the nuns you settled in that place
Have burned to death in awful, cruel shame!"

EUDON REPLIED: "By God, can this be true –
Has Origny been burned by Count Raoul?"
"Fair brother, yes, my own son brought the proof;
Just yesterday he met me with the news;
He saw his mother burn, and with her too
One hundred nuns in awful shame and cruel."
Eudon replied: "Then it must be the truth;
I know Bernier to be an honest youth."

YBERT REPLIED, his whiskers white and heavy:
"Fair brother, whom, for God's sake, shall we send for?"
Eudon replied: "There's many who will help us –
Send first of all for Herbert, lord of Hirson;
He holds in strength the halls of the Thiérache,
Some thirty keeps and castles all together;
He is our brother and always will defend us."
And so they did; Bernier was sent as envoy
And soon returned with some one thousand levies;
They pitched their tents on land below Saint-Quentin;
Count Raoul of Soissons they also sent for,
And he led forth one thousand of his Frenchmen;
Beneath Saint-Quentin's walls the sand was level,
And there they camped and flew their many pennons;
They swore to God – the song records their pledges –
That if they found Raoul, the reckless rebel,

He would regret the offer he'd accepted,
And Guerri too would have his whiskers severed.

THEY SUMMONED NEXT Bernart of Porcien;
He ruled Champagne on one side of that land;
He swore to God that he would bear their flag;
One thousand knights he and Gerard both had
And led them forth, each one a gallant man;
They camped apart upon Saint-Quentin's sand;
They swore in rage by good St Leonard that
With Raoul or Red Guerri in their hands,
The bolder man would quake or quiver as
They drained the blood from inside of his fat!

THEY SUMMONED THEN Riquier, the noble vassal
Who held the land towards the Rinier valley;
One thousand knights came with him, keen for battle,
With noble arms and good, fleet-footed stallions;
They camped apart upon the sand and gravel.

UPON THE SAND their weapons shone and shimmered
So splendidly across the lovely river
That everywhere the waters glowed and glittered;
They swore to God, Who suffered Crucifixion
To save the world from all its sins committed,
That if they found Raoul in town or village
Of their estate, he'd lose his head, the villain!

EUDON OF ROIE then led out from his palace
One thousand knights, their silky pennons flapping;
They rode at once to join the other vassals
Below Saint-Quentin's walls in their encampment;
They swore to God, our Everlasting Ally,
That if they found Raoul, the reckless bandit,
They'd all rip out his lungs and liver gladly!
"King Louis, lord of all of France, in madness
Hands out our land as if it were a lamprey!
But while we live, by God, he shall not have it!"

THEY SUMMONED THEN Sir Louis, their young brother –
Of Herbert's sons he was indeed the youngest,

But brought with him one thousand knights of courage;
Well-armed, he rode a steed called 'Paris Thunder';
They made their camp below Saint-Quentin's turrets
And swore to God, our Everlasting Comfort,
That Count Raoul and Red Guerri, his uncle,
Would rue the day they left Aalais his mother!
"By St Denis, whichever one we come to,
We'll strike him down and tear his limbs asunder;
They'll both regret they ever sought our country!"

AT LAST, YBERT, whose heart was ever brave,
The eldest brother, the father of Bernier,
Brought forth his men, whose help had never failed;
Well-armed, they rode fine Gascon destriers;
They made their camp upon Saint-Quentin's plain –
How many rich and splendid tents they raised,
Then swore to God, Who bore the Cross's bane,
That Count Raoul would rue the day he came!

16. Gerard's embassy

COUNT HERBERT'S SONS broke camp when it was morning;
They turned for Origny and rode towards it –
Eleven thousand strong, astride good horses,
With swords of steel and armour strong and stalwart;
One league away, or so the song records it,
They made their camp from Count Raoul's own forces,
And pitched in rows their tents and sundry awnings;
Then Eudon said: "Good nobles and supporters!
A reckless man is worth less than a straw-stalk!
The Cambrai Count is not an ill-bred pauper,
But nephew of the King, whose men we all are;
If he should die, it will be our misfortune:
For then the King would hate us now and always;
He'd seize our lands and then he would destroy them;
He'd hunt us down, and if he ever caught us,
Be sure of this, he'd have us drawn and quartered;
So let us send a knight as envoy for us
To urge Raoul to draw back from our borders
Inside his own, and pray the Lord restores him

His rightful land and grants him its enjoyment;
If we give cause for any spite before then,
We'll make amends for any trouble caused him;
We do not seek his land, let us assure him,
But some of ours we'll cede on his withdrawing;
We shall restore the church and holy order
Which he was wrong to set ablaze and slaughter;
And we will help him wage his other war then,
To claim his shire from Sir Giboin the Mansel;
Bernier's amends we are prepared to forfeit."
"God!" said Ybert, "Whose wisdom can perform this?"
"I'll go, my lord," Bernier replied, undaunted;
On hearing this, his father stormed towards him:
"You fool, Bernier! By God, are you so thoughtless
That you'd you run back to arms that scarred and scorned you?
Son, if you went, your fists would do the talking
And harm at once the justice of our cause here."
He looked and saw Gerard of Poix before him:
"You go, fine lord, I beg you and exhort you!"
"Most willingly," said he, "nor shall I loiter!"
And to his tent he went to don his hauberk.

SO TO HIS TENT went Gerard, famed in Spain;
Upon his back he donned his Eastern mail,
Then laced his good Pavian helm in place;
They led him forth his Danish destrier
And by the rings he mounted straightaway;
Around his neck his sturdy shield was draped,
Then through the marsh he quickly rode away;
He came to where Raoul's own tent was raised
And filled with knights from Artois and Cambrai;
He saw Raoul, sat there in pride of place,
And nobly dressed in silk of Grecian make;
Gerard himself was both well-bred and brave:
He leaned upon his lance of steel and made
No show of fear with what he had to say:
"May God the Lord, Who bore the Cross's pain,
And gave us laws to rule our lands in Faith,
Save Count Raoul and all his men the same,
And save the King, your uncle, on this day."
"God save you too!" replied Raoul with grace:
"So help me God, you seem more knight than knave!"

"RAOUL," REPLIED Gerard the gallant-tempered,
"I urge you please to listen to my message;
Without delay I ask your leave to tell it."
"You may, at once, then hurry back, good envoy,
Lest I suspect you've come to spy our levy!"
Gerard replied: "I have no such intention."
Then he began to say what he'd been sent for,
And spoke aloud until his speech was ended;
Raoul heard all and, as he did, reflected;
"In truth," he said, "I ought well to accept it;
But first I must discuss it with Red Guerri."

HE WENT TO SEEK his uncle's sound advice;
He told him that an envoy had arrived
And what he'd said before them all inside;
On hearing this, Red Guerri praised the skies
And said: "My boy, your heart should swell with pride,
That Herbert's sons would all appease your might;
For Heaven's sake, I urge you to comply;
What gain is there in governing their shires?"
On hearing this, Raoul's great rage revived,
And, staring him straight in the face, he cried:
"I took their glove before all Louis' knights;
You urge me now to drop and let it lie?
Each one of them would mock me, and do right!"

RAOUL SPOKE ON, he couldn't hold his peace:
"They used to say of noble Red Guerri
That all the world held none so bold as he;
But now I see he has a coward's streak!"
On hearing this, Red Guerri's words were brief:
For all the gold, he said, of Abbeville,
He would not hear again so vile a speech,
Nor have Raoul regard his honour cheap;
With all his rage he swore by St Géri:
"Since you have laid a coward's charge on me,
One thousand men shall have their hauberks pierced
Ere they and I will ever live in peace."
To Sir Gerard he said: "Be gone from here!
Tell Herbert's sons to arm themselves with speed
For their defence against us in the field!"

The envoy said: "By God, so let it be!
I challenge you upon the part of each!
You will regret the nuns of Origny,
And pay the price the next time that we meet!
Each one of us is dressed to fetch the fee!"
At this he turned and grasped his buckler near –
The wonder was he didn't use the shield –
But nonetheless he brandished forth his spear;
Recalling then that Ybert, white of beard,
Awaited him, he turned around to leave.

17. Bernier's embassy

GERARD RETURNED and neither did he loiter;
On spurring in, Ybert made haste towards him:
"What cheer, Gerard? Tell all you said and saw there!"
"In truth, my lord, Raoul is very haughty!
There's nothing more that we can do by talking;
Prepare yourself and all our men for warfare."
"Thank God for that!" Bernier cried out, rejoicing;
Eudon spoke up: "Lords, once again I warn you:
A reckless heart soon loses fame and fortune;
Select a man and send him forth one more time
To make again our offer of accordance,
As did Gerard when first he spoke this morning;
Perhaps Raoul has been advised or cautioned
By others since and his response has altered;
We should be glad if war can be avoided."
"God!" said Ybert, "This troubles me most sorely;
What man is left whose courage can perform this?"
"I'll go, my lord," Bernier replied, undaunted;
On hearing this, his father's rage was awful:
"By God, Bernier, you're far too high and haughty!
But as you've put your name and service forward,
Then go you will, and no one will forestall you!"
Bernier replied: "My lord, I thank you for it."
He laced his helm and donned his shining hauberk;
His shield was new as he bestrode his war-horse;
His father felt great pity when he saw him:
"Go forth, good son, and hurry, I implore you!

Do not neglect the justice of our cause here."
Bernier replied: "You have no need to warn me;
No word or deed of mine will disappoint you."

BERNIER RODE OFF and left his men behind;
He did not leave his steed when he arrived,
But made his words of greeting most precise:
"May God on High, Who never fails or lies,
Who blessed Adam and Eve in Paradise,
Save many lords I see before my eyes,
Who've nurtured me most kindly all my life;
I have no fight or quarrel with those knights;
But may he damn Raoul of Cambrai shire,
Who burned my mother and all her nuns alive,
Within their church, which was a shameful crime;
Who struck me too, so fiercely in his pride,
That crimson blood flowed down my face and side;
God, let me live to pay him back in kind,
For so I shall, I swear by Jesus Christ,
And St Géri, if but the chance arise."
Raoul replied: "This envoy is unwise!
Is this Bernier, white-haired Ybert's own child?
You harlot's son, you've gone too far this time,
You by-blow of an old man's concubine!"

RAOUL SPOKE ON, for he could not keep silent:
"You bastard rogue, I tell you without lying,
Your duty is to be back here beside me,
In company with all my squires and hirelings;
But they're too low for one so high and mighty!"
Bernier heard this and felt his anger rising.

"RAOUL, MY LORD," Bernier responded then,
"Let be this talk of duty and respect;
So help me God, I'm not so greatly led
By food and drink to join your meals again!
No taunt of yours shall force me to relent;
I've not come here to barter taunts or threats;
Count Herbert's sons have sent me on this quest:
To ask once more if you will now accept
The offer made this morning in your tent

By Sir Gerard of Poix at their behest;
My feud with you has naught to do with them;
You burned Marsent, my mother dear, to death,
Then with a shaft you struck and cut my head;
I'll not deny you tried to make amends:
You offered me fine horses to forget,
One hundred steeds both strong and fleet of step,
One hundred mules and palfreys finely bred,
One hundred swords and hauberks double-meshed,
One hundred shields, one hundred golden helms;
I was enraged to see the blood you shed
And would not think of compensation then;
I went instead to seek advice from friends;
And I agree with what they all suggest:
By St Riquier, if you renew your pledge,
I will accept and pardon your offence –
Provided this brings peace between our men."

RAOUL PAID HEED and heard Bernier's suggestion,
Then as a friend beheld him and addressed him:
"So help me God, this offer shows true friendship;
By Jesus Christ, Who died for our redemption,
Your noble words shall not go unattended."
He made his way to where his uncle's tent was,
And seized his arm as soon as he beheld him,
And told him all that young Bernier had said there –
How both of them had fixed upon a penance,
With nothing false, omitted or embellished:
"Fine uncle, lord, for love of God I beg you:
For friendship's sake, and peace, let us accept it!"
On hearing this, with all his temper's venom,
Red Guerri said: "You called *me* weak and feckless!
Your Arab steed, Fauvel, is saddled ready,
But now the wealth of all Ponthieu won't tempt you
To mount its back and face a fearsome mêlée!
So run away to your Cambrai, young nephew!
All Herbert's sons, I tell you, are my enemies!
They'll have a war – I'll fight them all together!"
Said young Bernier: "Then I thank God in Heaven!
Raoul, my lord, I see our bond has ended
For one offence – and you were the offender!

Until that time I served you well and ever,
But your reward was villainous and dreadful:
You burned Marsent, my mother, in God's dwelling,
Then struck at me in your relentless temper,
Till crimson blood was running from my temple."
He plucked three hairs out of his ermine vestment
And pulled them through his coat of mail and rent them;
He threw them down in sign of disaffection
And then he said: "Henceforth, I am against you!
You cannot say I ever failed my pledges."
The Frenchmen said: "Be gone now from our presence!
You've rendered clear to all men here your message."

SAID BRAVE BERNIER "Raoul, my lord, this fight
Will surely be most desperate and wild;
But I'll know you and all your friends by sight,
And seek your death at any place or time."
"This saddens me, in truth," Raoul replied,
"But no reproach shall blight our children's lives:
I will vouchsafe you challenged me and mine;
If on this field we fought, just you and I,
Then one of us, alone, would lose his life."
Said Bernier then: "That's all that I desire;
For I would prove to any doubting mind
That you were wrong to claim my uncles' shires,
And pay me back with treachery most vile."
On hearing this, Raoul was filled with spite
And felt disgraced before his band of knights;
He knew full well what young Bernier desired,
But was unarmed, and so made no reply.

BERNIER COULD SEE his challenge was received,
And at his back he turned his sturdy shield;
He dug the spurs well in his Niort steed
And went to strike the Count at once, though he
Stood in his tent and not upon the field;
Bernier spurred on towards him at a speed
More rapid than a roe runs through the trees;
On seeing this, a knight of great esteem
Leapt up between Bernier and Cambrai's liege,
And took the spear full on, from front to rear.

THE LIEGEMAN WAS as rash as he was brave;
He flung himself directly in the way
And took the spear to save his lord that day;
He wasn't spared – the point was deftly aimed:
From front to rear the shaft went true and straight
And struck him dead and thrust his soul away;
On seeing this, Raoul called out in rage:
"Pursue him, men! Don't let him get away!
My name and fame are dead if he escapes!
That blow was aimed at me, whose life he hates!"
One hundred knights, at this, with zealous haste,
All leapt astride their Orcan destriers,
Each challenging as one the young Bernier;
He heard and saw it was no jest or game
And turned in flight along the path he came;
They chased him hard, but never reached his reins –
His Orcan steed was swift and knew the way;
Ybert stood there, beside the leafy glade,
And saw it all, the clash and the escape;
He called aloud on God Almighty's name:
"Behold my son, in need of urgent aid!
If he should die, I'll never smile again!
Bold men of mine, assist him, for my sake!"
Some fourteen horns they sounded straightaway;
How many shields on doughty breasts were braced!
How many spears were brandished forth and raised!

YBERT THE COUNT addressed his men and vassals:
"The right is ours; ride forward and attack them!
My son returns at faster than a gallop –
He must have told our message like a madman!
In hot pursuit one hundred knights harass him:
I see the spears and javelins hurled at him!"
On either side men broke their ranks in anger;
Whoever had the right or wrong, no matter:
Young Bernier's ride had brought both sides to battle!

18. Battle's beginning

BOTH ARMIES WERE well armed, and, to begin with,
Held many knights in serried ranks close-knitted;
The boldest men, on both sides, wept for pity,
All well aware that friendship then meant little;
The weakest men were down at heart and dismal:
To those that fell no comfort would be given,
Except to die in desperate affliction
And need no more the comfort of the living;
But all the youths were in the highest spirits
And more than one, dismounting more than swiftly,
Re-armed themselves with noble knights' equipment,
And then made sure their mounts had shortened stirrups!
Young Bernier's ride had brought a fight so bitter
That many men still living then were smitten
Of limb and life before that day had finished.

BOTH RANKS APPROACHED, each dreading what would be,
And taking stock of all that could be seen;
The weakest men began to shake with fear,
The boldest men to fill with joyful zeal;
Raoul's men swore, all very sure indeed,
That they would bring such grief to Herbert's breed
That fathers first, then orphaned sons would weep;
Their small and great were armed, both all and each,
And led in front by fearsome Red Guerri,
With both his sons, courageous in the field:
Renier was one, whose heart with valour beat,
And young Garnier, whose sword-play had no peer;
Raoul himself bestrode his fiery steed
And placed his men behind Red Guerri's lead;
His barons rode so closely, I believe,
That any glove tossed up above their spears,
Would not have touched the ground for one whole league;
Their horses' necks were resting on the rears
Of those in front, the rows were set that near.

RAOUL HAD BROUGHT a force which was immense:
Ten thousand strong, with Guerri at their head,

All mounted men, well-armed and nobly dressed;
I tell no lie, Count Herbert's clan and friends
Were tallied at eleven thousand men
By young Bernier, whose ardour knew no lengths;
From every side they rushed with fierce intent,
And, as they did, each man with pity wept,
And promised God that if he cheated death,
He never would commit a sin again,
And, if he did, would steadfastly repent;
And many lords took Lay Communion then –
Three blades of grass, with no priest there to bless,
Then pledged their souls to God, their sins confessed;
Raoul swore fast, and Guerri made a pledge,
To fight this war and nevermore to rest
Till they had won by force all Herbert's realm
And slain his sons till not a one was left,
Or at the least had rid the land of them;
Ybert, he swore to cede them not one step,
And every one of all his liegemen pledged
To stand by him till all their blood was shed:
"What loyalty, by God!" young Bernier said:
"A curse on him, I say, who first relents
Or breaks his word and flees before the press!"
Then Bertolai said he would write a *geste*,
The like of which no *jongleur* chanted yet.

THIS BERTOLAI was very wise and brave,
Both born and bred in Laon itself and raised
Of noble stock, of highest rank and race;
He saw it all, he witnessed all the fray
And wrote this song, whose like was never made,
And which I've sung in countless halls of state,
Of Guerri, called 'The Red', and fair Aalais,
And Count Raoul, the liege lord of Cambrai,
Whose godfather was bishop of Beauvais;
By St Gervase, I swear Raoul was slain
At Bernier's hand, and Ernaut's of Douai.

THERE NEVER WAS so loud and fierce a clash;
No Norman lord fought here with English hand,
But peer with peer from France and Vermandois,

And many knights from Cambrai and Artois,
With Brabantines and many Champenois,
And many too from Louis' household ranks;
Count Herbert's sons were fighting for their lands –
And how much blood was shed and bled for that
By all their men, and how it cleft their clan!
Bernier spurred forth his Nordic steed and slammed
His spear against a knight from Avalois,
Whose armour then was worth no more than rags
Against the weight of hate Sir Bernier had!
A full lance-length he flung the fellow flat;
He cried aloud: "Saint-Quentin, curse the slack!
Raoul shall rue his proud and evil act!
If with my sword I cannot pay him back,
May I be cursed and earn a coward's tag!"
Then on both sides they rushed to the attack;
How loud their horns and all their bugles rang!
Not since the day God gave His Word to Man
Was there a fight with spite like this one had!

WHEN BOTH ATTACKED how mighty was the uproar!
No threats were made, no menaces were uttered;
They hurled themselves so wildly at each other
That for a league you'd not have heard God's thunder!
See Count Ybert go spurring through the struggle:
He called aloud, in tones aglow with courage:
"Come here Raoul, by God Who dwells above us!
So many men, why should they die or suffer?
Turn round your steed and face me, one to one here!
If your own sword can fairly overcome me,
Then all my land shall be your own to govern,
And all my men, their children and their mothers,
Shall flee their halls and have recourse to nothing."
Raoul, I think, could not have heard the summons –
He was away among the cut and thrusting,
With Red Guerri, his fierce, grey-bearded uncle;
On seeing this, Ybert's resentment doubled;
He spurred his steed, whose speed outsped its brothers,
And struck Fromont in front, upon his buckler;
Beneath the boss he broke its boards asunder
And ripped the mail till it availed him nothing;

He drove his lance straight through the vassal's stomach
And threw him down upon the ground, all bloody;
Ybert called out: "Saint-Quentin, curse the sluggard!
These Cambrai curs shall not return so smugly!
Raoul will rue he ever seized our country!"

WELL-ARMED FOR WAR upon a Gascon bay,
Eudon of Roie spurred swiftly to the fray,
Count Herbert's son, an uncle of Bernier;
On Simon's shield a mighty blow he laid;
This Simon was of Count Raoul's own race;
Beneath the boss he pierced the blazon's paint
And through his guts he thrust the pennon's tail;
A full lance-length he flung him to his grave;
He cried aloud: "Saint-Quentin, curse the knave!
Raoul shall rue he stole our lands away;
These Cambrai curs shall one and all be slain!"

YOUNG LOUIS THEN went spurring through the field,
The youngest son of Herbert's four, indeed,
But one whose fame outshone the other three;
He rode on 'Paris Thunder', his fine steed –
A gift he gained at court in Saint-Denis –
King Louis was his godfather, you see;
He called aloud, in tones aglow with zeal:
"Come here Raoul, by God our Loyal Liege!
Turn round your horse and set your course for me!
If you should win, what honours you will reap:
I would renounce all claims upon my fief,
With no recourse for any friend to seek."
Raoul, I think, could not have heard the speech,
For had he come, he'd not have shunned to meet;
He was away among the battle's heat,
His hacking sword beside fierce Red Guerri's;
On seeing this, young Louis' rage increased;
He turned his shield and then he turned his heels
Against his mount with all his angry zeal
To strike Garnier upon his sombre shield,
Red Guerri's son, born in Arras, his fief;
Beneath the boss he broke the boards with ease;
No hauberk made could save the flesh beneath,

As through the guts he thrust his shining spear;
He flung him dead, then turned towards his peers.

WHEN LOUIS HAD laid low the young Garnier,
He cried aloud: "Saint-Quentin, bless the brave!
Raoul shall rue the day he ever came!"
Red Guerri rode his horse among the fray,
His buckler clasped, his sword of steel upraised;
The man he struck was past all surgeons' aid;
Fourteen and more he had unhorsed and slain;
But when he glanced along a woodland glade
And saw his son, he reeled with grief and pain;
He never stopped till, coming where he lay,
He leapt straight off his rapid destrier;
All bloody as he was, he kissed his face:
"Fine son, I loved you so," he wept and wailed:
"My ears shall hear no word of peace again
Till I have slain and torn apart the knave
Who took your life, so help me St Riquier!"
He raised the corpse to take his son away,
But saw their force approaching through a vale;
His heart was filled with anger and dismay,
As on his shield instead he left him lain:
"My son," he said, "I cannot stop or stay,
But with God's help I will avenge your fate;
May Jesus Christ receive your soul with Grace!"
He hurried back to mount his destrier,
And with his heart filled up with pain and hate
He struck the press with fearsome blows and great;
If you had seen how he unleashed his rage
Upon their ranks with his unstinting blade –
How heads and arms and chests he chopped away –
You'd not have called him cowardly, I'd say;
One score and more of Vermandois he maimed,
As through their ranks he cut a mighty swathe.

HOW HARD THEY HACKED and grappled each with each!
Red Guerri spurred his war-horse at full speed
And met Ernaut, of Douai lord and liege;
Both filled with hate, then urged along their steeds
Until they struck each other's Beauvais shield;

Their lances bent, their wooden boards were pierced,
But neither's coat was ripped or rent beneath;
The strength of each threw both upon the field,
And, neither loath, they leapt up on their feet,
And in delight pursued the fight with steel.

THE TWO OF THEM were brave and noble men;
How fine a knight was Guerri called 'The Red',
How bold and strong in any joust or press!
He clasped his shield, he swung his sword's sharp edge
And struck Ernaut upon his golden helm,
So that its stones and floral emblems fell;
If old Ernaut had not drawn back his head,
It would have slit and split him to his belt;
The blade of steel sliced over to the left
And sheared one field upon the shield he held
And then one skirt upon his hauberk's mesh;
The blow was huge and very much to dread;
It stunned Ernaut and buckled both his legs;
His spirits fell to feel his strength grow less,
And, crying out to God above, he said:
"Blest Mary's Son, support me with Your strength!
I will rebuild Origny church, I pledge!"
Upon these words behold Renier, my friends,
The second son of brave Guerri the Red;
He saw Ernaut upon his knees and sped
His horse along, his buckler firmly clenched;
He would have slain Ernaut right there and then,
When who should come but young Bernier again,
Who stopped him, as with ringing tones he yelled:
"Most noble knight, for love of God, relent!
Turn round your steed and challenge me instead,
For if you dared, I'd willingly accept!"
On hearing this, Renier's great anger swelled
With his desire to fight and see him dead,
And gain revenge for his dear brother's death;
They spurred their steeds and, charging in, they met
With mighty blows against each other's breast;
Beneath the boss their bucklers broke and rent,
But not the mail which bound their bones and flesh!
Their lances broke as both men rode ahead

With neither one unhorsed or in distress;
On seeing this, Bernier went mad himself.

WITH ALL HIS RAGE, with all his strength and temper,
He drew his sword, whose blade was sharp and heavy,
And struck Renier upon his pointed helmet;
The blow laid low its stones and floral emblems
And split the coif upon his coat's fine meshing,
Through skin and skull, through brain and brow it cleft him;
Red Guerri said: "I've seen one blow too many;
I'd be a fool to wait here for the next one!"
Upon him then so many men descended
That all the blood froze in his veins with terror;
He reached his horse, still waiting there untethered,
And mounting up, his shield held at the ready,
He spurred away and left his son, his second,
Spreadeagled there in death upon the meadow.

RED GUERRI LEFT – what else could he have done?
He crossed a slope and spurred his stallion up;
What grief he felt for his two slaughtered sons:
He tore his hair with rage and sorrow wrung;
He met Raoul and spoke of nothing but
The awful loss of his own flesh and blood:
"Count Herbert's clan are villains every one!
So help me God, they've murdered both my sons!
They'll pay the price, then twice, then thrice as much!
God let me live till they have paid enough!"

19. Raoul's prowess

"FINE YOUTH RAOUL," Red Guerri cried and called:
"By St Denis, to whom my faith is sworn,
Count Herbert's clan are very fierce in war!
My sons are dead – they've slaughtered both my boys!
Just yesterday I never would have thought,
For all the gold in Paris, when we fought,
That they would hold against our might at all;
We have misjudged both their and our support!
They'll slay us all, unless God helps our cause!

By Jesus Christ, Who bore the Cross's gall,
I beg of you to stay with me henceforth;
I swear to you, as loyal kinsman ought,
That if you fight with ten of theirs and fall
Beneath their blows from your fine battle-horse,
Then with main force I'll lift you up once more!"
On hearing this, Raoul's great heart rejoiced.

COUNT RAOUL NOW, his eyes aglow with valour,
Beheld all round so thick a throng of vassals
That he could not manoeuvre well his stallion
Nor wield his sword with freedom to attack them;
He sweated hard to vent in vain his anger;
With great prowess he strove to hack them backwards;
But in one thing I think he acted rashly:
He broke his word to Guerri and abandoned
His uncle's side, whose valour was his standard,
And all the lords who would have helped him gladly;
Among the press he swung this way and that way;
The man he struck was past all surgeons' salving:
He took the heads of more than twenty barons,
And many more took flight before his challenge;
But then Ybert came spurring at the gallop
And struck Morant upon his buckler's panels;
And then Bernier spurred up in haste and harried
To bloody death one more of his companions;
Then all the sons of Herbert came to back them,
And how they raged through Raoul's liege- and landsmen!
The horses fled across the field, abandoned,
With dragging reins and girths ungirt from saddles;
How many knights were slaughtered in that battle!
Count Herbert's sons were neither fools nor madmen:
They set aside one thousand of their clansmen
To stop his men if any fled or scattered;
See Raoul then, whose ardour never slackened
To win his way and see revenge exacted!
He met with Hugh, a brave Vermandois vassal:
From West to East no count was half as handsome,
Nor half as bold to challenge as this champion;
Not old at all, he was a knight who travelled
In search of fame through feats of daring action;

Across the field with battle-cries and sallies
He wrought alarm and loss of life and panic;
Raoul looked up and spurred his war-horse at him;
With cutting blades what blows they gave and parried!
Raoul attacked his helmet with such passion
That all its stones and floral-emblems shattered;
The coif was hit, the hauberk slit to tatters,
And Hugh's young head split open like an apple;
He flung him dead and cried "Cambrai!" his rally:
"Count Herbert's sons shall never leave here bragging!
They'll never leave at all, while I am standing!"

THE NOBLE COUNT, his eyes aglow with pride,
Beheld all round so thick a throng of knights
That he could not manoeuvre well to ride
Nor wield his shield as freely as he liked;
He sweated hard to vent in vain his ire;
If you yourselves had seen him raise on high
His cutting blade against them left and right,
You'd not forget what true prowess was like;
Yet in one thing I think he was unwise:
He left Guerri, his uncle, far behind,
And all those lords who'd come to help him fight;
He forged ahead and hacked with all his might;
The man he struck was past all surgeons' guile;
Some seven lords he cleft and left to die;
Then young Richier rode up, a gallant knight
Who held the fief of Rinier vale and shire,
And Ybert's flag, for he was of his line
And cousin to his son Bernier alike;
With fifty score he'd come to aid his kind,
And had, at once, claimed many Cambrai lives;
Raoul looked up and longed to end his life;
He seized a spear which proved its worth in time:
He brandished it with all his rage and spite,
Then spurred along the steed he sat astride
And struck the youth upon his shield's device;
Beneath the boss he burst the buckler wide
And ripped the mail upon his coat aside;
From front to rear he rammed the lance's iron
And flung him down one lance's length to die;

The flag he held fell on the ground nearby;
Raoul, at this, was filled with great delight:
"Cambrai!" he cried, "Fight on, good men of mine!
These lying rogues shall not at all survive!"

HE SET THE SPUR once more to his good horse;
He looked ahead and saw the giant John
Who ruled Ponthieu and Ham, the song records;
In all their host was none so big or broad,
Nor was there one Raoul had dreaded more:
No Saxon stood, no giant stood as tall;
One hundred men had fallen to his sword;
Raoul looked up and stared at him in awe;
Upon his steed he towered with such force
That all God's gold would not lure Raoul forth;
Then, suddenly, his memory recalled
The Rending-Iron, his father, brave in war;
And when it did, his own bold valour soared,
And forty men would not have made him pause;
He turned his horse and urged it on towards
The giant John, not flinching now at all;
He lifted up his lance's point and scored
A mighty blow against his buckler's boards;
Beneath the boss he split the shield in four;
The hauberk proved no stronger then than straw:
From front to rear he rammed his lance's point
And flung him down to die in all his gore:
"Cambrai!" he cried with loud and ringing voice:
"Good men of mine, fight on and never halt!
Count Herbert's sons must never leave to vaunt!
While I'm alive, they'll never leave at all!"

20. Raoul's recklessness

RAOUL SPURRED FORTH his worthy horse again;
Upon his shield he struck young Bertolai,
A cousin of Bernier, well-born and bred,
Who held a fort down in the vale of Metz;
He'd struck to ground a mound of Cambrai men
And, striking him, Raoul filled with content;

He smote his shield, which like a mantle rent,
And ripped aside his hauberk at the neck;
From front to back he thrust his pennon, then
Upon the valley's slope he flung him dead:
"Cambrai!" he cried, 'Young vassals, forge ahead!
By God Who saved brave Daniel in the den,
I'll not be caught in any trap they've set!"

THE GROUND WAS SOFT beneath the falling rain;
The mud and slime were thick with blood that day,
And only I know who survived the fray,
Who won, who lost, the slayers and the slain;
Their weary steeds were worn out with the strain –
Their fleetest ones went now at walking pace;
The losses of Count Herbert's sons were great.

THE RAIN CAME DOWN and turned the ground to mud,
And all the steeds, both grey and bay, were stuck;
Ernaut, the count of all Douai, rode up
And saw Raoul of Cambrai in the crush;
I know full well Ernaut reproved him thus:
"By God, you're one I'll never love or trust,
Until you yield your sword or life to us!
You've slain my nephew Bertolai for one;
And Richerin, whom I most dearly loved,
I'll see no more, and countless other ones."
Raoul replied: "Their deaths are not enough!
I'll slay you too, if but the chance should come."
Ernaut replied: "My blade shall drink your blood!
I challenge you, by good St Nicholas;
The right is ours, so help me God above."

"ARE YOU IN TRUTH, the Cambrai Count, you blackguard?
I've not seen you since you began my sadness:
I had two sons, by holy, happy marriage,
And sent them both to Louis' royal palace;
From Vermandois I saw them leave for Paris;
You killed them both in foul and faithless fashion;
You struck no blow but stood and watched them stagger;
I hate you now because you let that happen –
But my good sword will see revenge exacted!

Your head will fall, or so will all my valour!"
Raoul replied: "You pledge yourself too rashly!
If I can't make you eat your words, you braggart,
In Cambrai shire I'll cast no more my shadow!"

WITH TAUNT AND VAUNT both nobles showed no measure;
They spurred their steeds and swiftly came together,
The bolder heart afraid of mortal peril;
Great blows they swapped on shields from Piacenza,
And though their coats proved able to deflect them,
Both knights at once were thrown upon the meadow;
They leapt aloft, so very great their strength was,
And struck again with blows of sharpest metal –
The bolder heart still beating hard with terror.

BOTH COUNTS HAD LOST their stirrups and their steeds;
Raoul, who was a wondrous knight indeed,
Both strong and bold with any arm to wield,
Was first to draw his sword-blade from its sheath,
And struck Ernaut's gold helm a blow so fierce
That all its stones and floral-gold flew free;
Without the coif upon his coat beneath,
It would have split his skull from top to teeth;
The blow slid off towards the left and sheared
One quarter of Ernaut's well-crafted shield;
His hauberk lost two hundred links at least,
And he was stunned and fell upon the field;
His spirits sank to feel his strength grow weak,
And, crying out to God upon his knees,
He said: "Sweet Lord, support me in my need!
I shall rebuild Your church at Origny!
Raoul, in truth, your ardour has no peer;
But with God's help I'll make you suffer dear
For killing those whose deaths so saddened me!"

HOW FINE A KNIGHT Ernaut of Douai was:
Both strong and bold with any arm to clutch!
His heart aglow with courage, he stood up
And, like a lord, a mighty blow he struck
Upon Raoul's embellished helmet's front;
The fleurs-de-lys upon its crest were cut;

Had not the coif beneath it borne the brunt,
From top to teeth he would have split his skull;
Raoul was stunned and felt his strength grow numb;
Then, crying out, he said: "By God above,
Whoever wins, you've struck me well enough!
You want revenge, you say, for those you loved;
I say this not to justify what's done,
But, by the Lord, Who died for all of us –
For good or ill, I never knew your sons."
Raoul was struck so hard by Ernaut's lunge
That all his cheek and mouth ran red with blood;
In Paris, where he'd gone when he was young,
He'd taught the skills of sword-play's cut and thrust:
Against Ernaut he used them all at once.

HOW BRAVE A KNIGHT he was, how great his strength!
He raised his arm and swung his sword's sharp edge
To strike Ernaut upon his pointed helm;
The precious stones and floral-emblems fell;
The blade of steel slid over to the left,
But with great skill he forced it to deflect
And slice Ernaut's left wrist in its descent;
The hand fell down and took the shield it held,
The strap of it still in its clasp well clenched;
Ernaut could see his chance was at an end:
Upon the ground his shield had come to rest,
And from his arm the blood ran out unchecked;
In great despair he mounted horse and fled
Beside the wood which stood there green and dense;
To blame Ernaut would make or show no sense;
In hot pursuit Raoul harassed him yet.

ERNAUT, HE FLED as young Raoul gave chase;
Great terror filled the liege lord of Douai
To know his horse was dropping with the strain,
While Raoul's steed was closing with each pace;
Ernaut resolved to beg the youth for grace,
So on the path he stopped and turned his reins,
Then hailed Raoul in ringing tones this way:
"Have mercy, knight, for our Redeemer's sake!
For any hurt I've done you, scar or scathe,

I yield to you my life and my estates;
I yield Brabant and all Hainault the same,
And any rights my heirs henceforth might claim."
But young Raoul swore nothing would avail
Until the hour he'd slain him with his blade.

ERNAUT, HE FLED as fast as he could go;
Raoul gave chase, with malice in his soul;
Ernaut looked up and saw a sandy slope,
And saw Rocoul, the noble lord who owned
The land near Soissons Vale, both high and low;
A kinsman of Bernier and of Ernaut,
He had with him one thousand knights all told;
On seeing them, Ernaut at once approached;
He urged Rocoul to save him from their foe.

ERNAUT CRIED OUT in very fear of death:
"Rocoul, fine youth, protect me with your men
Against Raoul, who will not let me rest;
He's robbed me of my means of self-defence –
The hand with which I held my shield is cleft –
And now his sword is raised against my neck!"
Rocoul heard this and anger filled his breast:
"Fine uncle, you shall flee no more," he said:
"Raoul shall feel the battle's heat instead;
He'll have a fight as hot as his own head!"

ROCOUL, HE WAS a knight of peerless merit,
Both brave and bold when holding any weapon;
"Fine uncle, you shall fret no more," he pledged him;
With spurs of gold he pricked his horse's belly
And, brandishing his spear, he charged directly
At Raoul's shield and struck it in the centre;
Raoul struck too, a blow so full of menace
It split his shield beneath its boss of metal;
Their coats were strong and took the blows they rendered;
As both men passed their lances broke together,
But neither knight was felled upon the meadow;
On seeing this, Raoul was driven senseless:
He seized his sword with all his strength and temper
And smote Rocoul upon his golden helmet;

The stones were dashed and all its floral-emblems;
Towards the left the blade of steel deflected
And rammed against the sturdy shield and rent it;
The blow drove on and slit his stirrup-leathers;
Below the knee Rocoul's right leg was severed,
And in the sand both foot and spur were buried;
On seeing this, Raoul was filled with pleasure,
And taunted both Ernaut and his young nephew:
"What wondrous work I have for you two wretches,
One-armed Ernaut and you, his one-legged nephew,
As watchman one, and one as gate-attendant,
Both nevermore to venture or have vengeance!"
Rocoul cried out: "That pain is worse than any!
Ernaut, my lord, I thought that I would help you,
But now my aid is of no use for ever."
Ernaut, he fled, in great dismay and terror;
Raoul gave chase with unrelenting frenzy.

21. Raoul's madness

ERNAUT, HE FLED and spurred his steed non-stop;
Raoul gave chase with unrelenting wrath;
He swore to God, Who suffered on the Cross,
That all earth's gold would never turn him from
Pursuit of him and cutting his head off;
Ernaut looked down a slope of sand and rock
And saw again Count Herbert of Hirson,
Count Louis, Samson, and Eudon of Roie,
With Bernier's father, Ybert of Vermandois;
On seeing them, he spurred his stallion on
And sought their aid in his most pressing want.

IN FEAR OF DEATH Ernaut called out again:
"My noble lords, protect me with your blades
Against Raoul and his relentless hate!
So many men of ours his hand has slain
And cleft in hate the very hand this day
With which I held the shield that kept me safe!
He threatens now to hew my head the same!"
On hearing this, Ybert was filled with rage.

YBERT SPURRED ON his noble Gascon steed;
He raised his lance, the pennon flying free,
And struck Raoul on his emblazoned shield;
He pierced the paint beneath its boss of steel
And sheared the mail upon his coat beneath;
He thrust the flag along his ribs – indeed
I'll never know how he survived the spear;
Two score and more came round him then to seize
And slay Raoul or lead him off at least,
But all at once, upon his raging steed,
Red Guerri came with some four hundred peers,
All noble lords and knights of gallant breed;
What pains they took, and gave, to save their liege:
How many men were felled upon the field!

RED GUERRI HAD assembled all his race;
Four hundred strong they were, the record states;
He spurred his steed and in unstinting rage
He struck Bernart of Rethel, wise of face,
Upon his shield with beaten gold inlaid;
Beneath the boss his spear-point burst its way
And ripped apart the byrnie's ancient chains;
From front to rear the spear rammed through his waist
And flung him from his golden saddle slain;
If you had seen the fierceness of that fray!
How many shields and shafts were shorn in twain,
How many coats were cleft and reft of mail,
How many feet and fists were sliced away
And vassals slain, left lain with mouths agape!
The field was filled with all the slain and maimed,
And all the grass with crimson blood was stained;
They saved Raoul, whose face with valour blazed,
And when they did, he made his pleasure plain:
He drew his sword with all his heart and hate
And struck the fight's most fierce and crowded place;
How many souls he severed on that day!
How many wives he widowed with his blade!
As fourteen lords were hastened to their graves,
Ernaut looked on, aggrieved for all their sakes;
He called aloud on God our Saviour's Grace:

"Sweet Mary, Queen of Heaven, blessed Maid:
My mortal life is past all mortal aid,
For there's no drop of mercy in this knave!"
He turned once more in flight along a dale,
And, seeing this, Raoul looked up and chased
Upon his heels in hot pursuit again;
In ringing tones he shouted as he came:
"Ernaut, by God, I yearn to see you slain!
My naked blade has sworn to bleed your veins!"
Ernaut replied, who felt his spirits fail:
"My strength has gone; whatever is my fate,
To fight it now would be of no avail."

ERNAUT, HE FLED, not knowing where to fly,
And so afraid that he could scarcely ride;
He watched Raoul draw nearer with each stride
And cried aloud for pity and for fright:
"Show mercy, Count, if mercy you can find,
For I'm not old – I do not want to die!
I'll be a monk and tend God's holy shrine;
I'll cede to you my lands and all my rights."
"In truth you've done with them!" Raoul replied:
"This sword of mine will sever every tie!
No ground or grass can shelter you this time,
No hand of man, nor hand of God on High,
Nor all the Saints who served Lord Jesus Christ!"
Ernaut heard this and heaved a heavy sigh.

RAOUL THE COUNT was like a man insane:
Those words of his, once spoken, sealed his fate,
For he denied Lord God and Christian Faith;
On hearing this, Ernaut raised up his face
And said aloud, his spirits high again:
"By God, your proud and overweening ways
Have shown me now that you're an apostate!
A rabid dog has no less hope of Grace,
Since you deny our Saviour's power to save!
The ground, the grass, can save us any day,
If God above takes pity on our pains."
He turned in flight and drew his naked blade;
He looked ahead, and when he'd gone some way,

He saw Bernier approaching him in haste,
Most nobly armed and splendidly arrayed
With shield and spear, in helm and hauberk's mail;
On seeing him, Ernaut felt whole again;
A surge of joy went flowing through his veins,
As, spurring forth, he greeted young Bernier
And urged him thus, in their great friendship's name:
"Take pity on me, lad, for our love's sake;
Behold again the justice of Cambrai:
Raoul has cleft my left hand like a knave."
On hearing this, Bernier's bright visage paled;
From head to toe he shook with dread and rage;
He saw Raoul, whose face was charged with hate,
Yet, ere he struck, he tried to speak again.

22. Raoul's death

SIR BERNIER WAS a knight of great noblesse,
Both strong and brave and full of bold prowess;
In ringing tones he called aloud and said:
"Ernaut, my lord, no longer be distressed,
For I will speak with Count Raoul myself."
So, leaning hard upon his horse's neck,
He hurried forth and shouted as he went:
"Raoul, my lord, so nobly born and bred:
You dubbed me knight, I know this very well;
But what a price you've made me pay since then:
You've slain and maimed so many of our best!
You've burned my mother, fair Marsent, to death,
Then with a shaft you struck and cut my head;
I'll not deny you tried to make amends:
You offered me fine horses to forget,
One hundred steeds both strong and fleet of step,
One hundred mules and palfreys finely bred,
One hundred shields and hauberks double-meshed;
I was enraged to see the blood you shed
And went to seek the counsel of my friends;
I still agree with what they told me then:
By St Riquier, if you renew your pledge,
I will accept and pardon your offence –

If you make peace with all of Herbert's men;
I'd gladly bring this fighting to an end
And never seek to harm your cause again;
I'll cede to you my lands and all my wealth,
Each ounce of it and every lance's length!
The dead are gone, we cannot rescue them,
But Lord Raoul, as God will judge us hence,
Have pity now and let your rage relent!
Let be Ernaut, whose spirit you have bled:
Without his hand he stands as good as dead."
On hearing this, Raoul raged more instead;
He lunged so hard his stirrup-irons bent –
His war-horse bowed with all the weight it felt:
"You bastard-knight, your tongue is most adept,
But all your words or wit won't help you hence!
You'll not escape me this time with your head!"
Bernier replied: "You spur me to revenge!
I shall no more bow down to your contempt!"

BERNIER COULD SEE that he was past all measure,
And knew that words would be no use whatever;
So with his spurs he smote his horse's belly
As Count Raoul came charging in against him;
With mighty blows both nobles came together;
Beneath the boss the shields of both were severed;
Bernier was first, whose right was far the better,
And thrust his spear, and all its flowing pennon,
Against Raoul, which stopped him short, I'll tell you;
But in return he took a blow so heavy
That neither shield nor hauberk could protect him;
He would have died, this is beyond contention,
But God and Right were on his side to help him;
The lance-head grazed against his ribs then left him;
Bernier, at this, swung round with all his temper
And struck his sword against Raoul's gold helmet;
Its precious stones and all its floral-emblems
Were cleft away, as was the hauberk's head-piece;
Through brain and brow the mighty blow descended;
My worthy friends, no singer in his senses,
Since mortal things and every man must perish,
Would tell a tale wherein men live for ever:

His head awry, Raoul fell on the meadow;
Count Herbert's sons could not contain their pleasure;
Yet there were some whose joy would soon be ended –
As you will hear, while I am here to tell you!

RAOUL STROVE HARD to rise and stand erect;
He drew his sword and with his utmost strength
He raised it high above his broken head,
Not knowing where to land his blow or when;
His arm came down, he struck the ground instead
And drove the blade right in to its full length;
How hard he tried to raise it even then!
His handsome mouth began to purse and set;
His sparkling eyes grew dark and dim with death;
He called aloud on God Almighty's help:
"God, Judge of all, and Father of all men!
How weak my body grows, how frail the flesh!
Just yesterday no man on earth I met
Could stand against whatever blow I dealt!
Alas the day I took this land in pledge –
This land or that shall never help me hence!
Sweet Heaven's Queen, come swiftly to my help!"
On hearing this, Bernier's own heart was cleft:
His eyes wept tears beneath his shining helm;
In ringing tones he cried aloud and said:
"Ah, Lord Raoul, so brave and nobly bred!
You dubbed me knight – I never could forget;
But I have paid most dearly for the debt:
You burned Marsent, my mother, as she slept,
And struck my head so viciously it bled;
I'll not deny you tried to make amends;
Now all is done; I seek no more revenge."
Ernaut the count cried out at this and said:
"Let this dead man avenge the hand he rent!"
Bernier replied: "I'll not prevent you – yet
Why strike again at one already dead?"
Ernaut replied: "Have I no rage to vent?"
He turned his horse and circled to the left;
He raised his sword in his right hand and then
With all his hate he swung at Raoul's head;
He smote the helm, not sparing him one shred;

He struck clean off the helmet's largest gem,
Then split the coif upon his coat's strong mesh;
In blood and brain he bathed the sword's sharp edge;
Not satisfied, he raised the sword again
And plunged it through his body, end to end;
The Count expired; his soul rose up and left;
Friends, let us pray God took it to His breast.

23. Red Guerri's grief

BERNIER CRIED OUT: "Saint-Quentin and Douai!
Raoul is dead, the liege lord of Cambrai,
By my own hand and by Ernaut's the same!"
As Count Ernaut spurred off upon his bay,
Bernier invoked St Nicholas to say:
"It breaks my heart that he should end this way;
But none, by God, could say I was to blame."
Then Guerri came on his great destrier:
He saw Raoul and staggered in dismay,
Then mourned him thus, or so the song maintains:
"Raoul, fine youth, my heart is filled with pain;
Your murderers have left me naught but hate; .
I'll never rest or sue for peace again
Till all of them are hunted down and slain,
Strung high and hung like common thieves and knaves!
What heavy news to bring the fair Aalais!
How shall I dare to tell her of your fate?"

UPON HIS STEED Red Guerri came, all stunned
To see Raoul lain on the meadow thus;
His nephew's sword was still so tightly clutched
Within his hand that it was hard enough
To prise it from his fingers and his thumb;
Around his neck his painted shield still hung;
Across his breast Red Guerri swooned and slumped:
"Raoul, fine youth, how cursed our coming was!
I see ahead Bernier, the bastard son
Who by your hand in Louis' court was dubbed;
His hand has slain the lord he should have loved!
I'll never rest, I swear by God above,

Until I've cleft his liver and his lungs;
My name's not worth a spur until that's done."

WHEN GUERRI SAW that many men had died,
And watched as death closed up his nephew's life –
Across his brow the brains ran in his eyes –
His grief was such it nearly drove him wild:
"Raoul, fine youth, what shall I do?" he cried;
"By God above, Who bore the Cross's spite,
I'll never cease to harry those whose crime
Has taken you, fine nephew, from my side!
I'll never rest till I have claimed their lives
Or driven them, at least, from shore and shire;
But if I can, I'll seek a truce meanwhile,
To bury you with every due and rite."

HOW FULL OF GRIEF was brave Guerri the Red!
He called aloud: "Sir Peter, come, my friend,
And you Berart, and you Harduin as well!
With every haste ride to my enemies
And seek a truce between us, not to end
Till we have laid my nephew's corpse to rest."
"Most willingly, as always, lord," they said,
And seized their shields and rode off there and then;
They had no need to search for any length:
Upon their steeds they found all Herbert's men
United in delight at Raoul's death –
Though some rejoiced who later would lament;
Red Guerri's men rode up and spoke to them,
Their sombre shields still hung around their necks:
"By St Denis, your laughter is ill-led!
Was not Raoul a lord most nobly bred?
Were not his kin the King of France himself
And Red Guerri, a lord of great noblesse?
Some here rejoice in safety and content,
Who soon will lie of limb or life bereft;
Brave Red Guerri, by whom we have been sent,
Would make a truce, by St Denis, that's kept
Till we have laid his nephew's corpse to rest."
"We grant it," said Ybert, the white of head,
"Though it should last till Judgement Day itself!"

THEY MADE A TRUCE before midday had rung;
Across the field they turned the dead face-up –
And you can guess how deeply they were struck
Each time they found a father or a son,
A nephew, uncle, or companion;
Red Guerri sought his fallen men at once,
But even he forgot his own two sons
For Raoul's sake, so valiant and young;
He saw Big John, who lay there in his blood,
The biggest knight in all of France – he was,
Till slain by Raoul's hand, as I have sung;
He saw him there, and laid his corpse at once
Beside Raoul's, then with a rapid thrust
He plied his sword and opened both men up
And took their hearts, or so the song instructs;
Upon a shield whose gold shone in the sun,
He placed both hearts, and in comparison
Big John's was small, more like a child's it was,
While Raoul's heart outstripped an ox's one –
This famous fact is known to all of us;
Red Guerri wept when he beheld it thus,
And called aloud on all his warriors:
"Come forward, friends, and by Lord God above,
Behold the heart that drove the lord we loved!
Compare it with the giant of Ponthieu's!
My worthy knights, you all have sworn in trust
To fight for me while breath lies in your lungs;
Then you must know our foe are those in front
Who've slain Raoul, the youth I loved so much!
Without revenge, my name's not worth a glove;
Ride back to them, Sir Peter of Artois,
And end the truce; in truth, their hour has come!"
That lord replied: "Most willingly, at once."
He spurred his mount in haste to Herbert's sons
And called aloud to each and every one:
"By St Amant, Red Guerri warns you thus:
The truce is up – with any chance or luck
He'll slay you all for all that you have done."
On hearing this, Count Herbert's men were hushed
With deep dismay, for they had had enough,
And all their mounts had lost the will to run;

The messenger returned across the mud
And Guerri placed his men in ranks at once;
One thousand men would die before the dusk.

RED GUERRI PLACED his men in ranks directly:
Five thousand seven hundred lined the meadow;
Count Herbert's sons alike then reassembled
Some seven thousand men in fighting fettle;
Then Guerri charged, his banner high and steady;
Bernier grew pale and said as he beheld him:
"How wrong we were to grant a truce to Guerri,
For he has joined Raoul's support against us,
Attacking us the way he'd planned already!"
Red Guerri spurred with all his speed and menace
And struck young Hugh, whose visage glowed with merit;
So hard he struck this cousin of young Bernier
Upon his shield he burst it through the centre
And broke the rings upon his byrnie's leather;
From front to rear he drove the spear and emptied
The golden saddle-bows and flung him headlong;
Bernier grew pale and said as he beheld him:
"Ah, Red Guerri, you grizzle-headed devil!
You sought a truce, and when we have accepted,
You break it like a traitor at your pleasure;
But now I vow, before this day has ended,
That countless shields of yours shall split and sever,
And countless souls leave flesh and blood for ever!"
When this was said both armies came together;
Red Guerri drew his sword and proved its temper
In countless blows upon their shining helmets –
From point to hilt its blade was all blood-reddened;
Some thirty men upon his sword-point perished;
Bernier grew pale when he beheld the frenzy
Of Guerri's blade and how it slew so many;
He pledged aloud to Mary, Queen of Heaven:
"Though I should die, wide-mouthed upon the meadow,
Both he and I must fight to end this mêlée."

BERNIER THE YOUTH, in truth, had great prowess;
On seeing Hugh, his cousin, sprawled in death,
Son of his aunt, his anger grew unchecked;

He mourned for him and called his life ill-blest:
"Ah, woe is me! Guerri, you've slain my friend!
A curse on you, you villainous old wretch!"
He goaded forth his long-maned war-horse then
And, seeing this, so did Guerri the Red;
So hard and harsh the shock was when they met
That both their shields beneath the boss were cleft;
Their coats were strong, they neither ripped nor rent;
Old Guerri's lance threw Bernier with its strength,
While he held on around his horse's neck;
How Guerri grinned to see the youngster felled!
He drew his sword and rushed to strike him dead;
He would have hewn his head, I swear it, when
Ybert rode up and saved him with his men;
To see this done, Red Guerri raged again:
"I've borne with you too long, you knave!" he said:
"You slew Raoul, whose life was so ill-blest;
By Jesus Christ our Saviour, I confess
I shall not feel one jot of joy myself
Till I have torn your bare heart from your breast!"

"MY NOBLE KNIGHTS," said Guerri in his wrath,
"I'll never bear the blame or shame hereon
That men of mine did treachery or wrong!
Bernier, you bastard son, where have you gone?
One moment since I had you at a loss:
Towards the sky I sent you, legs aloft!
I would have sent you all the way, had not
Your father come, Ybert of Ribemont."
Red Guerri spurred his steed and hastened off
With brandished spear and streaming gonfalon
To vent his wrath on Herbert of Hirson –
An uncle of Bernier and Herbert's son;
His mighty blow broke through the buckler's boss
And rent his ermine coat and never stopped:
One half of him, his lungs and liver, dropped
Upon the sand, the other half stayed propped
Between the saddle-bows till Guerri knocked
It off the steed whose breed was Aragon;
Then Louis came, together with Eudon,
And Count Ybert, the sons of Vermandois,

And saw him there, the butt of Guerri's wrath;
To see his fate they filled with grief and shock;
Bernier, he spurred his Gascon steed straight off
And smote the shield of Cambrai's Count Faucon;
And Louis rode to strike the knight Samson,
And Count Ybert the Breton Amauron;
Not one had time to rue his sins or wrongs;
Ybert's support grew larger as they thronged
Round Guerri's men, who grew less sure and strong;
Count Herbert's sons had forced them back ere long
Much further than a mighty arrow's shot;
So many knights were slaughtered on the spot
That none could pass, each passage-way was blocked,
And all their steeds, without a lie, by God,
Their fastest breeds, were slowed down to a trot.

RED GUERRI SAW his forces giving way
And felt such grief he almost went insane;
Upon his shield he struck the young Gautier;
Sir Peter of Artois alike was brave:
He struck Gilmer of Poix without delay,
While Harduin of Nivele struck Elier;
No armour made could save them from their fate,
Nor any priest confess their lives' mistakes;
Count Herbert's sons began to win the day,
As Guerri's hopes began to fall and fade;
His noble knights were all cut down or slain
But seven score, and most of those were maimed;
One final time they charged, resolved to pay
The final price and not to run away;
Red Guerri gazed upon the sandy plain
And saw his men as on their backs they lay
In bloody death, and his despair was great;
He blessed them all, his right hand gently raised:
"Alas for you, fine nobles of Cambrai!
Ill-starred indeed your lives I could not save!"
Bereft of sense he wept for pity's sake;
The teardrops fell upon his belted waist.

RED GUERRI STOOD beside the wood, regarding
Those knights of his, just seven score, all charging;

He looked and saw Bernier across the marshland,
And Louis too, on his Castilian charger,
With Count Ybert, who held his father's marches,
And Count Eudon of Roie, and all their army:
"What shall I do," said Guerri, "Heavenly Father?
My enemies are all around in armour;
I see Bernier, the cause of all my heartbreak,
Who slew Raoul, whose visage glowed with ardour;
If I should turn, and leaving all, departed,
Then all the world would scorn me ever after."
With all his strength he spurred his Nordic charger;
And yet, my friends, it was to no advantage:
It stopped, worn out, as soon as it had started.

RED-HAIRED GUERRI was wild with desperation;
He couldn't force his horse to make more pace than
A ploughing-mare, and that would overtake it!
On seeing this, it almost sent him crazy;
He swung to ground at once, and without waiting
For any squire, he took the saddle's weight off
And walked the horse to cool it and to aid it.

RED GUERRI WALKED his horse across the field;
It rolled three times then got back on its feet
With neighs so loud they echoed far and near;
On seeing this, Red Guerri's joy was fierce;
He saddled up, then swung upon the seat
And laid the spur most gently on the beast;
That noble horse set off at greater speed
Than swallows make in flight from tree to tree;
Red Guerri looked and saw Bernier appear:
"You bastard-knight, you're still too far from me!
Your hand has slain Raoul most wrongfully;
He dubbed you knight and loved you as a peer;
But if you come a little closer here,
Then I myself will set your conscience free!"

WHEN YOUNG BERNIER heard Guerri's threats and charges,
He raised his flag and spurred his steed the harder:
"My lord Guerri, you're wrong in this," he answered:
"Raoul the Count was reckless in his ardour,

But I see you more false and evil-hearted;
Since God sent Gabriel to guard the Garden,
No man has lived without the need of pardon;
To make amends I'll go as far as Acre
And be a Templar Knight for ever after."

RED GUERRI SAID: "Your vow is of no use;
While I've a shield and lance both strong and true,
I value it no more than shirt or shoe,
If I can hang you high or run you through!"
The youth replied: "You sing a hollow tune!
"You wrinkled wretch, I'll be too hot for you!
So help me God, my hand will slay you too!"

THE GALLANT YOUTH spurred on his battle-steed,
But it was loath and very slow indeed;
Red Guerri spurred his freshly-rested beast
And struck Bernier upon his sombre shield;
Beneath the boss he cleft the boards and breached
The coat of mail and ripped it like a leaf;
Against his ribs he drove the sharpened spear;
The wonder was it missed the flesh beneath;
Old Guerri's blow was so immense and fierce
It threw Bernier at once upon the field;
How Guerri grinned to see the youngster reel,
And, wheeling round, he charged with sword unsheathed;
In truth, the youth was doomed to die, it seemed,
When suddenly two friends of his appeared,
Two cousins, one Gerard and one Henri,
Who stopped the fight by riding in between;
The sight of them made Guerri's rage increase;
He struck Gerard, whose face with valour gleamed,
Upon his helm adorned with fleurs-de-lys;
The golden orb helped no more than a sheet:
He split the coif of chain-mail triple-weaved
And drove the blade right down to Gerard's teeth,
Then flung him dead from his fine saddle's seat;
On seeing this, Red Guerri grinned with glee:
"Cambrai!" he cried, "There's one has all he needs!
Now where are you, Bernier, disloyal fiend,
You bastard rogue who always run from me?
While you're alive, I'll know no joy or peace."

BERNIER, WHEN HE could see Gerard was slain,
He felt such grief he thought he's go insane;
But then his men arrived in ranks so great
That Guerri's force could see that they must fail;
Red Guerri looked, and almost died of rage;
To hold his men he boldly charged the fray,
Then so did they, with all their heart and hate;
If you had seen those final blows exchanged!
How many shafts and shields they broke in twain!
How many steeds would never neigh again!
How many coats were cleft and reft of mail,
And feet and fists and heads were hacked away!
Two score and more were slaughtered straightaway;
When Guerri knew that if he chose escape,
His knights might live to fight another day,
He grieved aloud for all his army's sake:
"My worthy men, I sorrow at your fate
If, as I must, I turn now for Cambrai!"

WITH SEVEN SCORE Red Guerri left the mêlée;
Ten thousand more had been the sum he'd led there;
He gazed upon the valley where they'd perished
And saw them all, their entrails spilt and spreading –
The jokers there had nothing now to jest at;
And Guerri wept, his face in both hands buried;
He bore away Raoul, his grief relentless,
And as he left along the sloping meadow,
He saw again the dead and hailed them gently:
"My worthy men, I cannot even rest you
In churchyard or in chapel-walls, God help me!
Ah, fair Aalais, what news have I to tell you!"
He wept such tears that all his face was wetted,
And in his breast his heart was full and heavy;
He swore to James, the Saint of Compostella,
That he would not make peace for all Tudela,
Till his own hand had torn out Bernier's entrails.

COUNT HERBERT'S SONS themselves were far from joyful;
Eleven thousand men they had beforehand,
And of these men and local reinforcements
Just fifteen score remained, the song recorded;

Upon their side the losses were enormous,
Their boldest men were stunned at such a slaughter;
Upon the ground they found their brothers' corpses,
And kith and kin all round in mounds appalling;
With great lament to Saint-Quentin they bore them;
And Guerri too rode home, bereft and mournful,
With Raoul's corpse upon a bier before him;
Below Cambrai his men stepped from their horses.

24. Cambrai's grief

THE FAIR AALAIS was in Cambrai her fief;
For three whole days she'd had no food or sleep
For Raoul's sake, with whom she'd disagreed,
And whom she'd cursed, to her regret and grief;
Worn out at last she fell asleep and dreamed
A heavy dream with omens all too clear:
She saw her son returning from the field,
Clad all in silk whose cloth was rich and green,
But which Bernier had rent at every seam;
She woke at once and started up with fear,
Then fled her room and met with Amauri,
A gallant knight whom she had raised and reared;
On seeing him, she cried aloud in tears:
"Where is my son? For God's sake, answer me!"
But he could not, for all of Ponthieu's fief,
For he himself was wounded from a spear,
And, swooning now, he clutched his Arab steed –
A townsman's arms upheld him as he reeled;
When this was said, a shout ran through the streets;
On every side they cried so all could hear:
"Raoul is dead and Guerri has been seized!"

AALAIS COULD SEE their sorrow grow more great,
As noble steeds came through the city-gates,
Their saddles cleft, with nothing left to break,
Bereft of knights who'd left them for their graves;
The aides and squires ran forth to grasp their reins;
Then through the gates rode hoary-haired Gautier,
His old head stooped in sorrow as he came

With young Raoul upon his buckler lain,
And borne by knights, each one well bred and brave;
The took the corpse to St Géri and laid
The body out upon a bier straightway,
About its head four golden crosses placed
And many censers too, of silver made;
The learned clerks did all that appertained;
Before the bier, upon a seat, Aalais
Was filled with grief, with pity and with pain;
Then she addressed her noble knights this way:
"My lords," she said, "you know, the other day
I cursed my son when in a fit of rage;
Yet neither Roland nor Oliver, I say,
Were better men when friends besought his aid;
When I must think that one of them, Bernier,
Has slain him now, I feel my heart will break."
Aalais, she swooned, and women wept and wailed
In pity as they helped her stand again.

RECOVERED FROM HER SWOON, Aalais once more
Wept tears unchecked as for her son she mourned:
"I loved you much," she cried, "my lovely boy,
And brought you up to bear the spear and sword;
My brother dear, who rules all France's soil,
He gave you arms which you received in joy;
A bastard son was knighted at the court
At your request, whom I, alas, had brought
From such neglect that none would help his cause;
How evil he to give me this reward,
To slaughter you beneath Origny's walls!"
Then Guerri came, whose face with valour stormed;
Upon the bier he went to lift the pall,
But, filled with grief, he swooned upon the floor;
Aalais began to censure him with taunts:
"My lord Guerri, the blame and shame are yours!
I placed my son beneath your watch and ward,
And yet you let him leave you when you fought;
What worthy man will trust in you henceforth,
If your own flesh and blood find no support?"
On hearing this, Red Guerri's anger boiled:
He rolled his eyes and scowled upon them all,

His face more fierce than any angry boar's;
He fixed Aalais with such a look, I'm sure
That had she been a man, they would have brawled:
"Aalais," he cried, "have I no loss to mourn?
Because I cared to bring home your son's corpse,
I left behind my own sons whom I saw
Cut limb from limb and slain by Herbert's force;
I thought my heart would break apart, I'm sure."

FIERCE-FACED AALAIS replied: "My lord Guerri,
I placed my son within your care and keep,
Your brother's son, whose love for you was deep;
Yet when you fought you left him faithlessly."
On hearing this, Red Guerri's anger seethed:
"Aalais," he cried, "you're wrong, by St Denis!
I could not halt Bernier the bastard's steel!
Its mortal blow I felt as though on me!
But I made sure his friends paid very dear!"
"God!" said Aalais, "My heart is filled with grief;
If some high count who was a royal peer
Had struck him down, my grief would be less keen;
How did Bernier the Bastard gain the means
To lift his hand against his lawful liege?
Whom shall I now bequeath my land and fief?
I have no heir, I swear it faithfully,
Except Gautier, whose father was Henri,
My daughter's son, a youth of noble breed."
When word was sent this young lad went indeed,
His mother too, and reached Cambrai in brief;
With heavy hearts they stepped down from their steeds;
The boy was brave and fearsome for his years.

THE YOUTH GAUTIER dismounted on the steps;
With joyless heart inside the church he went;
He raised the pall upon the corpse again,
As many lords once more for pity wept:
"I've learnt grief early, uncle," then he said:
"Whoever brought our friendship to an end
Shall fear my hate till I have made him beg,
Or burnt his bones or forced him to have fled;
What grief you've caused, Bernier, you bastard wretch!

You've robbed me of a strong support, whose help
Was there for me and would have served our friends!
But by the Saints who pray to God, I pledge
That if I live to lace my shining helm,
I'll give you not one moment's peace or rest
In any fort or tower of Louis' realm,
Till I have drawn the heart out of your breast
And torn it to one hundred tiny shreds!
And all your friends alike shall meet their death!"
On hearing this, Red Guerri raised his head,
And to himself, so none could hear, he said:
"If this one lives, then we shall have revenge."

THE FAIR AALAIS was lost in grief and rage;
Her daughter came and fell down in a faint,
But staggered up, assisted by Gautier;
In doing this, he knocked to ground the veil
With which the bier that bore Raoul was draped;
He saw once more his uncle's bloody face:
How wide the wound which had destroyed him gaped!
He cried aloud: "How foully was repaid
The debt incurred to you by vile Bernier,
Who in your hall was loved by all and raised!
If God prolongs my life until the day
When I may close the visor's iron and lace
My helmet on and take in hand my blade,
No peace shall reign in his or your domain
Till he has paid most dearly for your fate."
On hearing this, Red Guerri raised his gaze
And spoke aloud these fighting words: "In faith,
I'll gird you with a sword, in Lord God's name!"
Aalais replied, both brave and wise the same:
"My nephew fair, I name you heir this day!"
And so it was, ere long, he ruled Cambrai.

HOW MIGHTILY the knights and barons mourned!
No man could say, however far abroad
He may have been, in countries south and north,
That in his life he ever saw before
Such grief displayed for such a noble lord;

Then Heloise, his sweetheart, who by law
Of true descent held Abbeville, came forth;
How rich and rare a robe this maiden wore –
Pavian silk made up the weft and warp;
Her skin was white as blooms in summer warmth,
Her cheeks as red as roses on the thorn –
Her laughing eyes would light each face they saw;
There never lived a fairer maid, I'm sure;
But now she came inside the church distraught,
And straightaway she cried aloud and called:
"A cruel farewell this is for us, my lord!
My handsome love, kiss your beloved once more!
How evil is the head that shattered yours!
When you bestrode your noble Orcan horse
You were a king who led a mighty force!
And when you girt your bright and shining sword
And laced your helm with its well-strengthened coif,
You were the fairest, finest vassal born
To any shire of France or foreign shore;
Alas, that we should have our love cut short!
Ah, wicked death, how greedy are your jaws,
To have consumed so soon the best of all!
Because I was the sweetheart of your choice,
Until I die I'll love no other lord."
At this she swooned, she was so overborne;
The barons rushed to raise her from the floor.

"RAOUL, MY LORD," once more the maiden said,
"In chapel's ward you swore that we would wed;
My hand was sought by Harduin of Nivelles,
Who holds Brabant, which is a lovely realm;
But I said 'not for all Tudela's wealth';
Ah, holy Mary! Maiden ever-blest,
Why does my heart not break within my breast,
Since he whose wife I was to be is dead?
These tender cheeks shall wither uncaressed,
These sparkling eyes grow dim with hopelessness;
How sweet and dear was my beloved's breath!"
She swooned again, the maiden so well bred;
Beneath her arms they raised her up again.

"AALAIS, INDEED, in our Redeemer's name,"
The maiden said, so fair of form and face,
"I know and see that your own grief is great;
The other day you set events in train
Which will torment and haunt you to your grave;
Now leave your son; I came here straightaway
To see to him, for he is mine, I'd say –
I would have been his wife in thirty days;
My lord Guerri, in our Redeemer's name,
I beg of you, my noble lord, to take
Away at once his coat of Eastern mail,
His helm of green, so bright in sunlight's rays,
His costly arms and armaments the same;
A sad farewell is all I have to take."
And Guerri did the bidding of the maid,
Who kissed Raoul again, and then again,
As front and back she held him in her gaze:
"My dear, sweet love," she said, and wept, "I'll take
No husband else, I swear it, on my faith;
Our loyal love has met a tragic fate!"
They clad and clothed him like a prince and gave
A wealth in coin to prayers for his soul's sake;
The bishop sang a mass and then they placed
Rich offerings beside the altar-rails;
They laid to rest Raoul, Count of Cambrai,
Where many men still know he lies today.

GIRART OF VIENNE

(c.1190–1200)

Introduction

The *chanson de geste* known today as *Girart de Vienne* is preserved in five manuscript copies, four of them part of large cyclic compilations, which date from the middle of the thirteenth to the middle of the fourteenth centuries. The poem itself is considered by most scholars to have been composed towards the end of the twelfth century, and remains of first importance, both historically and artistically, to the study of baronial revolt as it appears in the Old French epics written during the reign of King Philippe-Auguste (1180–1222) of France. *Girart de Vienne* is also a poem of pivotal significance generically, as it establishes and itself forms a link among the three main cycles of contemporary and subsequent *chanson de geste* composition – a feat achieved through the author's highly original and influential recreation of the life, family relationships, and bellicose exploits of a leading Carolingian nobleman.

Gerardus (819–877), count of Vienne in the Dauphiné region of south-eastern France, played an important role in the struggles of the regional barons against the Normans in Provence during the latter stages of the reign of Charlemagne's son, Louis the Pious, and that of his successor King Charles the Bald. In the year 870, Count Gerardus was besieged by King Charles in Vienne, and although he was forced into an eventual retreat, his heroic stand before the king's forces soon made him a legendary symbol of local resistance to the arrogant but weakening Frankish monarchy. From the moment of his exile in Avignon to his death and interment at Pothières – where, as at Vézelay, he and his wife Bertha had founded a monastery – there is evidence to suggest that popular chants lamenting his misfortune and extolling his stubbornness had already sprung into existence. Scholars such as A. Lognon (1878) and R. Louis (1947) have traced the spread of these chants from the foothills of the Pyrenees along the length of the Rhône valley to the northernmost limits of Burgundy. An elaborate oral and written tradition surrounding the count was fostered and developed particularly in the anti-royalist enclaves of Burgundy, Dauphiné and Provence, Gerardus becoming known variously as Girart of Roussillon, of Vienne, and of Fraite (or of Eufrate), as the first epics in his honour proceeded to confuse and then consciously fuse geographical and biographical fact and fiction in their regional exploitation of his name and his fame.

Only one other *chanson de geste* having Count Girart as its central character has come down to us today – *Girart de Roussillon*, thought to have been written around 1150. This poem and other surviving epics which feature him offer substantial internal evidence of narrative composition within a well-established framework of traditional "Girart material" inherited from earlier *chansons de geste*. These works, if ever they were written down, are lost to us now. There is, however, sufficient testimony from the considerable corpus of Old French epic writing which *has* survived, as well as from later collections in verse and prose of the epic materials of French and other European writers, to indicate that during the tenth and eleventh centuries a negative change in Count Girart's legendary status had taken place. It is clear from a perusal of the extant epics that, even as his name had crystallised in the national imagination to become that of a powerful peer of Charlemagne's, so his most famous exhibition of this power had been broken down provincially to a popular representation of Girart as an arrogant baron, whose refusal to render vassalage to his liege lord had led him into treason and even into apostasy. Both the *Chanson de Roland* and the *Chançun de Willame*, two of the oldest extant epics, make mention of Girart as of a figure well know to their audiences. In the *Roland*, as Gerard de Russillon, one of the Twelve Peers of Charlemagne, he is mentioned four times and three times referred to as "the old." In the *Willame* he is known as Girard de Viane and we are told that William's jongleur sings of him and of Oliver "who were his (i.e., William's) relations and ancestors." In *Girart de Vienne* the poet specifies Girart as the uncle of Aymeri (and hence as the great-uncle of William of Orange) and of Oliver and Aude (Roland's betrothed), but his general relationship to these, the most famous and beloved characters in the Old French epic tales, seems to have been well established in the popular mind by at least the beginning of the twelfth century. Radulfus Tortarius (d. 1114) for one, records his knowledge of it. Nevertheless it is this negative conception of Girart as an arrogant and disloyal baron which pervades the mid-twelfth century *Girart de Roussillon*, and the much earlier and now lost major source poem(s) for the present composition, referred to by scholars variously as the *Chanson de Vaubeton*, *Girart de Fraite* or indeed *Girart de Vienne,* the contents of which are known to us through the records of the Scandinavian *Karlamagnús Saga* (1230–50) and the *Chronique Rimée* (c.1260) of Philippe Mousket. The *Chanson d'Aspremont*, probably written in the same decade as *Girart de Vienne* itself, presents the count also in this unfavourable light, as a rebellious baron without a real cause. It is against this background, therefore, that the intent and originality of the author of the present work should be understood and appreciated. He tells his audience (ll.81-89) that although they have heard Girart's story often enough from other singers (meaning doubtless the story of his insubordination), only *he* is aware of its origins "*la començaille dont la chançon oisi.*" It is clear from what follows that his artistic purpose is to cast his rebellious hero in a much more favourable light. He achieves this by giving to his source poem(s) a moral bias that will typify the epics of baronial revolt.

Girart de Vienne is one of the very few *chansons de geste* in which the author identifies himself. In lines 91–101 he gives his name as *Bertrans*, describes himself as a *gentis clers* (noble clerk), and says that he wrote down this song while sitting in a budding grove of the noble town Bar-sur-Aube. The language and dialectic traits discernible in the versification of the poem we possess are indeed those of a cultured Champenois. At the end of his work he announces that his next song will recount the deeds of Aymeri of Narbonne:

> '*Of Hernaut's son I'll tell you next, whose name*
> *Was Aymeri, that hero who became*
> *The liege lord of Narbonne.'*   (ll. 6927-29)

Although such linkage verses are common in works of cyclic compilation, at the initiative of the scribal hand itself, these very words occur in three of the four manuscripts extant, followed immediately by the tale of *Aymeri de Narbonne,* and most scholarly and literary research has concluded that Bertrand de Bar is the author of this second work also. Little remembered today, it does appear that Bertrand de Bar-sur-Aube was a *trouvère* of some celebrity at the turn of the thirteenth century. The author of the *chanson de geste* called *Doon de Nanteuil*, for example, which dates from that period, can best praise another *jongleur* by stating that "he learnt more in a single year than Bertrand de Bar knew in all his life." Although all biographical details concerning Bertrand remain conjectural, two further epics which have come down to us, the *Département des Enfants d'Aymeri* (which forms the first half of the final *chanson de geste* translated in this collection) and one version of *Beuve de Hantone* have also been attributed to him by most scholars. That this noble clerk must have travelled widely in the south of France is indicated not only by his attested fame in Gascony and Provence particularly, but also by the frequency, variety and accuracy of the topographical references to the Midi region which he makes in these works. That he may also at some stage have enjoyed the patronage of the court of Champagne under Henry the Liberal and the Countess Marie has also been considered (Benton, 1959). The poem's most recent editor, Wolfgang van Emden, has indeed suggested a connection between the composition of *Girart de Vienne* (a poem written by a Champagne poet in praise of a Burgundian duke) and the marriage of Henry and Marie's daughter Scholastique to William, the son of Girart I of Vienne and Mâcon. In the political atmosphere of the coalition against Philippe-Auguste, which began in the years 1181–83, it is known that the house of Champagne took several steps to align itself with this contemporary rebel Girart. It is certain that Bertrand's poem, where the responsibility for civil war is thrown back upon an indecisive, ungrateful and vindictive monarch, would have prospered at such a moment.

Artistic Achievement

In *Girart de Vienne* Bertrand de Bar has created an interesting range of psychologically credible characters whose relations, both cordial and hostile, are depicted with considerable dramatic and comic skill. His narrative is well crafted, varied in style, and centred on a fresh and strong conception of the protagonist. The author has also created an influential work that consciously constructs a bridge between the William of Orange and Charlemagne cycle of epics by providing an *enfances* poem which interrelates for the first time the principal characters of each, e.g., Roland and Oliver, Roland and Aude, Charlemagne and Aymeri, and, of course, Girart and them all.

   Bertrand's portrayal of Girart as the ideal liegeman and lord, "well-bred and brave", an epitome of the courtly and the chivalric ideal, is carefully and consistently maintained with deft allusion and open illustration throughout the entire poem. It serves both as the measure against which the qualities of all the other characters are to be judged and as the mainspring of the personality conflicts that advance the composition. Throughout the first and most original section of the poem Girart, although the youngest of Garin de Monglane's four sons, is clearly distinguished as the "first among equals." It is *his* plan, to waylay a Saracen caravan, that subsequently relieves his father's sufferings at the hands of Sinagon the Moor. It is Girart who, in a famous aside, deplores the use of a bow as being a cowardly weapon for knightly combat, and who, as the poet directly says, "brags the least, but achieves the most." When he and his brother Renier are received most condescendingly by the arrogant barons and toadying courtiers in Paris, and when their subsequent services go virtually unrewarded, it is Girart who continually strives to keep the peace between his increasingly insubordinate elder brother and an increasingly arrogant Charlemagne. Girart's steady loyalty to the church and state is contrasted sharply with the emperor's selfish whim in marrying the widowed duchess, whose hand he had promised to Girart, and with the duchess's own opportunistic acceptance of the emperor and the capricious and malicious revenge she exacts upon Girart's forthright probity. The new queen's insulting treachery, when she tricks Girart into setting the kiss of fealty upon *her* foot instead of the king's, is the author's original narrative justification for the legendary hostility between Charlemagne and Girart. It is Charlemagne's unwillingness to punish the queen, which as Girart's liege lord he is bound to do, which puts him fairly and squarely in the wrong.

In the course of the long siege of Vienne, and even more so in the scene which brings it to a conclusion, Bertrand adds subtly and ingeniously to the moral weight of Girart's cause. For example, whereas Charles is intransigent in his demand for Girart's submission and even death, Girart himself is devastated to discover that he has mistakenly struck his liege, the king, during one of the skirmishes outside Vienne. He even sends his beloved nephew Oliver to Charles's camp in the company of Lambert of Berry (the emperor's captured but freely released godson) to justify his right to rule Vienne through hereditary claim – but their embassy is met with royal rebuke and violence. The long single combat which ensues between Oliver and Roland transposes the moral balance of the conflict exactly but not simply onto a physical plane – for the counts are both the human and idealised champions of their respective causes, whose opposition requires a metaphysical resolution, inspired by divine love, to be found. The introduction of young Aymeri as Girart's other nephew provides the narrative with a more down-to-earth avenue of human appeal, and proves the artistic master-stroke of the poem. Firstly, enormous prestige and sympathy are added to Girart's character and cause among the audience through their alignment with the famous father of the even more famous William of Orange and all his much-loved clan. Secondly, the fiery Aymeri's character provides a credible catalyst to the final progressions of the plot. Thirdly, his rash actions illustrate by contrast the virtues of the more temperate Girart. For example, the uncle first urges his ebullient nephew to serve in Charles's court, as he himself had done, affirming:

> *"You could not serve in any finer place*
> *Than Charles's court, whose honour is so great,*
> *And who has raised us all through his own fame*
> *And through his gifts of lands and great estates."* (ll.1690-93)

Then it is Aymeri who, discovering the insult of the queen's deceit, and reacting most violently in its revenge, jeopardises the reconciliation that Girart eventually seeks. He slays a royal office-bearer and urges the slaughter of Charlemagne, when the emperor is caught at last in a clever ambush. When this, the real climax of the poem, is reached, it is Girart the rebel whose personal solution to the secular struggles between Paris and the provinces most closely resembles the divine resolution proffered earlier. By submitting the personal compromise of a vassal wronged as a challenge to the honour of a monarchy at fault, Girart gains the ultimate moral victory over the king. To the hot-headed Aymeri's pleas for revenge, in the presence of all, he replies:

> *"May God forbid the deed!*
> *No King of France shall be ill used by me!*
> *If he forgives my part in what has been,*
> *I'll be his man and hold his land in fief;*
> *If he will not, by blessed St Maurice,*
> *I'll set my sights on Arab lands and leave;*
> *I'll bear the blame but men shall lose esteem*
>   *For Charlemagne's own honour."* (ll. 6421-28)

Neither that of the idealised patriarch of the earliest epics, nor that of the burlesque greybeard of several later poems, the character of Charlemagne in *Girart de Vienne* is carefully constructed to serve as both a functionary and foil to that of Duke Girart himself. As a result, the portrait of the emperor which gradually emerges in the narrative is one of the best of him in Old French epic writing, presenting a much more credible mixture of human strengths and weaknesses against which those of Girart can be weighted and consequently weighed. He is shown to be both majestic and foolish, an unwavering ruler of many but an unstable wooer of one – generous and mean, conciliatory and antagonistic, humorous and sombre. He is openly brave and caring for his beloved queen and nephew Roland, while the former deceives and embarrasses him and the latter blames him for starting the war with Girart and for showing poor military tactics in its conduct. On the other hand Girart's wife, Guibourc (true, no doubt, to her prototype and namesake Orable/Guibourc, wife of William of Orange), is a reliable partner, religious, loyal, supportive and enterprising, while his nephews Oliver and Aymeri are unwavering and uncritical in their uncle's support. Both Charlemagne and Girart are high-hearted and high-handed in their dealings with each other and with others in their courts, but it is Charles's breach of faith, his broken promise of the duchess's hand, and even more his failure to avenge his liegeman's humiliation at her hands, which prove and move the moral balance of the pair at war.

Some of the finest and funniest verses of Bertrand's poem are those in which he relates his version of the *enfances* or youthful exploits of several of the genre's most famous individuals or pairs. Part of his artistic purpose in doing this lies undoubtedly in his desire to produce a work which might stand at the narrative heart of the genre's cyclic productions by interrelating the principal characters of its three established *gestes*, as expressed in his famous prologue. These narrative excursions are equally a means of deepening and lightening the basically simple and sombre texture of his work, to widen its appeal by introducing some traditional and original motifs and episode of humour, romance, and social criticism. The ready fists and tongues of Garin's sons, for example, particularly those of Renier and Girart, shock both the refined sensibilities and physical senses of Charles's Parisian courtiers. Their regional pride and much of the spirited sarcasm with which they express it produce moments ranging from slapstick comedy to anti-élitist diatribe, both extremes balanced by the egalitarian notion found time and again in the *chansons de geste* of this era, that:

> *'The heart's not clad in grey or ermine clothes*
> *But in the breast where, heaven-blest, it grows.'* (ll. 607-8)

Considerable generation-gap humour is present in many of the dialogues between Girart and his nephews Aymeri and Oliver, and between Charlemagne and his nephew Roland. The teasing of the younger heroes by their elders, especially in the latter relationship, where the actions and burgeoning affections of the maiden Aude are involved, presents some of the best *enfances* comedy in the entire genre, and certainly the most cleverly expressed. The first flowering of Roland's affections for the siblings Aude and Oliver is equally well wrought in dialogue that is both graceful and tongue-in-cheek.

Around such well-known and well-drawn protagonists Bertrand describes only a small circle of honourable and dishonourable minor characters to relieve them or set their actions into relief. Their cameo appearances form brief diversions and simple subplots at regular intervals in the story. Some are traditional anonymities such as unhelpful porters or villainous robbers, while others are famous personalities such as wise Naimon and bitter Ganelon, both acting in type. The original creations of the Duchess-Queen, Count Lambert of Berry and Joachim the Jew, are convincing embodiments of a woman scorned, an honourable enemy, and an honourable non-Christian, appealing as real people, not just as types. Bertrand's other original characters in *Girart de Vienne*, his hero's father Garin of Monglane, his brothers Miles of Puglia, Renier of Geneva and Hernaut of Biaulande, and his wife Guibourc, serve two distinct but related narrative functions. Firstly, by aligning Girart ever more closely with the honour and fidelity attached in all the Old French epics to the clan of William of Orange (Hernaut, for example, is presented as the father of Aymeri and thus the grandfather of Count William, making Duke Girart William's great-uncle), they each become symbols of his moral justification. Secondly, they serve the narrative purpose of linking the two major epic song cycles, when Renier of Geneva is introduced as the father of both Oliver and Aude.

Bertrand de Bar's greatest artistic talent, it is generally agreed, lies in his ability to present clashes of will and feeling with genuine psychological insight and dramatic skill. Conflict through direct dialogue is the major narrative technique of the earliest and most 'epic' *chansons de geste*. The poet excels in presenting this traditional skill within a more 'courtly' framework, through the verbal media of violent quarrels, protests, justifications, arrogant rejoinders, sarcastic insults, and through more tender exchanges of pity, friendship and love. He is also more skilful than many of his contemporaries in the presentation and valid participation of female protagonists in these 'heroic' works. The scenes in which the Duchess-Queen debates her feelings for Girart and Charlemagne, and in which Aude analyses her fears for her brother's safety when he must fight her lover, are written with a subtlety which is rare, if not unique in the genre's extant productions. The heightened importance and participation of female characters in the plot overall are features common to most epics of this era, as are the depiction of supernatural forces and the significant role of visions and dreams. Such elements betray the genre's attempt to compete with the more elaborate and sophisticated style of the increasingly popular *romans courtois*.

The versification techniques exhibited in *Girart de Vienne* are likewise of a type and talent common to many epics in French written towards the end of the twelfth century. Although the emotive qualities of the oral-based epic formulas, when used in descriptions of battles, knights and weapons, are still evident in the lengthy and ritualised accounts of duel and warfare, the strong dramatic possibilities of the old, short, assonating *laisses* are virtually abandoned in these later narrative poems. Here rhyme, of a limited and banal sort at that, replaces assonance and the *laisses* lengthen, even as the work progresses.

One small but significant feature of the versification of *Girart de Vienne* in which Bertrand de Bar displays extraordinary skill is in his use of the so-called *vers orphelin*, the shortened, unrhyming line which terminates each *laisse*. A common feature of late twelfth century *chansons de geste*, this stylistic feature is used variously in the present poem to sum up a proceedings, locate an action, highlight an irony, underline a sarcasm, establish a conflict, to censure conduct or to praise it.

Similar *vers orphelins* are often used at the end of consecutive verses to counterpoint actions, establish oppositions, underline hatreds or to consolidate loyalties. Uniquely, Bertrand de Bar uses them to adopt an ironic attitude to some of his characters, to point out to his audience some tragic or comic contrast both unperceived and unperceivable by the protagonists themselves. Most frequently, however, the author openly employs the *vers orphelin* to establish and embellish the basic opposition between King Charlemagne the Frenchman and Duke Girart of Vienne and to manipulate his audience's sympathies for both.

Sources and Influences

The most obvious source for the overall narrative conception of *Girart de Vienne* is the *Chanson de Roland* itself. Indeed, all of the earlier poem's most salient features of plot (the defeat at Roncesvalles), relationships (the friendship of Roland with Oliver and with the latter's sister, Aude) and character (reckless Roland, courteous Oliver, jealous Ganelon), are so often interwoven, either through allusion or lengthy illustration, with the description of Girart's struggle with Charles, that it seems evident that Bertand de Bar was attempting, in the present poem, to write a prequel to Turoldus's masterpiece. That he should have achieved this through the interrelation of the two major song cycles of his time, and furthermore, brought about their fusion through a totally fresh conception of an infamous rebellious baron, Girart of Vienne, making his new poem itself a source for so many subsequent Old French epic narratives, is also, surely, a masterly accomplishment.

Despite the undoubted breadth of invention displayed by Bertrand de Bar in his desire to present a moral re-evaluation of Girart de Vienne's relationship with the King of France, it is still clear that his poem is a composite work, incorporating many elements of earlier 'epic Girart material' preserved in folk-imagination or in actual written chant. The poet himself relates on three occasions (ll. 81–89, 107–109, and 6562–69) that his purpose is to reveal only the unknown beginning and ending of an earlier popular tale. That the long section dealing with the actual siege of

Vienne owes much to details from traditional sources is confirmed by internal differences, discrepancies, and downright contradictions within the major sections of the poem, and between them and later compilations, such as the *Karlamagnús Saga* and the *Chronique rimé*, which preserve versions much closer to the actual source poem(s) of *Girart de Vienne*. The events and people crucial to the poet's new purpose dominate the work's first one thousand or so lines, and some of them – Garin, Miles, the Duchess-Queen, the kissing of the latter's foot – are completely absent from the siege section of the text. Again, in the opening and final stages much emphasis is laid on the fact that Girart is *given* Vienne in fief and that he remains therefore a vassal of his equally bound liege lord King Charles; yet, in the central section of the poem, several characters, including Girart himself, maintain that Vienne is an *allod*, land won from the Saracens by Girart's ancestor Beuvon the bearded, and which Girart therefore rules independently and by hereditary right. It is interesting also that Roland and Oliver appear only in this second, less original part. Van Emden has in fact suggested that their famous duel and reconciliation are patterned on a similar confrontation between Count Oliver and the pagan Fierabras highlighted in the popular *chanson de geste* bearing the latter's name, which was written around the year 1170. Two further significant narrative details of *Girart de Vienne* that can be found in the earlier Old French epic called *Girart de Roussillon* are the loss to the hero of a promised bride and a decisive battle halted by divine intervention. The episodes of the quintain, the capture of the courtly Lambert of Berry, and Oliver's embassy to King Charles, have each been identified as borrowings from an earlier poem (now lost) transmitted to us through the record of the Norwegian saga.

In all the contemporary or later extant *chansons de geste* which feature, to a greater or lesser extent, the imposing personage of Girart de Vienne – most notably the stirring *Chanson d'Aspremont* (c.1190), the mid-thirteenth century *Auberi le Bourgignon*, and the expansive, late-thirteenth century Franco-Italian epic called *L'Entrée d'Espagne* – the duke is represented as the disloyal, arrogant baron of the source poem(s). A similar view of him is taken by the historical compilation of Jean d'Outremeuse (d. 1400), the *Myreur des Histors*, where Girart de Vienne, Girart de Fraite, and Girart de Roussillon are considered to be three different people, and by the Italian Renaissance work called the *Viaggio di Carlo Magno in Ispagna*. However, several of Bertrand de Bar's narrative innovations in *Girart de Vienne* reappear also in these and other works of the epic genre. For example, the *Chanson d'Aspremont* makes mention of four brothers called Hernaut, Milon, Renier, and 'Girardet le menor,' all sibling names originating in the present poem. The epics called *La Chevalerie Ogier, Renaud de Montauban, Les Narbonnais, Anseis de Cartage,* and *Le Moniage Guillaume* (the so-called second version) likewise name one or more of the brothers given to Girart by Bertrand de Bar. The several manuscripts preserving late twelfth century rhyming versions of the *Chanson de Roland* not only make much greater allusion to the figure of Girart de Vienne himself but also to certain relationships of his which are established only in Bertrand's work, e.g., his guardianship of the maiden Aude, she being his niece, and his particular affection for his brother Hernaut de Biaulande. Above all, there are so many narrative allusions and recapitulations to the text of *Girart de Vienne* to be found in the succeeding copies of *Aymeri de Narbonne,* and so many shared stylistic features, that not only are common authorship and consecutive recital considered almost certain, but also a conceptual companionship as prequel and sequel respectively to the genre's most celebrated and enduring heroic tale.

The continuing popularity of Bertrand's *Girart de Vienne* both in France an further afield is attested by the considerable number of prose adaptations which have survived either in fragment (e.g., a Dutch version of the thirteenth century) or in full (e.g., the fourteenth century Arsenal 3351 manuscript, the quasi-historical *Croniques et conquestes de Charlemaine* of David Aubert, and the several *Garin de Monglane* incunabula of the fifteenth, sixteenth and seventeenth centuries). The legend of Girart de Vienne, like that of Roland himself, enjoyed a revival among nineteenth-century poets of the Romantic school. In his 1811 edition of *Altfranzösische Gedichte* the German scholar and poet Ludwig Uhland faithfully and elegantly translates from *Girart de Vienne* the first meeting of Count Roland and Aude. In the section called *Le Mariage de Roland* of his own epic cycle *La Légende des Siècles,* first published in 1859, Victor Hugo recreates the celebrated duel between Oliver and Roland in lines very similar to those of Bertrand de Bar.

The contemporary and lasting influence upon the whole *chanson de geste* genre of Bertrand de Bar's inventive genius and artistic achievements as witnessed in *Girart de Vienne* both were and remain immense. His poem stands at the crossroads of Old French epic writing, interrelating with skill, humour, and grace the legendary protagonists of the three major heroic song cycles of its time, its prologue introducing a narrative cohesion respected by all subsequent poets and scholars of the genre.

GIRART OF VIENNE

Prologue

FRIENDS, WILL YOU HEAR a worthy tale that tells
Of lofty themes and deeds of great prowess?
A better one could not be sung or said;
My song is not of pride or foolishness,
Of treachery or of deceitfulness,
But of a clan whom may Lord Jesus bless,
As fierce a breed as ever yet drew breath;
At Saint-Denis' great abbey-church, my friends,
It's written down, don't doubt me now or hence,
Inside a book, a very ancient text,
That in old France three clans surpassed the rest –
I do not think that any will object;
The best contained the kings who ruled the French,
And after that the one of greatest strength
Sir Doon reared, of hoary beard and head,
Lord of Maience, whose valour was immense;
His sons and heirs were fierce and fearless men
Who could have ruled the whole of France itself
And been the first in chivalry and wealth,
If pride and spite had not ruled all of them;
Of this same line, wherein such evil bred,
Was Ganelon, who by his treason led
Almighty France to grief and great distress:
Whose treachery unbounded doomed to death
On Spanish soil, among the Saracens,
    The Peers Twelve of France.

IN COUNTLESS SONGS, my friends, you've heard the tale
Of how the line of Ganelon contained
High knights untold of bearing bold and brave,
Both fierce and proud, of great renown and fame;

295

They could have held all France beneath their sway,
If pride and sin had not held them enslaved;
But pride it is, don't doubt of what I say,
Which brings to grief so many of the great:
As were, in truth, those angels by God's grace,
Who through their pride at last were cast away
From Heaven's hall to bide inside Hell's Gate,
Where evermore they suffer grief and pain;
Through arrogance and through their foolish ways
They lost their place in Heaven's blest domain;
And Ganelon's proud clan was just as they,
Who could have been so rich and so well-famed,
If pride and sin had not flowed in their veins;
Of such a man the second clan was made,
    That never did but evil.

THE THIRD DESCENT they praised in times of yore
Was Garin of Monglane's, that fearsome lord;
And to his line, which I can witness for,
There never was a cur or coward born,
No lying rogue or renegade at all;
They were, indeed, both true and wise in thought,
And very brave and noble warriors
Who never harmed a King of France's cause;
They strove instead to aid their rightful lord
And to increase his fame at every point;
They battled hard to spread the Christian Law
And to expel and quell the Pagan hordes;
Four sons were born of fearsome Garin's loins,
And braver knights there never were before;
In one whole day I never could record
The tally of the merits of all four;
The oldest son, I tell you nothing false,
Was fierce Hernaut, the ruler of Biaulande;
The second son, as I have been assured,
Was Miles of Puglia, who won such laud;
Renier was third, who ruled Geneva's shores,
And brave Girart, our hero, was the fourth;
No man could plead a case for finer lords:
They never earned reproach for any fault;
Yet ere these four were made full knights at all,

While they were all still young, unproved and raw,
Misfortune struck their father with great force:
For Sinagon, a hostile, heathen Moor,
Whose hand ruled Alexandria's great port,
Attacked their land, to win its wealth in war,
To scorch its fields and torch its towns and forts;
Outside their gates they soon had next to naught,
Unless they fought to fetch it with their swords;
God help them all, whose Judgement day will dawn,
    With such a threat to counter.

SO MANY TIMES you've heard the stories told
Of Duke Girart, Vienne's brave lord of old,
And Hermenjart and Aymeri the bold;
But all the bards who've served you leave unknown
The best there is to tell about all those;
For they don't know the story I'll disclose:
The origin from which their story flows –
Who Girart was, his father and his folk;
But I shall tell, who know the truth alone;
Lord Garin of Monglane, as now you know,
Was father to four sons who all were bold;
As knights there were none better to behold;
Yet ere their arms or armour were bestowed
Or any wealth or land to call their own,
Great poverty drove all of them from home,
As you will hear, unless you let me go!
The month was May, with warmth and peace aglow,
The grass all green and buds upon the rose;
Inside the walls of noble Bar-sur-Aube
Bertrand sat down, a gentle clerk, and wrote
This story down within a budding grove;
When leaving church, one Thursday, he'd approached
A pilgrim there, a hale and hearty soul,
Who'd prayed in praise before St James's bones;
Returning through St Peter's church in Rome,
This man it was who told Bertrand the whole
Of all he'd heard and learnt upon the road
About Girart, his struggles and his woes,
    Before he owned Vienne.

1. How Garin of Monglane bewailed his lot

ONE EASTER DAY, a joyful feast decreed
By Lord our God for man on earth to keep,
A day which fills each Christian with good cheer,
Old Lord Garin, of hoary head and beard,
Was at Monglane, his strong and wealthy seat,
Beside his wife, for whom his love was deep,
And with his sons, of mighty merit each,
Lithe-limbed and strong, and very brave indeed;
Yet his content was ruined by this grief:
Between them all they had no bread to eat,
No drop of wine nor any salted meat;
Two peacocks and three cakes were all their means
Within that hall of vaulted walls and steep;
Of these their cook and servants made a meal;
In all Monglane they owned no more than these:
One battle-steed, one Syrian sumpter-beast,
Three buckler-shields and three well-burnished spears;
No other wealth was left, nor property;
Garin looked round and, sick at heart, he grieved
And groaned aloud and wept most bitterly;
The tears fell down upon his hoary beard;
Hernaut looked on and anger burned his cheeks;
He cried aloud and could not hold his peace:
"For Jesu's sake, what causes you such grief?
I see you weep, which seems most strange to me;
Don't hide it, lord, but tell me why you weep;
By St Elijah's bones, if you won't speak,
My life henceforth will know no joy or peace,
    For I would deem it treason."

"MY NOBLE LORD," his son Hernaut implored:
"So help me God, the giver of our laws,
 I see you weep and I would know the cause;
Don't hide it, lord, or I shall be distraught;
My life henceforth will know no peace or joy."
His father said: "My son, I'll tell you all;
So help me God, our everlasting Lord,
 It is for you that I am so forlorn;

To see my sons in clothes so drab and worn,
You seem no more than any townsman's boys,
Of lowly rank, of means and manner small;
Son, don't you think that I've a right to mourn,
To see you all, despite my rank, so poor?
All this the Pagan Sinagon has caused,
Who has destroyed our manors and our forts
And held us back from our own land by force,
So we receive no wealth of worth at all;
Our food supplies have dwindled down to naught;
We've nothing left to last us three days more,
    And for our lives I'm fearful."

2. How Garin's wealth was restored

"MY NOBLE LORD," said wise Hernaut, "to grieve
So much for that is shame enough for me!
There's none on earth, if they persist in grief,
Whom their own kin won't hold in less esteem;
And what is more, I'll tell you how I feel:
So help me God, such folk who always grieve
At present woes and speak of future ease,
Will not survive as far as St John's feast;
No city wall or fort allays their fear,
Nor any towns at all worth twopence each;
No vair, no grey or ermine cloaks they'll keep;
The faithless Jews in this way met defeat
On Abilant's hot sands in Egypt's heat,
When God above in love had seen their need:
For days he fed them Heaven's bread to eat;
But they got naught when they lost their belief,
Instead they lost His helping hand, and He
Was right to stop, since they all disbelieved;
And so it is with wicked folk and weak,
Who do not love Lord God or heed His creed
To save themselves, survive or thrive indeed;
And Easter Day it is, a joyous feast,
When both the high and humble make good cheer;
Be happy, then, and let us share our meal,
For no one knows tomorrow's woe or weal."

"Son," said Garin, "there's wisdom in your speech;
A priest himself could not so well have preached!
God strike me down, if any more I'll weep."
They washed their hands and then they took their seats –
Though not for long – so little did they eat;
When all were done, each son made haste to leave –
The oldest one, Hernaut, upon a steed,
The other three content upon their feet;
They took their bows, with arrows sharp and keen,
For none of them had knighthood's arms to wield;
Outside the hall they hurried with all speed;
Before its walls a river ran whose stream
Was very fast – both broad enough and deep
To carry boats and barges to their feet;
Before the war brought by the Moor emir,
How rich Garin and all his clan had been!
Girart it was, that day, who from the East
Beheld a band of Saracens appear
Along the road they stood on and between
Two rising hills, beside a row of trees;
With treasure trussed, they drove some twenty beasts,
    Ill-timed from Spain arriving.

AS EACH OBSERVED these mules upon the road,
With one accord they planned a daring stroke;
Girart, who was the youngest of them, spoke:
"I'll not conceal my thoughts from you – behold
Those sumpter-mules approaching us! I know
That each is piled with silver and pure gold!
Garin, our lord, is in great need of both,
Our mother too, with no more food at home;
This day I saw their teardrops freely flow,
And we must strive to end their bitter woe!
Let's win this wealth and have it for our own."
Hernaut replied: "Let all of them approach,
And by the Saint that pilgrims seek in Rome,
I'll cleave the first as soon as he draws close!
From front to back I'll drive my arrow's bolt."
But Girart said: "Renier, I hope he won't!
Like common boys, if we use archers' bows,
We shall be held in nothing but reproach;

But if we use our fists or solid poles,
Then we can show our strength and courage both;
A curse on him who shoots upon his foe;
A cur alone is loath to fight up close!"
Then Miles spoke up, both proud of heart and bold:
"I too won't let my thoughts lie undisclosed:
I'll challenge both their leaders on my own!
If I'm too weak to meet and beat them both,
So help me God, then I'm not worth a groat!"
Renier spoke up: "My lords, if I alone
Can't cope with three of these pernicious folk,
A curse on me and may I never hope
For food and drink from any noble host!"
"I'll take the rest," said fearsome-faced Hernaut;
"Men!" said Girart, "You'll leave me one, I hope!
If I can meet and beat just one of those,
So help me God, my own renown may grow!"
When this was said, those sumpter-mules approached,
Impelled and poked by good-for-nothing rogues;
Hernaut looked up and hailed them in these tones:
"You sons of whores, halt there your heathen bones!
You have to stop until you pay our toll!
You cannot leave until you pay what's owed!
I want one half in silver or in gold
Of all the wealth that's in your sumpters' load –
No, I'll not give you half, I'll have the whole!
We'll take the lot, whoever grieves or groans."
On hearing this, the heathens' anger glowed
And one replied, who made the fiercest show:
"A curse on him who'd give you that, and woe
To any man who dares to strike a blow
Or take from us the smallest coin we own –
No fort of his will boast a standing stone!
And once we take the man himself in hold,
He'll find his neck suspended from a rope!"
Hernaut heard this and in a rage half-choked
He ran at him, his manner brave and bold;
His left fist struck the villain on the nose
And then his right joined in with such a blow
He snapped his neck right back and broke the bone;
Against the ground he laid the villain low;

His brothers ran at once to join Hernaut,
And went to strike, with no more challenge thrown,
The very first each met of all those rogues;
They flung them dead upon the open road;
The youngest one, Girart, was nothing loath;
He bragged the least, but he achieved the most:
Beside his feet he laid two villains low;
They slew them all and laid the cowards cold,
Then took in hand their sumpters which they drove
Along the road, well-guided by their goads,
Towards Monglane and through its gates of old,
Not stopping once until they reached their home;
Garin looked out and gladness filled his soul;
He ran outside to kiss and hold them close,
      Now all once more were wealthy.

3. How Garin's sons departed from their home

NOW GARIN'S HALL was rich and well supplied
With noble coins and all that coin could buy,
They each returned, those noble household knights
Who'd gone their ways about the countryside;
When Wednesday came and Easter time was by,
His noble sons, not wasting any time,
Stepped out from church when Mass was said and signed,
And, as a band, decided with one mind
That they would leave their famous town behind
To win domains and fame in foreign climes;
The eldest one, Hernaut, of valour high,
Called on Garin, whose beard was tousled white,
And on his wife, the duchess shrewd and wise:
"My lord," he said, "and mother fair and fine:
Your home is here among the heathen tribes,
And all around they've scorched your land with fire;
But old Monglane was so well built betimes
That no assault or siege can harm its might;
Thank God above, Who made the dew and sky,
We've brought to you this morning such supplies,
Reclaimed from those who are the foes of Christ,
That you can live one year upon and thrive;

With your consent my brothers three and I
Will leave to win our spurs in foreign climes."
"Good father, lord, it's true enough," said Miles,
"I cannot hide my wish and my desire
To ride for Rome; as soon as I arrive,
I'll pray its Saint to guard and bless my life
With land and fame to match my heart's desire!"
His words were true, not one of them a lie –
For blest he went and won Apulia's shire,
Romagna and Palermo's wealth besides,
    Becoming Duke of Sicily.

THE BROTHERS BROOKED no more delay or let;
They mounted horse and made no more requests;
To all their friends, in tears, they bade farewell,
And noble Duke Garin made great lament,
As did his wife of face so clear and fresh;
Hernaut set out and reached Biaulande at length,
A noble town of much renown and wealth;
On riding in, he found his uncle dead,
Who'd ruled the town and its surrounding realm;
Good people all, God bless you, hear me well!
Hear what befell that worthy youngster then:
He took a wife of very high descent –
Her father was a duke of great noblesse,
Who held Marsone in fief, as I know best;
And in her womb Count Aymeri was bred,
Whose noble clan outshone all of the rest:
    I sing of its beginning.

NOR RENIER, NOR GIRART, the youngest born,
Sought any squire or men to serve their cause;
Each mounted up a mule and, setting forth
Upon their way, they rode without a pause;
Up countless hills they went, through many a gorge,
Through many a wood and many a watercourse
To reach Vienne, wherein they called a halt
And sought repose, those young, courageous lords;
A townsman there, Hervi, as he was called,
Gave rooms to them beside the wide Rhône's shore,
And richly too he served them from his board

With vension and wine and mead galore;
When this was done they took their ease outdoors
And saw Vienne, the city and its fort,
Whose marble walls were very wide and tall;
Girart spoke forth, whose heart was strong and sure:
"Renier, how fine this city is!" he called:
"I've not seen one as fine as this before!
This city's liege must be a mighty lord:
With nothing else he'd still be far from poor!"
On saying this, they turned around once more;
Their beds were made, so with the greatest joy
They both retired and slept until the morn;
They took their leave as soon as day had dawned,
Commended by their host to God the Lord,
Whose Son was born in Bethlehem for all;
They mounted mules and both of them set forth
Upon their way without delay or pause;
I'm loath to sing of everything they saw
Until they came to Cluny's cloister-walls:
They lodged that night in Abbé Morant's hall,
And ate and drank most nobly at his board;
Whatever dish they wished for they enjoyed;
That worthy priest received them with great warmth,
And when they'd done, he looked at them once more
And then he asked: "Where have you come from, lords?
Whose sons are you? Don't keep me uninformed!
And if you both are squires in service, or
Knights newly-dubbed in search of lord and court,
Then tell me so, if you don't mind of course!"
Good Renier said: "My lord, I'll tell you all –
To tell the truth to trusty men's no fault!
We both are sons of worthy Garin's loins,
Lord of Monglane, in Gascony the broad;
With Pagan tribes each day he wages war;
Within his town, behind it and before,
He lies besieged by Sinagon the Moor;
We ride for France and Charles the Emperor;
With his assent, we'll serve him and his cause;
One year or two, or three indeed or more,
    We'll serve beneath his banner."

4. *How Renier and Girart approached the King*

ABBÉ MORANT, with goodness in his soul
Heard Renier speak until his tale was told,
Then answered thus in kindly, loving tones:
"My sons, by God, I see that you are both
Of noble clan with honour in its bones!
How many times I've heard its deeds extolled!
But tell me this, which truthfully I'd know:
Have you as yet been dubbed as knights or no?"
"My lord, we've not, through poverty alone,
Which drove us both to leave our father's home,
That noble knight whose blood flows in our own."
On hearing this, the abbot's pity showed;
At once he bade his seneschal approach
And said: "My friend, do not delay, but go
And fetch these two a change of shirt and hose;
For friendship's sake let both of them be clothed
And shod so well that their good breeding shows
And earns respect wherever they may roam."
"As you decree," said he, and bowing low,
He went and brought each item he was told
So both the boys were freshly shod and robed:
"God," said Girart, "majestic Lord of Hosts,
We two are now both rich and wealthy folk!
Good Abbot, may St Peter bless your soul
For these fine goods which you have loaned us both:
And on my word, by God, it is a loan,
For if I live, I'll pay back all I owe!"
When this was said two beds were made, and so
When evening came, they slept in peace on those
The whole night long, until the bright dawn broke;
When both arose they donned their noble clothes
And sought their leave, then mounted mules to go,
Then started out upon the metalled road;
Beyond Palatre's ford they passed through Beaune
And then Dijon, so strongly built of stone,
And after that through Châtillon the old;
Through Burgundy, not halting once, they rode
With firm intent, like vassals true and bold,

For Paris bound, that wondrous town and throne;
They sought the King, yet he was not at home
But gone to Rheims, that much the pair was told;
They waited days until their patience broke
And they left town for Rheims upon their own;
And Charles was there, the monarch crowned in gold,
So there they stopped and, lodging, sought repose;
You've heard, my friends, and it's the truth I know,
That poverty is held in great reproach;
For one whole week Girart and Renier both
Remained at Rheims but didn't once behold
The King at court, nor share his board or bowl;
When Sunday came, and once the sun arose,
So did Girart and hailed his brother so:
"Good brother, lord, speak up and don't be loath!
We've been here now for seven days all told
And haven't heard one word from Charles the bold,
Nor been to court or seen a courtier close,
Nor gained a groat, nor any grain of oats!
If we remain within this town, I know
We'll soon have naught that we can call our own,
No padded mules, no weapons and no clothes!
The Living Fiend has led us to this woe,
For this whole realm is filled with spiteful folk!
We're better off back in Monglane our home;
Let's make our way – we've overstayed our hopes."
Renier heard this and in a rage half-choked
He looked Girart straight in the eye and groaned:
"The Living Fiend has lodged inside your soul!
If we return right now, as you propose,
Then when we reach Monglane, our worthy home,
The people there will welcome us, I know,
Then ask us where we've journeyed on our road;
And I will say: 'To Paris and the throne,
And then to Rheims and Charlemagne the bold
With all his court, but didn't once behold
The King nor share his board or bowl,
Nor gain one groat nor any grain of oats.'
Then all of them will treat us both as dolts,
And make us two the butt of all their jokes!
I'll go to court, God curse me if I don't,

And claim our dues before this day is old;
And by the faith I owe the Lord of Hosts,
If any man is rash enough to slow
Or bar my way, he'll pay more than he owed
   Ere ever I depart there."

SO OFF THEY WENT, the two of them together
To Charles's court, unheeding all or any,
And passed the gate despite the porter's presence;
They asked for drink and sat down at the benches;
A little bread was brought, though nothing better,
And one sole drink, most grudgingly presented;
On seeing this, great anger filled their senses;
The seneschal of Charles himself addressed them,
In ermine clad, a cloak most rich and precious,
And in a gown from town just made to measure;
A new-dubbed knight had given both as presents
And made the man more arrogant than ever;
He held a staff of apple-wood and bellowed
These words aloud in tones more fit for menace:
"Squires, take your oats exactly as I tell you,
Or by the Cross that pilgrims seek in blessing,
If you incur the rod of my displeasure,
You'll not receive one grain, by God in Heaven!"
"Give me some oats, my lord," Renier requested:
"Since yesternight my mules have not had any;
So help me God, you'll make a mighty error
If you refuse to offer us a welcome!
If you would like our services to help you,
We'll willingly assist, if you'll accept us."
The rogue could see that they weren't local Frenchmen,
But thought, therefore, that they weren't worth a penny,
And turned on them with taunts and vaunting temper:
"Get up and go, you sons of whores, you shepherds,
You foreigners, you double-talking Bedouins!
No trotting squire or ribald-looking fellow
Who comes and asks for oats to feed the belly
Of mule or hack or steed in his possession,
Will get good oats doled out to him by any –
Such rogues expect their noble host to lend them
A fireside seat and then good board and bedding!"

He raised his staff and moved to strike young Renier
And then once more to curse and to condemn him:
"You harlot's son, you slippery young beggar!
By Saint Riquier, you will regret your efforts
To rob our stores for your own cause and credit!"
Renier replied, with waves of anger welling:
"You harlot's son, you double-talking felon,
I'd rather die than leave you unrepentant!"
With fierce intent he stormed up from the benches,
Then seized the rogue and dragged his haughty head down;
He raised his fist and swung a blow so heavy
It shattered all the dotard's jaw past mending
And spun him down bereft of all his senses;
Not done, he seized the wretch's foot and wedged it
Against the door where Charles's stores were tended:
"Be gone, you rogue, God rot your bones for ever!
You don't know how to spare oats or to spend them!"
He took a hod and then he took to yelling:
"Those needing oats, come forward now and get them!
The smallest pleas shall earn ten times the measure!
God strike me down, if I demand one penny!"
Girart made sure that those with least had plenty –
And their own mules were sure to rest contented,
For Girart sent one load to their own dwelling;
The servants fled from Garin's sons in terror,
For any who approached them there, attempting
To repossess King Charles's grain, learnt better!
There were, that night, some forty war-steeds tethered
Within the town with no oats in their bellies!
A messenger raced off to Charles directly:
"In God's name, Sire, great evil has beset us!
Down in your barn your seneschal lies senseless
Upon the floor, attacked by two young felons!
I think his neck was broken when they felled him,
For from his mouth I saw his life-blood ebbing!
Without revenge, what man will serve you henceforth?"
On hearing this, the King cried out for vengeance;
He called Gilemer and Gautier to attend him –
The provost one, the other one his second:
"Close all the gates, bar each and every exit!
When morning comes, search every house and dwelling!

There is no squire, however rich the wretch is,
If he did this, will not live to regret it,
For you will slice both ears upon the felon,
And pluck his eyes and have his nose half-severed,
So nevermore he'll venture to offend me,
To harm myself or any who attend me."
They both replied: "Your bidding is our pleasure."
The youths, meanwhile, returned to their own dwelling,
And both their mules ate oats to their contentment;
That night Girart and Renier took their leisure,
And ere they slept, ate figs and dates a-plenty,
   Rejoicing much indeed.

MY WORTHY FRIENDS, you've heard it said enough:
When someone dies and all his days are done,
Folk soon forget the things he did and was;
At dawn next day, and with the rising sun,
Both brave Girart and bold Renier got up
And dressed themselves with no delay or fuss;
Renier called out and hailed his brother thus:
"Girart," he said, "we must return at once
To Charles's court – we've tarried here enough!
We must find out what's being said and done."
Girart replied: "In truth, by God above,
I fear we've slain that haughty seneschal
Whom yesternight in Charles's barn we struck;
If dead he is, then we may curse our luck;
Across his beard I saw his life-blood run;
We broke his neck; he lay there more than stunned;
We'll both be blamed and shamed, I fear it much;
We've no one here who'll speak a word for us."
"Don't fret for him," his brother cried at once:
"The King is served by far too many such!
You can be sure, if he is robbed of one,
   He's rushed by fourteen others."

THE PAIR OF THEM were nothing if not brave,
And went to court without the least delay;
The Emperor, when dawn lit up the day,
Went off to church and chapel, there to pray;
The Mass was sung by his own priest Guimer,

And many lords and peers were in the train
Which followed him to hear God's word proclaimed;
Outside the church one hundred came to wait,
Who all had suits to plead with Charlemagne –
But none of them could even state their claim;
And Renier saw them all in that one place,
And saw the door shut firmly in their face –
And with his boot he kicked it with such weight
It shook and gave and opened up half-way;
The guard saw this and, overwrought with rage,
He raised his staff and brought it down again
On Renier's head and cut an ugly graze;
The youth was stunned, and filled with hurt and hate
As insult next was added to his pain:
"You harlot's son, you do not know your place!
How did you dare, you foreign-looking knave,
To come this near and shake King Charles's gate?
Can you not see around you in this place
These many lords so worthy to be praised,
Who all are dressed in shining ermine drapes
And foreign furs of miniver and grey,
Who still cannot advance their cause or case?
And yet you thought you had more right than they –
   Dressed in your shabby mantle?"

RENIER, THAT WORTHY LORD, responded so:
"Whore's son yourself, you wretched, worthless rogue!
May Heaven's King, Lord Jesus, curse your soul!
The heart's not clad in grey or ermine clothes,
But in the breast where, heaven-blest, it grows!
Some men are rich whose courage is but low,
And some are poor who yet are brave and bold,
Of sturdy limb, stout heart and noble soul!
Now by the Saint whom pilgrims seek in Rome,
I'd rather die, by St Denis, God knows,
Than not pay back the blow that you are owed!"
Renier was fierce, a gallant friend or foe,
And back he stepped, then rushing forth he smote
That door again so angrily he broke
Its boards in half, and with a crushing blow
He struck the guard across the face and nose;

So fierce a rush it was, so fierce a stroke,
It drove both eyes straight out their socket-holes;
He fell to ground, against the door he groaned
While over him ten haughty nobles strode,
Who never asked if he were dead or no;
Then from the church fierce-visaged Charles approached
And heard the row and roaring as it rose;
He said aloud: "By St Denis's bones,
What rogue has dared to burst inside my home,
Break down my door and lay my porter low?"
Said Geoffrey, lord of Paris: "On God's oath,
Those two young lords in their grey-hooded cloaks
Have broken through the door you ordered closed!"
Said fearsome Charles: "Take both of them in hold!
    They must be brought to justice!"

5. How Girart and Renier were received at court

FIERCE-VISAGED Charles was filled with spite and rage;
With ringing voice he cried aloud and railed:
"By St Riquier, which rogue of you's to blame?
Within my hall whose gall has been so great
As first to break my door and then to slay?"
"In God's name, I'm the one," Renier exclaimed:
"I'll never hide my right to do the same!
God curse the soul of such a wretched knave –
He raised his staff and struck me, Charlemagne!
The fellow was so arrogant and vain,
So full of pride for his smart tunic's sake,
That he cared naught for any Jack or James!
But thanks to God I paid him his true wage –
Upon the ground he found it, in his grave!
True Emperor, for God our Saviour's sake,
Be sure of this: in any court of state,
Of Emperor, of king or prince the same,
When worthy men arrive before your gate,
They should be met with good and noble grace,
And not with blows or punches to the face!
For some are poor whose hearts are bright and brave,
And some are rich whose hearts are weak and pale;

True Emperor, I'm blunt of speech and plain,
But it is right and proper, by the Saints,
For you to let and hear me state my claim,
To tell you who I am and what I crave,
Before you have me flogged or flung in chains!"
"By St Riquier, he's right!" the French acclaimed:
    "Fine lord, grant him your pardon!"

THE EMPEROR allowed his rage to fall,
When he observed how bravely Renier talked;
He saw the youths to be most handsome boys,
And asked of them: "Where are you from, young lords?
Whose sons are you? Don't keep me uninformed!"
And Renier said: "My lord, I'll tell you all –
To tell the truth to noble men's no fault;
We both are sons of worthy Garin's loins,
Lord of Monglane in Gascony the broad;
With Pagan tribes each day he wages war,
Though held in siege by Sinagon the Moor
Within his town, behind it and before;
We're here to learn the language of the North,
And with your leave we'll stay here at your court;
With loyal hearts we'll serve both you and yours;
One year or two we'll serve you and your cause,
Then, if you will, a third or fourth or more,
And win ourselves both honour and reward."
The King replied: "Your speech is wisely wrought,
And, by the Lord, indeed, you're nobly born
Of gallant clan and fighters fierce in war;
Yet at this time I have no wish or cause
To lodge you here for years within my hall;
I'll give you both fresh clothing to be worn
And thirty pounds in gold and silver coin;
You can return to old Monglane with joy
And speak of me with honour and with warmth."
On hearing this, Renier's hot temper boiled;
He hailed Girart in tones of wild remorse:
"Go saddle up my ambling mule," he roared,
"And yours as well, with no delay or pause!
I'm not some merchant's son, in love with coin!
Upon my faith in God, Who governs all,

If I possessed the wealth within these walls,
I'd keep no part of it, much less a hoard!
My loyal knights and men would have it all,
My priests and monks and others who were poor;
No kin of mine has longed for wealth before,
Nor ever kept a shop or market-stall,
And nor shall I while I have breath to draw!
This King, I see, refuses the support
And services we two would have performed,
So we must seek another lord henceforth,
Who'll cherish us and our true service more."
Among themselves the Frenchmen spoke their thoughts:
"By God above, and by His love and law,
How wise they are, these youths, and how well-taught!
If they could stay at length within this court,
They would outdo the Norman Huidelon,
Old Gaydon and Sir Droon of Vincent."
At this Gaudin, a German lord, spoke forth:
"Retain them, Sire – they have both brain and brawn!
Bestow your grace and favour on them, lord,
For both have left a distant home and soil
And in good faith have pledged that they will toil
To do your will in times of peace and war."
The King replied: "Then let them both come forth
    And swear to be my liegemen!"

THE TWO OF THEM behaved with every grace:
Before the King they moved to kneel and make,
In front of all, their pledge of loyal faith;
Then, when the King had made them rise again,
He hailed the knights attending him that day:
"My lords," began the King so fierce of face,
"First I shall dub as knight the youth Renier,
And make Girart, the younger one, my page;
His service done, I'll dub Girart the same."
"Well done, my lord!" the Frenchmen all acclaimed;
A shirt and hose were brought to clothe Renier,
Made both of silk, and shoes from Montpellier;
Across his back they laid an ermine cape
And tunic cut to fit his size and shape;
A noble cloak worth many a coin they draped

With great address across his shoulder-blades;
Then off they went to hear a Mass proclaimed,
Which is the rite when any knight is made:
Before his arms may strike a blow for Faith,
He must hear Mass and pray to God for aid
In doing right and winning knightly fame,
And winning land to guard and guide the same;
When Mass was said they led the lad away
To dub him knight in Charles's hall of state;
They brought him forth new armour made of mail:
To shield his shins good iron greaves well made,
To guard his breast a hauberk double-chained,
To guard his face a helm with golden lace;
The King himself girt on a noble blade,
Then touched his neck and shoulders, fierce of face,
And said to him: "Renier, be ever brave!"
"Much thanks, my lord," the gallant youth exclaimed,
"With God's good help I shall be, to the grave!"
They brought him next a war-horse, swift of pace,
Which by the left he leapt on straightaway;
Against his breast a quartered shield they braced
And in his hand a spear of sturdy weight;
Upon his steed a sudden charge he made –
If you had seen how well he spurred away,
To speed his horse, to turn it and to aim,
Then lift his shield and lower it again,
Then raise his spear, then toss and catch the same,
Then I am sure you would have praised Renier,
As did all those of honest heart that day,
Who said aloud: "This youth was born for fame!"
But spiteful knights were filled with jealous hate:
"True Emperor," said Renart of Pevier,
A wicked rogue, God curse the fellow's fate,
"I see ahead the price that you will pay
For granting these two lads too much today!
The time will come when they will earn your hate!
Garin, the lord who's sent them on their way,
Has never had one meal in peace, they say;
When your own lord, Pépin, wed in his day
The lovely Berthe, that worthiest of maids,
Garin was still an arrogant young knave;

I saw him sail the open seas in wait
For pilgrims' ships – he knew the routes they'd take –
And he would steal from monks upon the waves
And rob the priests inside their churches' naves;
For this they chased him out of France in shame
And made him flee from all his French estates
To Gascony, and there he drew his rein;
He gained a wife from Yon the king, who gave
As dower-lands one quarter of his state –
A due he'd rue in time as a mistake!
My lord, this man whom I accuse and blame,
Most foully slew my uncle with his blade;
Now by the Saint whom pilgrims seek in praise,
Since my revenge upon Garin must wait,
His sons shall pay most dearly in his place!
True Emperor, I've reason to complain:
My son has served you well and without fail,
For countless days with no reward or gain –
No penny-piece, no hack or destrier;
May God, the Lord of Justice, curse Renier!"
       How endless is man's envy!

TO HEAR RENART, the traitor's, evil speech,
So galled Renier he almost burst with grief;
He cried aloud, blood rushing to his cheeks:
"My lord, who is this fat old dotard here,
Who by his paunch must hail from Lombardy?
He must have had such piles of pork to eat
He's swollen up like some old sumpter-beast!
He's born of Bernart's clan, the wretched thief
Who robbed Aymon of Autemere his fief;
A rogue he is – his look shows that at least!
True Emperor, do justice to my plea:
By St Médard, I beg at once for leave
To fight this knave no later than I need;
With this, my sword, I'll render blows so fierce
As evidence against this wicked fiend
Of Lord Garin, my father's, honesty!
If I don't make this jealous dotard yield,
Then have me burnt or hang me from a tree!"
Said young Girart: "Good brother, let this be!

By good St Leonard's soul, whose faith I keep,
If I'd not thought the King would be aggrieved,
I would have plucked the whiskers off this beast!"
On saying this, he seized Renart's long beard
And bared a patch where grey hairs once had been!
In pain and shame the old rogue ground his teeth:
The Frenchmen laughed, who looked upon the scene,
For they alike disdained Renart indeed;
     A curse upon his kindred!

6. How Renier served the King

"MY HOARY LORD," said good Renier once more,
"Your arrogance would never be the cause
If in a rage I left the court henceforth;
Nor would I take this armour or this sword;
But by the Cross for which our fights are fought,
If you persist, I'll pay you in such coin
As, when I do, you will not thank me for!"
When this was said they let the matter fall
And Charles the King kept both young men at court;
And when a plea or some complaint was brought,
Renier it was who judged the case by law;
He served the King as knights of courage ought:
All Vermandois he freed from vicious hordes
Of thieving rogues, foul outlaws each and all,
Who'd held the shire to ransom theretofore;
He set three traps in one combined assault
And at a bridge he caught three score and more;
And when at last the lot of them were caught,
He never locked them up three days or four,
But hung each one, to end it once for all;
     Which is both right and proper.

RENIER WAS BOTH a handsome knight and fierce;
He rid the King of countless foes and fiends
Within the King's own land and wide demesne:
No man could go from Paris to Senlis
And not be cut to pieces in between,

For in Serval there lay a nest of thieves
Who hid there in the wood below Senlis;
No traveller alive could pass unseen
And, once detained, was slain or chained at least;
Complaints of this at last reached Charles's ear,
And brave Renier alike was there to hear;
One hundred knights he took, all armed with steel,
And hid them all among the forest trees;
Then he prepared ten monks of Saint-Denis
To travel through that wood below Senlis;
So through they rode, with courage and with zeal,
Upon their mules, their habits plain to see,
And, as they went, all chanting loud and clear;
Their lungs were strong, their singing reached the thieves
Who from their lair leapt forth with every speed;
Those pilgrim-monks began to shout and scream
And, filled with rage, Renier sprang in between
With all his knights, five score of noble breed;
How fiercely then they fell upon those thieves!
How many times they struck with blade and spear
And slit their throats and left them there to bleed!
And worse it went with those who fled the scene,
For they were caught and hung with no reprieve;
From branch to branch they swung them in the breeze!
This set the land, so long held ransom, free,
And fearsome Charles was filled with joy indeed;
He held Renier in friendship so esteemed
That he was made, above all other Peers,
    His personal adviser.

7. How Renier chafed at the King's ingratitude

NOW AT THIS TIME of which my tale is speaking,
Charles held a court that never would be equalled;
At Pentecost, which is a time of feasting,
The King convened his noblest knights and liegemen
And made himself much honoured at this meeting;
He bade Girart to wait on him when eating,
Renier as well, whose deeds had so succeeded –
They both obeyed, not wishing to displease him;

One brought the plates for Charlemagne to eat from,
The other held his shining, golden beaker
Of spicy wine well strained in proper season;
Then, all at once, a messenger appeared there;
Up all the steps he ran, and when he reached there,
He greeted Charles in ringing tones and cheerful:
"May God the Lord, Who is the world's Redeemer,
Protect the King, of breed and deed so fearsome,
And guard the knights whom at his side I see here!
My noble lords, inform me, I beseech you,
If young Girart from Gascony has been here,
He and Renier, of whom the news has reached me
That Charles has made a household knight to keep him;
I've sought them both, each morning and each evening
For such a time, that I'm worn out and weary!"
"Behold us both!" said Renier, fair of feature:
"Fair brother, friend, what reason makes you seek us?
Have you some news of all our friends and people?"
"Indeed, fair sir, and now I shall reveal it:
Your brother Miles is now in Apulia
And has a wife of worthiest demeanour,
And two young sons whom everyone loves dearly –
You could not fine more handsome, noble creatures!
And Lord Hernaut, at Biaulande on the seaboard,
Has wed alike a woman of that region
And rules through her its land and all its people;
He has a son, and none has seen his equal –
Young Aymeri's his name, and lords, believe me,
If he grows old, that name will be a feared one
And raise his clan among the best of heroes!
And you, what news have you of your achievements?
What land to rule or honours have you reaped here,
That I may tell your brothers when I meet them?"
Renier replied: "Companion, you are speaking
Most foolishly to ask me this, believe me;
But tell them all, for I would not conceal it,
That we are here, still serving Charles in fealty;
Tell them Girart commands the cooks so keenly
To speed the meals, we cannot make him leave there;
He washes plates, then wipes them dry and cleans them;
I clear away the tablecloths and beakers

And guard them well so nobody can steal them!
King Charles, in turn, looks after us and treats us
Like hired hacks put out to graze the greensward;
    And so we serve the King."

THUS SPOKE THE YOUTH of noble face and mind,
Then, looking straight ahead of him, he cried:
"Fine brother, friend, God bless and let you thrive!
So is it true and no word of a lie
That Miles is lord of Apulia's might?"
"Yes lord, indeed, by blessed Mary's child!
And he has wed a slender, well-bred wife,
And has two sons of noble heart and mind;
And you, my lord, have you at least acquired
An ancient town or tower, fief or shire?"
"How mad of you to ask!" Renier replied:
"My brother here, God bless and let me thrive,
Knows nothing yet of what befits a knight;
But you've not seen a kitchen-boy his like!
To see him work, you'd not believe your eyes!
I guard the realm of tablecloths and knives;
But by the faith I owe to Jesus Christ,
If Charles, the King of every shore and shire,
Won't give to me some part of France as mine,
I'll serve his will no more until I die,
    But seek another liege lord!"

UPON THE BOARD King Charles's sword-hand moved;
He cried aloud to all within the room:
"My loyal lords, did you hear that rebuke?
And did you see Renier and mark his mood
Towards this man who stands in front of you?
Guirré, my good Archbishop, spoke the truth,
As did Renart, that worthy, well-famed duke
Of Peviers, whose heart is brave and true:
Whatever grace I granted them or boon,
They never would show fitting gratitude;
I've heard it said, and now I've had the proof,
That when a thief is rescued from the noose,
He'll rob the lord who saved him from his doom!
From poverty and want I've saved the two,

And now, for thanks, it seems I earn abuse!
    Their breed is far too lowly."

AS SOON AS CHARLES had started on this speech,
With utmost rage the blood burned Renier's cheek;
He raised his head so all of them could hear
And said aloud: "My lord, what do you mean?
From your rich hand what land have I received,
What region have you given us in fief?
You've dubbed me knight, and there you're right indeed,
But I have gained no other thanks or fee,
Though I have freed your realm from countless griefs;
The worthy land of Vermandois was seized
By outlaw bands and in the grip of thieves,
But forth I rode and gave them no reprieve:
I hanged them all, yet gained no thanks or fee;
But by the Saint they seek in Nero's field,
If this same day you give no land to me,
Then all the love I have for you shall cease;
When morning comes, without delay I'll leave
    For Garin of Monglane."

8. How Renier's service was finally rewarded

CHARLES LISTENED HARD to what he had to say –
But, as he did, his lip curled up with rage;
In angry mood he hailed the youth again:
"Vassal! You chose to be my man!" he railed,
"You bore my flag in countless fights and frays
And won much wealth in coin and kind that way:
Whate'er we won was there for you to take;
But still you bragged before my men and claimed
That you would take, no matter what I'd say,
Estates of mine and make them your domains,
In Burgundy, in France and Alemayn,
In Friesland and in Flanders just the same;
You said this like a lordless renegade;
I order you to show me your good faith:
For good or ill my will you will obey!"
Said good Girart: "Fine King, we thank your grace;

With your consent we'll journey whence we came;
With hair-shirts on, unshod and bearing staves
As penitents, we'll leave your land this day."
"Upon my soul, we'll not!" cried out Renier:
"Girart, you speak as if we were to blame!
Let Charlemagne say what he will or may!
Since we must plead the justice of our case,
God damn us if we've not the will to wait
    And hear the final judgement!"

THE EMPEROR was filled with rage and spite
To hear the words with which Renier replied;
To all the knights within his court he cried:
"Have you all heard, my worthy lords and knights,
These wretches speak, whom I have raised so high?
They've paid me back today in wretched kind,
And with their words have filled my heart with ire;
Now by the Saint for whom God shows His might,
I swear if they're still here in three days' time,
I'll have them hung upon a well-branched pine!"
Renier replied: "My lord, please tell me why!
But first recall not long ago, when I
Observed you fall, unhorsed amidst a fight;
I gave you then my flowing steed to ride,
While I remained on foot, prepared to die;
I struggled hard and with my blade of iron
I won a horse, thank God, and I survived;
Now by the Lord and everlasting Christ,
If this is how my service is misprised,
Men silent now shall loose their tongues and cry,
    Before we leave your kingdom."

"TRUE EMPEROR," said bearded Do at this:
"This pair of knaves, where do they think this is?
Such scorn for you has fallen from their lips,
And insults which have raised my anger's pitch,
That I advise you give them naught but this:
Let forty sous be each one's parting gift,
And two old hacks, unshod and with a limp;
Let all of us be quit of them forthwith!"
Renier heard this and almost lost his wits:

"You wretched, mad old fool!" he said to him:
"Do you forget I pulled you from a ditch
Which two young rogues had thrust and thrown you in?
The smaller one had fetched you such a hit
With his great staff, a long and sturdy stick,
That you fell back from its attack and slipped;
You never would have clambered from that pit,
But I came by and saved your wrinkled skin!
It grieves my heart that you should serve me ill!
But by the Saint they seek on Nero's hill,
If we were not in court and with the King,
I'd grab the hair upon your cheek and chin
And hurt you more than any ruffian did!"
On saying this, he strode in front of him
And struck old Do so firmly with his fist
That from his mouth he knocked five teeth of his!
Upon his back at once he slumped and slipped;
Renier looked round and saw the court's ill-will:
He saw Renart of Peviers, who, ere this,
Had shamed his name when Charles had knighted him;
The villain was a weakly, haggard thing,
With straggling beard and whiskers all grey-tinged;
Renier the brave strode up in front of him
And grasped his beard with both of his great fists;
For fourteen steps he dragged the wretch like this,
Who slipped and tripped, not wanting this one bit!
As Renier led, their bodies bumped until
They reached the hearth, where Renier threw him in!
His beard was burnt, his whiskers seared and singed,
And he'd have died, his hide burnt to a crisp,
But Charlemagne ran up and rescued him
With all the rest assembled there within,
     Who broke apart the mêlée.

"HAVE MERCY, SIRE," Girart began to plead,
"For love of God, Who bore the Cross's grief!
Renier indeed is angry and aggrieved,
But he remains a knight of high degree:
In forty lands there's none as brave as he;
May Christian love, which Longinus received,
Convince you, Sire, to keep my brother here!

I'll be your man; my freedom I will yield
And all my life I'll serve you willingly
Without relapse while life is left in me."
Girart knelt down before King Charles's feet,
But felt a hand on his grey-furred pelisse
Which hauled him up then slapped him on the cheek!
"Away, you wretch," he heard his brother scream,
"For by the Saint they seek in Nero's field,
I'd rather lose my limbs or life than be
A purchased slave and nevermore be free;
Our noble clan would always be held cheap;
By all the faith I owe my friends and peers,
If Charlemagne, the King of Saint-Denis,
Won't give me now a town or land in fief,
I'll spurn him too, while I have breath to breathe,
   And go to my own brother!"

"TRUE EMPEROR," said Henry of Orleans,
A gallant knight of high resolve and breeding:
"Do you forget the German Geoffrey's speeches?
He came to court, insulting and conceited,
And made his boast, with all the French to hear him,
That in Senlis and Paris and the regions
Your touted wealth was nothing but a mean one;
You had no knight among all those convened there
Within your court, no Frank or Fleming either,
Who'd stand against this Geoffrey's proud demeanour,
Except Renier – my lord, you know that he did!
He armed himself and went at once to meet him;
Across the field he sent his war-horse speeding
And struck the rogue with his Viana spear-point;
The German's arms nor armour could redeem him –
He lost the stand, by Renier's hand defeated;
You gained from this the land around Orleans,
Le Perche in part and all Laon's outer regions;
Give Renier land, lest you are charged with meanness!
If you agree, my lord, give him Geneva:
Its duke is dead these past two months and leaves there
No son as heir, fine Emperor believe me;
A daughter lives, a fair and courtly creature;
Let both be wed and Renier be received as
   The guardian of that land."

THE KING'S RESPONSE was very fair indeed;
He grew more calm and willing to concede
What Henry's words had tried to make him see:
Renier had served him well, with little fee;
At last he said to all of those convened:
"My noble knights of France and Hungary,
Of Normandy and Berry – hark to me!
I know the truth and cannot but agree
That Renier here has helped me in my need;
Yet he today has sold his service dear
And spoken words which have affronted me;
But now I wish this bitterness to cease:
I'll give to him Geneva, with your leave."
"Most willingly, my lord," said all and each;
Then, turning to the youth, they made this plea:
"Renier, my lord, go now and thank your liege!
Approach the King and kneel down at his feet!
His gift is great and much to be esteemed."
Renier replied: "Good barons, hold your peace!
To clamour thus is wrong and makes you seem
Like common folk with nothing left to eat!"
He said to Charles: "I thank you much, my liege;
But take good care, my lord, I do beseech,
That with this gift you practise no deceit;
For by the God Who judges all and each,
    You'd very soon regret it!"

RENIER, HE STOOD before King Charlemagne;
The King looked up and gave him straightaway
The right to rule Geneva's rich domains;
The Frisian lords and German knights exclaimed:
"Renier, my lord, for God Almighty's sake,
Kneel down before your liege, King Charles the great!"
But he replied: "Good barons, peace, I say!
You sound like boys to clamour thus and shape
Your whining pleas like warnings and complaints."
"Much thanks, my liege," he said to Charlemagne,
"But take good care that you uphold this claim;
Let knights of yours ride with me all the way
Until I reach my realm and its estates,
And let them all bear charters full and plain

Wherein my rights are proven and maintained."
"God bless all this, indeed," the King proclaimed:
"On leaving court, you'll lack for naught that way:
The Archbishop of Besançon, Renier,
Hoel of Nantes and Geoffrey, Anjou's brave
And noble lord, whose beard is white with age,
And seven more will ride with you as aides."
So while Girart remained with Charlemagne,
His brother left, without the least delay,
And set the spur to his swift destrier;
I'll not spin out their journey – safe to say
He galloped on with all his heart and haste
Until he reached Geneva, as did they!
And there he took the noble, orphaned maid
And married her without one moment's waste,
Their bows and vows within the hall exchanged;
This maid it was, I tell you in all faith,
Who bore brave Oliver, so fair of face,
Count Roland's friend until that fateful day
Their bond was rent by Ganelon the knave
  In Spain among the passes.

9. How Girart came between the King and Queen

THIS MAID IT WAS, in faith I tell you all,
Who bore the brave and noble Oliver,
And then the fair and lovely-visaged Aude
Whom Roland was betrothed to wed henceforth –
But never did, God's will be done in all;
So Renier ruled Geneva's shire and shore
And soon began to arm his land for war,
Constructing moats and strong defensive walls
And sturdy towers and mighty castle-forts;
In all his land there lived no peer or lord
Who failed to serve his word, for all were forced
To be his men, with faith and pledges sworn:
And those who baulked were driven from their halls;
King Charlemagne remained inside his court
With young Girart, who served him as before,
And earned esteem from every peer and lord,

Until the day whose deeds I'll next record: (1202a)
One day King Charles went hunting on his horse
And took with him his huntsman, who led forth
The hunting-dogs and hounds upon their course
Within the woods, where soon they were employed;
The party took two stags and one wild boar,
Then loaded up four sumpters with the spoils;
Towards midday, returning from their sport,
The wind picked up and whipped along a storm;
The lightning struck, it thundered and it poured,
So Charles withdrew beneath an oak and paused;
While there, a horseman came, who'd ridden forth
From Burgundy to bring his sad report;
He saw the King and hailed him as he ought:
"God bless you Sire, Who is the King of all!
I've hastened here to tell you this, my lord:
In Burgundy the duke survives no more –
His widowed wife would speak to you, therefore,
And bids you choose a time when you may talk."
The King replied: "Then listen to my choice!
Return at once and say she can be sure
That when the day of St John's feast has dawned,
My court will be most certainly at Sens."
The rider said: "I'll tell her, rest assured!"
He asked for leave and turned around his horse;
The Emperor was lost a while in thought
About the duke whom he had loved of yore,
And from his eyes the tears began to fall;
But by and by he stopped and wept no more,
For there is naught that sorrow can restore;
He raised his head and saw Girart and swore
Upon the shaft his bow would next have drawn,
Girart should wed the duchess in due course;
The day would come when he'd regret the choice!
So Charles returned to court at royal Laon
And clothed Girart in robes most richly wrought,
And then had arms and worthy armour brought
To dub him knight with no delay at all;
For love of him, he knighted twenty more
And gave to each new armour and a horse,
The finest found within his kingdom's bourne;

Girart received much honour and rejoiced –
But all would turn to treason and remorse
  When Charles took back the lady.

SO WHEN THE FEAST I've specified was nigh,
Of blessed John, when Christian joy is high,
King Charlemagne arrived at Sens to find
The widowed wife of Burgundy arrived
With two archbishops standing by her side;
On seeing this, he raised his voice and cried:
"I welcome you, good duchess fair and fine!"
"Almighty God, our Father, bless you Sire!"
"Your noble husband's death," the King replied,
"Is living death for you, his loving wife."
"My grief is great, indeed," the duchess sighed,
"But there is naught that sorrowing revives;
I need and seek another husband, Sire;
The law has said, since Moses and his time,
That widowed wives may wed a second time;
My lord is dead and I need one alive
To guard the laws my great domain requires;
If not, I'll lose too much of what is mine."
The King replied: "I know that you are right,
And have at court a fair and fitting knight
Who is Girart, of noble birth and mind,
Both brave and bold and strong of wit and wise;
He is a son of brave Garin, the sire
Of old Monglane in Gascony the wide."
"My lord," she said, "as Lord our God desires;
I shall accept whatever you decide,
  For I owe you my fealty."

KING CHARLES BEHELD the widow of the duke
And saw her grace, her charm and beauty too:
Her eyes were green, her face was fair to view,
Her skin more white than snow on ice in hue;
He said: "By God and Mary, in all truth,
Within my realm I've found no woman whom
I ever liked above the rest hereto;
And yet, this one I find so fair and pure
That no one else could match her looks or mood;

By God above, Who makes the sky and dew,
I'll take to wife this widow of the duke's!
Girart will find another somewhere soon."
He wished it thus, and so the wish came true;
And what he gained Girart was made to lose;
How fierce a feud between the pair ensued!
How many men were slain because of two!
Charles tarried not but summoned to his room
The duchess then to win his purpose through;
He said to her: "I'll not conceal my mood;
If all agree, and you will grant it too,
Then I shall wed – and she I'd wed is *you*!"
On hearing this, the duchess hardly moved:
"My lord," she said, "you jest, I'm sure you do!
No King should look to his own vavasours
To find a wife – you know I speak the truth;
You should address a Princess, born to rule,
Or dowager beyond the least reproof;
Give me Girart, the gallant-visaged youth
And lord to whom I first was introduced;
If he were spurned, then I should earn rebuke;
Fine King, my lord, I cannot hide the truth:
    I've no wish to be Queen here."

"YOUR WORDS ARE RASH," King Charlemagne replied:
"Good duchess, all would blame you, and be right!
I won't deny I think you most unwise!
Which course is best – to falter or to rise
And to exalt the honour of your line?"
"Don't jest with me, I beg you," she replied,
"For you can wed whatever queen you like,
Or princess of the highest royal line;
But I, in truth, should marry with my kind;
Give me Girart, whom I have heard admired
As one most brave and handsome and refined;
Give me Girart, whom I shall not decline,
For if I did, my name would be maligned;
Now grant me leave, I beg you, to retire
Inside my lodge and speak with men of mine
For their advice on both proposals, Sire,
To be your Queen or Sir Girart's new wife."

"With all my heart," King Charlemagne replied:
"Much benefit may come from good advice."
So with four counts in consort at her side,
The duchess left and to her lodge retired;
She bade Girart to come and he contrived
Without delay to do as she desired;
Across his back he draped a fur of white
And cape of silk with Oriental signs;
Most nobly dressed, Girart then leapt astride
An ambling mule well-saddled for the ride
With finer gear than any you could find:
One hundred pounds alone the bridle's price;
Along the street, as he began to ride,
Each man and maid looked up at once and cried:
"That's Sir Girart, the gallant Gascon knight!
How well they fare who serve a worthy Sire!"
Girart rode on, not wasting any time;
He reached the house, dismounted, then he climbed
The steps to find the duchess there inside;
She stood to meet and greet him fair and fine:
"Most welcome here, well-bred and bravest knight!
I asked for you to come, so help me Christ,
And come you have and in your debt I lie;
I'll not conceal from you the reason why:
I met the King within his palace high,
And such a thing he urged me to which I
Would neither then consent with nor comply;
Now *I've* a plea, Girart, that I'll not hide:
Come marry me, if that is your desire!
I'm not a one for speeches, worthy knight;
I've never heard a speech so very wise
That parts of it could not be criticised!"
Girart replied, not even thinking twice:
"My lady, I have never heard the like!
But now I know with my own ears and eyes
That God's good world is fated soon to die,
When women press the men to walk the aisle!
By all the faith I owe the Saving Christ,
The world will see two summers live and die
Before I'll wed a shrew or you alike!
Ask someone else, if someone you can find!

You'll not have me, on that you can rely!"
On hearing this, the duchess almost died:
   She'd never felt so humbled.

10. How the Queen came between Girart and the King

GIRART, HE LEFT, he'd no desire to be there;
He asked no leave but took it as it pleased him
And left her there, her breast with anger heaving;
She could not eat, nor could she drink that evening,
And spent the night in restlessness unceasing
Until the dawn and light of day appearing,
Whereon she dressed to look her best, ere leaving
To go to church and chapel at St Stephen's;
Upon the steps of its high altar kneeling,
She prayed to Christ our Saviour to redeem her
With Sir Girart, who'd spurned her frank entreaty –
For she loved him more than the King, her liege lord;
Her praying done, she went and sent discreetly
A squire of hers to urge Girart to see her;
But Sir Girart disdained to do so fiercely:
Not then, he said, and not for two weeks either;
On hearing this, she almost lost her reason,
Her thoughts confused as she reviewed her feelings:
'I'll have the King, as Girart has deceived me!'
And so she asked for Charles to come and meet her,
And come he did, most willingly and fleetly;
When he appeared, she greeted him most sweetly
And said: "My lord, I tell you very freely
That I am glad that you have deigned to see me;
   It fills me with great joy."

KING CHARLEMAGNE of France, the widely famed,
Came willingly within the hall well-paved
Where Burgundy's fair duchess was that day;
When both were in a private room and place,
He greeted her with tenderness and grace,
And, wisely, she acknowledged him the same;
She said: "My lord, hear what I have to say,
For you should know my feelings, Charlemagne:

Now, truly, you surprised me yesterday!
But I was not aware then of the state
Of certain things which now have been explained;
I've been advised, in truth and in good faith,
Concerning the proposal you have made;
And all my clan agree I should obey,
And I agree myself with all they say:
I'd rather be a Queen for fifteen days
Of royal France, which is so widely praised,
Than duchess still for fourteen years again!"
On hearing this, the King's delight was plain;
He called aloud to those he had retained:
"My lords, why should I hide the plans I make?
This lady, whom I've met and heard so praised,
Upon my life, shall be my wife, I say!"
"But you gave her to me!" Girart exclaimed,
"With all her lands and all of her estates!"
But she replied, as one quick with a phrase:
"I swear to you by Jesus and His Saints,
I'd rather feel my body rent and maimed
By rapid steeds, or drowned or set ablaze,
Than let some part, Girart, feel your embrace!
For on that day, in truth and in good faith,
When I was pledged to you by Charlemagne,
'Twas I complied and you who then complained!
    The shame of that still galls me!"

THE EMPEROR behaved in worthy wise,
As by the hand he held his courtly bride
And with these words addressed his band of knights:
"This lady is of noble birth and mind:
If you agree, then she shall be my wife."
"My lord and King," the young Girart replied:
"You do me wrong, and this I cannot hide;
The other day you said that she was mine,
And mine to rule was all her land alike;
But you're my lord, I'll not contest your right."
He showed no wish, did Charles, to change his mind,
And had his bride led off to church nearby,
Where both were wed in bishop Renier's sight;
Their wedding-feast filled up the palace high,

And all that day they passed a joyful time;
I'll not relate the plates of food supplied,
Such plenty flowed I'd never get it right!
As evening came and Charlemagne retired,
The bishops there all blessed the nuptial night
And Charles's men in this request combined:
"True Emperor, by God the Lord on High,
The noble knight Girart is filled with spite;
Bestow on him a fief to rule and guide
So no man hence may slander you or slight
Your name and fame for snubbing your best knights."
"Most willingly I shall," the King replied:
"For love of you, whose embassy I prize,
And for Girart, whom I esteem in kind,
I give to him Vienne and all its shire;
Its walls are high, its moat is deep and wide,
The city rich and much to be admired;
He'll have his fill of food and drink for life;
Against his foes his fort will be supplied –
But he must fight for me, should need arise."
The German and Bavarian lords all cried:
"Go kiss his foot, Girart, you worthy knight;
The gift is great – your thanks should be as high."
"Most willingly, by God," Girart replied;
For Charles's sake, who then had just retired,
His servants had turfed down the only fire;
So Girart came before the bed that night
And knelt to kiss the foot of Charles, his Sire;
The duchess, though, in her malicious pride,
As if The Fiend had got into her mind,
Put forth her foot just as Girart arrived;
He kissed the Queen, which was a mortal crime!
If good Girart had known of her design,
He would, instead, have struck her with a knife
Than deigned his lips to touch her foot that night!
God, what a war that kiss would cause in time!
How many lords and knights it doomed to die!
    In truth, *she* should have perished.

SO SIR GIRART, whose face with valour stormed,
Received Vienne, that city famed and sure,

From Charlemagne the mighty Emperor;
But when he left he never knew at all
Of the deceit performed the night before
By Charles's bride, in her unbridled scorn,
To his disgrace in Charles's very hall!
But what a price that kiss would cost henceforth!
How many souls from bodies would be shorn –
The Queen's one should have been the first of all!
But she was now revered by all and called
Your Majesty from every shire to shore;
When morning came, as soon as day had dawned,
Girart the duke was keen to journey forth,
And after Mass he left the royal court;
Charles offered him a noble household force
To garrison his new domain and forts,
And gave him too a wealth in goods and coin
Which Charles himself had won in lands abroad;
So off they rode, without delay or pause,
Until they came that night to Cluny's walls
And abbey-church, so richly built of yore,
        Where they would ask for lodging.

THE ABBOT LODGED Girart with him that night:
"Good Abbot, do you know me?" he inquired;
"No friend, in truth," the worthy priest replied,
"I've never met or seen you in my life."
"You have, by God," Girart said with a smile:
"The knight Renier, my brother brave, and I
Some fifteen years ago were passing by,
And you yourself received us at that time:
You gave us robes for our worn-out attire,
And your largesse has never left my mind;
Now I shall give to you a gift of mine:
One hundred marks and cloths of silk designed
To serve your needs and this great church of Christ."
On hearing this, the Abbot's thanks were high,
And all his monks bowed down in thanks alike;
Girart rode on, next day, at dawn's first light,
To reach Vienne as swiftly as he might;
His envoy spurred ahead till he arrived
Before the gate and galloped straight inside;

Throughout the town he spread the news and cried
That their new lord was on his way, a knight
To whom King Charles had granted all their shire –
And they should go to show their great delight
At this new lord who ruled them now by right;
On hearing this, they weren't remiss or shy;
They thronged the streets then rushed along outside;
The bishop too, the holy clerks and friars
Moved out to meet Girart in loyal lines;
They welcomed him with noble pomp and pride
Before the gates, rejoicing all the while;
They sang a mass at St Maurice's shrine,
Then all the folk of old Vienne combined,
Both high and low, with true and willing minds,
To pledge him faith and homage all their lives;
Then all the knights with great rejoicing climbed
    The steps inside the palace.

11. How Duke Girart met Aymeri his nephew

GIRART, INSTALLED within his hall of state,
Was loved by all who lived in his domains;
That very year, just past Ascension Day,
Upon the feast of John the blessed Saint,
He took a wife of high repute and race –
A sister of King Othon, Guibourc her name;
And it was she, this Lady I have named,
Who bore Beuvon and then Savariez,
Those youths whom in his evil Pagan jail
King Achatanz henceforth would cruelly chain;
One day, Girart, returning to my tale,
Was in his hall, when through the window-pane
He scanned the road that travelled through a dale
Between two hills to Lyons on its way;
At once he saw a gallant, gay young blade
Approaching with two others of his age;
On splendid mules of Aragon they came:
Their saddle-bows of gold were all engraved
With painted flowers and animals ornate,
And studs of gold were set along their reins;

Dismounting soon on blocks set in the shade,
They left their mules for good Guion to take,
The porter there, or so the record says,
And climbed the steps to reach the hall in haste;
The princely youth was Aymeri by name,
And he was first inside the hall of state;
On seeing him, Girart's complexion paled:
   He looked so like a kinsman!

YOUNG AYMERI strode up the steps and boards
Inside the hall whose walls were high and broad;
Upon his wrist he bore a sparrowhawk
As white as the alburnum's leaf and more;
Girart the duke behaved as well he ought:
When he beheld this youngster swaggering forth
He called his knights together in the hall
And said: "My lords, be silent, one and all!
For I see here a young and carefree lord
With eyes alone for sport and sparrowhawks!
Let neither squire nor man-at-arms step forth
And dare to speak one word with him before
I first have had my own words with the boy."
His men replied: "We will obey, my lord."
And so the youth strode up before them all
And in a clear and ringing voice he called:
"May God the Lord, Who Judges each and all,
Protect and bless this home of gallant lords!
Where is Girart, whose face with valour storms,
The noble duke whose fame I have been taught?"
No knight or squire replied or made a noise
But stooped his head and gazed upon the floor!
On seeing this, the youngster filled with scorn
And in a rage began to curse them all:
"You worthless rogues, you boors, you sons of whores!
A curse on him by whom you have been taught,
If I alone can scare you with my voice!
I've fifteen pounds of gold I can employ
To pay my way within this town of yours –
I'll find a bed and food and drink galore,
In spite of you, you weak and woeful horde!
You all display the manners of a boor

With naught to say until his gut is gorged!"
Girart heard this and with a laugh he roared:
"And who are you, young hero-with-a-hawk?
These nobles here have heard a matter brought
Of high concern and they must judge its course;
Your vaunting words weigh little on their thoughts!
Speak up, my lad, then seek your bed and board,
Then come back here and dine with us at court;
If you're a bard, we'll hear you then perform;
And if you want to sell that hawk of yours,
Then I'll make sure you get one copper coin!"
Girart then bade his treasurer come forth:
"Put on the perch this youngster's sparrowhawk;
He has no skill in holding it at all."
On hearing this, young Aymeri was galled;
He cried: "You rogue, you boor's son of a whore!
No serving-man of birth or worth so poor
Was ever kept in my good father's court!
I cannot bring myself in word or thought
To call you uncle – I shall return therefore
        To Hernaut of Biaulande!"

ON HEARING WHAT the youngster's lips disclosed,
Girart rejoiced to meet his nephew so;
Yet still he strove to keep the youth provoked,
So he could see his temper fully blown:
"Come on," he said, "let's hear you play a note!
If you're a bard, then sing a song of old!
I'll give you then an ermine fur-lined robe,
And with his gift no lord here will be loath."
The lad heard this and never felt so wroth;
The anger burned his cheeks like flaming coals;
He raised his voice, with rage and hate aglow:
"Now by the Saint in Nero's field at Rome,
Such service as I have been taught to show
I'll render now, to your delight or no!"
He raised his hawk, at this, and let it go
To strike the brow and bridge of Girart's nose;
His chin was skinned and blood began to flow
Upon the front of his fine ermine coat;
Girart called out: "Men, take this rogue in hold

And let him hang upon the gallows-rope!"
Three score and more rushed up as they were told;
Said Aymeri: "Get on your feet, you rogue!
I am the son of noble Sir Hernaut,
Lord of Biaulande, whose hair is white as snow,
And nephew of Girart – as here is shown
Upon a script inside this parchment's folds!"
Girart heard this and, unrestrained, he strode
To grasp the boy – then, lifting him up close,
On mouth and chin he kissed him sevenfold:
"My nephew fair, your heart is brave and bold!
        Well may you be my kinsman!"

12. How Aymeri learnt of the Queen's deceit

SAID AYMERI, of spirit bright and brave:
"Girart, my lord, it wasn't wise, I'd say,
To hide from me your proper self that way!
For by the Lord and all His blessed Saints,
If I had held, just then, when in my rage,
A staff or stick which my hand could have raised,
I would have struck your head a blow so great
It would have split your head and spread your brains!"
Said Duke Girart: "Good nephew, I had aimed
To test your worth and your prowess that way!
I love you now above the rest, in faith!
But tell me how my brother fares this day,
Hernaut the brave, whose name has won such fame."
"In truth, my lord, my father's wise and brave,
A wealthy man in high content and hale,
Both fierce and bold and by his friends well praised;
I've journeyed here to see your own estate,
To know your wealth and learn your noble ways."
"Lad," said Girart, "I'm very glad you came;
I'll dub you knight before you leave again,
With armour bright and rapid destrier!"
The youth replied: "In truth, I'd hoped you may!"
Soon after this Girart's command was made
And well obeyed throughout his wide domain,
To build new towers and barbicans and lakes;

At first Neuville was fortified this way,
Then Lyons' keys upon the Rhône he claimed
And made its walls more strong and tall the same,
And truly thought that he and his were safe;
Yet ere six months had spent their span of days,
His hands were full of warfare, and its pain
Was great enough to fill his heart with hate;
That winter all within his hall he lay
Till Easter time and summer came again,
When Aymeri had this request to make:
"My lord, I'd have you hear the plan I've made:
With your consent I wish to undertake
A journey to the court of Charlemagne;
My father, who is wise, advised the same."
"And so do I," Girart said straightaway:
"In highest courts your honour can but gain;
You could not serve in any finer place
Than Charles's court, whose honour is so great,
And who has raised us all through his own fame
And through his gifts of lands and great estates."
So Aymeri prepared without delay;
Girart was rich and gave him much to take
In silver, gold and many deniers;
He took with him two youths of matching age
To tend his needs and serve him in good faith;
Through Burgundy they started on their way,
Those worthy three, through Brie in such a haste
From dawn to dusk they never drew the rein;
They crossed the Marne at Saint Maur-des-Fossés,
Then saw the towers of Paris, tall and straight;
At length they passed the gardens and the gates
And sought the King but found he was away:
"The Emperor you seek, bright youths and brave,
Has gone this day to Saint-Denis to pray."
On hearing this, they neither stopped nor stayed
But strode along the metalled road again;
Outside Lendit they met with 'Big Gautier'
And Gilebert, two ruffians and knaves
Who on that road had robbed at will and slain,
As leaders of a gang that did the same:
Some ten of them were with the pair that day;

They saw the youths and didn't move away,
But passed them by and hailed them with 'good day';
But then they said: "We must have lost our brains!
These three are lords of noble birth and name:
The one in front, so splendidly arrayed,
Is some young count or prince of high estate;
If we could hold all three of them in chains,
Then we could win a ransom-fee so great
That four strong mules would stagger with its weight!"
And so all ten turned back upon their way
And stopped the youths by grasping at their reins,
With firm intent to drag them from the lane;
But Aymeri was not the least afraid;
With ringing voice he hailed them in this way:
"My lords, is this in earnest or in play?
If you're in need, then from our purses take
One hundred sous or more in deniers."
Their leader said: "Young fool! Your vaunting's vain!
We've come to take all three of you away!
For seven months you'll not escape our jail –
Until we get a full two bushels' weight
Of bezant coins and bags of deniers!"
Said Aymeri: "You ask too much, in faith;
We don't possess the riches that you crave;
But by the Lord and all His blessed Saints,
If we allowed ten thieves to block our way,
In every court we'd earn reproof and shame!"
While Gautier roared and wrenched the youngster's reins,
The sword he wore showed plainly at his waist –
So Aymeri, he seized it from its case
And struck the rogue who held him thus detained!
From top to teeth the sword-blade cleft his face;
At this his gang all tried to get away,
But Aymeri pursued them with the aid
Of both his squires, who joined him in the chase;
Not one of all that vicious gang escaped –
Each one was caught, cut down at once and slain!
The noble youths rode on their way again
And came at last to Saint-Denis that day;
Before the King sat down to dine, they'd placed
Their steeds in care within the town and made

Their way to court to speak with Charlemagne;
Arriving there, they found the first course laid,
The water brought, the courtiers at their plates,
Yet no one spoke one word with them or phrase;
Young Aymeri had been most nobly raised
And took a share of all the fare displayed;
He gave his friends a part of all he gained
And shared with them whate'er they cared to take;
The courtiers said, with lowered voice and gaze:
"This courtly youth is high of heart and grace;
He must be born of noble loins and race;
How rich he'll be if he should reach old age!"
When all had supped and all the cups were drained,
The courtiers rose, the cloths were cleared away;
Then Aymeri, not wishing to delay,
Approached the King and hailed him in this way:
"May God our Lord, Who bore the Cross's bane,
Protect our true and strong King Charlemagne,
The noblest Prince in Christendom's domains!"
"My friend," said Charles, "God prosper you the same!
What journey brings you here to me this day?
But tell me first your name – don't hide it, pray!"
"My lord and King, Count Aymeri's my name;
      Son of Hernaut of Biaulande."

THE QUEEN SPOKE UP: "Well here's a fine young fellow!
None half as fair came from Auvergne ever!
Youths full of spite and treasonable wretches
That duchy spawns, without a lie, I tell you!
Girart himself, Vienne's much feared protector,
I'll never prize for honest faith one bezant!
And who are you? Don't hide it or dissemble!"
"Count Aymeri I am, and proud to tell you
That I'm the son of Biaulande's lord, Sir Hernaut,
And am, madame, Girart of Vienne's nephew!
Don't speak of him with ill-regard, I beg you;
So help me God, good Queen, that would upset me!"
Across the hall a monk ran with a message
And told the King: "My lord, good news and merry!
Those thieving rogues whose evil deeds were many,
Have all been slain, thank God the Lord in Heaven!

This very day three noble youngsters met them,
Including one of peerless mood and merit
Who looks indeed like this one in your presence!"
The King heard this and straightaway he questioned
Young Aymeri: "Were you that gallant fellow?"
"By God, my lord, I was, I must confess it;
They set on us, without a lie I tell you;
In self-defence I struck them and they perished."
The King replied: "And stoutly I'd defend you
Against the charge of any who'd condemn you;
        You've done a gallant deed."

SAID CHARLEMAGNE: "Fine knights of high esteem,
This noble youth is very brave indeed:
With heart and hand he's felled a band of thieves
Who in our land had done such evil deeds;
Fine, noble youth, are you then truthfully
Sir Hernaut's son, of Biaulande by the sea?"
"Yes Sire, in truth," repeated Aymeri:
"The noble count appeals to you through me,
To dub me knight and arm me, noble liege;
His love for you will grow and never cease."
"If you can stay alive that long, indeed
I swear that I shall knight you in two weeks!"
The youth replied; "Much thanks for this, my liege;
Farewell until that happy day is here!"
That very day, ere daylight disappeared,
The King returned to Paris, while the Queen
Stayed where she was, at noble Saint-Denis,
As did the young and gallant Aymeri;
When evening came and all sat down to eat,
The Queen began to be more free of speech:
"Give ear to me, brave knights well-bred and free,
And hear a tale I've never yet revealed:
My husband died, the duke of Burgundy,
And I was left with all my lands to keep;
I came to Charles, the King of Saint-Denis,
And bade him find a husband fit for me,
And he named Sir Girart, who then was here;
I summoned him to ask if he agreed;
To my dismay, he said he would not meet,

But asked instead for me to wait two weeks!
I tell you all, I was aghast with grief,
So I asked Charles the fierce to come to me,
And come he did, at once and willingly;
Thank God above in Paradise the sweet,
Charles married me with everybody's leave;
When day was done upon our marriage-feast,
The King was urged by knights of high esteem
To give Girart Vienne with all its fiefs;
The King of Saint-Denis lay next to me
And Lord Girart approached our bed to kneel
And thank the King, his liege of visage fierce,
By kissing Charles's foot – or so it seemed!
Before the King I placed one of my feet
Upon the top of our grey blanket-sheet
And made Girart mistakenly kiss me –
He kissed my flesh, I pledge this faithfully!
No man alive divined my trickery;
I took revenge on proud Girart's deceit;
I paid him back for making light of me –
  And took delight to do so!"

TO HEAR THE QUEEN, with pleasure in her voice,
So pride herself upon the shame she'd caused,
Young Aymeri, whose heart was fiercely wrought,
Was sure his mood could never stand the taunt;
For life nor limb, he swore he'd eat no more,
And, leaping up in anger from the forms,
He spoke aloud, with vengeance in his voice:
"My Lady Queen, by good St Riquier's corpse,
If you did this of which you have made vaunt,
I have to say, you acted like a whore!
For brave Girart's a good and worthy lord;
I'll die of rage, if my revenge falls short!"
He held a knife with sharpened blade and point;
Before them all, at dinner in the hall,
He took his aim and hurled the dagger forth;
Between her breasts the weapon would have torn
But down she swooned upon the cushioned floor;
The dagger slammed against a roof-support;
Fierce Aymeri approached where she was sprawled

And would have slain her still, no doubt at all,
But he was chased and charged by several lords;
They clutched and clawed around him as they sought
To catch the youth, who hurried out the door;
And they went close to taking him, I'm sure,
But Aymeri was in no mood to pause;
He hailed his friends with this command and call:
"My worthy lords, each one of you, to horse!
This land is cursed and this a wicked court –
And I'll be damned if I'll remain here more!
    I'm off, back to Vienne!"

13. How Girart's clan united in Vienne

YOUNG AYMERI had left them on the run;
The Frenchmen said: "By God the Lord above,
What evil strife can come from woman's tongue!
My Lady Queen, you've brought the court ill luck!
Why did you speak of what was known to none?
If yonder knife, embedded in the truss,
Had found its mark, and you, the Queen, been struck,
Your bragging tale would dearly have been spun!"
"My lords," she said, "such terror filled my blood
That I shall feel it throbbing for a month!"
But Aymeri had lost none of his pluck:
Upon the road he set his steed at once
To reach Vienne the same way he had come;
From morn till night they kept their journey up
Till they arrived one evening at dusk;
Girart looked up with joy in heart and flung
His arms around his nephew's neck with love
And said: "Fine youth, most welcome back to us!
So have you seen great Charles the Emperor?
Have you received fine gifts and knighthood's glove?"
The youth said naught, his anger was too much,
And for a while he hailed or spoke to none,
But then, at last, he answered clear enough:
"By God our Lord, my quest met with ill-luck:
My face shall not be seen in France by such
    As love the Lady Queen there."

"BY GOD, MY LORD," said Aymeri the fierce:
"What evil news from France I bring with me;
At Charles's court your stay was cursed indeed,
For you've been shamed most foully by the Queen,
And all your clan will feel the shame and grief:
When Charles had wed the duchess, as he pleased,
That night when he and she retired to sleep,
 His mighty lords approached him to beseech
That you should have this land to rule and keep;
To thank the King you came on bended knee
Beside his bed; but in her spite the Queen
Put forth her foot, and this your kiss received!
The other day she boasted of the deed
In front of me and more at Saint-Denis;
I tried at once to slay her with my steel,
But I was forced to turn around and flee."
On hearing this, Girart's good conscience reeled:
"By St Maurice," he cried, "whom I hold dear,
If I can call my clan and liegemen here,
We'll go to France and fight them till they yield!
I'll leave behind no castle in one piece,
No fort or town, nor church or monastery!"
Said Aymeri: "By God, Who judges each,
If what you pledge you truly would achieve,
Then I'll be first to help you in your need!
Then there's Renier, my uncle full of zeal,
And Lord Hernaut my father fine and fierce,
And Miles the duke, whose valour has no peer."
"We'll ride to Renier first!" Girart decreed,
And straightaway he set about to leave;
He seized his arms of gold and silver steel,
Then turned to go with every show of speed;
From morn till night they rode until they reached
Geneva town as evening drew near,
And once inside dismounted from their steeds;
Renier was filled with joy when they appeared
And welcomed them to stay with hearty cheer;
Inside his hall they all of them perceived
A noble youth whom Renier bade them meet:
"Behold," he said, "fine knights of gallant breed,
The noble son who has been born to me!"

Said Duke Girart: "His look is fierce indeed!
You should, in truth, thank God for such as he!
But what's his name? Don't hide it or conceal!"
"His name is Oliver," Count Renier beamed;
Girart replied: "In truth, I hold him dear,
  For he looks like a fighter!"

THE BROTHERS MET within his hall of tiles,
And Duke Girart, of features fierce and wise,
Addressed Renier, then drawing him aside,
Revealed the news and told him of the slight
That he'd received from Charles's spiteful bride;
On hearing this, his brother's cheeks turned white;
He swore to God, Who makes the dew and sky:
"Her villainy shall pay an awful price!
We'll devastate all France with sword and fire
And lead away in shame great Charles's wife,
If they themselves won't give her up betimes:
For she must bear our vengeance for this crime;
If this affair should be revealed to Miles,
Our brother fair, of features fierce and wise,
He'd hurry here and never ponder twice;
So would Hernaut, of gallant heart and mind,
And Lord Garin, our father bearded white;
When all our clan has rallied forth its knights,
They'd gallop to the Sea of Ice to fight!"
Girart replied: "I know that you are right;
Without delay dispatch three men to ride
And seek them all and bid them from their shires,
  In Vienne to assemble."

BETWEEN THEM BOTH Girart and brave Renier
Affirmed the hour and fixed the day and date
When their great hosts, with all their haste and hate,
Would meet before Vienne upon the plain;
When this was done, without the least delay,
Girart set off with Aymeri the brave
Until they came to old Vienne again;
Girart was rich and ruled a wide domain:
He gathered stores from all of his estates
And slaughtered meat and garnered wheat and grain

For all the troops arriving as arranged;
Awaiting in his keep, Girart one day
Looked out towards Lyons, and, as he gazed,
One thousand knights came spurring hard his way;
He called young Aymeri to see the same:
"Fine nephew mine, attend to what I say!
I do not know this folk upon the plain;
They are, I hope, the Moors or Pagan knaves,
Or some such folk whom we must fear and face!"
On hearing this, the youngster laughed to say:
"Good uncle, I'll not hide from you their names!
That is Hernaut, his whiskers white with age,
My father dear whose life has won such fame:
Consider now where all his men can stay,
For there are more than fifty score in pay
 And service of my father."

GIRART LEAPT UP without one moment's pause,
With Aymeri, whose face with valour stormed;
They left Vienne by street and gate to join
The army come from Biaulande's shire and shore;
Young Aymeri beheld his father's force
And knew at once the ensign that they bore;
As you can guess, the noble youth rejoiced;
Then from a copse came Hernaut with his corps;
On seeing him, Girart advanced his horse
Towards the spot and left his reins to fall;
He reached Hernaut and greeted him with warmth:
"So, brother, will you lend me your support?"
"I will, by God Who made the sky!" he called:
"Ill-starred the hour that mighty wrong was wrought;
The Queen shall pay most dearly for her taunt –
We'll slay the wretch and bring her name to naught!"
Then, as Girart and he embraced and talked,
Sir Miles appeared, who too had brought his force
To help Girart, ten score they were in all;
And Girart went to greet him with great joy;
Then from another side came surging forth
Renier the duke – he'd not delayed at all;
And at his side how fine a band he'd brought
Of noble lords, and some less nobly born,

But all equipped and fully armed for war;
  Girart now had an army!

THE BROTHERS RODE inside Vienne in brief,
Where all were lodged, the mighty and the mean;
As all began to take their rest and ease,
Then old Garin, their sire himself, appeared,
Lord of Monglane, whose heart was high and fierce;
Within his ranks rode seven thousand peers
On crested steeds which stumbled with fatigue:
His force's coats were cleft of mail and seam,
Their helmets split and all their bucklers pierced,
Their bodies worn, for all had fought with zeal
Against the foul and evil Pagan breed;
Thank God above, they'd brought their foe to heel,
But not without great loss and injuries;
When these arrived, how glad and joyfully
They welcomed them and greeted all and each;
Inside the hall with marble all a-gleam,
  Garin the duke went striding.

GARIN THE DUKE strode up and came inside,
And all his sons rushed forth to kiss their sire;
They led him off to bathe and be attired,
And, coming back, he wore a mantle fine
And held a staff of apple-wood peeled white;
The court agreed his presence had no like;
When all had dined they left the hall that night,
Except Garin, his sons, and with those five,
Young Aymeri, whose face was brave and bright;
Girart spoke out, of heart and honour high;
With old Garin and all his brothers by,
Whom he most dearly loved, he spoke his mind:
"Give ear to me, my good and noble knights;
You've ridden here to help me with your might,
But none of you know yet the reason why;
I served the King, great Charles, the fierce of eye,
Until one day he went to hunt the hind;
Upon our way a messenger arrived,
Who came to him with tidings from his shire:
The worthy duke of Burgundy had died;

And then, good men, Charles took his arrow's iron,
And with it pledged the widow as my bride,
And all her land he pledged to me alike;
But what he pledged became too rich a prize,
For he himself reclaimed her as his wife!
When both were wed and to their bed retired,
The King was urged by all his lords and knights
To offer me this town and land entire;
To kiss his foot I went in thanks, that night,
But his new Queen, in her malicious pride,
Put forth her own, which took that kiss of mine;
Since then she's made a boast of this, in spite;
Young Aymeri, whose heart is fierce and high,
Was there to hear and many more besides;
Without revenge despair will end my life:
  The shame of it's so heavy."

ON HEARING THIS, Garin the old got up
And looked around as he addressed them thus:
"You are, my lords, each one and all, my sons;
Hernaut and Miles, you were the wisest ones:
You went to win your fiefs with blade and blood;
Renier, you went to France, there to become
A household knight; Girart, you did as much –
Like shepherds guarding sheep, you ended up!
I tell you this: if Charles has wit enough
To swear to you, in front of everyone,
That he knew not and it delights him none
To learn about this shameful thing she's done,
Then he'll not bear, I swear, our anger's brunt!
For it's not long, so help me God above,
That I clashed arms with pagan Sinagon;
I was besieged by hordes of Saracens
Within my town, behind it and in front;
I do believe if I had peace for once,
I'd be struck down by sickness in a month,
Some plague or ague or leprosy or such!
Yet when I see the whinnying war-steeds plunge
With worthy knights inside a battle's crush,
And see those spears and cutting blades well struck,
There's naught on earth my old blood loves as much!

But I repeat: if Charles has wit enough
To swear to you in front of everyone
That he knew naught of this most grave affront,
He shall not feel the angry steel of us;
But should he not, my worthy knights and sons,
He'll have a fight whose like there never was,
    And we shall overrun him!"

WHEN AYMERI had heard his grandsire speaking,
He sought Girart and said what he was feeling:
"Good uncle, did you heed the old man's preaching
And proud account of all the fights he's been in?
You would be called a fool, and with good reason,
To lead him forth to more, if he's so weary!"
Garin heard this and thought his wits would leave him!
He held a rod, to grace his age and please him,
But now, in rage, he brandished it to beat with!
The youth ran off, Garin could never reach him:
"You harlot's son!" he cried, his visage gleaming:
"No worthy man will change his plan on hearing
A wilful youth whose words are overweening,
And not be called by one and all a weakling!
    We'll pay no heed to you!"

HERNAUT THE COUNT, a man of boldest vigour,
Leapt up at this and showed a gallant visage;
He spoke aloud and all his brothers listened:
"Good men," he said, "we need no lengthy discourse!
King Charlemagne is at Chalon this minute,
And nearby lies Mâcon and all its district;
Let's ride at once and seize upon that city!
From Charles's hand with our own band we'll strip it!"
But Garin said: "By Jesus, I forbid it,
For then not he but we would be the villain!
Let's speak with him and that way we may win him!"
But then, my friends, upon that very instant,
Two riders of King Charles came striding in there –
Sir Baldwin and Sir Hugh their names – and swiftly
They sought Girart and spoke to him as bidden:
"Give ear, Girart, to Charlemagne's own wishes!
Five years and more at least have run their limit

Since from his hand you gained this land and city;
But you've not sent one spur to him in tribute;
Now he sends you his word, which we deliver:
Come straightaway and pay for this omission!
For if you don't, St Simon be our witness,
He'll come to you and bring his army with him,
To burn your fields and turn your fief to cinders!
You'll not have left one button's worth of riches."
Girart heard this and all his whiskers bristled:
"Upon my soul, we'll go," Garin said quickly,
"And we shall take some twenty knights there with us,
The fittest we can find, the wisest-witted,
    To judge the right and wrong."

14. How Girart's clan clashed with the King at court

THEIR COUNCIL CEASED as I have told you here;
Hernaut spoke up: "Will you come, Aymeri,
To speak with Charles the King, abiding near
With all his knights? Among them you may see
Those knights and lords who heard the tale revealed
To you in boast that evening by the Queen."
"In God's name, lord," replied young Aymeri,
"I guarantee I'll find at least thirteen!"
When this was said their party made to leave;
But Aymeri, whose mood was never meek,
Spoke privately into an envoy's ear:
"My friend," he said, "I bid you with all speed
To tell our men that they must arm with steel
And follow us some distance in the rear;
For I am sure, as now I live and breathe,
That we shall leave the King as enemies!"
The man replied: "I'll do it willingly."
When this was said the party rode their steeds
With rein unchecked until Chalon was reached;
Outside its wall they sought a hall to sleep
Then went to court all mindful of their need;
Charles greeted them with grace when they appeared;
"I welcome you, fine knights and noble peers;
I am obliged that you have come to me!"

Hernaut replied: "You don't deserve to be!
No friend of yours can say the same, I fear!"
On hearing this, the King was most aggrieved;
He looked askance and said to Aymeri:
"Fine, noble youth, I welcome you indeed;
Not long ago you were at Saint-Denis!"
The youth replied: "In Jesu's name, my liege,
Some thirty blows my welcome face received;
I'll not forget that warmth for many a year!
The Queen herself displayed such loving cheer
That I was nearly slain – for it was clear
I had no friends among the friends she keeps;
With every haste I turned around to leave
    And rode back to Vienne."

THE EMPEROR then heard what she had said,
While at his side she showed untold distress;
He looked at her and his regard was dread;
He looked across at fierce Girart and then,
Before his court, he called to him and them:
"My lord Girart, hide naught from me yourself!
Are all these knights your family or friends?
Who is that lord so old and white of head?"
"True Emperor, as Jesus is my strength,
That is Garin, my father, whom I bless,
And those three are my brothers, all brave men;
Fine King, my lord, as you have heard from them,
Do right by me and punish the offence
Your Queen confessed with foolish, proud contempt,
Inside the rooms of good Abbot Heles."
The King heard this and, in no mood to jest,
He called his reeve, with ringing voice, and said:
"Inquire for me and do not hide your quest,
If there is truth or mad deceitfulness
In this complaint which I have heard alleged;
By all my faith in Mary's son, I pledge
To do more than would any, if it's correct;
But if it's not, then let men know it hence
That charity can breed great wickedness!
For since the hour I gave Girart Vienne
And gave Renier Geneva's wealthy realm,

They've paid me naught in service or in wealth;
But now I swear by Heaven's King Himself,
I shall not leave this land or take a step
Till someone's paid for their deceitfulness!"
Said Aymeri: "Amen to that! And let
Revenge be done ere this day's sun has set!
Lord Emperor, I'll not leave this unsaid:
By God, the Lord we all adore and bless,
I swear that there is none, alive or dead,
No King or Prince of pride or such prowess,
Whom I would rate a rotten apple, when
He'd served me well to shame me better hence!
Though you gave me Romagna's wealth itself,
I'll make no truce nor any truce accept,
Until the Queen shall show and know regret!
    Ill-blest was her proud gesture!"

"MY LORD GIRART," spoke up the wise Duke Naimon,
"Take wealth in coin by way of reparation!"
Girart replied: "Your words and wit are wasted;
For by the Saint whom sinners seek and pray to,
Though you gave me Milan, I'd never take it;
Pavia, Rome, Toulouse – not one would make me
Agree to peace or any way placate me
Till such revenge as I deem fit is taken
Upon this Queen, whose arrogant behaviour
Has shamed my name and filled my heart with hatred;
And by the Saint whom sinners seek to save them,
I'll never stop while I have breath remaining,
    Till she herself knows shame."

"MY LORD GIRART," Duke Naimon said forthwith:
"Allow the Queen atonement for her sin
By bearing forth your saddle rich of stitch
Upon her head to walk a league therewith,
Unshod and in a hair-shirt, if you wish."
Garin replied: "You speak of pardon still;
But by the Saint they seek on Nero's hill,
We shall accept no peace or truce until
Her head and heart are split for what she did."
Said Do of Laon: "My lord, the Devil this!

Who is this boor of hoary beard and lip,
Who speaks to us so wildly of his will?
I challenge him in place of Charles the King!"
And forth he strode like one of wicked will;
He seized Garin, and from his bearded chin
He plucked away one hundred hairs forthwith,
    With all the barons watching.

SIR MILES'S CHEEK burned up at once with rage
To see Garin, his father's, pain and shame;
He looked at Do with eyes of deepest hate,
While Renier flung away his noble cape
And Duke Girart unsheathed his shining blade;
But Aymeri brought forth a mighty mace
And, running up to Do at rapid pace,
He struck the man, he didn't hesitate,
For having plucked his grandsire's beard away;
He split his head and out ran all his brains;
In ringing tones the King at once exclaimed:
"My household knights, take hold of him, I say!
If you do not, you have betrayed your faith;
Try what he may, this time he'll not escape!
    He has disgraced my presence!"

SOME TWENTY FIVE stood up in front of Charles,
All clansmen of the gallant knight Girart,
And each well armed with sturdy sword or staff;
They swore to fight right through the French and pass,
Unless the walls should fall and block their path!
Hernaut the count struck Oton first and fast
And forced his head and shoulder-blades to part!
Then Miles the count struck one Sir Haguenan
Upon the skull with two blows of his staff;
And Renier struck Hoel, who breathed his last;
Girart swung then his axe in mighty arcs,
Whose blade in length was one foot and a half;
They left the hall, whoever grieves or laughs;
And if the Queen had been where they went past,
Then their revenge would surely have been harsh;
But to her room she'd run in great alarm;
The gallant knights ran out into the yard

Where they had left their stallions in advance,
And mounted up without a backward glance;
On every side the Frenchmen seized their arms;
But Girart's men had mocked the court of France,
   And showed no will to linger!

15. How Aymeri was knighted

IN GOOD CHALON the Frenchmen seized their weapons
As Girart's men rode off in ranks well-serried;
Yet ere they'd gone one half a league together
The Duke looked up between a plain and meadow
And saw his men arriving in great plenty,
Led by the lad to whom they were commended!
They flew the flag of St Maurice, their emblem;
Girart looked up and couldn't hide his pleasure
As, calling all his brothers and his men there,
He said: "My lords, I see this as a message!
God's will is shown by sending them to help us!
These troops are ours – our comrades and our brethren
   Who've ventured from Vienne!"

GIRART MET UP with all his household force,
And greeted all with laughter in his voice:
"My worthy men, who set you on this course?"
Said Aymeri: "I brought them here, my lord,
Through word I gave a messenger at dawn."
Girart replied: "I love you more and more!
If not for you, we'd all be killed or caught."
His worthy band rode onward as before,
As fearsome Charles pursued them with his force
Of well-armed knights and men one hundred score,
With Hermer, knight of Paris, to the fore,
Who hailed Girart with anger in his voice:
"My lord Girart, where are you running for?
And you Renier, I challenge you to halt!
You've shown contempt for France's Christian Law,
And proven false to Charles, who rules us all!"
On hearing this, Renier was angered sore
And shouted back: "You harlot's son, that's false!

I'm well prepared to prove to you and all
That I have not betrayed the Emperor!"
When this was said they waited nothing more
But with their spurs drove both their stallions forth;
On Hermer's shield the shaft of Renier bore
Above the boss and broke apart its boards,
His coat not worthy a lily-leaf once torn;
Between his ribs he thrust the lance's point
And flung him dead upon the meadow gorse;
As Hermer fell Renier secured his horse
And then rode back as knights of breeding ought;
Young Aymeri called out: "By God, my lord,
I'll love you more than e'er I did before,
If you'll give me this worthy horse you've caught,
So I may arm and mount it fit for war,
And as a knight may fight for our good cause;
    I truly think it fitting!"

AND SO THEY STOPPED, beneath the shade of trees,
To make a knight of noble Aymeri;
Girart the duke and all his brothers three
Placed on his back a mail of triple weave
And on his head a helm of burnished green;
Girart girt on a sword of polished steel
And with his palms upon the youngster's cheeks
Said: "Aymeri, be brave and think of me!"
The lad replied: "I thank you much, my liege;
I shall, as long as God puts breath in me!"
They led him then that captured Arab steed
Which he bestrode with no delay indeed!
About his neck they hung a curving shield,
And in his hand he gripped a burnished spear,
Then ran his horse across the florid field:
"How fine a knight he is!" they all agreed
And straightaway gave blessings all and each,
    With joy and great rejoicing.

16. How Mâcon was taken and Vienne put to siege

SO AYMERI the youth was dubbed a knight;
He bore his arms and wore his armour bright
As all rode on, not wasting any time,
For now the King was very close behind,
With twenty score and more there by his side;
Young Aymeri was brave and bold alike:
He turned at once his Norway steed to strike
One Jocerain, who ruled in Albi's shire;
He split his shield and ripped his coat awry
And rammed his ribs with solid Vienne iron!
He speared him well and flung him dead and cried:
"You'll nevermore creep up on me or mine!"
He turned his reins, not wasting any time,
But first he seized the war-steed as his prize
    And gave it to his uncle.

THEY HURRIED ON and made no more delay –
For now the King, whose beard was white with age,
Was gaining ground with every pace he made,
And in his ranks rode knights of highest fame;
Through vale and dale in hot pursuit they came:
Renier, for one, had run his horse all day,
And spurred it hard and harder yet again;
But now he looked at those who gave them chase
And turned the head of his good horse to face
One Eliot with all his strength and hate;
Before the rest he charged him straightaway;
He split his shield without one moment's waste
And cleft his coat of countless chains of mail;
Between the ribs he thrust his battle-gage
And threw the knight from saddle bright to grave
In front of Charles, whose beard was grey with age;
Then, taking hold of both its golden reins,
He called Girart and spoke this prudent phrase:
"We must escape – their numbers are too great!"
When this was said they spurred ahead and raced
    In haste to reach Vienne.

KING CHARLES'S KNIGHTS pursued them hard and well;
The King held up a broken lance's end
And, as he rode, he called aloud and said:
"Girart, where are you running to, you wretch?
You shall not see this very season end
Before I'll take your castle at Vienne!
If you are caught, there'll be no ransom set –
I'll drag you out with chains around your neck!"
Said Aymeri: "Now that's a foolish threat!
Know well, instead, my uncle's own intent:
He'll strike your hide with his whole lance and send
Its gonfalon right through your royal flesh,
Whoever grieves at this or grins instead!"
The knights of both attacked when this was said
And Girart's ranks lost fifty there and then;
The King turned back to Vaudon river's edge,
Whose waters flow with mighty tow and depth,
While Duke Girart rode on to reach Vienne;
The Queen herself, of visage fair and fresh,
Returned to France, and at the King's behest
Called forth at once its mighty regiments;
From all around they came when summoned thence,
From every rank, some fifteen thousand men;
The Queen herself then led them back again
  To Charlemagne her husband.

INSIDE VIENNE, as evening drew near,
Girart arrived with all his men of liege;
With every haste dismounting from their steeds,
They climbed the steps to reach its mighty keep;
To all his clan Girart began to speak
And said: "My lords, it's very plain to see
That Charlemagne has turned his wrath on me:
He's slain today so many of my peers,
The loss of whom can never be redeemed."
Renier replied: "I swear by Christ's own creed,
King Charles shall not, I pledge you truthfully,
Set foot in France or have one moment's peace,
Till he has paid for this and for the Queen!
And by the Saint they seek in Nero's field,
When we have slain and laid them in their biers,

As King of France we'll crown young Aymeri!"
But Miles replied: "Good brother, hold your peace!
Majestic God forbids us all and each
To show contempt or make a foolish speech;
For all men know that Charles remains unique:
No King on earth is half as fine as he!
If he should die, I swear by Christ's own creed,
The whole of France would rise up in its grief;
To rob the King of Burgundy's rich fiefs
Would be revenge enough, it seems to me;
To go to France would be a foolish scheme –
   It's full of fearsome fighters."

AT CRACK OF DAWN, well-armed, their armour on,
Girart's whole force of knights and men set off
And left Vienne, his sturdy town well-stocked;
They rode in ranks some twenty thousand strong;
Between the woods and their surrounding rocks
They seized the herds belonging to Mâcon,
Then took the town itself by force and shock;
What wealth they found behind the city's locks –
Almerian silks and sundry precious cloths,
With silver, gold and steeds of Syrian stock!
Girart's whole force led all this booty off
Towards Vienne, his sturdy town well-stocked;
An envoy left Mâcon and rode non-stop
To find the King, so white of beard and long,
   And tell him what had happened.

THE ENVOY LEFT and rode with anxious mind
Upon a steed which sweated head to hind;
At rapid pace he raced along the heights,
Not slowing till the royal tent was nigh;
He asked for Charles and then was shown inside;
As soon as he could see the King he cried:
"Great Charlemagne, I bring you tidings dire!
Your town Mâcon is taken from you, Sire;
Of all its wealth the little that survives
Would not amount to twopence all combined!"
On hearing this, the King was filled with spite:
"Who did this thing?" cried Charlemagne the wise:

"By God, my lord, I know without a lie!
Girart the duke and Count Renier and Miles
Of Apulia's land and all their kind!
From Tarentaise to old Genèvre's heights
No faithless lord endures or Lombard knight
Whom they have not secured to their own side,
    To help them and support them."

THE MESSENGER continued with his message:
"Fine King, my lord, pay heed to what I tell you!
Girart and his own brother Miles together
Have openly and with all haste assembled
Each man of theirs from every town and dwelling;
And what is more, Hernaut, old Garin's eldest,
Has brought a host from his own coast to help them;
They all have sworn in highest rage and temper
To take from you no reparation ever,
But one by one to waste all your possessions
And render you both penniless and helpless,
Unless you give the Queen, of fair complexion,
To them alone so they may take their vengeance."
On hearing this, the King was far from merry;
He summoned forth Sir Droon and Sir Hervi,
And said: "My lords, how foul a wrong besets me!
Girart the duke, whom in my hall I welcomed,
And made a knight, has proved a thankless felon!
I urge you both to go to France together
And bring Sir Hugh and Baldwin here to help me;
Bring Roland too, my brave and handsome nephew:
In all of France let there remain no Frenchman
Who doesn't come to old Vienne directly,
On foot or horse, with any sort of weapon –
And those with none, we'll give them one, God help me!"
The pair replied: "With God Almighty's blessing;
True Emperor, your will shall be our pleasure."
So back they rode, as fast as spurs would fetch them,
To seek from France the aid that Charles had sent for;
The Emperor, with no delay whatever,
Had brought to him St Simon's chest of relics;
And all his knights and he swore solemn pledges
That they'd besiege Vienne's well-built defences,

For fourteen years or more, however many,
    Until that fortress fell!

HIS MESSENGERS rode back to France the sweet
And mustered there a mighty host indeed;
But in Vienne the men were set to leave:
Sir Miles set off and left for his demesne;
Hernaut the count, whose face with valour gleamed,
Set off alike for Biaulande by the sea,
And Renier too for his Genevan seat;
Inside his hall Girart remained, at ease,
Not thinking once, for it was past belief,
That Charles would come and lay Vienne to siege;
And yet, my friends, within that very year,
One hundred died who had decried the deed;
Those messengers, whose names I have revealed,
Who went to France at Charlemagne's decree,
Stayed long enough within the land to lead
So great a force of men to help their liege,
That never yet had France sent forth its peer –
One hundred thousand strong, the song reveals,
Some dukes, some counts, some knights of high degree;
They tarried not but mounted up their steeds
And journeyed forth in ranks at rapid speed;
One Tuesday night they entered Burgundy,
And by a slope they pitched their tents to sleep;
With dawning day, the morning bright and clear,
Towards Mâcon they made with merry cheer,
    And Charles advanced to meet them.

THE KING RODE ON through Burgundy's great shire;
Towards the west he turned and set his eyes
On lovely France, the worthy and the prized,
And saw his ranks upon a hillock's rise;
He blessed them all with God Almighty's sign:
"Ah God," he said, "Earth's Sovereign and Sire,
How lucky he, like me, to be alive
And in command of such a force so fine!
Now by the Saints whom sinners seek to find,
Since I have pledged my word and sworn to Christ,
I shall not turn to France again till I
    Have taken back Vienne!"

KING CHARLEMAGNE that night slept in the field
Till dawning day and morning bright and clear;
On every side the army woke from sleep
And packed its arms upon their sumpter-beasts;
Towards Mâcon they rode with rapid speed,
For they themselves, without a doubt, believed
That it was there they'd find young Aymeri;
But he was wise and when he first perceived
The mighty ranks which Charles had commandeered,
And all the knights and barons he'd convened,
The youngster left, with every haste indeed,
To reach Vienne, his only safe retreat;
In hot pursuit the King chased at his heels,
In serried ranks with all his knights and peers;
He ordered carts to carry wines and wheat,
And on all sides he laid Vienne to siege:
How many tents and canopies they reared!
Yet any siege would last five years at least,
Before it took that mighty castle's keep;
The town itself was full of food to eat,
　　And those inside were gallant.

17. How Aymeri went close to capturing the Queen

A MIGHTY SIEGE they laid around Vienne:
No man of them had seen a greater set;
The King of Saint-Denis spoke forth his pledge
To never leave till all were caught or dead;
Girart the duke saw all his walls beset:
Small wonder then that he was filled with dread:
"Lord God, fine King of Paradise," he said,
"I'll surely die if I can gain no help;
For Miles is back in Apulia's realm,
And fierce Hernaut is in Biaulande again,
And Renier in Geneva with his men."
So, calling forth three envoys to attend,
He said to them: "My friends, now hear me well!
Tomorrow, when the dawn's first light is shed,
You each must leave without delay or let
To seek support from all my clan and friends;

Tell all of them that Charles has sieged Vienne;
For love of Him whom Longinus confessed,
Request them all to come to my defence!"
"My lord," they cried, "we'll do as you have said!"
"By God, my lord," young Aymeri said then,
"I shall not eat, you have my solemn pledge,
Till I have slain some knight among these French
And captured one, or two, through my prowess!"
Girart replied: "God bless you with His strength!
Without you here my heart would be distressed."
The noble youth took up his arms and left;
He donned his mail and laced his shining helm;
A curving shield was draped around his neck
And in his hand a shining spear was set;
He summoned forth one hundred knights and ten
And through the gates, with fierce intent they went;
In Charles's host they heard them coming thence
And arms were seized by twice the sum of them;
No cries were made in challenge or contempt,
But every man spurred forth with fierce intent;
On every shield the shock of war was felt;
The spear-shafts hit and bits flew in the air;
The fight began and bitterly it spread;
Stout lances broke and solid shields were bent
As noble knights from noble steeds were rent;
Young Aymeri stood firm among the press,
His ringing voice heard high above the rest:
"God shame the man who shuns to strike his best!"
Girart the duke was in his tower when
He heard him shout with every ounce of breath,
Then heard the blows as fighters fought to death;
So straightaway he armed his bravest men,
Some twenty-seven whose courage was the best,
And through the gate they raced with fierce intent;
They saw the French, but *they* did not see them,
As in a rank they rushed towards their tents
And swung their blades at random, right and left,
To start a second fight, more bitter yet!
How many shields were split apart or bent,
How many coats were ripped awry and rent,
How many counts knocked from their mounts to death!

They hacked to ground the Frenchmen's biggest tent,
Where Charles himself was lying on a bed;
But when he heard their war-blades' whirring edge
And saw them strike upon his sentries' helms,
He left his couch and went to Bernard's tent,
    Calling for arms and armour.

TO BERNARD'S TENT the Emperor escaped;
He left his bed to save his head that day;
The Queen alike, of bright and shining face,
To save her skin fled after him in haste;
But Aymeri was there and caught her waist,
To her despair, but to his uncle's praise!
Girart the duke unsheathed his cutting blade
To strike her down with all his rage and hate;
But then the lad, with ringing voice, exclaimed:
"For Jesu's sake, don't let her end this way,
But drag the slag still living to your jail,
Where we may wreak such vengeance as we crave!"
Girart replied: "There's wit in what you say."
See Roland then, the bravest of the brave,
And Baldwin too, well-bred and brave the same,
Both nephews of the mighty Charlemagne;
Young Baldwin was the first to call his name:
"True Emperor, we tarry here too late!
The Queen is lost to you and us this day,
For she was caught and kidnapped in that raid!
Go after her, my lord, in Jesu's name!"
"Most willingly I will," said Charlemagne,
And leapt astride his Gascon destrier,
Equipped but half, he left in such a haste;
He bore a shield with lion-figures faced,
While in his fist he held a spear well made;
He left the tent and spurred with every haste,
In hot pursuit of Duke Girart, whose aim
And plan it was to place the Queen in chains;
Young Aymeri he saw, who held her waist,
And smote his shield with lion-figures faced;
He broke its boards beneath the blazon's paint;
He didn't pierce the sturdy hauberk's mail
But struck him well and flung him on the plain;

He took the Queen, of bright and shining face,
And bidding her mount up his destrier,
He led her back to Bernard's tent again,
    And from a death most certain.

18. How Oliver first met the young Sir Roland

GIRART RODE BACK from this attacking sortie
With Aymeri, whose bravery was dauntless,
And all of those who'd left with him that morning;
They'd put some fright all right in Charles's forces,
For they had slain or put in chains some forty!
Girart at last dismounted from his war-horse
And, sick at heart, went back inside his hallway;
He prayed aloud: "Sweet Jesus, I exhort you –
Without support my life and fort are forfeit!
My brother Miles has left for his own borders,
Hernaut alike is back on his own shoreline
And Renier too in his Genevan fortress!
The time has gone for their men to support me."
But he was wrong to be so dismal-thoughted!
The following day, with daylight barely dawning,
His brother Miles arrived with reinforcements,
One thousand men whose shields were wielded for him;
Then good Hernaut appeared and guided forward
One thousand men again, well-clad for warfare;
Renier alike had mustered forth more forces
To right the wrong, as noble fighters ought to,
Two thousand men on rapid, long-maned horses;
And one of his own sons this time had joined him:
Young Oliver, Count Roland's friend henceforward;
To come in time his brothers had not halted,
But now they did, dismounting when they saw him;
The sight of them filled Girart with rejoicing
And from his gate he galloped out towards them,
Embracing each as each arrived before him;
He looked with pride on Oliver and also
On lovely Aude, whose presence made him joyful,
And straightaway he kissed and hugged them warmly;
The squires ran off to ready lodgings for them

And stable well their rapid, long-maned horses;
Girart the duke stepped up inside his fortress
With all his clan, well-blest and cherished always,
Then all of them climbed up the highest storey
And there surveyed the host encamped before them;
Now Roland, friends, had ridden out beforehand
Below Vienne, with just his hunting-falcon,
And seen some drakes upon the Rhône's swift waters;
The dauntless youth had launched his hawk towards them,
Which straightaway took two, and then two more there;
But then the bird had vanished in an orchard;
From where he stood young Oliver saw all this
And cried aloud, for he could not ignore it:
"By God, my lord, how fine a stroke of fortune!
Some noble youth has wandered from their forces
Beside the Rhône beneath Vienne on horseback;
His hunting-hawk has downed two drakes in sport there,
Then flown away inside the leafy orchard:
I'll catch the bird – if not, then I'm a poor one!
And on my word, as soon as I have caught it,
    It won't fly back to Charles!"

GIRART REPLIED: "Fine nephew, let it be!
If *you* were caught, my heart would fill with grief!"
Said Oliver: "Don't talk of that, my liege!
I have to go, though I lose hand or feet!"
So on his horse he jumped, with utmost speed,
And through the gate in haste he disappeared,
Not stopping once until he reached the trees
And found the bird upon a branch well-leafed;
He set the hawk upon his left-hand sleeve;
On seeing this, young Roland raged indeed
And shouted out in ringing tones and clear:
"Are you an envoy, boy? Don't lie to me!
Just give me back the falcon I hold dear
And you'll be paid some fifteen pounds in fee."
Said Oliver: "Your fee's a wasted plea!
One hundred pounds in gold won't set this free!
Are you a Jew, for judging by your speech,
You think that coin can get you all you need?
Go buy a bird! This one belongs to me!"

On hearing this, young Roland's senses reeled;
He rode his horse straight through the river's stream
And up the bank and on to reach the trees;
By both its reins he grasped the other's steed
And spoke these words, with every courtesy:
"Fine youth, what is your name? Don't hide it, please!"
"In truth, my name is Oliver," said he,
"Count Renier's son, who rules Geneva's lease;
And brave Hernaut's my uncle, as indeed
Is Duke Girart, the noble lord and liege
Whom Charles intends to harry from his fief,
    Most evilly and wrongly."

WHEN OLIVER heard Roland's gallant voice,
He answered him with equal grace and more:
"Now I have told my name, my noble lord,
Please do the same, with nothing feigned or false."
"I am Sir Roland, friend, and I was born
The nephew of great Charles our Emperor;
And by the Saints of holy pilgrims sought,
I tell you straight that with God's will, my horse
And I will come again upon this shore
And put to death Girart, Hernaut and all
Your faithless clan – I'll hang them all with joy!
Give back my bird! Don't take it one step more!
I will not have some trifling youngster vaunt
Of robbing me in property or coin!"
Said Oliver: "Your boastful words mean naught;
But follow me and serve in my employ;
If I am pleased with what you do henceforth,
Then in a year, I'd say, you may be sure
That I shall make some town or region yours,
A city's wealth or fortress in reward,
    As you seem worthy of it."

WHEN ROLAND HEARD him taunt him in this way,
He raised his fist to strike him straightaway;
But suddenly he had a thought which made
Him drop the fist and speak to him again:
"Good vassal, one more time I ask and crave
That you return my falcon with good grace,

But with this pledge that you shall hear me make:
If you require some grace of me one day,
It shall be yours, I'll grant it, come what may."
Said Oliver: "This bargain is well made;
Upon these terms the bird is yours to take!"
He freed the straps with which it was restrained
And gave it back without the least delay;
Young Oliver called out to him again:
"By all the faith you owe to Charlemagne,
The lord for whom your loyal love is great,
If I had tried to take your bird away,
Please tell me now, how would you have behaved?"
"Most gladly and most truly," he exclaimed:
"I tell you straight, by God and all His Saints,
I would have hurled my fist against your face
With so much strength, whoever wept or wailed,
It would have smashed and dashed your eyes away,
 With all your kinsmen watching!"

YOUNG OLIVER was stung on hearing this
And straightaway the anger crossed his lips:
"And would I just have stood there while you did?
You're no more tall than I, more strong or big;
And by the Saint they seek on Nero's hill,
If ever we two fought, I tell you this:
You'd never boast in France that you had stripped
This Oliver of any stud or stitch;
Nor would I need to wield a sword or stick,
I'd punch your nose so hard with my strong fist
That crimson blood would flow down fast and thick,
 With all your siege-host watching!"

SAID ROLAND: "WRETCH, God curse you for your lies!
By Lord our God, Who lives in praise on High,
I tell you this: when I'm equipped to fight,
Then Count Girart and all his breed will die!
I'll hang the lot before four months are by,
And all your hair we'll shave and shear awry
For you to be the butt of jest and jibe!
And yet, my friend, I'll pay your grace in kind,
For giving back this hunting-hawk of mine:

I'll let you live – I'll give you back your life!"
On hearing this, young Oliver replied:
"By God our Lord, I promise that if I
Live long enough to be received a knight,
And meet with you in siege or battle's strife,
I'll strike so hard with my nielloed pike
That you will die – if not, I'll wonder why!"
On hearing this, young Roland laughed outright,
Then spurred his steed to cross the river's tide,
And, riding through, arrived the other side;
He rode along past lodges pitched in lines,
And leapt to ground before his uncle's eyes;
Around him came the King's most noble knights,
And Charles himself spoke out when he arrived:
"Attend to me," said he, "my nephew fine!
Just who was that, do not conceal or hide,
To whom you spoke beyond the waters wide?"
"You'll hear the truth, by God," his nephew cried:
"Count Renier's son, he is, Geneva's sire,
And nephew of your Duke Girart the wild!"
On hearing this, Charles almost lost his mind:
"You foolish youth, why did you spare his life?
By God, Who is our Saviour Jesus Christ,
I have no wish that he should live and thrive,
And that his deeds should glorify his line!"
"In God's name, Sire," said Roland in reply,
"I had no armour on or steel to strike
A blow at him or take his blow alike."
Said Charlemagne: "Good nephew, that was wise;
   But ride no more unready!"

19. How Oliver was knighted

INSIDE THE HALL, without a pause, returned
Young Oliver, so high of worth and birth;
On seeing him, Girart addressed these words:
"My nephew proud, has your prowess been curbed?
Your luck was in, thank God and His good works,
Or you'd have been a prisoner or worse!
I saw you by that bridge where you were first,

And on your fist you bore a falcon-bird;
From Charles's side I saw a youngster surge
Across the flow, and like a prince he spurred
And took the hawk, whatever you preferred;
How good's a hound whose heart is of a cur?
No man henceforth should prize your valour's worth."
On hearing this, the youth's complexion burned,
And to Girart he said, enraged and hurt:
"In Jesu's name, you speak of valour, sir,
Like one so old and bold, but in your turn
You kissed the foot of Charles's wife, when urged!
She boasted this and countless barons heard
At Saint-Denis in Abbot Heles' church;
By good St Simon's bones, I call that worse!
    The shame of it destroys me."

WHEN GIRART SAW his nephew so distressed,
He took him to his father, Count Renier,
Who greeted both and kissed the two of them:
"In God's name, lord," young Oliver said then,
"I need a horse and arms for my prowess;
For I am lithe and have good health and strength,
And in a joust should like to prove myself
And be a knight and fight for life and death!"
"Good nephew, so be it!" his uncle said:
"You shall be armed a knight at my behest."
And so it was with no delay or let
That Oliver was stripped and newly dressed
And shod in shoes that were Montpellier's best;
Upon his back an ermine fur they set
Above a gown of fitting width and length,
They led him off to church where Mass was said,
As is the way when budding knights are blessed:
Before they wield their weapons on a quest,
They must attend a Mass to pray for help
In gaining fame or earning brave success
Or ruling lands with good and noble sense;
When Mass was said, they led him back again,
Investing him with knighthood's noble dress:
Upon his back a coat of mail was set,
And on his head a green and golden helm;

Girart girt on a shining blade sharp-edged,
And, with his palms upon his cheeks, he said:
"Be brave and think of me, Sir Oliver!"
"My thanks, my lord," the proud youth said: "I shall,
With God's good help, as long as I draw breath."
They brought him then a stallion swift of step
Which he bestrode by mounting on the left,
While on the right the stirrup iron was held;
When this was done a quartered shield was fetched
And in his fist a cutting spear was set,
Which bore a flag fixed firmly at its end;
If you had seen how keen he was right then
To wield his shield! He seized the straps and sent
His noble steed across the courtyard's length,
Then galloped on to gaze upon the French!
"How fine a knight!" cried all inside Vienne:
"God keep him safe, the guardian of all men!"
Above the rest Renier replied: "Amen!"
Sir Oliver did not delay, instead
He hailed Girart and made him this request:
"I cannot hide, my lord, what I'd attempt:
Outside these walls I want to prove my strength;
In some brave act I may achieve success
Which in your eyes will raise my estimate!"
His father said: "My noble son, not yet!
If I lost you by any chance ill-met,
No man alive would make me smile again."
"Yes, let him go!" Girart the warrior said:
"No man alive should hold back his prowess;
God keep him safe, the guardian of all men."
Young Oliver turned round when this was said,
And through the gate he ventured from Vienne;
Beside the walls he spurred his horse ahead
And hadn't gone an arrow's distance when
He saw a knight leave from the siege-host's tents,
Who was the praised and much prized Guinement;
Beneath Vienne he rode, on pleasure bent,
Astride a steed both sure and fleet of step,
To prove his worth, his bravery and strength;
On seeing him approach with no one else,
Sir Oliver spurred forth with fierce intent;

He never deigned to challenge him, instead
He struck him hard upon his buckler's edge;
Beneath the boss he split the shield to shreds
And ripped aside the heavy hauberk's mesh
And rammed his spear against his bones and flesh;
He smote him well and flung him to his death;
Upon the sand he rammed his helmet's edge,
Then by the reins he took the horse he'd left
And galloped back as fitted one well bred;
Renier the duke was filled with deep content,
As was Girart, the liege lord of Vienne;
But in the camp what mighty anger spread
Among the host in fearsome Charles's tents –
For Guinement was one among their best
And they had lost in him a worthy friend!
But now I'll leave Sir Oliver to rest,
And in due course recount his deeds again;
I'll tell you now how Roland acted next:
He called for arms and for his battle-dress,
Which willingly they found for him and fetched;
Upon his back a shining coat they set
And Durendal, his sword, upon his left;
And then they brought a steed of rapid step,
Whose stirrup he swung into from the left;
A quartered shield they hung around his neck
And in his fist a sturdy lance they set;
A worthy knight he looked in every sense;
The Frenchmen stared, all knights of high prowess,
And each one said: "This youth deserves respect!
There's none on earth who looks so fierce or dread;
God keep him safe, the Guardian of all men;
   How noble is his manner!"

20. How Roland fought with young Aymeri

YOUNG ROLAND BORE his arms in noble manner
And spurred his steed across the Frenchmen's campsite;
Young Aymeri looked on in Vienne's palace,
His heart on fire to joust the foe in battle;
He called for arms and armour from his vassals,

Which willingly they found for him and carried;
They placed his helm and laced his hauberk's strapping
And girt his blade which had a golden handle;
They led him forth a strong and lively stallion
And straightaway he leapt astride its saddle;
Against his breast a heavy shield he gathered
And in his grip a cutting spear he brandished;
Straight through the gate he made his stallion gallop
And on his way met Roland fierce and gallant;
They spoke no word of greeting or of challenge,
But struck at once upon each buckler's panels;
Beneath the boss the boards of both were shattered;
Their coats were strong and neither's mail was damaged;
But Roland was a knight of fearsome valour,
And struck his foe a blow so mean and massive
It flung the youth from his beloved stallion!
Young Roland grasped its silver reins, to catch it
And claim it in a most accomplished manner,
    With all of Vienne watching.

WHEN AYMERI was felled upon all fours,
He started up and grasped his buckler's cord;
Then, drawing forth his shining, sharp-edged sword,
He cried aloud: "Sir knight, why now withdraw?
If you depart, your fame will surely fall!"
Young Roland said: "Be gone yourself, young lord!
I've felled you once, why should I fight you more?
I'll claim instead this lively, long-maned horse!"
On hearing this, young Aymeri was galled,
For he was forced to face the town and walk!
On seeing this, young Oliver rejoiced
And sought Girart and brought him this report,
Well heard by all, in ringing, singing voice:
"By God, I've seen my cousin well outfought!
But, truth to say, I'm not dismayed at all –
His victor was the one who took my hawk!
I've never seen, nor has there been before,
    A knight of France his equal!"

21. How young Roland raised a quintain as a lure

ATTEND, MY FRIENDS! May Jesus bless you all,
The glorious God of blessed Mary born!
This song contains no lies or foolish thoughts,
But gallant deeds and true, performed of yore
In battles fierce and fearsome heavy wars!
In all his life Charles never suffered more,
Except in Spain among the heathen Moors,
Where Roland died, betrayed by jealous scorn,
With Oliver, that gallant-visaged lord,
And knights and men of France one thousand score;
King Charlemagne made no delay or halt;
Before Vienne, its ancient town and fort,
He set up camp with all his sieging force;
The land around was razed and fierce assaults
On countless towns were made with fire and sword;
They wasted vines and gathered any spoils
In cattle, oxen, and wealth in kind or coin;
The people fled; not daring to endure,
They left their homes, their native soil and toil,
Till all around was soon reduced to naught;
Charles took it all to serve his army's cause –
But couldn't take the city or its stores;
For seven years his army sieged the walls,
Not budging once, for any wind or storm,
    One lance-length from the city.

ONE EASTER DAY, with summer just beginning
To green the woods and grass the fields, and in them
To set the birds with merry sweetness trilling,
The King sat down inside his royal pavilion
Beneath Vienne, that admirable city;
And, as he sat, young Roland galloped thither
From hunting game within a wood, and with him
Were many knights of noble strength and visage;
They'd taken stags and one wild-boar within there;
He rode straight up to where the King was sitting
And said at once, when he beheld the King there:
"My lord and liege, I urge you please to listen!

Some seven years have run their seasons' limit,
Since you laid siege to this most worthy city;
Like ordered monks the men inside are living,
While we outside like straying stags are milling!
Sire, if you please, allow me your permission
To raise outside the city-walls a quintain;
The budding knights will strive to show their fitness,
And agile youths within our host will hit it,
While you and I with our own eyes can witness
And know for sure which one will prove most skilful
When battles come and wars are for the winning!"
But Charles replied: "No, nephew, I forbid it!
I know too well Girart and his proud kinsmen!
Though limb or life be lost, he'd leave the city
With all his clan, the best could not resist it,
And he'd demand first joust against the quintain!
A worthy man's oft thwarted by a villain!"
Young Roland said: "Don't baulk at that, I bid you,
By all the faith I owe to you and give you,
For I shall take one thousand fighters with me;
So if Girart or Oliver comes hither,
They'll not return inside Vienne so quickly!
With blades of steel we'll block their journey thither!"
Said Ganelon: "My lord, he speaks with wisdom;
You'll never have a better chance than this one!"
Old Naimon too approved the plan so swiftly
That Charlemagne at last gave his permission
For him to take whatever men he wished to
    And set the quintain up.

OLD NAIMON BACKED the plan with so much weight,
With Ganelon and good Ogier the Dane,
That Charlemagne at last agreed the same;
At this, the youth, without the least delay,
Amid the field set up three sturdy stakes
And on them sat three suits of double-mail;
When this was done, the budding knights in haste
Threw saddles on their swift-paced destriers
And seized their spears, which cheerfully they raised;
Inside Vienne stood Oliver the brave,
With lovely Aude, so worthy to be praised;

The noble knight looked out upon the plain
And on the field he watched the quintain raised;
The sight of gold could no more cheer his face,
And, like a man, he started straightaway
Upon a plan to strike it first that day!
He called his squire, who was Garin by name:
"Go saddle up my stallion swift of pace
And bring me here my gear of dearest make!
I'm off to seek some sport outside the gates!"
On hearing this, Aude ran to his embrace:
"My lord," she said, "and where are you away?"
"To join the French in joust, my pretty maid!"
But she replied: "Don't go, for Jesu's sake!
The King will have your head, so great's his hate,
Or Roland will, his nephew fierce and brave;
A world of gold would be of no avail
If you were caught – they'd hang you straightaway!"
"My pretty maid," he said, "don't be afraid!
For by the Lord, Who governs all our fates,
If Girart finds I've gone, and you're to blame,
My love for you will die in any case!"
"My lord," she said, "no more of this, I pray;
No word of this shall pass my lips again,
     For you are my dear brother."

HE ARMED HIMSELF like one most bravely bred:
Most splendidly indeed he dressed himself
With silver spurs and iron greaves, and then
A coat of mail and then a shining helm;
A cutting sword he girt upon his left;
They led him forth a stallion swift of step,
Clad all in iron from hind-quarters to head;
The reins were worth some fourteen marks themselves;
He mounted up without the pommel's help;
A heavy shield he draped about his neck
And took a spear of stout and cutting edge;
Through postern-gates with every haste he sped
And spurred along to join the throng of French,
And merged among the surging mob of men
Before the King could pick him out from them;
The maiden Aude, of worthy heart, was left

To weep alone, against a window-ledge,
Her tears and fears for her dear brother's quest:
"Lord Oliver, brave count of high prowess,
May God, the Lord of trust and truthfulness,
Defend your life from torment and from death;
For Charlemagne, the King so fierce and dread,
Hates all our clan and holds us in contempt."
A witness went to Duke Girart and said
That Oliver, of worthy heart, had left
The town upon his stallion swift of step,
Without a guard of soldiers or of friends;
On hearing this, great anger filled his breast;
With fearsome rage he swore this solemn pledge:
"No knight or man who will or can show strength
Enough to bear an arm or armour well,
Shall bide inside, but ride with me instead!
It will be clear who loves me here the best!
Let any man who seeks my favour hence,
Arm straightaway, with no delay or let,
And let us ride once more towards their tents!
For I would show the strength of my intent
To Charlemagne, the King of all the French."
His men replied: "We'll do as you have said;
A curse on him who fails his honour's pledge!"
On saying this, they donned their battle-dress,
Their coats of mail, their solid, shining helms;
They girt on swords of sharp and shining edge,
And sturdy shields they hung about their necks;
Stout, cutting spears they seized in hand, and then,
With every haste through street and gate they went;
Girart the duke rode fiercely at their head,
Upon a steed which reared indeed and leapt;
Their lances streamed with gonfalons, and when
They caught the wind they billowed forth and spread;
Girart the duke led all his knights and men
Within a glade of shade beneath Vienne,
Three thousand strong, to watch and wait events;
The bushes glowed with rays of gold they shed;
Ere nones was sung or vespers rung, my friends,
A mighty loss was certain to descend
On one of them – Girart or Charles himself,
    In joust below the city.

22. How Roland lost his heart upon the field

OUR EMPEROR, the King of Saint-Denis,
Called up to him two knights of high degree:
Entelme was one, the other was Gaudris:
"My lords," he said, "now listen well to me!
Ride forth to guard our quintain in the field,
So that Girart does not deride us here."
"My lord," they said, "we'll do as you decree."
But they'd not stop young Oliver at least,
As by the grips he grasped his sturdy shield
Against his breast and held it up so near
That no one else could pick him from their peers!
The gallant youth spurred forth his lively steed
Towards the mark and struck it lustily!
He split the shields and slit the coats beneath
And broke in half the holding-posts all three!
The quintain fell, collapsing in a heap,
As on he rode with his unbroken spear,
His skilful blow for friend and foe to see!
Charles signed himself when he beheld the feat,
Invoking God, Who never fails the need:
"Almighty God! In truth, I've never seen
So stout a blow as I've just witnessed here!
Ride forth and see just who this man can be!
If he's a knight, or fights for any fee,
There's wealth of mine that he can earn and keep!"
His men replied: "As you desire, my liege."
On saying this, some ten broke rank to leave,
All noble dukes they were and marquises;
When Oliver beheld them coming near,
It's no surprise his blood should rise with fear;
He turned the reins upon his noble steed
And raised his lance, its gonfalon released;
He struck the first who faced him with such zeal
He pierced his shield and tripled mail beneath;
Between the ribs he rammed his cutting spear
And flung him dead – what more could he achieve?
He cried: "Vienne – for God and St. Maurice!
I'm Oliver, no friend of yours, dead Peer!

My father is Renier, the fine and fierce,
Girart, Hernaut, the uncles I hold dear,
My sister Aude, of visage fair and sweet;
And where are you, Sir Roland, brave of deed?
I'll vie with you on any battlefield!
Young Aymeri would have you know through me
That he will not forgive or give you peace
For that fine steed which yesterday you thieved!
He'll have revenge, while he has breath to breathe!"
Young Roland bowed, but Ganelon, he beamed!
Charles spoke aloud: "Ah God, our Heavenly Liege,
Full seven years have run their seasons' lease
Since first I set Girart's domain to siege;
In all that time no Oliver I've seen,
But now he jousts my barons with such ease
That he has felled before my eyes a Peer
Whom all the gold of Paris can't redeem!
Ride after him, fine youths of high degree,
And capture him and bring him back to me –
But make quite sure he takes no injury!"
When this was said, one hundred sped to leave,
Each calling out: "Mountjoy, for Saint-Denis!"
The first of them was Entelme of Senlis;
With hauberk on and helm, he raised his spear
Before the rest and pressed his noble steed
In hot pursuit to stop the youth's retreat –
    Which was a mortal folly!

BEFORE THE REST, an arrow's range or more,
He chased the youth, well armed upon his horse:
"Men, follow hard!" he cried, with ringing voice:
"Pursue Girart while I take Oliver!
If we can catch these traitors one and all,
A world of gold will never help their cause,
We'll hang the lot like robbers foul and false."
On hearing this, young Oliver was galled,
And nothing then would halt his angry scorn
From challenging Entelme with all his force:
He raised his spear, like any gallant lord,
And struck Entelme upon his buckler's boards;
Beneath the boss he broke them through and tore

To tattered shreds the hauberk's threaded coils;
Between his ribs he rammed the iron's point;
He speared him well and flung him on the floor;
The helmet's edge was wedged against the soil;
He galloped on, like gallant fighters ought,
And never thought to take the vassal's horse;
But then he turned, and riding to the corpse,
In sharp reproof he spoke this sentence forth:
"You'll ride no more, you blighted good-for-naught!
Ill-blessed you raised those quintain-posts for sport;
I've made you pay a heavy price for all
    Who've sinned against this parish!"

WHEN HE HAD FELLED Entelme and slaughtered him,
Towards Vienne he turned his steed forthwith;
Charles saw the deed and almost lost his wits,
As to his men he turned and uttered this:
"My noble lords, you all are witnesses!
Did any king as kind as I exist
Who was repaid and disobeyed like this?
Spur forth at once and never stop or stint
Till you are sure you have him in your grip!
Fine nephew mine, Sir Roland, bring him in!"
When this was said one hundred did as bid,
Each one of them a landed count or prince;
Attend, my lords, God bless you as I sing
Of how mischance missed those of France and hit
Count Oliver, so strong of mind and limb:
Across a ditch, below a narrow hill,
His lively horse trod awkwardly and tripped;
Young Oliver fell off and in the ditch!
The French arrived and soon surrounded him;
The youth exclaimed: "Dear God and St Maurice!
To your safe hands my body I commit!"
His horse jumped up, as did the youth, to swing
His shaft aloft, which by the haft he gripped,
So all could see he sought to joust them still!
Accursed indeed the first who came full-tilt,
Though he was Count of Burgundy the rich,
For Oliver stood firm and never flinched;
He grasped his spear and dealt him such a hit

He broke his shield and burst the hauberk's rings;
Between his ribs he rammed the lance's tip
And threw him dead one lance's length therewith;
On seeing this, the men still hiding in
The shady glade came riding like the wind,
With Duke Girart astride that steed of his;
Beneath Vienne, amid the meadows big,
Both forces met – Vienne's and Charles the King's;
Hernaut was there, well known for fighting's skill,
And feared by all who fought against him still;
Young Aymeri as well, so strongly built!
The younger there spared elders not a bit,
The lowest born but scorned the highest prince
   When blade and blood were mingled.

AS OLIVER bestrode his steed again,
His spear in hand, his shield around his neck,
Girart rode up to lend his nephew help;
One arrow's range he rode before the rest
And went to strike old Naimon's hoary head;
Against his shield a mighty blow he sent;
And Naimon too struck through with such prowess
That shaft and haft on either's spear was cleft;
Their worthy steeds, at pace, raced on unchecked;
How fierce a fight flared up between them then,
Which boded fair to end in grief and death;
Duke Roland saw Count Oliver and said:
"True Emperor and friend of all true French,
Sire, can you see that fighter over there
Whose shield is green with bands of gold inset?
He bears a flag in quarters with a crest
Whereon an eagle flies each time it spreads;
So help me God, that's Oliver himself!
No better knight now fights before Vienne,
   Or anywhere around it!"

"TRUE EMPEROR," young Roland said again:
"Sire, can you see that fighter on the plain
Who bears a shield with bands of gold inlaid?
That's Oliver, the son of Duke Renier –
Geneva's his, where Oliver was raised;

Within Vienne there's none more widely famed;
Two cities' gold won't hold me back, I say,
From matching strength with Oliver today –
For then I'll know how bold he is and brave,
How fearsome too for any foe to face."
But Charles replied: "No, son, for Heaven's sake!
I'll not allow a combat to be waged
Between the best in Christendom's domain!
If you and he should joust with lances raised,
While one would win, the other would be slain
And nevermore increase his name and fame."
"Sire, nonetheless," said Roland, unrestrained,
"Two cities' gold won't make me stop and stay,
Lest I be called and earn a coward's name;
Where hear it hence, if here it lies in wait?
With lances' iron our merits will be weighed,
And one fall short – and so be it, I say."
"Then go," said Charles, "and may God's will prevail;
May Jesus Christ defend your life this day,
And may He tend young Oliver the same
And send him back both whole of limb and safe
To his own kin behind the city's gate."
When this was said young Roland turned in haste
And spiked his steed with golden spurs to chase
Young Oliver with all the speed it may;
While this occurred, the ladies made their way
Outside Vienne to watch the jousting made;
Among them came young Aude, so fair of face,
A maiden of great beauty and high grace;
That day she had put on a cloak, a cape
Quite short in length and tailored to her shape;
She'd slipped it off her shoulders, neck and nape,
Till as she rushed it brushed upon the plain;
Shall I describe the beauty of this maid?
Upon her head a diadem was placed,
Of precious stones which shed a dazzling ray;
Her hair was fair, in ringlets all arranged;
Her eyes were green as falcon-bird's encaged,
Her skin more white than meadow-flowers in May,
Her visage bright with glowing cheeks that made
Her face as fresh of bloom and lovely grace

As is the rose that's plucked on summer's day;
Her hands were white, her fingers long and straight,
Her hips were low, her feet were finely shaped;
In Christendom there lived no fairer maid;
Young Roland looked and couldn't look away,
His heart on fire to hold her in embrace;
The lusty youth, in truth, was so inflamed
That he forgot the joust he'd gone to make!
He spurred instead towards the maid, whose waist
He seized in haste to carry her away
To Charles's tent, where his intent was plain:
To do his will and have his passion's way;
The maid herself began to cry for aid:
"Sir Oliver, my lord, where are you, pray?
The nephew of King Charles intends to rape
And ravish me to our eternal shame,
The blemish mine, but yours the lasting blame!
May God forbid, with His majestic grace,
That I be used in such a shameful way!"
On hearing this, her brother came in haste
And called aloud to Roland when he came:
"Most royal son, for so I hear you named,
For mercy's sake, release my sister's waist,
For when she weds the Church must bless the day,
And Lord Hernaut, whose deeds deserve your praise,
And Duke Renier, who rules Geneva's waves,
And Duke Girart, whose deeds alike are great,
And Aymeri, the youth well-bred and brave –
And my own hand may give what you would take!"
On hearing this, young Roland filled with rage:
"You serf!" he said, "Give your bravado rein!
I'll take her now, whoever weeps or wails,
To Charles's camp, and none shall say me nay!
I'll do my will and have my passion's way!
I don't care less about your clan's dismay!"
Said Oliver: "Give *your* bravado rein!
Your words alone deserve the highest blame;
By God above and all His blessed Saints,
If someone else had boasted in this vein,
I would have proved the fool a lying knave!
But if, in truth, you'd play this ruthless game,

I'll set the fee that you will have to pay –
A joust with me – if still you want to play!"
Young Roland said: "That price is quickly paid!
Ride over there and give me jousting space!"
Said Oliver: "Most gladly I'll obey,
For you're a duke and I'm a count the same;
This joust of ours is not unjustly made,
For both of us are scions of our states."
With spurs of gold they spiked their destriers,
Against their breast their worthy shields embraced;
With all the speed their lively steeds could make
They made their charge across the meadow's plain;
What mighty blows they swapped on shields ornate,
Which shattered both nielloed spears in twain;
Their coats were strong, they never ripped the mail,
And neither fell as on their stallions raced;
On seeing this, young Oliver, enraged
That in the joust young Roland was unscathed,
Withdrew his sword, and with its shining blade
Struck Roland's helm a blow so very great
It struck its gems and floral hems away
And crushed the dome and cracked it lace to lace;
The mighty blow stunned Roland, and I'd say
That had the Lord not shown His saving grace,
And had the coif upon his coat been frail,
It would have sent young Roland to his grave!
His war-horse fell beneath the blow's great weight,
And when it stood, it bolted straightaway!
Young Roland rode four acres in a daze,
Not knowing where he went or when he raced
Towards Vienne or then to Charlemagne!
And that was how young Oliver the brave
Saved lovely Aude, his sister fair of face,
    In joust before Vienne.

YOUNG ROLAND, WHEN he came to his right senses,
Was filled with rage and flushed with deep displeasure
That men should know the blow that had been dealt him;
In all his life he'd never been so bested!
His bolting horse fled back to join its fellows,
And Charles himself came forth to meet his nephew;

From Roland's head he raised the broken helmet
And sighed for joy to find no mortal head-wound;
"Fine youth," he said, "my heart was filled with terror
Lest such a blow had lain you low forever;
By God above and all His Saints in Heaven,
Girart the duke has vexed me past all measure,
And once he's caught, I'll hang the haughty felon,
    In front of all and sundry!"

23. How Lambert of Berry was captured

KING CHARLEMAGNE was mightily aggrieved
At Oliver for all the woe he'd wreaked;
But then, my friends, a well-armed knight appeared,
A Berry count, who, born in Burgundy,
Was godson of the King and kin indeed;
One hundred knights were rightly his to lead,
On honour bent in deeds of daring zeal;
He dropped the reins and let his horse run free
To strike in joust young Oliver's strong shield;
Beneath the boss he bored so big a breach
A falcon could have soared right through with ease!
On seeing this, the lad was filled with grief
And swore an oath in rage between his teeth,
By old Vienne's own Saint, the bold Maurice,
That he would make the Berry count pay dear!
Garin his squire brought forth a solid spear
Which bore a flag clipped on by golden cleats;
He armed himself and turned around to leave,
When lovely Aude came running through the field,
Her mantle's hem raised up above her feet;
Her shoulders too, in running, were revealed;
She hailed Lambert between the ranks of each;
The knights all said: "Now there's a sight to see!
Have you beheld a maid as fair as she?
The man who weds and beds so fair a queen,
Can bless the hour that he was born to breathe!"
She hurried on and only stopped to seize
The Berry count's gold-banded buckler-shield;
She drew it near and he stooped down to hear,

As lovely Aude addressed him with this plea:
"Fine, noble knight, please fight no further here
With Oliver, my brother brave and dear!
Lay down your arms and yield yourself to me!
Within Vienne your penance will be sweet:
To come and go within my rooms at ease
And share with me in laughter and in glee;
And if you wish, I'll summon there and leave
A lovely maid of noble birth and breed
For your delight and pleasure as you please:
And none shall treat her hence with less esteem –
For love of you, I'll have her wed in brief."
Lambert replied: "Let all this talking be!
Though I lose life or limb, I'll not agree!
I would be called both cowardly and weak,
And all my clan would hold my honour cheap
To know a maid had made a fool of me!
Both he and I must fight with lance's steel
Till one of us is forced to own defeat!"
"My lord," she said, "then what will be will be!
If you should fail, no blame shall fall on me!"
And back she stepped to watch the joust proceed;
Lambert the count was very strong and fierce:
He brandished forth his heavy-headed spear
And, golden-spurred, he spiked his worthy steed
At Oliver and smote his golden shield
A blow which burst the boards to smithereens;
His coat was strong, the chain-mail didn't yield,
And not to fall showed stubborn gall beneath!
But Oliver returned what he'd received,
A mighty blow, on his opponent's shield;
Against his breast he struck so lustily
That, legs aloft, he flung him on the field;
The plucky youth pursued him, sword unsheathed,
And would have slain the Berry count in brief,
When Lambert cried, despite his pride: "I yield!
Accept my sword, but let me live, and lead
Me with you now inside Vienne to meet
With Duke Girart, your uncle and your liege!
My life is worth a hefty ransom-fee:
Four sumpters, each with gold and silver heaped,

One hundred helmets jewelled and hauberks sleek,
One hundred spears and richly banded shields,
One hundred hacks and rested battle-steeds,
And bears and hounds and leopards on the leash,
Or wealth in coin, if such is what you seek,
For my supplies are very great indeed."
Said Oliver: "Then I can guarantee
That in Vienne we'll guard you well at least
For two long months, before we let you leave!
Girart, my lord, will thank me heartily
For bringing him a guest of such degree!"
And, grasping then his helmet's nasal-piece,
He called his knights and told a score of these:
"Escort him well inside Vienne for me!"
And so they did as he had bid them each;
They led him forth and headed for the keep;
On seeing this, the King was more than piqued,
    And showed it to his liegemen.

"LOOK THERE, MY LORDS!" said fearsome Charlemagne:
"The youth's own men have led Lambert away,
Who is, in faith, a godson of my race!
I fill with grief to think he may be slain!
Ride after him, my worthy knights well-raised,
Before he's brought within the city's gates!
If we could take a prisoner the same,
I could reclaim Lambert in fair exchange."
When this was said, five score and ten made haste:
"For St Denis, Mountjoy!" the French exclaimed;
"For St Maurice!" Vienne's own men proclaimed;
"Hernaut and Aymeri!" yelled Biaulande's brave,
While Oliver cried out: "Geneva, hail!"
Vienne's brave men were bold again that day,
As on the French they turned their reins in rage;
How fierce a fight this second time they waged!
The fragments flew as spears began to break
And solid shields were hit and split in twain,
And burnished helms of green knocked clean away;
They hacked and hewed with shining steel-edged blades,
And in the heat and heart of battle's fray
Stood Oliver, the count and marquis brave;

Without God's help, Who bore the Cross's bane,
Ere evening came, he'd need his fellows' aid!
He looked to ground and saw a lance still lain
Beside a knight who'd fallen to his fate;
So, leaning down, he grasped it forth again,
Prepared to tame whoever came his way;
To see him thus, in all his strength and rage,
The French were loath to turn and face him, save
One knight alone, a baron bold and brave
From Brittany, a count of high estate:
Young Oliver o'erwhelmed him just the same:
He split his shield and slit the hauberk's chains,
As through the ribs he ran his lance's blade;
The helmet's edge he rammed against the plain:
"Vienne – with God and St Maurice's aid!
I'm Oliver, no friend of yours!" he railed;
He looked around and saw Ogier the Dane,
Who came upon Flori, his destrier;
On seeing this, the youth turned straightaway
To joust with him, preparing on the way;
The King looked on and called his nephew's name:
"Young Roland, look! By St Rémy, I swear
You'll see a joust whose like was never made!
By Jesus Christ our Lord, who will prevail?"
The youth replied: "Young Oliver, I'd say;
I've never seen his like in all my days,
For harassing his foe with mortal hate!"
"Protect my knight, dear God," said Charlemagne,
"From death itself and agony and pain;
And spare alike young Oliver, the brave,
And send him back both whole of limb and safe
Within Vienne, whence he among us came!"
The youth, in truth, was spotted by the Dane,
Who raised aloft his burnished spear and aimed
A mighty blow upon his shield well-shaped;
Beneath the boss it smote the boards away;
The coat was strong, the chain-mail didn't break,
And not to fall showed stubborn gall the same;
But Oliver gave back what he had gained:
He struck his shield and split it through the grain;
Against his breast its impact was so great

It slammed the Dane past horse's rump and tail
Till helmet's rim went ramming in the plain!
The youth was fierce, and fast enough to take
The horse from which he'd dashed the Dane away!
Then, looking right, he saw a lad whose name
Was Poinçonet, and came from his domains;
One month had yet to run its span of days
Since Lord Girart had dubbed this Poinçonet;
Young Oliver called out to him: "This way!
Come, take from me this noble destrier!
I've captured it, my friend, by brawn and brain;
It's yours to have! Come, ride it whence you came!"
"Much thanks indeed, my lord!" said Poinçonet;
Alas, indeed, he ever grasped its reins –
For very soon that doomed him to be slain!
How great a hue and cry the Frenchmen raised
When Ogier's steed was taken from the Dane,
And Vienne's men rushed homeward to the gates!
Count Roland rode his steed in angry rage
Around the walls and saw young Poinçonet
Still riding back in pride that destrier
Which had belonged to strong Ogier the Dane;
At once the Count spurred forth at rapid pace
To strike the youth with all his strength, and laid
A mighty blow upon his shield well-shaped;
Beneath the boss it smote the boards away;
He ripped apart and wrecked the hauberk's mail
And through his ribs he rammed the lance's blade;
He speared him well and felled him on the plain;
Then Roland seized the war-horse by its reins
And led it back and gave it to Ogier;
The Vienne knights rode back inside the gates
And, as they closed, the drawbridge chains were raised;
Upon the walls the maiden Aude remained;
When Roland came, she hailed him in this vein:
"Sir knight, your spear has served us ill this day:
A novice knight lies slaughtered by your rage;
If Lord Girart and Oliver had stayed,
You'd not have dared to touch young Poinçonet,
For all the gold in Paris, I would say!"
On hearing this, young Roland dropped his gaze;

The French withdrew, as light began to fade,
And reached the tents which each of them had raised;
The King himself, fierce-faced, rode back the same,
While in Vienne Girart the duke remained;
Within a porch of old Maurice, their Saint,
They stripped Lambert of weapons when he came;
Girart strode up, well-bred and ever brave,
And to his care Lambert gave up his blade
And his own self in hope of mercy's grace;
The burnished helm was lifted from his face,
And from his back the coat of tripled mail;
With samite silk they robed him in exchange;
His skin was bruised; his hauberk-chains had chafed,
And with them there his captive air was plain;
But Aude the fair did not forget his claims;
About his neck she draped a costly cape,
Then took his hand and led him straightaway
From porch and wall to Vienne's hall of state;
Upon a seat she bade him take his place
Beside her there, with this consoling phrase:
"My lord Lambert, do not be too dismayed!
For love of God, Who never lies or fails,
Know that Girart is both well-bred and brave,
A noble lord of good and gallant grace,
Both rich in birth and in the friends he's made;
He'll never seek, I swear to you in faith,
A ransom which will leave you poor when paid."
Lambert replied: "I thank you for your grace;
No need of yours, however far away,
That's known to me, while I am free and hale,
Shall not be met with all my forces' aid,
In shining arms on Arab destriers!"
"Much thanks indeed, my lord," replied the maid;
With water brought, they sat at tables laid
    Along the walls and hallway.

24. How Lambert was received in Girart's hall

WITH WATER BROUGHT they all sat down to eat,
Brave Oliver and Duke Girart between

Hernaut, the lord of Biaulande on the sea,
And all their men of fine and famous deeds;
Lambert the count sat next to Aude the sweet,
While further down sat other knights and peers;
I'll not attempt to tell you of their feast,
Except to say that each appeased his need,
Save Count Lambert, who'd no desire to eat;
Girart the duke called out to him indeed:
"My lord Lambert, take food and drink at least!
You can't have all that's in this hall to see!"
Lambert replied: "Is that a certainty?
You say this, lord, about fair Aude your niece;
But she and I are closely matched in years,
And my descent should not prevent my plea!
My riches nor my holdings are so mean
That I should shun to marry such as she –
And if not her, there's countless others here:
Let God decide the proper bride for me!"
Girart replied: "Let all this talking be!
There's something else that I would have you hear:
If you can bring great Charles and me to peace,
I'll set your free before tomorrow's eve,
For hostages, if you can muster these."
Lambert replied: "Much thanks for this reprieve;
My wealth is yours to garner as you please;
Some thirty mules with riches shall be heaped,
Or, if you wish, this sum can be increased,
For my supplies are very great indeed."
On hearing this, young Oliver fell deep
In thought, then called Girart aside to speak
A quiet word, so none could overhear:
"My lord Girart," said Oliver the fierce,
"Have you before heard such a captive's speech?
Do not accept one peck or penny piece
Of any wealth Lambert has talked of here!
Release him, lord, and Charles will pay with peace!
If not, the world would hold his honour cheap!"
On hearing this, Girart at once agreed;
With nodding head, he said that he'd proceed
Exactly as his nephew had decreed!
When all had had their fill of meat and mead,

The squires moved up and all the cloths were cleared;
With no delay the knights began to leave
For lodge and bed, to rest their head and sleep;
Lambert was not forgotten there; indeed
A bed was made within the hall, complete
With costly silks and rugs from overseas;
They bade Lambert to slumber there in peace,
As lovely Aude once more addressed the Peer:
"My lord Lambert, do not dismay or fear!
For Jesu's sake, be strong and of good cheer!
Girart the duke is brave and high of breed,
A noble lord of good and gallant deeds,
And very rich; I swear, he'll never seek
A ransom which, when paid, will cause you grief."
Lambert replied: "I thank you, lovely queen!
You've brought my heart much comfort and much ease;
I pledge to you, in turn, my loyalty;
However far you are, if you're in need,
Three thousand knights shall speed to your relief!"
"My lord," she said, "much thanks for such a speech!"
And then she turned towards her rooms to sleep;
Lambert was not forgotten there, indeed!
Within the hall they made a bed, complete
With fourteen candles to light his head and feet;
Ten knights were dressed and armed in all their gear
To guard Lambert, while he was there asleep,
Until the dawn and morning light appeared,
To make quite sure he never rose to leave!
When morning came and all the bells were pealed,
Girart the duke, his knights and men of liege,
His wife Guibourc, and lovely Aude the sweet,
Her brother and Lambert the brave of breed,
Went off to church with all their company;
When Mass was said, with prayers and sermon preached,
They left the church, proceeding till they reached
The hall again, where at his highest seat
    Girart sat back and rested.

THEY LEFT THE CHURCH, with prayers and sermon read,
And in his hall Girart sat back at rest;
Lambert the knight addressed him there and then:

"My lord Girart," the noble fighter said,
"What ransom has been placed upon my head?
What fee will set me free, what hostages?
From Charles's host the ransom will be sent
By worthy knights whose honour is their crest."
"You're wrong in this," replied young Oliver,
"For by the Saint besought by knighthood's best,
For all the gold in Montpellier itself,
We do not want one penny of your wealth;
Although you fight for Charles against Vienne,
No noble here would censure your prowess;
For every knight should serve his lord's behest,
Who governs land through such a lord's largesse,
And be prepared to show his faith and strength
With shining arms of sharp and cutting edge –
Unless it be to rob the Church and vex
The lowly poor and cause them more distress;
No man should war with God the Lord Himself,
For he would fall before he'd gone one step."
Lambert replied: "I honour your noblesse!
How wise he was who taught your heart so well!"
"Fine sister Aude," young Oliver said next,
"The Berry knight returns to Charles's tent;
And what is more, he should be recompensed
With some rich gift of silk to carry hence,
Which he may show with pride to Charles's men."
"My lord," she said, "I readily assent;
I have, I think, an item to present
That's peerless here to Montpellier itself,
      In king or count's possession."

THE MAIDEN AUDE was high of birth and thought;
With every haste she hurried from the hall
To reach her rooms without delay or pause;
She opened up, inside, a chest of drawers
Where countless flags of silken cloth were stored,
And seized at once the richest one of all;
From edge to edge it shone, with gems adorned
And golden bands, and silver threads galore;
With this in hand she headed back once more
Within the hall and laid it out before

The Berry knight upon the marble floor;
How wondrously the eyes of all were drawn
Towards its hue, of many colours formed;
In truth, the Twelve Apostles of our Lord
Were each depicted on it, and it bore
In finest gold, most delicately drawn,
The face and form themselves of lovely Aude;
No man who bore that banner to the wars
Would need to fear the power or the scorn
Or evil hatched by heathens for his fall!
And it was this she gave the Berry lord,
Who, taking it, gave thanks with ringing voice,
Then clipped it to his spear and, rushing forth,
Climbed up the steps to reach the castle's fort
And showed the flag to all of Charles's force;
It billowed from the window so that all
Of Charles's host could see Lambert rejoice;
Young Roland saw it too, with sagging jaw,
And showed his friends, who came to see the cause;
"Behold Lambert, my worthy friends well-born!
Fair Aude and he have come to some accord,
And Count Lambert has earned a fair reward!
He's pierced my heart without a spear or sword!
If Duke Girart is party to it all,
   We're finished ere we started!"

GIRART THE FIGHTER SAID: "My noble nephew,
On my behalf equip Lambert of Berry:
Return his clothes, his war-horse and his weapons!
Ensure his loss amounts to not one penny
Of all the wealth with which he was attended;
Give back to him each one of his possessions
And give him more, if he will but accept them."
Young Oliver replied: "My lord, with pleasure."
Without delay they hastened forth to fetch him
His armour and his costly arms directly;
In hauberk white of double-weave they dressed him
And then they laced his green and golden helmet;
Girart held forth his sword of steel well-tempered,
Which he himself, upon his left side, tethered;
They led him forth his destrier, well rested,

Which straightaway he mounted from the left side;
They laid a shield around his neck and tendered
His sturdy spear, to which they had already
Affixed the flag that lovely Aude presented,
That maiden wise, of fierce and fine complexion;
Girart spoke forth: "My lord Lambert of Berry!
I free you for no fee in gold whatever!
When you return take Oliver, my nephew;
By God above, Who judges all, I beg you
To let no low or evil blow be dealt him!"
Lambert replied: "This plea needs no requesting,
For by the Lord, Who judges all in Heaven,
There's none so fierce among the host of Frenchmen
Whom, if he tried to be a fool or felon,
I would not force to stay his hand directly –
And if he won't, I'll teach him to regret it –
Unless it were the King of France himself, or
The warrior Sir Roland, his own nephew:
These two alone I couldn't dare to censure."
Count Oliver moved off and then he dressed in
A hauberk white with mail of double meshing,
On top of which he then had tightly tethered
A costly gown cut deftly to his measure;
He clasped a cloak around his neck, and then he
Bestrode his steed, the stirrup held to help him;
They left the town, Lambert and he together,
And hastened forth until they reached the Frenchmen,
      With news and views to tell.

WHEN LOVELY AUDE beheld her brother leave,
Most tenderly the maid began to weep:
"Sir Oliver," she cried, so fair of cheek,
"I pray to God the Lord, our Heavenly Liege,
Who in the Virgin's womb deigned once to be,
And deigned alike upon the Cross to bleed,
That He may guard your life from mortal grief!
I pray that Charles the King may show you peace,
And Roland too, whose valour is so fierce."
She called Garin, his squire, and he appeared:
"My friend," she said, "now pay good heed to me!
Go gather up your master's battle-gear

And with the lot ride hard upon his heels,
So all are close, if ever he's in need;
So help me God, you'll earn a princely fee!"
"I'll do at once," he said, "as you decree,"
And took the arms, departing with all speed;
Among the French he stole so stealthily
And hid so well beneath a leafy tree,
That no man there of mother born to breathe
　　Could see he was among them.

25. How Oliver was received in Charles's camp

BENEATH A TREE Garin hid well away
And held the arms of Oliver, in case
He needed them without the least delay;
Before the tent of fierce-faced Charlemagne
Lambert arrived, dismounting in great haste
With Oliver, whose face with valour blazed;
He drove his spear before the entrance-way,
Like any knight of high prowess and praise;
The worthy flag that Aude, the fair of face,
Had given him, unfurled at once and waved;
The gallant knights all gazed at it, amazed,
But none as much as Roland, jaws agape,
Who showed it to his friend Manesier:
"Who brought it here?" Manesier exclaimed;
"Lambert of Berry," said Roland straightaway:
"With brave Girart a private peace he's made
And, doing this, has met with Aude the maid,
And from my love has led her heart astray!"
"Lord, have you seen," his comrade said again,
"The maiden Aude, that you should sing her praise?"
"Indeed I have! I'll not conceal the same –
When riding forth I went upon the plain
Before Vienne to joust the other day;
I seized the maid on my swift destrier
And would, I know, have brought her back unscathed,
When Oliver, her noble brother, came
And rescued her with his well-burnished blade."
Manesier exclaimed: "My lord, in faith,

The maid must be a worthy prize, I'd say,
For there is none whom I have heard more praised."
When this was said, the two of them made haste
Inside the tent of noble Charlemagne;
The Frenchmen said: "What is this prince's name,
Who's led Lambert from where he was detained?"
Said one who knew: "He's Oliver! The same
Who led the fight around our quintain raised,
And labours still to kill us when he may!
Attend his needs, or we'll indeed be shamed!"
Ten score and more ran forward to his aid,
But squire Garin outran them to his reins,
Sir Achart's son, the lord of River Vale,
His cousin too, whose love for him was great;
One hundred knights of highest rank and rate
Among the French, lined up to form a train
Which came with Oliver to Charlemagne;
The tent was filled with France's best, who came
To hear the speech young Oliver would make;
Before the King, fierce-visaged Charles the Great,
   He stood to speak his message.

BEFORE THE SEAT of Charlemagne the King,
Young Oliver the brave came striding in;
He freed the clasp that held his mantle clipped
And from his back the costly garment slipped –
He didn't ask for any to assist;
Then, kneeling down, he lifted cheek and chin
To greet the King of Saint-Denis like this:
"May God, Who pardoned Longinus his sin,
Protect you, Sire, from evil acts or ill,
And save Girart, my uncle that he is,
And gallant liege, from treachery and tricks!
True Emperor, hear what I seek and bring:
Girart the duke, who was your friend ere this,
Returns to you Lambert, of ransom quit;
For all the gold in Paris, he insists
That he'll not hold your man against your will!
Girart himself is yours, by oath and kiss,
And holds his land from you and all that's his;
Take care, my lord, that you do not permit

A further woe which makes a foe of him!
Return to France, or anywhere you will,
And Duke Girart will follow you forthwith,
With fifty score who all are knights of his,
Which is the sum this duchy's standing gives;
He'll serve you there in any way you wish."
On hearing this, the King dropped cheek and chin,
And then replied, as one who pondered still:
"What is your name, my proud and handsome prince?"
The youth replied: "Sir Oliver, fine King."
Fierce Charles replied: "I well believe it is;
Speak on, brave youth! Use all your wisdom's wit,
Then hurry home to those who gave you it!"
The youth replied: "I'll do as you insist,
But lift your head and mark my look and lips!
I'll tell you all I know and think of this;
    No man alive shall stop me!"

"TRUE EMPEROR," said Oliver the fierce,
"I give you back Lambert, of ransom free,
Without the loss of weapons or of steed,
Or anything that's worth a penny-piece;
On his behalf Girart has sent me here
To tell you this: he charges you, through me,
That you are wrong to put Vienne to siege,
To waste his realm and devastate his fiefs;
He bids you leave at once for France the sweet;
And he will go there with you, when you leave,
With fifty score to keep him company;
He'll serve you there most willingly indeed,
And any wrong be ready to redeem."
The King replied: "His pride has angered me!
Without revenge, I'll never be appeased!
I've summoned here a mighty host indeed,
And we have laid this siege for seven years,
Which you ask me to lift so easily!
By God the Lord, to Whom our prayers should reach,
I tell you straight, before I ever leave,
Girart the brave shall know he's met defeat!
I'll have him come to me on bended knee,
In hair-shirt clad, unshod, to sue for peace;

Across his back I'll make him bear and feel
The saddle of some nag or sumpter-beast."
Said Oliver: "Sire, that will never be,
For Lord Girart is very proud and fierce,
 And from a powerful family."

YOUNG OLIVER, the brave and wise, spoke forth:
"True Emperor, attend to me once more!
So help me God, in majesty adored,
I'll tell you all the message I have brought,
From start to end, for I would have it all
Well heard and known by every knight of yours:
Vienne was my grandfather's land before,
And his grandfather's too, you know it, lord!
Beuvon 'Longbeard' my grandfather was called,
Who ruled Vienne one hundred years and more;
No king of France opposed his right or law;
It seems to me you have no right at all
To force Girart from what was ours of yore;
If you succeed, then you will be at fault!
And by the Saint in Nero's field besought
At holy Rome, wherein he is adored,
Before you lodge inside this city's walls,
And long before you have secured its fort,
I'll sail across the sea to foreign shores
And summon forth another uncle's force,
King Afloaires', a fearsome warrior;
No man alive would make him even pause:
He'd arm his men, some twenty thousand score,
For me to lead within this land to war;
In truth, I say, I'll summon here all four
Of Garin's sons, each one to valour born;
And when all these have come with their support,
Our sum will be some forty thousand more!
And we shall ride astride our steeds of war
From here to France in one relentless course;
We shall not leave one town of yours unstormed;
No tower of stone, no wealthy fort or hall
Shall even stand, each one of them shall fall!"
The King exclaimed: "You fool! What raving taunts!
I do not give two shelled eggs for your vaunts!"

When this was said, or so the song records,
Inside the tent strode Roland, who was joined
By Charles's Peers, in pairs appearing all;
Beside the King he leant upon the boards;
What stinging words would soon be heard and sworn,
Which led to his and Oliver's crossed swords,
    In duel on Vienne's island.

YOUNG ROLAND SAID, whose face with valour blazed:
"True Emperor, this vassal's gall is great,
To throw such taunts directly in your face!
Go, Oliver! Your speech has lost its way!
Can you deny, brag wildly as you may,
That Duke Girart has failed to keep the faith
He pledged and swore before King Charlemagne?"
Said Oliver: "You have no proof to lay!
I would to God, Whose mother was the Maid,
That you would pledge your own word straightaway
To ride alone, as soon as morning breaks,
Below Vienne until you reach the lake,
Then cross it to the island it contains,
Well armed astride your Syrian destrier!
And there we'd fight with our well-burnished blades,
I for Girart, whose face is bright and brave,
And you for Charles, whose beard is grey with age."
On hearing this, young Roland's visage flamed
    With shame for Charles's barons.

"SIR OLIVER," the gallant youth replied,
"How has Girart not broken faith and lied
To Charlemagne, his King by royal line,
To whom he pledged his loyalty and life?
Girart himself has no God-given rights
To any towns or castles, fiefs or shires!
He ought to flee and dwell in foreign climes
Beyond the sea among the Pagan tribes!"
"Sir Roland, lord," the gallant Lambert cried:
"You're wrong in this, so help me Jesus Christ!
Girart the duke is very fine and wise,
A noble lord, a brave and gallant knight,
And Oliver is very bold alike;

If you had been upon the field of fight,
You wouldn't think or judge them otherwise."
Said Oliver: "Say nothing more, sir knight;
Count Roland likes to talk, but I surmise
That doing more is far from his desire!
Sir Roland, lord, attend these words of mine:
Are you a woman, to argue all the time?
Come, pledge your word and honour as a knight,
To ride alone, as soon as dawn arrives,
Below Vienne until you reach the isle
Amid the lake, which you must cross astride
Your Syrian horse, with no one by your side,
And there we'll fight with our well-burnished iron,
I for Girart, the noblest duke alive,
And you for Charles, the King by royal line;
We'll fight alone and let Lord God decide
Who has the juster purpose, you or I."
On hearing this, young Roland filled with spite
And moved to strike him there – but thought in time
That, if he did, it would be judged a crime:
An envoy should be free to speak his mind;
So, thinking thus, the youth controlled his pride,
Not wishing blame to fall upon his side;
He drew his glove, inlaid with gold designs,
Approached the King, and seen by every eye,
Presented it in pledge that he would fight
With Oliver, of heart and valour high;
They pledged again that both men would arrive
Below Vienne upon the water's isle,
      To fight in single combat.

SO NOW YOU KNOW of their agreement, sworn
Before the King of mighty France and all
His barons there and all his knights and lords;
The pledges and the arguments set forth
That Roland claimed the city and its fort
For Charlemagne, whose beard and hair were hoar,
While Oliver, the gallant-visaged lord,
Defended Duke Girart with his sleek sword,
Of treachery to Charles in deed or thought:
And if he won, in single combat fought

Against the Count, whose face with valour stormed,
Then all the French would journey home once more
And make no claim upon Vienne henceforth;
But if young Oliver should fail and fall,
Then Duke Girart, however strong his force,
Would leave Vienne and all behind its walls
And lay no claim to any goods or coin,
 But flee to Apulia.

COUNT OLIVER spoke up: "So help me Jesus,
The righteous God, it's you who've shown the treason
And haughty pride, I cannot hide my feelings,
Since you have come to siege Vienne and seize it,
To chase Girart from land you gave him freely!
But if the Lord, Who judges all, so pleases,
You will not take one penny-piece so meanly,
While I may fight with my good horse beneath me!
I trust so much in God to judge the evil,
That if it comes to this one fight between us,
I'm very sure I shall disprove and beat you –
If God above, in His great love, will heed me;
But truly, Sire, once more I do beseech you
To stop this fight which we have both agreed to,
By calling off the business of this siege-host
And going back to France with all your legions;
I and Girart, the uncle I love dearly,
Will follow you most willingly and meekly,
And serve you there as our most honoured liege lord,
As well we should in any good way needed;
But if you don't, by St Riquier, believe me,
I'll nevermore endeavour to appease you,
But to defy – and I shall not conceal it,
In Jesu's name, Whose mighty Hand may teach you
To stoop your proud and arrogant demeanour!"
On hearing this, young Roland lost his reason
And raised his hand, although he dared not wield it!
The other Peers, who saw his anger seething,
Held back his arm, then straightaway proceeded
To lead him back within his tent and leave him;
Young Oliver still faced the King, unyielding
In his resolve to state what he believed in,
 Before all Charles's knights.

HERNAUT OF MONGENÇON rose to his feet;
With ringing voice he gave a wretched speech:
"True Emperor, my lord, attend to me!
By old St Simon's bones, this villain here
Should hang, I say, upon the gallows-tree!
With no delay, as soon as dawn appears,
Let us assault this town Vienne and seize
Girart himself and force the rogue to yield;
He has no force which we cannot defeat;
And when he's caught, allow no ransom-fee
    To free him from your justice!"

TO HEAR HIS LIFE attacked and threatened so
With hanging, like a thief or common rogue,
And then to hear alike the menace thrown
Of thrusting forth Girart from hall and home,
Young Oliver was almost mad with woe!
Without revenge, he'd hold his honour low,
And so he moved towards the wretch Hernaut
With fierce intent which grew each step he strode,
Till by the hair he dragged the villain close;
Hernaut was stooped, so heavy was the hold,
And Oliver's strong fist dealt such a blow
Upon his neck it broke the collar-bone;
The crimson blood escaped his mouth and flowed
Upon the ground as he was laid out cold;
When Aimart saw his wounded uncle roll
Upon the ground and heard him moan and groan,
His temper flared – small wonder, friends, I know,
And forth he rushed at Oliver the bold,
Till by the hair he caught and brought him close;
The youth was stooped, so heavy was the hold:
"God!" said Lambert, "My help may be too slow!"
He drew his sword, as fast as it would go,
And struck Aimart, not holding back the stroke,
Which took his head – before the King it rolled –
And flung him dead beside his kin Hernaut;
On seeing this, the King's impatience broke;
He cried aloud: "Take both of them in hold,
And if they move, then cut their faithless throats,
    For both have shamed me greatly!"

"TRUE EMPEROR," Lambert the brave spoke forth,
"So help me God, the shame and wrong are yours!
Accursed the court where men cannot report
Their honest thoughts or message they have brought –
And woe betide who cannot bide their talk!
You know full well, my lord, that I was caught
Before Vienne, where I had gone and fought
With Oliver, who stands before you all!
And I was brought inside Vienne by force,
But treated there with courtesy and warmth;
In France itself, or shire where I was born,
I never lacked for less or came by more!
Now I'm released so freely from their hall
That I've not lost in all two denier coins!
I've ridden back, as you can see, my lord,
The very horse I'd ridden forth before,
And with my arms and armour all restored;
Young Oliver the wise has led me forth,
And I, in turn, stand here his guarantor;
For his goodwill he's earned a poor reward,
Held up at once to insult and to scorn
By all these rogues, God curse them one and all!
I took his part – this surely is no fault."
On saying this, he lifted up his voice:
"You knights of mine, where are you now, my lords?"
Five hundred cried: "We're here for your support,
Equipped and armed with our well-burnished swords!"
The count replied: "Thanks be to God the Lord!
From Berry shire I've led you from your forts,
And urge you now, who love me as you ought,
And hold your fiefs and lands from me in law,
To serve my need and not to play me false,
Nor Oliver, who stands before you all
As he who set me free from threat and thrall."
They all replied: "We're with you! Rest assured,
We shall not fail, though life or limb be shorn!"
When this was said no Frenchman dared to talk
Or move against Lambert and vex him more;
    And so the madness lessened.

WHEN OLIVER saw all the French step nearer,
He thought at once that he would never leave there!
The press was thick with noble knights and liegemen,
And up they came, surrounding him to seize him;
They ripped aside his samite silken bliaut
And then the grey and rich pelisse beneath it;
The count dismayed and, filled with rage to feel it,
He lunged to reach a pole that he could see there,
By which the tent was held aloft and even;
He pulled it free, his gallant anger seething,
Which broke a rope and sent to ground the sheeting!
He raised the pole and then began to wield it:
The man he struck was robbed of breath to breathe with;
Lambert looked on and called so he could hear him:
"Escape at once, brave marquis, I beseech you!
I can no more be certain of your freedom!
For all the gold in Paris, I'd not see you
Abused, ill-used or slaughtered here by treason!"
The youth replied: "My lord, I thank you deeply."
And turned around, not asking leave, but leaving
The tent with all his enemies still reeling!
Garin the squire was his good friend, believe me,
And he'd made sure his noble horse would be there;
Young Oliver leapt straight astride the creature
And wasn't slow to use the rowels either –
His noble horse began at once to feel them!
Throughout the camp young Oliver went weaving,
His life in doubt, unless the count could flee them!
He looked and saw, at once, beneath the trees there,
The squire himself, whom Aude had sent to meet him;
He spurred the horse and turned that way to greet him;
The squire himself was unafraid and eager
To help him don the armour that he needed,
Which he put on like one of noble breeding:
Upon his back the coat of triple weaving,
And on his head the helmet green and gleaming;
He girt the sword, whose burnished blade was gleaming,
Then, once again, bestrode the horse, while seizing
A solid spear of burnish rich and recent,
Which good Garin had kept in his safekeeping;
When Oliver was fully armed, believe me,

No mortal knight more loved to fight than he did!
He rode downhill and out upon a clearing,
As did the squire, both fair of face and fearless;
But then, my friends, Girart came riding fiercely
With Hernaut of Biaulande, whose look was fearsome,
And Aymeri and Renier of Geneva;
He called aloud, when Oliver came near him:
"Fine nephew, friend, your quest! Has it succeeded?"
"No lord, indeed; I pledge you most sincerely,
I said your words and added mine most clearly
For Charles the King of Saint-Denis to hear them,
With all his knights, but Roland called them treason;
We two shall fight to prove the right between us;
Before the King I pledged that I would meet him."
"Dear God above, Who judges good and evil,
Assist us with Your grace!" Girart entreated;
"My friend, did you not speak or seek agreement
By peaceful means between the French and me here?"
"By St Maurice, I couldn't, lord, believe me!
They chased me off – look up, my lord, and see them!
Let's turn about, for God's sake and for Jesus,
And welcome them like knights of noble breeding."
Girart replied: "I grant your wish most freely!"
When this was said they spurred their steeds beneath them,
With bucklers pressed against their breasts to shield them;
They saw the French who, armed to fight, were eager,
And dropped the reins of their good steeds to speed them;
Without delay, as fast as they could reach them,
They struck their shields with sharp and shining spearheads;
The fight was fierce and full of zeal and feeling:
See lances split as shields were hit and beaten,
And hauberks cleft and left in little pieces
As knights were felled from steeds of Arab breeding;
Before the rest, see Aymeri appearing
To strike a Frank upon his sombre shield there!
Beneath the boss he broke the boards completely:
The coat was strong, he didn't part or pierce it,
Though from his steed he sent the fellow screaming!
"Vienne!" he cried, "For St Maurice and freedom!
Men, use your might like knights of noble breeding!"
And so they did, most gallantly and keenly,

Though Aymeri among them all was peerless!
They drove them back and then attacked the siege-camp;
They hacked them down and slew them on the field there;
Girart himself approached the campsite, seeing
Fine steeds galore and weapons piled in heaps which
The French had seized from all parts of his region;
The Duke himself had never seen their equal,
And with a sigh and cry he sorrowed deeply:
"By God above, our One and True Redeemer,
I do not think I've ever seen such people!
Ah, Charlemagne, fine King and mighty leader,
How wrongfully you've come here to besiege me!
May God and St Maurice not let you leave here
Until you too have had your share of grieving –
If I survive and thrive, you will receive it!"
He cried aloud so all his men could hear him:
"Return with me, brave knights of gallant breeding,
To Vienne town, whose glory is unequalled!"
"My lord," they said, "most gladly we will heed you!"
And turned the reins upon their steeds to leave there,
As all the French rushed forward to impede them
With every force and fibre of their being!
Within the press, where fighting was the fiercest,
Strove Oliver, of peerless mood and fearless,
But even he would need his friends ere evening,
Without God's help, Who died for all believers!
A Frenchman went from fighting in the meantime
To tell the King, so proud and fierce of feature,
That all Vienne had come in force and fiercely
    To fight them in their tents!

26. How love and war were blent before Vienne

BEFORE THE KING a messenger arrived
And cried aloud: "My lord, now you shall find
Who has the heart to help you in a fight:
Girart the duke, I'll not withhold or hide,
Has charged our tents upon the other side!"
On hearing this, King Charlemagne turned white;
He called Girbert of Tarragone aside,

Who hastened forth, not wasting any time;
And Roland too, well armed, came forth alike;
On seeing him, the King at once inquired:
"Fine nephew mine, by God, Who gave us life,
Are our men fit to fight, without a lie?"
"Indeed we are, and we are many, Sire;
Sound out your horns so all may heed the sign!"
And so he did: they sounded far and wide;
The King himself put on his armour bright
And mounted horse, not wasting any time;
He grasped a spear, whose blade was made of iron,
And spurred his steed which leapt to hit its stride;
He rode ahead, in front of all his knights
The distance of a well-drawn arrow's flight;
Girart addressed the nephew by his side:
"Young Oliver, do you not recognise
This rapid steed and he who sits astride?"
"My lord, I don't, by God Who gave me life;
But curse the cur who'd turn from him in fright!
Let's test his worth and see how he replies!"
Girart agreed: "We'll do as you desire."
And, turning round, spurred neither left nor right,
But straight ahead, not wasting any time;
He didn't know his foe, and that is why
    He rode at Charlemagne.

BENEATH VIENNE they gathered on the plain;
With all his zeal Girart spurred straightaway
To meet in joust the noble Charlemagne;
Upon his shield he laid a blow so great
That where it hit it split the boards in twain;
The coat was strong, the King himself unscathed
As Girart's lance in splinters split away;
With all his rage Charles struck him back and shaved
The saddle-bow behind Girart away,
Which flung him back and laid him flat against
The croup and rump of his good Gascon bay;
Girart was shocked, he rocked in fear and strained
With all his might to sit upright again;
He plied the rings with all his might and main,
Then drawing forth his golden-hilted blade,

He smote the helm of noble Charlemagne;
Without the help of God in Heaven's grace,
And sturdy coif upon his coat of mail,
The noble King would surely have been slain:
"Dear God, Who rescued Lazarus," he prayed,
"A score of years or more have passed, I'd say,
Since loyal France became my royal claim;
Since then I've met no prince so high in fame
Who ever struck my helm with so much rage,
Unless the blow was from some Pagan knave!
But now this lord has struck me with such hate
That all my head is spinning in a daze!
God, let me live to see him well repaid –
So help me God, he's earned a hefty wage!"
When Duke Girart heard this and it was plain
That he had struck his liege lord Charlemagne,
He leapt straight off his Spanish destrier
And ran to Charles without one moment's waste
To kiss his foot and stirrup-rings the same;
He begged the King, in Jesu's blessed name,
To pardon him for striking by mistake;
Charles heard the plea, but no reply he made,
And seeing this, Girart was filled with pain;
He saw the French approaching him in haste,
The Emperor's great host, in full array –
So, mounting up once more his Spanish bay,
He spurred again and turned its rein to race
　　Straight back towards the city.

BENEATH THE HALL and walls of old Vienne
There ran a wide and noble field back then;
An ancient wood was planted at one end,
And there it was that both those forces met –
King Charles's knights, so white of beard and head,
And Duke Girart's, with all his clan and friends:
"Mountjoy the fierce!" cried out aloud the French,
While "St Maurice!" was called by Girart's men;
If you had seen the spears they held erect,
With splendid flags of Eastern silk bedecked!
How well they struck with every ounce of strength!
How many shields were shorn apart and cleft,

How many coats all ripped awry and rent!
How many steeds were left bereft of men –
Lone horses roamed throughout the meadow's length,
With none to take or none to notice them;
Girart cried out with ringing voice and said:
"What holds you back, my gallant-hearted men,
Whose wont it was to vie with knighthood's best?
Strike hard and well – don't spare the likes of them!"
When this was said, his men took heart again:
If you had seen how many spears were spent,
How many steeds of France left riderless!
The man who fell had no time to repent
Ere he was crushed most awfully to death;
But Girart's men themselves were hard beset:
By force of arms they fell back from the press,
For Charles's side had overwhelming strength;
The battle's tide soon turned against Vienne,
    And heavy were their losses.

ANOTHER YOUTH was there, called Nevelon,
Among the best of Girart's clan he was;
He raised his lance and showed the gonfalon;
Upon his shield he struck one Eslion,
A counsellor of Charlemagne the strong;
He hit the shield and split it by the boss;
The Frank survived, his hauberk bore the shock,
But Nevelon struck well and down he dropped;
He drew his sword, whose hilt was gold-embossed,
And struck again upon his helmet's top
And sent him down, this time, where he belonged:
"Vienne!" he cried, "You gallant knights, lay on!"
He saw Girart and raised his voice aloft:
"Girart, my lord, how feeble is our wrath!
But I shall fight beside you from now on
    Amidst the blows of battle."

BELOW VIENNE, beside the leafy trees,
How fierce it was, my friends, believe you me!
The Poitevin Hernaut spurred hard his steed
To vent his spleen on Oliver the fierce,
Who saw him come and welcomed him indeed

With brandished spear and spurring hard his steed
To land a blow upon Hernaut's stout shield;
He hit the boards and split them piece from piece;
Hernaut survived, his hauberk bore the steel
And saved the knight from death or injury,
Though from the shock he dropped upon the field;
Count Oliver drew rein and turned to leave:
"Vienne!" he cried, "Geneva! St Maurice!"
He saw Girart and drew his war-horse near,
Then asked of him, in ringing tones and clear:
"Girart, my lord, don't hide it or conceal:
What happened when you fought that haughty Peer
Whom both of us before saw charging here?"
Girart replied: "The worst thing that could be,
For it was Charles, who gently cared for me!
To strike him thus has filled my heart with grief!
He'll never show me mercy now or peace!
Ride back at once, fine knights of gallant breed;
If we delay, I tell you truthfully,
We'll never reach the gates in time, I fear!
Charles never will forgive what's happened here!"
But Oliver replied, his anger deep:
"Fine uncle, lord, we cannot turn and leave!
By God above, let's gallop through the field
And strike again for all the pain we feel!"
Girart replied: "Good youth, most willingly!"
And, saying this, they quickly turned their steeds;
If you had seen that bitter fray proceed!
So many shields were split from front to rear,
And any man who tumbled from his steed,
Ne'er stood again, without a comrade near;
But Girart's men, at last, were forced to yield
The field; they couldn't bide the tide of steel
On Charles's side, or so the song reveals;
Girart the duke, of courage high and fierce,
And Lord Hernaut and his son Aymeri,
Regrouped their force upon a hillock's peak;
Their boldest knights then thundered down with zeal
And led with blows which cheered their slower peers;
Through Charles's ranks they forged and forced a breach;

The King looked on and groaned in disbelief
   And grief and rage most heavy.

THE CLASH WAS GREAT and fearful was the fray;
Charles summoned Elinant and young Gautier:
"My lords," he said, "pay heed to what I say:
Select at once and lead off straightaway
Four hundred men of courage fierce and great!
Turn round your steeds and head them with all haste
Towards Vienne and beat them to their gates:
If you do this, these traitors won't escape!"
Young Roland cried: "Are you in earnest, pray?
Are not these rogues before us, face to face?
Why seek to fight them in some other place?
Since they are here, may God confound the knave
Who'd ride away to find them once again!
Let's strike at once, together in our rage,
And stop the mouths of those with most to say!"
On saying this, young Roland spurred away
To strike the press with Durendal's sharp blade;
In hot pursuit the French all did the same;
Some seven thousand men, the song maintains,
Pursued Girart, whose ranks began to break;
If he had stopped to make a stand or stay,
He would have lost the bravest of his race;
So, sounding out his horn without delay,
He called back all his men across the plain;
He captured too his nephew's horse's rein,
Lest he should think of fighting on that day;
They left the fight, as well they might, in haste
To ride again inside Vienne's strong gates;
Behind them ran their gallant clan and race,
   Who closed the gates behind them.

THEY REACHED VIENNE and rode directly in;
The gates were closed, the drawbridge raised forthwith;
The King looked on and almost lost his wits;
He called aloud his proud and fearsome will:
"My worthy knights, assault these walls and bridge!
Who fails me now, shall lose what's mine to give:
No town in France that any knight thinks his,

No port or pass or fortress strongly-built,
Shall fail to fall, if I am failed in this!"
When this was said, they jostled to begin;
The squires first approached the walls and hit
The solid stones with hammers and with picks,
While those inside stood side by side and tipped
Upon their heads great stones and sharpened sticks;
Three score and more were struck at once and killed;
One hundred squires in service of the King
Fell off the walls and landed in the ditch;
"True Emperor," said Naimon, "do you think
That you can take so fine a town like this,
The sturdy walls and towers tall of which
Were long ago and strongly so rebuilt
By Pagan hands with all their strength and skill?
They'll never fall as long as you shall live!
Send back to France and have your envoys bring
French engineers to help you conquer it:
When they arrive, then they can start to build
Machines of war to their design, wherewith
To fell this town right down to its last inch!"
On hearing this, Charles blanched from cheek to chin,
    He was so heavy-hearted.

OLD NAIMON SAID, the wise and hoary-bearded:
"True Emperor, I will not hide my feelings;
So help me God, your mind has lost its reason,
If you believe this town can be defeated
By storming it with climbing and with leaping!
The walls are high and have been raised by heathens;
By all my faith in Jesus Christ, believe me,
You'll never take this town in seven seasons!
Send back to France for the assistance needed
From engineers who know how to besiege it;
They have the skill to fell these walls or breach them."
On hearing this, the King fell first to grieving,
Then cried aloud once more: "Mountjoy, the fearsome!
What holds you back, my good and gallant liegemen?"
And their attack began again, and fiercely
The force inside hurled stones and sticks to meet it;
But then fair Aude, the lovely, slender creature,

Dressed in a silk made up in Almeria,
With golden thread of perfect stitch and seaming,
Her eyes of green between her rosy features,
Appeared atop the walls for all to see there;
When she beheld the fierce assault proceeding,
She quickly stooped to seize a stone, then heaved it
To strike a Gascon's helm, made in Pavia:
She broke the brim and rim of it to pieces
And almost killed the Gascon lad beneath it!
Brave-faced and bold, young Roland laughed to see it,
And called aloud, so she as well could hear him:
"We'll never take this town or ever seize it
At this one point, so help me blessed Jesus,
For I refuse to fight with maids, believe me!
But I shall not forsake this rampart either,
Before I ask the name of this fair creature!
Take no offence, fair maiden, I entreat you;
I do not ask with any evil meaning."
"My lord," she said, "then I shall not conceal it;
My name is Aude – thus called by those who reared me;
I am the daughter of Renier of Geneva,
And sister of Sir Oliver the fearless,
And Girart's niece, who scorns a coward's weakness;
My noble clan is of the best and fiercest;
I've never had a lord to bow or kneel to,
Nor shall I have, so help me blessed Jesus,
If Lord Girart decides I do not need one,
And Oliver, who is our honour's beacon!"
Young Roland said, but so she could not hear him:
"By Jesus, born of Mary, how it grieves me
That I am not the lord that you pay heed to!
Without God's help I know I'll never be that,
For I must win the battle I've agreed to
    With her own Oliver!"

FAIR AUDE, THE MAIDEN wise of heart, remarked:
"Sir knight, my lord, I have for my own part
Replied in truth to everything you asked;
Now, if you please, reveal on your behalf
Where you were born, and who your kinsmen are;
How well you bear that shield upon your arm,

And wear the sword about your waist enclasped,
And hold the spear, its gonfalon held fast!
How well you sit that steed which in the charge
Can match the speed of any crossbow's shaft!
How many men this day you've slain of ours,
More fierce yourself than all the force of France!
I think, indeed I know it in my heart
That your true love has all of beauty's charms!"
On hearing this, the youth said with a laugh:
"My lady fair, you speak the truth, I'll grant!
She has no peer in beauty near or far,
From here to Rheims or Rome, in home or hearth,
   Nor elsewhere that I know of!"

WHEN ROLAND HEARD her speaking in this tenor,
He didn't tell her all he felt directly,
But nonetheless his manner grew most friendly:
"My lady fair, without a lie I tell you
That I am called young Roland by my fellows."
On hearing this, the maiden filled with pleasure:
"Are you the same whose name I've heard them mention
As he who's pledged to test my brother's mettle?
You little know his gallant strength and temper,
If you have sworn to meet in joust against him!
I swear to you, I truly do regret it,
For you are thought to be my friend by many,
Or so I've heard and had so many tell me!
Now by the faith you've pledged to Charles the Frenchman,
If you had caught me yesterday and kept me,
Would you have had the courtesy to let me
Return unharmed from hostile arms that held me?"
On hearing this, young Roland's senses trembled;
The youth replied: "My lady fair and gentle,
Don't mock me if you hold me dear, I beg you."
At this, the King called forth the count of Berry
And said: "Lambert, take care not to dissemble!
Who *is* that maid upon those ancient crenels
That speaks with him and whom he too addresses?"
The count replied: "Without a lie, I tell you
That she is Aude, a maiden fair and gentle,
The daughter of Geneva's brave Duke Renier;

The Lombard Enseis has sworn to wed her!"
King Charlemagne replied: "He'll never get her!
Young Roland's pledged his heart to her already!
One hundred men well armed in iron would perish
Ere Enseis and she could leave together!"
As this was said, young Roland turned, farewelling
The lovely maid, who turned around and left there;
The King looked on and teased the youngster gently:
"What vow," he said, "have you made now, fine nephew,
To that young girl I saw you just addressing?
If anything she's said or done has vexed you,
Forgive her 'if you hold her dear', I beg you!"
On hearing this, young Roland shook and trembled
    And bowed his head abashed.

"FINE NEPHEW MINE," said Charles in earnestness:
"Whoever gains the maid you spoke with then
At such a length, I've made no gains myself!
For Oliver has ridden from Vienne,
Together with one hundred knights and men,
And stormed our ranks along the campsite's edge;
They've hewn the heads of twenty of our best,
And taken more to sore imprisonment;
The maiden Aude, she knew this very well,
And made of you a butt of joke and jest!"
On hearing this, young Roland almost wept;
With utmost rage his chin and cheek turned red;
But when the King observed his great distress,
He said again, with noble tenderness:
"Fine nephew mine, allay your wild regrets!
Because of her on whom your heart is set,
We'll turn our steeds and speed back to our tents;
For fair Aude's sake, we'll break off this attempt."
The youth replied: "My lord, at your behest."
They blew their horns and turned their horses' heads;
The King returned to camp, then all the French
Throughout the host disarmed in high content
To take their ease and seek repose and rest;
They ate and drank in plenty, then they went.
With dying day, to lie upon their beds;
King Charlemagne, of fierce and high prowess,

Lay down to rest, his body worn and spent:
From dawn to dusk he'd fought with all his strength;
He fell asleep, and as he slept he dreamt
A vivid dream, which filled with mighty dread
    The Emperor of France.

27. How Charles dreamed a portentous dream

THE EMPEROR lay in his tent asleep;
The noble lord, his body worn indeed
From bearing arms and fighting in the field,
He dreamt a dream both full of dread and fierce;
He saw himself spur forth to take his ease
Beside a stream upon a mighty steed,
Upon his wrist a hawk he held most dear;
One hundred squires were with him, blithe of cheer,
When from Vienne he saw a falcon leave
To reach the isle – it flew there at great speed,
And reaching it, took rest upon a peak;
Three times it cried and made so loud a screech
That Charlemagne and all his men could hear;
If he could catch that falcon, all agreed
Montpellier's gold would never set it free,
    For he would love it dearly.

IN DEEPEST SLEEP the mighty King dreamt more:
It seemed to him that in his sleep he bore
Upon his wrist his lovely hunting-hawk;
He let it rise upon that falcon's course
Which he has seen depart Vienne before;
Upon the isle, whose grass was green and tall,
Both birds came face to face and claw to claw!
Then in a rage the two of them lunged forth
And struck away so fiercely in assault
Till both of them had lost much blood and force;
With brutal wings they beat each other raw;
The King looked on, in awful fear, and fraught
Lest he should lose the hawk which he adored;
And, as he looked, he turned his mind and thoughts
In fervent prayer to the Almighty Lord,

Beseeching Him to save his hunting-hawk;
So fervently the mighty King implored
That both the birds resolved on an accord
And mutual peace, so lovingly what's more,
They seemed to kiss in fond embrace and warm;
On seeing this, the King himself rejoiced
So fervently that he awoke with joy;
His body shook and started up, distraught
From top to toe that he had dreamt it all;
His right hand raised, he signed the Cross and called
Upon the Grace of our Almighty Lord,
To turn the dream to good account and cause;
He summoned then a very wise man forth
And told him everything, omitting naught
Of how, in slumber deep, he dreamt and saw
Two noble birds in fearsome contest caught,
Who then made peace, their friendship sweetly sworn;
On hearing this, the wise man was enthralled
And said aloud: "O mighty Emperor,
Be in no doubt about this dream of yours!
For I am sure, without one moment's thought,
That I can tell you well what this purports!
The falcon-bird, of this you may be sure,
Which flew down to the isle from Vienne's wall,
Is Oliver, the gallant-visaged lord,
Who will, I'd say, ride very shortly forth
From Vienne's gates, well armed upon his horse,
To keep the joust with Roland, as he swore,
And, falcon-like, will swoop upon the shore;
The fearsome hawk, I swear to you, my lord,
Who grappled with the hunting-falcon's claws,
That's Roland, Sire, that gallant kin of yours,
Who'll lunge and plunge with his sharp-cutting sword
At Oliver, whose valour is his ward;
And both shall wound each other sick and sore
Ere making peace in love and friendship born
At God's command, Who is the Lord of all;
These two shall be fond comrades evermore,
 And both shall make you joyful."

28. How Oliver and Roland armed for battle

FIERCE-VISAGED CHARLES was very glad indeed
To hear so good a meaning of his dream;
He had no wish that night for further sleep,
But was, instead, both shod and dressed in brief;
The night grew light as dawning day appeared
With rising sun and sunbeams bright and clear;
Below Vienne the birdsong filled the fields,
As in the town Count Oliver appeared,
Attending first the church of St Maurice
To hear God's word and blessings from the priest;
Then he returned inside the hall, where he
Called squire Garin, the man who served his needs:
"My friend," he said, "make haste and bring to me
My noblest clothes and finest fighting-gear,
So I may dress without delay and leave."
The squire replied: "Fine lord, most willingly!"
And went to bring the things that he would need;
The noble youth took off immediately
His ermine cloak and nobly-trimmed pelisse,
So that he stood in just the shirt beneath;
But then he donned a doublet, friends, that gleamed
With cloth of gold and feared no arrow's steel
Or any weapon's piercing of its weave;
He took his mail, but then looked up to see
Girart the duke arrive in company
With Elinant and young Gautier his peer;
His uncle seized the mail and made to speak
In ringing tones but very courteously:
"For Jesu's sake, my noble nephew dear,
Forgo this fight to which you have agreed
With Roland's might, who as a knight is fierce
In his prowess with weapons in the field!
A master carpenter, who cuts his beams
To make a room or dwelling, never wields
His axe aloft as skilfully as he!
For all of Gaifier's gold I'm loath to see
Him joust with you and cause you injury;
My happy heart would nevermore be cheered."

The youth replied: "Although you offered me
Bavaria or all of Poitiers' fief,
I'll not forgo this fight for any plea!
Now I must arm myself with every speed –
   I've wasted time already!"

"FINE NEPHEW MINE," said Duke Girart the brave,
"For Jesu's sake, Who suffered mortal pain
Upon the Cross to keep all Christians safe,
Forgo this fight, I urge you once again,
With Roland's might, who's fearsome in his rage;
There is no knight his equal in the fray."
Said Oliver: "My lord, I'm not afraid;
No fear of losing limb, no offer made
Of gaining wealth, will cause me to refrain
From riding forth to fight the Count this day;
I've pledged to go and cannot break my faith;
I trust in God to guard me as He may;
No blow can harm the man His arm keeps safe!
My lord Girart, I must put on my mail!
Already I've delayed too long, I'd say;
   It's high time that I left here."

AGAIN, JUST AS he armed himself to fight,
An ancient Jew called Joachim arrived!
On cheek and chin his beard was lily-white;
When Pilate, friends, was captured for his crime
Of letting Christ our Lord be crucified –
Although I think revenge was wrought in time
By Emperor Vespasian the wise,
Who rounded up and hounded, so they write,
All Jewish men his soldiers then could find
In old Jerusalem so fair and fine,
And marched them from the town and took their lives –
Friends, ever since that day, without a lie,
Vienne had housed this Jew and all his tribe;
And rich he'd grown, in coin and goods alike,
But gave so much to barons of the shire
That they were glad to let him live and thrive;
He saw the youth and came to speak his mind:
"Sir Oliver," he cried, "good friend of mine!

Accept these gifts and use them in your fight!
King Charlemagne of France has none so fine!"
On looking up, the youth knew he was right;
He clasped the Jew and would have kissed him twice,
If only he had loved Lord Jesus Christ!
The noble count most courteously replied:
"Much thanks for this, Joachim, friend of mine!
If God above, the King of Paradise,
In His great love allows me to survive,
Then your own son at once shall be baptised
And dubbed a knight ere seven days go by!
I'll give him arms and noble steeds to ride,
And ample share of my own shore and shire!"
"May God forbid," old Joachim replied,
"That my own son should ever be baptised!
By God's own voice, I swear I'd rather die
And cast my son upon a blazing fire!"
When Oliver heard this, he laughed outright,
As did the counts and marquises and knights;
The worthy Jew picked up his gifts meanwhile
    And brought them to young Oliver.

THIS JOACHIM did not delay or stop;
He gave his gifts to Oliver the strong,
Displaying them upon a table-top;
A bishop there blessed each and every one
In Jesu's name and signed them with the Cross,
Because the Jew, of hoary beard and locks,
Had held them all within his house so long;
Joachim said: "Let's put his armour on,
For you can see that this is what he wants!
In these, my lords, these shoes, let him be shod –
No pair was e'er so fair since Solomon's!
Then fit these spurs of peerless value on:
I bought them from a Slav in lands far-off –
One hundred pounds in mangons was their cost!
Behold the gems with which they are embossed:
They're worth far more than is the town Mâcon,
Or so I've heard, and do not think it wrong!"
Girart replied: "I'll gladly help, by God!"

And took the spurs without one moment's loss
And clipped them to the young man's heels, which on
His ermine cloak he held to do the job;
And while he did, he counselled him non-stop,
   As elder knight to younger.

THEY DRESSED HIM IN a coat of Eastern mail
Both strong and light, the lightest ever made:
A serving-man could carry twelve the same;
No arm on earth, no dart or cutting blade,
Could damage in the least this hauberk's chains,
So strong they were – none better could he crave;
Aeneas won this coat from Eliné
Upon the plains of ancient Troy, that day
When Paris, son of Priam, met his fate,
And Hector too, his brother dear, was slain;
They all were killed, defeated or enslaved,
Their buildings cast upon the ground and razed –
No tower tall or soaring wall remained,
Each brick of them lay broken on the plain;
No mortal man escaped that battle, save
Aeneas, whom the Lord loved with His grace:
He fled with his own father – both escaped
Upon a barge across the ocean's waves;
Aboard he cured with skill his wounds and pain;
Aeneas wore this coat of Eastern mail
But lost it near Maràdant in a fray
Fought in a wood with Roboant, they say;
This giant slew Aeneas on that day,
A soldier from the ranks of France the brave,
And that was when he won this coat of mail;
He brought it to Vienne, and when he came,
He sought the Jew, who bought it straightaway;
He'd hidden it since then to keep it safe!
But on this day he gave the coat away
To Oliver, the offspring bold and brave
   Of Renier of Geneva.

YOUNG OLIVER girt on his blade sharp-edged,
A sturdy sword – too solid in its strength:
It broke in half too soon below Vienne

And Aude the maid was filled with mighty dread
And great distress, who feared her brother's death –
As you will hear, in time, if you attend
And heed the song as I proceed, my friends!
A rounded shield was hung about his neck,
Of gold and blue its painted hue, whose crest
Portrayed a fish among the ocean's depths;
The boss and boards were anvil-hard themselves;
This Joachim, of hoary beard and head,
Obtained it from a Moor in Valsoret,
And paid him well for what he had to sell:
A goblet full of coins, so says the text;
Girart the duke, without delay or let,
Told all his squires to seek out and to fetch
A noble steed with golden saddle set
For Oliver, who liked it very well;
How many tears by lovely Aude were shed,
As Girart tried to comfort her distress;
The gallant duke addressed his nephew then:
"May God, Who made the sky and dew, direct
The victory to you and to our quest;
    And may His hand protect you!"

"FINE NEPHEW MINE," proclaimed Girart the bold:
"To Lord our God, Who suffered mortal woe
Upon the Cross to save all Christian folk,
I place in trust your noble life and soul!
You do not fight for riches of your own,
But to defend your uncle from reproach;
Take this good horn, fine nephew, as you go,
And drape it on your shield, where it may show;
Ride from Vienne, and when you reach below,
Then sound it high above the sieging-host
So Charles may hear and all his knights may know
That you have come to fight for me alone."
Said Oliver: "My lord, it shall be so."
He took the horn and feared none as he rode,
Except Lord God on His majestic throne,
And Roland too, so fierce and brave a foe –
Though in the field he felled him when he drove
An awesome thrust right through his horse's bones!

The worthy count struck countless worthy blows –
May Jesus Christ have mercy on his soul!
He mounted horse and wound the buckler's rope
Around his neck, the horn below his throat,
And seized his spear, whose point was finely honed
And bore a flag affixed with nails of gold;
Renier, Count of Geneva, wise and bold,
Bemoaned his son with gentle tears and low,
As did the lord of Biaulande, brave Hernaut,
And Aymeri, whose face with valour glowed;
Fair Aude commended him to Heaven's hold,
And he delayed no more, but turned to go
Beyond the gate on his appointed road;
Beneath Vienne he rode down to the Rhône,
Where, stepping down, he crossed upon a boat
To reach the isle, and, landing there, he rode
At rapid pace upon its grassy slope;
He took the horn and gave it three long blows
With such a force and with such fearsome notes
That in their tents the French all heard below;
They saw him there, three thousand knights all told,
And cried at once: "He is bewitched! Behold
How every inch of his fine armour glows!
If Roland seeks a fight, then one is close,
And fiercer far than any yet he's known!"
And envoy turned with every haste to go
And tell the Count of Oliver's approach:
"Well armed, he rides upon the isle alone,
With fervour deep to keep the pledge he spoke
In Charles's tent, when plighting you his troth."
On hearing this, what joy young Roland showed;
He cried aloud: "All praise the Lord of Hosts!
You've granted me what I desired the most!"
At once he called for weapons and for clothes,
And those in charge without delay brought both;
He donned the best of everything he owned:
A jewelled helm, a sturdy hauberk-coat,
And then his sword, whose handle shone with gold,
Called Durendal, as all among you know;
He won it from Aumon, a Pagan rogue;
King Charlemagne addressed him in these tones:

"Fine nephew mine, attend and be not loath!
For Jesu's sake, Who bore the Cross's woe,
Forgo this fight! I urge you not to go!
And Oliver the wise will then, I hope,
Ride back inside Vienne among his folk;
I do not wish, for two whole cities' gold,
To see him lose a limb or be laid low,
Or witness you struck too by some ill stroke!"
"You wish in vain," said Roland, "for I won't
Restrain my hand for all the land you own!
I've pledged my word to this, as well you know,
And will not be forsworn or break my oath;
There's nothing more that you can do or hope
That will prevent me riding at my foe!
If I, in truth, should break my plighted troth,
   The shame of it would kill me."

"FINE NEPHEW MINE," said fearsome Charlemagne:
"Since you desire it so and it is plain
That you will fight whatever I might say,
Then I commend your life to Jesu's grace!
May he defend you life and limb this day
And spare alike your foe from grief and grave."
"Fine uncle mine," said Roland, ever brave,
"For Jesu's sake, Who bore the Cross's bane,
Let no one here ride after me this day;
For all the gold in Paris, my good name
Shall not be blamed for wronging him this way."
Said Charlemagne: "None shall – I pledge the same."
Young Roland said: "Much thanks, upon my faith."
His Arab steed was led there straightaway
And up he swung, without the stirrups' aid;
Around his neck a curving shield was draped
And in his hand a burnished spear was laid,
Which flew a flag affixed with golden nails;
Across the camp he rode with every haste
To reach the Rhône without the least delay;
He waded through on his fine destrier
And reached the isle without a stop or stay,
Where Oliver was waiting, ever brave;
The gallant Count came forth at rapid pace

And Oliver rode forward just the same,
His heavy shield held up before his face,
   With all his strength and temper.

WHEN OLIVER saw Roland's fierce intention,
He rode at him, his shield up to protect him;
Duke Roland rode till they were close together,
And then he cried: "Disclose your name and tell me:
Are you a Hun, Bavarian or Frenchman,
From Normandy, from Flanders or from Berry?"
Count Oliver replied at once: "God help me,
Sir Roland, don't you know me or remember?
I'm Oliver, the son of noble Renier,
Geneva's lord of such prowess and merit;
My uncle is Girart, the fierce of mettle,
My cousin, I am more than glad to tell you,
Is Aymeri, of fierce and fiery temper,
From whom you stole the other day a destrier!
I've ridden here, in some part, to avenge him;
The other day, I also well remember,
Your seizing Aude, my sister fair, intending
To bear her forth on horseback to your shelter!
Thank God above, our Lord Who lives in Heaven,
My burnished sword came swiftly to her rescue;
I'll not forget how well your spur-points helped you
When you escaped to Charles's host and fled me!
I say this not to blame or to offend you –
Instead, indeed, to offer this suggestion:
Make peace for us with Charles, and then I pledge you
That you may have my sister Aude and wed her."
The Count replied: "Your plea to me is senseless,
For soon I'll drag you by my horse, well tethered,
To France itself, where you will be arrested,
While I take Aude with or without your blessing!"
Said Oliver: "That will not happen ever,
   While I have breath to breathe."

YOUNG OLIVER was full of gallant zeal,
At every point opposing Roland's speech,
Addressing him, in truth, most angrily:
"By God, the Son of Mary, I repeat

What I have said: it's mad of you indeed
To even think, in your great knavery,
That you will make my uncle bend the knee
Or bow his head while he has breath to breathe,
Or be your slave for all of Normandy!"
Young Roland said: "This makes no sense to me;
I do not care a jot for plots or pleas!
If God preserves good Durendal's sharp steel,
I'll have your head before day disappears!"
Said Oliver: "You'll not, for I believe
Girart the duke, my gallant-visaged liege,
 Would be too much the loser."

THE GALLANT YOUTHS stood facing on the isle;
There never were two fighters half as fine;
King Charles's knight addressed Sir Renier's child:
"Young vassal, let us leave all pleas aside!
I've ridden here to stoop this city's pride,
Whose hall and wall and ramparts are so high,
For Charlemagne, who is your liege and mine;
He'd honour you, if you did him alike!"
Count Oliver, the well-bred youth, replied
With words for which he should be praised and prized,
And cherished well by all of noble line:
"Ah, Roland, lord, most noble, gallant knight!
For Jesu's sake, Who suffered mortal spite
Upon the Cross to save all Christian lives,
Make peace for us, I urge it one last time,
And you shall have fair Aude to be your wife,
And all Vienne itself to rule in time;
I shall convince Girart he should comply;
And from this day, in fearsome frays and fights,
I'll bear your flag and never leave your side."
But Roland said: "Your sermoning's ill-timed!
When you are slain with my good blade, then I
Shall take Vienne and then fair Aude besides,
 In spite of all your kinsmen!"

SAID OLIVER, of bold and gallant heart:
"My noble lord, for love of God, hold hard!
What you have said can never come to pass;

Instead, do what for love of you I've asked:
For Jesu's sake, Who never fails the task,
Make peace for us and let us never part!
For all Ponthieu I would not see you harmed
Or captured here, for at the least and last
I know that then there would be every chance
That all my friends would face the wrath of France;
And then the King and my uncle Girart
Would nevermore be friends by choice or chance;
Adopt instead the plan I have advanced,
Then I and my good uncle, brave of heart,
Will be your men, with loyal hands enclasped."
But Roland said: "In truth, you'll be well grasped,
For I shall slay you here or hold you fast,
And hand you on to him who gave me arms –
And he will hold you in his jail in France,
Where you'll be chained and never be discharged
Till you are banned from your own land and ours;
I'll have Vienne and lie in Aude's fair arms;
Your uncle, who has broken faith with Charles,
Will flee in fear and walk a beggar's path!"
"What crazy lies!" cried Oliver, aghast,
"And I'd be mad to ask more than I've asked!
Good God above, why did I even start?
I was a fool and made a craven cast!
I place myself, henceforth, in Jesu's charge!
Sir Roland, lord, since things are as they are,
And I can find no mercy in your heart,
Do not say hence I failed my plighted task;
I've challenged you, so now be on your guard!
I've warned you well, so let the contest start!"
Young Roland said: "I've heard you out at last!"
If you had seen how hard they looked and harsh!
Each spurred his steed upon a speedy path
Which parted them one furlong and a half;
Then, turning round, each raised aloft his lance,
And lifted up his shield with his left arm,
Then galloped hard across the flowering grass,
    The one against the other.

29. How Oliver and Roland fought before Vienne

IF YOU HAD SEEN how stubbornly they raised
Their sturdy spears and aimed their cutting blades,
Then dug the spurs to speed their destriers,
You would have said they were the best men made
In all the world to justify their claims!
What mighty blows on either's shield they laid
Beneath the boss, which broke their boards away
And made each spear to split apart and break!
Their coats were strong, they couldn't pierce the mail,
But as they met, they hit with such a weight
That both their steeds fell down beneath the strain
Upon their knees, then staggered up again
As both men passed and then at last drew rein;
They turned at once, like falcons after prey,
    To come again and harder!

COUNT ROLAND CAME, astride his Gascon stallion;
With Durendal, his sword, unsheathed, he landed
A blow on his opponent's helmet-panels
Which knocked to ground the garland-jewels they carried
And, driving on, upon its downward passage,
Struck Oliver's good steed behind the saddle;
It split the felt of its vermilion padding
And hit the steed across and through its backbone;
Deep down inside the horse's bowels it travelled
And smote his spur, while slicing in its angle
The tip away beside the youngster's ankle;
The wretched steed was cut in half exactly;
The blade went on until it struck the paddock;
Count Oliver the brave was left there standing!
Young Roland cried: "Mountjoy for Charles the gallant!
This day Vienne shall be destroyed and captured,
Which false Girart has held in rebel fashion!
He will receive a bitter wage to thank him –
Like any thief he'll hang upon the gallows!"
Said Oliver: "You are a foolish braggart!
Lord God, Who pardoned Longinus his action,
Decides on all; He may put forth His hand here
To fight for me, despite you and your valour;

I've ridden here and face you in this battle
To save Vienne, its people and its palace;
You will not gain one spur of all its value,
Unless you pay one hundred pounds in mangons!"
He drew his sword, a lion in his anger,
Advancing like a most courageous vassal;
Girart the duke was fraught with fear and anguish
Within the tower of his most splendid palace;
No treasure or no pleasure could distract him:
He stood and watched as silent as a shadow;
But when he spoke, he cried out with a clamour
To God on High, our Everlasting Ally:
"Immortal God, Who suffered mortal Passion,
And from the grave brought back and saved St Lazarus,
And pardoned all the sins of Mary Magdalen,
And saved old Jonah when the great fish had him,
As this is true, and we believe it gladly,
Redeem this day the life of my young champion,
From Roland's hand, King Charlemagne's captain –
    Or I shall die of grief!"

FAIR AUDE LEANT AT a window-ledge to see;
She cried and sighed, her hand upon her cheek,
When she beheld her brother cast afield,
From saddle-bows thrown down upon his feet
When Roland struck his stallion from Castile;
Within her breast the maiden felt such grief
Her heart well nigh was cleft in two beneath;
She ran to church and fell upon her knees
Before the rails and made this private plea:
"Immortal God," the maiden prayed, unseen,
"Who in the Maid took on mortality,
Whom, sinners all, we call on in our need,
Send word to me of both men which will please
Both Duke Girart and noble Charles's ear,
    The Emperor of France."

THE MAIDEN SWOONED upon the marbled stone;
Her lovely gown and noble ermine cloak
Were wet with tears, for she had fretted so;
She begged the Lord, in gentle, honest tones,

Who came to earth to bring His people hope:
"Immortal God, let Your great mercy flow
On both who fight, for I do love them both!
Let neither one be maimed or slain as foes!"
My worthy friends, we'll leave poor Aude alone
And hear again of Roland, famed of old,
And Oliver, whose heart was strong and bold,
And who, on foot, moved up to strike a blow!
He raised his sword, whose hilt was seamed with gold,
And struck young Roland's helm so well, he smote
Its garland-jewels away with just one stroke!
The worthy blade went on, and, down below,
It struck his steed beside the saddle-bows
And split the beast between its shoulder-bones,
As on it fell till in the field it drove
And in a heap both horse and rider rolled!
On seeing this, what gladness filled his soul!
If half of France had lain in his control,
And Orléans and Rheims been his to own,
He'd not have been, I think, so glad of those,
As of the count just then unhorsed and thrown
    Upon Vienne's own island.

IF YOU HAD BEEN beneath Vienne, my lords,
When Oliver and Roland faced and fought!
There never were two knights as brave before,
So bold of heart or skilled in arts of war!
How well they struck each other with their swords
And landed blows upon those bucklers' boards!
From both their helms the precious gems were torn
And sparks flew off and lit the land abroad;
No man alive in these days ever saw
A fight to match the combat I record!
And those who saw it then would nevermore
Behold a duel wherein such blows were scored;
Girart the duke stood on his castle walls
With Lord Hernaut, the ruler of Biaulande,
And Aymeri, whose face with valour stormed;
Geneva's lord, Renier, stood there distraught
For Oliver, the son whom he adored:
"Most blessed Maid," he prayed aloud and called,

"Keep Oliver this day in watch and ward,
Lest he be made to yield the field or fall!"
And Charles alike most earnestly implored:
"Most blessed Maid, defend young Roland more,
        For he is my successor!"

BENEATH VIENNE, upon the sandy isle,
Those gallant youths were locked in mortal strife;
Like champions they raised their swords to strike
And showed no mercy upon each other's life,
Both fiercer than the leopard or the lion;
I do not know which one to praise the higher,
For both of them were of such fame and pride
That neither one would flee from any fight
One spur in length, for all of Samson's might!
What lusty blows with naked steel they plied!
Their shields were split, their jewelled helmets sliced,
Whose golden hoops were useless in the fight –
They sundered them like saddle-blanket ties!
The clash of steel flung forth a blaze of light
As all the sparks flew off to every side;
The two of them were so intent and wild
That neither feared the other person's might;
With such a rage and such rampaging strides
They stalked each other, it was a wondrous sight!
Their lion-blazoned shields were broken wide
As were the rings upon their hauberks bright,
So underneath their actons showed inside;
If neither won the help of Jesus Christ,
Then neither one would leave that fight alive;
Within Vienne, inside its hall on high,
Guibourc was filled with bitter grief and spite,
As was the sweet, fair-visaged Aude alike;
They tore their hair, with constant tears and sighs,
And wrung their hands and wailed aloud and cried:
"Alas, Vienne! How better far that fire
Should burn your walls on each and every side
Until no tower or any room survived,
Than that for you such knights should risk their lives!
For we know well, if one of them should die,
The whole of France will rage with civil strife,

And all this land will be destroyed thereby."
The maiden Aude made every haste to find
Hernaut the count, whose name and fame were high,
And spoke this way to Biaulande's worthy sire:
"Fine uncle mine, please give us your advice:
How may we, with no blame or shame, contrive
For these two knights to stop their fight in time?"
"My hands are tied," the worthy man replied:
"It is Girart and Charles the King who fight –
With common fault and common hate and pride!
Our ancestor, we know this to be right,
Old Duke Beuvon, of beard and whiskers white,
Gave not one ounce, in coinage or in kind,
Of fealty to Charles in all his life,
   For Vienne and its region."

FRIENDS, LOOK AGAIN! Both men were face to face –
On foot the pair, for both their destriers
Were on the ground, cut down by ruthless blades!
Count Roland spoke, whose heart was ever brave:
"Sir Oliver, by all my Christian faith,
I never saw a man who had your grace!
We two oppose each other in this place,
Where we shall fight for right with all our rage
Till one of us is made to yield or slain;
No mortal man is here to lend us aid;
And yet I swear, in God's majestic name,
That I can see two ladies far away
In Vienne's hall, lamenting for our sakes,
Both fraught with fear, in anguish at your fate;
So help me God, I pity their complaints!"
Said Oliver: "You speak the truth, in faith;
Guibourc is one, whose heart is wise with age,
The other Aude, so fair of form and face;
They sorrow both for me and what awaits;
But if Lord God, Who made the world, dictates
That I return alive, then I shall say
So much to Aude before the close of day,
That if her wish to marry you must fail,
She'll wed no other lord, but take the veil
   Until in death she joins you."

THE NOBLE KNIGHTS stood facing on the field,
Prepared to strike with all their strength and zeal;
See Roland there, whose face with valour gleamed!
What blows he struck with his great blade of steel
Called Durendal, whose valour well was seen
At Roncevaux, upon that morning bleak
When it was cleft by death from Roland's keep!
See Oliver, who raised his own to deal
A mighty blow at Roland's circled shield;
It struck the boss, but what a loss indeed!
When drawing it, he found it stuck too deep,
And snapped it by the hilt as it was freed!
Before Vienne the cry went up in brief
That Oliver, whose face with valour gleamed,
Had snapped his sword and bore a paltry piece!
On hearing this, Aude swooned away with grief;
She moaned aloud, when rising to her feet,
And called upon the Virgin's help in need:
"Fine brother mine, how hard your destiny!
If you are lost, the Lord's forgotten me!
I never shall be Roland's wife, it seems,
The best of men to gird a sword of steel!
A convent nun, alas, is what I'll be!
St Mary, blessed Maiden, must I see
My brother fight to death on Vienne field
With my beloved, who spoke his love for me?
Whoever dies, I'll lose my mind for grief!
Blest Heaven's Queen, I beg you, intervene!"
On hearing this, the blood left Girart's cheeks;
He raised her up and bade her with all speed
To go to church with noble company;
With greatest strain they strove to calm her fears;
When news of this arrived for Charles to hear,
One thousand showed their grief throughout the siege;
The King himself, in private, showered tears
    Upon his furs of marten.

WHEN OLIVER beheld his sword-blade severed,
The bits of which lay useless on the meadow,
And when he saw his horse struck through the centre,
And saw his shield pierced through past any mending,

Then, rest assured, my friends, his heart was heavy,
For he could see no mortal means to help him;
He looked around to all parts of the meadow
And saw himself enclosed in each direction,
With no means of escape from there whatever;
His grief was such he almost left his senses;
But then his mind displayed its gallant temper:
He chose to die with honour on that meadow
Than have it thought as cowardice by any
That, in his need, he'd thought to flee from death there;
So up he moved, his fists held at the ready,
Prepared, within the sight of all, to wrestle;
But Roland saw the noble lord's intention
And, like a knight well-bred and raised, addressed him:
"Lord Oliver, how proud your great prowess is!
For I can see that your good sword has severed,
And I have one which is so fine and splendid
That it cannot be chipped or broken ever!
I am the King of noble France's nephew –
If I should wound or kill you when defenceless,
Then all my life I'd bear the blame and blemish
That I had slain a man who had no weapon!
Go, seek a sword, fine lord – you have my blessing –
And find some wine – a cask, if you can get it!
My thirst is great, I'm not afraid to tell you!"
When Oliver heard this, he thanked him gently:
"Sir Roland, lord, much thanks for this expression
Of your noblesse in warfare for my welfare;
Now, if you please, for your own body's pleasure,
Seek rest a while upon this island's meadow
Till I have seen the ferryman who led me
Across the flow below upon his ferry."
The Count replied: "Most willingly I shall do!"
And Oliver, of gallant mood and mettle,
Delayed no more to reach the shore, intending
    To hail the boatman there.

COUNT OLIVER strode forth without delay
And called upon the ferryman in haste:
"Attend to me, my friend! Go straightaway
Within Vienne on my behalf and say

To Duke Girart, my uncle bold and brave,
That by its hilt I've snapped my silver blade,
And he must send a second in its place
So I may fight for all the rights he claims
In Lord God the Almighty Father's name,
And St Maurice, in whom I set my faith;
And bid him send a cask of wine the same,
For Charles's nephew Roland's thirst is great."
The boatman said: "My lord, I shall obey."
He turned his boat and, leaving straightaway,
He sailed across and landed on the plain;
With every haste he reached the city-gates,
Aware that he could brook no moment's waste,
For Oliver had urgent need of aid;
He raced at once inside the hall of state
And saw Girart, whom loud and proud he hailed:
"My lord, for God our great Redeemer's sake,
Brave Oliver, through me, bids you this day
To help his need, as best you can and may:
Below its hilt he's snapped his silver blade
And bids you send a second straightaway,
And spicy wine, a cask of it, he says,
For Charles's nephew Roland's thirst is great."
Girart replied: "God works in wondrous ways!
    How fine is Charles's nephew."

GIRART THE DUKE made no delay at all,
But straightaway addressed the good man's call:
"My friend, may God defend you evermore!
Return in haste to noble Oliver
And you will earn, by God, a rich reward!
Go, take this key, which is my cellar-door's,
And take ten times the wine you asked me for,
And bid them bring my golden goblet forth,
While I arrange for two swords to be brought –
One is my own and one is Renier's sword,
Who is his father and brave Geneva's lord."
The boatman said: "I'll gladly take it all!"
Now Joachim was still inside the hall,
That worthy Jew of noble deed and thought,
Who gave the arms to Oliver before;

He heard the cries and sighs from every voice;
He heard as well the boatman's grim report
   And hastened to his dwelling.

THE JEW, WHO'D HEARD the cries and sighing made,
And grim report the boatman's news contained –
That Oliver had snapped in two his blade –
Went back at once to his own home again
To fetch a sword of great renown and rate,
Which he had kept one hundred years encased;
It once was Closamont's, whose fame was great
As Emperor of mighty Rome the praised:
He lost the sword in woodland grass the day
Of that most fearsome fight and dreadful fray
When he was slain by Malque of Valsegree;
His head was cleft, and as he fell, the blade
Was tipped awry and slithered from its case;
The grass was thick where it was lost and lay;
Some reapers then, long after, found the place:
The scythe of one was shattered by its blade;
On seeing this, they picked it up again
And took it to the Pope in Rome, who gazed
Upon its craft – its shaft with gold inlaid,
And hilt and haft ornate with gold the same;
And in the words he saw thereon engraved
He found, in truth, a text which made it plain
That Halteclere was this fine weapon's name,
And that it came from Rome, where it was made
By one Magnificans, who formed its shape,
An artisan of high repute and fame;
The Pontiff had it sharpened well again
And kept it at St Peter's from that day;
King Pépin took it forth, of France the famed,
When first he wore the crown which he had claimed;
Then, in reward, old Beuvon gained the blade
And sold it to the Jew in fair exchange
For goods and gold of pounds untold in weight;
For years on end the Jew had kept it safe
And not one word was heard of it again
Until that day the Jew gave it away
To one, I'd say, most worthy of such grace –
   To Oliver of Geneva.

THE WORTHY JEW, of noble heart and mind,
Brought forth at once that burnished blade of iron
And gave it to Girart, the warrior-knight,
Who in his turn then gave it to a squire,
With yet one more, before that youngster climbed
Astride his mount and turned about to ride
Without delay to reach the riverside;
The ferryman soon took him through the tide,
For Oliver to meet when he arrived;
The squire, at once, held out the blades of iron
For Oliver to choose the best – who tried
Fine Halteclere, and never changed his mind –
The other ones he left there with the squire;
He quickly filled the golden cup with wine
And knelt before Sir Roland on the isle,
Who took the cup and drained the goblet dry
To slake his thirst, until the worst was by;
My friends, as Roland drank, that eager squire
Could see his neck inclined as he imbibed,
And thought to help his lord in lowly wise:
From his own sheath he drew a sword of iron,
With full intent to strike the noble knight
Across his neck and that way take his life;
When Oliver looked over, and his eye
Beheld the glint of bare steel in the light,
He hastened forth and, rushing on the squire,
He raised his fist and with a mighty swipe
He knocked him flat before them in a trice!
When this was done, he railed at him and cried:
"You harlot's son! I loved you well betimes,
But now you've lost whatever love was mine!
At Pentecost I would have dubbed you knight,
But now be gone forever from my sight!
If you're still here tomorrow, when I've dined,
I'll have you flung in flames or strung up high,
Like any thief, the noose around you tight,
Or have you dragged by horses till you die!
You'll rue your wish to harm a worthy knight
    In such a wicked manner!"

COUNT ROLAND DRANK, and having slaked his need,
He hailed Count Oliver, his anger keen:
"Let be your speech with that low wretch! If he
Had struck me down, what loss there would have been
Of Frenchmen's lives, and others' far and near!
And all the knights of Charlemagne the fierce
Would, in their woe, have lost their noble zeal!
But let us speak no more of his deceit –
To hell with him, where he can meet his peers!
Sir, take your arms and hasten to the field,
For we have stayed too long at leisure here!
This day Girart shall know dismay and fear,
This lord who holds Vienne against his liege!
When all is done, the payment he'll receive
Will be to hang for his great treachery!"
Said Oliver: "How bad and mad a speech!
God governs all, Who made us all and each,
Whose gentle Hands can save the man they please;
I trust in Him with all of my belief,
And in my arms and in my flashing steel,
To give me strength and every might and means
    To champion my uncle."

WHEN OLIVER knew plainly what was meant
By Roland's words, who answered him with threats,
He gripped his shield and grasped it to his breast –
But had it not been shameful to relent,
He'd not have fought for all of Hungary's wealth;
He raised his sword, the shining Halteclere,
And Roland raised bright Durendal again;
Once more he rushed at Oliver and sent
A mighty blow at his Pavian helm,
Which split apart and splintered all it met,
Then slipped to hit the rings around its edge;
Without the help of Jesus Christ Himself,
From hair to ear it would have split his head!
But slip it did, and slid towards the left
So forcefully it struck his shield instead,
Which wasn't worth a clove of garlic then –
It split apart and cleft it end to end;
The byrnie's skirts alike were cut to shreds,

As Durendal drove on and on unchecked;
On feeling this, young Oliver saw red,
And said: "Dear God and Mary ever-blest,
Defend my limbs and guard my life from death!
By Roland's blows I know he's not in jest!
How weak I am, if I can't wreak revenge!"
He raised his sword, his trusted Halteclere,
And struck the Count on his Pavian helm,
Which split apart, well cleft upon the left;
But God looked on and rescued Roland next:
He stopped the blow from splitting Roland's head,
Deflecting it below with so much strength
It struck his shield and severed all it met,
The boards, the boss, as on and on it went
In its descent and struck the ground at length;
Count Roland said: "You've not held back, my friend!"
This barter done, they moved up once again
To trade more blows with firm and fierce intent;
They braced their shields, each one, against their breast,
And swung their blades with all their skill and strength;
So fierce a duel was never seen again,
For both these knights were of such great prowess
That neither one would ever cede one step
Before his foe, although it meant his death;
   So dauntless was their courage.

THE COURAGE SHOWN by both of them was great;
No leopard or no lion was as brave;
No armour made could take the blows they rained:
I don't know how they fought so long, in faith;
The maiden Aude was very much afraid,
Inside Vienne, in Girart's hall again;
With loving heart on bended knee she prayed:
"Immortal God, Who in their glory made
The earth, the seas and all that they contain,
And Heaven high, according to Your ways;
Who here on earth made Adam out of clay,
And made his wife, whose name was Eve, and gave
All Paradise for their enjoyment, save
An apple-tree, the fruit of which they ate,
Against your wish, and all their gain was pain,

For which their heirs still bear the shame and blame;
Who in the womb of Mary, blessed Maid,
Came down to earth in mortal birth and lay
In Bethlehem, we know this from our faith;
Who in the arms of Simeon the Saint
Went in the house of Solomon the sage;
Who caused Three Kings to leave their rich domains
In search of You and Your all-loving grace –
Throughout his realm King Herod, in his rage,
Took every child and slew the blameless babes,
And thought that he could murder You this way –
Who lived on earth for thirty years and stayed
With Your Apostles, to preach and teach Your name;
Who pardoned Mary Magdalen her shame,
When she confessed in Simon's dwelling-place;
Who by the hand of Judas were betrayed
For thirty coins, which bought him naught but shame;
Who to the Cross by wicked Jews were nailed
And suffered death to save the human race;
Who three days thence arose from death again
To batter down the gates of Hell and save
The friends of God from its infernal jail,
To dwell with You in grace and glory framed;
Who rose to Heaven upon Ascension Day;
Immortal God, as we believe and state
The truth of all these things I have proclaimed,
Defend, I pray, Lord Oliver the brave
From Charles's nephew Roland's deadly blade!
Fine God, my Lord, in Your most blessed name,
Make peace between these rivals and their claims!
If one should die by any stroke of fate,
     Then I, alike, would perish."

30. How God brought Oliver and Roland together

FAIR AUDE WAS FRAUGHT with fear – and by her side
Renier was too and Duke Girart alike,
And all of those up in the palace high –
For Oliver, that fine and gallant knight,
In combat with Count Roland for their rights;

The bravest there were filled with dread and fright,
For Roland had prowess to match his pride;
But Oliver was brave, and quick and lithe:
He aimed a blow between Count Roland's eyes,
Which broke the ring upon his helmet bright
And robbed the nasal-knob of half its iron,
Then slid along his hauberk triple-lined
And severed more than sixty links the while;
It struck the ground, embedding with its might:
"Sweet Mary mild!" the marquis Roland cried:
"How great a sin! How great a wrong, that I
     Should be beset so badly!"

THE YOUTHFUL COUNT was filled with wrath to see
His helmet shorn of half its nasal-piece,
And then his coat bereft of rings and breached –
Five score and more lay severed on the field!
With Durendal, which he knew how to wield
Full well, he stalked Count Oliver with zeal,
And swung a blow upon his helmet's peak;
The blade of steel drove downwards and it sheered
His hauberk of one hundred rings at least;
Upon the left the crimson blood ran free
As Renier's son was forced upon his knees;
He fell with shame, you may be sure indeed,
And leapt at once, most bravely, to his feet
In self-defence, with all his might and means;
He called on God, the Judge of all and each,
To save his life from death and from defeat
And let him see once more his fearsome breed –
Girart the duke, who did such worthy deeds,
His sister Aude, his father Duke Renier:
"Count Roland, lord, don't hide it or conceal:
Is that Joyeuse, fierce-visaged Charles's steel,
With which you lay such lusty blows on me?"
"No, noble lord," said Roland, frank and free:
"It is gold-hilted Durendal you feel,
Whose burnished steel will bring you soon to heel
So ruthlessly that Girart's heart will heave
For sending you to battle with me here!"
Said Oliver: "It's your heart that will grieve,

For you will pay for Charlemagne's deceit,
    If God commends my weapons!"

WHEN OLIVER beheld his hauberk torn
And cleft of rings by stinging Durendal,
Count Roland's sharp and shining battle-sword,
His gallant heart was sad and angered sore;
With Halteclere, which had no peer before,
He struck so hard on Roland's helm once more
That all its gems and garland-stones were shorn;
The blow went on, unhindered in its course,
And sliced the skirts upon his coat of war –
They fluttered up, then fell upon the floor:
"Good God above!" said Roland, "Now I'm sure
That blade of his can slice with deadly force,
And he himself has strength enough for four!
But I can see he loves me not at all."
Count Oliver replied with this retort:
"I hear you well, fine Count! But rest assured,
So help me God, our everlasting Lord,
In all of this your thoughts of me are false!
I did not come to fight you out of choice;
But if I have, with Jesus Christ's support,
In some small way allayed that pride of yours,
    Then I would be most happy."

THERE NEVER WERE two knights of such prowess;
Upon the isle how gallantly they met
With mighty blows from blades of burnished edge!
Behold Girart upon his battlements!
The worthy duke spoke out before his men:
"God strengthen you, fine nephew Oliver!
To his command your courage I commend –
Though if this day you master Roland's strength
And make him yield, in honour or in death,
We'll never know the King's goodwill again,
Nor evermore shall our two clans be friends"
Strong Charlemagne, meanwhile, before Vienne,
Was knelt in prayer in his most splendid tent;
With all his heart he called on God to bless
And guard the life of him he loved the best,

His nephew fine, lest by defeat or death
  His life should be dishonoured.

HOW GALLANTLY they met upon the field!
They fought on foot with blades of naked steel;
So ripped apart their armour was and pierced,
The wonder was how still they lived and breathed!
Inside Vienne the cries and sighs were clear,
And on the plain the French were fraught with fear;
In Charles's host, the King so white of beard,
One hundred knights with no delay or leave
Seized armour forth and weapons secretly;
Beneath Vienne, in ambush there concealed,
They lay in wait for Oliver, agreed
To have his head as soon as he appeared;
But news of this was brought to Charles's ears,
And in a rage he swore by his white beard
That there was none, however proud a peer,
Whom he'd not hang upon a spreading tree,
If he performed so foul an infamy;
On hearing this, they beat a fast retreat,
And watched the duel in silence and in peace,
  And put aside their weapons.

HOW GALLANTLY they met upon the isle!
What blows they lent upon those helmet-stripes,
And sparks they sent from sharp-edged blades of iron!
The shields of both were crushed and cleft aside,
Their coats of mail so wrecked and ripped awry
That not even one half of one survived;
Sir Roland then considered in his mind
How best to test Sir Oliver and try
His loyalty, so praised by other knights:
"Sir Oliver," the fearsome Roland cried,
"My body aches, I can no more deny,
And I should like to lie down here a while
And seek repose, which greatly I require."
"This saddens me," young Oliver replied:
"I'd rather that this cutting blade of mine
Should lay you low, than something otherwise;
But, if you wish, attend your need and lie

Upon my shield, whose boards you've broken wide;
I'll fan your limbs to cool your body's fire
Until your strength and valour have revived."
The Count heard this and marvelled in his mind;
With ringing voice he made him this reply:
"Sir Oliver, your wit is far from wise!
I told a lie to test your faith – for I
Could fight like this for four whole days and nights
And never think of food and drink the while."
"And I alike!" young Oliver replied:
"So we may start and finish with this fight!"
The Count replied: "Most willingly, say I,
Though it should last until tomorrow night!"
Their fearsome swords began once more to strike,
But then the sweat, which bathed them left and right
From brow to waist, oppressed them both so nigh
They couldn't hold or wield their arms on high;
On seeing this, Count Roland filled with spite:
"Sir Oliver," the warrior said, "my eyes
Have never yet beheld so strong a knight,
Who could endure so long the blows I strike!"
"Sir Roland, lord," Count Oliver replied,
"I know, as long as I am helped by Christ,
That mortal blows will never take my life;
 No man alive can harm me."

HOW HARD THEY FOUGHT! How fiercely and how well
They lunged and plunged and struck with greater strength
Than ever known before between two men!
They'd never stop or stint of their prowess
Till one of them lay on the island dead;
But God, you know, would turn these foes to friends,
Their bond so fond that it would never end
Until the day when it was closed and cleft
At Roncevaux, in land most desolate,
By Ganelon, a curse upon the wretch!
He sold them to the Pagan forces there
Of King Marsile, may Jesus curse his breath!
In mighty France there dawned no morning hence
 When such a loss was suffered!

THEY BATTLED ON, they fought each other fiercely
Till daylight waned and it was nearly evening;
Their mood was not for halting then or yielding,
Both spurred along by anger and ill-feeling,
With naked blades still in their hands for wielding,
And willing hearts to sell their honour dearly –
When from the sky a thick cloud fell between them,
Which formed a mist that stopped them both from seeing;
No sound they made nor any movement either:
The braver there was filled with dread and fearful,
And both were sure that death was coming near them;
Then from the cloud an Angel stepped, who sweetly,
In God's good name, addressed them with this greeting:
"My noble knights, you have been honoured deeply!
This feud of yours shall last no more – believe me,
Not one more blow must be exchanged – for Jesus,
The Lord our God, forbids you to proceed it!
In Spain henceforth, against the race of heathens,
Your fierce prowess shall yet be proved and needed;
All men shall know your valour there, and see it
     In service of God's love."

THE PAIR INDEED were very much afraid
To hear the will of God the Lord proclaimed;
The Angel said: "My lords, do not dismay!
Lord God on High commands you both this day
To stop this rivalry of clan and claim!
In hostile land, upon the heathen race,
Throughout the realm of King Marsile in Spain,
Is where you'll see who is or is not brave;
Go there and win that kingdom with your blades,
By force of arms against his Pagan knaves!
Exalt the Lord and glorify His faith,
And your reward shall be most grand and great:
Your souls shall earn true pardon and true grace;
In Heaven high, in His great dwelling-place,
     Your souls shall live in glory."

WHEN BOTH HAD HEARD the Angel-envoy's speech,
Forbidding them to fight by God's decree,
Our glorious Lord, the King of Majesty,

They said: "True King of Heaven, may You be
Revered as Lord and Judge of all and each,
Since you have sent your envoy, making clear
Your will by word of Your own Angel here!"
The Angel left, it tarried not, indeed
And neither did those two upon the field;
The Holy Ghost had filled them with new zeal;
They sought repose beneath a spreading tree
And there they pledged in love and loyalty
To live as friends through all their coming years;
Then Roland spoke, of courage high and fierce:
"Sir Oliver, this much I'll not conceal:
I pledge to you my lifelong loyalty;
I love you more than any man that breathes,
Except for Charles, who is my noble liege;
Since God decreed that we should be at peace,
No fort henceforth or fortress that I seize,
No town or city, nor any castle-keep,
Shall not be shared with you, if you agree;
I'll wed fair Aude, if you will give her me,
And if I may, within four days from here,
I shall unite King Charles and you in peace;
But if he turns a deaf ear to my pleas
And still withholds his friendship, I shall leave
And come to you within the town in brief;
Then all his life this warring will not cease."
When Oliver heard this, his thanks were deep;
He clasped his hands towards the sky to speak:
"Immortal God, all praise to You indeed,
Who have this day allied this man to me!
Sir Roland, lord, I too shall not conceal:
I love you more than any man that breathes;
My sister Aude I give you willingly,
Upon this one condition you shall hear:
My uncle's rift with Charles must first be healed!
Now, lord, unlace your jewelled helm of green,
So we may kiss in sign of friendship sealed."
The Count replied: "I willingly agree."
So both took off their helm most willingly
And, glad of heart, they kissed each other's cheek;
Then, sitting down upon the grassy field,

Their mutual faith they pledged most loyally,
And comradeship to last their lifelong years;
    Their loyal pact had started.

31. How war and peace lay finely in the balance

WHEN ALL WAS DONE as you have heard me say,
They kissed once more, then went their separate ways,
Close comrades now until their dying day;
The French looked on and filled with deep dismay;
The Emperor looked on and felt the same;
He called on God, Who never lies or fails:
"Immortal Lord of mercy and of grace,
I never saw a vow as now exchanged:
The nephew, whom in my own house I raised,
Has kissed the man he knows I can but hate!
I greatly fear he has betrayed my faith
By breaking his, to his eternal shame!
If this is true, then he has proved more base
Than Judas was, when Jesus was betrayed!"
Said Ganelon: "He's done it for Aude's sake,
Whom he adores – I'm certain of the same;
He's come to terms with them to win the maid!"
On hearing this, old Naimon came in haste
And spoke aloud this way to Charlemagne:
"True Emperor, my lord, do not dismay!
Let Roland come and make his actions plain,
Then you will know what pledges have been made
    To warrant this close friendship."

"TRUE EMPEROR," said old Naimon the wise:
"Let Roland give account when he arrives!
What can you know of all he has in mind?
For by the Saint whom sinners seek to find,
I would endure the trial of truth by fire,
Or fight a great emir to prove the lie
That he of all could have betrayed you, Sire;
He never would for all Milano's might!"
The youth himself made straight towards their lines;
He sailed the stream and to the ferry's side

They led him forth a palfrey-horse to ride,
Which he bestrode by stirrups silver-bright;
He rode in haste and back in camp the knights
Surrounded him with happy grins and smiles,
   All overjoyed to see him.

YOUNG ROLAND LEFT the isle behind, where he
And Oliver had fought with all their zeal;
Their shields were split from edge to edge and breached,
Their lances cleft and sharply-pointed spears;
Their helmet-rings were crushed about their ears;
Upon the field lay both their battle-steeds,
Whose backs were broke by strokes of slashing steel;
Before his tent, beneath a leafy tree,
Stood Charlemagne with some two hundred Peers,
Who had beseeched Almighty God to keep
Both knights from death upon that battlefield;
Before them all young Roland left his steed,
And thirty youths ran up to serve his need;
The Emperor moved up, in company
With many lords, who hailed him heartily;
The King spoke up: "Lad, welcome back, indeed!
It's many hours since you departed here;
And Duke Girart – does he not come to yield,
Or will he still not give Vienne to me?"
Young Roland said: "I have not heard him speak;
No word of that was spoken where I've been;
But every bald and bearded man agrees
That your own pride began this span of grief!
Sire, let us leave! There's nothing for us here!
True Emperor, if you will but agree,
Girart will be a friend to France the sweet,
And we may ride to our own shires in brief!"
On hearing this, the blood left Charles's cheek;
He looked at him as though his wits were weak:
"You fool!" he said, "How cursed your quest has been!
Why is your foe not here on bended knee?"
"I have not made him yield at all, my liege,
For God Himself decreed it not to be!
Within a cloud, which hid both him and me,
An Angel came, forbidding us proceed;

Young Oliver, most truly, has no peer;
There's none alive, however strong, he fears;
I struck him well, he stood there proud and fierce
And paid me back whatever he received!
I have endured such pounding from his steel
I feel it still and will for seven years!"
Young Oliver, meanwhile, had reappeared
Back in Vienne, to everyone's relief –
The brothers Miles and Hernaut, white of beard,
And Renier, and his cousin Aymeri,
All welcomed him with great delight and glee,
Disarming him with every haste and speed;
They took his helm of beaten gold and seized
His hauberk-coat, which Roland's sword had pierced;
Upon his side the wound was wide and deep;
On seeing this, Guibourc was filled with grief –
But never was a wife as wise as she!
She had some cream, which Jesus had bequeathed,
And rubbed it on, until he said that he
Felt better then than he had ever been!
They led him up inside the mighty keep
    Where Aude made haste towards him.

INSIDE VIENNE how joyful were the knights
For Oliver, who had returned alive
From such a fight and fright upon the isle;
And when the count within the hall arrived,
His sister Aude ran up and hugged him tight;
Young Roland went to Charles's tent the while,
Where once again great Charlemagne inquired:
"Fine nephew mine, what happened in the fight?
Where is he now, this youngster brave and wise?
Don't lie to me! Did he regret his pride?"
"No, he did not, nor should you think so, Sire!
There's no man here who could defeat this knight;
But, thanks to God, we two are reconciled;
Within the town, unharmed, he has retired;
An Angel came, forbidding us to fight,
In Jesu's name – if not, one would have died."
"Thank God for that, at least!" the King replied:
"For any gold I would not have desired

Young Oliver to lose his limbs or life."
When this was said, each noble there retired
Till morning came, when with the dawning light
The Emperor got up and, once attired,
Betook himself to an erected shrine
To hear the Mass with faithful heart and mind;
When this was said, the service read and signed,
He left the shrine and, turning back, arrived
Before his tent, where in he went to find
His nephew, who then urged him in this wise:
"Fine uncle, will you heed my words a while?
You have besieged this city with great might
Till seven years and more have passed us by;
The Pagans built these walls so strong and high
That we possess no pick or bar of iron
That can unstick or prise one brick aside,
They are secured so solidly and tight!
And in between the Rhône goes streaming by!
A score of years could run their course of time
Before you took the strongholds you desire;
Instead of this, make peace with those inside!"
"You waste your breath!" the Emperor replied,
"I'll not return to France in all my life
Until the walls before us lie in piles!
And woe to those my foes I seize inside:
Not one of them shall keep his limbs or life!"
The Count replied: "Your threats are fierce and high:
But time will show if words and blows unite!
One thing alone is certain, noble Sire –
I'll not be here to help you win this fight!"
On hearing this, the King was filled with spite:
"Give ear to me a while, my nephew fine!
I know full well, young Roland, what's transpired!
When, bearing arms, you rode off to the isle
Whence you have just returned, then, in my mind,
I was quite sure you would defend my rights;
But Aude the maid has made you friends for life
With Oliver, whose glove you bear in sign."
"You speak the truth," said Roland in reply:
"Count Oliver's the noblest knight alive,
A handsome, fine, well-bred and skilful knight;

In all of France you'd not find three his like;
To win a friend is life's most precious prize!
If he and I can thus be reconciled,
Then so can you and Duke Girart alike;
For by the Saint they seek in Rome to find,
I shall not gird my sword to help you, Sire."
"I shall not ask you, wretch!" the Emperor cried:
"Begone from here, for you have too much pride!"
"I shall not go," the noble youth replied,
"I shall not leave as long as you abide –
But I shall see how your endeavours thrive
    With Girart of Vienne."

IN MANY SONGS you've heard, my worthy friends,
Each one of you, both old and young as well,
How Charles's rage at Girart was so dread
He sieged Vienne for seven years on end,
With four more kings and fourteen dukes, who went
With thirty counts of mighty power and strength,
Whose fighting force could not be reckoned less
That one hundred and sixty thousand men;
The rearguard troops from France arrived at length
And saw the siege-machines and mangonels;
Girart himself was at a window's ledge,
The coat he bore worn sore against his flesh;
His wife Guibourc stood by him on a step:
A fairer wife no king or duke possessed;
She looked at him and spoke aloud and said:
"How is it with you now, my noble friend?
There's many now would say this was the end!
Old Charlemagne has got you so hard-pressed
And ravaged such a parcel of your realm
That any steed could run ten leagues unchecked
And still not find sufficient fodder left
To feed itself from morn till night again;
If you had done as I advised you best,
Your realm would not be wasted now and bled,
Nor would this allod, this conquest of Vienne,
Be taken as the King's or rendered yet!"
Count Oliver came up when this was said,
    And spoke with them together.

THE MONTH WAS MAY, with roses on the thorn;
The oriole sang out, the blackbird called;
The woodlands bloomed, the grass was green once more,
And every stream flowed back between its course;
The lover longed for his beloved's voice,
And sighed away each day it never called!
King Charlemagne, of beard and whiskers hoar,
Sat in his tent of Spanish silk before
The well-stocked walls of old Vienne, with all
His knights of liege around him, and his lords;
Both kings and counts were in his mighty force,
And mighty dukes with all the knights they'd brought,
And barons too, or so the song records;
"Ah, Lord," he cried, "Who governs each and all;
Immortal God of blessed Mary born,
I have, ere this, felled seven kings in war;
By force of arms and daring deeds I've forced
Each one of them to serve me and my cause;
Each one of them obeys my will and voice,
And holds from me whatever he enjoys;
Yet here I see a duke whose claim is small,
Whose holding here lies in my realm and law,
Who will not heed or bow to me at all!
I'd rather die than leave him in his hall!"
Old Richard, duke of Normandy, spoke forth:
"True Emperor, do not dismay, my lord,
But send your word, your final word what's more,
To Duke Girart, who treats you with such scorn,
That he must cede this ancient town of yours,
With all its towers and all its wealth and stores,
And he, and all his breed, must heed your law!
By Jesus Christ, should he refuse once more,
Then turn from siege and launch a fierce assault!
The French are bold and daring with their swords,
And very skilled in all the ways of war:
From Vienne field, while some besiege the walls,
We'll strike the gates with unrelenting force;
While any live we never shall withdraw
Until the town and all within it fall!
Seize forth Girart to punish in accord
With judgement passed by all your mighty lords!"

The King replied, of beard and whiskers hoar:
"Well said, Richard of Normandy, my lord!"
Inside Vienne, within its vaulted hall,
Stood Duke Girart, the gallant-visaged lord,
While at his side was his good wife Guibourc;
She said to him, as any good wife ought:
"For Jesu's sake, of blessed Mary born,
Take counsel now, my gallant-visaged lord,
From all the knights and barons that are yours
Within this land, abandoned to the sword,
And in this town so long beset by war;
This foolishness has cost too dearly, for
From Burgundy to here and further forth
To Lombardy, your land is scarred and scorched;
Make peace with Charles, for God's sake, I implore!"
Said Oliver, whose face with valour stormed:
"You speak the truth, my Lady, best of all!
With your assent, fine uncle, we shall talk
       With Hernaut of Biaulande."

NOW AT THE TIME of which my tale recites,
Vienne contained two palaces of might;
The smaller one, itself most rich and fine,
Was where Hernaut had chosen to reside,
While Duke Girart was in the one nearby;
No man alive would have the skill or time
To catalogue their wealth or to describe
The lovely things they both contained inside;
Behold Guibourc, of noble form and fine,
As down the steps of stone she went outside
And strode along the street till she arrived
Before the palace-door, the same which I
Have told you of, to see Hernaut the wise;
She climbed the steps inside the hall to find
The good man there, so fine and feared a knight,
While he was playing at backgammon and dice;
He stood at once, on seeing her arrive,
And with his arm around her neck inquired:
"My Lady fair, do you seek help of mine?
What troubles you, or what do you desire?"
"My lord," she said, "please let me speak my mind:

We are besieged by mighty force outside,
And so have been for seven years entire,
By Charlemagne the strong and all the knights
Of royal France – you know this is no lie;
Now he has called his rearguard forth to fight;
There's not a man of woman born to life,
Save clerks or priests, who serve Lord Jesus Christ,
Who has not come to join his army's lines –
And maidens too, of noble form and fine,
To whom he gives rich husbands from the knights
Prepared to stay each day until they die
To see Vienne cast down and set alight!
Girart my lord will lose his limbs and life:
He's sure to die, if he is caught inside,
And so will you, and so, I'm sure, will Miles
Of Puglia and brave Renier the wise,
And Aymeri, of such prowess and pride,
And Oliver, whose face with valour shines;
And both my sons will lose what's theirs by right –
Both Beuvon and Savariez – while I
Shall be the butt of shameful sport and spite!"
"You speak the truth, Guibourc," Hernaut replied:
"But I shall do whatever you desire;
Though all my deeds earned shame in others' eyes,
And men should blame my name in after-times,
I'll act in this as God directs my mind,
And at your will, good Lady, fair and wise."
"My lord," she said, "God bless and let you thrive!"
They left the hall and down the steps they climbed
To wend their way along the road outside;
They met Girart, of noble loin and line,
Who from his hall withal had stepped alike;
　　　Now all would speak together.

32. How the balance was tipped towards peace

WHILE GIRART HAILED his wife and made to speak
With her and with Hernaut of visage fierce,
Renier arrived with one Moreheier;
Young Oliver was also there, and keen

To bring about the peace with utmost speed;
My friends, a plan would soon have been agreed
By envoys sent to sue the French for peace,
Had it not been for Aymeri's rash deed:
As evening came, he rode off with his spear
To Charles's tent and slew a high-ranked Peer,
And Guielin, his treasurer-in-chief;
On seeing this, the King was angered deep
And called aloud: "Knights, after him! If he
Escapes you here, I'll hold your honour cheap!"
When this was said, they didn't drag their heels,
And neither did young Aymeri indeed!
Three hundred knights pursued him, swearing each
To hew his head with sturdy swords of steel!
They chased him hard until the Rhône, where he,
On reaching there, at once leapt off his steed
And in a boat, which fourteen sailors heaved
With heavy oars to take him through the stream
Without a pause until the boat was beached;
To reach the hall he climbed the stairway steep,
But when he did, Girart, enraged, appeared
And said: "You wretch! God damn your reckless deeds!
Why go to Charles and use your spear to speak?
By doing this you have put back the peace
Which we this day have chosen to achieve;
We were about to give an envoy leave
To sue for peace and have it signed and sealed!"
When this was said, a messenger appeared,
Whose wont had been to spy upon the siege;
And he had heard the news with his own ears
That Charles had planned to go out hunting deer;
He saw the Duke and called aloud and clear:
"My lord Girart, and you my lord Renier,
And you Hernaut of Biaulande, called 'The Fierce';
You used to be most daring knights, more feared
Than any storm or striking lightning-streak!
But now the French don't fear you in the least –
Their fiery steeds are grazing in your fields!
Tomorrow Charles has planned to hunt your deer
Within Clermont, your forest wide and deep,
With seven knights, no more or less, it seems;

Duke Otto of Bavaria will be
With Didier the Lombard, so I hear;
Another one I know is Duke Gaifier;
So help me God, my lords, not one of these
Has in his heart one spark of bravery
To save himself or help another's need!"
On hearing this, Girart was greatly cheered;
They talked it through and soon they all agreed:
"My worthy lords, prepare at once to leave!
If we should miss this chance to vent our spleen,
Then curse the hand that gives us food to eat!"
Some twenty knights made ready with all speed;
They donned their mail and laced their helms of steel;
They girt their swords, then leapt with every zeal
Upon the backs of their good battle-steeds;
Around their necks they hung their quartered shields
And in their hands they gripped their sturdy spears;
Then, lighting up bright torches all and each,
They rode inside a tunnel dug beneath
The city gates by Moors in former years:
More white its walls than snow upon a beach;
Some twenty knights rode in there on their steeds;
They left the town and rode beneath its streets
Till just before the light of dawn appeared;
They saw Berart the woodsman's dwelling near;
His job it was to guard the woods and streams;
They left their mounts beneath some leafy trees
To graze the grass and cool down in the breeze,
Then clutched their spears and climbed a laurel-tree;
When morning came, with sunlight bright and clear,
The King got up, put on his hunting-gear,
And bade a squire put boots upon his feet;
His horn was brought, his hounds put on the leash;
He mounted horse, as did his knights, to leave
Upon a hunt within the woodland green;
Without God's help, no swift return there'd be
     For Charlemagne the Emperor.

THE EMPEROR, arriving where he thought to,
Unleashed his hounds and when they all ran forward,
Attacked a boar, a fearsome beast and awful;

The greyhounds yelped and helped the huntsmen stalk it;
With all their skill the hunters raced towards it
And Charles the King, upon a long-maned palfrey,
Outran them all, the bearded and the bald ones;
But then the King encountered great misfortune:
He lost his men from view across a moorland
And didn't know which way their hunt had brought them;
Along a path, an ancient and a worn one,
The boar escaped, the greyhounds chased undaunted,
With Charles behind the chasing pack on horseback,
In hot pursuit, until the beast was cornered;
Beneath a tree, beside a fount of water,
The boar had stopped to make a stand before them;
Charles looked at it and, lighting from his palfrey,
He struck the beast, as gallant hunters ought to,
Till it was slain with his well-tempered sword-blade;
He drew a knife and, cutting out the offal,
He threw it to the greyhounds to reward them;
He'd kept his horn and blew it now, rejoicing;
Berart, the guard of Girart's woods and waters,
Had stalked the King so closely all that morning
He'd seen it all and knew him unescorted;
So, riding off without delay or halting,
He called aloud the moment that he saw him:
"Fine Duke, my lord, you'll not be disappointed!
I have pursued the King of France so surely
That I know all about his morning's fortunes!
Beneath a tree, beside a stream, he's slaughtered
A wild boar – and now, alone he pauses!
He has with him no young or older courtiers,
For all his men have lost him, I assure you –
Not one's aware that he is there before them!
Girart, my lord, do not delay or dawdle!
Without a blow I know he can be caught there
     And made to pay your price!"

THE GALLANT KNIGHTS, on hearing Berart speak,
With one accord and voice cried all and each:
"My lords, to horse, by blessed St Denis!"
And none were loath, but mounted willingly:
"Make haste to ride!" cried out fierce Aymeri,

As all set off among the woodland trees,
With good Berart to guide them and to lead;
The King, he blew, who knew not they were near,
Till from all sides they barred his way and seized
The rein-straps of his fine Arabian steed;
Girart knew well how brave the King could be
And hurried forth to take his burnished spear,
And then he said: "Sir King, Girart is here!
You thought that I would still be fast asleep
Inside Vienne, with hunger wan and weak!
But, as you see, I'm wide awake indeed!
You blew your horn, I heard it loud and clear,
And every word you've said has reached my ears!
This boar is mine, you've slain it wrongfully!
And now my knights shall have it served to eat,
As will my wife, of face and figure sweet;
And you, my lord, shall come back home with me!"
Said Aymeri: "Fine uncle, kill him here!
Cut off his head, right now with sharpest steel,
And then this war and your dispute will cease!"
Girart replied: "May God forbid the deed!
No King of France shall be ill used by me!
If he forgives my part in what has been,
I'll be his man and hold this land in fief;
If he will not, by blessed St Maurice,
I'll set my sights on Arab lands and leave;
I'll bear the blame but men shall lose esteem
    For Charlemagne's own honour."

WHEN CHARLEMAGNE heard such a fine reply
From Duke Girart, who showed himself contrite
And spoke with grace and not revengeful spite,
Then he looked up in joy towards the sky:
"Ah God, the King of everyone," he cried:
"You have performed such wonders in my sight!
This war against Girart within this shire
I've hated more than any other strife!
May I be damned if I pursue the fight!
Come forward, Duke Girart, you worthy knight!"
"What does this mean, my lord?" Girart inquired;
The King replied: "Attend these words of mine:

Our peace shall rest on terms that you decide
And with such land in France as you desire;
I pardon you the payment of all fines,
And grant to you one third of all my tithes;
The men you love shall all be friends of mine,
And those you hate I shall alike despise."
"May God forbid," the noble Duke replied,
"That you should lose whatever's yours by right;
And Lord Hernaut, my brother, at all times,
Should profit first, for he's the older knight."
Then Hernaut knelt before the King to plight
His loyal word to be his man for life,
And then Girart wholeheartedly complied,
As did the lord of Puglia's land, Sir Miles,
With Oliver, that brave and courtly knight;
No fiercer heart than Aymeri's you'd find,
For all this time he'd stood upon one side
And watched them all, to judge the wrong and right
Of the amends they made to Charles's might:
"Young man," said Charles, "and what is your reply?
Will you make peace or war with me and mine?"
"I do not know, in truth," the youth replied:
"My father and my uncle, to my eyes,
Are trapped by you like gentle birds in lime –
While I, who said to hew your head, will bide
The curse or worse of all who heard me cry!
But since you have these others tamed and tied,
I have no wish to stand alone and fight;
I will comply with any pledge they plight
And serve you hence as my good faith requires;
And when I do, I shall observe you, Sire,
For my rewards shall add to yours in time."
"Well spoken, friend," the King of France replied:
"Both Oliver and you shall be my knights;
With Roland, you shall be, all three, my pride!
And you shall bear the Oriflamme, say I!"
"Much thanks, my lord," young Aymeri replied:
"Wretch! On your knees before him!" Girart cried:
"Can you not see the love this trust implies?"
Said Aymeri: "My lord, you do not lie."
He went and knelt before the King this time,

And Charles leant down and helped the youth to rise;
Hernaut spoke out: "What will you do now, Sire?
Will you return to camp or at our side
Be honoured in Vienne when we arrive?
Let Alemans and Germans hear it cried
   That Charles does hold the city!"

33. How Charlemagne was welcomed in Vienne

HERNAUT SPOKE OUT: "Good King, attend to me!
Will you return to camp or with us here
Be honoured in Vienne when you appear?
If we should ride beside your mighty siege
Before the French have had the truth revealed
Of our accord and how we've made our peace,
We should be slain and slaughtered all and each!"
The King replied: "You speak the truth, indeed!"
Said Duke Girart, the wise of heart: "My liege,
Ere evening comes we'll ride, if you agree,
Below the ground upon our battle-steeds
Along a vault of great antiquity
Which leads us to my wondrous city's streets!
The Pagans dug this way in former years."
The King replied: "Fine noble, as you please –
But sir, beware of any treachery!"
The Duke replied: "That's foolish talk to me;
For life or limb I'd never use deceit."
When this was said, they started underneath;
The forester Berart was wise indeed:
With torch in hand he cantered in the lead
As underground they journeyed on their steeds;
King Charles himself was stunned beyond belief,
And, as he went, approached Girart to speak:
"Fine Duke Girart, my lord, attend to me!
I've won in war so many towns and keeps
And all the land from here to Balaguer;
But such a vault or road I've never seen!
For seven years we've held Vienne in siege
And never knew this passageway was here!
We could have stayed another seven years
Before, at last, your hunger made you yield!"

Girart replied: "In all your life, my liege,
You'd not have forced my men to leave the keep,
For I'd have left my city by this means
To hunt for boar or fatted woodland deer,
And gathered wealth from foreign realms and fiefs
To give to all within Vienne, so each
Would be well fed and live in health and ease."
The King replied: "I'm sure you would, indeed!"
When this was said, they joined the city streets;
Upon the square, beneath two leafy trees,
The King stepped down and was at once received
Within the hall of marble walls a-gleam,
Where he was served with joy and glad esteem;
Guibourc the wise, whose face with valour gleamed,
And lovely Aude, whose beauty had no peer,
Returned at once from prayer at St Maurice,
Where both had been the while upon their knees,
Beseeching God, the King of Majesty,
To save Girart from death and from defeat,
And all the knights he led beneath the streets
Along the vault to reach the woods unseen;
Guibourc, his wife, was wise of wit indeed:
She saw the King and knew him instantly –
His face, his nose, and his regard so fierce,
His royal brow, so lofty and so clear;
She saw Girart and said immediately:
"How did you bring this noble King to heel?
I urge you not to treat him cruelly
Or in a way to make him more displeased!
Submit yourself instead at Charles's feet
And give him back this city as a fief."
The Duke replied: "You speech is in arrears!
At dawn this day I did as he decreed;
I have become his loyal man of liege,
With kiss of faith and pledge of fealty,
As have the rest of all our gallant breed!"
His wife replied: "All praise the Lord of peace!
If we receive the King with honour here
For just one night, and serve him rightfully,
Our clan will rise in honour and prestige."
Girart replied: "You have my willing leave
    To render him this service."

ATTEND, MY FRIENDS, may Jesus bless and keep you!
Not everyone knows well the song you're hearing!
Some singers have not learnt or kept the details
Of what is true, as I've told you, believe me:
How Charlemagne, the Emperor white-bearded,
Was captured as he hunted in the greenwood,
Just like a bird encaged, and led in secret
By Duke Girart inside Vienne the fearsome;
The day he came, how joyful was the cheering
Of all the knights and all the common people;
Guibourc the fair came forward there to meet him,
And when she did, how noble was her greeting;
And nobody before saw such a feasting
As Charlemagne the King received that evening;
Both high and low attended him between them;
Nor did he have a lonely cell to sleep in;
But all the due that Charlemagne received there
Was still unknown to those within the siege-host;
When those who went to hunt within the greenwood
With Charlemagne the Emperor white-bearded,
Though searching long, could neither see nor hear him,
They turned around and to their tents went speeding;
The knights in camp came forward there to meet them
And asked for Charles, their mighty lord and leader:
"My noble lords," said Naimon hoary-bearded,
"I curse this land, this wretched realm, by Jesus!
The hills are high, the rocks are sharp and piercing,
The valleys long and overgrown the greenwood;
When Charlemagne surprised among its trees there
A heavy sow, a boar or some such creature,
He gave pursuit till he could kill and keep it;
But since he left, we've neither heard nor seen him;
Nor do we know which way he took when leaving;
If he has met with people of the region
Whose mighty lands his hand has seized, believe me,
They'll take revenge with every sort of evil!"
On hearing thus of Charles's disappearance,
How bitter, friends, was all the army's grieving!
So great a loss spread all across the siege-host
That nobody could eat or drink that evening,
Or lift the reins from any war-horse either;

From night till morn, with light of dawn appearing,
The army's knights, its followers and leaders,
   Lamented Charles's loss.

THE NOBLE KNIGHTS and men-at-arms the same
Throughout the host were filled with deep dismay
At Charles's loss, so grand a King and great,
Whose whereabouts they knew not, nor his fate;
And yet their gallant Emperor was safe
And well at ease inside Vienne, I'd say,
Attended there by counts of noble rate,
Girart himself and many of his race;
Before the King so rich a feast they raised,
With torches bright to light the hall of state,
That none before had witnessed such display!
I'll not describe the food, except to state
They had as much as appetite could crave;
And so much spiced and claret wine was drained
To tell you more would make a thirsty tale!
With Charles himself Girart took every pain:
He served the food the King desired and bade
Young Oliver to pour his wine and wait;
They other counts were never far away:
Hernaut, the lord of Biaulande on the waves,
And brave Geneva's liege and lord, Renier,
And Miles, the lord of Puglia, ever brave;
Young Aymeri served all of them that day;
Guibourc herself, of gallant heart and ways,
Sat next to him, and next to her the maid –
The lovely Aude, so fair of form and face:
The hall there glowed with all her radiant grace;
The King looked once, then twice, and then he hailed
Girart the duke with voice and visage raised:
"Fine Duke, my lord, I've one request to make:
Bestow the hand of this most fair of maids,
So I in turn may make her fiancée
To Roland, my own nephew, ever brave,
The best of knights to live and breathe today!
How fine a match so fair a pair will make!"
Girart replied: "My lord, I've naught against
This wish of yours, and gladly will obey."

Before them all he gave his glove in gage,
And Charles the King returned his thanks the same;
Their feasting done, the servants made all haste,
With noble squires, to clear the cloths away;
Then in the hall a merry time was made
As tales were told and the *vièle* was played
Till all retired until the dawning day;
Within a room most richly made they placed
The mighty King and liege lord Charlemagne,
Inside a bed more lovely and ornate
Than any couch where any sultan lay!
If all the French who then bemoaned his fate,
Had seen him there in Girart's hall of state,
They'd not have been so ill at ease, I'd say –
For Charlemagne, whose face with valour blazed,
Was sound asleep, and slept in peace and safe,
Inside Vienne until the dawn of day;
In Charles's camp, before the dawn-light came,
The knights arose, and infantry the same;
Duke Naimon, he whose hair and beard were grey,
And Roland, with three thousand men, made haste
To scour the wood in search of Charlemagne,
Down every ride and valley it contained;
How sad they were when still they found no trace,
And, sick at heart, combed back along the trails;
But in Vienne how glad they were and gay
To have the King within their city gates,
Who only rose on seeing daylight break,
And when Girart, with all his barons, came
To stand before him there and nobly wait
To greet him fair in our Redeemer's name;
Then all of them went off to church to pray;
When Bishop Morant sang the Mass they gave
Rich gifts of gold in coin and silken drapes;
When Mass was said, without the least delay,
Both Charlemagne and Duke Girart the brave
Bestrode the backs of their good destriers,
As did two thousand fighting men the same,
All dressed alike in rich and fine array:
Good robes they wore and garments richly made,
And bore no arms, as in a blithe parade
        They trotted from the city.

34. How Girart's good name was restored

KING CHARLEMAGNE, of fearsome mood and strength,
With Duke Girart, his closest lords and friends,
Paraded forth in joy and high content,
Before, in all, two thousand unarmed men,
Who shouted out the happiness they felt,
While riding straight towards the Frenchmen's tents!
Duke Naimon and young Roland saw them then,
And panic seized the hearts of all the French –
The boldest there were filled with coldest dread,
As Naimon said: "I see our fate ahead,
Since Charles is lost, by whom we all were led!
Behold what force has ridden from Vienne:
It is Girart with all his lords and friends
Come forth in strength to send us to our deaths!
They must have learnt that we have been bereft
Of Charlemagne through our own foolishness."
On hearing this, the French, in great distress,
Both rich and poor, seized weapons forth and then
The knights bestrode their long-maned destriers
And blew their horns with long and lusty breath;
When all were armed, both young and old, they sped
On steed or foot towards the King himself!
On seeing this, Charles laughed aloud and said
To Duke Girart, who rode beside him there:
"Fine Duke, my lord, we've frightened all my men!
They come at us in all their battle-dress!
By Jesus Christ, if it were our intent
To barter blows, then we could do it well!
How things have changed – but they don't know it yet!
I'll ride ahead, so they may see and guess!"
So, spurring forth his long-maned destrier,
He left behind his entourage and met
With Naimon and young Roland, whom he loved best;
And when those two beheld their liege again
Their joy was such as both had never felt!
They left at once their battle-steeds and stepped
Towards their lord and raised his pointed helm:
Said Charlemagne: "Be not afraid or vexed!

You had no need to summon all these men;
Thank God above, our cause has prospered well –
We have the prize that has comprised our quest:
Girart and I are allies now and friends –
   This lengthy war is finished."

WHEN ALL THE KNIGHTS heard Charlemagne's own voice,
Which told them he had reached a peace accord
With Duke Girart, whose many blows they'd borne,
Their joy was such as none had felt before;
They called aloud: "All praise to God the Lord,
And bless the man whose hand has stopped this war!
Now we can turn to our own homes and halls,
Unseen by us for seven years and more."
When this was said, returning one and all,
They left their steeds and laid aside their swords;
Before his tent the King, dismounting, called
On all his knights, his princes and his lords;
Then, standing on his folding-stool before
This loyal band, he said to one and all:
"Attend to me, my gallant-hearted lords!
You know it well, I went out yestermorn
As one of seven to Clermont wood for sport;
In forest deep I chased a fearsome boar
And struck it well – but when I blew my horn,
Girart arrived with all his men in force!
I thought my death or capture was assured;
But he displayed such honour and remorse
That at my feet he yielded and implored
My mercy, as a sober vassal ought,
As did Hernaut, that brave and famous lord;
On seeing this, my rage began to fall,
For they had won and I was in their thrall!
I pardoned them with goodwill and with joy:
I've never seen such loyalty before;
And now I ask for your advice, my lords:
What means have I to recompense them for
This realm of theirs that we have scarred and scorched?"
Said Naimon then: "Your words are wise, my lord;
So help me God, I've told you once and more
That you had wronged Girart and were at fault!

So help me God, if your amends fall short,
You'll lose at once my friendship and support."
The King replied: "You speak as wisdom ought;
My lord Girart, I bid you hasten forth!
This land is yours and always shall be yours,
And you shall keep your Frankish fiefs and forts!
The men you love I'll cherish at my court,
And those you hate I shall alike abhor:
Bereft of land, they'll leave my palace poor!"
Girart replied: "My grateful thanks, my lord."
Despite his rise he knelt upon the sward
Before the King, who raised him up once more;
Across the land the message went abroad
That Charles's host would distribute its stores:
If merchants thought they'd lost by this at all,
In goods themselves or what they'd sold them for,
They could regain four times the losses caused!
The merchants, then, came once again, and all
Began to sell new merchandise they'd brought:
From morning light, as soon as day had dawned,
Until the dusk, as night began to fall,
They never ceased their going back and forth,
Until the town was bursting with their stalls!
Then in the fields they lodged outside the walls
And slept in tents and shelters of all sorts;
The knights and Peers were filled with mighty joy,
And all the clerks and tonsured monks rejoiced
  That peace had been restored there.

THE MONTH WAS MAY, aglow with warmth and peace;
The fields were green, the woodland-trees in leaf,
The birds in voice most beautifully and clear,
And maids content who held their lovers near!
Upon the day of St Maurice's feast,
The King held court with great largesse indeed
Inside Vienne, within the hall replete
With knights galore, whose face with valour gleamed;
They all were served with richest foods and meats,
And afterwards, before they rose to leave,
Guibourc appeared, and by the right hand she
Led forth young Aude, so fair of form and sweet,

Clad all in silk of peerless shine and sheen;
Her beauty glowed and all about her gleamed;
The knights looked on, bedazzled by the scene:
"God," said the King, "how beautiful a queen!"
Hernaut replied: "Fine lord, she is indeed;
You know, I'm sure, that she is my own niece,
The daughter of my brother Count Renier,
And sister of Count Oliver the fierce."
King Charles replied: "Please give this maid to me
For Roland's sake, the man I hold most dear;
I would not ask for any other Peer;
And when they wed, no future day shall cleave
The bond between your noble clan and me;
And if the Lord, Who never lies, decrees
That by His grace a son may be conceived,
What good may come from such a one as he!"
Hernaut replied: "My liege, I quite agree;
My niece could never hope to wed or seek
   A higher house than your one!"

THE KING STOOD UP, whose face with valour blazed,
And called the youth for whom his love was great:
"Fine nephew, you may wed fair Aude the maid!"
He took her hand and gave the maid away
In view of all within the hall of state;
The bishop there bore witness to the same,
Before them all declaring Aude engaged;
They named the day the wedding would take place –
Brave heroes all, they named the day, I say,
But soon the Moors, those evil Pagan knaves,
Would rend the knot, may Jesus curse their fate!
When all was said as I have said the same,
Two messengers approached the King in haste,
Whom Yon the king of Gascony the famed
Had sent to him with tidings grim and grave!
They saw the King and, greeting him, proclaimed:
"Ah, mighty liege, whom all of France obeys,
Your mighty throne is under threat today,
For fourteen kings of evil Pagan race
Have razed the walls of Tarragone in Spain,
Then run amok in Gascony, then laid

Bordeaux to siege upon the Gironde's wave!
May God, Who judges all of us, gainsay
Your right to rule a fief or realm again,
  If this escapes your vengeance!"

35. How the Spanish campaign was begun

WHEN ALL THE KNIGHTS had heard the envoys' speech,
The bravest ones were filled with dread and fear;
Seguin spoke up – Bordeaux was his demesne:
"Good messengers, is this the truth indeed,
That Saracens have struck inside my fief?"
"Indeed, my lord, they've ruined fort and field,
Laid waste the land and left us naught but need;
The first of May is when they have decreed
That they will sail across the Gironde's stream
To Orléans and on their rapid steeds
Ride on to Bourges, for they tell all and each
That it was theirs by right in former years."
"Immortal God, True King of Majesty,"
Cried Charlemagne, "Who by Your grace decreed
That I should wear the crown of royalty,
Have pity on me now and counsel me
How I may break this haughty heathen breed,
Who have no right to what You've given me!
Advise me now, the wisest of you here,
As you are all my knights and men of liege;
Some seven years you have maintained this siege
For love of me, I speak but truthfully,
And you have done your service willingly
For all the land I gave you formerly;
Now serve again the King of Majesty,
  So you may win His love!"

WHEN THIS WAS SAID, you should have seen the bishop!
Upon a stool he stood, where he'd been sitting,
And made to speak in noble tones and ringing:
"My gallant lords, give ear to me and listen!
I stand for God, Who made the world we live in,
And for St Peter, His regent in Rome city,

To whom He gave the power of forgiveness
To any man for any sins committed;
I tell you now, that any man who's willing
To go with Charles and fight for his religion,
Shall be absolved of all his years of sinning,
For love of God, Who made the world we live in!"
The French all said: "How mighty a remission!
How blessed born are we to journey with him
    And win so rich a grace!"

THE EMPEROR of France stood up directly
And called aloud once more for the attention
Of all his knights and mightiest of men there;
He gave them leave and bade them reassemble
On May the first, the day of summer's entrance,
Beneath Narbonne in force of arms together,
Whence all would ride against the Pagan menace;
Then, calling forth Girart, he thus addressed him:
"When I'm in Spain, you must remain, protecting
Bavaria and Germany's defences;
And you, Hernaut of Biaulande, I direct you
To guard Geneva and all its lands appended,
With Lombardy, against all misadventure!
Defend Alsace, as well as Piacenza,
And Rome itself, which is my empire's centre."
"In truth, Hernaut," the noble Guibourc said then,
"He trusts you much, who gives you such an empire!"
Hernaut replied: "That's true enough, God bless you!"
When this was said, the King strode forth and left there;
Young Roland went with Aude inside her bedroom
And kissed here there, his lovely bride intended,
And bade her keep his ring in pledge and emblem;
And she gave him that lovely milk-white pennon
He used henceforth to indicate his presence
And rally troops within the Spanish Empire,
When taking towers and making towns surrender;
But, friends, the Moors, God curse them all for ever,
Cleft Aude and him – that pair were never wedded
And never left that heir for France to treasure;
    Which was a grievous shame.

I'VE TOLD MY TALE of Duke Girart the brave –
How Charles and he made war then peace again;
When all was done as you have heard me say,
The King set off to reach the realm of Spain
And led his host against that evil race
Which had attacked and sacked his own domains;
My friends, you've heard the ancient song relate
How Ganelon deceived the French that day
When Roland died with all his Peers the same,
And thousands more, God bless them all with grace,
In Roncevaux to King Marsile betrayed;
But let us leave those heroes and their fate,
And leave Girart, for I have told his tale,
And Hernaut of Biaulande, the nobly famed;
Of Hernaut's son I'll tell you next, whose name
Was Aymeri, that hero who became
    The liege lord of Narbonne.

THE KNIGHTS OF NARBONNE

(c.1205–1210)

For Bygrave Makeham

Introduction

The complete text of *Les Narbonnais* is preserved in four composite manuscripts of the thirteenth and fourteenth centuries. The original poem is thought to have been composed in the early years of the thirteenth century, and is one of the twenty-four surviving *chansons de geste* of the William of Orange song-cycle. With *Girart de Vienne* and *Aymeri of Narbonne*, which precede it in three of the four extant copies, it constitutes a sub-cycle of its own, centred around the legendary father of the hero William, namely Count Aymeri of Narbonne, his capture and defence of the southern French town, and the youthful exploits of his seven famous sons.

It is clear from any analysis of the manuscripts themselves, or of the style and content of the existing narrative, that *Les Narbonnais* is itself a composite work, made up of two original songs almost certainly composed by different authors. The first half of the present poem, known traditionally as *Le Département des enfants d'Aymeri*, tells of the collective dismissal and individual adventures of Count Aymeri's seven sons, and may well have been written by Bertrand de Bar-sur-Aube, the author of both *Girart de Vienne* and *Aymeri de Narbonne*. The latter poem indeed not only foretells their dismissal but contains many narrative episodes either repeated or embellished in the present, much longer poem. The second half of *Les Narbonnais* recounts, in condensed form, the turbulent history of this far-flung outpost of Charlemagne's empire during the Moorish invasions of the eighth century, with the artistic purpose of relating the Narbonne sub-cycle more closely with the *chansons de geste* dealing specifically with the major heroic figure of William of Orange.

The legendary character of Count Aymeri of Narbonne cannot now be identified with any single historical prototype. From the eleventh century onwards some nine viscounts of that name ruled in Narbonne, and baptismal records reveal the local popularity of the name from one hundred years earlier still. The *Annals* of Einhard for the year 810 mention an 'Haimericum comitem olim a Sarracenis captum' (Count Aimeric at that time held captive by the Saracens), and indeed that Aymeri may well have been one of the early ninth-century viscounts of Narbonne.

Einhard's reference to his imprisonment suggests a biographical detail which is certainly matched by episodes in the narratives of two later tales which feature the epic count (*La Mort d'Aymeri* and *Guibert d'Andrenas*). Of greater significance for the treatment of the Aymeri legend in the composition of *Les Narbonnais*, however, is the fact that the Castilian royal house of Lara inherited the viscounty of Narbonne in 1168. The heroic history of that household itself contains the legend of *los infantes de Lara*, a family saga which details the dismissal and exploits both bellicose and amorous of seven princely brothers – a narrative construct which matches exactly that of the first half of the present poem.

Narbonne itself, exposed by its location to the first Saracen invasions of southern France, was in the hands of the Moors for forty years during the eighth century, until it was retaken by Charlemagne's father Pépin the Short in 751. In 793, the emir of Cordova, Abd-el-Mélek, led an invasion of Septimania, and his force set fire to the outskirts of the town. It was during this conflict that William, duke of Aquitaine, met and turned this force back at the river Orbieu, near Villedaigne – a deed to be immortalised in the *Chançun de Willame* (see pages 29–142 of this collection) – by which time the deeds and family relationships of one Aymeri of Narbonne were well-established facts as far as the poets were concerned. The epic poems *Coronemenz Loois*, *Charroi de Nîmes*, *Pèlerinage de Charlemagne*, *Girart de Roussillon* and *Aliscans*, all speak of him and know him as the father of Count William 'Hooknose' of Orange. By the beginning of the twelfth century the name and fame of Pépin's son, Charlemagne, had assumed the credit for Narbonne's deliverance from Saracen hands, and by that century's end it is *his* son, Louis the Pious, who, in the tales, helps Count Aymeri's sons, The Knights of Narbonne, to deliver their troubled city.

The detailed and accurate geographical references made to Narbonne in the narratives of both *Aymeri de Narbonne* and in the *Département* sections of *Les Narbonnais* raise the possibility that the author(s) of these works may have enjoyed for some time the patronage of Ermengard (d. 1197), daughter of Aymeri II, vicount of Narbonne (d. 1134), whose brilliant court was famous for its reception of both *troubadours* and *trouvères*. Not only had her father and her grandfather (Aymeri I, d. 1105) led and fought in enough campaigns against the Saracens to be equally deserving of the legend's patronymic, but she herself, in 1148, had ridden at the head of her troops to the aid of Count Raymond Bérenger IV of Barcelona, during the siege of Tortosa. The portrait of the wise, spirited and beloved Hermanjart, wife of

Aymeri of Narbonne and mother of the Knights, as she appears not only in these two tales but in several other contemporaneous *chansons de geste,* could certainly have been inspired by this imposing matron of the Narbonne dynasty.

Artistic Achievement

Whether or not the first half of *Les Narbonnais* was composed by the Champenois poet Bertrand de Bar-sur-Aube – a hypothesis in fact refuted by the poem's only editor, Hermann Suchier, in 1898 – it cannot be doubted that the present poem displays many of the artistic strengths which exemplify the work of the undisputed author of *Girart de Vienne.* Although, at just over 8,000 lines, it is the longest poem in this collection, *The Knights of Narbonne* represents the average length of the entire corpus of surviving *chansons de geste,* and, in its own right, affords us an interesting glimpse of the genre's aims and accomplishments in the last one hundred years of its development from an oral/aural to a written/read art-form. Its narrative is varied in style, energetic yet graceful in its movement, combining epic action with historical anecdote, satiric humour with romantic intrigue, to form a sustained tale which is both internally consistent and generically cohesive.

The protagonists of this tale are particularly clearly delineated as individuals, not just as character-types. In *Les Narbonnais* the hot-headed young Aymeri of *Girart de Vienne* has indeed become a patriarchal figure to rival Charlemagne himself, but his is certainly not a one-dimensional personality. 'Grey-bearded' yet still 'fierce-faced', he is impatient of challenge yet steadfast in support, and remains resented and admired for his indomitable will by both friend and enemy alike. The equally strong portrait of his wife Hermenjart, whose character matches that of her husband in energy, personal courage and family pride, is faithful to the image of her established in the poem's major source, *Aymeri de Narbonne,* and links her at once in the reader's mind to her literary progenitor, Lady Guibourc, from the *Chançun de Willame.* The Knights of Narbonne themselves, the seven male offspring of Aymeri and Hermenjart, come alive as individual personalities through an elaborate delineation and illustration of their differing natures that reaches far beyond the narrative compass of the earlier *chansons de geste.* Dismissed from Narbonne by their father, all but the youngest, Guibert, depart on individual or collective quests which demonstrate and develop their distinctive characters. Bernart, the eldest, the most sensible, and the best talker, goes with Hernaut, the least sensible and loosest talker, and with dour Aimer, who hardly talks at all, to seek Charlemagne in Paris. Garin is sent to his uncle Boniface in Pavia, while Beuvon is directed to Gascony and to the hand of its ageing monarch's most obliging daughter. Young Guibert, meanwhile, who stays behind, manages to get in and out of more scrapes than any of them.

It is, however, the character of Narbonne's second son, William, the hero of the entire cycle, which is most cleverly constructed by the poet of the first half of *Les Narbonnais,* and most extensively developed by the author of the second, to give the narrative its most unifying voice. It is William's inspirational speech upon the occasion of their departure that finds an immediate and prolonged echo in each brother's feelings and actions. William's own future fame is constantly alluded to in speeches and tokens presented by both his family and by the emperor himself, who entrusts him not only with France's symbol of military domination, the Oriflamme banner, but also with his own symbol of divine approbation, the sword Joyeuse. In the second half of the narrative young William plays an increasingly prominent role, not only in the defeat of the Pagans besieging Narbonne – he concocts and conducts the ruse which delivers food to the starving town, he saves his father's life in battle, he leads the attack which eventually puts the great emir to flight – but also in securing the succession of Charlemagne's chosen heir, Louis, after the French emperor's death. Collectively, the varied and various exploits of the Knights of Narbonne orchestrate as harmoniously as in the similarly expansive but much better known William-tale of *Aliscans* the mighty theme of 'kinship's bond', which dominates the entire song-cycle, and which acts like a great ground bass to the changing melodies of religious, romantic, humorous and heroic service that the individual personalities of this legendary family, in solo or in chorus, contribute to the rich texture of each *chanson* in which they appear.

Mockery of Pagan adversaries, the original source of comedy in the *chansons de geste*, is complemented by that of other racial groups, most notably Lombards and Germans, and by that of high-ranking officials of the Church from any country, in *Les Narbonnais.* The Lombard citizenry are portrayed as mercenary, their chivalry as fat and cowardly – this particular antipathy thought to have arisen from the business rivalry and jealousy of the southern French in particular towards the rising power and wealth of certain north Italian cities at the turn of the thirteenth century. The German knights accommodated in Roland's old lodge in Paris are also depicted in an unflattering light as mean and insulting drunkards, while certain prelates are presented as pompous and pampered hypocrites. The comic comeuppance received by these last two groups is almost exclusively meted out by the ready fists and tongue of Aymeri's most hot-headed offspring, Hernaut the Red, whose antics as unofficial seneschal of Paris provide the poem with its most successful moments of unabashed burlesque. An aesthetically satisfying narrative balance is maintained by the poets of *Les Narbonnais* in their treatment of all three target-groups, however. The Lombard leader, King Boniface, a somewhat weak character in *Aymeri de Narbonne*, is a courageous leader in the present poem, the Germans are gallant fighters, and it is the abbot of Saint-Denis who defends Aymeri's sons upon their arrival in Paris, when every other aristocrat there wants them dead. The *William* song-cycle's unusual tolerance for 'the noble Pagan adversary' can also be seen in *Les Narbonnais*, where two Pagan royals are permitted conversion to 'The One True Faith'.

As with *Girart de Vienne*, the text of *Les Narbonnais* displays the literary flowering of stylistic features firmly rooted in the oral tradition of *chanson de geste* composition and performance. The old *jongleur* is still and always present in the written text as an omniscient narrator, who controls the attention and emotion of his audience by frequent interjections of humour, horror and homespun philosophy. He establishes a lasting rapport with his public by constantly communicating his own enthusiasm for the tale through praise or censure of its protagonists. In the first, more dramatic half of the poem, the emotive qualities of the syntactically flexible epic formulas are still used to fine effect in short verses of dialogue, where tension and sentiment are intended to override narrative development. The opening episodes of the brothers' dismissal from Narbonne, and their subsequent knighting by Charlemagne in Paris, exemplify this ancient technique at its best. In the work's second, more narrative half, although the verses lengthen and the rhyme change plays little emotional role, the *chanson de geste* poet's ability to display this basic skill of his genre is still evident in the extended accounts of weaponry and warfare. The more detailed descriptions of luxurious objects, the elaboration of travel sequences, and a more self-conscious reflection of a 'courtly' lifestyle itself – in the pointed illustration of correct and incorrect modes of behaviour – bear witness to the heavy influence of the contemporary works of romance upon the development of the Old French epic tale.

Sources and influences

Although their common authorship may be disputed, there can be little doubt that the text of *Les Narbonnais* was intended as a continuation of that of *Aymeri de Narbonne*, which precedes it in all of the surviving cyclic manuscripts. The last two hundred or so lines of the earlier poem not only offer biographical sketches of all of Aymeri's children which are embellished faithfully in *Les Narbonnais*, but also conclude with the narrator's invitation to his audience to prolong its attention and hear at once of their subsequent dismissal from Narbonne and its consequences. During the course of the succeeding poem Count Aymeri's famous conquest of both the city and his Pavian bride Hermenjart are frequently alluded to, and moreover, specific episodes, such as young Garin's humorous adventures in the old Lombard capital, recall parallel scenes from the earlier poem. Other *chansons de geste* to which the present poem's only editor finds either brief or extended allusion in the text are the *Chanson de Roland*, *Coronement Loois*, *Aliscans*, *Aspremont*, *La Bataille Loquifer*, *Huon de Bordeaux*, *Le Moniage Rainouart* and *Girart de Vienne*.

The legend of Aymeri's dismissal of his sons seems to have enjoyed a huge popularity in the Middle Ages. Not only is specific mention of it made in other *chansons de geste* (e.g *Jourdain de Blaye*), but it seems also to have formed the basis of a *tableau vivant* or mimed play, for a performance of which, in 1351, the council members of Lille paid a certain troupe 'forty crowns'. An extant French prose version of the tale dates from the middle of the fifteenth century, while the derivative prose work of the Italian author Andrea da Barberino called *I Nerbonesi* dates from 1410 and itself exists in four further Italian manuscripts from the fifteenth and sixteenth centuries.

Generically, it would seem that *Les Narbonnais* was written principally to relate the exploits of the Garin de Monglane song cycle's greatest hero, Count William of Orange, to those of his legendary father, Count Aymeri of Narbonne, as detailed in his own sub-cycle, and also to those other popular epic tales which deal particularly with the exploits of certain of his brothers (e.g. *Guibert d'Andrenas*, *La Prise de Cordres et Sebille*, *Le Siège de Barbastre* and *Beuvon de Conmarchis*). The content of a *chanson de geste* dealing specifically with the youthful exploits of William Hooknose, Count of Orange, *Les Enfances Guillaume*, differs little from that detailing his early achievements in the narrative of *Les Narbonnais*, which pre-dates the better known poem in the opinion of most scholars.

THE KNIGHTS OF NARBONNE

1. How Aymeri of Narbonne dismissed his sons

ONE EASTER TIME it was, a noble feast;
The days were warm, the sunlight bright and clear;
The streams were full with waters swift and sweet,
And woods were green with growing bud and leaf;
The song of birds rang sweetly in the trees
As knights engaged in jousting-bouts beneath;
Young maids in love showed brighter eyes and cheeks
And dressed their best in gowns of finer weave;
Friends, many know the tale I'll tell you here
Is in the *gestes*, the best of which agree
That Charles of France, the Emperor, convened
His court in Paris at this time of the year;
His subject-kings, all seven, came to eat
With all the knights of Charlemagne's demesne,
Archbishops too, and abbots, priors and priests,
And many more who served the Christian Creed –
While fighting lords stayed in their border-seats,
To keep at bay the hated heathen breed!
No better man there was among all these
Than Aymeri in Narbonne's castle-keep,
A gallant knight of honour and esteem
And loyal faith to Charlemagne his liege;
He too held court to match his rank's degree:
Inside his hall he'd call one thousand Peers
And sit there, at the highest table reared,
His beard all white, his face alight with zeal –
And all could see that he was born to lead!
One day, stood by his window there to see
His town Narbonne and its surrounding fiefs –
The Moorish port, the vineyards and the fields,
And round them all the pounding, salty sea,
Which brought to shore so many ships whose yield

483

Made wealthy men of those who worked the fleets –
He saw his wife, fair Hermenjart, between
Their seven sons, whose face with valour gleamed;
With love and grace he turned to greet them each:
"My sons," he said, "I've loved you all these years!
You each are worth an Emperor to me!
I praise the Lord, for truly I believe
The least of you to match a king at least!
But now I think it far from wise indeed
That you should wait to share this land from me!
When I was young I never thought to keep
One half a foot of my good father's lease;
I rode away to serve a worthy liege –
King Charles of France, who in reward decreed
Narbonne and all its shores and shires to me,
Which I have held against the Pagan breed;
If I split up this realm in seven fiefs,
The largest one would be too small to please –
So I shall not! Go win yourselves a fief!
Ride forth to France and by your daring deeds
Serve Charlemagne, our mighty King and Liege,
As I did once, in my young, fighting years!
By God the Lord, I swear most solemnly
That none of you shall rule here after me,
Except Guibert: as youngest, I decree
　　That he shall have my holding."

THE DAY WAS FINE and summer-like the weather,
As in his hall sat Aymeri in splendour,
His beard as white as flowers of the meadow,
And long enough to overhang his belt-knot;
In Christian lands there lived no finer elder;
Within his hand a polished rod lay ready,
Well-bound in four with bands of silvered metal;
Upon the boards he brought it down so heavy
That through the hall in every nook it echoed;
It was his way to say they should attend him;
He saw his sons, all young and strong together,
And cried: "My boys, may Jesus Christ protect you!
These many years I've brought you up and bred you
To knighthood's call, and now you all are ready!

But now I think that you would be in error
To wait for land together when I perish!
This town alone is all I own, I tell you,
Which I received at Charles's hand and pleasure;
He offered it to all his barons present,
But none of them was willing to accept it –
So much they feared the mighty Pagan menace;
I asked for it and had it, with God's blessing;
And have, in truth, controlled it well and kept it:
I haven't lost six inches to those devils!
But, by the Lord, be sure of what I tell you:
This land is not enough for one young fellow!
I tell you this, Bernart, who are my eldest,
So you'll not wait for what I could have left you,
But go to France, the homeland of the Frenchmen,
And serve the King with all your strength and temper;
If you succeed, he'll give you lands a-plenty;
But, by St Honoré, I swear I'll never
Bequeath you land that lies in my possession,
No piece or part that's worth the smallest penny;
Guibert alone, my youngest, shall inherit;
   I'll not retract his right!"

THE MONTH WAS MAY, with roses blooming sweetly,
And oriole's song with nightingale's competing;
Fair Hermenjart, whose mind and heart were peerless,
Who'd wed the Count when Princess of Pavia,
Was in her room, of vaulted walls and ceiling,
Most richly clad in silk from Almeria;
But how she filled with deep dismay, on hearing
Her husband's speech, his face with valour gleaming,
Who said her sons, her pride and joy, must leave her!
Perplexed and vexed, her anger grew with grieving,
As Aymeri, whose beard was white and streaming,
Within his hall, among his knights and liegemen,
Beheld his sons and raised his voice up fiercely:
"My boys," he cried, "so help me, blessed Jesus,
I never had my father's land bequeathed me,
No penny-piece, nor half a piece, believe me;
I made my way, when I was young and eager,
To serve the King, our Emperor white-bearded;

By my prowess I made him know and heed me
Before Vienne, that mighty town and region,
Which he besieged with all his levied legions;
For seven years he fought but failed to seize it;
Then Lord Girart, who held it, gave it freely
To Charlemagne, before his town and people,
In loyal love and true noblesse of feeling;
Then Charlemagne, his face with valour gleaming,
Rode straight for Spain to strike the hated heathens,
Then left me here to rule this town and keep it;
Thank God above, I have so far succeeded
In doing so; I haven't lost or yielded
One inch of land to Moorish hands or scheming;
I tell you this, so help me blessed Jesus,
To make you see that all of you must leave here!
Bernart! You are the eldest; I'd not bequeath you
So small a part as this my little fiefdom;
Go forth and serve in France's many regions,
With William, your brother fierce of feature!
And take Hernaut, to make of you a threesome;
Tell Charlemagne, the mighty King white-bearded,
That Aymeri sends greetings and entreats him
To honour you as his own barons' equals,
And in his hall as counsellor to keep you;
And bid him give to William the wielding
Of Oriflamme, to bear in battles fielded;
And bid him make Hernaut, if so he pleases,
The seneschal of all he owns and eats there,
To store his wealth and share it out as needed,
And not be mean, but not be wasteful either!
In Charles's court these duties are the chief ones
And held as best above the rest, believe me;
Serve Charlemagne, the Emperor white-bearded,
So loyally that everyone who sees you
Will sing your praise; and honour all the peers there,
The sons of counts, the knights and other leaders;
They'll help you then to gain the heart and hearing
Of Charles himself, and with goodwill beseech him
On your behalf to give you wealthy fiefdoms
And lovely wives of noble birth and breeding;
I tell you straight, Bernart, you have no reason

To stay and hope that one day you'll succeed me;
By all the faith I owe to blessed Jesus,
You'll not receive one inch of land between you!
Guibert alone, my youngest son, shall keep it;
    I'll never change my mind!"

"BEUVON, FINE SON," said Aymeri the wise,
"You seem to me to be of gallant mind,
Of fearsome look, both strong of limb and lithe;
In this respect I think you waste your time
In waiting for a portion when I die;
I swear to God, Who made us in His like,
You'll never have one inch of what was mine;
Yet when you leave these noble walls behind,
I'll give you lands and wealthy halls besides:
Take Gascony and all its woodlands wide!
Possess the land, its shoreline and its shires,
As far as Spain, the mighty and the wild!
Through Gascony it is that pilgrims wind
Upon their way to James's blessed shrine;
I give you this in gift by gage and right:
And not because I ever in my life
Possessed the smallest inch of it or slice,
Or that its men were ever bondsmen tied
In fealty to me or to my line!
But its King Yon, who is a gallant knight,
Has in his hall a daughter fair and wise:
If you are brave and serve the King Yon awhile,
With all your strength, your courage and desire,
Then you can win this maid most fair and fine,
And all his realm will come to you in time
    As regent of that kingdom."

"BEUVON, FINE SON, my own sword I will give you;
Its fame is great, its name is noble Grisbay –
As long as you and wide as your five fingers!
No better blade was ever made than this one;
At Roncevaux Count Roland strove to win it,
But made it mine, not needing it with his one;
Those Saracens paid dearly when he did this,
For with this blade the blows I gave were bitter!

Take care, my son, to keep this weapon with you –
Don't barter it for any fief or kingdom,
Or take its price in wagonloads of silver;
It has no peer from here to Iceland's limits;
But by the faith I swore as a true Christian
To Hermenjart, when married in the minster,
There's nothing else of which you'll own one inch here!
    Seek elsewhere with the sword!"

"GARIN, FINE SON, attend my words and heed them!
Now, as for you, there will be little reason
But your own pride and lack of proper feeling,
If you remain and hope to gain my fiefdom;
You shall not have one bit of it, believe me!
But you shall have authority and wield it
In noble lands with wealth enough to please you!
Come forward, son, and take in trust Pavia,
Your uncle's realm, for you may soon succeed him!
Serve Boniface the king in honest fealty;
He has no son, no child or any regent,
And when he dies, he'll leave you Lombardia;
You'll rule alike that wealthy city Pisa
And all the land to where Romagna reaches,
    And so be rich enough!"

"FINE SON AIMER, by all the Breton Saints,
It would be wrong and foolish in your case
To stay in hope of gain from my estate:
You shall not have one bit of it, I say!
Come forward, though, and take in trust all Spain
And all the land from there to Moriayn,
With fifteen thousand men to serve your name!
Go first with them to mighty Charlemagne,
But, come what may, I swear you must not stay,
But rally there brave lords of Alemayn,
And Brittany and Normandy the same,
And of Anjou, to ride with you to Spain
And seek to slay the hated heathen race!
Take Cordova with all its towers great!
But first of all you must eliminate
The heathen Moors and Turkish hordes the same!

With you in Spain and Beuvon's rule obeyed
In Gascony, along its vast terrain,
And Garin's flag above Pavia's state,
And three of you in France with Charlemagne,
Then I, at last, may sleep at ease and safe
With Hermenjart, and be no more afraid
Of Saracen attacks and Pagan raids;
    My gallant sons shall guard me!"

2. How Hermenjart and others objected in vain

COUNT AYMERI, of courage fierce in war,
Saw all his sons and then dismissed them all
To promised lands and borders far and broad,
As suited him and satisfied his choice;
But while he spoke, the countess Hermenjart
Paced up and down, her lovely face distraught;
She wrung her hands, she pulled her hair and clawed
Her ermine cloak until its seams were torn;
She saw the Count and said with weeping voice:
"My worthy lord, you steer a foolish course
If you dismiss like this from their own hall
The noble sons I've nurtured and adored!
For what will pass among the Persian Moors
When they find out you have dismissed them all?
Without a doubt their hearts will fill with joy
That you have grown so weak in deed and thought!
They'll summon forth their armies and set forth
Across the sea in sailing ships of war;
We Narbonnese shall be outfought and caught
And forced to leave the Faith of Christ our Lord,
To serve Mahom and worship Tervagaunt!
What shame for me, while your good name will fall,
    With all our family's honour."

"FINE SON GUIBERT," the Count continued speaking,
"Whatever else I've said, you'll not be leaving,
But live within this hall and all this region;
For it is said in ancient texts and precepts –
King Alexander did himself decree it,

As did the brave and noble Julius Caesar,
That youngest sons should run their family leases;
So you shall have Narbonne and Biaulande's beaches
And all the land and fiefs around Geneva;
Four noble towns and twenty-three strong keeps there
Will raise for you one thousand knights when needed;
But while I live, your service in the meantime
Is needed here by me and she who reared you!"
Guibert replied: "By all my faith in Jesus,
I'll do as you require me to, believe me –
Although I grieve for my six brothers deeply,
    That they must leave this land."

SAID AYMERI, his face with valour blazing:
"My noble sons, by all the Saints we pray to,
What do you hope to gain if you remain here –
Some plot or tract, through acts that will disgrace you?
Or will you seize young Narbonne girls and rape them,
Or rob the folk of this good town and shame them?
By all the faith I owe our blessed Lady,
There's none of you, however strong he may be,
If he should find the poorest, sleeping maiden,
And even do as little as to wake her,
Or cause alarm or any harm to shake her,
Whom I would not seek vengeance on, far greater
Than any other lord or noble neighbour
From here to Normandy, God bless and aid me,
Save Charlemagne, whose beard is white and trailing;
I do not match my will against his greatness;
So gird your loins, my sons, and never waver!
Farewell this town as soon as you are able –
If you do not, by Jesus Christ our Saviour,
Tomorrow night, before the light has faded,
I'll drive you out, with steel nor steed to aid you!
    How shameful that would be!"

WITHIN THE HALL how great a grief was felt
For Narbonne's sons and their dismissal hence!
Throughout the town the news began to spread
Among the rich and worthy citizens,
Who heard the word with droop and drop of head;

Five score of them rushed up the castle-steps
To find the Count that moment playing chess
For his delight, against a pillar leant;
A spokesman for the deputation said:
"Lord Aymeri, attend our strong request!
We've hastened here to speak to you yourself,
And this is why, although you well might guess!
We're merchants all and all our days are spent
In travel here and there to buy and sell;
We bear our goods to many towns and realms:
Rich silken cloths and cloaks of ermine fresh
And steeds of war praised highly everywhere;
We work the land and vineyards hard and well;
While making sure that your half-share is kept,
We strive to make our profits with the rest;
Lord Aymeri, we bid you take our wealth
And give it to your sons, each one of them,
But do not make them leave Narbonne, nor let
Them ever quit this city on some quest!
You must know why we urge you to this end:
When we transport our goods the length and breadth
Of lands to sell and buy where fairs are held,
The local folk come up and ask us then:
'Where are you from? Come, tell us, worthy men,
Who rules the land where you good people dwell?'
Then we reply, most readily as well,
That we are bound to Aymeri, the best
Of knights, whose laws we all of us respect,
Who with his sons protects us in his strength;
On hearing this, they leave us to ourselves
And never seek the smallest coin in rents,
For there is none that dares cause us offence!
Thus we rejoice in our good lord's prowess;
Sire, do not let your sons leave us bereft,
For love of God, Who saved us all from death!"
Bernart replied: "Men, do not waste your breath!
Allow my lord his leisure and his bed,
And let him hunt and fish to his content,
Then drink a toast and boast of his success –
Without a doubt he has well earned his rest!
All we his sons are sturdy, strong young men

Who should henceforth secure Narbonne ourselves
By making war on those who pose a threat –
The Pagan Moors across the sea! Their wealth
We'll win in war and bring in to this realm
For his delight and for his honour hence,
And Hermenjart's, so fair of face and fresh."
On hearing this, his father laughed unchecked;
He called upon fair Hermenjart and said:
"My lady wife, I know beyond a shred
Of doubt he is a son whom I have bred!
    A true and noble scion."

3. How Aymeri's sons refused their mother's help

WHEN HERMENJART heard Aymeri dismissing
Their sturdy sons, her own beloved children,
To other lands according to his wishes,
And make Guibert the heir to all their riches,
She sought him out and spoke to him with spirit:
"Fine Count, my lord, give ear to me and listen!
So help me God, Who made the world we live in,
While I'm alive I'll not stand by and witness
Our youngest child inherit all this kingdom!
The monarch Charles has never ruled in this way!
Let young Guibert, by all means, have the city,
But let him find fit honours and positions
For all our sons within our fiefdom's limits,
And fitting lords for all his noble sisters;
    French custom has it so."

WHILE HERMENJART the fair spoke out her thoughts
To Aymeri the Count in Narbonne's hall,
Guibert himself was roaming through the court,
Perplexed and vexed and very much distraught;
As soon as beheld the Count, he roared:
"My noble sire, by St Denis, I'm sure
You hold me cheap and set my name at naught,
Since from my side you send my friends abroad,
Whom I should serve in this domain of yours –
Whose brotherhood I always should exalt!

But by the faith I owe to Christ the Lord,
I'll not be rich while all of them are poor!
I'd rather live in exile, lost and lorn!
We'll never part while I have breath to draw!"
"Wretch, hold your tongue!" the mighty Marquis roared:
"By Christ, Who pardoned Longinus his fault,
Were you as old as they are, rest assured
You would not have one foot of Narbonne's soil –
Aymerillot, my godson, would have it all!
And hear the rage that fills your mother's voice!
Ah womankind! I truly think, my boy,
That if I died, by St Denis, before
One month were past, she would be wed once more
To any duke or count or vavasor."
On hearing this, the Countess fretted more:
"Sir Aymeri," she cried, "my noble lord!
By God above, your words are most ill thought!
I'd never wed another husband, for
I want our sons to share Narbonne henceforth;
But there's one thing of which you can be sure:
Without God's help, those failing eyes of yours
Will never see all six here any more!"
My worthy friends, how truly she foresaw!
The noble Count was nearly at death's door
Before they met again, and then because
Guibert himself went searching for them all,
Each one by one, in foreign shires and shores –
When twenty thousand Moors besieged the walls
    Surrounding Narbonne city.

"LORD AYMERI," said Hermenjart the wise,
"Attend my words, for what I prophesy
May very well prove true enough in time!
So help me God, have I not cause to cry,
Since you dismiss the children from my side,
With whom God blessed my womb and both our lives,
And who should now protect me till I die?
When this is heard by all the Pagan tribes,
That you have sent our children far and wide,
They'll raise at once a host of massive size;
And when their ships have sailed, and they arrive,

They'll fall upon Narbonne and all its shires
And drag us back in chains across the tide!
What pain for you and shame for me your wife,
With no defence from you against their crimes,
Now you're too old to gird your sword and fight;
So help me God, Who saved us all through Christ,
Now I perceive how true it is and right
That if a man outlives his strength's decline,
He spends his days both wretched and reviled!"
When Aymeri heard this, it stung his pride:
He raised his hand against his lovely wife
And struck her face so fiercely in his spite
That down she fell upon the marble tiles;
But straightaway she nobly made to rise,
And when she did, she made this wise reply –
Few ladies now would show themselves so wise –
In ringing tones she answered with a cry:
"Lord Aymeri, your blow has served me right!
May God above, Who made the dew and sky,
Reward the arm and let its valour thrive,
With which my cheek was checked with so much might!
Now I myself have felt the strength it hides,
I know full well that your prowess abides!
I went too far in speaking out my mind;
The boys are yours, this cannot be denied,
And I am but their mother and your wife;
So give them lands where sturdy hands may thrive,
And near or far, as fits your heart's desire;
God grant them all good fortune in their lives,
So every land this day to them assigned
May prosper well beneath their enterprise."
Red-haired Hernaut had seen with his own eyes
His mother struck by Aymeri's great ire,
And, turning white with anger at the sight,
He gripped his sword and slid the shining iron
Six inches from its leather sheath and cried:
"Old man, you grow too arrogant and wild,
To hit and harm our mother with us nigh!
So help me God, Who saved us all through Christ,
If you so much as touch her one more time,
You'll feel yourself how well I too can strike!
    And all this court shall see it!"

AND ALL THE COURT, the wise and weaker-witted,
The seven sons and all the barons witnessed
Count Aymeri in anger strike the visage
Of Hermenjart, that paragon of women;
Red Hernaut did and, angered past his limit,
He crossed the floor, his breast with passion brimming:
"Old man," he cried, "the Devil has bewitched you!
To strike your wife is shameful and most wicked,
For she is one whom you should honour richly;
I do not know what others may be thinking,
But by the Lord, Who made me in His image,
I tell you this: if you could even give me
Apulia, Calabria and Frisia,
And all the ports and trading-routes of England,
And Normandy, with all its coast and rivers,
I would not stay within your walls to win it!"
He called the rest: "Why waste another minute?
Retrieve your arms and let us leave this prison!
Let each of us be bold and fierce of spirit,
And let us seek for finer lands to live in!
This dotard's mad and drives us from his city;
Before he dies may he alike be driven
To feel the hurt and smart when he is smitten
By friends' and knights' desertion and dismissal!"
And so he was – both wise and weaker-witted
Know well enough how Pagans nearly killed him,
    When they besieged Narbonne.

WITHIN THE HALL how high was all their grief!
With moan and groan they cried aloud indeed!
The sons themselves knew well they had to leave,
And turning round, with Hernaut in the lead,
Made no delay but left the palace, keen
To be away, not lingering the least;
Before the tower there grew a grove, well-leafed
With laurel, yew and fine laburnum trees;
And as the youths paused briefly underneath,
Their mother came, who hastened on their heels!
If you had seen the love she showed them each!
I couldn't say which son she most esteemed:
"My sons," she said, "wait briefly here for me,

And I will ask the noble Aymeri
To let you stay within Narbonne at least
Till I have shared my wealth out for your needs."
Bernart, he laughed to hear his mother speak,
And then he said: "Fine Countess, fair and sweet,
I swear by God, in Whom there's no deceit,
We'll never take your smallest penny-piece!
For if the Lord in His high grace decreed
That we should serve a worthy lord and reap
A just reward for our good faith and deeds,
Count Aymeri would say at once, I fear,
That we had bought whatever we'd received
With all the wealth that you would give us here."
When Hermenjart could see they all agreed,
She left them there and made her way, in tears,
    To speak to her fine husband.

FAIR HERMENJART did not delay or wait
But climbed the steps inside her hall again;
Her youngest son, Guibert, still wept and wailed,
And she began to comfort him this way:
"Fine son," she said, "do not be so dismayed!
King Charlemagne will welcome such as they,
And give them gold and silver in good faith,
And noble lands, for service that they make;
But in one year they will be here again."
For comfort's sake she spoke to him this way,
Then saw the Count against a pillar there
And said to him with courtesy and grace:
"Lord Aymeri, God bless you with His grace,
Although, by God, today you are to blame!
I had six sons whom everybody praised,
Yet three must go to France the sweet, you say,
Beuvon to Gascony, Aimer to Spain,
While good Garin must cross the mountain-trails;
And none of them has anything to pay
For any meal when daylight starts to fade,
Or any food at all when morning breaks."
Said Aymeri: "No more of your complaints!
I've battled hard for everything I've gained!
I swear to you with all my love and faith

I shall not give them anything this day!
To conquer land and win the wealth they crave
They must ride off to fierce-faced Charlemagne,
As I did when I was a knight their age!
For, by the Lord, I swear once more that they
Shall never rule one inch of my domain!"
On hearing this, the tears ran down her face,
And young Guibert began to fall and faint;
The noble Count went swiftly to his aid
And raised him up and tried to soothe his pain;
The other six were in no mood to stay;
Throughout the town they had the word proclaimed
That any man who rode with them that day
Should have his share of any common gains
In land or goods which their prowess attained;
If you had seen how many youngsters came
With laden mules and harnessed destriers;
Some twenty-seven came there straightaway,
Who all were sons of counts and peers of state,
Or citizens of highest rank and rate;
Before the sun had journeyed half its way,
Five hundred youths had come to them and prayed
To be allowed to follow in their train;
Whatever road the six of them might take,
The others swore to follow it the same;
When this was done, without one moment's waste,
    They parted from the city.

THE BROTHERS LEFT, without one moment's pause,
And with them went those twenty-seven more
Who were the fruit of Narbonne's noblest loins;
There wasn't one among them, short or tall,
Who didn't ride a mule or palfrey-horse;
Their gallant squires rode bravely to the fore,
And led by hand their masters' steeds of war;
The noble Count farewelled them, lost in thought,
As to their backs he raised his voice and called:
"My noble sons, I trust the lives of all
To Lord our God, Who, of the Virgin born,
Was put to death upon the Cross's boards;
Who felt the blow that Roman soldier scored,

From which His blood ran down the spear towards
Those blinded eyes, which opened to the Lord
And sought His grace, and gained a soul reborn!
As all of this is true and nothing false,
I say farewell to you in surest joy!"
He sighed again, but turning to withdraw,
Saw once again those citizens come forth,
Whose sons had left; and seeing him, they roared:
"White-haired old man, your dotage dooms us all!
You should be in an abbey, or its vault!
You rob us now of all we labour for –
The lovely sons we've nurtured and adored."
He heard them roar, but he ignored their taunts,
For he could see their sorrow and remorse;
He never raged against their bitter scorn,
　　But walked away in silence.

UPON THAT DAY their gallant sons rode off
And left behind their homeland of Narbonne,
Each knight of liege lamented for his loss
And rode with them a little way along,
Then took his leave and left them riding on,
Commending each and every one to God;
The sons farewelled their mother fair and fond,
Then turned their mounts towards sweet France beyond,
Their spirits high and hopeful in their bond –
Young William addressed the rest thereon:
"My lords," he said, "let honour be our song,
As it was theirs who rose in days bygone –
Who sung it well and from its strain grew strong!"
On hearing this, his brothers said, as one,
　　That they would heed his wisdom.

WHEN AYMERI, whose face with valour blazed,
Had said farewell and sent his sons away,
He stepped inside his mighty hall of state
And found his wife in such a sorry case
Inside her room, as if she'd swooned away;
Upon a quilt of rich and precious make
She sat alone, lamenting at her fate;
To God above how loudly she bewailed

Her sorry plight and made her sad complaint
And called aloud the blessed Mary's name:
"Ah! Heaven's Queen, most blessed Virgin Maid,
Whom God Himself illumined with His grace,
Light up my mind or I shall go insane!
Alas Narbonne, that you were ever raised!
I wish Greek fire had brought you down in flames
Till not a stone or stick alone remained!
And as for me, I wish I had been slain,
My bosom cleft with sword or dagger's blade,
Than been bereft of my six sons this way."
On saying this, she swooned away again;
Count Aymeri, he held her round the waist
And made her stand, with great distress and strain,
As tenderly he sought to soothe her pain:
"My lovely wife, what purpose can you gain
In grieving so for your good children's sake?
And what will Charles, whose beard is white with age,
On learning of your sorrow, have to say?
And will he judge our sons by your display,
These gallant youths that you and I have raised?
Let France be lit and glitter in their rays!
Each land on earth will bless the day they came!
And do not fret for your fair daughters' fate:
Each one will wed and raise our name and fame –
The least endowed shall win so high a place
As Lady of some wealthy land or state;
The youngest one will fare so well, in faith,
That she will rule the whole of France one day,
And wear the crown as Queen of France the great!"
On hearing this, his wife put by her pain,
    To please the Count her husband.

COUNT AYMERI consoled with all his might
The heavy grief of Hermenjart his wife;
Then, climbing up his tower's tallest height,
He saw Bernart before the other knights,
And from the stones in ringing tones he cried:
"Sons, wait for me by that clear fountain's side!
Do not ride on beyond St Helen's spire!"
Bernart spoke out: "Our father bids us bide!

Our mother has rich gifts to bless us by!"
But Beuvon said, his voice as firm as iron:
"By God, Who fasted for forty days and nights,
And gave to Mary Magdalen new life,
We shouldn't take the smallest coin, but strive
To win our way through hardship and through trial
    To wealth we may rejoice in!"

COUNT AYMERI came down his tower and ordered
His equerries to lead him forth his palfrey;
He mounted up, without one moment's pausing,
And Hermenjart, her mother's heart in mourning,
Bestrode a mule worth twenty marks in coinage;
Before the town they rode and hastened forward
Towards their sons and those of other courtiers
Until they came where all of them had halted
Beside a park for pleasure and enjoyment;
Said Hermenjart: "Bernart, are you so thoughtless?
Will you desert your father in his fortress?
And what of me? Will pity never halt you,
Or will you leave, with heathens on our doorstep,
Who pay no heed to what Lord Jesus taught us?
This year, I fear, shall not run half its portion
Before the Moors have overrun our borders;
They'll come at us from every side and quarter,
And leave us not six inches of our shoreline;
And we ourselves shall be attacked and cornered,
Then stripped and shipped in captives' bonds or slaughtered;
They'll sport with me and slit my nose in torture,
Then sever all my lower lip to taunt me."
On hearing this, Bernart was angered sorely;
He said: "Indeed, you chide and charge me falsely!
In all the days that I have lived before this
Since I was born, I've never felt so joyful
As on this day, in truth I do assure you,
That Aymeri has sent us from his portals;
We'll not return before the Lord rewards us
With what His grace may grant to our good fortune,
And what His hand has planned and readied for us!
But do not fear, dear mother, I implore you,
That we shall let the heathens be so haughty

As to besiege this city and assault you,
Or chase you from the land our father fought for!
I swear by God, Who never fails or falters,
That while your sons have life and strength to call on,
We'll never stray so far from Narbonne's borders
That, should you send a messenger to warn us,
We cannot come at once with ready sword-blades,
     To save you in Narbonne."

WHEN AYMERI heard from his eldest child,
The brave Bernart, of heart and honour high,
That if the Moors attacked their native shire,
Then all his sons would hurry back to fight,
Friends, rest assured it filled him with delight:
"My noble wife," he said and laughed outright,
"Behold our sons! How strong they are! How fine!
How full of cheer, how full of lusty life,
With sword to wield and rapid steed to ride!
When they arrive in France and pledge their lives
To Charlemagne, our liege lord in his might,
He'll soon attach a good sword to their side
And dub them knight for love of me and mine!
And I am sure that any knights more fine
Will nevermore be dubbed and dressed in iron!
Now give them gold and silver if you like,
Four sumpter-loads, as much as you desire!"
Bernart, who won Brabant soon after, smiled,
And spoke his mind to Beuvon by his side:
"The old man still insults us in his pride,
Presenting us with wealth that he's acquired!
By all the faith I owe Lord Jesus Christ,
We'll leave with naught, if you are of my mind;
For I am sure, before this year is by,
That at the court our William will rise
To bear the flag of royal France in fights,
And govern lands, exalting all our line,
With tributes raised from all the German tribes:
     Soon all our clan will cheer him!"

"FAIR HERMENJART," says Aymeri her husband,
"Let be this bitter grief that you indulge in!

Behold your sons, all full of life and courage,
With arms of steel and steeds so full of running,
And let them strive, as I did as a youngster!
By St Denis, I swear not one among them
Shall ever have a holding in my country!"
"My lord," she said, "I bow before your judgement;
God guide them all, Who died for all and suffered."
The fair Countess turned back, her tears still running,
And told her seneschal, who was Anfelis:
"Load up for me four sturdy, noble sumpters,
With silver, gold and mantles vair of colour,
And send these mules to follow my six sons there;
For all the gold in Paris I'll not suffer
My sons to bide in foreign lands with nothing."
And he replied: "Your wish shall be my comfort;
So help me God, in Heaven's hall above us,
I would be glad to pack and stack six others,
　　To serve you and your sons."

SAID AYMERI: "Good Lady, fair and gentle,
In Jesu's name, I swear you act in error
By sending wealth to help our sons, whose temper
Would fight for it; it isn't right, I tell you,
For each one has a nimble steed to help him
And noble robes and armaments a-plenty!
They'll all proceed with joyful speed and merry
As far as Rome, to gain the Pope's own blessing;
Then, when they ride inside sweet France together,
There is no lord who will not make them welcome
And willingly provide them food and shelter;
But by the Saint whom sinners seek in penance,
I swear that ere this evening comes, I'll test them
To see if they are strong of mind and mettle;
If they accept your goods, by God in Heaven,
Then I shall say, whoever may contest it,
That they are all some braggart's sons or beggar's,
Who in your bed has slipped by trick and slept there!
But if at once they utterly reject them
With all their strength, their anger and displeasure,
And beat the men in whose good hands you send them,
Then I will swear, by Jesus Christ in Heaven,

That it is I, Count Aymeri, who bred them,
The Narbonne knight, of fearful might and temper!
For they will show that in their soul and senses
   They're scions of my clan! "

SAID HERMENJART of noble mind and soul:
"Lord Aymeri, whoever tells me 'no',
So help me God, I still believe you show
A foolish pride and recklessness to hope
That you can tell your gallant sons to go
To France itself, which is a rich abode,
When they themselves take nothing of their own;
For when each day the vespers-bell has tolled
And they must seek for lodgings on the road,
They'll never have one coin to pay their host;
And he will come with all his hostel-folk
To sell them half of all the goods they own,
And all the food provisioned in his home,
Supposing them as rich as they are bold!
By Mary's Son, if they have naught to show
The following day, when they must pay and go,
They will awake each time to greater woe!
For they will pay in Syrian steeds and robes
Three times the debt that ever yet they owed!
And when, at last, in France they all approach
King Charlemagne, whose beard is white as snow,
They'll not have left one penny or one cloak!
His wealthy lords will stand around his throne
And all our sons will seem like country dolts!
By God above, our Everlasting Hope,
I could not bear, for all of Russia's gold,
That mocking tales about them should be told!"
On saying this, the Lady, nothing loath,
Called Anfelis and said in ringing tones:
"Make haste to do as I have told you so!"
The seneschal was neither slack nor slow,
But hastened to the hall and went below,
Where all the wealth of old Narbonne was stowed;
He filled a sack with finest, purest gold,
And on a mule he packed the heavy load;
Then on three more Pavian silk and robes
   Were stacked up high together.

THE SENESCHAL was brave and noble-blooded;
He stacked a mule and packed three other sumpters
With cloths of gold and goblets richly-studded;
Then, calling forth two brave and noble youngsters –
Foucon was one, and Renier was the other –
He bade them take this booty to the brothers;
Hernaut the Red was first to see them coming
And said aloud: " My brothers, see this couple
Sent after us on Aymeri's instruction!
Like shepherds first he sends us forth with nothing
And then, at once, he follows us with money!"
Said Jocerain, a noble squire among them:
"May God the Lord of Justice, bless your mother!
We'll surely need these noble sumpters' luggage,
To shoe our steeds and to provide enough of
Good wine to drink and food to fill our stomachs,
Good, salted fish and fattened ducks and plovers!"
Hernaut heard this and fearsomely he thundered:
"By Jesus Christ, our Saviour and our Comfort,
We'll never keep two coins of all this money,
But send it back to Narbonne's hall abruptly
And give those squires who brought it here a drubbing!"
Said William: "We shall accept your judgement
And willingly obey your word and summons;
For Aymeri himself said you should govern
As seneschal in France, dispensing justice!
From this time on commit yourself with courage
　　To act with sense and wit!"

WHEN HERNAUT SAW the manner and the smile
His brother showed when making this reply,
Then he was sure he meant it as a gibe;
He swore to God, Who made the cloudy sky,
That he would do a deed before that night
Which would be known to people far and wide,
To rich and poor, to high and low alike;
The sumpters came, each beaten from behind
By scourges held by both of those young squires,
Who used them well, in haste to reach the knights;
Foucon was first and with a burst arrived
Before them all and hailed them fair and fine:

"May God above, Who in His love supplied
Eternal Life through His Son Jesus Christ,
Protect you all, and let your valour thrive!
Fair Hermenjart, your mother sweet and kind,
Has sent you this in her distress of mind;
Her grief is such that she despairs of life,
But sends you this to help you in your plight;
No street or town will fail to let you thrive
When you ride up so wealthily supplied,
    In any foreign country."

HERNAUT THE RED was first to move and speak:
"Foucon, my friend, attend to me," said he:
"By St Clément, we brothers have agreed
That Aymeri shall not make boast that we
Have won the wealth that we shall win in brief
Through his own wealth that you have brought us here;
So turn around these sumpter-mules you lead
And take them back with all dispatch and speed!
Return this wealth at once to Aymeri!"
The lad replied: "My lord, this cannot be!
By God above, we dare not but succeed!
If we do not, fair Hermenjart will seethe
With hate for us and make us feel her grief!"
On hearing this, Hernaut was angered deep;
He held a rod and swung it high and steep
Then struck Foucon so fiercely on the cheek
He knocked him flat and flung him at his feet,
As crimson blood flowed freely on the field;
Hernaut looked on and shouted in his ear:
"You harlot's son, do you hold me so cheap
That you should dare to baulk or challenge *me*?
By Jesus Christ, Who never fails our need,
I swear to you that but for our good Creed
I'd beat you more than any bear or beast!"
On hearing this, Foucon regained his feet
And took to flight with all his might and means,
And all the while he said between his teeth:
"Good riddance, then! The Devil take you, fiend!"
The brothers laughed to see the youngster leave;
Said William: "Hernaut was born to lead!

Beware henceforth who dares to disagree!
The seneschal we have among us here
   Knows how to mete out justice!"

FOUCON RETURNED in anger and distress,
And with those mules who well had earned their rest!
If you had been and seen in Narbonne then,
As Aymeri came up to him and said:
"So where's the wealth which you transported hence?
Don't tell me lies – did sons of mine relent?"
The lad replied: "My lord, that's foolishness!
They never kept two pennies for themselves;
I curse the hour you sent me on that quest –
Hernaut went close to beating me to death!
Behold the blood and bruises on my head!"
On hearing this, the Count was most content;
He laughed aloud, then saw his wife and went
To throw his arms in joy around her neck;
He kissed her thrice with all the joy he felt:
"My dear," he said, "now I know very well
That six of them are sons that I have bred!
   They'll never shame our family!"

4 How Aymeri's sons were received in Vauguyon

MY FRIENDS, IT'S TOLD in histories of old,
And in the *gestes* the best of them all show
That of the sons of Aymeri the bold,
The wildest one whom people feared the most,
The proudest and the loudest was Hernaut;
He struck Foucon and his companion both,
And in his rage sent back with angry oaths
The mighty wealth his mother had bestowed
In coin and silk, in mangons and rich stones;
Hernaut refused the smallest grain or groat;
And when his lord, Count Aymeri, was told,
The brave man laughed and knew him for his own;
And so they left and journeyed down the road
Until they reached the town called Vauguyon
And entered through its gate called Porte Milon;

They took a room within the well built home
Of Simon, a rich citizen and host;
Throughout his house the marble flooring glowed
And pillars gleamed all round with polished stone;
His cellar's stock was worth a wealth of gold –
And there they sat, the brothers, in a row,
Till Hernaut stood, the rod still in his hold!
How strong he was, and how his visage glowed!
His hair was long and bright-red to the bone –
No man resembled Aymeri as close!
He rose to speak and said: "Lords, let me know
What we should eat – the dinner-bell has tolled!"
Said William: "We look to you, Hernaut!
You hold the rod! You are the seneschal!
We never would usurp your royal role!"
Hernaut replied "God willing, no, you won't!"
He called across to Simon, their good host,
And said: "Good man, attend what I propose:
Bring wine and fish, and bring us bread and bowls
Of meat to eat, both salted, fresh and smoked,
And poultry too, if some is to be sold;
We'll pay the bill, as God's our help and hope,
When morning comes and we prepare to go."
The worthy host stepped out of his fine home
And went to stalls which traded all they chose;
He bought so much it made a wondrous load
Which thirty boys brought back with them on poles;
Young William spoke up as they approached:
"By all the Saints, our Hernaut's very bold –
Our father's like in body and in soul!
His tastes are grand and we don't have a groat!
I must speak up, by good St Simon's bones."
He grasped the sleeve of Hernaut's fur-trimmed robe
And said these words, in worthy, well-bred tones:
"Hernaut, my friend, was it still wise or no
To beat those squires who brought us goods and gold,
And send them home with nothing left to show?
Your purse has spent ten pounds this night alone!
So tell me, friend, just how do you propose
To pay for this which we already owe?
When morning comes, fine brother, I suppose

That you will say, just as we mount to go:
'We give our word as bond to pay this loan!'"
Hernaut heard this, his face like burning coals,
And raised his rod to punish this reproach –
But didn't dare, for William was bold!
"So help me God," he moaned aloud and groaned,
"The very day we set out on our own,
No sooner stopped, we lose all heart and hope!
Be strong in Faith, my brothers, for I know
That we shall gain the wealth that God bestows."
When this was said, they filled their plates and bowls
With fish and bread until they overflowed;
And no young man or maid in Vauguyon
Who wanted food, was left to starve alone;
A man went off to see Sir Gui, who owned
All Vauguyon, to say its walls enclosed
Six youths whose purse out-spent the Emperor's own,
When from St James he stayed there, going home!
On hearing this, Sir Gui left his abode
And took with him his seneschal Milon,
And closest friends, called Andrew and Othon;
They mounted mules, beside the mounting-stones,
And, singing songs, they rode to Simon's home,
     Where each man rose to greet them.

LORD GUI OF VAUGUYON strode in the dwelling
And they all rose to greet him as he entered;
They said their names and so great was his pleasure
He hugged them close and kissed them all in friendship:
"Young men," he said, "God bless the hour that bred you!
God bless the hour that I have found and met you,
And that you rode for my abode together!
But in one way you have behaved in error:
You never came to me when seeking shelter!
It would have been more friendly and much better
If you had sent a messenger to tell me!
You could have shared my hall and all with pleasure:
My men and means stand ready still to help you,
For Aymeri's sake, of noble strength and temper,
The best of men in all the Christian Empire,
Whom I do love above all men and cherish!

He dubbed me knight and I shall not forget it:
My father died and then, when he was buried,
I was besieged by my own blood and brethren,
Who tried to seize the very lands he left me;
But when your lord was told of their intention,
With all his knights he rode here to my rescue;
Through his prowess and noble-hearted efforts
My land was freed from what their greed had threatened;
I never lost one city to their envy,
Nor any fort, nor silver pound or penny;
He pitied me, and he was so relentless
That soon he forced the fiercest to respect me!
My fighting force, since then, has not been less than
The thousand knights he left here to protect me;
So I thank God, the mighty King of Heaven,
That all his sons have journeyed here together!
Now I insist that you become my guests here;
Within my walls your every wish I'll welcome,
And have your needs before my own attended;
My goods and wealth are here to serve your pleasure;
To your desires my own shall rank as second."
Said William: "In truth, you are most generous;
In Jesu's name and in our own we bless you;
But you should know, and we are bound to tell you,
That just before we left Narbonne together,
Brave Aymeri was strict in his direction:
Young Aimer here must ride for Spain directly,
While Beuvon seeks a Gascon fief and wedding!
We others go to dwell among the Frenchmen,
In Paris at the court of Charles the Emperor;
You know that if we showed ourselves so headstrong
As to ignore our father's strict direction,
　　We'd all be more than mad!"

SAID GUI OF VAUGUYON: "It would be wise,
I'll not deny, to do as he desires!
You should obey, and none would be surprised,
For there is no more noble prince alive
Than Aymeri, and none more feared or fine;
For love of God, Who judges all our lives,
How fares the Count, do not conceal or lie,

And Hermenjart, his loved and lovely wife?
I am amazed, this much I can't deny,
That he or she has let you leave their side!"
"Sir Gui, my lord," the brave Bernart replied,
"So help me God, Who judges wrong and right,
The city wept when we began to ride;
Our mother dear, the Countess fierce of eye,
Was filled with grief that cannot be described;
But none of this would change our father's mind
To let us stay within our native clime;
He urged us more to leave his shore and shire
And seck out fame and fortune far and wide!
We left today, and with unslackened stride,
Till this good host received us for tonight,
For we are worn and weary from our ride
And soon must sleep until the morning light."
Sir Gui replied: "This cannot be denied!
God bless you all through His son Jesus Christ;
I shall return as soon as dawn arrives."
His set his foot upon his stirrups' iron
To mount his steed, the other three alike,
And to his hall they all of them retired;
And all our youths, so worthy to be prized,
Went straight to bed and slept throughout the night;
When all awoke they sought a church nearby
Where Renier said a Mass for them and signed;
When this was done, not wasting any time,
They ate the meal their worthy host supplied,
Where there was much of anything they liked;
When each had had whatever he required,
Beuvon stood up, his face with zeal alight,
And saw his brothers, around him on all sides,
And said: "My lords, I must be gone, for I
Must ride at once for Gascony the wide,
To greet King Yon and serve with him a while!
Hernaut, fine lord, now pay our host his price,
For he has seen our needs well satisfied
And done for us whatever we desired."
But to himself he softly said and sighed:
"My God, with what? Must we now leave behind
The robes we wear and horses that we ride?
　　We must, without God's favour."

"HERNAUT, FINE LORD," said Beuvon, wise of speech,
"Do not forget to pay our host his fee
In recompense for what we have received."
On hearing this, Hernaut was vexed indeed;
But then, at once, the door swung wide and Gui,
That noble count, strode in and with good cheer
He cried aloud: "My lords, how are you each?"
Bernart replied: "My lord, we're well indeed
And well prepared to journey forth and leave,
When we have paid good Simon for our keep;
He's served us all with generous esteem."
"My friends," said Gui, "no more of payment, please,
For you'll not pay two pennies while you're here;
Though you might owe one hundred marks apiece,
I'd pay it all, and more, most willingly;
Because he's served you nobly, I decree
All Simon's lands of future taxes free;
Nor shall he pay two broken eggs to me
For any land or field he holds in lease."
On hearing this, the host fell at his feet
And cried aloud: "Much thanks, my lord and liege!"
All saddled up, they led the brothers' steeds
Before the door to mount them at their ease;
To Jesu's care the host commended each,
And Gui the count rode with them down the street;
Before the town they halted when they reached
The highway road, where Beuvon made to speak:
"My brothers, lords, attend a while to me!
This lengthy road we see before us leads
Direct to France, where you must all proceed,
While I myself must ride to Gascony;
For Jesu's sake, show wisdom in your zeal!
Let none of you be brutal to the weak,
Nor arrogant nor open to deceit;
Accept no bribes to change your mind or cheat,
Nor rob the poor of what is theirs to keep;
If you must fight against the Pagan breed,
Then show your pride and not one inch of fear,
And you will be both dreaded by those fiends
And loved by God and all our Christian peers."
He blessed them all and wished them all Godspeed,

Then with a kiss and an embrace for each,
  For Gascony he galloped.

5. How young Beuvon fared in Gascony

YOUNG BEUVON TURNED his steed without delay;
He wished them all Godspeed and Jesu's aid,
Then kissed them all and galloped on his way;
Sir Gui the count, whose love for each was great,
Sent twenty youths with Beuvon, whom he gave
Two sumpter-mules with gold and silver lain;
And so he left, with every speed and haste,
And came at length to Gascony's domains;
Thank God above, it proved his lucky day,
For Yon the king was journeying the same –
Just riding back from raiding land in Spain,
Where he had sacked a town and made it pay
In gold and silver, and taken in the raid
A gang of Moors his soldiers led in chains;
On seeing this, young Beuvon turned his reins
Towards a knight in charge of this parade;
He showed him Yon, at which the youngster made
His way across and greeted him with grace:
"May God, Who made the world, and then of clay
Made Adam and made Eve and all their race,
And made the sun and moon to light their way,
Bless mighty Yon to whom I've come in faith."
On hearing this, Yon asked him for his name,
And whence he'd come and what his quest entailed;
The youth replied: "I'll never hide the same,
For I'm a son of Hermenjart, who says
My father is Count Aymeri the brave!
Of seven sons, the youngest one remains
Within Narbonne; the rest he's sent away:
Garin has gone to rich Pavia's state,
While Aimer rides to reach the wilds of Spain;
The other three he's sent to Charlemagne,
And me to you in Gascony the great;
Now I would know, if you are pleased to say,
If I may love and serve you with my blade."

King Yon replied, a smile upon his face,
That this would need some counsel and debate;
But when they heard, his men said straightaway
To keep Beuvon, for all their honour's sake;
He could employ no better man, they claimed,
To fight his wars and captain his campaigns,
He had no son – what better one to take
His daughter's hand and rule his land one day?
King Yon replied: "Your counsel shall prevail."
On hearing this, in gratitude and grace,
Young Beuvon kissed the monarch's feet, in praise
    For such a mighty honour.

KING YON OBSERVED the sturdy youth up close,
Then spoke to him in noble, friendly tones,
Inquiring first of Aymeri the bold;
Beuvon replied, whose face with valour glowed:
"There's none so brave from here to Barcelone
As Aymeri; and no man that I know,
From Port Bayonne to Tarragona's coast,
Would dare to pass the borders of his home
And pose a threat to what my father owns;
His noble grace deserves a kingdom's throne;
The great prowess which fills his heart and soul
Shall not be matched, though men search high and low;
On faithful men his bounty flows the most;
One day alone my father will bestow
    More than their yearly earnings."

"MY NOBLE LORD, I tell you nothing false,"
Said young Beuvon, whose face with valour stormed:
"My father is a nobler, finer lord
Than I have said or ever could report."
On hearing this, King Yon was filled with joy;
When this was said, once more they journeyed forth;
Across old fields and country lanes of yore
They galloped, side by side, till in due course
They reached Bordeaux as night began to fall;
They passed the gates, not drawing rein at all,
Until they reached its noble fort and court;
Upon the stones King Yon dismounted horse,

Then climbed the steps to his well-painted hall;
Young Beuvon's squires sought lodgings near the court,
And he himself, whose face with valour stormed,
Showed great largesse so they should want for naught;
And from the hall they sent supplies galore
Of anything they lacked or asked them for;
At Yon's command this service was performed,
And bread and meat and claret-wine were brought
To where they lodged, and laid upon the board!
And young Beuvon enjoyed it, like a lord,
As did they all who'd come with him by choice –
They thought no more of when they once were poor!
The following day, as soon as day had dawned,
Beuvon got dressed with no delay at all
And climbed the steps to Yon's most noble hall
With all the youths Gui'd given him before;
He saw the king and greeted him with warmth;
Yon raised his head and said with ringing voice:
"Beuvon, fine youth, of this you may be sure:
I hold you dear and cherish you the more
For Aymeri's sake, that wise and gallant lord
Whose great prowess I personally saw:
When Charlemagne first saw Narbonne and called
On all his lords to win it with their swords,
Not one of them responded to his call;
But Aymeri, your father, did with joy!
He fought his way inside it with great force
And ever since has kept it from the Moors,
Not yielding up one inch to their assaults;
I was but young when we attacked those walls,
And now I'm old and all my hair is hoar!
I have a child whose beauty passes all:
She shall be yours, with all my fiefs and forts,
If Charlemagne does not oppose my choice;
I'll go to him, for I am summoned forth
At Pentecost this summer to his court;
And you shall too, in rich array adorned."
On hearing this, young Beuvon thanked him more:
"Most willingly and gratefully, my lord,
I'll wed and love this fair Princess of yours,
     If she herself will have me!"

"MY NOBLE LORD," Beuvon the youth replied,
"May God above, Who never fails or lies,
Bless all you've said and all you have in mind;
But there's one thing that cannot be denied,
And Aymeri himself told us outside
Our city walls, when we were set to ride:
That none of us should ever take a bride
Until we knew that she herself complied;
So, by your leave, I'll speak with her a while."
"Most willingly," the noble king replied;
He called Davee, his seneschal, aside
And said: "Bring here my loved and lovely child!"
"Most willingly, my lord," the man replied;
He went at once, and as he opened wide
Her chamber door, he saw her there and cried:
"My fair princess, arouse yourself and rise!
Your father bids, who in his hall abides,
That you should come to meet a gallant squire
They call Beuvon, whom Aymeri has sired;
I never saw a youth so fair or fine!
They've talked of you and now the king desires
That this young lord and you be man and wife,
To rule his land together when he dies."
On hearing this, she filled with great delight:
"Ah God, indeed!" the lovely maid replied,
"Count Aymeri, whose face with valour shines!
If his own son were truly to be mine,
And by the grace of our Lord Jesus Christ
A son and heir were born to us in time,
    How brave would be his breeding!"

THE LOVELY MAID prepared herself to go;
She put on first a robe of woven gold
And then a cape, a costly silken cloak;
Three noble maids attended to her clothes;
If you had seen how radiantly she glowed!
She saw Beuvon and, as she came up close,
He said to her, with loving voice and low:
"Fair maiden, hear what I would have you know;
I am Beuvon; Narbonne has been my home;
I am a son of Aymeri, more bold

Than any man the world has ever known!
Your father Yon, who truly loves you so,
Has talked with me at length upon our road,
And wishes now that we should plight our troth
To marry soon in Christian love, and hope
Of God's esteem, Who governs all below;
I ask you now, while we are both alone,
To tell me if you share his wish or no,
Lest I should give, or take in turn, reproach,
And other folk behind our backs should joke
At our expense and blame or shame us both."
"Good sir," she said, "by all the faith I owe
To God on High, I'll gladly plight my troth;
If we are wed in Christian faith and hope,
I'll love you well with all my heart and soul,
   As liege lord and as husband."

THE KING STOOD UP, so all could hear, and hailed
His fair princess, on seeing her again:
"My lovely child, attend to what I say!
See here Beuvon, a gallant youth and brave,
Who is a son of Aymeri the famed!
If you agree, I'd have you wed and make
This man the heir to all of my estates."
"My lord," she said, "in our Redeemer's name,
I'll wed this man – no other's hand I crave!
I swear to you, unless this match is made,
I'll go unwed until my dying day
At St Amand's, where I shall take the veil!"
"So help me God," the worthy Yon exclaimed,
"This wedding-day should happen soon, I'd say!"
As all looked on, Beuvon gave straightaway
His solemn word, and so did she the same;
Throughout the court what joy and gladness reigned!
The maid herself went back with every haste
Inside her room and carried forth a blade
Called Weepingblood, or so the song maintains;
She hailed Beuvon and said, with laughing face:
"I give to you this sword, and with it pray
That God will give you courage all your days
And victories against the heathen race!"

He took the blade, his heart with joy aflame,
  And thanked the maiden for it.

HOW GLAD THE COURT, how full of happy cheer,
For Beuvon's sake, whose face with valour gleamed,
And for the pledge their princess had received;
The maid herself was very wise indeed,
As at his side she made this loving plea:
"My noble lord, in Jesu's name, I hear
That you must leave for noble France the sweet
In two weeks' time, when my dear father leaves!
For love of God, show nobly there and treat
With grace and love, with honour and esteem,
King Charles's knights, both bachelors and Peers;
I shall ensure some seven sumpter-beasts
Are packed for you with gold and silver each."
The youth replied: "My princess, never fear!
So help me God, Who governs all our deeds,
You'll never hear a bad report of me!"
On hearing this, the slender maid was pleased
And kissed him thrice, each time most tenderly;
The courtly maid then turned away to reach
  Once more her vaulted chamber.

THE FAITHFUL MAID was very fair and wise;
Within her room, as soon as she arrived,
She went and called her chamberlain aside:
"My loyal friend, hear what I have in mind;
You too shall go to noble France beside
My lord Beuvon, whose face with valour shines;
Load seven mules with gold and silver high
For you to lead, and as your party rides,
Let your largesse be shown on every side
And shared among the old and young alike!
Let Beuvon's name be carried far and wide,
So I may hear and others be apprised
Of what good cheer the Gascon court provides!"
He said: "My dear, I'll do as you desire;
By all the faith I've borne you all your life,
If God will bless our way and let us thrive,
No man shall seek our aid and be denied,

Nor shall our door be closed to low or high;
Both rich and poor may take from our supplies
   Whatever wealth they wish for!"

6. *How young Garin fared in Pavia*

THE SENESCHAL made no delay or pause
But straightaway did everything and all
The fair princess advised him that he ought;
He saddled mules with gold and silver coins
And bowls untold and silken cloths galore;
King Yon himself was keen to journey forth
And readied all to visit Charles's court;
He left Bordeaux with many knights and lords
And young Beuvon, whose face with valour stormed;
The princess blew a kiss as he rode forth,
Commending him to God, our loving Lord;
They reached the port before midday to board
The boats which took them over the Gironde;
When all their craft had reached the other shore
They disembarked and each remounted horse,
Then spurred away, and took the highway north;
I'll leave them there, a while, and tell you more
Of wise Bernart and all those other four –
Young William and Hernaut, strong and sure,
And young Aimer and Garin, wise in thought;
The good Sir Gui, whose name you've heard before,
Had led the five towards his mighty fort
And brought them wealth from his well-hidden hoard;
Then Garin sought his leave to journey forth;
He hailed the rest and said, in ringing voice:
"My noble lords, I'll never hide my thoughts;
I must depart, with your goodwill's accord,
And ride for rich Pavia's royal court,
As Aymeri commanded in his hall."
His brothers said: "Your words are nothing false,"
And loaded up one sumpter with the stores
Supplied to all by Gui of Vauguyon;
So Garin left, not waiting any more;
He took with him some twenty youths, who all,

As they farewelled their brothers in the force,
Commended each to God Almighty's ward;
Then Garin's band went bounding on their course!
From break of dawn each day they journeyed forth
To Great St Bernard's Pass, and thence towards
Pavia town and passed within its walls;
They lodged inside a wealthy merchant's hall,
Where Garin soon addressed his seneschal:
"Young Geoffrey, friend, attend upon my thoughts!
It's Friday now and we have eaten naught!
Procure us food, enough to feed us all,
Some good-sized fish, if any can be bought
Within this town, whatever price is sought."
"My lord," he said, "I shall do, rest assured;
You'll have a fish, so help me God the Lord,
If one exists within this town at all
Which can be bought for any cost in coin!"
Their host was kind and took him to the stall
Where soon they found a huge one, which is called
A sturgeon-fish on coasts where such is caught;
Three days ago this one was brined and brought;
The king's own seneschal four times before
Had priced the fish and prayed the price might fall!
A Lombard man, a mean and haggling sort,
He hadn't bought the sturgeon to that point;
One Guirré was the noble Narbonne lord
Whom Geoffrey, Garin's seneschal, employed
To go with him and help him at the stalls;
The fishmonger beheld them and was sure
That neither man had been brought up or born
In Lombardy, nor locally at all,
And so he raised his price to one half more!
Good Geoffrey asked: "What's this fish selling for?"
"For thirty sous, so please you, my good lord;
The fish is fresh, of this you can be sure –
They brought it here this morning from the port."
Good Geoffrey said: "God bless me! Thank the Lord!
It's worth the price! We'll buy and bear it forth!"
Inside his purse he put his hand to draw
A fist of coins, some forty sous or more:
"My friend," he said, "count out these copper coins,

While I go back to where my master boards;
I cannot wait until you count them all –
If they fall short, I'll willingly pay more,
Until you have the asking price you sought;
If there are more, then gladly keep them all –
I'll not take back what I have said is yours."
"Much thanks, my friend," the man said, overjoyed:
"It's clear to see that you are nobly born;
I've never done such noble trade before!
I bless the hour that brought you here, my lord!"
They raised the fish upon a mule and walked
With happy hearts towards their lodging-hall;
While this was done, a man went to report
Their purchase to the king's own seneschal:
"My lord," he said, "there's wickedness abroad!
Within our town a brazen youth has waltzed
And commandeered that sturgeon at the stall!
He paid the price they'd raised it to, and more!
King Boniface will suffer now and all
His band of knights who dine with him at court:
There's no more fish within Pavia's walls!"
On hearing this, the steward was appalled:
"My friend," he said, "we can't wait any more;
Come take me now to where these bullies board:
They shall not keep that sturgeon, by the Lord!"
And so the man led off the seneschal
Towards the house, then straight inside its door!
They'd placed the fish upon a sturdy form
And gutted it when they had scaled it all
And cleft the head and tail and cast them forth;
The seneschal and his companion stormed
Inside the room where young Garin and all
His men were lodged, and in a haughty voice
The marshal said: "This fish cannot be yours!
It must be borne to Boniface's court,
To feed the men now gathered in his hall;
A curse on him who stole it from its stall!"
"I *bought* that fish!" cried Geoffrey in retort,
"And you weren't there, by God, as I recall,
When from my purse I paid the man in coin!
If you insist on taking this, the fault

And foul offence, without a doubt, are yours!"
Despite these words the local man still hauled
The fish upon his back to bear it forth;
On seeing this, good Geoffrey filled with scorn:
He grasped the rogue with all his rage and forced
His head so hard against a stone support
That he was stunned and, starry-eyed, stopped short!
The seneschal was filled with haughty gall,
Because he was the king's own seneschal;
He raised his fist, both fat it was and broad,
And in revenge struck Geoffrey on the jaw
So viciously he stunned him even more!
Garin saw this and his hot temper boiled:
"Ah God," he cried, "I'll stand for this no more;
What? Shall I watch my men struck down and fall?
I'll never win a foreign shire or shore
If they are killed and I myself do naught!"
He saw the fire, which at that moment roared,
And seized a brand and raised it like a torch,
Then swung it round and flung it with such force
Against the head of that proud seneschal,
It spun him round and flung him on the floor;
A second blow soon matched the one before,
And almost knocked his brains out where he sprawled;
When he had thwacked and smacked the rogue some more,
They seized his hair and dragged him out the door
And in the mud they cast and kicked him sore:
"You went too far," the noble Garin roared,
"To strike my man without the slightest cause!
This fish has cost much more now than you thought!
You've paid the price for something never bought,
And something that you'll never taste, what's more!
By all the faith I owe to God the Lord,
No Lombard lips shall lick this fish's sauce,
Unless they may by my own say and choice."
"For love of God, my lord," the host implored,
"Pavia's king is proud and fierce of thought;
Without a blink he'll throw me out of all
I ever had and throw you in his vault!"
Young Garin said: "My friend, do not be fraught!
I'll see him soon and when we two have talked,

You will not lose whatever dues are yours!
  So do not be down-hearted!"

THE SENESCHAL whom Garin thus had struck,
Was racked with pain but struggled from the mud
And went to see King Boniface at once;
The king looked up and knew him well enough;
He asked him: "Have you suffered some bad luck?"
"I have indeed, my lord, and more than some!
For I have met, I know not whence he comes,
A foreign rogue as strong as he is rough;
He stole from me your Friday fish and struck
Me with a stick and hurled me in the muck;
Without redress, I'll die of this affront
And nevermore support you as I've done."
On hearing this, the king was angered much;
His Lombard knights came round him in a crush,
Their hauberks wide but very short in front;
They grasped an axe or cutting sword and rushed
To long-maned steeds, and mounting swiftly up,
They rode away to Garin's rooms at once;
And he was there to greet them fair enough,
In amber clothes most richly sewn and cut!
King Boniface knew not his sister's son,
For he'd not seen the lad since he was young,
And since that time he had indeed grown up!
Garin looked up and hailed him nobly thus:
"My worthy lord, I welcome you with love."
The king replied: "Upon my side there's none!
You have attacked my royal seneschal
And stolen fish which wasn't yours to touch!
No grace you show will stop you being hung,
Nor will I take your gage for trial by blood!"
"No, lord, you won't – for I'll not offer one,
While I've a sword whose blade is far from blunt,
And twenty men whose bravery I trust,
Who've come with me and left the land we love!
Your Lombard lords will never make us run,
They're all too fat and slack – just look at them!
If all of them came at me, all at once,
I wouldn't fear their strength the smallest crumb!

Their hearts are weak, their boasting all a bluff!
By all the faith I owe Lord God above,
If one of them, however old or young,
Should dare to lay a hand on one of us,
I'll strike his head straight off his wretched trunk
With my own sword, whose blade is never blunt!"
On hearing this, the Lombards held their tongue,
Their boldest one not daring then to budge;
Each said to each: "What madness we've begun!
Behold this lord! How strong he is! He must
Be sent from Hell by fell Beelzebub,
To fetch his price out of our seneschal!
Well, so be it! We'll not contest the sum!
The buyer must beware of bargains struck!
We'll not speak out against so fierce a dun,
Nor take up arms for some supposed affront!
For, truthfully, the custom always was,
And known to be by each and everyone,
That any soul who has sufficient funds
May purchase goods without rebuff or snub;
And when they pay for something, they may trust
It cannot be reclaimed by anyone!
Our seneschal must surely have been drunk;
Though he has met a little with ill luck,
  We knights shall not avenge him."

IN FEARSOME MOOD Garin the youth replied:
"Lombardians, by God, you are too kind!
How dare you come to challenge me and mine?
Such chivalry is not the skill you ply,
But selling goods or lending money, while
Your backs are watched by all your noble squires!
My kith and kin don't drag or lag behind,
But bear the flag most gallantly for Christ
In Spanish lands against the Moorish tribes."
Said Boniface: "You set your banner high!
You seem to me to be a reckless squire
Who's come in here with others, running wild!
For one of you, there's fifty score of mine!"
Garin replied: "I couldn't care a mite,
For I myself have seen so many times

One hawk put thirty partridges to flight!"
"Who are you, man," the noble monarch cried,
"With such a skill to argue and to skite?
Are you some fool come here in hope of hire?
I need to know, without deceit or lies,
What realm you've left and where your party rides."
Garin replied: "I never meant to hide:
I am a son of Aymeri, and child
Of Hermenjart, his fair Pavian bride,
The daughter of King Didier the wise!
In truth, you are my uncle, and I defy
Another man to boast a finer line!"
"Thank God above!" the king said with a sigh:
"Be vexed no more, my nephew fair and fine!
Embrace me now, in peace and friendship's sign."
"With all my heart," Garin replied and smiled;
And when they kissed, all Boniface's knights
　　　Were filled with great rejoicing.

7. How the other four fared on the road to Paris

WHEN GARIN MADE his peace with Boniface,
The seneschal made peace with him the same,
Then told the host that most of them would stay;
They asked for water to wash their hands and face,
Then all sat down at tables low and raised;
And, friends, the dish they wished them first to taste
Was that great fish, which caused such row and rage,
Well-served upon Narbonne and Lombard plates!
Their feasting done, the king left straightaway
With happy heart to reach his hall of state;
Garin remained and showed each day such grace
That soon the king was lavish in his praise,
Awarding him, in less than thirty days,
His pick of land from all in his domains;
Now I shall tell of brave Bernart again:
He rode with just three brothers now, whose names
Were William, who suffered hence such pain,
And Hernaut called 'The Red', so quick to rage,
And young Aimer, whose every thought was aimed

At Pagan death in service of the Faith,
Each time he drew his bright Viana blade;
They took their leave of good Sir Gui the brave,
Who loaded up four sumpters bred in Spain
With silver, gold, and Grecian silk brocades,
And lovely robes and weapons richly made;
He rode with them for two or three leagues' space,
Then kissed them twice and watched them ride away;
They turned their reins and, as they did, he prayed
Lord God above to bless and keep them safe,
    Then turned back to his castle.

SIR GUI OF VAUGUYON turned round to leave,
Farewelling all and wishing them Godspeed –
And forth they rode, with bold and gallant zeal,
Until Hernaut looked down upon a heath
And saw a bishop upon the road beneath,
Who led with him some thirty clerks and priests;
Red-haired Hernaut rode straight towards all these
And by the reins pulled up the bishop's steed
And asked of him: "Where are you taking these?
Who are you all? Confess without deceit!"
"Fair brother, friend," the bishop made to speak,
"So help me God, Who made the air we breathe,
I am a bishop; my name is Amauri;
Know well and true I hold the church and see
Of Saint-Viel, beloved of the Creed;
The King holds court, the richest ever seen,
Which I'd attend with these good canons here!
I head for, and, God willing, we shall reach
Auvergne first, and Berry, then we'll need
To journey on for four more days to reach
King Charles's land, where this grand court's convened."
Hernaut replied: "What luck for all, indeed,
For we're a score of noble youths who seek
King Charles as well, the lord of Saint-Denis;
But we have lost our way, I fear, for we
Were neither born nor bred in this land here;
I charge you now to take the road that leads
The quickest way to where we all would be!"
"My gallant friend," the bishop said in pique,

"By all my faith I tell you honestly
That Cluny's Abbot has such dislike for me
That I don't dare go near his monastery
Or journey through his borderlands or fields
For all Ponthieu, which is a wealthy fief!
But one thing, son, I'll tell you without fear:
I take you for a foolish rogue to seize
My reins like this and check me with such cheek!
You have deserved to lose your hand indeed!"
On hearing this, Hernaut was more than peeved!
"By God," he cried, "in Whom bides no deceit,
"You'll rue your slight before this night is here!"
He raised his rod, a stout and solid piece,
And would have struck the bishop from his seat,
Had William not seized his arm and squeezed!
He said to him: "What are you doing, fiend?
Have you become the Lord God's enemy,
That you would strike a bishop of His Creed?"
Hernaut replied: "He's earned it with his speech!
He wouldn't ride the way that I'd decreed!
Don't you recall our father Aymeri
When bidding us to leave, appointing me
As seneschal-elect of France the sweet?
This vassal here mocked my authority,
And disobeyed my order out of fear!"
The bishop heard and answered, most relieved:
"Fair brother, friend, by God the ever-near,
Since Aymeri himself has sent you here,
And since you are that hero's son indeed,
And Hermenjart's, whose face with beauty gleams,
I pledge to you henceforth that I shall heed
Your every word – don't doubt my honesty,
For Heremenjart, I tell you truthfully,
Is my own cousin! We must be friends, you see,
By God our Lord, Who made the air we breathe!
Since you are all the sons of Aymeri,
Let us unite and ride to France the sweet!
I'll keep from you no part or penny-piece
Of all I have – take what you want, for we
Are richly stocked with wealthy goods and gear,
Which you may have to furnish those you lead

With richest clothes and leather for their feet."
Hernaut replied: "My lord, much thanks indeed;
With such largesse, your soul is safe with me."
So in this way the two bands made their peace,
   And rode for France together.

WHEN PEACE WAS MADE between red-haired Hernaut
And that good priest, who was a noble soul,
They rode for France as fast as they could go;
In front of them their well-stocked wagons rolled,
While in the rear they rode in serried rows;
They passed the rocks and ridge of Ricordone
And urged their mules along the routes and roads
To reach Clermont before the vespers tolled;
They spent the night inside a rich man's home,
Where their largesse, once more, was nothing loath;
What costly food they paid for with their gold –
Three plates and more they took, both hot and cold,
With noble wines and bread as white as snow,
And venison and fish, both fresh and smoked,
Their bill as great as any monarch's own –
   As was their sport in spending!

INSIDE CLERMONT our brothers and their landsmen
Retired to bed and slept content and happy;
When morning came they saddled up their stallions
Then swung astride and slid aside their saddles;
They left the town, with no desire to dally,
Then up a hill and on its crest they cantered;
As William looked down, along its valley,
He saw a band of evil-looking bandits,
Three score in all, a lawless, robbing rabble:
"My lords," he said, "by God, Who is our gladness,
I see a band that's set its hand to malice!
But if we hide or let them ride unchallenged,
In France itself we'll never win our battles!"
On hearing this, they lighted from their saddles
And armed themselves like noble, fighting vassals,
With coats of mail and helmets of enamel,
And solid pikes of Poitou steel and handle;
The thieves approached in most aggressive manner,

Well-armed themselves with armour they had captured,
And lances too, held ready in their hands there;
Without a word, both sides began attacking,
As on they spurred their rapid-footed stallions;
Head-on they met, with dread and deadly valour,
As good and bad began to hack and hammer!
My worthy friends, if you had seen that battle!
As saddles snapped, and as their breast-plates shattered,
The horses fled across the valley, dragging
　　Their reins across the grass.

ACROSS THE VALE they faced each other fiercely,
Those evil thieves and our young band of heroes!
My worthy friends, if only you had seen them!
The brothers struck with all their force and feeling,
As did the youths they'd brought with them on leaving;
Their fierce attack, their hacking and their cleaving,
Soon drove them back and many soon stopped breathing!
What more's to say? They fought them, never yielding
Until the lot lay dead upon the field there,
Save one they called Gonbaut, their evil leader;
The Narbonne youths surrounded him and seized him,
Then tied him up as tight as cord could keep him;
Towards a hut, whose secret he revealed there,
They dragged him forth, still loath at all to free him;
What wealth it held, that cabin, when they reached it,
In coin and cloths and horses tethered near it!
Hernaut the Red surveyed the spot, ere speaking
In outraged tones to him who led this evil:
"So tell me, rogue, whom did you rob or steal from
To gain such wealth as all of us can see here?"
Gonbaut replied: "My lord, I'll not conceal it;
A year has come and gone, my lord, believe me,
Since I cast off King Charlemagne's allegiance;
Since then all men who've passed across this region
Have served my needs so swiftly and so sweetly
That I'd have been content for life and easy,
Had you not come and managed to defeat me;
Just yesterday, this is no lie or secret,
At morning-light there cáme here through the greenwood
A noble priest, a high-born churchman, leading

Some thirty clerks, their shaven heads all gleaming,
An abbot too, with four monks of his teaching;
Their load was great with wealth that they were eager
To give to Charles in Paris at their meeting;
But with our strength we very soon relieved them
Of all that weight, so nothing could impede them –
Unless they found more wealth as they proceeded!
We hid the lot, and no one knew our secret."
Said William: "But you've committed treason
And sinned against the faith our land believes in!
You've murdered men without regard or reason,
And you must pay this very day as dearly!"
The bishop then spoke up with this entreaty:
"My noble youths, in service of Lord Jesus,
Let me collect, if this does not displease you,
The stolen goods your prowess has retrieved here,
And share them out among the poor and needy."
Hernaut replies: "Most willingly and freely."
They took the wealth and packed it all ere leaving,
Upon the main and metalled road proceeding;
Gonbaut the rogue was led along on leashes
    To gain his just reward.

IN HIGH CONTENT they went along the road;
On leashes held, they led the rogue Gonbaut
To reap ere long the harvest he had sown;
Upon their way they looked and saw a home
Where loyal folk had lived not long ago,
Before those rogues had come and laid it low,
With nothing left, no rafters and no posts,
Save corner-beams and one great ridging-pole;
They made a noose by twisting up some rope
And hung Gonbaut upon it, nothing loath;
He'd nevermore cause honest people woe;
And when they'd strung and hung that evil rogue,
The Narbonne youths continued on their road;
Through Berry shire, as fast as spurs could goad,
They sped their mounts; not stopping, they approached
The bridge at Orléans, and boldly strode
    Within sweet France's kingdom.

8. How the four brothers fared on reaching Paris

THE NOBLE YOUTHS arrived and spent the night
In Orléans, that city fair and fine;
Next day at dawn, with morning's early light,
Their steeds were brought and they prepared to ride;
At Holy Cross, with all their heart and mind,
They heard the Mass and prayed to Jesus Christ;
When this was done, they left the town behind;
They crossed La Beause and rode without respite
To reach Etampes, and there they spent the night
In peaceful sleep, which each of them required;
The following day, as soon as dawn arrived,
They rode again and passed Etréchy by;
They spurred so hard until at last they spied
The town of Paris, and wondered at the sight
Of all its spires and belfry-towers so high,
Its abbey-halls and all its splendid shrines!
They saw the Seine, its banks so deep and wide,
With all its mills in rows both left and right,
And all its boats weighed down with wheat and wines
And bags of salt and wealth of every kind!
Young William saw Hernaut by his side
And called to him in noble tones and fine:
"Dear brother, hear the plan I have in mind!
You are in charge of all before our eyes,
As seneschal appointed by our sire!
So let us see before this day declines
How you employ the honour that implies!
If you agree, then hasten to acquire
Some noble house where we may lodge tonight,
And food and drink for us and more besides –
For I have heard, and hold it to be right,
That worthy men are never truly prized
Unless they show largesse each time they dine!"
Hernaut replied: "By all my faith in Christ,
Without a lie, you'll have what you desire,
If there are rooms and there is food to find
That silver coin or rowelled silks can buy."
When this was said, an abbot ambled by,

Most richly robed, from Cluny's abbey-shrine;
With fifteen monks he'd left the town behind;
Hernaut the Red caught hold his rein and cried,
In ringing tones, with all his force and pride:
"Hold hard, Sir Monk! What lodge have you resigned?
And whom did you pay visit to, and why?
Did you see Charles, the monarch strong and wise?"
"Indeed I did," the worthy priest replied:
"The King holds court with many wealthy knights;
So large a crowd has come here from the shires
I couldn't count one half of those arrived;
The city-walls contain so many knights
Whom Charlemagne has summoned to his side,
That there's no hall at all or palace fine,
No house or vault, nor solar-room up high,
That's not full up already, swollen tight
With dukes and counts and princes richly prized,
With bishops and archbishops, abbots and friars,
With priests and provosts of our Lord Jesus Christ!
And that's the cause and reason why I ride,
For there's no way that I may lodge inside!
In some poor cell I hope to spend the night
Until the dawn, and with the morning light
I'll hasten back inside the town in time
To meet with him who is our King by right;
I've journeyed here to counsel and advise
In certain things the Emperor desires."
"A curse on this!" Hernaut the Red replied:
"I am the seneschal of France, and I
Shall only heed or cede to Charles the wise;
You'll never lack for lodgings, worthy friar!
By all the faith I owe Lord Jesus Christ,
You'll soon have rooms, as many as you like,
Fourteen, fifteen, whatever you require,
If you'll ride back to Paris at my side."
On hearing this, the abbot laughed outright
And said: "My friend, your will outwits your mind!
For you yourself will find it hard to find
   A lodging in this city."

THE ABBOT LOOKED at Hernaut hard indeed
And said again, with every courtesy:
"My worthy friend, by all the faith I preach,
There *are* no rooms within the town still free;
So many kings and princes have convened
With bishops and archbishops of their fiefs,
So many dukes and knights and noble peers,
There are no rooms for others such as we!
The galleries have all been commandeered;
Six hundred men are sleeping in the streets!
By all the faith I owe to St Denis,
Retrace your steps some half a dozen leagues,
For seven leagues from here lies Montlhéry;
The castle there is well supplied with meat,
With wine and bread, with everything we need;
So let's go there, we'll both be well received;
Then, with the dawn, we'll simply ride back here."
But Hernaut said: "You hold your honour cheap!
What you intend seems foolishness to me!
In truth, you monks are cowardly and weak!
But good Sir Monk, your mind may rest at ease;
I'm seneschal of Charlemagne, you see!
I swear by good St Felix that I'll free
A room for you in any place you please;
So ride with me, and soon you will receive
Five rooms or six for every two you need!"
Said William: "Enough, you foolish fiend!
How do you think your boasting will succeed
Where this high man of God has not, though he
Rules all the land of Cluny's abbacy,
And spends in pounds each day he lives and breathes
Much more than we in Paris pence each week?"
On hearing this, the blood left Hernaut's cheek;
He raised his staff, a stout and sturdy piece,
And would have struck, his anger was so keen,
But checked himself from such a churlish deed;
He spoke instead with fierce intent indeed:
"Young William, you act most shamefully
When you dispute the power I've received
From our own father, the noble Aymeri;
Do you dispute the rank he gave to me?"

"Not I, in truth," said William the fierce:
"I'll stand by you, so help me St Denis,
With every ounce of all my strength and zeal."
As this was said, they reached the Paris streets,
With no intent to ask for but to seize
The rooms they sought with every force and speed;
Without God's help, Who bore the Cross's grief,
Some living then would die before they'd leave
    The lodgings that they'd sought there.

THE ABBOT TURNED his steed – he had no choice:
He didn't dare refuse or bid them halt!
Along Grande Rue the Narbonne youths rode forth
Until they saw a splendid-looking hall,
Most richly built and on each side adorned
With crenelled walls and columns for support;
Hernaut went in, still sitting on his horse!
He saw in rows well-polished coats of war
And burnished blades and newly-hilted swords,
And glossy steeds with water for them all,
And food galore behind the kitchen doors;
A splendid rug was spread upon the floor
Which forty knights were seated on or sprawled,
For they'd set up both chess and checker-boards
At which they played for their delight and sport;
Hernaut the Red beheld them all then roared
Most fiercely, in a domineering voice:
"Whose men are these, installed within these walls?"
Their seneschal stood up without a pause
And straightaway replied with this retort:
"You foolish knave, you'll soon find out, I'm sure!
The noble duke of Burgundy you call,
Whom Charlemagne has summoned to his court;
This very hall will host their private talks!"
Hernaut replied: "Oh no it won't, my lord!
Our fathers were sworn enemies before,
Nor shall the sons be any less or more!
I have this town in my control and ward,
At Aymeri's command as seneschal;
The duke was mad to settle here before
He'd come to me and asked me as he ought!

You cannot stay, so off you go, my lords,
And seek for rooms where others may be sought!
Leave straightaway! You must renounce this hall!"
"You foolish knave!" the other steward roared:
"I've heard before, and you've not proved it false,
That red heads hold no good or noble thoughts!
All rogues they are, I know it now for sure!"
On hearing this Hernaut's hot temper boiled!
He raised his rod and straightaway he scored
A mighty blow on that poor seneschal,
Which knocked him down and left him dazed and sore;
On seeing this, those young Burgundian lords,
Who were at ease and playing games, leapt forth
And threw themselves at Hernaut and his horse;
They clutched the reins and tried to make him fall;
He would have died, unable to withdraw,
When in the hall his Narbonne brothers stormed!
They saw him seized, and then well nigh unhorsed,
And ran to him as wild as savage boars;
Bernart was first, with William in support,
And Aimer too whom nobody could daunt;
They took in hand whatever help they saw –
A staff or stick – to swing upon that swarm!
The scarlet blood seeped through Burgundian coifs
As they all fled before that fierce assault!
The hall was cleared and, glad or sad, they all
Were forced to find some other beds and board;
Their host was loath to show his face abroad,
But climbed the stairs and with his wife crept forth
To watch the blows in his own home and hall!
Hernaut looked up and, seeing him, he roared:
"The Living Fiend should hang you for your gall!
By St Denis, this hall is mine, not yours!"
The host called out: "Don't harm me, I implore!
I'm just the host placed in here and employed
By Charles himself to oversee it all!
I'll not deny that I am far from poor,
For I have gold and silver coin galore,
And cloths of silk and sendal from abroad,
And rapid steeds in stables by the score,
And vineyard fields where many are employed;

If you desire to stay within these walls,
I'll serve you all most richly, rest assured –
But save me from those other men, my lord!"
Hernaut replied: "God has redressed your fault!
I ask of you no more than to install
This abbot here and serve him as you ought,
Together with this bishop we have brought."
The landlord swore by good St Omer's corpse,
And St Denis, so worthy of our laud,
That there would be not one desire at all
Their lips could speak or hearts could hanker for,
That would not be fulfilled as soon as thought,
If coin could pay and it could still be bought:
"You have my thanks," replied Hernaut with joy:
"Good monks, dismount at once, my noble lords!"
Not daring else, each one dismounted horse,
And so it was that bishop was installed
With all his monks, their comfort well assured,
So they could sing all day and praise the Lord;
That splendid rug was spread across the floor
And there they sat at rest and in the warmth,
While food galore was readied for them all;
Hernaut the Red was in no mood to pause:
He said farewell and then set off once more
    To seek out further lodgings!

RED-HAIRED HERNAUT farewelled that fair abode,
His brothers too, whose fellowship was close;
In every street they met with throngs of folk,
As Hernaut led with lofty tread and showed
His steward's rod which Aymeri'd bestowed;
But God surprised their gallant eyes when, lo!
They looked ahead and saw upon the road
King Boniface beside Garin the bold!
Garin saw all his brothers too and showed
Them to the king and said: "My lord, behold
The valour born to Aymeri the old
And Hermenjart, your sister, in Narbonne!"
On hearing this, the king was glad of soul
And hastened up to hold each brother close
And kiss them all four times before he spoke

To ask them news of Aymeri the bold;
Hernaut replied that he was hale and whole
When they set out to venture on their own:
"Before we left he promised me the role
Of royal seneschal; now I control
The whole of France, its guest-halls and its homes!"
The king heard this and looked a little wroth,
And then complained of finding none of those!
Hernaut replied that soon he'd give him both!
"Just follow me wherever I may go!"
He turned his steed and started up the road;
The mighty staff his father had bestowed
He held erect, then tossed it to and fro;
Throughout the town they rode till they approached
The Petit Pont, near which a palace glowed –
The best in town, save Charlemagne's own,
With cellars deep and stable-rows of stone;
How skilled he was who built it long ago:
He made its rooms with vaulted roofs and domes,
All painted with mosaics and in gold,
With soaring stone to bear the mighty load,
And crystal tiles which glowed at dawn's approach;
The river Seine flowed round it like a moat;
Hernaut just rode inside it, even so,
And found within two bishops, and from Rome
A legate sent as envoy of the Pope;
Each room he saw was brightly lit and glowed
With candles that were long alight at nones;
He saw at once that they had wealth untold,
And that no pike or salmon would be sold
To any folk except this legate's own!
Hernaut rode up, upon his rapid roan,
And, seeing them, he cried, with ringing tones:
"And who are you? I have a right to know!
A curse on him who gave you this abode
Without my leave, who hold its lease alone!"
One bishop stood and glared at young Hernaut:
"A curse on you," he said, "for raving so!
Who gave you wine? He too must be an oaf –
Too strong it was for your weak head to hold!
You need a man to shake your wits, you dolt,

For Charles the King has called us to his throne
And he himself installed us here – and so
I'm damned if we will move for you, you rogue!"
But Hernaut swore that they had better go
Before his staff broke all their holy bones –
    Which would indeed be foolish.

HERNAUT THE RED was very proud and fierce;
He saw the priests inside there at their ease
And tried once more to move them with a speech,
Ere he was forced to drive them out with deeds!
"My lords," he said, "I wish you all Godspeed,
For willingly or not, you all must leave!
A king comes here, of highest rank and deeds,
King Didier's own son from Lombardy,
Called Boniface, with many knights and peers."
The clerics' host, observing all, could see
Hernaut advance, and no more held his peace:
"Young wretch, you are too arrogant for me!
Turn round and take your ravings to the streets!
These godly lords are noble men of peace;
By St Richier, I swear if you don't cease,
My own two hands will drag you from your steed
And fling you in the nearest bog I see!"
On hearing this, Hernaut's hot temper seethed,
And with his staff he struck him fast and fierce
Upon the skull, not stinting in the least;
The blood flew out and flowed down both his cheeks
As on the hearth he crumpled in a heap;
On seeing this, the prelates' rage was deep;
Their men-at-arms and servants rushed to seize
Hernaut's red head; and then their cooks appeared,
And from his mount they dragged him by the beard;
He would have died, there is no doubt indeed,
Without God's help, Who judges all and each,
And William's too, his brother fine and fierce,
Who heard the din and shouted, loud and clear,
To all the rest: "We're wasting time out here!
Our seneschal and brother's in great need!"
On hearing this, they rushed with angry zeal
Inside the hall, not pausing in the least;

One swung a pole, another flung a beam
As all laid on, right, left and in between!
The fighting's tide soon turned against those priests!
Their men and squires were mauled – more than fourteen
Took mighty blows and mighty injuries;
With broken heads they lurched about and leaned;
With broken arms they beat a fast retreat!
The legate, when he saw his men's defeat,
Was filled with fright, as well you might believe;
With ringing voice he cried aloud in fear:
"Good Christian men, for God's sake let us be,
For we're not men of war, but men of peace,
Who spend our time in prayer upon our knees!
You shouldn't harm Christ's servants such as we!
For if you do, I tell you truthfully,
That when the awful Judgement Day is here,
Lord God will cast your sins back in your teeth,
     With all Creation watching!"

THE LEGATE SAID: "Good Christian men and brave!
We are all priests and prelates shorn and shaved,
And humble clerks, who serve the Lord God's name;
We have prepared our meal here and, in faith,
It would be cruel to drive us out today!
The Lord Himself would say you were to blame;
But if you seek our charity and grace,
Then you may share with pleasure from our plates:
But then depart – you'd not be wise to stay!"
On hearing this, Hernaut went wild again!
He swore aloud with all his heart and hate:
"For this alone that you have dared to say,
You'll pay the price before you run away!"
He swung his staff with all his might and main
And would have dashed the fellow's brow and brains
But William held back his arm again
To halt the staff before it found its aim;
He spoke aloud in heavy blame and shame:
"Hernaut!" he cried, "Have you lost all your brains?
You're striking men who serve the Christian Faith!"
The legate, when he saw how close he came
To Hernaut's wrath, ran off in swift escape,

As did the priests and all their clerks ordained;
They left the hall and all they had in haste,
Each crying out: "Our journey was ill made!
The Devil's brood inhabit all this place;
Both friend and foe they torment just the same!"
To Charles's court they cantered straightaway,
And took with them those servants in their pay
Who suffered most from injury and pain;
They each complained to mighty Charlemagne:
"My lord, we call for justice in God's name!
We all are priests and prelates of the Faith,
Who've journeyed here to Paris for your sake:
We did not come to be deprived or shamed!
Behold the men we brought here in our train –
Each bears a wound and wears a bloodied face;
Within your town there bides a band of knaves
Unknown to us, but they are all insane!
They've driven us most cruelly from the place
Where you yourself directed us to stay;
Our men-at-arms have been so badly maimed
That some of them will never be the same;
If you deny the vengeance that we crave,
Then we shall bear this sorrow to our graves."
On hearing this, the King was filled with rage;
He swore to God and good Denis the Saint,
That those to blame would suffer for their ways;
He cried aloud: "I'll find them straightaway!
Close every lane and every city gate!
No mortal man shall leave this town today!
For all the gold a mule can bear in weight,
Not one of them shall leave this town, I say,
Until my thirst for vengeance has been slaked!
Good, holy men, depart in peace and take
Whatever rooms within the town remain;
Tomorrow morn, upon the dawn of day,
Return to court and do not be afraid:
I tell you truly, the bodies of those knaves
Who did you wrong and wrought your men such pain,
Will each be here for you to meet again!"
The legate said: "Much thanks, in Jesu's name!"
On saying this, they left King Charlemagne

But didn't dare return to that fine place
From which our youths had chased them all away!
Before the town a mighty tent they raised
Upon a field which bordered on the Seine,
And this is where they stayed till break of day;
The Narbonne youths kept nothing of their gains –
The goods and gear, the treasures small and great
Those clerics left within their hall of state
When they had had their residence curtailed,
Were sent to them, with nothing kept or claimed;
They never took one item of it, save
That noble feast their kitchen-cooks had made!
Hernaut spoke out and hailed King Boniface:
"Good uncle, these are *your* rooms now, in faith!
"If you're prepared, dismount and take your place;
The table is already richly laid!
You won't be short of food and drink, I'd say;
It was the clerks' – their charity has made
It everyone's, as every man and maid
Gives all they have to *them*, in Jesu's name!"
"God bless us all!" the Lombards there exclaimed,
And they all laughed, and everyone proclaimed
In tones as low as honest throats could make:
"By St Fermin, Hernaut deserves our praise!
In heart and pride he's Aymeri again!"
Dismounting then, with all his barons brave,
The king sat down upon a silk brocade;
The Narbonne youths farewelled him in God's name
     And left to seek more lodgings!

HERNAUT THE RED departed from that lodge,
His brothers too, whose noble fame lives on,
And with them went that happy, gallant throng
Of noble youths all nurtured in Narbonne;
Along the streets they rode without a stop
Until they saw before them young Beuvon!
Hernaut called out in greeting fair and fond:
"By all my faith in God the Lord above,
"Fine brother mine, did you not find King Yon?"
"Indeed I did, my lord, by grace of God!
He bade me stay and at his court I've stopped;

His barons' praise has so advanced my lot
That I shall wed and rule his land ere long!"
"God bless the day!" Hernaut said in response:
"Now, have you found fit lodgings here or not?"
"Indeed we have, a very noble lodge;
But let us ride together from now on
Till evening comes and all we from Narbonne
Have spoken with great Charles the Emperor."
On saying this, they spurred their horses off
And trotted on until they reached Grand Pont,
    And crossed the river Seine there.

AND SO ALL SIX whom Aymeri had sired
Traversed the bridge and on the other side
Exchanged their mounts and gave their steeds to squires,
Who, in the lead, held these upon their right;
The soldiers there looked on, as did the knights,
And each one said: "How proud and fair a sight!
We never saw six men so much alike
In handsomeness as they! Just see them ride!
They hold themselves so proudly and so fine
That they must be the sons of someone high!"
And all agreed who saw them there alike;
The noble youths rode on till by and by,
As they progressed in serried rank and lines,
They came across a bishop meek and mild,
Called Morant of Le Mans, as he arrived;
Young William addressed him first and cried:
"Good day, my lord! For love of God on High,
Please bless our band with your own hand in Christ!"
And so he did, with happy heart and mind;
And on they went, past every street and sign,
Till vespers rang and daylight turned to night –
And *they*'d no beds and soon bewailed their plight!
Young Hernaut said: "Whoever seeks shall find!
Which lodging here did Roland use in life,
That Paladin whose deeds will never die?"
An ageing priest raised up his glove and sighed:
"My son, up there before your very eyes,
A pommel glows, and where the street divides,
Old Anchetin the Norman lives inside;

There Roland dwelt when he was still alive;
And Anchetin, a wealthy man, supplied
The Count with all he needed and desired;
The Paladin, whose valour never died,
Repaid his host and his largesse in kind:
He gave him gold and silver won in fights,
And robes galore to Anchetin's good wife,
And coats of fur so long they dragged behind;
The Count is dead; alas the day he died!
But there, good friend, is where he lodged in life;
The mansion now is full of German knights."
"But not for long, good friend!" Hernaut replied:
"They have no leave to live there and no right;
Brave Roland's lodge should not be theirs to hire!"
He found the hall and rode inside to find
The Germans there, just sitting down to dine;
He hailed them all most graciously and cried:
"Immortal God, Who took on mortal life
In Bethlehem as Jesus, Mary's child,
Bless all of you and keep you, worthy knights!
You are indeed a noble, gallant sight!
Enjoy the meal that our Lord God provides
And at your ease enjoy those worthy wines –
Without excess, for that would not be wise;
But then, my lords, prepare to leave and find
Another house where you may spend the night:
For this was Roland's lodge, and now it's mine!"
A German knight, at this, began to rise,
His hand around a long, sharp-bladed knife;
He swore to God, the King of all Mankind:
"If it were not against our Faith, I'd strike
Your breast with this, before you'd spoken twice!"
On hearing this, the brothers filled with ire;
Young Aimer spurred his ambling horse to smite
The wretched rogue who'd threatened Hernaut's life:
He seized, at once, his whiskers, left and right,
And wrested forth one hundred hairs in spite!
The blood shot out and trickled down his sides;
Then Aimer drew his blade of cutting iron
And swore to God, the King of Paradise:
"If you don't leave this dwelling now, then I

Shall flay you out, with this to speed your flight!"
Beuvon looked on and added with a smile:
  "You Huns had better hurry!"

THE GERMANS THERE were filled with rage and grief
That such a youth should seize their leader's beard!
They all jumped up and, with their arms unsheathed,
Enclosed the lad, advancing front and rear;
They clawed his cloak and ripped it piece by piece,
While Aimer writhed and tried to struggle free!
How quickly then his brothers all appeared –
Beuvon, Bernart and William the fierce,
Garin – and Red Hernaut, I guarantee!
How well they struck those Germans in their zeal!
They smote their coifs till blood seeped out beneath;
That German band just couldn't stand the heat!
Whoever grieves, they chased them out to seek
Another lodge to eat in and to sleep!
My friends, it's said, and oft in blame indeed,
That might is right and fortune flees the weak;
Those Narbonne youths with every haste and speed,
Prepared the lodge for their delight and ease;
They sent out men to find good fish to eat,
As best they could, freshwater fish and sea,
And ordered squires to purchase fowl and meat,
To buy wild-boar and venison and deer;
They brought in mint and rushes freshly sheaved
To make the lodge more fragrant and more clean;
Hernaut engaged the worthy host in speech:
"Good Anchetin – for thus you're known to me:
My noble friend, advise me, for we need
A minstrel's skill to fill us with good cheer,
Until the cooks have made our evening meal!"
Their host replied: "You'll have it, gallant peer!
So help me God, if there are minstrels free
In Paris now, then I shall bring them here!"
Throughout the town he sent his men to seek
Good minstrels out and hire their minstrelsy;
If you had seen how they pricked up their ears
And came at once, as soon as it was clear
That Anchetin had guests of high esteem!

For minstrels shun the villainous and mean –
You'll never see them hurry forth to these!
But where there is largesse that's where you'll see
Performers come with skill and will to please;
And come they did, in ones and twos and threes,
To please the sons of brave Count Aymeri!
They plucked their harps and played so joyfully
Upon *vièles*, they filled the house with glee;
And while they strove with song and sundry feats
To entertain their hosts and bring good cheer,
In their domain the cooks prepared a feast;
They stoked the fires to cook delicious meats:
Some scalded pork and flayed the sides of beef,
While others plucked the fattened fowls and geese;
If it had been four kings they'd had to feed,
The food they cooked would well have met their needs!
When he beheld the joy of such a scene,
The worthy host took heart enough to speak
His feelings forth, as at his door he leaned:
"For shame on you, you knights of Germany!
Good riddance to you all and to you each!
To lodge your like was no delight for me;
For thirty days you took your lodgings here
And in that time you left me not one seat
That you could find to fuel the fire's heat;
So mean you were, so grasping and so cheap,
You'd never pay for tinder you could steal!
I never gained from you one penny-piece;
May God forbid, Who judges all and each,
That you come back to lodge again for free!"
Young Beuvon said: "Good host, put by your grief!
There's nothing gained lamenting what has been;
But rest assured, in lodging such as we,
You'll make up all your losses, never fear!
Put on this noble fur of mine, and keep
My mantle too, a gift to you from me;
For friendship's sake, please wear it at your ease;
Accept as well, in friendship and esteem,
This palfrey-horse, an admirable beast,
Which you can ride when you survey your wheat!"
The host replied: "Much thanks for both of these!

Ah, mighty God, Your wonders never cease;
You have at last restored my wealth and weal,
And brought me back brave Roland from the field."
My friends, we'll leave our gallant youths to eat,
And look upon those Germans as they reached
King Charles's court to protest and appeal;
They climbed the steps, all wounded, wan and weak,
Then, for them all, their spokesman made to speak:
"Sir Emperor, attend our plaint and plea!
You summoned us to meet and greet you here,
And we all thought to come and go in peace;
But certain lords, six braggarts young in years,
Have treated us most brutally indeed;
From our own lodge they cast us in the street,
And beat us black and blue, as you can see!"
On hearing this, the blood left Charles's cheek;
He asked them all, with dudgeon in his speech:
"Who are these knaves? Can you give names to me?"
"We cannot, Sire; but there are six, all fierce
And arrogant and wild in word and deed,
And all alike in looks from head to feet!
Without a doubt one father sired them each;
Men cannot look so matching and not be
One father's sons, on this we all agree;
They made us stand from our own evening meal;
We didn't dare oppose their raging zeal!
Against our will we all stood up to leave,
And, as we did, they struck us with their steel;
We didn't know where else we should appeal,
Except to you, who should protect us here;
We seek redress, true Emperor and liege."
The King, he pledged, by blessed St Denis,
And St Omer, whose honour he revered,
That all the six, however proud or fierce,
Would soon be tamed by his authority,
And pay in blood for those they'd made to bleed;
He swore revenge, as well he might indeed,
With ringing tones so all his court could hear:
But when, himself, he heard those brothers speak
And name themselves as Aymeri's own breed,
His heart and mind would be inclined to yield
    To other thoughts and feelings.

THE GERMAN KNIGHTS sustained their sorry song:
They showed their wounds, which they had plenty of –
Some struck with sticks, some laid about with logs!
The saddest there and maddest of the lot
Had only half his beard left, having lost
The left-hand side when Aimer wrenched it off
And shed his blood and left him red with shock!
He showed the King, complaining loud and long;
The King himself turned fiery red with wrath
And cried aloud: "But, in the name of God,
Who are these rogues, these dregs of vilest stock,
Who in my town have dared to do such wrongs?
My name and fame will die if I do not
Avenge my guests with justice swift and strong."
"True King," said one Tibert of Orion,
"Take neither wealth nor ransom from these dogs,
Or all your house will bear the shame and shock."
"Be still, you rogue," replied Lanbert of Laon:
"Your own house bears the lasting blame and blot
Of Ganelon's foul schemes and wicked plots
With King Marsile, which slew Roland and robbed
Our Peers Twelve of life at Roncevaux,
And twenty thousand more, slain on the spot;
By Simon's bones, I'd never rest or stop
Till all your race were put to death and gone!
Hear my advice in this, true Emperor!
Have summoned here inside your hall the lot
Of them who thus are charged with doing wrong,
And let us hear their reasons in response;
Then we may judge the right and wrong thereof,
By knowing why they gave these blows and knocks;
Let their own words confirm their guilt or not."
"Lanbert," said Charles, "your heart is true and prompt;
In any need you never fail my want;
By this my beard, so white of hue and long,
I shall not err from your advice one jot!
   Let no one doubt my justice."

KING CHARLEMAGNE was lost a while in thought,
Then to his side he summoned forth three lords,
One from Anjou, Count Geoffrey he was called,

Gui of Beauvais and Gautier of Etampes:
"My lords," he said, "attend the Norman's hall
And bring me back at once these braggart boys
Who treat my town as if it were their toy!"
All three replied: "We shall, my lord, with joy."
They mounted up on Spanish mules adorned
With harnesses of most resplendent sort,
While they themselves wore silk from Grecian shores
And ermine-cloaks, snow-white, to keep them warm;
They started forth and, while upon their course,
Old Anchetin was standing by his door,
Inside of which our heroes were installed;
While looking round, he saw a German lord
Whom he had lodged in his fine house before;
He grasped an axe of Danish steel and stormed
Upon the rogue and struck him with such force
He cleft his head, which left him dead, of course;
Young Beuvon said: "You'll slake his thirst no more!
By St Omer of Blois, that blow of yours
Will bring the King upon our heads, for sure!"
The host replied: "By God, Who made our Laws,
Don't doubt the worth of what my wealth affords;
I have at hand a hogshead of Mans coins
Which you may use for any need or cause;
We'll give them this, if summoned to the court,
And this will pay the German's price, I'm sure;
I slew him now for slanders made before;
He called me oft 'you cuckold of a whore!'
And once, in pride, he killed a cub I'd bought;
I never liked his patronage at all;
He angered me so many times with taunts."
Beuvon replied: "He's had his just reward;
    Ill-blest he left his homeland!"

THOSE ENVOYS SENT by Charles of Saint-Denis,
Who, as I said, set off on splendid beasts
To seek our youths where they were seen to be,
Then came across that corpse left in the street:
"This goes from bad to even worse!" said each;
"My noble lords," said Geoffrey, moved to speak,
"So help me God, Who bore the Cross's grief,

These villains' guilt is plain for all to see!
If Charlemagne won't heed his wisest Peers,
Or will not do as Paris law decrees,
No honest man will live here in a week!"
As this was said, the Norman's house was reached;
Inside, at chess, our heroes sat at ease –
The men outside could hear them in good cheer;
Before one word could be exchanged in heat,
From Saint-Denis the Abbot strode between,
Who'd been sent off by Charles to guarantee
That our good lads would come to court in peace!
He saw them sat around their games on seats,
And hailed them all in ringing tones and clear:
"My lords, what land has bred and brought you here
To treat our town with such disdain and greed?
We here don't teach such merry ways and means!
King Charlemagne is outraged at your cheek;
He orders you to come to court with me."
Young William and Hernaut laughed indeed,
As Beuvon said: "Sir Monk, by Christ's own Creed,
We are resolved to go to court and see
Great Charlemagne, the King of Saint-Denis!
We've journeyed here, all six of us, to greet
Him in our father's name, Count Aymeri,
And Hermenjart's, our mother proud and dear."
On hearing this, the Abbot laughed indeed
And raised his hood, to see and to be seen:
"My noble sons," he said to them with glee,
"Embrace me now! You have a friend in me!
I am in truth a cousin near and dear
Of Hermenjart, the Countess fine and sweet!
From Mont-Cenis I hail, in Lombardy,
And my own clan held land from Aymeri;
My sons, I'll always love you and your breed;
By all the faith I owe to St Denis,
What wealth I have is yours to share and keep,
        As children of such parents!"

THE ABBOT, WHEN he heard they were the children
Of Hermenjart, the lovely Lombard Princess,
And Aymeri, who never loved the timid,

The noble Count whose hair with grey was grizzled,
Yet ruled Narbonne with robust health and vigour,
And mighty blows for Pagan foes and villains,
The Abbot, then, exulted deep within him:
He hastened first to hug Bernart and kiss him,
Then William, who won Porpaillart city,
And then Beuvon, then Aimer, standing with him:
"My sons," he said, "at last I see you princes!
By all the faith I owe St Médard's spirit,
I fill with joy to see your noble figures!
You don't at all look like your Lombard kinsmen,
But are, each one of you, the very image
Of leopard-hearted Aymeri the grizzled!
By all the faith I owe St Leonard's spirit,
You can rely on me and all my riches,
    To sponsor you as knights."

THE ABBOT LOOKED at all of them with gladness
And saw each one to be both strong and handsome;
They all were dressed in fresh and clean apparel:
In ermine gowns and snowy ermine mantles:
"Ah God, our Heavenly Father," said the Abbot,
"How fine a band of blooming youth these lads are!
How blest the tree that bears such noble branches!
Their service here should make the King most thankful,
For he may go with hunting-dogs and falcons
To look for game and hunt with his companions,
While these bestride their sturdy battle-stallions
To conquer towns and castles with their valour,
To scourge and purge the Saracens and hammer
Their heathen heads till they repent their madness!
When these are dubbed new knights inside his palace
The King at last may rest from all his travels:
These youths shall go and show the Christian banner
In any land where Christian Law is challenged,
And conquer towns and Pagan forts in battle
    Against the Spanish Moors."

THE ABBOT FILLED with joy as he surveyed
The noble youths and saw in every face
The fierce prowess that each of them displayed;

Within his heart he knew, for it was plain,
That there could be no fiercer knights than they;
With ringing tones he solemnly proclaimed:
"I swear by all my fealty and faith
That these young men shall light up France again
From all its gloom since Roland's doom in Spain;
Let Charles be sure, without a doubt I say,
That when he girds their loins with knighthood's blade,
They will avenge his grief at Roland's fate,
    Who died in Spain a martyr."

9. How Narbonne's pride met with France's King

THE ABBOT SAID: "My children, keep your heads!
Persist no more with foolish recklessness!
Though you are all most brave and nobly bred,
This doesn't mean that you may show contempt!
The King is fierce, his heart is proud and dread,
And he is served by knights of great prowess;
Some thirty counts are his in homage pledged,
And pay him tithes of all their tolls and rent;
No man alive could hope to match his strength;
The Emperor has sent us here to fetch
You all to him without delay or let;
For Jesu's sake, I urge you once again:
When you are there before the King himself,
Take care to speak with wisdom and respect,
The eldest first, with due regard and sense;
I'll go there first and make a short address
To Charles's knights; if you need hostages,
I'll summon forth one hundred noble men
    To Charlemagne's palace."

WITH THANKS TO GOD for what he hoped would be,
The Abbot turned with happy heart indeed
To speak with Charles in counsel with his Peers;
He came to court and said with joyous mien:
"My lord, by my old hood of grey, I feel
You should rejoice and praise good St Maurice!
Count Aymeri, who loves you as his liege,

Has sent his sons to serve your wish and need,
Abroad or here, wherever you decree;
They are, in truth, the bravest youths that breathe
From Apre's heights to faraway Tubize;
All six are sons of Hermenjart the sweet,
Who's taught them well to love the laws of peace
And to respect the Church and all its priests!
We may avenge, through their prowess and zeal,
The men who died by Ganelon's deceit,
For which he paid in awful pain and grief."
The King replied: "By God, I cannot see
Good done or won by villains such as these!
No sooner here, they have dishonoured me!
They stake their lives on my good will, it seems;
I have good cause to treat them all as thieves!"
The Abbot said: "My lord, by St Maurice,
Show mercy, Sire, as God shows such as we!
They will atone for any wrong they've wreaked,
And I shall pay their first amendment fee:
One thousand marks of my lord St Denis
    I'll give in reparation."

AS SOON AS CHARLES heard talk of reparation,
His visage flamed with anger and vexation;
He eyed the priest with such high indignation
That he began to quiver and to quaver;
As you can hear, he answered him most plainly:
"Sir Monk, it seems you sanction their behaviour!
Your best advice is that I look with favour
On braggart rogues who come here to obey me,
Yet treat my town as if it were a plaything,
And sack my streets, attack my men and slay them!
So weak a king should never rule a nation!
He would deserve his subjects' scorn and hatred;
Will you dispense the Church's wealth to save them?
By all my faith in Jesus Christ our Saviour,
I scorn your wealth and never shall I take it;
However much you pay will not dissuade me
From seizing them and making prison tame them,
Or, failing that, some other means more painful."
The Abbot said: "Your will shall be obeyed, Sire;

I much regret that my words have dismayed you;
Since nothing I can say or do will save them,
Or make amends for them with compensation,
Your will be done; I'll seek no more to change it;
But one thing must be said and I must say it:
You should respect and never doubt the faith of
Count Aymeri and Hermenjart his lady;
If they have sent their sons to serve and aid you,
For that alone no harm should overtake them;
When they took back the lodge that Roland stayed in,
The Germans there refused to leave in safety;
On hearing this, the Narbonne brothers made them;
Why should they pay, my lord, for acting bravely?
I shall attend the German who was slain there
With every care and honour he has claim to;
It is my lot, and I shall not evade it;
I urge you, Sire, to let these youths remain here;
Their service hence may yet assist you greatly."
The King replied: "My duty will not fail them,
    For their brave father's sake."

FOR ALL THIS TIME the Abbot spent in talking
With Charlemagne, to soothe and to exhort him,
The Narbonne youths remained within their quarters;
Young Beuvon turned to Anchetin the Norman:
"Good host, come here, for I have something for you!
Come, take this gown well-trimmed with ermine borders,
And have this coat, which is a long and warm one;
Accept in gift this sturdy ambling palfrey –
It has no peer for comfort, I assure you;
This pouch contains one hundred bezants also."
Then Beuvon called to one of his supporters:
"Make sure that he receives all this henceforward."
"My lord," said he, "I shall do, I assure you."
The noble youths took off the clothes they'd worn there
And put on robes of even richer order:
No great emir or king had robes more royal!
Then they bestrode, each one, an ambling palfrey,
And through the streets all six of them rode forward;
Along the way they never reined their horses
Until they came to Charlemagne's courtyard;

They climbed the steps to reach the marbled hallway
And saw the King enthroned among his courtiers,
And all the knights and lords of most importance
Throughout his realm, from every shire and shoreline;
The gallant youths went straightaway towards him,
The eldest first, in fine array and order;
Each one unclasped his coat of fur, while walking,
And let it fall as soon as all had halted,
For any there to gather what they scorned to;
Bernart spoke first, who best was versed in talking;
He hailed the King most courteously and warmly:
"May Jesus Christ, of Mary born for all men
In Bethlehem, by God Almighty's order,
Bless Charlemagne this happy day and always,
The best of kings that day has ever dawned on!"
The King was mum; he sat there, very thoughtful,
But not a word he uttered in rejoinder,
And all the time he stared at those before him
To mark their look, which never flinched or faltered;
Then he replied, most solemnly and surely,
To brave Bernart, his brothers and supporters:
"Proud youths, approach! I bid you to inform me
Which lord gave you the leave and the assurance
    To treat me with contempt?"

"TRUE EMPEROR," they said, "we ask for grace!
We had no wish, we swear in Jesu's name,
To show contempt to you in any way;
The only leave and surety we claim
Is that we have in Jesus and our Faith,
And in your self, whose honour we obey;
We brothers are the sons of the most brave
And noble knight your mighty realm contains:
Lord Aymeri, the Count to whom you gave
The town Narbonne, which lies upon the waves,
And which you won from kings of Pagan race;
He's held its land so strongly since that day
That not one foot or fistful has been claimed
By heathen hands in never-ending raids;
The fief, instead, has grown with Jesu's aid;
He greets you, Sire, in homage, and he prays

And urges you in love and faith the same
To honour us, his sons, with those domains
And offices within the Frankish state
That our house held from yours in ancient days."
The King, this time, replied with no delay:
"God bless and keep Count Aymeri and save
Good Hermenjart, so fair and fresh of face!
But as for you, by God, I say again
I greet you not and owe you naught but hate!
For you are knaves and full of roguish ways
Which you must suffer for, make no mistake!
And nonetheless you strut in here and claim
Estates and ranks that once were yours, you say!
What lands are these and titles in my state
To which the Count has pledged his children's names?"
Red Hernaut said: "I'll tell you straightaway!
Young William requests the Oriflamme
And right to guard your lands which border Spain;
Bernart requests that he himself remain
Here by your side as counsellor-in-state;
And I would serve your table every day
As seneschal of mighty France the great;
Our father made these promises and claims
　　When we began our journey."

"TRUE EMPEROR, my lord," Hernaut went on:
"In word or deed we'd never do you wrong;
These offices which I have told you of,
Were promised us the day we left Narbonne;
And furthermore, he said, when we set off,
That my young brother here, the brave Beuvon,
Should go at once to Gascony's King Yon,
And wed his daughter, whose face with beauty shone,
And rule his land, when he was dead and gone;
He's done all this and won the things he wants;
And Aimer here was told to fight non-stop
Till he had won all Spain and Cordova
With Jesu's help, Who died upon the Cross;
He also said that with the will of God
Garin would rule Pavia and Monbaldon
And all the realm of Didier the strong –

For he himself has neither heir nor son."
"That much is true," the King said in response:
"So far, I see, you've made but little loss!"
With ringing tones he hailed young William:
"To you alone I give my gonfalon!
Your brothers' hands may take the lands whereof
Count Aymeri possessed them in Narbonne!"
"Much thanks, my lord," they said in swift response,
And all knelt down without one moment lost
Before the feet of Charles the Emperor –
All save Aimer, who stood there like a rock;
He never bowed, nor yet allowed a nod;
The King was shocked and raised his voice aloft:
"What trick is this?" he cried aloud in wrath:
"Will you declare your faith to me or not?"
"Great Charlemagne," said Aimer in response,
"So help me God, Who pardoned Longinus,
I want no fief, no large or smaller plot
Within your realm and borders large and long,
No city tower or fortress richly stocked;
I claim alone the right to fight non-stop
And conquer lands in Spanish hands for God,
And hence for me, against the Infidels!
With blade and blood I'll fight them my life long."
On hearing this, the King's reply was prompt:
"Fair brother, friend, your heart is true and strong;
God guide you then, and guard you with His rod,
     As you perform His service."

"FINE BROTHER MINE," said Beuvon, hearing that:
"Don't leave the King against his wish or plan,
But serve him here a year with your strong hand
And in return earn wealth in coin and land!"
"So help me God," said Charles, "he would be mad
To leave me now before he's gained my thanks!
I offer you this promise, brave young man:
So help me God, Whose laws we heed and have,
Serve sixteen months with me and, after that,
I'll give to you both Melun and Samois,
And Béthisy, and Crépy in Valois,
And all the land which makes up Tardenois;

This very day receive Château-Porcien
And borderlands beside the Alemans."
Young Aimer said: "Great King, you have my thanks,
But Sire, I swear by St Omer of Blois,
That if you gave me Chartres and Orléans,
With half Le Perche and all of Le Dunois,
If you gave me half Paris and Etampes,
And filled this hall with every coin in Mans,
   My lord, I couldn't stay here."

AS AIMER SPOKE Charles looked at him and listened:
Within his heart the King was moved to pity,
For he could sense the young man's faith and spirit;
With ringing voice, the noble youth continued:
"True Emperor, my lord, if you are willing
To hear me out, I'd like you as a witness:
I make a vow before you, as a Christian,
To God the Lord of Heaven's glorious kingdom,
And to yourself and all these nobles with you:
While I am gone from lands of our religion
And must abide in kingdoms of the wicked,
No roof or eaves of any Pagan building
Shall shelter me from storm or winds of winter,
Unless it be, by force, some Pagan prison;
I'll seek the heights, the woods or banks of rivers
To pitch the tent which I alone shall live in;
My mangonels each day shall storm their cities;
My catapults and picks each day shall hit them
Until their towers and crenelled walls are smitten
Upon the ground so Christ may gain admittance;
We'll storm them all and strike the Moors within them
Until they yield, or die if they resist us;
And you, my lord, shall have their lands and riches."
On saying this, he hailed the knights within there:
"Where are you then, young knights of daring vigour,
Who wish to prove your prowess to the limit?
To all who come with me upon this mission,
I give my word, most truly, as a Christian,
That any wealth or goods that we shall win there
Will all be yours, shared out in fair division;
For I seek naught except your sworn admission

To be my men and fight as you are bidden."
They all replied: "You speak with grace and wisdom;
If you do all that you have pledged your will to,
Not only we but many will assist you!"
Young Aimer said: "Don't doubt of me one instant!
I'll treat you all as you yourselves would wish it,
If you'll obey and never fail or trick me,
But be my men and fight as you are bidden."
They all replied: "We shall be, true and willing."
When this was said they swore to journey with him
And pledged their word as well as they could give it;
Before the bell at noon had ceased its ringing,
Some fifty score and more *en masse* were milling
Along the streets to meet outside the city,
Where, in a field, young Aimer bade them listen:
"My lords," he said, "attend the thoughts I'm thinking!
Two further weeks are needed to permit us
To fully arm and seek the best provisions
That we can find in horses and equipment;
For this expense I'll give you gold and silver."
They all replied: "We'll do as you have bidden."
And full of cheer they charged back to the city;
Inside his hall King Charlemagne was sitting
With all his knights of great renown and wisdom;
The King was sad and to himself he whispered:
"Ah, God above, Who made the world we live in,
I've lost a lot and still my loss continues!
Two score and more of years have not diminished
My memory of Spain and pain co-mingled!
My losses there were greater than my winning,
For there it was I lost my finest kinsman,
My nephew dear, whose death has stopped me living,
And Oliver, his breast with valour brimming,
And many knights of fearless might and spirit;
And must I watch this callow knight, this infant,
Ride off again to Spain so keen and quickly,
And men of mine in serried lines ride with him?
Almighty God, true King of all, forgive me:
I'm sore afraid my eyes again shall witness
    Scarce one return from Spain."

KING CHARLEMAGNE was mightily afraid
For Aimer's sake, whose valour won such fame,
As he prepared to journey into Spain
And fight the Moors, that savage, heathen race;
If only you had seen him on that day
Come striding forth before King Charlemagne!
The King looked up and hailed him in this vein:
"Brave youth, it seems too reckless, I must say,
"For you to rush so rashly into Spain!
So little time has passed since I campaigned
With many men in Spain to serve the Faith;
My losses there were greater than my gains,
For all my best and bravest knights were slain;
This makes me very fearful for your sake!"
"True Emperor, for good St Simon's sake,
You went to Spain a King of might and fame,
And would have won that realm and all its claims,
Without the crime of Ganelon the knave;
But I am still a youth, whose fame and name
And property, are nothing at this day;
But in God's name and with His loving grace
There's all to win, if I am strong and brave;
Most noble King, accept this pledge I make:
By God, Who pardoned Longinus's blade,
I swear to you that every town I take
From Gate of Spain to Cordova the great,
I'll battle hard with all my strength and faith
To have and hold for God and you the same!
I'll send to you each tribute that I raise."
On hearing this, the King's delight was plain;
He swore at once, by Simeon the Saint:
"By God, Who pardoned Longinus's blade,
How fine and fair a promise you have made!
And I pledge this: however far away
Your quest may lead, if you are caught or gaoled
By Saracens, I'll hasten to your aid
With all my knights on rapid destriers."
"Much thanks, my lord," the youth said straightaway:
    "It makes me glad to serve you."

YOUNG AIMER STOOD upon the marble floor
Of Charles's hall, the mighty Emperor;
He pledged his faith to Charles the King for all
The help and aid that Charles himself had sworn,
And filled at once with great content and joy;
Then all the sons of Aymeri stepped forth
And bowed to Charles without one moment's pause;
See then, my friends, that legate rushing forth,
That bishop too – we met the pair before,
When our good youths deprived them of their board!
They'd come again to Charlemagne's high court
To see the King and seek recourse in law;
The legate said: "Most mighty liege and lord,
These very youths who stand here, proud and tall,
Are vicious rogues who drove us from our hall
And flayed the skins of those in our employ;
We ask, lord, that you give us justice, or
Give up these men, we ask for nothing more:
You promised us, last night, your full support."
The King replied: "These men are mine, not yours!
In all good faith, I cannot harm them, for
Fair Hermenjart would say I served her false,
And Aymeri, who's never failed my cause;
    Nor will I hand them over."

ON HEARING THUS the high and haughty legate,
Hernaut the Red with heavy rage turned redder!
He strode to him and almost struck the fellow,
But stayed his hand as he beheld the Emperor;
He swore to God, Who lies or fails us never:
"If it were not for Charlemagne's presence,
I'd make you pay a full and fearful penance!
True Emperor, by St Rémy, I tell you,
These tonsured thieves have seized the lands of many
And stolen wealth to make their own selves wealthy;
Their vestries bulge with gold and silver vestments!
From here up to Ponthieu these lustful prelates,
If they live near some honest man, are ready
To shame his wife and blame him for the error."
The King replied: "No more of this, young fellow!
We all should serve with honour and should cherish

The chosen men of God the Lord in Heaven;
Make peace with him, I order you directly."
Hernaut replied: "I shall obey you ever."
He drew his glove and held it to the legate;
The priest, when he observed King Charles's pleasure,
Though glad or sad, came forward to accept it;
    He dared do nothing else.

WHEN PEACE WAS MADE between Hernaut the strong
And that old priest, against his will or not,
The next to come before them was King Yon,
Who by the coat enclasped the young Beuvon;
He saw the King and raised his voice aloft:
"True Emperor, I greet you here in God!
My lovely wife, whose face with beauty shone,
Gave birth to none save fair-faced Elisant,
Whom I would wed, in truth, before too long
To this fine son of Aymeri of Narbonne,
A gallant youth and worthy called Beuvon;
While I still live he'll help me like a son
And rule my realm when I am dead and gone."
"That's wise indeed," said Charles the Emperor:
"As wedding gift I'll give Château-Landon."
"Much thanks for this," said Beuvon in response;
So, saying this, and other things thereon,
The King decreed that, with the death of Yon,
    Beuvon should rule his kingdom.

WHEN YON SHOULD DIE, whose heart with courage beat,
All Gascony would be young Beuvon's fief;
He pledged the King his faith and fealty;
When this was done, King Boniface appeared
With young Garin, whose face with valour gleamed;
He strode his way to Charlemagne's gold seat
And hailed the King with wisdom, as was meet:
"True Emperor, my lord, I bid you hear!
Behold Garin, a youth who's kin to me,
As son of brave and wise Count Aymeri;
I have no son or daughter to bequeath
My kingdom to, and so, if you agree,
I'd make Garin the heir to all my fiefs;

He is my sister's son, and brave indeed."
"By God," said Charles, "Who gives us breath to breathe,
I do agree – it fills me with good cheer!"
The pledge was made, and then at Charles's feet,
Young Garin swore his love and loyalty;
Now all the sons of Aymeri the fierce
Had won the place he'd sent them forth to seek,
    Before all France's barons.

10. How Aymeri's sons were knighted

HOW FINE A DEED the King performed that day!
Now all the youths had won their honour's claim,
The King resolved to crown their quest and raise
All six of them to knighthood's high estate,
Before his lords returned to their domains;
With happy heart he hailed them all this way:
"My youthful lords, your ardour has prevailed!
Because of this, and for your father's sake,
I'll raise you all to knighthood's high estate,
Before my lords return from whence they came;
But go to your good lodgings now and wait
Until the dawn, when, as the morning breaks,
I'll knight you all and give you destriers
And arms to bear for me in Jesu's name."
"My lord," they said, "we thank you for this grace."
Then all retired, his lords and Peers the same;
And our young men, whose face with valour blazed,
In high content sought out their lodging-place;
Through every street the word ran like a flame
From north to south, as each new mouth proclaimed
That Charles the King would dub the coming day
Six noble sons of Aymeri the brave;
The minstrels heard and hurried forth again!
No *jongleur* there or harper who could play
Or sing a song or somehow entertain
Did not attend the lodgings where they stayed!
Nor did Hernaut dismiss them in a rage,
But told his host and bade him to obey,
That none whom came to ply his merry trade

Should be denied but brought inside to play!
Friends, I'll not try to tell you all they ate:
Without a lie, their bounty was so great
I couldn't count one half of all they paid!
To Notre Dame the youths then went to pray
And keep their watch until the dawn of day;
When Charles awoke, without the least delay,
He went to church to hear the Mass proclaimed;
The noble sons of Aymeri the brave
Attended too, with fervent hearts and grave;
How rich indeed the offerings they gave!
When Mass was said they left with Charlemagne
To reach his hall where all his knights were ranged;
Such lovely gowns he gave the youths to take,
As nowadays are never seen or made!
Then squires were told to bring them destriers
And noble arms, each one of highest rate;
The King performed his duty well that day:
He clipped the spurs upon their heels, then raised –
As you all know, for such is still the case
When men are brought to knighthood's high estate –
A noble sword of much renown and praise,
And girt Bernart, the eldest, round the waist:
"My friend," he said, "I give to you this blade
Upon these terms, which I shall clearly state:
That, using it, in service, all your days,
Of God and me, with loyalty and faith,
You never cease to fight the heathen race
And conquer land and honour for your name –
And, doing this, to earn eternal Grace!
Sir Bernart, rise! I order you to stay
Here at my side as counsellor-in-state;
God let you thrive in all you do and say,
    So you may win great honours."

THE SECOND SON of Aymeri the wise
Was dubbed a knight by Charles the fierce of eye;
Young William this was, whose heart was high
And who was called 'Hooknose' in later life;
Charles girt the sword Joyeuse about his side:
This was the blade whose blows put such a blight

Upon the Moors, that hated heathen tribe,
And harvested so many souls for Christ,
So many homes, so many towns and shires:
"My gallant friend," said Charles, the fierce of eye,
"I give to you, with joy, this blade of mine,
To fight for God, Who made us in His like;
There's never been a better sword, besides
Brave Roland's own, who was a peerless knight;
Be ever brave and fierce in every fight,
And serve your liege with faithful heart and mind;
Be bold and strong against all heathen kind
And you will be a true son of the line
    Of Aymeri of Narbonne."

WHEN THIS WAS SAID, King Charlemagne received
The third-born son of gallant Aymeri,
The youth Garin, of strength and temper fierce,
Whom Boniface entrusted with his fief;
Charles girt on him a sword of graven steel
Whose mortal blows so many Moors would feel!
"My friend," said Charles, "God prosper all your deeds!
Be ever brave and love our Christian Creed,
And honour God, the King of Majesty;
With faithful heart and mind serve me, your liege,
And you will be a true son of the breed
That bred your sire, the fearless Aymeri,
Who all his days has filled with gallant feats!
If you can tread the track your father beat,
Then when you die your sons shall never hear
Songs sung of you in blame or mockery;
May God, Who dwells in blessed Trinity,
Reward your life with honour and esteem,
    And death with life eternal."

KING CHARLEMAGNE the Emperor called forth
The fourth-born son of Narbonne's mighty lord,
The youth Hernaut, of stubborn will and force:
He suffered more than all the rest in war;
Charles girt his sword with no delay or pause,
Whose blade in time would bleed so many Moors!

What noble deeds that sword and he performed!
"My friend," said Charles, " I give to you this sword,
Upon these terms, which shall be heard by all:
Be ever brave, each day for evermore!
Love mighty God, the Father of us all,
And serve your liege with loyal deeds and thoughts,
And you will be a true son of the loins
Of Aymeri and all his line before;
May God on High, Who holds the world in ward,
     Confirm your heart with courage."

WHEN THIS WAS SAID, the King turned to Beuvon,
The fifth-born son of Aymeri the strong;
Upon his left he girt the sword-blade on –
Its name Grisbay, its hilt of gold embossed,
Which Aymeri bequeathed him in Narbonne:
No other one, he said, he'd ever want;
"Beuvon," said Charles, " work hard each day for God,
So that your deeds and fame live on in song,
As Aymeri's do; though grizzled grey his locks,
He's slaughtered Moors in scores his lifetime long!
Your fief will be the Gascon realm of Yon,
Which you will rule when he is dead and gone;
But wed at once his daughter Elisant!
May God, Who pardoned Longinus's wrong,
Give victory to you and to the Cross,
     Against our foes in battle."

WHEN THIS WAS DONE he dubbed Aimer a knight,
The sixth-born son of Aymeri the wise;
The Emperor, who showed his great delight,
Girt on a sword whose blade was shining bright;
How well that sword was used in Aimer's life!
How many Moors it slew in countless fights!
How many lands it won for Jesus Christ!
"My friend," said Charles, "attend these words of mine!
Receive this blade of perfect, peerless iron,
In God's own name, the King of all mankind,
Upon these terms which you must pledge and plight:
That, loving God, you'll serve Him day and night!
If you do this, the Lord will be your guide,

And give you strength in every need and strife;
Your fame will grow each day, and when you die,
Your soul will live with God in Paradise,
    If you perform His service."

SO ALL THE SONS of Aymeri the brave
Were dubbed as knights by mighty Charlemagne;
You never saw such worthy knights as they!
Through their prowess they raised the King's own fame
And made him feared in every land and state;
And when at last the King went to his grave,
His son and heir, King Louis, took his place,
But would have been dethroned without their aid;
They fought for and supported his true claim,
And they controlled his borders every day
Against the Moors in service of the Faith;
In Charles's hall what joy and gladness reigned
As all our youths were raised to knighthood's state;
For love of them the King's largesse was great:
One hundred knights were newly armed and gained
New gowns and gear and rested destriers;
Throughout the town flags filled the squares and ways
And bunting flew in every street and lane;
From window-frames they hung out quilts and drapes
And cloths of gold and rowelled silks and capes
With trims of fur and collars of brocade;
Inside the hall the splendour was the same
That Charles displayed for Aymeri's sons' sake:
A feast was laid which all could share and take –
Both high and low, with no one turned away;
So many foods there were and wines to taste
That no one now could name them all, I'd say;
When Charles had supped with all his barons brave,
They raised a pole outside the city-gates
So novice knights could test their skill and grace!
If you had see those lances split and break
And splinters fly from bucklers split in twain!
But our six knights – by now you know their names –
Not one of them, in truth, joined in the games:
For they all thought it was a shameful waste
To strike at boards when there were Moors to slay!

When all the rest, their jests and jousting made,
Returned inside, our brothers did the same;
What music, friends, they bade their *jongleurs* play
And what rich gifts they gave them for their pains –
Fine robes and steeds and bags of deniers
They gave to all who came and entertained;
Not one could say he wasn't richly paid!
The Narbonne knights were full of joy and praise
And feasted thus for three most happy days,
    Before they thought of leaving.

FOR THREE WHOLE DAYS the Monarch and his knights
All feasted thus in joy and praise alike;
And Sir Hernaut performed his role with pride,
Sir William assisting, fierce of eye!
How many cups and goblets full of wine
They carried to the tables where they dined
And served before the worthies there aligned!
The minstrels too were paid a noble price:
One hundred marks for one day and one night;
With no delay, when three days had expired,
The barons left, returning to their shires;
King Yon set off for Gascony the wide,
His entourage behind him, and beside
Him Sir Beuvon, his face with valour bright,
Who'd wed and bed fair Elisant in time;
King Boniface and all his Lombard knights,
Departed for Pavia, and at his side
Rode Sir Garin, the heir to all his might,
Which he would wield with honour all his life;
And forth to Spain and all its heathen tribes
Sir Aimer rode, whose valour was his guide;
A noble band of youths he led in lines,
Three thousand strong, each one well-armed with iron;
My friends, what pains that party would abide,
What hunger, thirst, what agonies and trials!
Throughout all France the word spread like a fire
That Charles, at last, had had his hopes revived,
Which all were dashed the day his Peers had died
At Pagan hands in Roncevaux's divide;
The court dispersed, and yet our six new knights

Did not forget their duty and desire:
They bade a man as messenger to ride
And reach Narbonne, not wasting any time,
To tell the Count, their father fierce and wise,
And Hermenjart, their mother fair and kind,
How Charlemagne, whose beard was tousled white,
Had welcomed them to France and to his side;
And how he'd dubbed each one of them a knight,
And granted them much land and wealth besides;
On hearing this, imagine the delight
  Of Narbonne's Lord and Lady!

11. How the great Emir invaded Narbonne

ON HEARING OF his gallant sons' good fortune,
Of all the things the King had done there for them,
Count Aymeri was filled with great rejoicing;
But listen well, and you shall hear henceforward
How Pagans came to threaten and destroy him!
You all have heard my honest words before this,
How Aymeri dismissed his sons one morning
And gave them lands, with promises of glory,
Which at that time they never could be sure of!
Well, on that day they left their father's fortress,
There was a Moor within the city walls there
Who'd journeyed there at the Emir's own orders
To spy upon the Count and all his forces;
And so it was, when on that fateful morning
The brothers left, the Pagan heard and saw them,
And followed them through hill and dale undaunted,
Until they came to Charlemagne and halted;
And he was there when Charles received them warmly;
And when the King made knights of them, he saw it,
And watched again as three of them rode staunchly
Their separate ways, while three remained at court there;
His time had come; he swore upon his altar
That he would ride within a month, reporting
  To the Emir of Spain.

AND SO THE SPY, God curse the heathen devil,
Rode back again, through hill and dale and meadow,
Not stopping once until Aix-la-Chapelle;
Then, riding on from dawning day to vespers,
He reached Narbonne upon its rocky headland;
And there he stopped, for one whole week, to measure
The city's force, its traffic and defences,
Observing too, at anchor by the jetties,
The many ships and sundry craft which ferried
Within its port from every land and empire,
Expensive silks, fine taffeta and sendal,
And pepper, cumin, both silverware and metal,
Fine swords and spears of Poitou steel, together
With burnished mail and fine enamelled helmets;
When up and down he'd spied the town intently,
He journeyed on – what else is there to tell you?
He journeyed on until one day at vespers
He rode inside the Spanish town Biterno;
He rested there, then with the dawn he readied
And rode non-stop to reach the town Tudela;
It's there he found the daughter of that felon
The great Emir of all the Pagan empire;
Three sons she had, God curse the brute who bred them,
　　Who much desired Narbonne.

ALL THREE WERE THERE, within a grove, that day:
King Esplandoin sat next to King Forrez;
The eldest one was Anfelis by name;
Cornuafar, their uncle, was the knave
Who'd just arrived, the spy, with much to say
Of what he'd seen since setting off from Spain
To spy the land and hand of Charlemagne!
He had returned, and not through Balaguer,
But through Narbonne, that city grand and great;
Said Anfelis: "Fine uncle, tell us, pray,
About Narbonne, that wealthy town and state!"
The Moor replied: "There's much I can relate:
Before the town lie fields and fertile plains
Where wheat is grown, and vineyards full of grapes;
On one side of the town the ocean waves
Bring iron boats and barges to its bay

And galleys full of costly goods to trade;
In summertime or winter, every day,
They barter silks and ermines with brocade
And rested mules and Spanish destriers;
Within the town there's one great palace raised
By Pagan hands and hearts in bygone days:
Their skill and art are shown in how it's made –
Its size and shape and all that it contains;
Its walls depict, in brightly-coloured paint,
A world of birds and beasts in their domains
Of sky and earth, of ocean, air and lake,
And all of them so skilfully portrayed
As if they lived and looked you in the face!
And on one wall a calendar's displayed
With seasons set, and every month and date,
So cleverly that none can tell the way!
And battle-scenes they drew, of fearsome frays,
With all the men who fought them and prevailed;
A picture of Mahomet still remains,
But Christian hands have marred its form and face;
On seeing this, I stormed away in rage."
Said Anfelis: "Your mission was well made;
By great Mahom, in whom I set my faith,
If they're still there in two months from today,
    I swear they all shall perish!"

THE SPANISH KING heard well his uncle's speech,
And to the spy he turned aside to speak:
"My friend," he said, "now listen well to me!
You must set off for Babylon and plead
With our grand Sire, the fierce and great Emir,
To come to us and help us in our need –
For we'd regain Narbonne and all its fiefs,
Which Charles of France took from us in his greed –
And, with his help, cast out Count Aymeri."
The spy replied: "My lord, most willingly!
But I must board a ship prepared to leave!"
The king replies: "You shall do, never fear."
Without delay they left their shady seats
And strode the streets that led down to the quays,
To bid a ship to be equipped to leave;

And when it was, it set out on the sea;
They raised the sails and strove to pick up speed;
The wind blew hard – God curse the Living Fiend –
And never dropped, and so, in just a week,
They crossed the sea and Babylon was reached,
    Where the Emir was waiting.

CORNUAFAR, King Aufarion's son,
Who ruled a town where Martroy's river runs,
Had come from France, where Charles's will was done:
His pilgrim cloak and staff still bore the dust;
He climbed the steps to where his master was,
One hundred Moors surrounding him, each one
A mighty lord and famous Saracen;
The great Emir looked up and hailed him thus:
"Cornuafar, good spy, whence have you come?"
"My lord," he said, "I'll tell you all, at once!
I come from France, where Charles's will is done;
From south to north I've journeyed, learning much;
At Paris, in the King's own citadel,
My eyes beheld the white-haired Emperor
Inside his court with all his courtiers;
I saw and heard their evils plans discussed;
If they had known, I would have been strung up
At once, upon Montmartre's bridge, and hung;
    No ransom would have saved me."

"CORNUAFAR, Mahomet bless you ever!
Let's hear of Charles, the King of all the Frenchmen!"
"Most gladly, Sire, with Mahom's will and blessing!
The King is old but still most hale and healthy;
His beard is white, like flowers in the meadow;
His face is fair, but proud his eye and dreadful;
His fearsome gaze filled all of me with terror!
Each day he rides to woods and streams for pleasure,
And yet, each day, he looks to Spain, lamenting
Count Roland's death, his bravest knight and nephew,
And all the men who perished when he perished;
And as their lord his barons all have pledged him
That they will take this land of yours in vengeance;
And Charles himself has made a start already:

Each day his cooks pack cauldrons, pans and kettles,
And engineers build sieging-towers and engines
Which they can haul and very soon assemble;
He's bringing ploughs to till your fields and meadows;
He'll seize our maids to wed the barons left here:
Each one of them shall have a wife to wed him,
The King himself and all of his lieutenants;
Against this land, and very soon, I tell you,
　　Comes Charlemagne of France."

THUS SPOKE THE SPY, and the Emir, who listened,
Was filled with hate as anger welled within him:
"My friend," he said, "is this your firm conviction:
That Charlemagne, the King of all the Christians,
Will challenge us with all his kith and kindred?"
"Indeed, my lord; without a doubt, he will do!
At Pentecost, when winter turns to springtime,
The King will call on all his lords and princes;
His gallant French will rally first, and with them
His Norman lords, Burgundians and English,
Who then will meet at Orléans and link with
The subject-kings and princes of his kingdoms!
Count Aymeri, whose beard with grey is grizzled,
Who holds Narbonne, a fief that's far from little,
Will be there too, with seven sons whose spirit
Is so renowned they fear no leader living,
No great Emir, no Pagan kings or princes!
With fierce contempt these Narbonne knights and kinsmen
Have sworn revenge for noble Roland's killing;
This Aymeri, their father, will be given
The Oriflamme and lead their army hither:
　　He is indeed a hero."

THE GREAT EMIR, to hear of Aymeri,
Was filled with hate, as anger burned his cheek;
With ringing tones he cried, so all could hear:
"I call on you, my men of breed and creed,
To slay this man who slew my father dear!
Cornuafar, you've shown great bravery,
To dwell so long among a folk so fierce!
For Mahom's sake, describe Narbonne to me,

Which Charlemagne allows this rogue to keep!
What source has he for all the wealth he needs
To pay the knights who serve him for a fee?
If I should call on all my bravest Peers
And muster forth a force that they may lead,
And if we bear Mahom upon the field,
Can we re-take Narbonne and slay this fiend?"
The spy replied: "My lord, you can indeed,
For at this time both he and it are weak!
Strike now, my lord, and all is yours to seize!
I tarried there for more than seven weeks
And my own eyes saw ageing Aymeri
Dismiss his sons and send them from his fief;
They're all in France, I swear to you, Emir,
With Charlemagne their Emperor and liege;
I've written down each fact and act I've seen;
    Lord, I know all about them."

OF FEARLESS HEART, the great Emir replied:
"Describe Narbonne to me, which is so prized;
If I attack, which is its weakest side?
Can I besiege and starve the Narbonne knights?"
"I'll tell you all," Cornuafar replied:
"I know the land and every road alike;
Outside Narbonne an ancient forest thrives
With trees whose trunks are more than six feet wide;
Make siege-engines of these when you arrive!
Within this wood run stag and doe and hind
Which Aymeri, whose face with valour shines,
Rides forth to hunt for venison and prize,
At dawn or dusk, whenever he desires;
If you make camp upon the plain close by,
Then all your host will never lack supplies
    Of game and other plunder!"

"MY LORD EMIR, I swear by my religion
That rich Narbonne's a town well worth the winning;
I truly think I never saw one richer;
The Count is old but full of vim and vigour;
One thousand men each day pay him a visit,
Who all are lords or vavasors or princes

With noble steeds and armour and equipment;
Three thousand troops he has who always live there:
On every side they guard the city's limits;
The city walls built by the Moors are thickened
With mighty towers of stone at equal distance;
Inside his hall are counts and barons with him
Who call him liege and serve him well and willing
For all the fiefs and honours that he gives them;
On any day all those within the city
　Would die to serve the Count."

"MY LORD EMIR, pay heed to what I say:
Four olive trees grow tall in Narbonne's square;
Beneath their shade each day a market trades –
When one is done, another takes its place,
And fills with folk who come and go all day!
There's not one day in Narbonne's market-place
Which isn't worth a full two bushels' weight
Of wealth in coin to Aymeri the brave!
The market trades in spices brought from Spain
And silk from Tyre and ermines with brocade;
Inside the town are mills which grind away
To make the wheat and barley-corn and grains
Which feed the town and livestock it contains;
In truth my lord, this trade it is which makes
The Count so rich and which he gives in pay
To all of those who gladly serve his name
　Inside this noble city."

"MY LORD EMIR, I'll not conceal the fact
That, in Narbonne, some fifteen churches stand,
Constructed by the Frenchmen's faith and hands;
With heavy lead their belfry-towers are clad;
Count Aymeri, and all his knighthood's band,
Go there to pray and praise the God they have –
Their Jesus Christ, Whom high aloft they hang
Upon a cross like some low cattleman,
But all in gold and silver, front and back!
If you can put this city to the sack
And fling to ground each cross and lay it flat,
Then you could strip the wealth that each one has

In gold and silver, and pay your men with that;
And if the Count were toppled too and dashed
To little bits, then all of Spain would clap!
   I swear this by Mahomet."

THE GREAT EMIR heard all he had to say,
Then called upon his envoys straightaway,
And messengers, whose sum alone was great;
"Go forth," he said, "without one moment's waste,
And call to arms the armies of my race,
With none exempt whose hand can lift a blade!
Tell all of them to come here under pain
Of certain death if they should disobey!
I go to win Narbonne upon the waves!"
His riders turned, not daring to delay,
And saddled up their camels in great haste:
Friends, these are beasts which, ridden well, will take
You all around the world and back again
Before four months have spent their span of days!
With letters sealed, which in their packs they placed,
The envoys left to summon help and aid;
From Durelande to mighty Montescler
No Saracen or Slav dared hesitate:
By land and sea they travelled till they came
To Mecca's fields in numberless array;
And there they prayed to Mahom and complained
Against the deeds of our King Charlemagne
And Aymeri, who had attacked their faith
And thrust them out of what was their domain;
Rich offerings upon a shrine they made
And then prepared to set out straightaway,
In ranks too large for me to estimate;
Their battle-gear on sumpters' backs they laid
As olifants gave forth their strident strains
And trumpets trilled and cornets whined and wailed
Till all combined in wild fanfaronade
From ranks so large that I could never state
How many men or kings each flank contained;
Yet there were two with a familiar face!
Behold again the strong King Desramé,
And his much feared co-ruler Baufumez;

You've heard of these, my friends, for they're the same
Who fled Narbonne that evening they escaped
King Charles's siege and Aymeri's sharp blade,
The year he wed fair Hermenjart the Maid!
They gathered now with strong King Cosdroez,
Mohan of Egypt, Mauprin and Giboez,
And Aquilant, lord of Lucena bay,
And the Emir, with Auciber the aged,
And other kings too numerous to name –
At least fifteen, or so the song maintains,
Led by the spy Cornuafar, the knave!
The mountains rang with all the shouts they made,
The neighing steeds and braying mules the same;
The force embarked on barges iron-based,
Which left the port and launched upon the waves;
The Living Fiend breathed wind to fill their sails,
And in two weeks they reached the coast of Spain;
They saw Narbonne, a prize so fit for praise,
As on they sailed for Tarragona bay;
They saw the coast, the cities and the plains,
And thousands wept for pity and for shame
That they were forced to leave so fine a place
To Charlemagne upon that fateful day;
They reached the port and disembarked in haste;
They seized their arms and mounted straightaway
On steeds of war, impatient for the fray;
They struck the towns and laid the country waste;
They captured men and placed them all in chains,
Then drove them forth and beat them, filled with hate,
Until they bled, then beat them once again;
The month was June, my friends, the very day
Of St John's feast, a day of joy and faith,
When the Emir and his accursed race
    Arrived before Narbonne

12. How the siege began and how Aymeri ran into trouble

THE MONTH WAS JUNE, with flowers on the rose,
And nightingales in song with orioles;
My friends, behold! The Pagans left their boats

And the Emir aligned them all in rows;
He called upon Mauprin to lead their host:
"Good man, lead forth the vanguard of my folk,
A thousand score, both nobly armed and bold!
Before Narbonne, that ancient town of stone,
Erect my tent where it can face our foe –
My mighty tent, whose colours flame and glow;
I won it once on Almeria's coast,
When Corsublez the Turk fell to my blows:
Its ropes alone are worth Pavia's gold;
The shining tent is like a silver bowl!
By great Mahom, who keeps us hale and whole,
I'll take Narbonne before this summer goes,
And add its gold and silver to my own!
Then Burgundy I'll take and seize the throne
Of Normandy and France from Charles the old!
I won't allow great Charlemagne a groat,
Nor Aymeri, whose hoary whiskers flow!
Narbonne the rich shall no more be his home!
    By right of birth I claim it!"

"ATTEND ME WELL, my lords," the Pagan said:
"We'll take this town with every speed and strength!
Gaudin the king, who built it, was himself
My ancestor and ruled here till some wretch
Approached his bed and slew him as he slept;
Old Julius Caesar put that rogue to death
Then led his troops to seek and take revenge;
He entered Apulia, where he was met
By Breton troops sent there to halt his steps;
Their armies fought a battle of such length
It carried on for one whole day and then,
At break of dawn, it broke out once again;
Fenicius, at last, was struck to death,
Great Pompey's nephew, by whom this host was led;
King Salemon, at once, urged on his men,
Who rallied when Fenicius fell dead,
And fought like mad against those Romans left;
They spared them naught until the night-time, when
The Romans knew they'd failed in their attempt,
And, giving up, they turned around and fled;

King Salemon pursued them long and well,
And those not killed were hauled away to spend
Their final days in Breton gaols and cells,
    As soon as he rode homeward."

HIS STORY TOLD, the great Emir stopped talking
And mustered forth his men in rank and order;
They left the shore and rode to hide their horses
One half a league before the city's fortress,
Within a wood, both very dense and broad there;
The vanguard troops were given to King Mauprin;
The Pagan said: "Without delay ride forward!
One thousand score are ready to support you;
Stop only when you see Narbonne before you!
Upon your way put every beast to slaughter!
If Aymeri should dare to ride towards you
And fight you with his knights, then I exhort you
To let him feel the anger of your sword-blade!
I want no man to tell me and to taunt me
That I mistook a weakling for a warlord!
    We all would feel the shame."

IN FEARSOME MOOD Mauprin bestrode his steed
And called to Gaudelin, who led Montclis:
"Your men and mine shall be those in the lead!
Call forth your troops and ride in front with me!
We'll start our ride well guarded by these trees,
Then, on our way, we'll slaughter every beast,
So Aymeri and Hermenjart can see!"
Said Gaudelin: "A worthy plan, indeed!
By great Mahom, the god of our belief,
I'd rather see my heart and liver pierced
Than have bad news of us reach the Emir!"
They crossed the Aude, its waters fierce and fleet,
And, with the wind behind them, made good speed;
They hurried on, with strength and temper fierce,
And saw Narbonne, which thrilled the hearts of each;
Upon their way they gathered prey to eat
By slaughtering and quartering each beast;
Inside Narbonne the Count was seized with fear,
    And climbed upon his ramparts.

THE MONTH WAS JUNE, the weather fine and warm;
As you have heard, my friends, before Narbonne
The fields were filled with Saracens and Moors;
Upon their way they slaughtered prey galore;
Mauprin, upon an Arab mule, rode forth
In fearsome mood before the city walls,
And reaching there, cried out with ringing voice:
"And where are you, pernicious Count and false?
Most wrongfully you rule what isn't yours;
The great Emir demands of you, and all,
To leave Narbonne, which was his town before,
And flee his land as Christian cowards ought!
By great Mahom, who is our Lord and Law,
Tomorrow, if he finds you, he has sworn
    That you will be beheaded."

BEFORE NARBONNE the meadows were alive
With Saracens and sundry Pagan tribes!
Mauprin the Moor, God blast his blighted life,
With ringing tones raised up his voice and cried:
"You wrinkled wretch! Bestir your horse and ride!
Escape at once, or you will surely die!
Forget Narbonne – this town and port are mine!
When morning comes, if you've not taken flight,
We'll string you up upon a gallows high!
And Hermenjart, your fair and lovely wife,
Will go to Spain and be the sport of squires."
"You lying rogue!" Count Aymeri replied:
"It's written down in charters sealed and signed
That Narbonne town is ours by lawful right;
A Christian fief it was in times gone by,
And thanks to God, Who makes the dew and sky,
It's ours again! We'll never lose it twice!
Narbonne is filled with churches and with shrines
Confessed and blest and freshly sanctified
For God and Mary, parents of the Christ;
No mosque shall raise its dome against their spires!
Be gone yourself, with all your heathen kind!
When news arrives in all of France's shires
That you have crossed the sea to steal and fight,
I know full well it won't take long to find

My worthy sons in France, who will unite
And hurry here with every Frankish knight,
    To meet you and defeat you."

SAID ANFELIS: "Old man, pay heed to me!
I have men here more fierce than any seen:
As black as ink they are and built like beasts:
Their spines are huge and twisted at the peak;
Their eyes are red, like coals aflame with heat,
Their noses long and razor-sharp their teeth –
Their bite is worse than any snake's can be;
Their heads are small but they have monstrous ears
Which shade their face at night from storm or breeze,
And, when they fight, protect them like a shield;
They fear no axe, no cutting sword or spear,
And use no arms or armour in the field:
They eat the foe that dares to go too near!
Old man and weak, how can you combat these?
If you attempt to fight with them, I fear
That they will crush and eat you up like wheat!"
Said Aymeri: "A curse upon such fiends,
For God decides and guides my destiny!"
Said Hermenjart, of visage fair and sweet:
"Lord Aymeri, we are bereft and weak;
My noble Count, ill-starred the day indeed
    That our fine sons departed."

BELOW NARBONNE, along the meadow's length,
The Pagans camped in noisy joy and jest;
King Esplandoin, with Mauprin and Borrel,
Raised up at once a very noble tent
Made for them by the wife of Fanoel,
A lord who lived and ruled in Aufalerne;
Upon one side a Moor called Yrael
Had painted scenes from Pagan Testament,
Of birds and beasts and history's events,
Of gallant knights and ladies and young men
In battle's strife or trials of skill and strength;
And when the ropes pulled up the sides to let
The sunlight shine upon the poles, they shed
A brighter glow than candles in a cell!

The Pagan ranks paraded their prowess,
As up and down they shouted as they went,
For Aymeri to hear, and all the rest
   That day inside the city.

THE PAGANS SAT in siege around the city;
Without a lie, so many tents they pitched there,
The very sky has no more stars within it
Than Narbonne plain had lodges and pavilions!
What happened next I'll tell you, if you'll listen!
The time went by, and one day, after dinner,
The Count looked out of his well-hidden window
Upon the camp, so very vast and busy –
Three thousand youths were running through the middle,
The noble squires of Pagan knights and princes –
And, as he looked, he cursed the camp's existence:
"God damn you all, you blighted heathen villains!
If Charlemagne, whose hair with grey is grizzled,
Could know our plight, who left me in this city,
Then he'd be here, or on his way, this minute,
With all his knights to free us from our prison!"
While Aymeri was lost in thought and wishes
The Pagans cheered, beholding in the distance
A raiding-gang returning from its mission:
They'd plundered shrines and houses of religion
And driven forth defenceless men and women,
Then chained them up and beaten them and whipped them;
The wretches cried, with hands and voice uplifted:
"Lord Aymeri, most noble Count and Christian,
Deliver us from shame and from affliction,
For you will bear the blame if they should kill us!"
On hearing this, Count Aymeri sighed grimly
And then cried out to all the nobles with him:
"Where are you now, you vassals of such vigour,
You new-dubbed knights who've promised to assist me,
And in my hall have boasted with such spirit
And begged me there so often for permission
To break this siege with which we have been smitten?
The day has come to prove your valour's limit!
If you can save these prisoners and bring them
By force of arms back here inside the city,

Then I would cheer and cherish those who did it."
On hearing this, they bowed and vowed to give him
  Their brave and hearty thanks.

ON HEARING THIS, his vassals and his knights
Cheered fearlessly and hurried to comply;
With every haste they armed themselves with iron
And through the gate, which porters opened wide,
They left the town, equipped and keen to fight;
The Count remained beside his window high,
But still he heard below the dismal cries
Of wretched folk the Moors had caught and tied
And dragged along in chains to flog and strike;
Among them was a Count Garin, whose wife
Had borne a son, called Romanz, then had died –
And he'd been called 'The Orphan' since that time;
He stood in chains at his good father's side,
Till, suddenly, they stripped him, in his sight,
And with their sticks they struck him with such spite
That blood was drawn with every blow applied;
Both son and sire were so beset they cried
Aloud to God, Who never fails or lies,
To guard their souls and pity them their lives;
With ringing tones they raised their heads on high
And cried aloud: "For love of Jesus Christ,
Sir Aymeri, defend us, lest we die
And you should earn a coward's name thereby."
Fair Hermenjart could not but hear their cries;
She hastened forth to reach her husband's side,
And at his feet, beseeching him, she sighed:
"Fine Count, my lord, for love of God on High,
Ride forth and save your people from these crimes!"
"By God above," Count Aymeri replied,
"If I should fail these people in their plight,
  Let fire and flame consume me!"

THREE THOUSAND MEN and more from Estrangor
Bestrode a red or brown or piebald horse;
Before his gate Count Aymeri rode forth
With all his knights in fierce array and force;
They slew at once one hundred of those Moors

And freed all those their raiding-band had caught;
The captives fled for safety's sake towards
The town itself with all its wealth and warmth,
While after them the Pagans sent a corps
Of ruthless men, strong-willed and skilled in war,
To stand between the Count and his own walls;
God help them all, and good my lord St Maur –
If captured there, they'd have no cause for joy;
No wealth or coin would save them then at all
    From shameful death and slaughter.

BELOW NARBONNE, upon the flowery meadow,
Rode Aymeri and all of his assembly –
One hundred knights, in bright and shining helmets,
Who ruled their fiefs through him as his lieutenants;
Each said to each: "Now let us earn the credit
Which Aymeri has lavished on us ever!
The time has come for us to prove our mettle,
And for the brave to show their valour's merit!"
When this was said they doubled their endeavours,
And as they met, and both sides came together,
They speared the Moors and spilled their Pagan entrails;
But on their side the loss alike was heavy;
Within the town they climbed the walls at vespers
And lit up fires and lanterns to direct them;
And yet, before the Count could ever get there,
More Saracens entrapped him with their weapons;
He fought them off with all his strength and temper,
And with their swords his men came to the rescue;
They fought so well that with the Lord God's blessing
The fields were filled with all the Moors that perished;
What use was that? Unless Lord God in Heaven,
Who makes the sky and dew alike, could help them,
They all would die; for there were just too many
    Of that accursed race.

THE NOBLE FRENCH fought on with all their zeal;
So many Moors they slew with sword and spear
That on the field their blood poured out in streams;
They never stopped till daylight disappeared,
When, turning round, they found they'd no retreat:

My friends, that night they had no rest or sleep,
For by their gates, before them, they could see
That corps of Moors who went there when their peers
Were fighting hard upon the open field;
So, spurring on and down a steep ravine,
They met the Aude, its waters dark and deep,
Its channel wide, and noisy as it beat
Against the town and any ground between;
They waded in until the waters reached
To each man's chest, and chilled them to their feet;
As best they could they held on to their steeds,
And stayed that way until the dawn appeared!
They swore that this would cost the Pagans dear!
With light of day they looked about to see
The mighty tent of Pagandom's Emir;
They knew it by the crystal on its peak,
And struck at once, to vent their raging grief!
How many gold enamelled cups they thieved
And silks from Tyre and sendal cloths and sheets
And pikes and spears of Poitou's finest steel;
With all they took they loaded up four beasts
To reach the town when all around was clear;
But this, I fear, would also cost them dear,
    Before they reached their city.

THE TENT WHEREIN our Frenchmen boldly entered
Was the Emir's itself, and full of treasure,
Which they purloined with great delight and pleasure:
Both silver, gold and cloths of silk and sendal;
They found a Moor, a courtly youth and clever,
Called Prince Forrez, so wise in law and letters
That he was their lord chamberlain already;
His father was a mighty king – however,
He shook with fear when he beheld our Frenchmen,
And cried aloud: "Good, noble knights, I beg you,
If I am slain, you may one day regret it!
In healing arts I have no peer or fellow;
There's none on earth, though he were on his death-bed,
If I were called before his breath had left him,
Whom I could not restore to health and better!"
Said Aymeri: "Then come with me directly

And live with me and help me live forever!
Not one of us will harm you or torment you."
They raised the lad upon an ambling jennet
And made for home in high content and merry;
And yet, my friends, before they ever entered,
  They'd pay a heavy price.

THE NIGHT BEFORE not one of them had slept,
But, come the dawn, they stormed the Pagan's tent
And found Forrez, so skilled in healing men;
A youth, in truth, more use than any wealth!
The Count addressed Girart and Gaudin then:
"My lords," he said, "escort this lad ahead
To Narbonne's walls and guard him right and left!
Inside my hall be sure that he is led
To no one else but Hermenjart herself;
Tell her, for love of me, to watch him well."
"My lord," they said, "we'll do as you request."
At this they turned, to do as he had said,
While he himself turned round to strike again!
How many blows he dealt, and felt no less!
If you had seen the clash that happened next!
How many shields were split and spears were cleft!
How many feet were shorn, and hands and heads!
How many Moors were floored and flung to death!
The great Emir appeared on horse himself
And Aymeri ran at him, rein unchecked;
He would have run his sword right through his flesh,
But, looking up, the Pagan filled with dread
And ran away – no gold would stay his step!
The raiding Moors all turned their mounts at length
And spurred them back directly to their tents,
Relieved as one that they had cheated death;
The great Emir was there, and with respect
They said: "My lord, is Forrez rescued yet?"
He answered: "No! His loss, I much regret,
  Will never be recovered."

THE PAGAN, WHEN he saw his raiding force
In full retreat, was filled with bitter gall;
His comrades said: "Do not dismay, my lord!

They've won this fight, but we shall win the war!
With good Mahom we'll flay and slay them all!"
They seized their arms without one moment's pause
And chased the Count, on seeing him withdraw;
They met again and fighting flared once more –
And this time, they'd have killed the Count, I'm sure,
When from the town a gallant band rode forth,
Their fighting strength some five and thirty score,
The very knights the King had left before
To serve the Count when first the town was stormed;
Girart controlled the rear, Garin the fore;
On reaching him, they struck without remorse
    Against the hated heathens.

IF YOU HAD SEEN those French and Pagan ranks
Swap blow for blow as both sides made a stand!
A Moor was there, his name was Cristomal,
With richer arms than any mortal man!
He pledged Mahom, whose evil ways he had,
That he would strike the first opposing Frank
So fiercely with his spear that he would ram
The shaft of steel and its vermilion flag
Through chest and chine and force it out the back!
God curse the knave for such a pledge as that!
Such awesome strength bode ill for all the Franks,
    And evil for the first one!

THIS CRISTOMAL had armour all of iron:
His mail was damascened, his helm alike;
God strike him dead, Who made of water wine,
Or we shall lose, if he should live and thrive!
This brute from hell impelled his steed to strike
Sir Garin's shield with his nielloed pike;
Above the boss of purest gold refined
He struck him well and flung the knight aside;
His son, Romanz the Orphan, filled with spite
    To see his father falling

GARIN THE DUKE was filled with shame and grief;
He sprang aloft and stood upon his feet;
He drew his sword and, raising forth his shield,

He hacked the Moors in scores upon the field;
His son Romanz came spurring up with speed,
His shield aloft, astride his sturdy steed,
And in his hand a strong and cutting spear;
Unless the Moors were on their guard, they'd see
The duke avenged with interest on the fee!
Romanz arrived to aid his father's zeal;
Against the Moor who met him first he reared
A mighty blow which battered through his shield
And bored a hole five fingers wide and deep
Inside the boards to bite the flesh beneath;
He flung him dead upon the flowery field,
     Before Garin his father.

ROMANZ THE LAD was sad and sick at heart
To see his sire in such a deadly pass;
Without revenge his honour shared the smart;
He spurred his steed, which galloped in the charge,
And struck a Moor head-on upon his targe;
He smote the boss and broke the boards apart
And through his ribs he rammed the sturdy shaft;
He flung him dead upon the flowery grass;
Then by the rein he grabbed within his grasp
The Pagan's steed to stop it striding past;
His father smiled, the danger past at last,
     And mounted it with pleasure.

HE MOUNTED UP, and with his son's support,
He seized a lance and gripped a buckler's cords;
Upon his shield he smote another Moor
And through the boss he broke his buckler's boards;
The hauberk's mail he ripped aside and bored
The heavy spear from front to rear and more!
A lance's length he flung him from his horse
And left him dead upon the flowery floor;
He galloped on and, lifting up his sword,
He cried: "Narbonne!" in clear and ringing voice:
"Good men of France, race valiant in war!
Lay on, I say, against this heathen horde!"
The Count himself, forever back and forth
Throughout the press, fought on with all his force

Against the Moors with no respite at all!
Upon his heels rode all his knights and lords;
The men they struck knew well their time was short!
At last Guibert was woken by the noise
From slumber deep within the ancient wards
    Of Narbonne's noble palace!

13. How Guibert fared against the Pagans

WHEN DAWN ARRIVED, the day was bright and sunny;
Within a room in which the sun came flooding,
Slept young Guibert, all mindless of the struggle;
He heard the noise and woke, his spirit troubled;
Without delay he jumped up from his slumber,
And through a hole made in the window's shutter –
God curse the rogue whose dart or arrow cut it –
The lad looked out and saw and heard the hubbub
Of men and steeds, of thumping blows and thudding,
As on the plain both sides displayed their courage;
He saw their spears, their cutting swords and bucklers,
And glowing arms which glittered in the sunlight,
And in his mind the lad was filled with wonder;
Invoking God with all his heart, he hurried
With dress and shoes, and then at once went running
    Towards the castle hall.

WHEN YOUNG GUIBERT beheld the Moors so near,
Invoking God, Who never fails the need,
He cried: "Dear Lord, look down and pity me,
And keep from harm my father Aymeri –
If he should die, I am bereft indeed!"
This said, he called his tutor, Aumari:
"My lord," he said, "by blessed St Géry,
Bring forth my arms and armour with all speed,
So I may join my father in the field;
I've heard the noise of many men and steeds!
The Devil must have drugged me in my sleep,
Or I'd have been there since the dawn at least;
For love of God, make haste and help me here."
On hearing this, his tutor blanched with fear:

"Guibert, my boy, for God's sake let it be!
I dare not act without your father's leave;
He'd have me hung or flung down in the sea
Or burnt alive for all the world to see!"
On hearing this, Guibert was filled with grief;
He raised his fist and struck him in the teeth;
Blood spurted forth and smeared his chin and cheek;
He fell to ground, all dizzy, in a heap,
But straightaway he staggered to his feet:
"Much thanks, my son; you too know how to teach!
For Jesu's sake, take up your arms and leave!"
Guibert replied: "Sir, bring them please to me."
And he replied: " My lord, most willingly."
He brought him first a hauberk stitched with steel,
Which Guibert donned, his manner proud and fierce,
Then on his head he laced a helm of green;
Then, in the stalls, Guibert led forth a steed
Which Aymeri his father held so dear
That never would he give or sell that beast
To any man, to friend or family;
Guibert puts on its saddle, then its leash,
Then swung astride with gallant pride and zeal,
And took in hand a shining, golden shield;
He had no lance but grasped a sturdy spear;
Through Narbonne's gate the porter watched him leave
And make all haste to join the battle's heat,
    To joust the hated heathens!

WHEN YOUNG GUIBERT rode through the gate, he sped
His long-maned steed to strike among the press;
Some fourteen blows he'd struck and smitten dead
Two Pagan kings and ten more rogues as well,
Before his shield was noticed by his men!
The Count, meanwhile, was very close to death!
All day the Moors had stalked him till at length
They'd cornered him against a chasm's edge;
With four great spears they'd pierced his shield and rent
The mail upon his hauberk's coat to shreds,
And maimed the Count – with heavy wounds he'd bled
And fallen down with pain, his war-horse fled;
The Pagans would have killed him there, my friends,

And, after that, have won Narbonne itself,
If young Guibert had not arrived just then!
He spurred his steed, which galloped on unchecked,
And went to strike the first he saw ahead
Upon his shield, which split in pieces when
He speared the boss and broke it end to end;
The coat beneath was ripped apart and wrecked
And, like a wedge, the spear-point split the flesh;
One lance's length it flung him to his death;
Guibert at once secured his horse and helped
His father mount, who, in his great distress,
Rode off at once, with nothing heard or said;
Without delay he spurred away instead
To reach Narbonne with all his knights and friends;
The gate swung wide, all rode inside – except
For young Guibert, himself now sorely pressed;
Upon the field, bereft of any French,
He faced alone the Pagans' fierce revenge,
And fought them off, again and yet again;
His spear all split, he drew his sword and sent
Relentless blows upon those heathen helms!
Like elder-logs he split them end to end,
Through skull and skin, through chest and chine and legs;
First one he slew and then his neighbour next,
Then, after those, a third with blows immense;
The Moors looked on, aghast at his prowess:
"Mahomet and Cahu!" they shrieked and yelled:
"Lay on, my lords! There is but one of them!
Don't stay your hand – his days are overspent!"
On saying this, they rushed at young Guibert
And cast their spears and wyverns sharply-edged;
Beneath his thighs his long-maned stallion fell,
And he was seized with overwhelming strength;
He called aloud in Jesu's name for help:
"Count Aymeri, my lord, where are your men?
Sweet Hermenjart, your seventh son is dead!"
But all his words, my friends, were wasted breath;
The youth was bound by cruel cords and led
To the Emir, who brooded in his tent;
    God curse those faithless felons!

THE LAD WAS LED upon a cruel leash
In sad distress to see the great Emir;
While Aymeri, with wicked wounds and deep,
Approached his hall of marble walls a-gleam;
Before its door, beneath a sycamore tree,
The noble Count dismounted from his steed
As knights ran up to help him with all speed;
They loosened first his helm of shining green
And then unlaced his hauberk of the East;
His body showed all red and raw beneath
From injuries the wretched Moors had wreaked,
When in his side they rammed four sturdy spears;
His crimson blood ran down, and suddenly,
He fell to ground with suffering so keen;
His noble knights were overcome with grief,
As Hermenjart returned from church to see
Her husband there, all lifeless at their feet;
She cried aloud, in noble tones and sweet:
"Lord Aymeri, how brave your life has been!
How wise you were in every word and deed!
How great a loss, your death, to chivalry!
Whose hand shall be so liberal and free
With gifts of gold and silver, arms and steeds?
The Saracens henceforth may live in peace
And do their worst, God curse them all and each,
And never fear reprisal or defeat,
     With you no more to match them!"

INSIDE NARBONNE how great a cry went forth!
Fair Hermenjart, of noble face and form,
Returned from church, where Mass had been performed,
To find the Count beneath the sycamore
And thought she looked upon her husband's corpse;
From where she stood she swooned upon the floor
Against the Count, and when she did, her jaw
Lay on a wound from which the blood still poured,
So when she woke, her face was stained with gore;
She stood again and raised her hands and voice:
"Ah, Blessed Maid, Who bore our Heavenly Lord,
Ill-starred the hour that I was ever born!
Alas, Narbonne, you noble town of yore!

How fine a lord no longer will be yours!
A better knight than he ne'er wore a sword –
Not even Roland, the greatest Frenchman, or
Count Oliver, both brave and wise withal;
Fine son Guibert, alas this day should dawn!
For you are robbed, and I, for evermore,
Of Aymeri, whose face with valour stormed,
Your noble sire, whose life has run its course;
Ah, blessed Maid, sweet Mother of us all,
    Restore to me my husband!"

BENEATH THE TREE lay Aymeri the brave;
Fair Hermenjart lamented for his sake,
And all his lords and barons hurried straight
To where he lay, displaying grief so great
As never was for any man displayed;
They wrung their hands, they rent their hair and wailed,
And some fell down around him in a faint;
Romanz spoke out, whose courage never failed:
"What have you done, fine Countess, with Forrez?"
"My lord," she said, "within the hall he waits,
In rooms well-locked to hinder his escape."
On hearing this, Romanz left straightaway;
He found the Moor and brought him in great haste
From where he was to where the Count was lain:
"My friend," he said, "attend to what I say:
Count Aymeri lies here in mortal pain
Your peers have wrought, all rent with wounds and maimed;
If by your skill you make him whole and hale,
We'll give to you such riches and estates
That nevermore will you be poor again."
The Pagan swore by gods whom he obeyed,
That he would not free any man from pain
Till they freed *him*, with no conditions made,
    So he could join his comrades.

COUNT AYMERI bled on beneath the tree;
Throughout Narbonne how awful was the grief
Of every knight and soldier, friend and peer;
Forrez the Moor observed all this indeed
And pitied much, like many of his creed,

The Lady's grief, who swooned without relief;
So, suddenly, he stepped down to the scene,
Unstopped a jar and, taking out some cream,
Stooped down and felt the body at his feet;
He turned the Count this way and that, then cleaned
His wicked wounds with wine most carefully;
He stopped the flow where blows had bitten deep,
Then laid the cream on every wound he'd seen;
Each wound, at once, began to close and heal!
Then with a knife he prised apart his teeth
And made him take a potion bitter-sweet,
More precious far than gold or silver each:
Its drops were drawn from Paradise's stream,
Below a fount which flows in Eden's East,
Where God Himself gave Adam life, and Eve;
Since then, in truth, no mortal born to breathe,
However maimed, however hurt or weak,
If they could drink one drop, then he or she
Would not become as healthy as could be!
Behold the Count! He sat up and decreed
A peacock cooked at once for him to eat!
When this was done, he slumbered, fast asleep,
And when he woke his pain and wounds were healed!
He saw Forrez and hugged and held him near –
He would have kissed the Moor but for his creed;
With ringing tones he raised his voice to speak:
"Forrez, my friend, by God our mighty Liege,
Above all men I ought to hold you dear,
For there's no doubt you've saved my life indeed;
My worthy knights," continued Aymeri,
"This morning when we fought with the Emir,
They brought me down from my fleet-footed steed
And I'd have lost my life or liberty,
If Lord our God had not looked after me,
And one rare youth, who raced to my relief;
I've never seen so fine a lad as he,
Nor one who bore his arms so skilfully;
His look was like my son Guibert's indeed!
Before my eyes he slew upon the field
A Pagan king and brought his steed to me;
I mounted up, for mighty was my need

To reach Narbonne with every haste and speed;
Now we are safe, but he's been caught, I fear,
And dragged away in chains to the Emir!
If I were sure that he would be released,
I'd pay in silver some fifteen ransom-fees!
By St Amant, my noble Countess, please
Bring forth my son so I may see him here."
His wife replied: "My lord, most willingly."
But coming where she'd left the lad asleep,
She only found his tutor, all in tears;
She cried at once: "Old fool, why do you weep?"
He wailed at once: "You'll hear no lies from me;
Though I should die, I'll tell you no deceit;
This morning, when the bell of prime had pealed,
Guibert could hear the fighting in the field
And then a shout of one in direst need;
He bade me fetch his armour instantly;
When I delayed and dared to disagree,
He raised his fist and hit me in the teeth
So fiercely that the blood ran down my beard;
He raced then to the stables for that steed,
The one your gallant husband holds so dear
That no one else may gallop it but he,
And harnessed it and saddled it to leave;
Then, putting on his mail and helmet green,
He mounted up in all his battle-gear;
Around his neck he hung his heavy shield,
Then in his fist he seized a solid spear
And left the town with every haste and speed;
Since then I've heard no news of him, I fear."
Cried Hermenjart: "Narbonne, you've murdered me!
     Now I have lost my youngest!"

AS HERMENJART was told of his escaping,
Her visage paled and all her blood went racing:
She swooned with shock and dropped to ground in fainting;
On coming round, she cried aloud and hastened
To Aymeri as fast as she was able,
And found him well, his wounds no longer painful:
"My lord," she cried, "my only son remaining
Is lost to me! He joined the fray at daybreak

To fight for you, and now I fear he's taken!
The Saracens will torture him and slay him!"
The Count replied: "He did as he was fated;
Our family is destined thus, my lady;
Not one of us lies buried in a graveyard
But on the field where death is always waiting;
And should it come, by Heaven, those it takes there
Shall never hear reproaches made against them
   On God's great Judgement Day."

WITHIN NARBONNE how deep a sorrow reigned
For young Guibert, that gallant vassal's sake;
But all alike rejoiced at young Forrez,
Who had restored the Count to health again;
Now in his hall a certain room of state
Had once been an emir's called Giboez;
Upon its walls the seasons were portrayed
And mighty fights and battles of great fame;
Around the room were pictures, done in paint,
Of harps and lutes the ancient minstrels played;
And histories, passed down from age to age
Since time began and God made man of clay,
Were written there in scripts of noble grace;
So sweet a smell the room itself exhaled
That anyone who entered thought that they
Were purified with every breath they'd take!
Count Aymeri made use of it this way:
He brought all those whose injuries were grave
Directly there, and in that lovely place,
On couches, side by side, he had them laid,
So each could have, at once, Forrez's aid;
The youth himself applied such tender care
That all were healed of all their hurts and pains
Before the sun had waxed four times and waned;
If young Guibert had been with them again,
They would have been content enough, I'd say;
But he was not; the Moors had brought him straight
To their Emir, who in his tent remained,
And there they'd stripped his armour straightaway,
Unstrapped his shield and lifted from his face
His helm of green with golden gems inlaid;

And as they raised his coat of saffroned mail
He stood there then, in just a gown, all chafed
And bruised in parts from his strong hauberk's chains;
His skin was white, like summer flowers in May;
His eyes were green and like a hawk's they blazed;
His hair was blond and cut with curls and waves;
The Pagans stared and all were moved to say:
"These Christians are, of all, the fairest race!
Alas, indeed, that they are false in faith!
This fighter here is proud and fierce of face,
A scion of some rich and noble race!
He's very like Aimer, that crazy knave
Who felt our wrath in lofty Valsegrez!"
They said these words to taunt the youngster's fate,
And friends, in truth, he rose up to their bait:
"Enough!" he cried, "You lying renegades!
I am indeed the brother of that brave
Young hero whom I love more every day."
"And whom I pierced with my most cutting blade,
From front to rear!" roared out King Cosdroez;
On hearing this, the blood left Guibert's face;
He raised his arm, both strong it was and straight,
And struck the Moor with all his might and main:
He split his skull and splattered all his brains
As down he fell and bled his life away;
They rushed Guibert, their hearts aglow with rage,
And would have torn him limb from limb, I'd say,
When the Emir with ringing tones exclaimed:
"By great Mahom, let no one touch this knave
Until I'm told the land from which he hails
And know whose blood runs hotly in his veins!"
The youth replied, with ready pride and hate:
"My lord Emir, I'll never hide my name;
So help me God, our Maker full of grace,
I am Guibert, in baptism so named
By Aymeri, whose son I am, the brave
And noble Count who rules here and has slain
Your mighty clan each time they test his claim!"
To hear this drove the great Emir insane;
He cried aloud, his fiery eyes ablaze:
"By great Mahom, he must return Forrez

With all his phials and vials that cheat the grave!
    Or you will meet your Maker!"

14. How the Emir made and then broke a promise

WHEN THIS WAS SAID the king of Loquifier
Spoke up and said: "Heed my advice, Emir!
The Narbonne knights are weary now and weak:
They spent the night wet through, forgoing sleep
Until the dawn, then struck us from the beach;
They had to fight in order to retreat!
The first I struck, indeed, was Aymeri:
I got him with my crossbow's sturdy steel
And struck his horse the same way to the field;
But with his sword he would have slaughtered me,
If great Mahom had not observed my need!
The time has come to arm your men and breach
Their city walls and reach the terraced streets!"
"Your words are wise," replied the great Emir;
Throughout his host the word was spread with speed
That every knight and soldier should proceed
To arm himself as quickly as could be;
So each bestrode and rode his rapid steed
As round his neck was laid a banded shield,
And in his hand a sturdy spear of steel;
Men moved to mount the engines they had reared,
And stormed the walls with all their wicked greed;
The French were roused, and with no thought of fear
They manned the walls and parapets between;
They hurtled rocks and wooden blocks and beams
To break the heads of all who came too near!
The Moors looked on, in helpless rage and pique,
And the Emir looked up at them and screamed:
"And where are you, Count Aymeri the fierce?
Why grieve me thus and thwart me uselessly?
You know full well that you are helpless here;
Yet, let us choose a champion for each,
A single knight to fight for you and me;
If yours should win, and mine admits defeat,
I'll give you back Guibert, of ransom free;

But if my man should gain the victory,
Then I shall have Narbonne and all its fiefs."
On hearing this, the Count rejoiced indeed;
He raised his head and said, so all could hear:
"My lord Emir, I willingly agree;
Without delay let this resolve proceed!"
So both men pledged to let stout lances plead
    Their case and cause in battle.

THE COUNT RETURNED within his banquet-hall
And summoned there his knights and all his lords;
Not daring else, they gathered, one and all:
"Attend me well," he said, with swelling voice:
"In single fight I mean to meet the Moor,
Upon the terms that he and I have sworn:
If I am slain or forced to yield, then all
Narbonne itself shall be my own no more,
Nor all its fiefs nor any shire or shore;
And if I win this test of lance and sword,
Guibert my son shall be released and brought
Here safe and sound and ransomless restored."
On hearing this, his wife was most distraught;
With ringing tones she cried aloud and called:
"Count Aymeri, my brave and noble lord,
For love of God, Who holds the world in ward,
Forgo this pledge and reckless plan of yours!
Not long ago death held you in its thrall;
I saw your wounds and all the blood they poured;
Alas indeed I ever saw the dawn
When you dismissed my children from our walls
And made them seek the King of France's court!
If they were here, then I am very sure
That William would champion our cause
And rid the realm of all this Pagan swarm!
But now you see what I myself foresaw
    When our six sons departed!"

SAID HERMEMJART, his fine and lovely wife:
"Lord, pardon me, for love of Jesus Christ,
But when our sons had left this town behind
And ridden forth to France at your desire,

They left you here bereft of friends and knights;
If they were here, you know it's not a lie,
Their valour would have saved us by this time!"
On hearing this, her husband heaved a sigh –
He knew full well that what she said was right;
He looked around and saw, upon all sides,
His loyal knights with sad, averted eyes –
Not one of them dared say a word the while;
But then, Romanz the Orphan made to rise!
Though very young, well-built and fierce of eye,
He faced the Count and raised his voice on high:
"I've heard you well, my loving lord!" he cried:
"If you agree, then suffer me to fight
On your behalf against this Antichrist!
For I'm a strong and newly-dubbed young knight,
And wish to prove my valour in your sight;
Before my peers I ask you for the right
To take your place against the Pagan's pride."
The Count was mum; he looked at him a while
And thought he seemed like William, his fine,
Beloved son, and so he loved the knight
     Who looked so like a kinsman.

ROMANZ stood up for all to see and witness
His firm resolve, his strong and gallant figure;
He faced the Count and spoke for all to listen:
"My lord," he said, "I call on you to give me
The right to fight against this heathen villain!"
On hearing this, the Count admired his spirit
And gave to him, in sign of his permission,
The glove and rod, and thanked him well and willing,
And then went forth to St Paul's of the City;
One hundred knights and young Romanz went with him,
For love of whom they swore to keep a vigil
Throughout the night until the sun had risen;
Then Mass was sung by good Morant the bishop,
And Romanz left behind him as a gift there
A cloth of silk, a candle and some silver,
And all the rest made offerings of riches;
The day was light and bright as prime went ringing –
But you must hear of the Emir, so listen!

He too had called together all his kinsmen
And there they were, with those in front the richest,
Fourteen emirs and fifteen kings and princes,
All keen to fight for him and their religion;
But the Emir just sat in silence, thinking,
When suddenly one Gadifer rose swiftly;
The brute was huge, his hue as black as pitch is;
His giant frame held up a loathsome visage
Whose eyes were red like flaming coals a-flicker;
He faced his lord and said, his voice uplifting:
"My lord Emir, I ask for you to give me
The right to fight with Aymeri the Christian!
If I should fail to make him yield or kill him,
Then I renounce all right to rule my kingdoms
Of Wieland Isle and those around Abilant;
I will not keep one foot of them or fistful."
On hearing this, the Pagan's brooding finished:
He gave the brute the rod of his permission
And Gadifer bowed low and left there quickly;
At Mahom's shrine he sought divine assistance:
"In your strong hands, great lord, I place my spirit;
Protect me now, your servant true and willing;
I pledge to you that if I am the victor,
You shall return this day to Narbonne city
And reign once more inside its golden minster,
From which the French once hauled and hit your image;
But you escaped through your almighty wisdom;
As this is true, I pray you will assist me
    And save me from all harm."

HOW GREAT A JOY those Saracens displayed
As Gadifer stepped forth to fight against
Count Aymeri, whose face with valour blazed;
The Pagan called for armour straightaway
And forth it came, without the least delay:
The spurs were gold, the leggings finely chained;
Upon his back the burnished coat of mail
Was white as snow upon a winter's day;
His coif was jewelled, his noble helm was laced –
A king drew down the visor on his face;
Then, girding on a golden-pommelled blade,

He took his steed, whose croup was speckled grey;
About his neck a banded buckler lay,
And in his hand a spear whose spike was great
And flew a flag clipped on with golden nails;
Across the field he drove his destrier,
Which leapt away in bounds across the plain;
With ringing voice he cried aloud and railed:
"Lord Aymeri, what cause have you to wait?
How long before you open Narbonne's gate?
Have you reneged upon the vow you made?
I challenge you to show me your good faith
And fight me now, so with its blows my blade
Can wrest from you your city and your state!
This day I shall avenge for all my race
Those noble hearts your haughty hand has slain!
By great Mahom, with whom my soul is safe,
    Your rule shall soon be over!"

WHEN AYMERI heard Gadifer's abuse,
He sweated hard, so angry was his mood;
Back in St Paul's, Romanz, the gallant youth,
Was blessed to fight by worthy Bishop Hugh,
Then left the church with firm resolve and true;
Beneath an olive tree a silk was strewn
And there they brought the armour he would use;
His legs were clad in solid chain and smooth,
And then his back, and front, inside a suit
Of mail too strong for spears to enter through;
His sword was King Corsolt's of Valperdue,
Which Aymeri acquired at Roche Ague
When he outfought the King of Bassemue;
He donned a helm of priceless wealth and proof –
Its nasal-piece was studded with a jewel
Which sparkled like the sun through clouds at noon;
Upon his chest he set his shield of blue,
The straps of which were gold- and purple-hued,
Then took his steed, more swift and fleet of hoof
Than is the hart when by the hunt pursued;
He gripped a spear that Aymeri had used
To sever mail in many former feuds;
It bore a flag atop it, fixed with screws,

Oft flown before and feared by not a few;
They swung the gate and Romanz galloped through
Towards the Moors and all their creedless crew;
He spurred his steed towards the Pagan who
Was waiting there to fight a mortal duel
    Upon the flowery meadow.

COUNT AYMERI climbed up his tower's height
To watch them through a window there and spy
Upon the tents of all those Antichrists;
Then through a glade, which sloped upon his right,
Within a wood of leafy boughs and wide,
He saw a band of Moors well armed in iron,
In sturdy mail and helmets burnished bright;
Fine, noble steeds they had between their thighs,
And in their hands held curving shields and pikes;
The Count looked on, and filled with rage and spite,
He called aloud to all his noble knights:
"Come, look at this, my worthy, well-bred knights,
And learn how Moors keep promises they plight!
Down there they've planned an ambush to surprise
And trick us with their treachery and wiles,
To slay Romanz should he defeat their knight!
My noble lords, let all of us alike
Put armour on and be prepared to fight:
For all the gold in Paris I'll not stand by
And see Romanz deceived and lose his life."
"Most willingly," his men-at-arms replied,
And hastened forth to do as he desired;
They donned their mail and helmets burnished bright,
And swords of steel upon their right hand sides;
Around their necks they draped their shields and climbed
Upon their steeds, not wasting any time;
With every haste they rode in serried lines
Outside the gate and passed the swing-bridge by;
Romanz rode up to meet the Moor meanwhile,
And, as he did, the brute looked up and cried:
"And who are you to bother me, and why?
Have you been sent by Aymeri the wild?"
"How wise you are!" Romanz the youth replied:
"I am his man and love him with my life;

I've ridden here to make you yield or die!"
On hearing this, the Pagan laughed outright:
"By great Mahom, you show prowess and pride –
But I gain naught from slaying callow squires!
Be off with you! I order you to ride
To my Emir, who rules the Persian tribes;
Let him decide your fate, as he desires;
He'll make the Count endure a double slight:
Before Narbonne we'll have you flayed alive
With young Guibert whom we have seized alike;
Fair Hermenjart shall have fair cause to cry:
We'll flay you both, then slay you in her sight;
    Your clan will come to nothing!"

KING GADIFER beheld him and perceived
A handsome youth with down upon his cheeks:
"Young man," he said, "I grant you this indeed:
You're very bold, for someone of your years,
To leave Narbonne and come to fight with me!
But now beware – your death is very near!"
Romanz replied: "Your sermon's badly preached!
In Jesu's name, the King of Majesty,
I'll fight you here until you die or yield!"
The Moor replied: "And I you, by my creed!"
Then both rode back one furlong in the field
And on their breast they braced their sturdy shields;
With levelled lance each charged at greater speed
Than feathered bolt when from the bow released;
What mighty blows their banded shields received!
The Moor struck first and such a blow he beat
Upon the boards that all its bands were pierced
And cleft apart like leaves upon a tree!
The coat was strong and stopped the blow beneath;
The lance flew off in splinters on the field;
Then Romanz struck, and struck him well indeed;
So fierce a blow he gave his golden shield
It broke, at once, the buckler's boards with ease,
And ripped aside the hauberk damascened;
The blade ran through to naked flesh beneath
And from his ribs the Moor began to bleed;
He turned the shaft and flung him on the field,

While riding through, as strong as any Peer!
The Pagan's heart was filled with shame and grief,
And straightaway he staggered to his feet,
Then drew his sword and grasped his buckler near;
He saw Romanz and strode towards his steed;
He struck the youth upon his helm, which gleamed
With precious jewels, and felled some on the field;
The blow went past the saddle-bows and sheared
The noble head of that most splendid beast;
The war-horse fell, as did Romanz, but he
Jumped up at once, and once upon his feet
He drew his sword and raised his banded shield;
He faced the Moor and strode towards the fiend;
Upon his helm, inset with stones, he reared
A mighty blow, which cast them low, and sheared
The coif upon his coat of white to reach
His skull beneath, and sever his right ear;
The blow went on and cut the coat beneath;
Five hundred rings it severed from the sleeve
And sliced away sufficient flesh to feed
The hunger of four hunting-hawks at least;
The Pagan swooned, headlong, upon the field;
On seeing this, the Count praised God indeed,
Invoking Him with this most tender plea:
"Almighty God, Who gives us breath to breathe,
Defend Romanz, whose heart with valour beats,
And keep him safe from death or injury
Against this Moor and all the heathen breed;
If he survives this day, then I decree
He shall, one day, be king of Lombardy;
    It is his land by birthright."

WHEN GADIFER had come back to his senses,
He filled with rage that such a page should fell him!
Without revenge his shame would last forever;
He drew his sword, and with his shield held steady,
He stalked Romanz, impatient for his vengeance;
He faced the youth and struck his pointed helmet
With such a force the stones fell on the meadow;
Enough remained within the helm, however,
To take the blow, absorb it and deflect it:

The youth was spared, thank God above in Heaven,
But still he swayed and almost swooned, so heavy
With hate and hurt the blow was that he dealt him!
His vision blurred and all his body trembled,
As blood escaped his mouth and passed the ventail;
He called on God, Whose help is ever present:
"Lord Jesus Christ, with Your great strength protect me
From death today against this heathen devil!"
He held his sword, whose blade displayed the message
'*For Jesus Christ our King*' upon the metal;
He saw it then and it was like a blessing:
His spirits soared as did his strength and temper;
He grasped the grip and with his shield held steady,
He strode towards the Pagan, sure and ready;
He struck so hard, with Jesu's strength to help him,
He slit right through the coat of mail and severed
The Pagan's arm, which fell, the buckler clenching;
The Moor was filled with pain and shame together
As he beheld the blood spurt from his breast-plate,
And saw his arm upon the flowery meadow –
No wonder, friends, if anger turned to frenzy!
He faced Romanz and struck him with a vengeance!
How fierce a blow his shining blade directed
Against the lad, but thanks to his good helmet
His skull survived without the slightest headache!
The blow slid off behind his head so deftly
That all its weight drove on beside the leggings
And struck the spur, dividing all it met there;
His foot was bared but spared from being severed;
Romanz looked down, but never stopped his efforts,
As through the field he stalked the Moor to end it;
He struck again, with strength inspired by Heaven,
And with this blow, you know, he struck his head off;
The Pagan fell and sprawled upon the meadow;
Within the woods those Pagans watched him perish,
And said as one: "What evil does this beckon?
Our king is dead, who never yet was bested."
Each dug the spurs against his horse's belly
And in a band they galloped from their shelter
Towards their king, determined to avenge him;
Romanz looked up and paled as he beheld them,

But called on God, the one true King of Heaven:
"Almighty God, I pray for Your protection
Against this band of faithless, heathen henchmen!
  Ah God, where are my friends?"

ROMANZ LOOKED UP with pale and pallid face;
He called on God, Who bore the Cross's pain:
"Lord God of Hosts, Who never lies or fails,
Deliver me from pain or death against
This evil band of faithless renegades
Who come at me with all their heart and hate!"
He turned his gaze towards a sloping glade
Upon his right and saw the destrier
That Gadífer had cherished all his days:
Jet-black it was, but with a white-flecked mane;
The youth ran up and, grasping both its reins,
He leapt astride the stallion straightaway;
King Alatriz the Saracen exclaimed,
With ringing voice: "You thief! You'll not escape!
Dismount that steed and meet your death, you knave!"
Romanz heard this, but never stopped or stayed;
He drew his sword and with its burnished blade
He struck the Moor with all his wrath and rage;
He smote the helm and cleft the coif away;
He cracked the skull and severed half the face,
Then turned the blade and flung him to his grave;
    May all his comrades follow!

THE YOUNG LAD FLUNG the villain to his death;
But ere he'd sheathed his blade's well-burnished edge,
The rest rode up, intent on swift revenge!
They charged Romanz and cast their spears ahead
As, for his part, he made a brave defence:
He battered one upon his burnished helm
And split his skull and all his face no less;
When Aymeri beheld him so hard-pressed,
He raised his horn and twice he gave it breath:
Inside the town they heard and knew it well;
The porter swung the gates apart and let
The city's knights swarm out with fierce intent;
They never stopped until they reached the press;

How fierce a fight they gave those villains then!
How many spears were split and bucklers cleft!
How many coats were ripped apart and rent!
How many Moors were smitten dead on dead!
The Count himself rode out there, worthy friends,
Well-armed astride his Arab thoroughbred!
He broke his lance against a Pagan's breast
Then in his hand he held his sword erect
And lopped the limbs and head of all he met;
He slaughtered ten and then did not relent;
You know it well: Count Aymeri was the best
Of all the knights of his proud clan, except
For William, the son he bred himself,
And Oliver, the noble count and friend
Of Roland, slain by Ganelon's foul pledge;
Both Oliver and Aymeri were bred
   And brought up by two brothers.

THE FIGHT WAS HARD, the press was thick and heaving;
A Pagan king called Aristant came speeding
With his command, ten thousand angry heathens,
Who'd seen Romanz and rode in haste to reach him;
How many darts they hurled, on coming near him,
And how he fought, as one of gallant breeding:
The man he struck knew well that death had seized him;
But there were just too many Moors to beat them;
Soon all his shield was shorn away, not leaving
Sufficient wood to guard the hand that reared it;
On every side he struck so hard and fiercely
That all his limbs were smeared with blood and bleeding;
The Pagans would have cut him down, believe me,
When Aymeri himself came to relieve him
And struck at once King Aristant their leader;
He struck him hard upon his helmet gleaming,
Which helped his head as little as a leaf would:
He split his coif and then his corpse completely;
The blade went on, embedding in the heathland;
The Pagans stood with sinking heart to see it,
And, filled with fear, ten thousand turned to flee him!
The Count's own men pursued them fast and fiercely:
With slashing blows they slaughtered those they reached there;

They chased the rest right back inside their siege-camp,
Then turned around, in high content retreating;
How fine a haul of heathen arms they seized there:
How many coats of mail and helmets gleaming;
How many steeds well-rested, fast and eager!
With no more lord to ride or guide them either,
They dragged their reins and roamed across the greensward;
His men could take whichever horses pleased them;
The Moors returned, those craven misbelievers,
And their Emir most foolishly received them:
"My gallant men, how glad I am to see you!
What news have you of Gadifer to cheer me,
That mighty king, whose valour is unequalled!
Come, bring him in, so I may see and hear him!"
"He's dead, my lord; your plan has been defeated;
Before Narbonne a youngster braved and beat him;
Then Aymeri himself came out to meet him
With knights of his, both fierce of heart and fearless;
They slew in all two thousand of our people
Who'd ridden forth to help the king, if needed."
On hearing this, how angry the Emir was!
He swore aloud, with all his strength and feeling,
That Aymeri would pay for interfering!
He bade Mauprin and Murgalant to heed him:
"Bring here that son of Aymeri, called Guibert,
And tie him to a target in the field there;
Let all who wish shoot arrows at this creature
From every side to prick his hide and pierce him!"
On hearing this, the Pagans' joy was fearful;
God curse them all and punish all the evil
        Of their unshriven souls!

WHEN THE EMIR had spoken thus, the mood
Of all his men most joyfully approved;
But then up spoke Pinel of Roche Ague
And Escorfaut, the king of Valperdue:
"Fine lord, Emir, our beards are grey of hue;
If you will hear and heed the words of two
Who love you well, then this is what to do:
Prepare at once to hang Guibert the youth!
Since Charlemagne took Spain from Pagan rule,

And Christian France seized power in Pampelune,
Narbonne has lain in forfeit to them too:
But here at last the chance has come to you
To seize it back: the youth can be the tool!
    The time is now or never."

CORSOLT OF MONTACLER was next to speak:
"My lord Emir, attend a while to me!
Dispatch a man as envoy with all speed
Who, at the walls, will order Aymeri
To open up his city gates and yield
His fort and port without delay, or we
Shall take Guibert, for whom his love is deep,
And hang him high upon a cross's beams;
We'll hammer nails to pierce his hands and feet,
Before the walls, so all can be well seen
By both the Count and his fair wife; her grief
To see him thus will doubtless be extreme;
The Count will not abide it long ere he
Will do whatever you ask of him, Emir."
Said Persia's lord: "I willingly agree –
And he who'd not, deserves to rot and be
    Remembered with dishonour."

15. How Aymeri rescued young Guibert

THE DAY WAS FINE; the Pagans armed themselves;
Five hundred Moors and more on horses went
Towards the walls and stopped before them, where
Interpreters among them spoke in French
To tell the Count the new conditions sent
By the Emir and all his host of men;
Whatever words they used brought no success,
For he agreed to nothing that was said;
Inside the walls they thought no more of threats
    Than promises he'd made them.

THE DAY WAS FINE, the morning bright and warm,
As the Emir prepared his host of Moors;
Interpreters among them rode towards

The city gate and stopped before the walls
To tell the Count the new demand they'd brought;
Whatever words they used had no reward,
For he replied in ringing tone of voice:
"Begone, you fools, and take your heathen hordes
Across the sea to your infernal shores!
If you remain, then you may rest assured
That you will keep no whit or bit of all
The wealth and coin your mighty lords have brought;
You race of curs! Despite your greater force,
We've taken much already that was yours!
All praise to you, blest Mother of our Lord,
Whose part in all shall never be ignored:
We shall repay St Peter and St Paul
   In Rome itself, I tell you!"

THE PAGAN SENT some fifteen thousand knights
Before the walls a third and final time;
Before them all one Clargis led the line,
Whom the Emir loved dearer than his life:
I've heard it said he was his sister's child;
Upon his lance he raised a glove in sign
That none should strike while he would speak his mind;
Before the walls he raised his voice and cried:
"Lord Aymeri, fine son of gallant knights,
Give up Narbonne and take your son alive,
For the Emir will name no other price!"
Said Aymeri: "Begone, you villain vile!
I've six more sons of Hermenjart's and mine,
Apart from him whom you would cheat of life,
And each of them rejoices more in fights
Than food or drink, and takes much more delight
In striking blows with blades of naked iron,
Than making love to ladies, safe inside!
If you are here when all of these arrive
Upon my shore, then you will surely die!"
The Pagan raged, on hearing this reply;
Amid the field he had a beam raised high
Then joined it with a crossbeam bolted tight;
On this they raised Guibert, whom first they tied,
Then nailed his hands and feet thereon with spikes;

Two Saracens, God curse them both, then climbed
Beside the cross to more torment the child;
Clargis was one, the other Matefier;
This evil pair then scourged him left and right
With heavy whips, which flayed the lad alive;
Inside the town the people wept and sighed;
With hopeless looks they helplessly stood by,
 Not knowing how to reach him.

BESIDE THE CROSS, upon his right and left,
With heavy whips they flayed the youngster's flesh
And bled him till his arms and legs were red;
The youth cried out in his extreme distress:
"Lord Aymeri, where are you and your men?
What shame for you if I am left for dead;
And all your sons will bear the censure hence
That you looked on while I was flogged to death!
Dear God above," the gallant youngster said,
"Who on the Cross were crucified Yourself
By jealous Jews, who knew not their offence,
I know indeed that You came down from Heaven
To save our souls, which sinning had condemned;
Immaculate, as Holy Scripture tells,
In Mary's womb You took on mortal flesh,
Who carried You in joy to her term's end,
When, sinless, You were born in Bethlehem
And taken to the temple by Simeon;
When Herod heard of You, in fear and dread
Of what You'd do, his soldiers took the heads
Of every new-born boy within his realm;
The Magi came to praise You, nonetheless,
And then for thirty years You lived and dwelt
With twelve Apostles, who knew and loved You well;
Then came the hour when Judas, robbed of sense,
Betrayed You to the jealous Jews for wealth –
For thirty coins, the Holy Scripture says;
They led You forth to Pilate's punishment,
And You were whipped and held in vile contempt,
Then on a Friday crucified to death;
Your blood fell on the blind centurion's head,
Called Longinus, who was the guard they'd set:

His spear-point pierced Your body on the left
And when Your blood ran down his spear it went
Upon his eyes and made him see again;
He saw the Light and fervently confessed
His sins to God and was absolved and blessed;
And then Your corpse was brought and laid to rest
Upon a couch within a sepulchre,
But in three days You rose again from death
And went at once to break the gates of Hell,
And rescued Adam and all of us as well!
As this is true, I pray You to protect
Me now, Lord God, among these godless men;
The blame is mine," he cried, "and I repent
Of all my sins and all my trespasses;
I have no priest to whom I may confess;
Lord, hear my plea and clasp me to Your breast!"
On saying this, he swooned, of sense bereft;
Inside Narbonne his mother cried in dread:
"Ah, woe is me! When will my anguish end?
My son has died and no one tried to help;
I truly think his noble heart was cleft."
The Count heard this and filled with wild regret;
Beside his wife he strode the parapet
And saw their son upon the cross outstretched;
The Pagan whips still flayed his naked flesh
And all his limbs and sides were raw and red;
Regaining sense, he raised his voice and said:
"Lord Aymeri, this day I meet my death;
God bless you, Sire, and bless the kind Countess;
I bid you both on my behalf to bless
My brothers, when you next shall meet with them;
You gave Narbonne to me the day they left,
And all the shires and shores within your realm –
But now you're free to honour someone else:
I'll never need two coins' worth of its wealth!
God save my soul, for I am close to death."
When this was said Guibert swooned once again
And Hermenjart was filled with such a dread
She almost fell to certain death herself;
The Count ran forth with all his knights and men,
    To comfort and console her.

WITHIN NARBONNE how great a sadness reigned;
Count Aymeri, his wife and men the same,
Were filled with grief for gallant Guibert's sake;
The Countess swooned, again and yet again:
"Lord God on High," the noble Lady prayed,
"As true as You were cruelly whipped and maimed
By jealous Jews and bore the Cross's pain,
As does my son Guibert this very day,
Be with him now and shield him with Your grace!
Let one so young not die in such a way!"
When this was said, once more she took her place,
And with her sleeve she wiped her weeping face;
The knights did all they could do to assuage
     Her awful grief and sorrow.

COUNT AYMERI stood on the battlements
With Hermenjart, the winsome wife he loved,
Consoling her and comforting her much;
Romanz the youth came forth and hailed them thus:
"Lord Aymeri, fine knight of noble blood,
For love of God, Who pardoned Longinus,
Save Guibert's life, so gallant and so young,
Which heathen spite expends in front of us!
I know a way it surely may be done."
"And what is that?" the Count said, looking up:
"By God, my lord, the plan is plain enough:
Arm all your knights and in a sudden rush
Attack the camp before they know we've struck!
Our shining blades will slaughter such a sum
That Narbonne's field with Pagan blood shall run!
If God permits, Who on the Cross was hung,
We'll carry off Guibert, your gallant son,
And hear our names when songs of deeds are sung!"
The Count heard this, his heart inspired at once:
"By St Denis, I love your plan and pluck!
I am prepared to try our skill and luck!
     Men, seize your arms and armour!"

WITHIN HIS HALL once more the hero went
With Hermenjart, so fair and nobly bred:
"My lord," she said, "it was great foolishness

To not exchange Forrez for young Guibert!
I wish Forrez were dead and gone to Hell!
If I'd a stick, I'd flay him to his death!"
The Count replied: "My love, where is your sense?
So many times you have advised me well,
But now it seems that all your wits have fled!
Do not mistake my feelings, fair Countess,
But by the faith I owe to God Himself,
And all those Saints whom I have loved the best,
I tell you now that if the Pagans held
Our eldest son Bernart as hostage there,
With William as well, and then had pledged
To fill this hall with gold from end to end,
I'd not exchange the lot for young Forrez,
    Whose knowledge healed and saved me."

COUNT AYMERI WAS in his hall beside
Fair Hermenjart, his loved and lovely wife:
"My lord," she said, "by God, Who never lies,
How strong you were, and brave, in times gone by!
The Pagan Moors beheld you with more fright
Than larks behold the mountain-hawk in flight."
"In Jesu's name," Count Aymeri replied,
"When I was young, you know that this is right,
No enemy withstood my will and might;
But now I'm old, and weaker in their eyes;
They fear me now no greater than a child;
But bring me here a crossbow and you'll find
That I can make it sing with more delight
Than David's psalms are sung by holy friars!"
"Most willingly, my lord," his wife replied,
And chose one that was close, of goodly size,
And brought it forth to do as he desired;
He set a bolt and looked along the sight;
"My lord," she said, "by God Who never lies,
Be careful of Guibert, for love of Christ!"
"In Jesu's name," Count Aymeri replied,
"He's safe enough, I swear it on my life."
He set his aim upon an Arab knight,
Released the lock and let the arrow fly;
It struck its mark and spiked the cross behind;

The arrow broke, the Pagan fell and died;
Their Captain cried: "I never saw the like:
So swift a death for one so much alive!"
His soldiers said: "A crossbow took his life:
The Christians are too cowardly to fight."
The Count had left his lookout there meanwhile,
And armed himself and all his men in iron!
Without a sound they left the town to ride
And reach the tents as silently as mice!
The Pagan host knew nothing but surprise
When gallant French attacked them from all sides
With all the strength of their prowess and pride!
If only you had been there, friends of mine,
And seen the spears they split, and splinters fly
As bucklers broke and knights were sent to die,
Bereft of feet or fists, on flowers of white!
The Pagans fled to save their wretched lives,
And Hermenjart called out aloud and cried:
"For love of God, my lords, Who never lies,
Bring back Guibert, for love of Jesus Christ!"
On hearing this, the Count, with fierce desire,
Rode off towards the cross and, once arrived,
He brought it down, not wasting any time;
Within his arms he grasped his son and sighed,
Then drew the nails which held him crucified,
And on his shield most gently let him lie;
He seized as well Clargis, who was the child
Of the Emir's own sister in Leutice;
Their quest achieved, the Narbonnese retired;
While in his tent the Pagan seethed with spite,
     What joy reigned in the city!

16. How messengers were dispatched to Charlemagne, and how the great Emperor died

THE FRENCH RETURNED inside the town together;
How joyfully they took Guibert to tend him,
While in his tent the Pagan's heart was heavy:
"Mahom," he cried, "why thwart my loyal vengeance?
Now I have lost my prisoner and nephew."

When this was said, some fourteen kings all entered:
"My lord," they said, "waste no more time lamenting!
Select two men, one younger and one elder,
To go to Laon, great Charlemagne's centre,
And learn at once if, as his lord, the Emperor
Intends to come to Aymeri in rescue!
When both are sure they know the King's intention,
Then bid them ride without delay to tell us;
If Charles the King is in no mood to help him,
Then we can stay and know that they are dead men!"
The Moor replied: "I hear you and commend you;
Your plan is good and will be done directly!"
On saying this, he called upon Danébru
And Matefier, a Moorish lord white-headed:
"My noble friends, to Charlemagne I'd send you;
Observe his plans and any plot or measure
Of his desire to ride and help his men here;
As soon as you are certain of his pledges,
Come back at once! Mahomet speed and bless you!"
They both replied: "Don't doubt us whatsoever!
We'll spy upon the King and all his Frenchmen;
With both Mahom and Cahu to protect us,
We shall fulfil your will, Emir, with pleasure."
Disrobing then, they changed to pilgrim dresses:
Hair-shirts and hoods of coarsest cloth those wretches
Were clad in soon, and marten-cloaks whose edges
Were trimmed with fur from creatures of the hedgerow;
They took in hand great pilgrim staves sharp-ended
And left their host with both their haughty heads down,
Bare-footed too, like palmers on a penance;
God damn the pair, the mighty King in Heaven,
     As they set off for France!

IN FERVENT HOPE that they would soon succeed,
The Pagan host watched both their agents leave,
While the Emir maintained the city's siege;
But those inside were in no mood to yield,
And when attacked fought back with every zeal;
The Countess spoke and said: "Lord Aymeri,
Send forth a man to Paris who can speak
With Charlemagne, the King of Saint-Denis;

Send forth a man both swift of plan and fierce,
A man well-skilled in skirmish and in speech,
And let him bear your letters signed and sealed,
To give the King, so Charlemagne can see
That in this far-flung land of his we need
His help against the hosts of the Emir;
If he declines, be certain, Aymeri,
　He has no right to rule us."

THE SIEGING-HOST, in truth, was filled with spite
At having lost their leader's sister's child;
While in the town they showed their great delight
At having gained Guibert, though scarce alive!
Upon a shield they brought the youth inside;
His hands and feet were swollen from the spikes,
And crimson blood ran down his beaten sides;
They laid him down upon a bed inside;
Fair Hermenjart, when she beheld him, cried
In shock and grief, my friends, without a lie;
Then Aymeri stepped up, both strong and wise,
And sent at once for Forrez, who arrived
Without delay as Aymeri desired;
The skilful Moor felt all his wounds for signs
Of mortal blows or promises of life;
On learning all, he called the Count aside
And said: "My lord, attend these words of mine;
If you will swear, upon your faith in Christ,
At once to free Clargis and me, then I
Will swear alike to save young Guibert's life."
If you do not, then he will surely die."
On hearing this, the hero, in a trice,
Unsheathed his sword and then he told a squire
To bring Clargis, not wasting any time;
The squire obeyed and brought the king well tied
With sturdy rope around him taut and tight;
The Count addressed Forrez a second time:
"And now, young leech, attend these words of mine:
I swear to you upon the Cross of Christ,
That if you fail to save young Guibert's life,
King Clargis here will die when Guibert dies,
And then I'll cleave your clever head alike."

This said, he seized the shining blade on high,
And, seeing this, Clargis spoke up and cried:
"For Mahom's sake, Prince Forrez, do what's wise,
Or we shall both be slaughtered by this knight."
On hearing this, Forrez knew what was right,
And said: "My lord, lay down your sword of iron!
Be sure of this: I can and will revive
Your son Guibert as quickly as you'd like."
On hearing this, with thanks the Count retired
And left the Moor to tend him day and night,
Who in a month restored him to such might
    That he could wield his weapons!

WHEN YOUNG GUIBERT was whole and hale again,
Within the hall what joy they all displayed!
Before the walls how loudly they complained
Of sitting there in siege so many days
And gaining naught in any wise or way;
Good Hermenjart, so fair of form and face,
Besought the Count again, and yet again:
"My noble lord, for God Almighty's sake,
Send messengers to France without delay,
So they may urge the gallant Charlemagne
To save our town from Infidels and knaves!"
Dear God, it would have been to no avail –
For noble Charles had died of his old age,
The mighty King, by all his race bewailed;
No death before caused Frenchmen so much pain;
But friends, you know that none of Adam's race
May live for long on this side of the grave;
The mighty King could not avoid his fate;
The King of Kings had called, and he obeyed;
But God, what wild lament his barons made!
They bore his bier and buried him at Aix:
Upon his throne they sat him, where he remains
This very day, as many can vouchsafe,
    Who've visited the vaults there.

KING CHARLES'S CORPSE was borne aloft then buried;
Upon his throne they sat him down and left him;
Then in the land they challenged his successor,

And many there bade fair to crown Erneis,
A wealthy lord and rich in friends to help him;
King Louis would have lost his crown forever,
Had it not been for William's endeavours,
Who saved him more than anybody else there;
With loyal strength he slew the fierce Pretender
And claimed the land for Louis to inherit,
Despite the plots of renegades and rebels;
And thus it was young William who rendered
The crown of France and all the Christian Empire
  To Louis, the true King.

WHAT LOYAL STRENGTH young William displayed!
He claimed all France in royal Louis' name,
Despite the plots of rogues and renegades;
But Aymeri knew nothing of the fate
Of Charles the King, his Emperor fierce-faced:
The Saracens, God curse the faithless knaves,
Had been in siege so long before his gates;
Behold him there! Within his hall of state
He bided time with all his barons brave;
They showed respect for clever young Forrez,
Who with his skill had healed Guibert and made
Him strong enough to ride his destrier:
"Lord Aymeri," the Countess said again,
"Send messengers to France without delay,
 So they may urge the gallant Charles for aid
To save Narbonne; our need of him is great;
If he delays, then we shall all be slain."
The Count replied: "By good St Riquier,
So many Moors are camped before our gates
That none of us could pass their lines unscathed,
Though bribes of gold a valley wide were paid!"
At this Clargis spoke up, of Valplenier,
The Moor they found and bound that other day,
Beloved above the others of his race
By the Emir, in whose house he was raised;
He saw the Count and hailed him in this vein:
"I have a plan which is direct and plain:
If you will let me keep my Pagan faith,
And let me pray as I am wont to pray,

Then I will show your messengers a way
To pass across our siege-host and escape
To France the sweet, unchallenged and unscathed."
Said Aymeri: "But you are proud and brave;
I do not dare put in your care this day
My son or nephew for whom my love is great;
    I am afraid to trust you."

CLARGIS REPLIED, his face with valour bright:
"Lord Aymeri, I swear I never lie:
I'll see them through, without deceit or guile;
In Mahom's name, whose strength keeps me alive,
And by whose will the sun shines in the sky,
And with whose help I hope to stay alive
To see once more my slim and slender wife,
And my own son and all my noble line,
My uncle, whom I love, and all his knights:
I swear I'm true to pledges that I plight."
He raised his hand and gave his word thereby;
Said Aymeri, his face with valour bright:
"Clargis, my friend, now I am satisfied;
You would not risk your honour with a lie."
"No, lord, indeed; I would much rather die;
Throughout our camp I shall conduct and guide
    Your messengers in safety."

"WE HAVE NO TIME TO WASTE," said brave Clargis:
"Unbind these bonds of mine and set me free,
Then mount at once your battlements, but keep
To hidden spots that stop you being seen;
I'll hail our men and make the guards believe
That I've escaped and am about to leave
With two of yours by whom I have been freed."
Said Aymeri: "You're brave of heart indeed;
If you abjured your faith in Mahom's creed
And loved the Lord with all your heart and zeal,
I'd give to you fine palaces and keeps
And hunting-grounds and towns to serve your need."
Clargis replied: "Let all these matters be;
Now's not the time to preach your faith to me;
The time may come when I shall hear and heed;

If your request to Charlemagne succeeds –
If he can meet and beat the great Emir,
And if your force survives to lift this siege,
Then I shall come to you on bended knee
    And beg to be a Christian."

COUNT AYMERI WAS FILLED with doubt and dread;
He saddled up a Syrian steed and then
Guibert his son strode forth to claim the quest
With young Romanz, of gallant heart and head;
If any could, then these would gain success –
But all the knights lamented as they left;
Guibert set off, with no delay or let,
With Clargis on his Syrian stallion next,
And then Romanz, his steed Hungarian-bred,
Not waiting once, as through the gate they went;
God guard them all and guide their every step!
If you had seen how fearlessly they sped
Inside the lines of all those Infidels!
So many Moors had pitched pavilions there
That our two youths would soon have been struck dead,
Had King Clargis not cried aloud instead:
"Good Pagans all, do not attack these men!
I am Clargis, king of Saloriez!"
What mighty joy they showed when this was said:
They cheered their king and chaired him to his tent!
His men leapt up to see their lord again
And serve his needs and heed each word he said;
He told them this: "My worthy knights and men,
This pair has saved my life! Attend to them!"
And so they did, with diligent respect;
They took their steeds to stables, where they were fed
A feast of fodder – I know no more, except
To say the oats and hay were of the best –
    Then waited on their owners.

THE PAGANS SERVED our counts with every speed;
Without delay they went to cook a meal
And brought fresh water in silver bowls for each;
They bade them sit upon their best of seats
And brought them swan and peacock meat to eat,

And claret-wine to drink, and jugs of mead;
Clargis himself assisted with good cheer;
Their eating done, the tablecloths were cleared
And beds prepared most handsomely indeed
For both our youths at once to take their ease –
And both were tired and soon they fell asleep;
But then, my friends, the Saracen Emir
Approached the tent, four monarchs at his rear,
Who all had come to welcome King Clargis
    And seek news of his captors.

THE GREAT EMIR, four monarchs all around,
Approached Guibert and Romanz, sleeping sound;
God, how their blades became their noble brows,
Their spears of gold and gold embroidered gowns!
"And who are these?" said the Emir aloud;
Clargis replied: "Two Frenchmen, brave and proud,
Who rescued me from death within the town;
They're bound for France, so they cannot be found!
I've pledged the pair to do all in my power
For their escape as your largesse allows."
The Pagan said: "Their goodwill merits ours."
On saying this, he moved up to the couch
Where Guibert slept and grasped his golden gown:
"Frenchman, wake up! Put off your sleep an hour
And give me news of Narbonne and the Count!"
Clargis spoke out: "Sire, if you please, not now!
Two weary nights they watched my prison-tower
Till they could break the bonds that held me bound!"
The Pagan said: "For love of you, I vow
    That no one shall disturb them."

THE GREAT EMIR, at this, turned on his heels
And left the tent, four monarchs at his rear;
Clargis went with them too till he could see
That all had gone, and then, with every speed,
Retraced his steps and woke them from their sleep;
How good and true King Clargis proved to be!
How well he kept his word to Aymeri
And both of those with whom he'd set him free!
Each pledge he'd made he carried on to keep:

He clothed them well and gave them all they'd need –
Two nobly-bred and sturdy-footed steeds,
And gold from his own country in the East,
And cloths of silk and cloaks of grey and cream;
Where'er they went, they'd both be well received;
He gave them too a spokesman who could speak
In many languages with fluent ease;
Then he himself and ten men from his fiefs
Led young Guibert and Romanz through the fields
Filled up with Moors, before he took his leave;
The youths rode on until at length they reached
    The road to France and took it.

OUR NOBLE PAIR rode on along the road
Which led to France, where both had sworn to go;
High-towered Nîmes they saw, then they approached
The hills of Ricordane, and through its slopes
They saw Vienne upon its ridge of stone,
Beside the wide and fiercely-flowing Rhône;
Now by the falls and channels of it grow
Both laurel-trees and pines in shady groves;
And sitting there they saw that pair of rogues
The great Emir had sent some while ago
To spy in France the threat from Charles's throne;
    This done, they were returning.

BESIDE THE FALLS, beneath a grove of pines,
That pair of rogues, one old, one young, reclined;
The great Emir had sent them forth to spy
On Charles of France and all his household knights;
He'd sent them forth in pilgrims' dress disguised,
Which still they wore, in part, although their pride
Had shown its hand now Charlemagne had died;
Young Romanz said: "Good cousin, there's a sight!
That pilgrim-pair is very fair attired
In marten-furs and tunics ermine-white!
The pilgrim-staves they hold are gold-incised!"
Young Danebru, God curse his evil life,
Looked up and said: "I fear we've been out-spied!"
The Moor who was interpreter and guide
Rode to and fro with questions and replies;

"Where are you from, my lords?" Guibert inquired:
And Danebru, the Pagan spy, replied:
"We're Frenchmen, lord; I am from Tours and my
Good brother here was born in Beauvais shire;
As penitents we've travelled far and wide;
At Aix in France, which sits upon the Rhine,
We've learnt with grief that Charlemagne has died,
The best of kings who ever drank of wine;
Upon his throne, as if he were alive,
    His knights have had him buried."

"GOOD PENITENTS," Guibert the noble said:
"Can this be true, that Charlemagne is dead?"
They both replied: "Upon our honour, yes;
Upon his throne his courtiers and friends
Have buried him as if he ruled them yet;
Upon his hand a golden glove they've set
And turned his face towards the Spanish realm,
To menace still the Moors and Saracens."
Said Romanz: "I cannot believe he's dead."
Said Danebru: "He is so, nonetheless,
His corpse embalmed, I saw that for myself;
Three sons that old Count Aymeri had bred,
Were with the King and heard his dying breath,
And they ensured his son Louis' ascent:
And yet, before the crown sat on his head,
    His realm was racked by rivals."

THE YOUTHS, ON BEING told this news, were shaken
With shock and grief that showed upon their faces,
And left their steeds, dismounting in the shade there;
They both lay down, their hearts and bodies aching,
Upon the grass where sleep soon overcame them;
On seeing this, young Danebru the Pagan
Addressed the Moor their guide and their translator:
"Come, tell me friend, are these two spies or vagrants?"
But he replied: "They're neither, Mahom aid me!
Both men are knights of Narbonne town the ancient,
Who left the walls with Clargis, having saved him
From Aymeri, and joined him on the plain there;
I do not know, but I think that their aim is

To go to France in hope of wealth and favour."
Said Danebru: "A curse on all who'd aid them!
My fellow Moor, allow my sword to slay them
And you shall have fine Syrian steeds in payment!"
But he replied: "To do so would be shameful!
For all the gold in Russia I'll not betray them;
The great Emir has guaranteed their safety,
And King Clargis, for whom I've undertaken
To be their guide and guard against all danger;
And I will die before I turn a traitor,
      For anybody's wealth."

SAID DANEBRU: "My fellow Moor, pay heed!
If you allow my sword to slay them here,
I'll give to you fine arms and Syrian steeds
And make your peace in this with the Emir,
So he himself will thank you for the deed;
They go to France for help against our siege!"
But still the fellow said: "All this to me
Is meaningless; I never will agree."
"You harlot's son! My staff should stop your ears
And start your eyes so you might hear and see!
I'll see you hang like any common thief!"
"Sire, you can try, but you will not succeed!"
Friends, while they urged the rights and wrongs of each,
Guibert slept on and dreamt a fearful dream:
That the Emir had captured him and heaved
Him in a pit where lions came to feed;
The lions sprang and he awoke in fear
And awful dread at what his dream could mean;
He bade the Moor interpreter to speak,
On pain of death, of what their talk had been;
The man replied: "I'll tell you willingly
Each word I've heard and spoken."

MY FRIENDS, IF THAT interpreter was willing
To tell him all, there was no wonder in it:
Guibert's sharp blade convinced him very quickly!
"My lord," he said, "I will not keep it hidden;
These men are Pagan spies disguised as pilgrims!
They've made and are returning from a mission

To France the sweet and Paris where the King is."
"God," says Guibert, "protect us from their mischief!"
He drew his sword and turned to use it swiftly –
But Danebru, his sturdy staff uplifted,
Stood facing him, already poised to hit him!
Guibert was brave, both lithe of limb and nimble:
He boldly strode towards the staff and hit it
A mighty blow which cleft it through the middle;
Romanz woke up, who heard it split and splinter:
"My friend," he said, "why strike a pious pilgrim?
Your sturdy arm should not alarm good Christians!"
"It doesn't, sir, as Jesus is my witness!
These men are spies and craven Moors, whose business
Was finding out what help King Charles would bring us!
We should string up the pair of them this minute."
Romanz replied: " Good brother, reconsider!
Instead, let's take these Pagan villains with us
To France again, where they may still assist us."
Guibert replied: "I grant your words their wisdom;
    Haul both these villains forth!"

17. How Louis learnt of Aymeri's distress

THEY SADDLED UP their rapid steeds to mount;
The Pagan pair and our two noble counts
Set off for France, together with their scout,
And as they rode the Pagans asked about
Their great Emir and how the siege was now,
And how he ruled his kingdom to the south;
And in return they told their captors how
King Charles had died and how at last the crown
Became his son's, because of William's power:
"In Paris now King Louis will be found,
Or Orléans, where all the court is bound;
Across his realm he visits forts and towns
    To hear his barons' homage."

TO ROYAL FRANCE the gallant vassals rode;
Not stopping once, and never slack or slow,
They met the King upon the metalled road

To Orléans as he and they approached;
Towards the King Guibert, as elder, strode
And greeted him in fair and loyal tones,
In Jesu's name and Aymeri's, the bold;
The King replied: "God's blessing on you both!
How far you've come! How fares the Count at home?"
Guibert replied: "The truth is quickly told:
The great Emir of Babylon has thrown
A mighty siege around us in Narbonne!
Some fifteen kings are with him, and their host
Is so immense we cannot count the whole;
Lord Aymeri has sent us to your throne
To seek your aid with all the knights you own;
The Count will die, if you refuse to go."
The King heard this and held his visage low;
On looking up, he spoke most wisely so:
"My lords," he said, "I swear to you this oath:
I first shall ask the barons here to show,
By their advice, if I should go or no;
If they agree, then I shall not be loath;
I'll muster forth my legions when I know
    My wisest men advise it."

AGAIN GUIBERT was urgent with his plea,
As men passed by and then the sumpter-beasts;
And even then the youngster never ceased
To urge the King with all his skill and zeal;
When all were past, he made this last appeal:
"Fine King, my lord, as you and I believe
In God above, Who judges all and each,
Make haste to help my father Aymeri!
Your own fine father, Charlemagne the fierce,
Who ruled all France so long and faithfully,
When he returned from Spain, he gave in fief
The town Narbonne to gallant Aymeri,
And promised then, before his knights and Peers,
That if the Count should ever be besieged,
He'd hasten back and help him in his need –
No cause at all should stop him, he decreed."
This said, he drew his sword of steel to wield
Its tip on high so that he could reveal

The graven hilt for Louis' hand to seize:
"My lord," he said, "the truth is here to see!
Count Aymeri, who is Narbonne's true liege,
Has sent this sword, with which he was enfeoffed,
With this request, made now for him by me,
That you should read what's written on its steel:
Thus plainly was the pledge he made received
By Aymeri, whose face with valour gleamed,
    When Charles gave him Narbonne."

KING LOUIS TOOK in hand the tendered blade
And looked at it and saw its lovely make:
With golden script the hilt was overlain;
A bishop there, of noble name and fame,
Received it then from Louis' hand to state,
In ringing tones, the words thereon engraved;
The King himself paid heed to every phrase;
Heed *me*, my friends, and you shall hear the same:
"True Emperor, permit me, if I may,
To read the words engraved upon this blade:
'When Charlemagne had liberated Spain,
He spied Narbonne, on riding home to Aix;
And when that town was taken and reclaimed
He offered it to fifteen counts that day;
Each one of them refused it straightaway;
Then Aymeri, whose face with valour blazed,
Requested it and gained it with God's grace;
King Charlemagne then solemnly proclaimed
That if the Moors or any heathen race
Should ever come within that land again,
He'd help the Count, his Oriflamme upraised.' "
This read and said the priest returned the blade
To Guibert's hand, which sheathed it in its case;
Then Guibert looked his brothers in the face,
And, staring hard, these stirring words exclaimed:
"And you, my lords, have you the need to wait?
Have you found here so wonderful a place?
You seem to me like lost sheep that have strayed
Upon a field so lush and green to graze,
That you are loath to turn for home again!
I cannot any other way explain

Why you should wait on hearing of the fate
Of your brave father and what he fights against!
He is besieged and soon he will be slain!
Have you forgotten too your mother's face
And gentle hands by which we all were raised?
In Pagan hands she will be maimed and shamed;
No food at all gets through the city's gates:
No wheat or wine nor any wealth or trade;
Inside Narbonne, which was so prized and praised,
Whoever owns the coarsest flour or grain
Can weigh it out with gold upon the scales!
But if the Moors, who are a craven race,
Could know the Crown has learnt the city's fate,
And that its host was met and on its way,
    Then they would leave the country."

IN PLEDGE AND PLEA Guibert spent so much time
That both the spies, who'd been some way behind,
Were now abreast and resting, side by side:
"True Emperor," said William, fierce of eye,
"Behold this pair! I swear the other night
You gave them food, as pilgrims passing by!
They said that they were penitents on trial!"
"By St Riquier, they lied!" young Guibert cried:
"They both are spies sent here by heathenkind!
The great Emir had sent them here to spy
Upon your court, your character and might;
As they returned, we took them by surprise
And made them keep us company a while!"
On hearing this, the King began to smile;
Upon a steed he bade them mount and ride
Each side of him, along the weary miles!
And all the time they whimpered and they whined
And cursed our Faith and criticised our Christ
And blessed Mahom and praised him to the skies!
"Above all things Mahomet is most high,
For he it is who gives us food and wine,
And drives the storm and makes the sun to shine."
Guibert replied: "You wretched rogues, you lie!
To bless Mahom you must be deaf and blind!
The truth is this: Our Lord loved him betimes

And sent him forth to preach and prophesy
And teach us men the way to Truth and Light;
But Mahom drank a barrelful of wine
Then slept it off upon a dunghill's pile
Till pigs arrived and ate the wretch alive!"
When Danebru heard this he filled with spite
And from his gown he drew a gleaming knife
Whose handle glowed with purest gold incised;
At Guibert's ribs he let the dagger fly:
Above the hips it ripped the cloth awry
But, thanks to God, it never reached inside;
When William saw this his blood was fired:
He drew his sword, whose hilt was golden-bright,
And would have slain the wretched Moor outright,
When Guibert called: "Good brother, do not strike!
We may, perhaps, still profit from his life!"
At this, the King resolved to waste no time,
But sent his word to every shore and shire,
To all his lords, in letters sealed and signed,
To say that every soldier and every knight,
On pain of death, if they did not comply,
    Should ride at once to meet him.

THE ENVOYS LEFT and soon performed their task:
At Louis' call knights came from all of France
And camped outside the town of Orléans;
Around the walls, on every side and part
For two whole leagues, they camped upon the grass
Four days and nights; and with their men-at-arms
And noble lords three further monarchs marched
To Louis' side and joined his entourage:
He said to all: "Hear what is in my heart!
Count Aymeri in Narbonne town has asked
For help against the Moors who hold him fast!
His envoys here have told us what has passed;
But from Cologne I've had, not three days past,
Sealed letters with a similar demand!
For Saxon troops beneath the fierce command
Of Witikind have ridden there to starve
The city out and capture it from France;
Which summons do I heed?" King Louis asked;

On hearing this from Louis, son of Charles,
That Aymeri, of valour unsurpassed,
So good and wise, was now oppressed so hard,
With one accord they answered in alarm:
"True Emperor, by God Who guides the stars,
You have no choice! Since Aymeri has asked,
You must help him before he comes to harm!
      Let's make all haste to leave here!"

WHEN LOUIS HEARD his counsellors agree
That they should ride to Aymeri's relief,
He bade his host prepare itself to leave
For old Narbonne and thence for Saxony;
And so it did: with every haste and speed
The army left, the soldiers in the lead,
With Louis next, of blessed France the sweet,
His heart inspired to help Count Aymeri,
And then his knights, whose valour had no peer;
For old Narbonne they steered their rapid steeds,
In serried ranks and long, league after league,
   To save the Count from slaughter.

THE EMPEROR was in no mood for weakness
As forth he led his mighty levied legions;
My worthy friends, what brave men were convened there!
Brabant's brave duke, from Flanders' wealthy seaboard,
With Boniface the rich king of Pavia;
Duke Geoffrey too, of Anjou's noble region,
And Salemon, who ruled the Breton people,
And Richard, duke of Normandy, all leading
Enormous sums of knights and lesser liegemen;
And with them too was Neustria's old chieftain,
With hardy men and knights most fierce of feature;
The army rode at rapid pace and, reaching
The river Rhône, made camp there for the evening;
My friends, when they arrived where the Emir was
With all his Moors, then all those craven creatures
Would soon find out that life can lose its sweetness:
      When mortal foemen meet!

BESIDE THE RHÔNE the host unpacked its tents
And slept till day, when dawn's first light was shed;
The Emperor, when he was shod and dressed,
Addressed four counts most praised for their prowess:
First William, so wise and bravely bred,
Then good Bernart and fierce Hernaut the Red,
And young Guibert whom Aymeri had sent:
"My worthy lords," said Louis, "hear me well!
My plan and plea is that you arm yourselves
And with all speed traverse your father's realm
Until you see the Pagan host ahead,
Who have besieged Narbonne with foul intent;
Observe their troops, their campsite and their strength,
And the approach that we should take to best
Attack their force with most hope of success."
Said William: "This fills me with content!
We shall depart with no delay or let,
      To spy upon the Pagans."

THE BROTHERS CALLED upon their loyal vassals:
A thousand score prepared themselves for battle;
In serried ranks they set off in the vanguard;
Atop his tower Count Aymeri was standing
With Hermenjart, his wife and wise companion;
She leaned and looked beyond the window's panels
Across the fields upon a distant valley,
Where she beheld a wedge of waving banners,
All purple-red, in threads of silk and satin:
"God help us now!" the Lady cried in panic:
"Lord Aymeri, whose visage glows with valour,
What race is this that sends its vanguard at us?
Alas for us, if they are heathen vassals!
Our strength is gone; we shall be slain and vanquished!"
But he, the while, looked closely at their ranks there,
And saw in front sweet France's battle-standard,
The Oriflamme, with William as carrier!
"My love," he cried, "for evermore be happy!
You have no cause for any further sadness!
Look closely there! Your own son is the captain
Who brings the Oriflamme and France's barons!
There is Bernart, whose visage glows with valour,

And our own Red Hernaut, aglow with anger,
And young Guibert whose pluck has brought them back here!
Behold your sons, for whom you grieved to madness,
When they set off for France to prove their manhood!"
"God!" said his wife, "How blest I am and thankful!
St Mary, you have comforted my anguish!
My gallant sons will drive these heathens backwards,
Who've plundered all and sundered all our lands here,
All our supplies and all our traders' travel,
So that our town has been struck down with famine;
     God grant us our revenge!"

FAIR HERMENJART looked out from left to right
And saw two thousand more all dressed in iron;
Beside the fence and at that vanguard's side
She saw the silk of all their pennants fly,
Grey-brown and green, and red and lily-white:
"Look there, my lord!" the noble Countess cried:
"So many men! I swear by Jesus Christ,
These may be men of Aupatris, arrived
For the Emir to call on when he strikes!
If this is so, then we shall surely die!"
But he the while looked closer till he spied
King Boniface's flag within their lines!
On seeing this, he said to his fair wife:
"My love, these men are friends of yours and mine!
It's Boniface himself, Pavia's sire,
With our own son, brave Garin, by his side,
To whom the king has willed his wealth and shires."
On hearing this, the Lady laughed and smiled:
"Ah God!" she said, "True King of Paradise!
My gallant sons will put these Moors to flight,
With their Emir who rules all heathenkind!
     They will regret they came here!"

FAIR HERMENJART surveyed the land once more;
From Spanish land, along the coastal shore,
She saw a band of many men ride forth,
With lances raised and flying flags galore;
Their arms were black, without a glint at all:
"Look there, my lord!" the noble Countess called:

"I am quite sure that these are heathen Moors;
The Living Fiend, where does he find such hordes?"
But he again beheld the force and saw
Upon their arms the Cross of God the Lord;
On seeing this, he couldn't hide his joy:
"My love," he said, "be happy evermore!
For these are led by that brave son of yours
Sir Aimer, called 'The Captive', who has sworn
Not once to sleep in any town or fort
Till he has slain in Spain each Spanish Moor!"
"Ah God!" said Hermenjart, "True King adored!
My gallant sons shall wield unyielding swords
    And shame these Moors forever!"

18. How young William made contact with the town

WHILE IN THE TOWER they watched and talked this way,
Young William and his vanguard lay in wait –
A thousand score well furnished for the fray;
They looked ahead and through a distant dale
They saw a band of mounted Pagan knaves,
All foragers returning from a raid
With wealth galore, and more ill-gotten gains
In oxen, cattle, and Christian folk in chains,
Who called aloud in great distress and pain
As all were scourged and scarred by sundry knaves;
When William first heard them weep and wail,
He hailed Bernart: "Good brother, bless the day
That's brought us back to our home town again!
Now we shall see whose birth is worth his blade,
Whose blows are best with spear and sword upraised!
The man who thrives will glorify his name,
And he who dies with valour shall be saved
To dwell with God in everlasting Grace."
"A gallant speech!" Hernaut the Red exclaimed:
"I've waited long to witness such a day!"
On saying this, he cried his battle-gage
And spurred his steed with all his heart and hate;
No word was said as each man sped the same –
But when they struck, how fierce a din they made!

If you had seen those bucklers bend and break,
And lances split while slitting coats of mail
And severing fists and feet and heads the same,
As dead on dead were spread, their jaws agape!
From light of dawn until the fading day
They bartered blows and neither side gave way,
Until the French, with God Almighty's aid,
Wore down at last that band of renegades;
The field was filled with all their maimed and slain,
And all the rest, as best they could, escaped;
The Frenchmen freed those captives straightaway
Then rounded up the plunder on the plain
Which they had fought so fiercely to regain;
They took the lot to Louis, who displayed
His great delight and thanks that they had gained
     First blood within the battle.

YOUNG WILLIAM did worthily indeed:
Hear how he made a plan of his succeed,
Which turned the tide against the Pagan siege!
Ten thousand men, all knights of high esteem,
Were made to don with every haste and speed
The Pagan gowns, the arms and battle-gear
His troops had won from those who'd fled the field,
Till soon they looked like Moors from head to feet!
And then he stacked two hundred sumpter-beasts
With sacks of wine and packs of food to eat!
If these supplies could cross their lines and reach
Inside Narbonne, its danger could be eased;
So setting off, with sumpters in the lead,
And all his troops, his vanguard, in the rear,
They rode and reached the tents of the Emir;
The first they passed belonged to Corsublis,
Who was a prince, the son of King Turfier;
The Moors themselves had risen from their meal
And with their swords disported on the field;
As our men came they raised their blades of steel
And asked: "Who owns these sumpters, worthy peers?"
Romanz replied, as did Guibert the fierce:
"They all belong to strong King Aufanier:
Four days ago we left the camp to seek

Fresh food and drink to satisfy our needs;
We've plundered towns and raided castle-keeps!"
"Well done!" said they, "In Mahom's name, proceed!"
    And so the French obeyed them!

THE FRENCH RODE ON, their visors firmly shut,
All armed and dressed just like the Saracens;
Across the camp they slapped those sumpters' rumps;
If they could cross the Pagan lines and come
Inside Narbonne, and reach its citadel
With all the food and drink they'd loaded up,
Then there'd be meat and wheat and wine enough
To fear no force outside for five long months!
So on they pressed, and soon, proceeding thus,
They reached the tents of King Alepatin;
"Whose food is this?" cried his Barbarians;
Guibert replied, as did Romanz, at once:
"My lords, this food is strong King Aufarin's,
On whose advice this conquest was begun!"
"Then welcome, friends," they answered, "and well done!
May Mahom and Apollo bring you luck!"
    The French passed on and thanked them!

HIGH COURAGE AND HIGH WIT the French displayed
In passing through those packs of Pagan knaves,
As I've described, my friends, as best I may;
With food galore their convoy made its way
Towards the gates of old Narbonne the famed,
And Mauprin's lodge, the lord of Valfondez;
He cried aloud: "Wherever do you take
The wealth of food upon these sumpters laid?"
Romanz replied: "Without a lie, this train
Is bound for King Felis of Valsegree;
We've raided forts and cities in his name,
With such success we've made enormous gains!"
"Well done!" they said, "Ride on, in Mahom's name,
Who saves our souls and blesses us each day!"
    The French did too, in passing!

THE FRENCH RODE ON in serried ranks and even
Until they came to where the king Clargis was;

He asked of them: "Whose are these beasts you're leading,
And all this wealth with which their backs are heaving?"
Guibert replied and brave Romanz repeated:
"My lord, we both are Frenchmen of this region,
Who went to France to see the King, our liege lord;
It was with us that you received your freedom
And led us past the guard-posts of your siege-camp
Till we were through in safety and could leave there;
We rode to France and have so well succeeded
That we have brought the King here with his legions;
This food is for the city's knights and people;
We shall confer with Aymeri white-bearded;
Sire, thanks to you, this siege will be defeated."
Clargis replied: "By all that I believe in,
Do not delay! Maintain your goal and reach it
Before you're seen, or you'll be cut to pieces!"
The French rode on, with all their sumpters leading,
Until they reached the tents of Aufarion
And King Mabon, the ruler of Toledo,
      And four more mighty kings.

IN PAGAN DRESS the gallant knights progressed
And talked their way through challenges and checks
Until they saw Narbonne's great gate ahead;
But all around were pitched the mighty tents
Of Pagandom's one hundred noblest men –
The Almanzors, with the Emir himself:
"God!" said Guibert, "What can we say to them?
No speech of ours will charm them with its spell!
Our cutting swords must do the talking hence!
We'll never pass these last pavilions else."
"Whose food is that?" cries the Emir to them;
Guibert replied: "Not yours at all, you wretch!
God curse the beast or iron-barge's deck
That ever brought you food or will again!
This food is bound for Aymeri instead!
So do your worst, or best, he'll have it yet!"
On hearing this, the great Emir saw red:
In Mahom's name he swore aloud and said:
"You'll hang for this before the sun has set!"
On hearing this, young William was incensed:

He drew his sword, of sharp and shining edge,
And struck Cordova's Almanzor down dead!
Then Guibert felled a Persian king, and then
A mighty fray broke out among the rest!
On seeing this, with no delay, the French
Drove all their beasts towards the gates ahead,
     Then turned to offer battle.

YOUNG WILLIAM WAS a brave and worthy knight;
Towards Narbonne he drove his sumpters' lines,
Then, turning back towards the growing strife,
He bade a horn be blown to those inside;
The Count heard this, inside his tower high,
And called Garin of Anseune to his side:
"I hear a horn blown in the host outside:
I do not know what ruse they have in mind:
They well may try some trickery or guile;
But at our gates are sumpters with supplies
We greatly need, if we're to stay alive;
If only we can get the beasts inside!
Arm all our men and be prepared to fight!"
"Your will is ours," they willingly replied,
As donning mail and lacing helms of iron,
They girt their swords upon their left-hand sides;
Around their necks they laid their shields and climbed
Astride their steeds, not wasting any time,
As through the gate they left the walls behind;
If you had seen those French and Pagans strike!
So many spears they split and shields alike,
So many coats they slit and ripped awry
And flung from steeds so many men to die!
Both Romanz and Guibert, on either side,
Brought Danebru to Aymeri meanwhile:
"My lord," they said, "see here the Pagan spy
Who went to France to plot against your life!"
Said Aymeri: "Then he must pay the price:
By St Denis, he'll suffer for his crime."
"Your words are wind!" young Danebru replied:
"By killing me, what fee do you derive?
Take gold and coin in ransom for my life –
I'll saddle up four camels high and wide

With cloth of gold and sendal highly prized,
And other wealth, as much as you desire!"
"Your words are wind!" Count Aymeri replied;
The heathen's hand was smitten off, his eye
Plucked out, and then his nose half-split and sliced;
His fellow spy was brought and taught alike;
Friends, how they wailed and railed against their plight,
And fled like hounds when both were flung outside!
The Moors looked on, in dark dismay and fright,
    And filled with deep foreboding.

19. How the Narbonne knights displayed their might

WHEN AYMERI had made his vengeance clear
And punished them like any pair of thieves,
He flung them out and, fleeing, they appealed
So loudly to Mahomet in their grief,
That all their host could hear them and took heed;
Throughout their camp the Pagans seized their steel;
Young William, meanwhile, was not asleep!
He and Bernart and both their brothers each
Attacked the camp with all their strength and zeal;
There never were four brothers such as these!
How many Moors their mortal blows received
From shining blades swung by these Narbonnese,
Who scythed their way right through them with their steel,
And all who saw were filled with awful fear!
Then from his gate the Count himself appeared
With all his knights, well-mounted on their steeds,
To thresh and thrash them too like stands of wheat!
Where'er he went he lent them no relief
But through their camp he cleft their ranks with ease
And ripped to shreds their tents and beds and sheared
The ropes all round the lodge of the Emir;
Then young Guibert came spurring up at speed,
To smite the helm of an Almoravide
Who held Biterne and Pampelone in fief;
Between his ribs he rammed his burnished spear
And threw him down upon the rolling heath
Before his uncle, the ageing Aupatris;

On seeing this, how much his comrades grieved!
His uncle cried: "How heavy is my grief!
Without revenge, I'll hold my honour cheap."
He gripped his shield and held aloft his spear;
With all his spite he spiked his Arab steed
And split the press to smite Guibert at speed;
How fierce a blow he smote upon his shield
Above the boss, which broke the boards with ease!
His coat was strong, the mail withstood the steel,
And he survived, not injured in the least,
But swung and swayed and almost fell indeed;
The lad was mad and anger burned his cheeks
To see his shield so broken and so breached;
With spear aloft, as fits a gallant Peer,
He spurred his steed to smite old Aupatris –
Apollo's face was pictured on his shield
In sky-blue paint upon a golden field –
And young Guibert so focussed on the Fiend
He broke the boards right through his ugly teeth!
The splinters flew and so did Aupatris:
With Satan's help the villain disappeared!
Guibert rode on and drew his sword of steel
To strike once more a fierce Almoravide:
So fierce a blow he struck between his ears
He flung him dead upon the sloping field,
Then turned his horse and set a course to leave;
But by this time the Moors were on his heels,
In hot pursuit to cut off his retreat;
Yet in defence he sold his honour dear:
The man he struck was lucky still to breathe;
But if the Lord had still ignored his need,
He would have died right then and there, I fear!
His mortal foes stood toe to toe and heaved
Great pikes at him and brightly-burnished spears;
Below his thighs they slew his snow-white steed,
And, seeing this, the courage fled his cheeks;
He cried aloud and shouted in his need:
"Count Aymeri, fine father, rescue me!
Knights of Narbonne, my brothers near and dear,
My cherished friends, I need your valour here,
    Or I shall surely perish."

IN RINGING TONES four times Guibert the brave
Cried out '*Narbonne!*' to summon help against
The Blackamoors who blocked him every way;
With all his strength he kept their blows at bay
And with his sword struck many to their grave;
So many men he slew, the song maintains,
That all around a wall of corpses lay;
Romanz the youth could hear the cries he made,
As did the Count, whose beard was white with age;
Both young and old spurred off to lend him aid
And cleft the press with sharp and shining blades,
As did the knights who served the Count the same;
No matter where they rode, what cries they raised!
If you'd been there and seen their lances break
On shattered shields and burst their boards away,
How you'd have liked those pikes whose massive blades
Sliced feet and fists and heads and sent in haste
So many Moors to Hell, their jaws agape!
They saw Guibert hemmed in by Satan's slaves,
And with a roar they rushed to lend him aid;
Young William could hear their voices raised
And saw the Count, his battle-helmet laced,
But with no shield to guard his breast or face,
As with both hands he swung his bloodied blade
Upon the Moors whose bodies blocked his way
In heaving heaps, like swelling, welling waves!
Said William: "By all the saving Grace
Of Jesus Christ! How foul a stroke of fate,
If I should lose my father on this day!"
With every speed he spurred his destrier
And rode across, his gallant heart ablaze,
    To help his noble father.

YOUNG WILLIAM spurred forth his rapid horse
To gallop to his father's swift support;
Guibert, meanwhile, still swung his cutting sword
Upon the press, which thought they had him caught;
So many Moors he slew, the song records,
That all around the corpses formed a wall;
The Saracens hurled darts and wyverns forth
Which ripped apart his hauberk with their points

And rent his shield till all of it was shorn,
And split his helm clean open to the coif;
They brought him down by sheer and brutal force,
Yet still he cried '*Narbonne!*' with ringing voice:
"Count Aymeri, I need you now, my lord!
Young William, I'll see your face no more!"
On hearing this his father's anger boiled;
He cried '*Narbonne!*' and blew aloud his horn
To call his men and rally his supports;
And so they did: they rallied to his call
And struck again behind them and before;
See William, astride his sturdy horse!
He gripped his shield and grasped his naked sword
To cut a swathe among those heathen hordes;
The blood they'd spilt would be most dearly bought!
Against his blows their armour served them naught
As on he went and slaughtered more and more,
Until he came to where his father fought:
He cried aloud: "What cheer, my noble lord?"
On hearing this, the Count looked up with joy
To see his son and said with ringing voice:
"Son William! I welcome you, my boy!
But see Guibert! The Saracens and Moors
Have brought him down by sheer and brutal force!
For love of God, go clutch him from their claws!
If not, I fear you will embrace a corpse."
On hearing this, young William, appalled,
Cried out '*Mountjoy!*' the King's own battle-call,
Then galloped forth and struck with so much force
He cleft the press like timber with a saw!
How well he swung Joyeuse, that royal sword!
So many fell before his fierce assault
It would have been too hard to count them all!
Upon the ground he saw his brother sprawled
And cried aloud: "True Father, mighty Lord,
Is Guibert dead, whose face with valour stormed?
If he is gone, then so is all my joy!
I swear to You that my revenge will fall
Like thunderbolts upon the heathen Moors!"
On hearing this, Guibert stood up once more,
And said aloud: "What's all this wailing for?

Good William, I'm hardly hurt at all!"
Count Aymeri, meanwhile, came spurring forth
And asked alike: "What cheer, my gallant boy?"
"In truth," said he, "I feel both rich and poor –
For I'm unhurt, but am indeed unhorsed!"
Said William: "That loss can be restored!"
He saw a king from Bocidant's wild shore,
Well-armed astride a fine and noble horse,
Before a band of some four hundred Moors
Sent off in haste to crush this French assault;
In ringing tones the heathen raged and roared:
"Count Aymeri, you grey-haired rogue, come forth!
Today's the day your glory fades and falls;
Ill-starred the hour you entered Narbonne's hall!"
On hearing this, young William spurred his horse
Towards the rogue and said: "You villain, halt!
I'll have from you that noble horse of yours
To give Guibert, whose face with valour storms."
He grasped a spear embedded in the soil
And spurred his steed towards the hated Moor;
He struck his shield with such a fearful force
Above the boss that he destroyed the boards
And proved the mail of no avail at all:
He pierced it through like brittle buckram-board;
From front to rear he speared the wretched Moor,
Then flung him dead and led his noble horse
To young Guibert, who watched him there in joy,
Then mounted up and mightily rejoiced;
And yet, my friends, his anguish wasn't small:
He'd taken blows that bled from every pore –
Though from his deeds he gave them little thought,
As through the press he thrust with spear and sword;
God bless Narbonne, as sons and father joined
    Their force once more together.

WHEN YOUNG GUIBERT was rescued and relieved,
And sat once more upon a warring-steed,
The Narbonne knights displayed their might indeed!
At once, my friends, the great Emir appeared
With his own force of twenty thousand Peers,
Who filled the air with awful cries and screams!

But Aymeri, with those who held him dear –
His gallant sons, whose loyalty was deep,
And Narbonne's lords, all barons brave and free,
And men of France, come at their King's decree –
Stood firmly there to face them on the field;
They blew their horns of copper and of steel
Which blared around the ground from vale to peak
And flared again to flame the battle's heat;
Young William spurred hard and grasped his shield;
He gripped the shaft of his good Poitiers spear
And struck the nephew of the great Emir,
Who led his force – but not for long, indeed!
The sturdy spear ran through from front to rear
And flung him dead upon the sloping field;
　　　'*Mountjoy!*' exclaimed the victor.

THE DAY WAS FINE, but light began to fade;
Those vanguard troops, whom William the brave
Had brought from France, their heads in helmets laced,
Had fought their best, contesting still the fray –
And yet, my friends, they would have all been slain,
Had it not been for gallant William's aid,
And Aymeri, whose beard was white with age,
And all his sons of such prowess and praise;
Young William, whose face with valour blazed,
Swung high Joyeuse, that blade so feared and famed,
Which Charles himself had girt about his waist;
Before them all an Almanzor of Spain,
Stood in their way, an axe in hand, whose blade
Was half a foot at least in width, I'd say;
A heavy toll of Christian souls it claimed,
And, seeing this, young William's anger flamed:
"By God the Lord and Mary, blessed Maid,
How many men this vicious villain slays!
I give my oath, in our sweet Saviour's name,
That he or I shall not survive this day!"
He spurred his steed, which ran at rapid pace,
And raised his spear of sturdy steel well made;
He dealt the Moor a mighty blow that staved
His rounded shield and ripped apart the chains
Across his coat of double-woven mail;

From front to rear the spear-point sheared the knave
And flung him dead from his red destrier;
On seeing this, that raiding-party paled
And turned in flight; with all their might they raced
Towards the tent which their Emir had raised;
Count Aymeri had horns blown straightaway
To tell his men to seize the booty gained
And hasten to the safety of the gates,
Which opened wide, and straight inside they haled
The food and drink that William had obtained,
So all Narbonne was well supplied again!
But Aymeri forgot in his great haste
That three of those whose blood ran in his veins
Were still outside, abiding in the dales
With all their men and those of France the praised
The Emperor had summoned to their aid;
The vanguard troops of royal Louis' train
Turned round at last and made to leave the plain:
But not one half of all of those who came
Would ever see their king or camp again –
The blighted Moors had sent them to their graves;
On seeing this, young William bowed his face;
In serried ranks the vanguard rode away
Until they reached their comrades' camp again;
King Louis looked and saw them all still laced
In helms of steel and clad in coats of mail,
And knew at once their foe had been engaged;
He mounted horse without one moment's waste
And spurred across to William, whom he hailed:
"My gallant lord, where are those fighters brave
I gave to you this morning? Tell me, pray!
You have returned much fewer than I gave!"
"My lord," replied young William, "in faith,
They lie in death upon the city's plain;
No men before bore battle such as they:
From break of dawn till light began to fade
They crossed the sword with mighty hordes in waves
     Of Saracen invaders."

"SIR WILLIAM," the King continued then,
"For love of God, can this be true, my friend,

That you have lost so many of my men?"
On hearing this, the youth in anger said:
"True Emperor, upon my oath I pledge
I fought my best – I couldn't help the rest!
When we set out this day, at your request,
Upon our road we saw armed Moors ahead;
Ten thousand strong, astride rich steeds, they led
Long lines of men and women prisoners,
And stolen steers and cattle herded hence
At the command of the Emir himself;
My noble lord, on seeing such distress,
We sought no truce but struck them with our strength;
Our blades of steel knew no respite or rest
Until we'd won and they were dead or fled,
    And we had claimed their plunder."

"TRUE EMPEROR," brave William replied,
"I speak the truth, for I have naught to hide;
We slew in fight that band of raider-knights
And freed all those whom they had chained and tied;
We stripped the clothes from all their heathen hides
To dress our men as them, and thus disguised
We brought Narbonne their plunder as supplies!
We had to pass right through their army's lines,
Which are immense – I've never seen their like;
To trick them we were all obliged to lie,
Our visors shut, until we passed them by;
We reached the walls, but found we had to fight
The great Emir with twenty kings besides;
When we could see no other way inside,
We drew our swords and we began to strike
Both left and right, so we could goad and guide
Those sumpters through – and we succeeded, Sire;
Before the Moors could seize their swords of iron,
Ten thousand fell to our prowess and pride,
    And died before the walls there."

WHEN LOUIS SAW he'd lost so many liegemen,
His visage paled, he grieved for them so keenly;
Inside his tent he sat upon the greensward;
But when he looked at all the men who'd been there,

Who'd fought so hard against the hated heathens
That all were hurt, and many still were bleeding,
He spoke at last with noble heart and reason:
"My lords," he said, "by God, Who makes the seasons,
Though we have lost good men in this first meeting,
We shall not sound our softest horn and leave here;
When morning comes, with light of dawn appearing,
Let each of you be dressed in hauberk gleaming
And ride with me as fast as spurs will speed him,
Till we may meet these blighted misbelievers
And with our blades and Jesu's aid defeat them!
Too many times they've brought and wrought their evil
Upon sweet France, its cities and its people;
Since I have called so many from my regions,
And they have come, as we have, to defeat them,
Then let us ride tomorrow with Lord Jesus
    And cast these demons out!"

20. How the final battle-lines were drawn

THE DAYLIGHT DIMMED and night began to fall;
Young William, and all that fighting force
Who went with him and fought the raiding Moors,
Sought out their tents and set aside their swords;
When each had drunk and eaten well, they all
Retired to rest and slept until the dawn;
Now hear again of Aymeri, and more
Of his good wife, the worthy Hermenjart!
Back in Narbonne how much they sorrowed for
Young William, whose face with valour stormed,
And for Bernart, who ruled Brabant by law,
And Red Hernaut, who spared no foe he fought,
Their worthy sons, who strove outside the walls
Of old Narbonne against the heathen horde;
The grey-haired Count, who'd seen them there, was sure
That all of them had been cut down or caught,
Since none of them had answered to his horn;
But he'd no need to fear for them at all:
All three were safe and sound asleep, what's more!
If Aymeri had known of this, what joy

There would have been among his men and lords!
Instead, he said to all, with ringing voice,
That every man should arm himself for war
And mount the walls on all sides of his hall:
So much he feared the great Emir's assault;
His men obeyed without a second thought,
And mounted guard until the morning dawned;
But in their camp the Pagans slept and snored –
    God curse the faithless felons!

ATTEND, MY FRIENDS, and all God-fearing people!
This song of mine should be well heard and heeded,
For all of it, in truth, in every detail,
Is found in noble histories and readings;
You all have heard how on the day I speak of,
The heathen hordes around Narbonne were beaten;
Look back with me and see there in his siege-tent
The great Emir with monarchs of his regions,
Some ten in all, with every legion's leader!
Hark back and hear the wailing cries that reached him
From every throat as each one started speaking!
The great Emir cried out, so all could hear him:
"You sheep and goats, I bid you cease your bleating!
That you have met with loss and woe last evening,
I know it well, for so have I, believe me:
Ten thousand Moors lie dead upon the field there;
It seems our god Mahom himself was sleeping
The moment when those Christian men came creeping
In search of us and all our raiders' reapings!"
On hearing this, the lord of Aquilea
Spoke up and said: "My lords, attend and heed me!
By great Mahom, whom all my race believes in,
Some news of whose these soldiers were has reached me:
Beyond that hill, camped in the dale beneath it,
So great a force of Christians has convened there,
It would be hard to tally half their legion."
Said Danebru: "This much is true, believe me;
The King of France himself has come there, leading
A mighty force of Frenchmen here to meet us;
Young William's there, his face with valour gleaming,
The Count's own son, that snowy-bearded demon;

The King has made young William their leader,
And it was he and they this day deceived us,
Who slew our men and dealt with me so meanly:
His father sliced my hand and nose and ear off!"
The great Emir, at this, turned white with evil,
And by his beard he swore with all his feeling
That Louis' force would rue its interference:
That very soon his vengeance would be fearful!
He bade Clargis, his sister's son, come near him,
And ordered him to ready every heathen
And guard the camp all night from sudden seizure:
"My lord," said he, "your will I well agree to!"
And straightaway they armed themselves completely
And sent out guards whose watch and ward were ceaseless;
From dusk till dawn they filled the air between them
　　With horn-calls and with cries.

CLARGIS THE MOOR kept watch throughout the night,
Until the dawn and morning's early light;
King Boniface was camped the closest by,
With men he'd brought from his Pavian shires;
Within a wood they slept till dawn arrived,
And then the king, not wasting any time,
Called young Garin, his nephew, to his side,
And said: "Fine youth, hear what I have in mind!
Bid all our men to dress in battle's iron
And be prepared, at any time, to strike."
The lad replied: "My lord as you desire,"
And straightaway did all the king required,
While Boniface himself prepared to fight;
When all were armed, they mounted steeds to ride
Towards the town in serried ranks and lines;
King Boniface looked down the road and spied,
Across the vale, a sea of banners bright,
And shields the same, that shimmered in the light,
As Louis' knights prepared themselves to ride;
"My God!" he said "How fierce a force of knights!
If they are Moors, we'll not escape alive!"
On hearing this, his Lombards filled with fright;
And then, at once, the French set off behind
Young William, the Oriflamme, held high;

On seeing this, and knowing France's sign,
The Lombard king rejoiced and gladly cried:
"Be cheerful, men, not fearful, for these knights
Have come from France to join us in the fight!"
On saying this, he galloped down the rise
With all his men, keen now to show their pride;
Pavia's liege saw Louis with his knights
And came to him, and hailed him fair and fine
Upon his steed, embracing him with smiles;
And then he hailed his nephews there alike
As both their ranks rode on till they arrived
Where William had fought for those supplies;
Each man was stunned to see the dead piled high;
King Louis said: "How great a swathe was scythed
By William at yesterday's first light!
How many Moors his brothers' mood and might
    Left lifeless on the meadow!"

WHEN BOTH HAD KISSED in Christian love and hope,
They joined their ranks with no delay and rode;
Their army then held thirty thousand souls;
They passed the Moors whom William laid low
And reached, at last, the vanguard of their host;
Then, looking up, they saw upon the coast
A band of knights approaching down the road;
The arms they bore displayed a sombre show:
Their shields were bent and some were rent with holes;
Their coats of mail were neither sleek nor whole,
But rusty from the rain and storms they'd known;
King Louis looked and said in ringing tones:
"King Boniface, my noble lord, behold
This fearsome force so strict of rank and close;
They look resolved to overcome all foes,
But I can't tell if they are Moors or no!"
Said Boniface: "Then we must seek to know!
If Moors they are, they'll pay a mortal toll!"
King Louis said: "Well spoken, on my oath!"
And called to him a learned knight who spoke
The languages of many lands and folk:
"Find out for us this force's native home!"
The man replied: "I will do, nothing loath,"

And spurred his steed ahead as they approached;
On drawing near and seeing them up close,
It soon was clear, from both their looks and clothes,
That they were of the Christian Faith and fold;
In Jesu's name he hailed them, young and old,
Then asked at once: "Which country is your own?"
Young Aimer says: "One close to here, good soul!
My friend, we all are from Narbonne, enclosed
In bitter siege by countless Pagan rogues!
I am a son of Aymeri the bold."
On hearing this, what joy the envoy showed!
"My lord," he said, "I have been sent to know
If you will join your forces with all those
Of France's King, whose face with valour glows,
And Boniface, who rules Pavia's throne;
Their force is great; I cannot state the whole."
At this, the youth addressed his soldiers so:
"My lords, we have a hearty welcome home:
Great Charles's son has come with sums untold!"
When this was said the envoy turned and showed
Them where to ride and meet King Louis' host;
     They all stepped down to greet him.

YOUNG AIMER STEPPED from his swift destrier
And straightaway unstrapped his pointed helm;
He saw the King and strode to him and then
In Jesu's name he greeted him and said:
"May God above protect you with His strength,
Who rules the world forever without end!"
The King replied: " I welcome you, brave friend!
How fares your quest against the Moorish threat?"
The youth replied: "We've slaughtered all we've met
Along this road to bring my father help!
If we can lift this siege laid by the rest,
I do not fear the men they may have left."
King Boniface beheld his nephew there,
Whom he had seen but once before he went:
"My boy," he said, "this fills me with content!
When first you left I feared much from your pledge."
Then they embraced in love and sweet respect,
     As did the other brothers.

THE FRENCH RODE ON until they reached the headland;
They saw Narbonne and all its lands together,
Its walls of stone, its tall and golden belfries,
The river Aude, the vineyards and the meadows,
All laid to waste and ravaged by those wretches
Whose tents they saw in such array erected
The fields were filled with nothing else except them;
King Louis said: "By God, the King of Heaven,
How huge a host of evil Pagan devils!
God curse the brutes and heathen hounds that bred them,
And curse the wombs that sheltered them and shed them!"
He summoned then his barons to assemble,
And said: "My lords, your good advice must help me."
Said Boniface: "Sire, this is my suggestion;
Do not delay, but arm your men and set them
In ranks to fight as soon as all are ready."
The King replied: "I willingly accept it!"
    And bade his men obey.

"ONE OTHER THING, my lord," said Boniface:
"Let William once more lead forth your race!"
The King replied: "Most willingly he may!"
And summoned him before him straightaway;
Young William came forth without delay
And Louis said: "My love for you is great;
I'd have you lead my vanguard troops again,
One thousand score, well armed for war and brave,
And keen to serve with all their heart and faith."
On hearing this, the youth said, unafraid:
"Much thanks, my lord, for this reward and grace;
May God on High, Who governs all our fates,
    Both strengthen and protect us."

BRAVE WILLIAM obeyed the King's behest,
Most willingly and with great thankfulness;
Without delay he hastened to his men
And said to them: "Fear not what lies ahead!
Today Lord God will fill us with His strength;
In Jesu's name prepare to fight your best!"
And so they did, without delay or let;
In shining mail they clothed themselves and then

They girt their swords and donned their pointed helms;
Each mounted up his long-maned steed and set
His spear in hand and buckler round his neck;
Brave William displayed his fierce prowess:
He grasped the flag which rallied all the French
And left the camp, not looking right or left;
His men and he, with slow and steady step,
    Rode down towards the Pagans.

THE EMPEROR did not delay or falter;
He told Hernaut: "My noble friend, step forward,
For you shall lead the second of our forces:
Ten thousand men shall fight upon your orders."
"My lord," said he, "I shall not disappoint you!"
Then all that rank prepared itself for warfare:
They seized their arms and swung astride their horses,
Then, easy-paced, they followed those before them;
The King looked on, in deep content rejoicing,
And praying God, Who governs all our fortunes,
    To grant them strength and victory that morning,
        Through His most blessed Grace.

THE KING CALLED UP his third rank into line
Behind Bernart, who filled with joy and pride;
Ten thousand men they were, well armed with iron,
All noble knights of France, with more desire
To battle well and win a worthy fight,
Than maidens have to wed and be a wife!
The King looked on, commending them to Christ
And God the Lord, Who makes the dew and sky;
They left in haste, not wasting any time,
Across the crest beyond the rest to ride;
To Garin's care, his face with valour bright,
Lord of Anseune, the fourth rank was consigned,
By Louis, lord of France, and held alike
Ten thousand men of strength and temper high;
Young Aimer led the fifth rank, which comprised
That hardy band who loved him with their lives;
How feared they were by Pagans of all kinds!
They never lay in castles or inside
A town or hall on curtained beds at night,

But in the fields, their heads in helms of iron;
Unending war they waged for love of Christ;
How well it was that they had come in time!
Behind Garin they rode in dogged lines;
Upon their heels the next rank was comprised
Of Boniface and all his Lombard knights,
Ten thousand strong, from every shore and shire;
They bore, each one, a leaden mace or spike
Of sturdy steel, or spear or shining pike;
Behind their peers they veered across the rise;
Duke Richard led the seventh rank, the sire
Of Normandy, with courage fit to guide
Ten thousand men of great prowess and pride;
Geoffrey Anjou led forth the eighth rank, while
Within the ninth, the strongest of all nine,
Were Louis' men, the finest French alive,
One thousand score and more, famed far and wide,
Who had no fear of any fray or strife;
When all these ranks were set in one long line
From front to rear they reached at least a mile;
The army moved in serried ranks and tight;
The day was fair, the morning warm and fine;
Before them all, the Oriflamme held high,
Rode William, his face with valour bright;
He led the way until the host arrived
Where all could see the Pagan host close by;
On seeing *them*, the heathens sent a spy
Who went at once with every speed to find
Their great Emir within his tent and cry
    The news of their arrival.

WITH EVERY SPEED he spurred along his horse
To the Emir, beside the city walls,
Within his tent, whereon an eagle soared;
The spy went in, God curse his evil course,
To the Emir, and, seeing him, he called:
"For Mahom's sake, are you awake, my lord?
The Emperor of France stands at your door!
Great Charles's son is now their Emperor,
And he has brought a host to vie with yours,
Of Christian men from every shire and shore –

There's French and Fleming, Breton and Burgund lords,
And Hennuyers and countless many more:
Beyond belief's the tally of them all!
And they are led in reckless rage by four
Of Aymeri's own sons, with the support
Of Boniface and his Pavian force:
A king he is of great renown, who's brought
His boldest knights, as fierce as lions' claws,
Not one a cur, a squire or callow boy."
The great Emir, at this, was filled with gall,
And for a while said nothing, lost in thought;
Then, suddenly, he cried with ringing voice:
"Sound out for war my largest, loudest horns!"
And so they did, with no delay or pause;
The land around resounded with the noise,
As all his men equipped themselves for war;
Count Aymeri, inside his mighty hall,
Heard all the calls that echoed back and forth,
And hailed his men before him in the court:
"My worthy knights, prepare to fight once more,
And mount again our parapets and walls!
The heathen host has armed itself for war;
If they attack, let our defence be sure!"
His men replied: "May Jesus bless us all!"
　　Then ran to seize their weapons.

INSIDE NARBONNE they armed themselves with zeal
Then mounted guard all round the castle-keep;
The Count looked out and all that he could see
Were gonfalons and countless golden shields,
And coats of mail and jewelled helms of green!
"Ah God," he said, "true King of Majesty,
What folk is this adorned as rich as these?
Have they all come to help the great Emir?
If they are Moors, then we are lost indeed;
Good Hermenjart, you spoke the truth to me
Upon that day when I dismissed from here
Six sons of ours and told them they must leave;
Now William has died for us, I fear,
With Red Hernaut, and brave Bernart – all three
We left outside among the Pagan breed;

They may still live, but not at liberty!"
Said young Guibert: "Do not despair, my liege!
King Louis' camp lies in our greenwood trees;
They may still live and be there as we speak,
With all the knights and noblemen and peers
In countless sums the King himself's convened;
Ere evening comes the truth will be revealed."
But while they spoke, in hope alike and fear,
Guibert himself saw William appear,
As, holding high the flag of France the free,
He rode in view, his gallant face a-gleam!
Friends, you can guess the joy that made him feel!
"Father!" he cried, "Lift up your eyes and see!
Lord God this day has pitied all our grief:
Since Adam's time, and his companion Eve,
So fine a force, I tell you truthfully,
Has never formed for any Christian need,
As that this day which gallant Louis leads;
I do not lie, fine father Aymeri:
Look there yourself! That's William who wields
The Oriflamme of mighty France the sweet!
Behold its lion, all golden, proud and fierce!
And that's Hernaut, there riding at his rear!
He has become just what you said he'd be –
The seneschal of Paris and its fiefs!
And there's Bernart behind him, who's revered
As Louis' friend and counsellor-in-chief!
I cannot see for certain him who leads
The King's fourth rank that rides to our relief;
But in my heart I truly do believe
That it will be Garin, who's journeyed here
With Boniface from royal Lombardy;
Nor can I tell by any sign or means
The leader of the fifth rank I can see
Approaching us; how sombre is their mien!
Their shields are bent and some are sundered clean;
Their coats of mail are neither whole nor sleek;
Because of this, in truth, they look more fierce
Than all the rest dressed in their noblest gear!
Fine father, lord, by all that we believe:
If, in His grace, the Lord our God could speak

To Aimer now, whose heart with courage beats,
And let him know how much we are in need,
His fearless mood would soon impel him here!
If *this* were him, by God in Majesty,
The Moors will curse this day for countless years!"
But even while they spoke this way, the field
Filled up with Moors, who, armed in iron and steel,
Bestrode at once their swift-paced battle-steeds;
Within his tent, upon a silken sheet,
The Pagans clad and armed their great Emir:
His coat of mail was white and damascened
With double chains of purest gold between;
No lance or spear would harm him in the least;
Upon his head they laced a helm which gleamed
With precious jewels of great antiquity:
Upon his skull it sat so skilfully
That nothing thrown or thrust at him would cleave
The stones apart or penetrate beneath;
With fifteen strips they strapped it round his cheeks;
Then at his waist they hung a sword of steel
Six inches wide, and six foot long at least,
Its hilt enclosed with gold and silver pleats;
His horse was huge, and yet it was as fleet
Across the rocks as others over fields,
And never tired of distance or of speed!
He mounted up without his stirrups' need –
A lesser king held forth his banded shield,
With Mahom's face upon its centrepiece,
In blue and gold, a noble sight to see,
Which gave each Moor who saw it greater zeal;
Within his fist they placed a mighty spear
Whose blade, in width, was one hand's span at least;
No man it rammed, they say, could help but feel
As if his heart were swollen with such heat
That it must burst – and so it did in brief;
The great Emir, once dressed, impelled his steed
Across the field in mighty, bounding leaps;
With ringing tones he called to all and each:
"My worthy knights, let your revenge run free!
Each man who fights with valour, I decree,
Shall have his lands and all his wealth increased,

When we have done and won back this our fief,
    And slaughtered all these Christians."

21. How young William led the way in battle

WHEN THE EMIR had spoken forth his thoughts,
He formed his men in fourteen lines for war,
In serried ranks, both very long and broad,
Each captained by a king or mighty lord;
The smallest rank contained ten thousand Moors –
Without a lie, I tell you nothing false;
The great Emir led off the last of all,
Whose mighty sum was some one thousand score,
Made up of Caananites and heathen hordes
Of Ethiops and Bedouins galore,
In longer lines than any arrow's draw;
Like savage beasts they screeched aloud and roared,
And the Emir was certain that their noise
Would fill with fear our smaller Christian force;
But, thank the Lord, Who makes the rain to fall,
Ere evening came he wouldn't be so sure!
If you had watched our men's relentless course,
And William, whose face with valour stormed,
As at their head he led King Louis' force!
He passed the flag to one of his supports,
Preparing then to open the assault:
He grasped a spear of sharp and shining point,
And turned his horse towards the Pagan hordes;
He drove his steed and dropped the reins to draw
One furlong clear of all his leading corps;
He steadied then in readiness for war;
Against his breast he pressed his buckler's boards
And turned his spear towards the leading Moors;
King Turfier was first to see his horse,
Who led the van of Pagans here by choice
Of the Emir, by whom he was adored;
How soon, my friends, that friendship would be shorn!
Behold the Moor! He spurred his steed towards
Young William with all his spite and scorn;
The youth saw all, but fearlessly he formed

The Cross's sign and spurred his stallion forth;
No words were said, in challenge or in taunt,
But charging in as fast as spurs could gore,
Their lances crossed with nothing spared at all;
King Turfier smote hard the buckler's boards
And through the boss a mighty hole he bored;
The mail was strong and stopped the lance-head short;
Lord God was there to lend His man support,
And snapped the shaft so it could smite no more;
Young William stood on his stirrup-points
And struck the Moor with all his faith and force;
He hit the shield and split the heavy boards
And all the mail just like a bale of straw;
From front to back he rammed his lance's point
And flung him dead one spear-length from his horse;
Then William stooped down towards the Moor
To draw the spear that sheared his sprawling corpse;
He turned his steed and cried aloud '*Mountjoy!*';
The Moors looked on; with heavy heart they mourned
And made lament, and then with rage they roared
And faced the French and set themselves for war!
Their ranks advanced and sounded thirty horns;
The vanguard troops in William's battle-corps
Moved boldly on against the vanguard Moors;
Their captain's blow, which slew the Pagan lord,
Gave added force to every blow they scored;
The strength of those who fought against them stalled
In equal part to see King Turfier fall:
    Who was their vanguard's leader.

THE DAWN WAS CLEAR and sunny was the day,
As fights began with knights and barons brave;
How many times the Pagan cornets wailed
And ranks advanced with all their heart and hate!
What clouds of dust the clashing horses raised!
No word was said, no cries or taunts were made,
Except the call of each side's battle-gage;
Upon the field, before the city's gates,
It came at last – the mighty hosts engaged!
Behold the haste that every knight displayed
To run his steed and strike with spear and blade!

And as they clashed how fierce a noise it made!
If you had seen those bucklers slit and break,
Those lances split right through their ash-wood grain,
Those hauberks reft of all their saffroned mail,
And faces cleft and feet and fists the same,
And horses left with dropped and dragging reins,
Their riders down in death, their mouths agape!
Young William held high Joyeuse, that blade
Bestowed on him by mighty Charlemagne;
With all his rage he smote those Pagan knaves,
Who knew, when struck, they'd spent their span of days:
Against his blows no coat of mail availed;
The vanguard troops rode swiftly in his wake
And struck great blows with all their might and main;
Through Pagan lines they scythed a mighty swathe
And drove them back well-nigh one crossbow's range,
Until they reached Morgant of Aquilez,
The king who led their second rank that day;
He blocked their flight and stopped their runaways,
Took stock of them and flew into a rage;
He blew a horn, then showed his rank their shame:
"Now we shall know the scions of our race!
Be proud and strong, with courage in your veins!
King Turfier of Valsegree is slain
And all his rank like cowards turned their tails!
By good Mahom, in whom I set my faith,
If one of you decides to flee the same,
I'll have his head myself, with my own blade!"
When Morgant's rank heard what he had to say,
The stirring words and awful threat he made,
They raised their hearts and voices to obey
And strike at William's vanguard straightaway;
Ten thousand strong they struck, in helmets laced;
On seeing this, young William, enraged,
Spurred forth his horse which sprang across the plain,
And swung his blade to strike the press again;
So fierce he was he cut a mighty swathe
One furlong wide inside the ranks they'd made;
With brutal strength he went a mighty way,
But if the Lord had failed to lend him aid,
He'd never have returned the way he came:

Their ranks reformed to cut off his escape,
And then they hurled sharp javelins his way,
    Which slew the horse beneath him.

COUNT WILLIAM was filled with rage and grief
To feel the steed fall dead beneath his knees;
But, like a lord, he leapt up to his feet
And drew his sword, then thrusting forth his shield
Took telling toll of heads and hands and feet;
The man he struck was lucky still to breathe;
The mound of Moors he slaughtered was too steep
To climb or breach to reach their living peers!
But there were still too many of those fiends,
And they began to hurl their burnished spears
And would have killed or captured him at least,
Had he not cried '*Mountjoy!*' for all to hear,
As did Bernart, who knew, across the field,
His brother's voice, beloved to his ears;
He told his men: "My brother's in great need;
I hear him call '*Mountjoy for St Denis!*'
If he should die, my heart will break with grief!
Now we shall see whose birth is worth his steel!"
He grasped his lance, its pennant flying free,
And pricked his steed with spurs both large and sleek;
Among their ranks he rushed at utmost speed
And flayed the press with all his raging zeal;
Upon his way he met a young emir
And rammed his spear against his grey-brown shield;
Above the boss he broke the boards with ease
And cut his coat just like a lily-leaf;
He speared the rogue right through from front to rear
And flung him dead upon the flowery field:
'*Narbonne!*' he cried, so joyfully and clear
That in the town his father Aymeri
Could hear the call and knew what it must mean;
Upon the walls the noble Count appeared
With all his knights, his noblemen and peers,
And Hermenjart, whose face was fine and fierce:
"My God," he sighed, "our true and heavenly Liege,
I hear the cry '*Narbonne!*' upon my ears!
Now I am sure our Emperor is near,
    The Lord of France, King Louis."

SAID AYMERI: "True God, the Judge of men,
How many knights upon Narbonne are met!
Now I am sure the Emperor himself
Has come to me with his support and help;
But he must think I am a craven wretch
To not be there before him and the rest!"
So then he said: "My noble son Guibert,
Tell all our knights to arm themselves again!"
His son replied: "I will, with no regret!"
They laced the mail upon their limbs and chest
And placed their swords about them on the left;
Then, seizing shields to hang around their necks,
They mounted steeds without delay or let;
Count Aymeri himself made haste to dress
In armour of the finest and the best;
How much indeed he'd need its virtue hence!
He took his steed, both strong and fleet of step,
And plied the straps and stirrups with such strength
The sturdy beast strove hard to stand erect!
The city gate was opened wide and then
The noble Count rode forward at the head
Of every knight that Aymeri possessed;
No serving-man or able squire was left
Inside Narbonne to guard it then, except
An archer troop, and women bravely bred;
When all had gone, they closed the gate again;
Count Aymeri rode straight towards the press
With all his men, one hundred score of them,
Who smote the Moors at random, right and left:
They had no time to joust like gentlemen!
Proud Aymeri displayed such wild prowess
That all his men, inspired, could do no less!
But William still stood in great distress,
Whose steed the Moors had stabbed and struck to death;
How well he fought in stubborn self-defence
Against those hated heathens!

WHEN AYMERI rode forth from Narbonne's gate
With all his men on long-maned destriers,
Their shields were braced to battle straightaway:
And so they did, with sharp and shining blades,

And slaughtered more than truly I could say;
What use was that? Young William remained
In great distress, surrounded by those knaves;
How well he fought in self-defence that day!
The Pagans cast great, sharpened spears his way:
In fifteen spots they rent his coat of mail,
And split his shield and slit its boards in twain;
He fought so long and showed himself so brave
That he was felled three times but stood again;
But when he saw no help arrive or aid,
He cried '*Narbonne!*' with all his might and main:
"Sir Aymeri, my lord, where are you, pray?
Your bravery and strength were once so great!
My brothers too, if I am caught or slain,
What will become of your renown and name?
They'll both be scorned and you will all be shamed."
Bernart heard this and galloped from the fray,
With boar-like rage at William's tirade!
With sharpened spurs he sped his destrier
And cleft the press his brother held at bay;
Some thirty Moors he felled in mighty rage
To reach the youth and help him in all haste,
     Against those hated heathens.

BERNART, LORD OF Brabant, a gallant knight,
Attacked the Moors so well he cleft their lines
And fought his way towards his brother's side;
He swung aloft his cutting sword to smite
A Pagan king who came at him too nigh;
From crest to coif he drove his sword of iron
And split his skull and all his teeth besides;
He turned the blade and flung him down to die,
Then grasped the reins before his horse ran by
And led the steed towards his brother's side;
The youth leapt up and, once astride, he cried:
"Good brother brave, much thanks for this respite!
I'm very sure, if you had not arrived,
These faithless fiends would soon have claimed my life."
Bernart replied: "So help me Jesus Christ,
I'll never fail to serve you till I die!"
When this was said they both spurred off to strike

The throng of Moors, their cutting swords held high;
They raised the blades and swung them round like scythes;
Behind them came their worthy vanguard knights,
All gallant men of great prowess and pride
And fierce desire to face the Moors and fight!
The Pagans reeled when William's men arrived
And beat them back one well-drawn arrow's flight,
Until they reached King Morgant's flag behind,
The Pagan lord who'd sworn to hold the line
And keep them safe – but, friends, they couldn't hide:
His royal pledge had lost its edge, they'd find,
As William and strong Bernart combined
Their fearsome blows without the least respite!
The faithless Moors were filled with pain and fright
To feel the strength with which our French could strike:
With sword or spear, through front or rear, they sliced
And slaughtered all upon one flank and side;
Their other side was hard oppressed alike,
For Aymeri, his face with valour bright,
Attacked again with all his city's knights;
I tell you, friends, with no word of a lie,
    Those Moors had got their hands full!

BEFORE NARBONNE, that town of ancient strength,
The faithless Moors were filled with pain and dread:
For Aymeri, whose face glowed with prowess,
Chastised them with his sword-blade's biting edge,
As did Guibert, with all the knights and men
Of old Narbonne who left the town with them;
Count Aymeri's bright sword outshone the rest:
The man it struck had no defence from death;
The Moors looked on and, one and all, they said:
"This living fiend will take us all to hell!
If we wait here, our lives will soon be spent!"
How well he struck those hated heathen heads!
And young Guibert gave everything as well,
As did Romanz, and all the knights who left
The city walls at Aymeri's request;
Upon one flank they flayed the heathens' best,
While, on another, the Frenchmen did no less;
Young William, his jaw with courage set,

And Lord Bernart, his brother and best friend,
Led countless blows, in no mood to relent,
While they were backed by Louis' noble French,
Who drove their mounts so fiercely in the press
That they threw back that second rank as well
Upon their peers one mighty furlong's length;
Our Christian knights, whom may Lord Jesus bless,
Had turned the foe – though far from finished yet:
Another rank of Moors rode forward, led
By King Butor, lord of Saloriez,
The fiercest knight of his benighted *geste*:
Beneath his roar one thousand score he led,
Who, at his word, once heard, outrode the rest
And drove upon our Frenchmen like a wedge;
The tide of war turned more from us to them,
As Butor's men swept over Christian flesh
And killed at once some thirty of our men,
Then murdered more, God curse their wickedness!
Butor, the king who led their evil quest,
Spurred hard and swung his spear above his head,
Then moved to strike a knight of great noblesse,
Gautier his name and Normandy his realm;
He smote his mail and ripped its rings to shreds;
From front to rear he speared him with contempt,
Then on the field he flung the fellow dead;
With ringing tones he cried: "Saloriez!
Strike on with me! Let Mahom be your strength
Against this race of cringing Christian men!
I swear to you they'll rue the day they left
Their wealthy land for poverty and death!"
He drew his sword, those wicked words expressed,
And moved to strike Girart, knight of Pontel:
Through skull and skin he split the fellow's head,
And then he slew Pavia's Guibouen,
And then four more, God rob him of his breath!
Young William looked on in great distress:
"By Jesus Christ and Mary mild," he said,
"We're bitten hard by this wild hound from hell!
Without revenge, my honour will be spent!"
He spurred his steed and sped across the press,
Not drawing rein until the Moor was met;

He had no spear but held his sword erect
And smote Butor on his Pavian helm;
Its golden ring, which gleamed aglow, he rent,
And then the coif upon the coat itself;
But Satan came to save his servant's neck:
The sword slid off and slipped along the left;
It split the coif down one side of his head
And then the blade dropped down to sever next
The leather straps upon his buckler's belt,
Then sliced the neck of his swift destrier,
    As Butor swayed and tumbled.

WHEN BUTOR FELL to ground, behold the fear
Upon the face of all his men of liege:
They shook with shock and groaned aloud in grief!
The fight was fierce and terrible their screams;
Such mortal blows our mortal foes received
Their corpses lay across the field in heaps;
So many Moors were felled from long-maned steeds,
With gaping wounds which bled upon the field,
That all their blood ran through the grass in streams;
But still their men in countless sums appeared!
Without God's help, Who governs all and each,
Young William would find he'd struck too deep
Within their ranks, Bernart the same indeed;
For while they struck King Butor's men with zeal,
Another rank came at them from the rear;
This troop was led by Isembart Greybeard,
A king who dwelt beyond the Vale of Tears;
His brutes of men had horns above their ears,
As long and hard as those of any deer,
And agony for any man they pierced;
As well as this, these warriors had spears
With giant hooks attached, whose vicious teeth
Gripped every foe and ripped them from their steeds!
The French looked on, aghast at such a breed,
And said aloud: "What fate has cursed us here?
These brutes aren't men, but servants of The Fiend!
    May Jesus Christ protect us!"

WHEN ALL OUR MEN beheld these brutal vassals,
As black as ink, with horns as big as antlers,
Their stoutest hearts were seized with sudden panic,
As each one said: "What curse has come to damn us?
These brutes aren't men but servants of Sathanas!"
Young William still urged along his vanguard,
While Lord Bernart blew forth his horn to rally
The King's supports behind them in the valley;
Hernaut the Red, whose visage glowed with valour,
The brother of Bernart, the Lord of Brabant,
Replied at once and spurred his battle-stallion;
And from his host so did their brother Garin,
Who held the large and wealthy land of Anseune;
Those noble sons of Aymeri went dashing
To aid their kin as fast as they could gallop,
To pit their strength and that of their battalions,
A thousand score of proven skill and valour,
On noble steeds, against the Pagan challenge;
They met at once that fearsome rank and savage,
Pitch-black of hue and hideous of aspect –
God curse them all, Whose might and right are matchless!
With sharpened crooks they hooked our men and dragged them
Across their steeds, and, as they left the saddle
And sprawled to ground, those Pagan monsters stabbed them
With shortened spears, whose tips were sharp as arrows;
On seeing this, the French were seized with anguish,
The bravest there not daring to attack them;
Young William saw this and filled with sadness;
He cried '*Mountjoy!*' to rally his companions
And spurred his steed in fearsome rage and rancour;
His blade aloft, he drove his stallion at them
And struck their ranks with fierce and wild abandon;
Not far behind rode brave Bernart of Brabant,
And Red Hernaut, who wasn't slow to back them,
Nor Sir Garin, the wealthy lord of Anseune;
They smote the press and smashed those devils backwards;
On seeing this, the others followed gladly,
With greater zeal to deal with such a phalanx;
With spear and sword they hit that horde and hacked them,
But took, in turn, great blows, which made them stagger;
They blew their horns across the hills and valleys

And beat their drums with such a burst of banging
They'd not have heard God's voice above the clamour!
Whoever fell had little hope of standing,
As horses' hooves trod over him and trampled;
The Frenchmen called on Jesus Christ, their Champion;
The Pagans called on Mahom and Tervagant,
       To help them win this war.

22. How the knights of Narbonne were reunited

IN TRUTH, MY LORDS, this battle was more fierce
And more widespread than any ever seen!
Our gallant knights struck mighty blows indeed,
Lombard and French, but more than all of these,
The noble sons of fierce Count Aymeri
Struck mortal blows with blades of burnished steel;
Red-haired Hernaut drove forth his Arab steed
And broke the ranks of those horn-headed beasts
To smite their king, Brohadas, with his spear;
Across the boss he broke his sturdy shield
And ripped apart the coat of mail beneath;
Below his steed he flung him on the field,
Where, if he lived, his doctor had no peer!
Hernaut rode on; he kicked his spur-clad heels
And drew his sword with all his angry zeal
To smite the helm of an Almoravide;
He split his skull right through from top to teeth;
His brother too, Garin, spurred off to meet
A royal foe for whom his hate was deep:
The Moor Butor, the king of Saloriez;
He smote his helm of shining gold and sheared
Its crown away and ornaments between;
He cracked it wide beside its nasal-piece;
The coif was strong and saved the skull beneath;
The blade slid down the monarch's mail to cleave
The noble head of Butor's Arab steed;
The Pagan swayed then dropped upon the field;
His men looked on and groaned aloud in grief;
They yapped and yelled and raised such piercing screams
That every man, both near and far, could hear;

Ten thousand more, their next rank, drove their steeds
With the Emir of Leutis in the lead;
They joined the fray with every haste and speed
And straightaway the toll they took was steep;
So many French they robbed of breath to breathe,
Who nevermore would greet their near and dear!
And those still left were wearied soon and weak,
And all fell back one furlong's length at least;
Young William looked on and groaned in grief;
'*Narbonne!*' he cried, in tones so loud and clear
That Aymeri his father stopped to heed,
Who was, himself, hard-pressed in combat fierce
Before the walls, with all his knights of liege;
He told his men: "The French are very near,
And need our help, without a lie, I fear!
My worthy knights, let us assist their need."
Guibert replied: "My lord, most willingly!"
And so they turned with every haste and speed
To join the fight which raged across the fields;
Count Aymeri broke through the press with ease
And cut a swathe with his bright sword of steel
Which swept the Moors aside like fallen leaves;
His men rode through the passageway he'd cleared,
Each spurring hard till one and all could see
Young William among the swords and spears;
Bernart, Hernaut and Garin too were near;
On seeing these, the Narbonnese all cheered,
But just before they met and welcomed each,
The Count himself was almost brought to grief:
For when they saw old Aymeri appear,
Five hundred Moors surrounded him with glee;
Those heathen brutes with horns above their ears,
Put forth their crooks to hook his hauberk's seams,
And hauled him down from his good Arab steed;
Guibert looked on and groaned aloud in grief,
     While spurring straight to help him.

THE PAGANS FELLED Count Aymeri by force;
Guibert looked on and groaned in great remorse;
With all his hate he drew his burnished sword
And struck Galafre upon his helmet's point;

The golden crown fell down, as did the coif,
And to his teeth he cleft the royal Moor;
He flung him dead upon the flowery floor
And cried aloud: "That blow was your reward
For what you've done to Aymeri, my lord;
I am his son; his death you've dearly bought!"
Young William could hear his brother's voice
And spurred his steed to where he saw the boy;
Upon the ground he saw his father sprawled,
Hauled down and mauled by those foul Moors with horns;
With every haste he left his long-maned horse
And in his arms he took his father's corpse –
For he was sure they'd killed him after all:
"Alas," he cried, "that this day ever dawned!
Ah, father dear, how reft we are and poor
Now your rich life is over, noble lord!"
On hearing this and knowing William's voice,
The Count revived and hoarsely whispered forth:
"Son, welcome home to old Narbonne once more!
These Pagan knaves have choked me with their claws!
What has become of my fleet-footed horse?
Son, I know this: if it could be restored,
These Moors would feel that I still have some force!"
On hearing this, how William rejoiced!
He grasped the reins of King Galafre's horse,
The Pagan whom Guibert had felled before,
And claimed it for his father's use henceforth,
Who mounted up with no delay at all;
Young William attended him, then soared
Once more upon his own strong steed of war;
Count Aymeri raised high his worthy sword,
And William rode by his side towards
The mighty press and struck with all his force;
If you had seen him then, so strong and tall!
He raised Joyeuse, which was the King's before,
And struck in rage one Malargu the Moor;
No steel he wore or bore was worth a straw:
From helm to hip he split him like a stalk;
And Aymeri, not stinting, struck one more
And flung him down to die upon the floor;
Again the Moors began to rant and roar;

They urged Mahom and Cahu to support
  And help them win this battle.

23. *How the Pagans were put to rout*

WHEN AYMERI once more bestrode a steed,
And with his sons ran rampant round the field,
So many Moors were slaughtered by their steel
That none alive could tell the toll achieved;
They slew the Moors with all the spite and speed
Of hungry wolves among a flock of sheep;
Their bravest knights took fright and turned to flee
Towards the camp and tent of their Emir;
He saw them come and groaned in rage and grief,
Then cried aloud so all of them could hear:
"Turn back, my lords! Trust in Mahom and me!
I'll know today my faithful by their deeds!"
And turn they did, when they had heard this speech;
See their Emir! He grasped his mighty spear
And swung astride his finest battle-steed
To lead his ranks as fit a noble Peer;
He still had left so many Moors to lead
The hills were filled and all the dales between;
Without God's help, our Everlasting Liege,
The Narbonnese would still have met defeat,
For such a sum opposed them in the field!
From every side they suddenly appeared
And struck with pikes and burnished swords of steel;
Three score at once they slew with greatest glee,
And heard once more the roar of their Emir:
"Lay on, my lords, for these men are the fiends
Who slew your peers and those you held most dear!"
When this was said, the blows and woes increased!
In self-defence the Narbonnese were fierce,
But, bit by bit, they couldn't help but yield –
Outnumbered there by six to one at least;
Those men, each one, were all but done, indeed,
When William raised up his horn and pealed;
Young Aimer, then, for one, pricked up his ears,
And Boniface, that king of high esteem,

And Richard, duke of noble Normandy,
And Geoffrey of Anjou, that worthy Peer,
And Louis too, the King of France the sweet,
Who all set out in answer to the plea!
Before the rest young Aimer's quest was keen:
"Lord God," he said, "our Everlasting Liege,
Maintain the fray and do not let it cease
Until my sword has struck the heathen breed!
I never was so slow before to reach
Your mortal foes – it was my wont to lead!"
With mighty spurs he urged his horse to speed
Towards the press with all his raging zeal;
He raised his spear of strong and polished steel
And struck a Moor upon his tawny shield –
Whose boards were worth no more than lily-leaves,
As down he fell, run through from ribs to rear;
Then Aimer drew his burnished sword to cleave
King Agolafre, the liege lord of Leutice;
He flung him dead, no more, no less indeed;
Felis, a nephew of the great Emir,
He slaughtered next, a cousin of Clargis;
Again he struck and one less Pagan breathed;
The Moors all said: "This youth's a living fiend!
    Mahomet, curse the villain!"

THE DAY WAS FINE, the sun shone clear and bright;
The heat and dust oppressed each knight and squire,
But Aimer still attacked the Pagan lines
And swung his sword against them like a scythe!
No bearded Moor, nor bald, could bide his might,
And fled his blade, both humble-born and high;
They would have sped, but their Emir arrived
Upon his steed with leaping, bounding strides,
And all his rank, some thirty thousand knights;
Fresh fighting flared, more stubborn and more wild,
As Pagans rushed our Frenchmen from all sides;
Their leader roared: "Take none of them alive!
With axe and pike bleed every Frenchman dry!
Avenge Mahom and all your friends and mine!"
The Moors broke rank and sprang at them like lions;
They blew their horns of brass and copper bright,

And all the bells their horses bore with pride
On bridles, reins and breast-plates, chinked and chimed
So loud and clear that every slope and height
And shore and wood rang out as they rode by;
Without God's help, Who governs all and guides,
That day could well have proved our worst of times;
Count Aymeri and all his city's knights,
His sons and friends, and all at Louis' side
Who fought that day, could well have lost their lives,
　　Had God the Lord not helped them.

THE NOISE WAS FIERCE, the hue and cry was great;
The Moor Emir had rallied all his race
And led them forth in hatred and in haste
To fight our knights in one almighty fray;
As he arrived two hundred bugles brayed
And every hill rang out and every dale;
King Louis heard the fearsome din they made,
Who held his line one crossbow's draw away;
He cried '*Mountjoy!*' and hailed his baronage:
"My lords," he said, "our waiting wastes the day!
In Lord God's name, Who rules the sun and rain,
Let's fight them now with all our force and faith!"
On hearing this, the knights of France the praised
Grew proud and dread and sped their destriers,
While on his side, with those of his domains,
Spurred off alike white-bearded Boniface;
Geoffrey Anjou, whose face with valour blazed,
Drove forth his steed and freely gave it rein;
Before the rest Duke Richard led the chase,
With flashing spurs, his visage flushed with rage;
Behind each lord the rank and file kept pace
And struck the Moors with all their heart and hate;
How fierce it is when mortal foes engage!
The Pagan lines were swept aside in swathes
When all our force attacked them thus in waves;
As rank on rank rode in, more gains were made,
Despite the herds and hordes of those they faced!
For all the French were strong in war and brave
And keen to fight for honour and for fame;
Each fighting man held in his hand a blade,

Or sturdy spear or axe or pike the same,
Through chest and chine, through breast and spine to break!
The Pagans cried: "This marks our darkest day!
Mahomet, lord, how awful is our fate!
    Your power serves us nothing!"

THE HEATHEN MOORS were put to sword and beaten;
They blamed their gods and, all the same, beseeched them;
Across the fray with flashing spurs went speeding
King Louis, son of Charlemagne the peerless,
And Boniface, Pavia's worthy Regent;
The Lombards, when they saw the Pagans fleeing,
Were keen to fight: you never saw them keener
To flay and slay as many as they pleased to;
King Boniface drove on his steed to lead them,
And in the rout he turned about to meet there
King Baligant of Bocidant the Eastland;
He smote the Moor with his well-sharpened spear-point,
Which pierced the mail as though no mail had been there,
And flung him dead, whoever jeered or cheered it!
He struck again and stopped another breathing;
With ringing tones he called aloud '*Pavia!*';
King Louis came with Geoffrey, count and leader
Of rich Anjou; Duke Richard too was near them;
Uniting soon, with all their might and feeling
They struck the Moors wherever they could reach them;
King Louis spurred his rapid steed, and wielding
His spear aloft, its snowy banner streaming,
He moved to strike the mighty King Aquilant –
A giant Moor he challenged for that reason!
With great prowess King Louis charged to deal him
A mighty blow with his well-burnished spear-point;
Like buckram-board his shield broke into pieces,
As did the chains of Eastern mail beneath it;
Inside his ribs he rammed the blade completely;
'*Mountjoy!*' he cried, his noble sword unsheathing;
Said William: "That blow was not a weak one!
So fierce a lord deserves our firm allegiance!"
The Pagans though, were further shocked to see it,
And would have fled, without the fierce Emir there,
Who joined the fight with fifteen thousand heathens;

He swung a sword of wondrous size and features,
And straightaway slew four who rode to meet him:
Counts Elinant, Droon, Fochart and Mielant;
The man he struck knew well that death was near him;
Count Aymeri saw this and, spurring keenly,
He smote the Moor with all his force and feeling
Upon his helm with gold and jewels gleaming –
But not a dent, much less a rent, appeared there,
For it was forged and tempered with such evil
That neither iron nor steel could ever cleave it;
The Count looked on with sinking heart to see it,
Lamenting as he turned his steed to leave him:
"Alas, fine sword! How sharp you were and peerless!
How many Moors before this day you've beaten:
Now, only now, you fail me when I need you!"
He looked ahead and saw their King Boidant,
Who'd slain Gautier of Tolosant on leaving;
Said Aymeri: "You'll never boast your deeds here!"
Against his helm a mighty blow he wielded,
Which cleft him to the saddlebows, believe me!
On seeing this, those heathen hearts stopped beating,
And all like sheep went flocking round their leader –
Though this would prove no safety for them either!
Our men were filled with fresh prowess and eager
To smite the Moors wherever they could see them;
Their heathen blood ran all across the heath-land;
Their horses fled and dragged their reins, unheeded;
See young Guibert and William, the hero,
With Bernart of Brabant and Aimer, leading
Hernaut the Red, his face with valour gleaming,
Geoffrey Anjou and Normandy's brave liege lord;
They met Clargis, whom the Emir loved dearly,
Still leading forth five hundred Pagans fiercely
Against our men, still striving to defeat them;
And young Guibert, as soon as he could reach him,
Attacked his shield with all his strength and feeling;
But God looked down and helped the Moor to meet it,
For He desired to save Clargis for Jesus:
The Pagan fell, as soon as Guibert's spear hit;
The Narbonnese rushed forward then to seize him,
And ten more lords, who all were rich and regal;

Then everyone attacked Clargis's legion
And slew as few or many as they pleased to;
But one escaped, and he, poor rogue, went speeding
To the Emir, to tell him of the seizure
Of young Clargis, his nephew, and his people;
On hearing this, how sad the great Emir was!
What taunts he threw the gods that he believed in!
"Ah, wicked gods, the Devil curse your weakness!"
But, saying this, he never lingered either:
He dropped his shield and turned his horse to flee there;
With those still left he galloped down the sea-road
    To reach his ships alive.

THE GREAT EMIR delayed no more, escaping
The fight he'd lost with every knight remaining,
To reach the boats and barges they had sailed in;
He thought his haste would guarantee their safety –
And yet, my friends, he'd sweat before he gained it!
For Louis, when he saw the Moor evade him
And turn his steed to flee defeat and danger,
Sent Aimer off directly to waylay him;
King Louis cried: "My lords, pursue them bravely!
If one escapes, our friends in France will blame us!"
If you had seen the way his barons hastened!
The great Emir spurred wildly to outpace them
And struck the beach to find young Aimer waiting!
Friends, you can guess his anger and amazement
To see that he was far from his safe haven!
He cried aloud to rally all his Pagans:
Some fifty score had fled who still obeyed him;
They reached the beach, to meet with further mayhem;
Young Aimer rode to the Emir and hailed him
In fearsome tones: "To pass me, you must slay me!
I am the son of Aymeri called Aimer!"
On hearing this, the great Emir was shaken,
And yet he swore that he would never waver
But fight to live, though he be captured later,
And take a life, although his own be taken;
Count Aimer spurred and sped his horse to face him;
The blow he struck was such a grand and great one
That all the jewels upon his helm were shaven,

But nothing else – the helmet's power saved him:
So strong it was that sword nor axe could break it;
It turned the blow towards the ground and aimed it
Through crest and breast of his good Arab racer;
The great Emir fell down upon the shale there,
But straightaway regained his feet most bravely;
He raised his sword and lunged towards young Aimer
To smite his horse upon its course in payment;
And so he did: from rib to rib he aimed it
And felled the horse, and so, perforce, young Aimer;
The Moor, meanwhile, beheld a stallion straying
Across the sand with no one's hand to claim it;
He grasped the reins and, once astride, he hastened
Across the beach to reach his mighty navy;
Whatever fate awaited those detained there,
He thought, at least, that *he* had made it safely;
Four Pagan kings, the last of his retainers,
And five score men, were all, in fact, who made it;
They galloped on and found his galley waiting,
So raced aboard as fast as they were able;
The great Emir gave orders to his sailors,
And left the bay, whose tide was in their favour;
And thus it was the great Emir escaped there;
To all his gods he swore that one year later
He'd set Narbonne a second siege and greater,
And seek revenge upon the whole French nation;
He gave his word, and, friends, he didn't break it:
Within a year what trials and tribulation
He caused the Count, whose son Beuvon was taken
To Barbastro and tortured in its jail there;
My worthy friends, I'll tell you that tale later:
    You'll not have heard its like!

THE GREAT EMIR escaped upon the tide
With four more kings and just one hundred knights;
The Living Fiend filled up their sails to drive
Their galley home to Persia's heathen climes,
With nothing saved, except their limbs and lives;
But as for those whom they had left behind,
How bitterly they paid for all their crimes!
Before Narbonne in countless sums they died,

As Christian wrath spared neither low nor high:
The fields were filled with all their fallen knights;
They slew them all, not one survived, besides
The youth Clargis, whose life they spared, alike
That youth whose skill had saved the Count's own life;
The two were saved to serve Lord Jesus Christ,
And both, next day, without delay, baptised.

24. How Narbonne was filled with rejoicing

WHEN FIGHTING STOPPED upon that fearsome day
And every Moor on field and shore was slain,
One thousand score lay scattered on the plain;
From everything the Pagans owned or claimed,
One thing was sure: they'd taken naught away!
Within their tents, what gold and silver plates
Our soldiers found in open trunks and trays!
What weapons too on sumpter-mules that strayed
Across the field with steeds and destriers;
I couldn't count the half of all they gained:
Each took as much as heart and hand could crave;
Then William blew forth his horn again
To halt the troops and bid them to remain
Within their tents, disarming straightaway;
They all were hot and weary from the fray,
And no one there unwillingly obeyed;
Each man had earned his meat and drink, I'd say!
Inside the tents of the Emir were laid
Large stores of meat they'd stolen in their raids,
Of bird and beast, and sacks of wine the same;
Good Hermenjart, so fair of form and face,
When she beheld the final blows exchanged,
Came running down the palace-steps in haste,
With three more maids, whose beauty too was great;
They mounted mares and, riding through the gates,
They reached the tents and only then drew rein;
Fair Hermanjart, with wisdom and with grace,
Hailed Louis first and thanked him for the aid
He'd brought which fought to keep their city safe;
Dismounting then, she held in her embrace
Each son in turn: first William the brave,

Then brash Hernaut, then all of them the same,
Her brother too, the good King Boniface;
    What joy she showed to see them!

WHEN THIS WAS DONE and all was won at last,
And every lord and lad had been disarmed,
The King of France, his knights and men-at-arms
Sat down to feast before they'd have to part;
Inside those tents, so richly made and marked,
The cloths were laid and fingerbowls were passed,
And those who wished devoured the dishes fast
And ate their fill without restraint or guard!
No serving-boy or menial was asked
To pay for theirs one penny or one half;
They crammed each crumb, they drained each drop and draught
Of everything those heathens stole from France
Or owned themselves, whoever groans or laughs!
They had no fear the great Emir would march
    His men inside to stop them!

THE KING OF FRANCE and all his men of liege
Enjoyed the tent that was the great Emir's;
They took their pick of all its wine and meat
And there was none who didn't slake his need;
Their fighting done, they had a right to feast!
But then the King stood up at last to speak,
In ringing tones, so all his men could hear:
"My lords," he said, "hear well what I decree:
That all this wealth that we have won and see
Should be shared out to all men equally,
Without complaint from commoners or Peers."
With no delay each one of them agreed,
And that was done and no one was displeased;
What goods were left became Count Aymeri's;
Then, mounting up and riding through the streets,
They met Morant the bishop with his priests,
And all his monks sang chants of joy and peace;
In high content the French and Narbonnese
Rode side by side to St Paul's church, and here
The King of France went first, as was but meet;
Then all his counts and barons did as he:

Rich offerings they made, both all and each,
To thank the Lord, Whose strength had intervened
   Between them and the Pagans.

WHILE IN THE CHURCH King Louis still was kneeling,
Fair Hermenjart did not delay, but leaving,
She reached her hall to deck and strew it freely
With fragrant herbs to make it smell more sweetly;
The Emperor then left the holy precincts
With Richard and King Boniface the Regent,
Then Aymeri, then William the hero,
His brothers next, their face with valour gleaming;
Throughout the town the ranks found rooms to sleep in,
While all the knights sought lodgings from their equals;
The barons rode to Narbonne's hall that evening,
Which Hermenjart had readied to receive them,
    That Countess without peer!

THE SUN WENT DOWN and daylight turned to night;
The Emperor then left St Paul's to ride
With Boniface and his most cherished knights
Towards the hall where all at last arrived;
Now Hermenjart had seen to all inside,
Count Aymeri called out for food and wine;
Upon a couch the Emperor reclined,
While Aymeri asked Hermenjart aside:
"My dear, why does our daughter wait and hide?
Go bring her here to greet, as is but right,
Her brothers home and greet your own alike!"
On hearing this, the Countess went to find
Fair Blancheflor within her room nearby,
And bade her dress in her most rich attire –
A lovely robe, close-fitting and refined,
And diadem of jewels all golden-bright;
Her beauty, friends, just couldn't be described:
She was, in truth, the fairest maid alive,
Who lit the hall with beauty when she smiled;
The knights agreed: "How fair she is and fine!
How happy he who takes her for his bride!"
King Boniface stood up when she arrived
And bade his niece be seated at his side;

Her beauty seemed the more for being shy;
King Louis looked and couldn't turn his eyes
From Blancheflor, who filled him with desire;
At length he turned to William and sighed,
Then spoke his mind: "Now hear me well, sir knight!
You told me once that she could be my wife!
Were you in jest or earnest at the time,
For truly I would take and make her mine!"
On hearing this, the Count filled with delight:
"Your will is ours, my lord," the Count replied,
And brought the maid before the King to plight
His solemn word, by kissing her three times
As hand in hand they stood, and side by side;
"We'll wed," he said, "as soon as day is bright!"
Fair Hermenjart shed tears of tender pride
And all Narbonne was filled with joy alike;
A herald called and water was supplied
For everyone to wash before they dined –
The King, good Boniface, and all their knights;
With bench and boards the banquet hall was lined,
And food brought in on platters richly piled:
I couldn't name the quantity or kinds!
Each man had more than slaked his appetite;
The cloths were cleared and Louis made to rise,
As beds were spread in which to pass the night;
Fair Blancheflor and Hermenjart alike
Accompanied the King when he retired,
Then, waiting there till sleep had closed his eyes,
They turned away together, side by side;
The palace slept until the dawn arrived
And Louis rose with morning's early light,
　　And everyone made ready.

WHEN MORNING DAWNED each one and all made ready;
The knights and lords prepared to look their best there,
While Blancheflor was dressed by her attendants
In noble silks to complement her splendour;
Then joyfully they led her to her wedding
Inside the church, where Louis and his men were,
And where the good archbishop duly wed them
In Jesu's name, then sang a Mass to bless them;

With loyal hearts the local knights and Frenchmen
Attended all and offered gifts a-plenty,
Then left the church to join in the reception;
Before they ate, they did with grace, however,
As Louis and King Boniface requested:
They searched the fields for all of those who'd perished
In Jesu's name, their Crown and Creed defending;
Without delay they searched the fields and meadows
And bade the folk within the town to help them
Recover those who'd saved Narbonne from peril;
They set apart the Christians from the rest there
And carried them before the town on stretchers;
Beneath the waves they tossed the heathen dead there,
Then dug some graves within a grove to bury
The Christian dead, whose souls the priests commended
To Lord our God, the Majesty of Heaven;
Then they returned to celebrate the wedding
Of Blancheflor with Louis, their true Emperor;
For life goes on, my friends, and it is better
To joy in life than to lament its ending;
The *jongleurs* came to play and give them pleasure:
Some played rebecs, some harps, and some *vièles* there,
While others sang or tumbled for the guests there;
The knights were sad, but these lads made them merry!
And then they washed, for soon the feast was ready;
Both kings sat at the table's head and centre,
While all their knights sat right and left together;
The food was brought and laid upon the trestles,
Whatever dish they wished, in plates of plenty,
To fulsome praise from every person present;
The cloths were cleared when every dish was empty,
And once again the merry *jongleurs* entered;
With fiddles, flutes and harps well-tuned and tempered
They played and, as they pranced around, they beckoned
The maids to sing and dance until the menfolk,
Both young and old, joined in the merry measures;
When all was done, the *jongleurs*, for their efforts,
Gained noble cloaks from all the nobles present,
  And left in high content.

INSIDE THE HALL how noisy was the feast!
When all was done, Guibert came from his seat
Towards the King and knelt down at his feet:
"My lord," he said, "please listen to my plea:
Within our cells we hold ten Pagan Peers
Who curse their fate, oppressed by loss and grief;
Among their ranks is one called King Clargis,
A noble Moor and nephew of the Emir;
I swear, my lord, he has done much for me;
By God, Who pardoned Longinus his deed,
I beg you now to set these Pagans free;
If they could turn and learn the Christian Creed,
They'd gain by this, my lord, and so would we."
King Louis said: "I willingly agree;
Without delay convey them here to me!"
Count Aymeri himself went off to lead
The prisoners, all ten men, from his keep;
Before the King he brought them on their knees;
King Louis bade them rise, addressing each:
"My lords," he said, "pay heed to me and speak!
    Will you become true Christians?"

KING LOUIS LOOKED each Pagan in the face:
"My lords," he said, "your answer straightaway!
Will you become true Christian men this day?"
Clargis replied: "I will, without delay;
Baptise me, Sire, for my desire is great,
As is my cousin's, the doctor, young Forrez;
I have said much to urge these Moors the same,
But Lord Mahom still rules their heart and brains."
King Louis said: "Then he has sealed their fate;
If they resist, they all can rot in jail,
While you, in joy and love, are led away
To Lord God's house and welcomed to the Faith."
When this was said, those other Pagans changed
Their hearts and minds, so all were taken straight
To St Paul's church, whose fonts were filled in haste;
The bishop came and in the fonts he bathed
Their sins away and made them whole again;
The names of all, except Clargis, were changed;
How fine a gift from Louis' hand he gained:

Auvergne's land would be his new domain;
Young William stood sponsor for Forrez,
And all the rest were blest with Christian names;
Towards the hall they turned in joy and grace,
Where all were dressed in lovely robes and drapes;
They ate and drank, and when their need was slaked,
And when they'd had what any heart could crave,
Clargis sat down at Louis' side to say
The thought that he had had in mind all day,
    And now would speak it nobly.

"MY NOBLE LIEGE and lords, give ear to me!
You all know well, you French and Narbonnese,
That I am nephew to Persia's great Emir,
Who rules the lands that lie across the sea;
In one of them lives his most lovely niece,
My sister, and her name, most truthfully,
Is Fair Gaiete, for fair she is and sweet;
Our father was a very fine Vizier,
Who, while he lived, ruled Andrenas in peace;
But now, my lords, without the least deceit
I tell you all, there's no one to succeed
My father's throne – they all have perished here;
I swear to you: you have but to agree,
And young Guibert shall wed Gaiete and be
The ruler of all Andrenas, bequeathed
By right of line and lineage to me;
He is my friend; these rights I freely yield."
"Much thanks for this," replied Guibert, "indeed,
You'll never want while I want not the means:
    Of this you can be certain."

INSIDE NARBONNE, that town of ancient might,
What noisy joy reigned in the hall on high!
Clargis's words had filled them with delight,
And he was served with honour on all sides;
The feasting went for four whole days and nights,
For love of her, the loveliest of brides,
To whom the King had sworn his love for life,
And in their midst had made his Queen and wife;
The fifth day came, and at the King's desire

The feasting stopped and all were dressed to ride;
King Louis left with Blancheflor his wife
And turned his steed to France the sweetly prized,
Together with his barons and his knights,
And young Guibert, his face aglow with pride
To be King Louis' seneschal a while;
Good Boniface, with Garin by his side,
Returned to his Pavian shore and shires,
Which Garin soon would rule in his own right,
    As his beloved succesor.

THE BRAVE KNIGHTS OF NARBONNE rode forth again;
Count Bernart for Brabant and his domains,
And Aimer left for Venice on the waves,
To fight the Moors and keep the pledge he'd made
Of waging war for Jesus every day;
Count Hernaut too, so fierce of mood and make,
Rode off to the Gironde and his estates;
Inside Narbonne, with heavy hearts, remained
The Count himself, whose courage never failed,
And Hermenjart, his Countess fair of face;
But when the rest rode forth upon their way,
And even Blancheflor, that lovely maid,
Was led away to France in royal state,
Young William resolved a while to stay,
For something more aggrieved those who remained:
They hadn't seen at all Beuvon the brave
Outside Narbonne, before or since the fray
They'd fought against the hated heathen race;
Their minds were fraught and very much afraid
That he had met some fierce and awful fate;
They watched in vain, then on the seventh day
An envoy rode inside the city gates;
Upon the stones he stopped and stepped his way
Inside the walls to reach the hall of state;
He found the Count sat down before his plate,
With William, his son of courage great;
The envoy spoke with courtesy and grace
To Aymeri of hoary beard and grey:
"May Lord our God, Who made the human race,
The earth and heaven and all that they contain,

The sun, the moon and shining stars the same,
And Whom we all in Christian love obey,
Protect you, sire, and bless you all your days,
And Hermenjart, the Countess fair of face!
I greet you thus in noble Beuvon's name;
He rides here now with all his baronage
And ten full counts of high prowess and fame;
At Beuvon's side ride both his sons and heirs,
Gui and Girart, most hardy youths and brave,
And other men of your own clan and race,
And friends of his, who've come to lend you aid:
Renaut and Eslinant of Monthermé,
Count Savari, Gaudin of Alemayn,
And Count Hunaut and noble Gautier,
Ten counts in all, of high renown and rate;
We've come to fight the Moors – but we're too late!
Had we been here before, I'm bound to say
We would have slain great numbers of those knaves!"
The Count leapt up, on hearing Beuvon's name,
As did the rest, when they all heard the same:
Count William, his face with joy ablaze,
And Hermenjart, so fair of form and face,
And all the knights inside Narbonne that day;
They hugged the man and held him in embrace,
    And filled with fresh rejoicing.

WHEN AYMERI, whose visage glowed with courage,
And Hermenjart, so fair of face and lovely,
Had heard him say that brave Beuvon was coming,
They both leapt up and kissed the man and hugged him!
Across the town of rich renown they hurried
To deck the walls and all the halls with bunting,
While on the fires the cooks and all their scullions
Prepared more meat and fish to feed their hunger;
Count Aymeri bestrode his steed and summoned
Young William to welcome home his brother
With every lord, their knights and sundry others;
They left the town and just outside, above it,
Upon the field they met him, filled with wonder
At all the men of such renown he'd mustered;
How joyfully they hailed both high and humble –

With open arms they clasped and clutched each other;
Sir Beuvon first ran forth to kiss his mother,
And then the Count, of hardy mind and muscle;
Then, turning round, they rode in joy and comfort,
The happy sons, the happy wife and husband,
    Inside Narbonne the great.

WHEN BEUVON CAME, the Count of Commarchis,
What joy was felt by old Count Aymeri
And Hermenjart, his wife of many years!
Within the hall once more the forms were reared
And on the fires the cooks prepared a feast;
When all had washed, the barons took their seats
Along the hall, where all would sit and eat;
Two noble youths served all the highest Peers –
Girart was one, the other one young Gui,
The noble sons that Beuvon's court had reared;
The rest were served by squires of high degree;
I cannot list the courses in their meal,
But there were five or six of them at least!
When all were done, at last Count Aymeri
Informed his son, Beuvon of Commarchis,
Of how the Moors had laid Narbonne to siege;
Of all their woes and all their daring deeds;
Of how Guibert had fought till he was seized
Then hung and lashed upon a cross's beams,
And how his friends had fought till he was freed;
Then he described how Louis' host appeared
And how his knights had routed the Emir;
On hearing this, Beuvon was greatly cheered;
He thanked the Lord, our great Eternal Liege,
Whose Loving Grace saves all who hold Him dear;
My worthy friends, Beuvon of Commarchis
Stayed at Narbonne for more than half a year,
To hunt and fish within its woods and streams;
But then his knights began at length to feel
That they had spent too many days at ease,
And that the Moors would nevermore appear;
Yet, after this, my friends, within a week
They all were filled with fresh alarm and fear:
For the Emir, whose humbled host and fleet

Had fled away before our Frenchmen's zeal,
Had sworn revenge and gathered, fief by fief,
Five thousand score more Saracens at least,
  To teach Narbonne a lesson.

Glossary

Acton	A quilted jacket worn under a knight's chain-mail armour.
Allod	An estate held in absolute ownership, without acknowledging a superior; the opposite of a fief (q.v.).
Almanzor	A Saracen chieftain.
Bezant	A gold coin of Byzantine origin.
Boss	A round metal knob or stud on the centre of a shield.
Buckler	A small round shield.
Byrnie	A long knee-length garment of leather, upon which metal rings were sewn in various patterns; for the protection of the body and the thighs in battle.
Castellan	A governor of a castle.
Chain mail	Armour made of small metal rings linked together.
Coif	A close cap worn under the helmet.
Compline	The last canonical hour of the day; around 6.00 p.m.
Crenel	An open space in an embattled parapet.
Demesne	A liege lord's own territory.
Denier	A coin of little value; a penny.
Destrier	A war-horse; a charger.
Emir	A Saracen prince or governor.
Fealty	A feudal tenant's fidelity to his lord.
Fief	An estate held in fee by a vassal (q.v.) from a superior. The opposite of an allod (q.v.).
Geste	1. A military exploit 2. An epic narrative 3. A clan.
Gonfalon	A banner with streamers.
Hauberk	A knee-length garment of chain mail (q.v.) which protected the body and the thighs in battle.
Jongleur	An itinerant musician.
Liege lord	A feudal superior.
Liegeman	A sworn vassal (q.v.); a faithful follower.
Mangon	A golden coin worth two bezants (q.v.).
Mangonel	A military engine for casting stones; a catapult.
Matins	A canonical hour of the breviary, ending at dawn.
Nero's Field	Site of the *Circus Neronis* in Rome; the traditional place of St Peter's martyrdom and the present-day site of the Vatican.
Nones	The ninth canonical hour of the day; around 3.00 p.m.
Olifant	An ivory horn.

Oriflamme	The sacred red banner of the abbey at Saint-Denis; the flag traditionally handed to French kings at the start of any war.
Paladin	1. One of the Twelve Peers of Charlemagne's court.
	2. A knight-errant; a champion.
Quintain	A jousting-post, often provided with a shield as a mark to tilt at and a sandbag to swing round and strike the unskilful tilter.
Rebec	A three-stringed, lute-shaped instrument, played with a bow.
Seizin	The possession or the taking possession of land by freehold.
Seneschal	A steward in a noble household.
Squire	A knight's attendant.
Sumpter	A beast of burden.
Targe	A small, round shield.
Vassal	A holder of land by feudal tenure.
Vavasor	A vassal holding of a great lord and having other vassals under him.
Vespers	A canonical hour of the breviary, ending at dusk.
Vièle	A five-stringed, lute-shaped instrument, played with a bow.
Wyvern	A snake-shaped dart hurled by Saracen warriors.

SELECT BIBLIOGRAPHIES

General

Bédier, Joseph. *Les Légendes épiques.* 3rd. ed., 4 vols. Paris 1908-13; rptd. 1914-21.

Bennett, Philip E .*The Cycle of Guillaume d'Orange or Garin de Monglane: A Critical Bibliography.* Woodbridge and Rochester, NY, 2004.

Boutet, Dominique. *La chanson de geste. Forme et signification d'une écriture épique au Moyen Age.* Paris 1993.

Calin, William C. *The Old French Epic of Revolt: Raoul de Cambrai, Renaud de Montauban, Gormont et Isembart.* Geneva 1962.

——. *The Epic Quest: Studies in Four Old French chansons de geste.* Baltimore 1966.

Crosland, Jessie. *The Old French Epic.* Oxford 1951.

Cook, Robert F. *The Sense of the Song of Roland.* Ithaca, NY, and London 1973.

Daniel, Norman. *Heroes and Saracens: An Interpretation of the Chansons de Geste.* Edinburgh 1984.

De Riquer, Martin. *Les chansons de geste françaises.* trans. I.-M. Cluzel. 2nd ed., 228-33. Paris 1968.

Duggan, Joseph J. *The Song of Roland: Formulaic Style and Poetic Craft.* Berkeley 1973.

Frappier, Jean. *Les Chansons de geste du cycle de Guillaume d'Orange.* 2 vols. Paris 1955-6.

Gautier, Léon. *Les Epopées françaises*, 2nd ed. 4 vols. Paris 1879-92, repr. Osnabrück 1966.

Heinemann, Edward A. *L'art métrique dans les chansons de geste.* Geneva 1993.

Hindley, Alan and Brian J. Levy. *The Old French Epic: An Introduction.* Louvain 1983.

Holmes, Urban T. *A History of Old French Literature.* 90-92. New York, 1948.

Jones, George F. *The Ethos of the Song of Roland.* Baltimore 1963.

Kay, Sarah. *The Chansons de Geste in the Age of Romance.* Oxford 1995.

Keller, Hans-Erich. *Romance Epic: Essays on a medieval literary genre.* Kalamazoo, MI, 1987.

Martin, Jean-Pierre. *Les motifs dans la chanson de geste.* Paris 1984.

Ramey, Lynn T. *Christian, Saracen and Genre in Medieval French Literature: Imagination and Cultural Interaction in the French Middle Ages.* New York 2001.

Rychner, Jean. *La chanson de geste. Essai sur l'art épique des jongleurs.* Geneva 1955.

Suard, François. *Chanson de geste et tradition épique en France au Moyen Age.* Paris 1994.

——. *La chanson de geste.* Collection *Que sais-je?* Paris 1993.

Subrenat, Jean. *La Technique Littéraire des chansons de geste: Actes du Colloque de Liège, sept. 1957.* Liège 1959.

Gormont et Isembart

1. Editions

Bayot, Alphonse. *Gormont et Isembart, fragment de chanson de geste du XIIe siècle*, 3rd. ed. Classiques Français du Moyen Age 14. Paris 1969.

2. Secondary Texts

Ashford, Josette B. "Etat présent des recherches sur *Gormont et Isembart.*" *Olifant* 10 (1984-5), 188-209.

Lonigan, Paul R. "Is Isembart's defeat inglorious or heroic?" *Neophilologus* 53 (1969), 1-7.

——. "Does *Gormont et Isembart* contain lyric elements?" *Neophilologus* 54 (1970), 119-122.

Luethans, Tod N. *Gormont et Isembart: The Epic as Seen in the Light of the Oral Theory.* Harvard Dissertations In Folklore and Oral Tradition 11. New York 1991.

Nichols Jr., Stephen G. "Style and Structure in *Gormont et Isembart.*" *Romania* 84 (1963), 500-35.

van Emden, Wolfgang G. "Isembart and the Old French Epic of Revolt." *Nottingham Medieval Studies* 8 (1964), 22-34.

The Song of William

1. Editions and Translations

Bennett, Philip E. *La Chanson de Guillaume*. 2 vols, London 2000.
An edition, study and prose translation of the poem.
Iseley, Nancy V. *La Chançun de Willame*. Chapel Hill, NC, 1961.
McMillan, Duncan. *La Chanson de Guillaume*. 2 vols, Société des Anciens Textes Français, Paris 1949-50.
Price, Glanville, ed. *William, Count of Orange: Four Old French Epics*. London 1975. Includes a prose translation of the poem.
Suard, François. *La Chanson de Guillaume*. Paris 1999.
Suchier, Hermann. *La Chançun de Guillelme: Französisches Volksepos des XI. Jahrhunderts kritisch ausgegeben*. Halle 1911.

2. Secondary Texts

Black, Patricia Eileen. "The gendered world of the *"Chanson de Guillaume."* *Olifant* 21, 3-4 (1997), 41-63.
Clifton, Nicole. "Adolescent knights in the *"Song of William."* *Olifant* 20, 1-4 (1995-6), 213-233.
Niles, John D. "Ring-Composition in *"La Chanson de Roland"* and *"La Chançun de Willame."* *Olifant* 1, 2 (December 1973), 4-12.
Schenk, David P. "The finite world of the *"Chanson de Guillaume."* *Olifant* 1, 2 (December 1973), 13-20.
Silver, Barbara Levy. "The death of Vivien in *"La Chançun de Willame."* *Neuphilologische Mitteilungen* 71 (1970), 306-11.
Urwin, K. "La mort de Vivien et la genèse des chansons de geste." *Romania* 78 (1957), 392-404.
Wathelet-Willem, J. *Recherches sur la "Chanson de Guillaume."* Paris 1976.

Charlemagne's Pilgrimage

1. Editions and Translations

Aebischer, Paul. *Le Voyage de Charlemagne à Jérusalem et à Constantinople: texte publié avec une introduction, des notes et un glossaire.* Geneva and Paris 1965.

Burgess, Glyn S., and Anne Elizabeth Cobby. *The Pilgrimage of Charlemagne and Aucassin and Nicolette.* GLML 47A., New York and London 1988. Editions and prose translations.

——. *Le Pèlerinage de Charlemagne.* British Rencesvals Publications, 2. Edinburgh 1998. Edition and prose translation.

Picherit, Jean-Louis G. *The Journey of Charlemagne to Jerusalem and Constantinople (Le Voyage de Charlemagne à Jérusalem et à Constantinople).* Birmingham, AL, 1984. Edition and translation.

Schlauch, Margaret. *Medieval Narrative: A Book of Translations.* New York 1969. Translation of the *Pèlerinage,* 77-101.

2. Secondary Texts

Adler, Alfred. "The *Pèlerinage de Charlemagne* in New Light on Saint-Denis." *Speculum* 22 (1947), 550-61.

Bates, Robert C. "*Le Pèlerinage de Charlemagne*: A Baroque Epic." *Yale Romanic Studies* 18 (1941), 1-47.

Burns, Jane E. "Portraits of Kingship in the *Pèlerinage de Charlemagne.*" *Olifant* 10 (1984-5), 161-181.

Grigsby, John L. "The Relics' Role in the *Voyage de Charlemagne.*" *Olifant* 9 (1982-3), 20-34.

Hatcher, Anna G. "Contributions to the *Pèlerinage de Charlemagne.*" *Studies in Philology* 44 (1947), 4-25.

Heinermann, Theodor. "Zeit und Sinn der Karlsreise." *Zeitschrift für Romanische Philologie* 56 (1936), 497-562.

Horrent, Jules. *Le Pèlerinage de Charlemagne: essai d'explication littéraire avec des notes de critique textuelle.* Bibliothèque de la Faculté de Philosophie et Lettres de l'Université de Liège, 158. Paris 1961.

Knudson, Charles A. "A Distinctive and Charming Jewel: *Le Voyage de Charlemagne à Jérusalem et à Constantinople.*" *Romanic Review* 59 (1968), 98-105.

Loomis, Laura H. "Observations on the *Pèlerinage de Charlemagne.*" *Modern Philology* 25 (1927-28), 31-49.

Neuschäfer, Hans-Jörg. *"Le Voyage de Charlemagne en Orient* als Parodie der Chanson de geste: Untersuchungen zur Epenparodie im Mittelalter (1). " *Romanistisches Jahrbuch* 10 (1959), 78-102.

Niles, John D. "On the Logic of *Le Pèlerinage de Charlemagne.*" *Neuphilologische Mitteilungen* 81 (1980), 208-16.

Paris, Gaston *"La Chanson du Pèlerinage de Charlemagne."* *Romania* 9 (1880), 1-50.

Schlauch, Margaret. "The Palace of Hugo de Constantinople." *Speculum* 7 (1932), 500-14.

Sturm, Sara. "The Stature of Charlemagne in the *Pèlerinage."* *Studies in Philology* 71 (1974), 1-18.

Walpole, Ronald N. *"The Pèlerinage de Charlemagne*: Poem, Legend, and Problem." *Romance Philology* 8 (1954-55), 173-86.

Raoul of Cambrai

1. Editions and Translations

Crosland, Jessie. *Raoul de Cambrai: An Old French Feudal Epic.* London, 1926; repr. Cambridge, Ontario 1991. A prose translation of the entire poem.

Kay, Sarah. *Raoul de Cambrai.* Oxford 1992. An edition of the entire poem, with an introduction, prose translation and notes.

Meyer, Paul and A. Lognon. *Raoul de Cambrai: Chanson de geste.* Société des Anciens Textes Français, Paris 1882.

2. Secondary Texts

Eisner, Robert. *"Raoul de Cambrai* ou la tragédie du désordre." *French Review* 45 (1971), Special Issue 3.

Levin, L. A, "The Epic Motivation of *Raoul de Cambrai."* *Philological Quarterly* 11 (1932), 374-84.

Lot, Ferdinand. "Etudes sur les légendes épiques françaises: I *Raoul de Cambrai."* *Romania* 52 (1926), 75-133.

Matarasso, Pauline. *Recherches historiques et littéraires sur Raoul de Cambrai.* Paris 1962.

Girart of Vienne

1. Edition and Translation

van Emden, Wolfgang. *Girart de Vienne par Bertrand de Bar-sur-Aube.* Société des Anciens Textes Français, Paris 1977.

Newth, Michael A. *The Song of Girart de Vienne by Bertrand de Bar-Sur-Aube.* MRTS Volume 196. Tempe, AZ, 1999. A verse translation.

2. Secondary Material

Elliott, Alison Goddard. "The Double Genesis of *Girart de Vienne.*" *Olifant* 8 (1980/81), 130-160.

van Emden, Wolfgang G. "*Girart de Vienne*, Epic or Romance?" *Olifant* 10.4 (1984/85), 147-60.

Frappier, Jean. *Les Chansons de geste du cycle de Guillaume d'Orange.* 2 vols. Paris 1955-65.

Gautier, Léon. *Les Epopées françaises*, 2nd ed. 3:94-114; 4:171-91, 218-32. Paris 1878-92.

Guidot, Bernard. "L'Empereur Charles dans *Girart de Vienne.*" *Marche Romane* 30.3-4 (1980), 127-41.

Longnon, A. "Girard de Roussillon dans l'histoire." *Revue historique* 8 (1878), 241-79.

Lot, Ferdinand. "La légende de Girart de Roussillon." *Romania* 52 (1926), 257-95.

Louis, René. *Girart, comte de Vienne, dans les chansons de geste.* Vol. 1. Auxerre, 1947.

Misrahi, Jean. "Girard de Vienne et la Geste de Guillaume." *Medium Aevum* 4 (1935), 1-15.

Tyssens, Madeleine and Jeanne Wathelet-Willem. *La "Geste des Narbonnais (Cycle de Guillaume d'Orange)* Heidelberg 2001.

The Knights of Narbonne

1. Edition

Les Narbonnais: Chanson de geste, ed. Hermann Suchier, 2 vols. Société des Anciens Textes Français, Paris 1898; repr. New York 1965.

2. Secondary Material

Combarieu (de Gres), Micheline de. "Une ville du sud vue du nord: Narbonne dans le cycle d'Aymeri." *Perspectives médiévales* 22 (1966), 59-77.

Haugeard, Philippe. "L'avenir des fils dans la chanson des *'Narbonnais'*." *Romania* 115 (1997), 406-433.

Scherping, Walther. *Die Prosafassungen des "Aymeri de Narbonne" und der "Narbonnais".* Halle 1911.

Tyssens, Madeleine. "Aspects de l'intertextualité dans la geste des *Narbonnais.*" *Medioevo romanzo* 21 (1997): 163-183.

——. and Jeanne Wathelet-Willem. *La "Geste des Narbonnais" (Cycle de Guillaume d'Orange).* Heidelberg 2001.

Other Old French Epics in Translation

Burgess, Glyn S. *The Song of Roland.* Harmondsworth 1990.

Einhorn, Elsabe. *Count William of Orange: Guillaume d'Orange.* Ampersand, 2005. This ebook presents abridged prose translations of seventeen of the most important poems from the William cycle.

Ferrante, Joan M. *Guillaume d'Orange: Four Twelfth-Century Epics.* New York and London 1974. Translated are *Li Coronomenz Loois, La Prise d'Orange, Aliscans* and *Le Moniage Guillaume.*

Goldin, Frederick. *The Song of Roland.* New York 1978.

Harrison, Robert. *The Song of Roland.* New York 1970.

Newth, Michael A. *Aymeri of Narbonne: A French Epic Romance.* New York 2005.

——. *The Song of Aliscans.* GLML 85B., New York and London 1992.

——. *The Song of Aspremont.* GLML 61B., New York and London 1989.

——. *The Song of Roland.* Sydney 2003.

Owen, D.D.R. *The Song of Roland.* Woodbridge 1990

Sayers, Dorothy. *The Song of Roland.* Harmondsworth 1957.

Sisson, C.H. *The Song of Roland.* Manchester 1983.

Some readers may also like to consult the webpage of the international *Société Rencesvals* for details of access to its journal *Olifant,* and to its annual *Bulletin Bibliographique* of the Romance epic.